To Nish.
[illegible]

THE HANDBOOK OF C VIOLENCE

The first of its kind, *The Handbook of Collective Violence* covers a range of contexts in which collective violence occurs, bringing together international perspectives from psychology, criminology and sociology into one complete volume.

There have been significant advances made in the last 25 years regarding how collective violence is conceptualized and understood, with a move away from focusing on solely individual forms of violence toward examining and understanding violence that can occur within groups. This handbook presents some of the most interesting topics within the area of collective violence, drawing upon international expertise and including some of the most well-known academics and practitioners of our generation. Structured into four parts: understanding war; terrorism; public order and organized violent crime; and gang and multiple offender groups, this volume provides academics and practitioners with an up-to-date resource that covers core areas of interest and application.

Accessibly written, it is ideal for both academics and policymakers alike, capturing developments in the field and offering a deep theoretical insight to enhance our understanding of how such collective violence evolves, alongside practical suggestions for management, prevention and intervention.

Carol A. Ireland is a Consultant Chartered Psychologist, Forensic Psychologist and Chartered Scientist. She is a Reader in Aggression at the University of Central Lancashire and Senior Research Lead at the Ashworth Research Centre. She is also the Director of Studies for the MSc in Forensic Psychology. She holds a visiting/honorary professorship at Charles Sturt University. She currently works at the Coastal Child and Adult Therapeutic Services, working with children and adults who present with offence concerns and/or are victims.

Michael Lewis is a Chartered Psychologist, Chartered Scientist, Associate Fellow of the British Psychological Society and Lecturer in Forensic Psychology at the University of Central Lancashire. He is the Research Lead for Policing and Security at the Ashworth Research Centre, Mersey Care NHS Trust, and as part of this role collaborates with numerous police forces across the UK. Dr Lewis is the Editor-In-Chief of the *Journal of Criminological Research, Policy and Practice*.

Anthony C. Lopez is an Associate Professor of Political Psychology in the School of Politics, Philosophy, and Public Affairs, at Washington State University. Dr Lopez serves as Associate Editor of *Politics* with the Evolution Institute and blogs regularly at *Psychology Today*.

Jane L. Ireland is a Chartered Forensic Psychologist and Chartered Scientist, holds a Professorial Chair at the University of Central Lancashire and is Violence Treatment Lead within High Secure Services, Ashworth Hospital. She holds three further (visiting/honorary) professorships at Abo Akademi University, Charles Sturt University and Cardiff Metropolitan University. She is currently academic lead for the Ashworth Research Centre.

THE HANDBOOK OF COLLECTIVE VIOLENCE

Current Developments and Understanding

Edited by
Carol A. Ireland, Michael Lewis,
Anthony C. Lopez and Jane L. Ireland

Routledge
Taylor & Francis Group
LONDON AND NEW YORK

First published 2020
by Routledge
2 Park Square, Milton Park, Abingdon, Oxon OX14 4RN

and by Routledge
52 Vanderbilt Avenue, New York, NY 10017

Routledge is an imprint of the Taylor & Francis Group, an informa business

British Library Cataloguing-in-Publication Data
A catalogue record for this book is available from the British Library

Library of Congress Cataloging-in-Publication Data
A catalog record has been requested for this book

ISBN: 978-0-367-18652-4 (hbk)
ISBN: 978-0-367-18654-8 (pbk)
ISBN: 978-0-429-19742-0 (ebk)

Typeset in Bembo
by Wearset Ltd, Boldon, Tyne and Wear

'This book is dedicated to Dr Peter Banister. A kind, caring, generous mentor and colleague who always found the time. We are forever grateful for him shaping our careers and his continual encouraging words.'
Carol A. Ireland and Jane L. Ireland

'To my parents, David and Deidre, for their kindness and support. I am forever grateful.'
Michael Lewis

'To my son, Nikolai, who always reminds me to play.'
Anthony C. Lopez

CONTENTS

CONTRIBUTORS

Dr Paul Andell has more than 25 years of experience of working in the criminal justice field. He has worked in the statutory, voluntary and private sectors undertaking criminal justice related work in practice, policy and research. He is a current advisor to the All Political Party Group on Alcohol, Drugs and Crime. His former practice was in Probation and Youth Justice in East London, he later worked as a Consultancy Manager for NACRO and Matrix Knowledge. He has worked as a Performance Advisor for the Ministry of Justice, Community Safety Manager for the Greater London Assembly and was Director of Communities for a Youth Leadership Charity, Brathay. For 14 years, he was Vice Chair of the Lambeth Community Police Consultative Committee, which was set up after Lord Scarman's Report following the Brixton Riots. His current research interests are focused towards youth gangs and illicit economies. He is the author of *Thinking Seriously About Gangs* (2019).

Laura H. Atuesta is an Assistant Professor and Coordinator of the Drug Policy Program at the Centro de Investigación y Docencia Económicas (CIDE – Center for Economic Research and Teaching) in Aguascalientes, Mexico. She holds a Masters in Economics and a PhD in Agricultural and Applied Economics from the University of Illinois at Urbana-Champaign. Her research interests are related to the economics of illegal drugs, the evolution of organized crime and the estimation of the social costs associated to the war on drugs in prohibitionist countries. She has published her work in *Global Crime*, the *Journal of Conflict Resolution*, the *International Journal of Drug Policy* and *Trends in Organized Crime*, among others. She teaches impact evaluation courses at the undergraduate and graduate levels and offers public policy evaluation training to public officers in Latin America. As coordinator of the Drug Policy Program at CIDE, she has published relevant data to study the effects of the war on drugs in Mexico and has co-edited a book about the consequences and the different types of violence caused by prohibition and repressive policies in Mexico.

Roger Ball was a founding member of the Bristol Radical History Group (BRHG) and subsequently received a PhD in History from the University of the West of England with a thesis entitled *Violent Urban Disturbance in England 1980–81*. From 2016–2019, he collaborated with social psychologists in researching the anatomy and dynamics of the urban riots of 2011 in England as part of the *Beyond Contagion* project. He is currently employed as a Research Fellow in the School of Law, Politics and Sociology at Sussex University working on British law and policy on the global death penalty. He has been involved in a number of research projects and written several books focused on local history in Bristol. These include labour history, the Victorian workhouse, the 1831 Reform "riots" and strikes in the British armed forces after the First World War. He is currently co-authoring a book on slavery and abolition in Bristol.

Daniel T. Beaumont is a Forensic Psychologist-in-Training working with Child Coastal and Adult Therapeutic Services (CCATS), and a PhD candidate at the University of Central Lancashire, Preston. His clinical practice focuses on the assessment and intervention of adult sexual offenders, some of whom likely operate within organized networks. He also works closely with police forces on various research projects, including his own PhD, which focuses on police officer mental health. He is a member of the British Psychological Society and Division of Forensic Psychology.

Sucharita Belavadi is an honorary Postdoctoral Fellow in the social identity lab at Claremont Graduate University. Her research has focused on the ways in which communication that flows within and between groups serves to clarify ingroup norms and shape social identity, especially when identity-uncertainty is experienced by group members. Specifically, she has examined collective victimhood rhetoric in the context of troubled intergroup relations and the implications an identity of victimhood has for intergroup relations. She recently defended her doctoral dissertation which examines the conditions that are ripe for ingroup leaders to exploit heightened identity-uncertainty and threat to ingroup high-status by employing collective victimhood rhetoric to fashion divisive, tight-knit identities.

Dr Philip Birch, B.Soc.Sci. (Hons); P.G. Cert. (HEP); P.G. Cert. (SSRM); P.G. Dip. (Soc. Sci.); MSc.; PhD, is a Senior Lecturer in Criminology in the Centre for Law and Justice at Charles Sturt University, Australia. He has previously held posts at the University of Western Sydney, the University of New South Wales, Sydney, Australia and the University of Huddersfield, in United Kingdom. Prior to entering academia he worked as a criminologist in the field holding posts in the UK prison service as well as in the crime and disorder field, which involved managing a specialist crime unit. He has published internationally, including books, book chapters, peer reviewed articles and Government reports in his main areas of research – offender management and rehabilitation; police, prisons and probation practices; gender symmetry violence with a particular focus on domestic family violence and sex work. He has secured over $830,000 in research funding and support grants, which has addressed a variety of themes within his areas of expertise. He holds an honorary research fellowship in the School of Psychology, University of Central Lancashire, UK, as well as a Senior Research Associate in the Ashworth Research Centre, Mersey Health Care, National Health Services, UK. He is also a Fellow of the Higher Education Academy. He was the co-founder and inaugural Editor-in-Chief of the *Journal of Criminological Research, Policy and Practice* (JCRPP, 2014–2017) and currently the Editor-in-Chief of *Salus: An International Journal for Law Enforcement and Public Safety* (2018–Present), he also sits on the editorial board of the *Journal of Aggression, Conflict and Peace Research.*

Laura Boulton, PhD, is a Senior Lecturer in Policing and is actively engaged in multidisciplinary research related to policing and criminal investigation. Her teaching topics include research methods using both quantitative and qualitative methods, as well as decision-making in the context of threat, risk and harm. She is the module lead in charge of policing related MSc research dissertations and she supervises doctoral students in research projects examining policing, violence and multi-agency working. Her research specialism surrounds police decision-making in various critical decision-making roles (i.e. armed policing and senior investigative roles), but she has also conducted research in other policing related fields such as organized crime, children who go missing from home, child sexual exploitation and police-public engagement. She works in collaboration with the Lancashire Constabulary's Evidence-Based Policing team, and is a member of RUSI's Strategic Hub for Organised Crime Research.

Dr Kurt Braddock (PhD, Penn State University) is an Assistant Teaching Professor of Communication Arts and Sciences and Homeland Security at Penn State University. His research focuses on the strategic communication employed by terrorist organizations for the purposes of recruitment and radicalization, as well as communicative strategies that can be employed to counter terrorist propaganda. His work has been published in several communication and security journals, including *Terrorism and Political Violence, Studies in Conflict and Terrorism, Dynamics of Asymmetric Conflict*, and *Communication Monographs*. He has also authored a book on persuasion in the context of terrorism and counter-terrorism titled *Weaponized Words: The Strategic Role of Persuasion in Violent Radicalization and Counter-Radicalization* (Cambridge University Press, 2020).

Fernanda Buril has a PhD in Political Science from Washington State University, where she specialized in Political Psychology and International Relations. Her research focuses on the links between gender, religious beliefs and extremism, and communication strategies used to motivate people into participating in violence. Currently, she works in the field of democracy and governance, designing and implementing projects to strengthen democratic institutions, combat disinformation and hate speech, and prevent and mitigate election-related violence.

Gianmarco Daniele is an applied economist with interest in political, public and development economics. His current research agenda focuses on political accountability and distortions of, and within, the political process. A central topic of his research concerns organized crime, and specifically its effects on the political arena. He works as postdoctoral researcher at Bocconi University (Milan, Italy). He previously worked at the Institut d'Economia Barcelona and at the University of Barcelona. He completed a PhD in 2015 at the Vrije Universiteit Brussel (Brussels, Belgium). He has been a visiting scholar at Universidad Autonoma de Barcelona, BI Norwegian Business School and Stanford University.

Mathieu Deflem is Professor of Sociology at the University of South Carolina. His research and teaching interests concern a variety of aspects of social control, including counter-terrorism, international police cooperation and law. His work also concerns the study of popular culture and sociological theory. He is the author of dozens of articles in journals and anthologies and has, to date, authored four books, including *The Policing of Terrorism* (Routledge, 2010), *Sociology of Law* (Cambridge, 2008) and *Policing World Society* (Oxford, 2002). He is the editor of *The Handbook of Social Control* (Wiley Blackwell, 2019).

James Densley, D.Phil (Oxford), is a Professor of Criminal Justice at Metropolitan State University, part of the Minnesota State system (USA). He has received global media attention for his research on street gangs, criminal networks, violence and policing. He is the author of two books, including the award-winning, *How Gangs Work* (Palgrave, 2013), and more than 50 peer-reviewed articles and book chapters. His writing has also featured for CNN, *The Conversation*, the *Guardian*, *HuffPost*, *USA Today*, and the *Wall Street Journal*.

John Drury is Professor of Social Psychology at the University of Sussex. He has published over 80 peer-reviewed journal articles on crowd behaviour. Some of the crowd events and campaigns he has researched include No M11 anti-roads campaign, the 2011 English riots, the London bombings of 7 July 2005, the Hillsborough disaster and the 2010 Chile earthquake. He teaches crowd psychology to the UK Fire and Rescue Service, and to crowd safety managers around the world. His research on mass emergencies has informed the training of over 2000 crowd safety managers and stewards across the UK and European football clubs. He heads the Crowds & Identities group at the University of Sussex, and is currently the editor of the *British Journal of Social Psychology*.

Rob Ewin is a Detective Sergeant and PhD candidate exploring the legislative and psychological effects of vulnerability in law enforcement responses. He has been involved with a number of successful prosecutions for serious sexual offences, supervised responses to county lines drug use and led a number of investigations for serious violence offences. He is involved with national working groups concerning witnesses and risk assessment, and is an advocate of evidence-based policing and research often operating as a practitioner-academic to seek understandings to key policing challenges.

Teresa Ferraz-da-Silva is a Forensic Psychologist and Assistant Professor in Forensic Psychology at Coventry University, UK. She worked for more than 12 years in the Portuguese prison system with young offenders. She completed a PhD in Forensic Psychology on multiple perpetrator rape (MPR). Her research in this area is ongoing and she has published papers in peer-reviewed international journals and contributed with a chapter in the first book on MPR. Her research interests include juvenile offenders and group offending.

Azar Gat is Ezer Weitzman Professor of National Security at Tel Aviv University. He is the author of nine books, including, most recently: *A History of Military Thought: From the Enlightenment to the Cold War* (Oxford, 2001); *War in Human Civilization* (Oxford, 2006), named one of the best books of the year by the Times Literary Supplement (TLS); *Victorious and Vulnerable: Why Democracy Won in the 20th Century and How it is still Imperiled* (Hoover, 2010); *Nations: The Long History and Deep Roots of Political Ethnicity and Nationalism* (Cambridge, 2013); *The Causes of War and the Spread of Peace: But Will War Rebound?* (Oxford, 2017); and *War and Strategy in the Modern World: From Blitzkrieg to Unconventional Terrorism* (Routledge, 2018). His books have been translated into Spanish, Japanese, Chinese, Korean, Greek, Turkish and Hebrew. He is the recipient of the EMET Prize for 2019, Israel's premier scholarly distinction.

Paul Gill is Professor of Security and Crime Science at University College London. He has conducted research funded by the Office for Naval Research, the Department of Homeland Security, DSTL, the European Union, the National Institute of Justice, CREST, Public Safety Canada and MINERVA. He currently manages European Research Council Starter Grant project entitled GRIEVANCE. These projects focused upon various aspects of terrorist behaviour including IED development, creativity, terrorist network structures, risk assessment and management, and lone-actor terrorism. His doctoral research focused on the underlying individual and organizational motivations behind suicide bombing. He has published in leading psychology, criminology and political science journals.

Amos Goldberg is an Associate Professor of Holocaust History at the Department of Jewish History and Contemporary Jewry at the Hebrew University of Jerusalem. He served as the

2018/19 J.B. and Maurice C. Shapiro Senior Scholar-in-Residence Fellow, at the Jack, Joseph and Morton Mandel Center for Advanced Holocaust Studies at the USHMM. He is a cultural historian whose work is interdisciplinary in nature. Part of it focuses on the history of the Jews in the Holocaust while other parts focus on Holocaust memory and historiography. Among his publications are: *Trauma in First Person: Diary Writing during the Holocaust* (Indiana University press, 2017) which was listed as an outstanding academic title for 2018 by "Choice" magazine of the Association of College and Research Libraries; and his co-edited volume, together with Bashir Bashir, *The Holocaust and the Nakba: A new Grammar of Trauma and History* (Columbia University Press, 2018).

Sören Henrich is currently working at the University of Central Lancashire (UK) as a Lecturer in Forensic Psychology. His research focuses on individuals on the fringes of prison culture: in the scope of his PhD, he is exploring the radicalization of vulnerable individuals in secure forensic settings. In his additional work at the High Security Hospital Ashworth Liverpool, he is supporting the service in the research about the assessment of transgender patients. Furthermore, he is specialized in the risk assessment and anti-aggression therapy of high-risk offenders, as well as a trained and enlisted crisis and hostage negotiator under the NHS. Previously, he has worked for several years in medium secure psychiatric settings in Germany and studied "Forensic Psychology" at the Maastricht University (NL).

Michael A. Hogg is Professor and Chair of Social Psychology at Claremont Graduate University, an Honorary Professor at the University of Kent, a former Australian Research Council Professorial Fellow and past President of the Society of Experimental Social Psychology. He received his PhD from Bristol University and is a Fellow of the Association for Psychological Science, the Society for Personality and Social Psychology, the Society of Experimental Social Psychology, the Society for the Psychological Study of Social Issues, and the Academy of the Social Sciences in Australia. His research on group processes, intergroup relations, influence and leadership, and self and identity is closely associated with the development of social identity theory. He has published extensively on these topics, and is the recipient of the Australian Psychological Society's 1989 Early Career award and the Society for Personality and Social Psychology's 2010 Carol and Ed Diener Mid-Career Award. He is Editor-in-Chief of the journal *Group Processes and Intergroup Relations*, an Associate Editor of *The Leadership Quarterly* and a former Associate Editor of the *Journal of Experimental Social Psychology*. Current research focuses on leadership and influence, uncertainty and extremism, and group fragmentation.

Dr Carol A. Ireland is a Consultant Chartered Psychologist, Forensic Psychologist and Chartered Scientist. She is a Reader in Aggression at the University of Central Lancashire and Senior Research Lead at the Ashworth Research Centre. She is also the Director of Studies for the MSc in Forensic Psychology. She holds a visiting/honorary professorship at Charles Sturt University. She currently works at the Coastal Child and Adult Therapeutic Services, working with children and adults who present with offence concerns and/or are victims. Her research interests are around aggression, including critical incident management, harmful sexual behaviour, trauma and sexual exploitation.

Professor Jane L. Ireland is a Chartered Forensic Psychologist and Chartered Scientist, holds a Professorial Chair at the University of Central Lancashire and is Violence Treatment Lead within High Secure Services, Ashworth Hospital. She holds three further (visiting/honorary) professorships at Abo Akademi University, Charles Sturt University and Cardiff Metropolitan University. She is currently academic lead for the Ashworth Research Centre.

Stuart Kirby, PhD, C. Psychol. is a Professor of Policing and Criminal Investigation at the University of Central Lancashire (UK). His academic interests surround crime reduction, investigation and organized crime, and acts as academic advisor to Her Majesties Inspector of Constabulary and National Police Chiefs Council (Crime). He has advised and presented to police agencies in the North America, China, India, UAE and Europe. Prior to academia he served with the Lancashire Constabulary, retiring as Detective Chief Superintendent in command of the HQ Crime & Operations Division. During his police career he commanded many overt and covert policing operations in relation to organized crime. He continues to act as a UK Behavioural Investigative Advisor (Offender Profiler).

Randall D. Law is Professor of History at Birmingham-Southern College in Birmingham, Alabama, where he teaches courses on modern Russian and European history and the history of terrorism. He is the author of *Terrorism: A History* (2nd ed., Polity Press, 2016) and the editor of *The Routledge History of Terrorism* (2015). His current projects are the history of white supremacist terrorism in the United States as well as terrorism, political violence and criminality in the city of Odessa in the Russian Empire in the early twentieth century. In 2009 he spent four months in Odessa as a Fulbright Research Scholar. He is frequently interviewed by national and international reporters on matters related to terrorism and Russian politics and history. He earned his PhD in Russian and European history from Georgetown University.

Dr Michael Lewis is a Chartered Psychologist, Chartered Scientist, Associate Fellow of the British Psychological Society and Lecturer in Forensic Psychology at the University of Central Lancashire, Preston. He is the Research Lead for Policing and Security at the Ashworth Research Centre, Mersey Care NHS Trust, and as part of this role collaborates with numerous police forces across the UK. His research interests include organized crime, aggression, child sexual exploitation and police wellbeing. He is the Editor-in-Chief of the *Journal of Criminological Research, Policy and Practice*, and he also sits on the editorial board for the *Journal of Aggression, Conflict and Peace Research*. He has a background in operational policing.

Neophytos Loizides is Chair in International Conflict Analysis at the University of Kent. He is the author of *The Politics of Majority Nationalism: Framing Peace, Stalemates, and Crises* (Stanford Press, 2015), *Designing Peace: Cyprus and Institutional Innovations in Divided Societies* (University of Pennsylvania Press, 2016) and *Mediating Power-Sharing* (Routledge, 2018, with Feargal Cochrane and Thibaud Bodson). He has authored more than forty academic articles and book chapters in the areas of forced displacement, nationalism and conflict regulation in deeply divided societies including most recently work published in the *European Journal of Political Research, The International Journal of Constitutional Law, Political Psychology, Ethnic and Racial Studies, and International Migration.*

Dr Anthony C. Lopez is Associate Professor of Political Psychology in the School of Politics, Philosophy and Public Affairs at Washington State University. He received his PhD from Brown University, and also received training as a research affiliate at the Center for Evolutionary Psychology, University of California, Santa Barbara. His research explores the evolutionary origins of warfare, as well as its constituent psychological dynamics, such as: revenge, the nature of deterrence, collective action problems of warfare, extremist violence, and distinctions between offensive and defensive aggression. He serves as Associate Editor of Politics with the Evolution Institute and blogs regularly at Psychology Today.

Clarissa Luttmann is an Honours student at Leiden University College, The Hague, where she pursues her studies in Governance, Economics and Development, and participates in Leiden University's Honours Academy Tackling Global Challenges. In 2018, she served as Research Assistant to Mark Tomass, Harvard University Extension School.

Zoe Marchment is a Post-doctoral Research Associate on the European Research Council-funded project GRIEVANCE, in the Department of Security and Crime Science, UCL. Her doctoral research examined the spatial decision-making of terrorist target selection, with a focus on lone actors and violent Dissident Republican activity. She holds a BSc in Psychology and MSc in Countering Organised Crime and Terrorism. She has worked on projects for the UK Defence Science and Technology Laboratory; Centre for Research and Evidence on Security Threats (CREST); FP7 Preventing, Interdicting and Mitigating Extremism (PRIME), MINERVA and the VOX-Pol Network of Excellence.

David Marshall is a serving UK Senior Police Officer. He has performed a number of uniformed and specialist roles as a Constable and Sergeant, operating in various geographic areas of the UK both in frontline operations and within the Crime Management Department. Promotion to Inspector saw him head up force operations in Edinburgh, Scotland during which time he was heavily involved in the policing of the G8 summit in 2005. As an inspector he also served as staff officer to the Assistant Chief Constable.

Promotion to Chief Inspector saw David assume responsibility for territorial operations and in that rank held command roles within Operational Support and Protective Services. He also served as the lead for Professional Standards. As Superintendent, he is head of divisional operations with overall responsibility for territorial policing, operational support, and crime and intelligence. He is an experienced senior leader, is a member of the Chartered Management Institute, and is an accredited College of Policing Gold and Silver Public Order Commander. He has a strong background in the planning and delivery of large scale events, as well as leading the response to spontaneous operations including terrorism incidents.

David holds a Foundation Degree in Arts in Policing, a Bachelor of Science in Crime and Criminology, and a Masters in Criminology and Criminal Psychology. He is an occasional guest lecturer in Criminology, and part-time Associate Tutor with the University of Essex Online where he teaches on the Criminology and Criminal Psychology course.

Marco Le Moglie is an applied economist primarily interested in organized crime, political economy and more in general policy evaluation. His current research focuses on mafia investments in the legal economy, the effect of organized criminal violence on society, as well as corruption and its impact on people's attitudes and beliefs. He received his PhD in Economics at the University of Turin in 2016 and works as a postdoctoral researcher at Bocconi University (Milan, Italy).

John Mwangi Githigaro is a Lecturer in Peace and Conflict Studies at the St Paul's University, Limuru (Kenya). He holds a PhD in International Relations from the United States International University Africa (USIU-A) Nairobi, Kenya. His research interests revolve around peace and security studies, refugee studies, and media portrayals of terrorism with a specific focus on the Horn of Africa. He was a Nextgen Social Science Research Council New York (SSRC) Fellow (2016–2019). He is currently a Co-investigator on a project titled "Examining Interpretations of Civic National Values: Advancing Shared Communications Through the Voices and Actions of Children in Post-Conflict Settings", which is an intercontinental comparative project involving researchers from the UK, Kenya and Nepal (March–September 2019).

Fergus Neville is a Lecturer in Organisational Studies at the University of St Andrews. His research is broadly focused on group processes and their pro-social and anti-social consequences. His research covers a range of phenomena which are central to understandings of groups and organizations, including leadership and influence, normative processes, social support and toxic behaviour in groups. Much of this research has been conducted within crowd contexts which represent a uniquely rich site in which to study processes of identity, organization, leadership and conflict.

Rebecca Phythian, PhD, is a Lecturer in Policing and Criminal Investigation at the University of Central Lancashire, teaching on research methods (quantitative and qualitative) and Criminal Justice to postgraduate students. She supervises MSc, PhD and Professional Doctorate students on topics including vulnerability, multi-agency working and female offenders, and is deputy chair for the School's Research and Innovation committee. She is a member of the Royal United Services Institute's (RUSI) Strategic Hub for Organised Crime Research, holds "Accredited Researcher" status with the Office for National Statistics and is actively involved in UCLan's Institute of Citizenship, Society and Change, and Criminal Justice Partnership. She continues to work in collaboration with many UK police forces and organizations. Her research interests include violent offenders, criminal exploitation and organized crime.

Dr Mohammed Rahman is a Senior Lecturer in the School of Social Sciences, Nottingham Trent University. His academic work concerns serious crimes, especially organized crime and gangs. His doctoral research required him to ethnographically investigate the nature, extent and meaning of fatal violence within various West Midlands, England, based organized crime groups. As a criminologist, he has used his teaching and research experiences to inform the public and international press about crime, harm and crime control. His book entitled: *Homicide and Organised Crime: Ethnographic Narratives of Violence in the Criminal Underworld*, is due to be published in 2019 with Palgrave Macmillan.

Stephen Reicher is Wardlaw Professor of Psychology at the University of St Andrews. He is a Fellow of the British Academy, a Fellow of the Royal Society of Edinburgh and a Fellow of the Academy of Social Sciences. His work is broadly in the area of social identity and group processes. He has written some 300 books, book chapters and journal articles covering such topics as crowd behaviour, collective action, collective solidarity and helping, leadership and political rhetoric, nationalism, intergroup hatred, the psychology of tyranny and obedience. Two constant themes that run through this work are (a) the way that groups provide power to powerless that allows them to achieve social change, and hence (b) the need to challenge the pervasive anti-collectivism in psychology.

Dr Shannon E. Reid is an Associate Professor in the Department of Criminal Justice and Criminology at the University of North Carolina at Charlotte. She received her PhD in Criminology, Law, and Society from the University of California, Irvine in 2013. Her research interests are focused on street gangs, youth and adults in the correctional system, and the integration of technology into policing. She is currently the Principal Investigator grant funded by the Office of Juvenile Justice and Delinquency Prevention (OJJDP) evaluating trauma-informed care for youth in community corrections. She is also a Co-PI on a National Science Foundation funded grant that is developing AI based video analytics to alert for suspicious parking lot behaviour for police deployment. Her work has been published in *Criminology*, the *Journal of Interpersonal Violence, Homicide Studies, Journal of Youth Studies, Legal and Criminal Psychology*, and *Deviant Behavior*. Her research has also received coverage in mainstream media outlets such as *National Public Radio, The Conversation, The Washington Post's The Monkey Cage* and *The Crime Report*.

Dr Imogen Richards is a Lecturer in Criminology and a member of the Alfred Deakin Institute at Deakin University. She specializes in the areas of surveillance, social media and counter/terrorism, and has published on issues related to online extremism, with a focus on comparative and cross-disciplinary approaches to online criminological research. Her work has appeared in the *International Journal of Cyber Criminology, Studies in Conflict and Terrorism, Critical Studies on Terrorism*, among others. Her wider research interests include the performance of security, theories of violence, and drugs and crime.

Mark J. Rinella is a doctoral student in the Basic and Applied Social Psychology program at Claremont Graduate University, where he previously received his MA. He is a current member and former manager of the Social Identity Research Lab at CGU. His research has included topics such as intergroup negotiation, shared realities and group fragmentation. His current research focuses on the derogation versus acceptance of group deviants. He has worked as a Lecturer at California State University, Dominguez Hills, and he is currently a Lecturer at California State University, Los Angeles.

Moritz Schuberth, for the past two years, has been working as Monitoring, Evaluation and Research Manager for the global humanitarian agency Mercy Corps in the eastern Democratic Republic of the Congo. Prior to this he has worked at the European Commission, the German Federal Foreign Office and the German Federal Office for Migration and Refugees. He completed his PhD in Peace Studies at the University of Bradford and consults the US Institute of Peace on the engagement of community-based armed groups. His research focuses on peacekeeping, non-state armed groups, security governance and urban violence. He is the author of recent articles in *Africa Spectrum*; the *Journal of Eastern African Studies, Conflict, Security & Development*; the *Journal of Peacebuilding and Development*; *Contemporary Security Policy*; *Stability: International Journal of Security and Development*; *International Peacekeeping*; and *Environment and Urbanization*.

Aaron Sell received his PhD in developmental and evolutionary psychology from the prestigious Center for Evolutionary Psychology at the University of California, Santa Barbara. His dissertation introduced the "recalibrational theory of anger", an evolutionary-computational model informed by models of animal conflict, game theory, criminology and anthropological cross-cultural reports of human conflict. His research focuses on human conflict including anger, aggressive facial expressions, formidability assessment, anger-based arguments and the importance of upper body strength as a psychological predictor in males. He uses multiple methodologies including classical psychological experiments, correlational studies, cross-cultural surveys, voice analyses, FACS coding and vignette studies. He is currently an Assistant Professor at Heidelberg University in the Department of Psychology and Criminal Justice, and an Adjunct Research Fellow in the School of Criminology at Griffith University.

Dr Djordje (George) Stefanovic is a Senior Lecturer at Department of Sociology, Criminology and Gender Studies, the University of Adelaide, Australia. He is a political sociologist who uses quantitative and historical methods to study ethnic conflict. His current research focuses on the post-war refugee returns and on the drivers of anti-minority sentiments. His research was published in *Ethnic and Racial Studies, International Migration, Journal of Refugee Studies, Human Rights Quarterly, Political Psychology, Europe-Asia Studies, Ethnopolitics*, and *European History Quarterly*. His research projects were supported by Social Sciences and Humanities Research Council of Canada; European Institutes for Advanced Study; Nuffield College, the University of Oxford; European Commission; the Faculty of Graduate Studies and Research, Saint Mary's University; and the Faculty Research Active Grants Scheme, the University of Adelaide.

Clifford Stott is Professor of Social Psychology and Dean for Research in the Faculty of Natural Sciences at Keele University. He is also Director of the Keele Policing Academic Collaboration, a Research Centre at Keele University designed to facilitate knowledge co-production and research impact. His research is primarily criminological and focuses on crowds, psychology and policing. He draws extensively upon the Social Identity Approach and Procedural Justice Theory as explanatory models to understand police citizen encounters across a range of contexts and seeks to utilize his research to drive progressive police reforms. He is predominantly a qualitative researcher who utilizes ethnographic and participant action research frameworks.

Mark Tomass is Instructor at Harvard University Extension School, specializing in using economic methodology for understanding monetary and financial crises, the working of economic systems, and violent group conflicts in the Middle East. His book *The Religious Roots of the Syrian Conflict: Remaking the Fertile Crescent* (2016) formulates economic concepts to outline mechanisms by which conflicts of secular nature often mutate into conflicts among religious groups. In his edited book on *Assessing the War on Terror: Western and Middle Eastern Perspectives*, he pairs his background as an expert in both international economics and Middle Eastern history with his personal upbringing in Aleppo, Syria to add unique value and deliver an unspoken voice to the vital study of counter-terrorism. He brings a pragmatic approach to the study, centred on deep-seated historic analysis critical in confronting the ongoing battle of international terrorism.

Dr Matthew Valasik is an Assistant Professor in the Department of Sociology at Louisiana State University. His research interests include the socio-spatial dynamics of gang behaviour (i.e. territoriality, group cohesion and violence), including comparing and contrasting the attributes of street gangs with other deviant groups (i.e. ISIS, Skinheads, Alt-Right, White Power Groups), and problem-oriented policing strategies (e.g. gang units, civil gang injunctions) used by law enforcement. His work has appeared in *Journal of Criminal Justice, Social Science Research, Homicide Studies, Theoretical Criminology, Journal of Youth Studies, Crime & Delinquency, Journal of Interpersonal Violence, Deviant Behavior, Statistics and Public Policy, Journal of Criminological Research, Policy and Practice, Oxford Bibliographies Online: Criminology*, and *The Oxford Handbook of Environmental Criminology*. His research has received coverage in mainstream media outlets such as *The Conversation, The Washington Post's The Monkey Cage* and *The Crime Report*.

Dr Mark Wood is a Lecturer in Criminology at the University of Melbourne, Australia. Most of his research falls within the field of digital criminology, and investigates how digital technologies shape the ways crime is experienced, understood and responded to. His first book, *Antisocial Media: Crime-watching in the Internet Age*, was published by Palgrave Macmillan (2017) in the publisher's Palgrave Studies in Crime, Media and Culture series. His work has been published in *Theoretical Criminology, Surveillance and Society, Crime Media Culture, The International Journal of Cyber Criminology, The International Journal for Crime, Justice and Social Democracy*, and *Feminist Media Studies*.

FOREWORD

Collective violence – the main question

Azar Gat

The use of violence in human relations – individual and collective – has constituted a puzzle throughout human history, and even more so in modern times. Much of the confusion during the past century is traced to the following: people habitually assume that if widespread deadly violence has always been with us, it must be a primary, "irresistible" biological drive that is nearly impossible to suppress. Many find in this conclusion reason enough to object to the idea that human fighting is as old as our species while others regard it as compelling evidence that war is inevitable. Both sides are wrong. Contrary to fashionable 1960s' notions, traced back to Freud's latter-day theorizing about a death drive or instinct, *Thanatos*, violence is not a primary drive that requires release, like hunger or sex. The Swiss or Swedes, to use the cliché, who have not fought for two centuries, show no special signs of deprivation on this account. But try to deny them food for more than a few hours or sex for more than a few days, and their reaction would be quite predictable.[1]

On the other hand, the fact that violence is not a primary drive does not mean that we are not hardwired for it. Studies on "warless" prestate societies usually intend to prove that, neither primordial nor natural to humankind, warfare was probably a late – and in any case, wholly contingent – cultural phenomenon. Margaret Mead's framing of the problem in her 1940 essay "Warfare is Only an Invention – Not a Biological Necessity" is the mother of all mistakes.[2] It expresses the widespread assumption that violence must be either a primary drive or entirely learned, whereas in reality its potential is deeply ingrained in us as a means or tool, ever ready to be employed. People can cooperate, compete peacefully, or use violence to achieve their objectives, depending on what they believe will serve them best in any given circumstance. In cooperation, the parties combine efforts, in principle because the synergic outcome of their efforts divided among them promises greater benefit to each of them than their independent efforts might. In competition, each party strives to outdo the other in order to obtain a desired good by employing whatever means it has at its disposal, except direct action against the other. Competition runs parallel. By contrast, in a conflict, direct action against the competitor is taken in order to eliminate it or lessen its ability to engage in the competition. If physical injury is inflicted, then a conflict becomes a violent one.

Cooperation, competition, and conflict are the three fundamental forms of social interaction. People have always had all three options to choose from, and they have always assessed the situation to decide which option, or combination of them, seemed the most promising. People are well equipped biologically for pursuing any of the above behavioural strategies, with conflict being only one tool, albeit a major one – the hammer – in our diverse behavioural tool kit. Furthermore, *Homo sapiens* is a social species whose local and regional groups – universally and uniquely bound together by ties of both kinship and shared cultural codes, including language and customs – cooperate within themselves in a variety of group activities. The latter include fighting, which is pursued for the attainment of collective goods – above all, hunting territory and other scarce sources of food.

Thus, neither a late invention nor a compulsive inevitability independent of conditions, group fighting is part of our evolution-shaped behavioural menu. It is in this sense that *both* war *and* peace are "in our genes", which accounts for their widely fluctuating prevalence in different sociohistorical contexts. As the "Seville Statement on Violence" (1986), issued by an international group of scientists under the auspices of the United Nations Educational, Scientific and Cultural Organization (UNESCO), rightly put it in rejection of the view that human biology makes violence and war inescapable, "There is nothing in our neurophysiology that compels us to react violently … We conclude that biology does not condemn humanity to war." However, the statement fell into the opposite fallacy, proclaiming that warfare "is a product of culture" and solemnly prescribing that "IT IS SCIENTIFICALLY INCORRECT to say that war or any other violent behaviour is genetically programmed into our human nature" (emphasis in the original). The statement carelessly concludes that "violence is neither in our evolutionary legacy nor in our genes."[3]

In reality, the potential for *both* war *and* peace is embedded in us. Although activated interchangeably and conjointly in response to the overall environmental and sociocultural conditions, all three behavioural strategies – violent conflict, peaceful competition, and cooperation – are not *purely* learned cultural forms. This naïve nature/nurture dichotomy overlooks the heavy and complex biological machinery that is necessary for the working of each of these behavioural strategies and the interplay among them. Certainly, these deep, evolution-shaped patterns are variably calibrated to particular conditions through social learning. However, the reason they are all there, very close under our skin and readily activated, is that they were very handy during our long evolutionary history. They all proved highly useful and advantageous, thereby becoming part and parcel of our biological equipment.

Wars have been fought for the attainment of the same objects of human desire that underlie the human motivational system in general – *only by violent means*, through the use of force. Politics – domestic and international – is the activity intended to achieve these evolution-shaped human desires at the intra- and interstate levels. It is also not true that all sides in a war lose, that they are "tragically" caught in some sort of a prisoner's dilemma. Although all sorts of prisoner's dilemmas are found in conflict situations, throughout human history there have been many winners and losers in war.

On the other hand, and here I take issue with Steven Pinker's *The Better Angels of Our Nature*,[4] with which I am otherwise in much agreement, particular human quests such as dominance or ideology are not "demons" with which the blame for war rests. Dominance or ideology, no less than the desire for love and sex, can just as well be counted on the side of the "angels" when pursued by peaceful means and for peaceful ends. Furthermore, the distinctions that Pinker draws between different categories of violence, respectively related to the above "demons", are also questionable. He cites studies showing that separate parts of the brain may trigger violent behaviour, which is true of nearly all behaviours. But this does not mean that all violent behaviours are not subject to, and regulated by, a unified evolutionary calculus originally designed to advance survival and reproduction.

The "problem" of war is not these or other human desires – desires that make us what we are, that are the stuff of life. Rather, violence and war occur when the conflictual behavioural strategy is judged to be more promising than peaceful competition and cooperation for attaining objects of human desire. *Both* our basic desires *and* the conditions that channel the efforts to fulfil them to the conflictual path are necessary for understanding why war occurs. Thus, state authority and coercion have tilted the menu of human behavioural strategies in the direction of the peaceful options in the domestic arena. Furthermore, changing economic, social, and political conditions are generating a similar effect in the international arena, most notably where a modern liberal economic and political order prevails and peaceful behavioural options become that much more rewarding than the violent option. Contrary to a prevailing opinion, wars have not become more lethal and costly under modern conditions (relative to population and wealth); it is peace that has become more rewarding. For this reason, both intrastate (civil) and interstate wars have disappeared completely within the affluent parts of the world: North America, Western Europe, Oceania, and the most developed parts of East Asia (Japan, South Korea, Taiwan). War survives only in the less developed parts of the world. Will they follow the peaceful parts as they modernize is one of the big questions of the twenty-first century. Even if they do, the threat of mass killing in the form of unconventional terrorism remains, potentially carried out by zealots who might find this an effective means to pursue their ends.

Notes

1 Azar Gat, *War in Human Civilization* (Oxford: Oxford University Press, 2006); Azar Gat, *The Causes of War and the Spread of Peace: But will War Rebound* (Oxford: Oxford University Press, 2017).
2 Margaret Mead, "Warfare is Only an Invention – Not a Biological Necessity," *Asia* 40, no. 8 (August 1940): 402–405.
3 "The Seville Statement" (Paris: UNESCO, 1986), www.unesco.org/cpp/uk/declarations/seville.pdf.
4 Steven Pinker, *The Better Angels of Our Nature: Why Violence Has Declined* (New York: Viking, 2011).

PART I

Understanding war

1
THE EVOLUTION OF WARFARE

Anthony C. Lopez

Introduction

The evolution and history of warfare has been investigated by philosophers, historians, practitioners, social scientists and life scientists. Common questions in this endeavour are: How far back into human evolution and history do we find evidence of warfare? How frequent was warfare in any given historical period? And how lethal was warfare? In short, scholarship on the evolution and history of warfare has focused on questions of origins, frequency, and intensity.

Despite the fact that scientific interest in these questions is perhaps broader and more methodologically sophisticated than ever, consensus on these questions remains elusive for at least two reasons. First, the archaeological record of warfare is incomplete. Second, we do not agree on what warfare is or how to unambiguously distinguish it from other forms of violence. Beyond an agreement that warfare is something more than violence between two individuals, there is little consensus on the proper scope of our main unit of analysis.

Given these hurdles, it would seem that an investigation into the evolutionary origins of human warfare is destined merely to perpetuate academic stalemates, in which old arguments are continuously repackaged with each new discovery of a mass grave or 'peaceful' society. Although this is a rather pessimistic view, I establish it at the forefront of this chapter since my argument will be that these hurdles (e.g. knowledge of ancestral phenomena and consensus on definitions) are not insurmountable. Entire disciplines thrive on their ability to successfully infer and model the unobserved past based on imperfect historical, geological and archaeological evidence. And the question of definitions must be placed in its proper scope – as a methodological, rather than ontological, consideration.

Again, most evolutionary approaches to warfare have focused on its ancestral or historical frequency and intensity, and although this has generated useful discussion, it is also incomplete. One of the core dynamics of the evolutionary process is natural selection, which is the only force known to organise biological design – that is; natural selection builds adaptations. Given that biological adaptations are solutions to recurrent and reproductively significant problems in an organism's environment, these adaptations themselves convey some information about the environment in which they evolved. In other words, the form and function of adaptations contains information about the (socio)ecology in which they were built. Therefore, if there is an argument to be made about the ancestral frequency and intensity of warfare, we should expect that the form and function of our evolved psychology should reflect the ancestral existence of such challenges. This is a way of saying that if warfare was evolutionarily recurrent and reproductively significant for our ancestors, evidence of this fact lies in our very brains.

An evolutionary approach to behaviour investigates the link between ancestral selection pressures and psychological design. In general, we are asking: what were the evolutionarily recurrent and reproductively significant challenges that confronted our ancestors, and how – if at all – has natural selection shaped the human phenotype, and specifically human nervous systems, to deal with these challenges? Given this perspective, the relevant questions for scholars of warfare are: (1) what ancestral selection pressures might have favoured the emergence of a psychology capable of intergroup violence, and (2) how specifically is that psychology designed to shape reasoning, motivation and behaviour in contexts of intergroup violence, such as warfare?

From this perspective, we immediately err if we begin by asking: what is warfare? Instead, we must begin by investigating the socio-ecology of ancestral landscapes based on known and inferred data about such environments. From this, we gain a reasonable estimation of the character of ancestral intergroup violence. If there are psychological adaptations that operate in modern contexts of intergroup violence then they were shaped in response to these ancestral forms. Whether we call those forms "war", "violence", "feuds", or "ritualised contests", is entirely irrelevant.

There is growing evidence the human brain possesses the psychological tools of intergroup violence. This evolved psychology is laden with adaptively contextual triggers and moderators, and it also sits alongside other evolved systems, such as systems that regulate sharing, cooperation and forgiveness, which are largely outside this scope of this discussion. However, if there is any one lesson that the evolutionary sciences have revealed regarding human behaviour, it is that human nature is a complex motivational web of competing desires and interests. We are no more rabidly aggressive than we are blindly altruistic. Our evolved psychology is material, knowable, and highly contextual.

In this chapter, I outline a case for the evolutionary origins of warfare. First, I begin by briefly reviewing several definitions of war in order to make the case that such definitions should be seen as methodological tools, rather than as ontological claims. In this section, I also compare arguments for a long versus short chronology of warfare, concluding that although the evidence is inconclusive overall, a long chronology of warfare cannot be dismissed, and we are justified in more rigorously exploring ancestral selection pressures for intergroup aggression. Second, I therefore evaluate the evidence for ancestral selection pressures that may have favoured the emergence of an evolved psychology of intergroup violence, and I sketch some of the general features of these evolved systems. Third, and to briefly conclude, I explain that although humans seem to possess the psychological tools of intergroup violence, the form of this violence has changed both quantitatively and qualitatively over history. Thus, it may be useful to distinguish between the *evolution of coalitional aggression* and the *historical emergence of warfare*. This distinction is meant to acknowledge two points: first, that modern complex warfare can indeed be very different from the behavioural patterns that prevailed in ancestral environments, and second, that as different as it is, modern warfare nevertheless remains influenced and shaped by our evolved psychology of coalitional aggression.

Definitions of war and its chronology

Scholars who study group-based violence among a range of pre-state people (i.e. forager, hunter-gatherer, farmer, etc.) tend to define war more broadly than scholars of international relations, which should come as no surprise (Lopez and Johnson, 2017). Yet, unlike scholars of modern international war, in which there is some consensus on measuring war (Gleditsch *et al.*, 2002; Sarkees and Wayman, 2010; Maoz *et al.*, 2019), the study of simple or "primitive" war is fraught with raucous disagreement on definitions and core concepts. Anthropologists and archaeologists who believe that war is relatively recent claim that their opponents' definitions of war are hopelessly all-encompassing, while those who see warfare as evolutionarily old claim that their opponents have simply defined war out of the ancestral record. What has emerged is a debate between two positions that Allen (2014) describes as a long chronology of war and a short chronology of war.

Short chronology of war

The short chronology can be summarised as follows: warfare is the cultural product of material necessity made possible by social complexity. It is a *cultural* product because it was invented, not inherited. It is the product of *material necessity* because it was not until historical developments relating to agriculture and sedentarism that the need to protect and the ability to seize resources became relevant. Finally, it was made possible as societies developed well-articulated *social complexity*, in the form of institutions such as political command and military organisation that made the practice of warfare available for the first time as an instrument of intergroup competition, or simply, "statecraft" (Ferguson, 1997; Otterbein, 2004; Kelly, 2005).

Advocates of the short chronology point to the fact that fossilised evidence of the weapons of war exists at most no earlier than about 40,000 years ago, and evidence of fortifications indicative of a need for defence against out-group aggression is even more recent. Furthermore, modern groups whose lifestyle and ecology are proposed to mirror those of our evolutionary ancestors are argued to be relatively peaceful and mostly egalitarian (Fry and Söderberg, 2013). In part because of this, advocates of the short chronology reject the comparison of humans to chimpanzees and instead suggest that the relatively peaceful bonobo is the more instructive comparison species (Fry, 2007).

How do proponents of the short chronology define war? Following Prosterman (1972, p. 140), Douglas Fry (2007), a leading example, defines warfare as:

> A group activity, carried on by members of one community against members of another community, in which it is the primary purpose to inflict serious injury or death on multiple nonspecified members of that other community, or in which the primary purpose makes it highly likely that serious injury or death will be inflicted on multiple nonspecified members of that community in the accomplishment of that primary purpose.

This definition seems fairly broad at first, but Fry and others (Fry, 2013) are quick to argue that when violence occurs between kin groups it should not be considered warfare, but rather should be called either homicide or feuding. Fry's review of the anthropological literature concludes that simple foragers exhibit high rates of homicide, moderate feuding, and little or no warfare. In sum, scholars of the short chronology date the origins of warfare to no earlier than that indicated in the fossil record, and see most forms of violence between groups as either kin-based (and thus feuds) or revenge attacks and raids that target single individuals (and thus homicide). If our ancestors engaged in anything close to warfare, it was extremely rare and of insufficient frequency to result in selection for biological adaptations for warfare (Ferguson, 1997; Otterbein, 2004; Fry, 2007, 2013; Fry and Söderberg, 2013).

Long chronology of war

In contrast to this position, proponents of a long chronology argue that warfare existed prior to the availability of military and social instruments to prosecute it. Warfare is a *behavioural* pattern of violence between groups, and does not depend on *how* (e.g. with fists; with weapons; with armies) or *why* you are fighting (e.g. for women; for territory; for revenge). The long chronology argues that pre-state and forager warfare was commonplace and lethal, rendering claims of the "peaceful savage" empirically false (Ember and Ember, 1992; Keeley, 1996; LeBlanc and Register, 2003; Otterbein, 2004). One common definition of warfare in this tradition is provided by Ember and Ember (1992, p. 172):

> Warfare is defined as socially organized armed combat between members of different territorial units (communities or aggregates of communities). In the ethnographic record, such combat usually involves groups on both sides, but a warfare event could involve the ambush of a single person of an enemy or group. Thus, the phrase "socially organized" means that there is a group of combatants on at least one of the sides.

In keeping with this broader perspective on warfare, Mark Allen and Terry Jones, following archaeologist Steven A. LeBlanc, define warfare as "socially sanctioned lethal conflict between independent polities", and acknowledge that "nearly any other definition would ... drive us quickly (and incorrectly) to a conclusion that hunter-gatherers did not engage in war" (Allen and Jones, 2014, p. 354). This definition is also close to Wrangham and Glowacki (2012) and the economist Sam Bowles (2009), who define warfare as "relationships in which coalitions of members of a group seek to inflict bodily harm on one or more members of another group" (Wrangham and Glowacki, 2012, p. 8).

Some in this camp argue that not only does intergroup violence precede its material instruments, it can also be traced back to our common ancestor with chimpanzees several million years ago (Pinker, 2011; Tooby and Cosmides, 1988; Wrangham, 1999; Wrangham and Peterson, 1996). Although the comparison with chimpanzees is imperfect (Wrangham and Glowacki, 2012), the similarities are striking and suggest that evolutionary analysis provides an additional line of inquiry for thinking about the origins of human warfare.

This brief juxtaposition of the long versus short chronology reveals that there are two major nodes of contention regarding the evolution of warfare. First is our ability to date the emergence of warfare with reference to direct fossilised evidence of its occurrence. Second is our ability to infer ancestral behaviour based on comparisons with non-human primates and modern-day simple forager groups. Both nodes of contention are worth elaborating in some detail.

The fossil trail

The problem can be put simply: if warfare is defined in terms of war-related instruments and impacts that fossilise, then the beginning of the fossil trail signals the origins of the phenomenon itself. In other words, the emergence of warfare dates to the earliest direct evidence of instruments and impacts. However, if warfare is not defined in terms of things that fossilise, then the archaeological record can reveal only instances of warfare that *happened* to involve those things that fossilise. In short, one's interpretation of the archaeological record as a reference to the origins of warfare is fully dependent on how one defines warfare. Although some behavioural patterns may leave unique archaeological traces in which there is a unique or singular interpretation, the case of intergroup violence is not so clear. For example, in the case of fossilised bone damage from weapon impacts, it is often difficult to distinguish between violence that is: accidental versus intentional; individual versus coalitional; and within versus between groups. Thus, Allen and Jones (2014, p. 354) complain that, "...the persistent problem with bioarchaeological evidence is that it can never be unequivocally attributed to warfare". This in part explains the preference of advocates of the long chronology to adopt a definition of warfare that does not hinge on its instruments, though this preference is perhaps better understood as a principled wariness of conflating the instruments of war with its behavioural occurrence (Lopez, 2016b). As LeBlanc and Register (2003) wryly notes: "The world was hardly peaceful until someone in China or Mesopotamia hammered out the first bronze sword."

Defining war in terms of instruments invariably leads one to conclude a shorter chronology of war. However, in isolation, this criticism is somewhat unfair because advocates of the short chronology do not define warfare exclusively with reference to weapons and forts, but also with respect to the ways in which groups are involved in the fighting. Thus, both short and long chronology scholars also rightly focus on comparisons with modern forager groups that are thought to mirror the socio-ecology in which humans evolved in order to infer whether our ancestors were likely to have engaged in warfare as well.

Modern windows into antiquity

The archaeological record provides useful data for examining the occurrence of warfare as early as the Holocene (~12,000 years ago – present), but is at best incomplete and is often subject to multiple interpretations. Furthermore, the long chronology of warfare presumes that even if it left no fossilised evidence, warfare at least in principle could have occurred earlier than the Holocene, into the Pleistocene (~2.5 million years ago to ~12,000 years ago), and can also be traced at least to a common ancestor with chimpanzees (Wrangham and Peterson, 1996). However, evaluation of this claim requires some method for inferring behavioural patterns aside from or at least in addition to paleo-archaeology. Generally, this is accomplished with comparisons to non-human primates – particularly, but not exclusively, chimpanzees – as well as inferences based on the modern ethnographic record.

Comparisons with non-human primates suggest that human forms of intergroup violence – particularly raiding – closely approximate the chimpanzee model (Wrangham and Peterson, 1996). However, relative to the chimpanzee model, human intergroup relations simultaneously entail greater risk-taking in violence and also broad cooperation, ranging from deadly battles and revenge killing to relationships of intergroup trade and alliance (Wrangham and Glowacki, 2012). Taken together, this in part suggests that an evolutionary biological explanation for human warfare should be complemented with cultural evolutionary dynamics that may help to explain the incentive structures that facilitate risky violence and intergroup alliance in humans (Glowacki and Wrangham, 2013; Glowacki *et al.*, 2017).

In addition to comparisons with non-human primates, scholars turn to the ethnographic record as a guide for inferring the ancestral prevalence of human intergroup violence. This line of inquiry proceeds in three steps. First, of course, one must define warfare. Second, one must identify which modern-day societies best approximate the lives and environments of our ancestors. Third, cross-cultural analysis can then reveal how prevalent intergroup violence is in these modern-day societies, which can then be used as an approximation of the nature and prevalence of intergroup violence in ancestral environments.

Definitions of war, some of which are described here, vary along three prominent dimensions: (1) the *targets* of violence; (2) the *scale and complexity* of violence; and (3) the *motives* of violence. The answers to these questions again reflect the long versus short chronology of war. Scholars of the short chronology (Kelly, 2000; Fry and Söderberg, 2013) argue that for an instance of group violence to count as warfare, it must target multiple individuals (e.g. most raids are not war), should occur between kin groups (otherwise it is labelled a "feud"), and should implicate the out-group as a community rather than targeted attacks on particular individuals. Kelly (2000) is even more conservative in his requirement that "true war" must involve not only collective liability but also a clearly established grievance. In this sense, Kelly implicitly argues that warfare cannot be merely opportunistic. In contrast, long chronology scholars allow warfare to target individuals, to occur within kin groups, and do not require that warfare must demonstrate a particular motive or set of motives (Ember and Ember, 1992; LeBlanc and Register, 2003; Gat, 2006; Allen and Jones, 2014; Lopez, 2016b; Glowacki *et al.*, 2017; Hames, 2019).

There is some disagreement as well in determining which modern groups most closely resemble their ancestral analogues and have been free from interaction with more complex societies. Such "contaminating" interactions could range from encroachment by sedentary farmer neighbours to outright imperial conquest (Ferguson and Whitehead, 1992). Such interactions fundamentally alter the calculus and prevalence of warfare in otherwise "primitive" societies, such that they would no longer be reliable proxies for ancestral groups. In attempting to identify such groups, anthropologists often turn to the Standard Cross-Cultural Sample (SCCS), which consists of 186 societies, and filter out the societies that do not fulfil the researcher's selection criteria (Murdock and White, 1969). Generally, the societies that are most likely to resemble our Pleistocene ancestors should be residentially mobile, relatively small in size, mostly egalitarian, and depend largely on resources that are not domesticated (Murdock and White, 1969; Hames, 2019). These general criteria are relatively uncontroversial. However, because such societies are increasingly rare, analysis often focuses on only a few dozen societies at most. Fry and Söderberg (2013) for example, examine 21 societies drawn from the SCCS, and, as indicated above, conclude that warfare is rare at best.

The anthropologist Richard Hames (2019) provides an in-depth evaluation of Fry and Söderberg (2013). Although scope limits a full review of Hames' valuable critiques, several are worth pointing out. First, Hames argues that Fry and Söderberg apply problematic selection criteria that lead to the inclusion of societies with "little detail on violence and conflict resolution", and also record incidents of violence "that are clearly a post-contact phenomena" – in other words, societies that have been exposed to impacts from more complex societies. Second, Hames points out that Fry and Söderberg report "lethal events" but do not report more fine-grained data that would be relevant for an evolutionary analysis, such as "deaths per 100,000, per year or proportion of causes of deaths as a consequence of violence". As Hames shows in a re-analysis of the data, "death counts from warfare and within-group homicides were nearly equal in terms of total killed".

Notwithstanding disputes about whether the sample of mobile forager bands includes or excludes groups that it should not – a significant criticism given the relatively small sample available – we again see that long versus short chronology proponents can often come to very different conclusions about the prevalence of warfare even though for the most part they are examining the exact same data (Fry and Söderberg, 2013; Hames, 2019). As constructed, this debate cannot be resolved because definitional criteria are so central to the interpretation of data, and there is no way, a priori, to establish what warfare objectively is or should be. Advocates of a short chronology are as justified in defining warfare conservatively as advocates of a long chronology are in defining it broadly. Furthermore, and perhaps more to the point, even short chronology proponents are willing to acknowledge that forms of intergroup violence such as raids and revenge killings do occur among modern forager groups and probably also occurred among ancestral human groups; however, they simply prefer not to call these things "warfare" (Fry, 2013). Again, there is no objective criteria for establishing whether this definitional preference is intrinsically valid; it is simply – or at least, should be seen as – a methodological preference.

In a sense, the short chronology is the easier and clearer approach to studying warfare, given its reliance on direct fossilised evidence and intuitive definitions of war that stress arguably popular notions of organisation, complexity and intention. The challenge for the long chronology is to defend the claim that what we "see" in the fossil record is merely a more recent manifestation of a much older behavioural pattern; i.e. that we have been fighting in groups for potentially millions of years, and only relatively recently in history did we take advantage of materials that left fossilised signatures in their wake. Given the mobile small-scale structure of ancestral human groups (but see Bird *et al.*, 2019), if any form of intergroup violence existed among them, it would necessarily be limited by this scale and complexity.

A reconciliation between both camps is possible and should begin by asking: if violence between groups existed in the Pleistocene, what were its likely forms and attributes? The goal is to establish what patterns could plausibly have existed, and to determine whether such patterns would have represented a selection pressure that could have shaped our species' psychology. If we can identify patterns of intergroup violence that could plausibly be said to represent ancestral selection pressures, then the next question is to ask: how is our psychology designed to shape reasoning, motivation and behaviour in these contexts? Finally, we can investigate the ways in which that evolved psychology would have interacted with important historical developments such as agriculture and sedentarism to produce increasingly modern variants of older patterns of motivation and behaviour. All of this is possible without any agreement on how to define "warfare".

The evolution of coalitional aggression

What are the conditions under which natural selection could have favoured a conditional propensity to engage in coalitional aggression? Given the definitional ambiguity surrounding warfare, I begin by examining two prominent forms of intergroup violence that are nearly unanimously agreed to occur and be very distinct: raids and battles. As noted above, raids may not qualify as warfare to some, but even if one prefers not to label them warfare, a psychology designed for raiding likely plays a prominent role in reasoning about warfare in modern contexts. Therefore, even if, for the sake of discussion, we exclude "raiding" from a definition of warfare, we would be ignoring a major component of our coalitional psychology that is likely active in contexts of violence between groups. For this reason, I consider its evolutionary origins here as a component of resultant adaptations for coalitional aggression and I remain usefully agnostic on whether this qualifies as warfare, per se.

Raiding

The most common form of violence between human groups is raiding (Gat, 2006). Raids are distinct in that they often occur by stealth, exploiting ambush and surprise, tend to occur at night and most commonly target individual out-group members before turning a quick retreat. Wrangham and Glowacki (2012) describe that this form of violence in humans closely approximates the chimpanzee model of warfare, which is best explained by the Imbalance of Power Hypothesis (Wrangham, 1999). This hypothesis explains that in the context of intergroup competition, chimpanzees readily seize on opportunities to attack and kill lone "strangers" in contexts in which the ratio of attackers to defenders is at least 3 to 1. These low-risk opportunistic attacks have been demonstrated to provide tremendous benefits in the form of territory, food, and reproductive resources (Wilson *et al.*, 2012, 2014).

Raiding in humans resembles the chimpanzee model in many significant ways, from mirroring the imbalance of power calculus of low-risk opportunistic aggression to also reflecting the presence of evolved heuristics specific to the use of weapons in human history, known as "Lanchester's Laws" of combat (Johnson and MacKay, 2015). There are, however, important differences between chimpanzee and human raiding. To the best of our knowledge, for example, chimpanzee raids seem fully opportunistic, while human raids can be motivated by both opportunism and grievance (e.g. revenge). The latter motivation means that humans, unlike chimpanzees, can become locked in intergenerational cycles of intractable violence that is (so-far) unknown in the animal kingdom. What this helps to reveal is that although chimpanzee raids are unequivocally a form of low-risk/high-benefit violence, human raids seem relatively riskier, which leads to the second major form of collective violence.

Battles

In contrast to raids, which are small-scale and common, battles are relatively symmetric engagements of larger groups of opponents from competing groups. Battles can occur as a consequence of "escalated conflicts between prepared opponents" or can occur somewhat more suddenly as when a raiding party is detected and defenders have time to organise (Wrangham and Glowacki, 2012; LeBlanc, 2014). With respect to our non-human primate cousins, battles are a uniquely human phenomenon.

Are raids and battles products of evolved adaptations?

The prevalence of low-risk/high-benefit raiding seems to unambiguously point to the existence of an evolved propensity to conditionally engage in opportunistic raiding in chimpanzees. Given that human raiding resembles the chimpanzee model in many ways, it is reasonable to assume that at least some of this propensity in humans is the product of an inherited adapted psychology that regulates raiding behaviour. However, as noted above, the contrasts are at least as striking; in short, revenge and weapons conspire to elevate the riskiness of nearly any scenario of human aggression (Keeley, 1996; Gat, 2006; Boehm, 2011). There are at least two explanations of this divergence that are not mutually exclusive.

First, Wrangham and Glowacki (2012) argue that greater levels of risk in human raiding, for example, suggest that some force other than natural selection must be invoked to explain a behaviour that seems so individually costly. For example, the *cultural* evolution of norms and institutions of reward might sufficiently incentivize behaviour toward participation in risky violence (Glowacki and Wrangham, 2013). Second, it is possible, even if counterintuitive, that natural selection can engineer a motivation to engage in risky violence as long as the rewards are sufficiently high, on average, over evolutionary time (Tooby and Cosmides, 1988; Enquist and Leimar, 1990; McDonald *et al.*, 2012; Lopez, 2016a, 2016b). Problematically, this would only shift the puzzle back to chimpanzees since we must then explain why chimpanzees do not engage in relatively risker violence.

At a minimum, therefore, given that there are substantial reproductive benefits to both chimpanzee raiding (Wilson *et al.*, 2014) and human raiding (LeBlanc and Register, 2003; Glowacki and Wrangham, 2015), and that even short chronology scholars acknowledge the likely occurrence of raiding (while not calling it "warfare") in ancestral environments, it is reasonable to conclude that natural selection has shaped an evolved psychology in humans that regulates behaviour in the context of intergroup raiding.

Whether adaptations for battles exist in humans is still very much an open question and is somewhat more problematic given (1) the absence of battles in non-human primate comparison groups, and (2) the relative rarity of battles in the ethnographic record. Nevertheless, battles are not entirely absent. Tellingly, perhaps the earliest "direct evidence" of human warfare is a ten-thousand-year-old site in which multiple victims from different territories are shown to have been killed by trauma from arrows or clubs (Lahr *et al.*, 2016). Battles may be relatively infrequent, but given that they occur as far back as we can record intergroup violence itself, and given that they can be particularly deadly, we are remiss in fully rejecting the possibility that battles can at least partly be explained as the product of adaptations for engaging in relatively larger symmetrical contests. Yet this remains an open and important question for future study.

Ancestral patterns of collective violence

Some patterns emerge from the archaeology and anthropology violence that are a necessary starting point for thinking about an evolved psychology of coalitional aggression. We have an increasingly fine-grained perspective on what ancestral coalitional aggression might have looked like. In addition to the clear reproductive benefits of raiding (notwithstanding an ambiguous case for battles), it is likely that ancestral collective violence often contained at least some of the following behavioural and motivational attributes: territorial stakes; occurring by ambush of vulnerable individuals; risky and often involving weapons; involving the exploitation of defensive locations; causing high death rates between groups; likely to involve or implicate intergroup alliances; most commonly motivated by revenge or women (Keeley, 1996; Kelly, 2000; LeBlanc and Register, 2003; Otterbein, 2004; Gat, 2006; Allen and Jones, 2014; Glowacki *et al.*, 2017).

Given that these common patterns suggest an evolutionarily recurrent and reproductively significant set of adaptive problems, it is possible to begin to sketch some of the features that may comprise an evolved psychology of coalitional aggression.

The psychology of coalitional aggression

Despite fierce debate on the origins, frequency, intensity, nature and definition of warfare, one element that is almost universally acknowledged is that coalitional aggression presupposes the presence of a collective action problem (Lopez, 2016b; Pietraszewski, 2016; Glowacki *et al.*, 2017). In principle, this collective action problem is at least minimally one of coordinating the behaviour of multiple individuals toward a shared goal, and can also involve efforts to incentivize and coerce participation. The evidence for an evolved psychology of coalitional aggression, therefore, can more usefully be described in the following way: is there evidence of psychological design for solving collective action problems in the unique domain(s) of coalitional aggression? There are three overlapping bodies of research that indicate that this may indeed be the case. First, the regular and powerful connection between intergroup violence and within-group cooperation; second, adaptively patterned differences in reasoning and behaviour in contexts of offensive and defensive coalitional aggression; third, the role of two emotions – anger and hatred – that organise patterns of motivation and behaviour in coalitional aggression.

Out-group threat organises within-group motivation and behaviour

One of the most robust findings in the study of intergroup conflict is that the presence or possibility of competition between groups reliably triggers a host of within-group motivations and behaviours that seem well-designed to facilitate victory in such conflicts. In other words, war is a cascading trigger of within-group cooperation. The presence or promise of out-group threat appears sufficient, within-groups, to trigger: increased cooperation; increased punishment of social norm violators; increased aversion to inequality; increased gratitude toward cooperators; increased support for dominant leaders (Burton-Chellew *et al.*, 2010; Gneezy and Fessler, 2011; Bauer *et al.*, 2016; Laustsen and Petersen, 2017). These effects can linger for many years after the conflict has ended. There are at least three caveats to this phenomenon, however.

First, this effect has been observed both in the field and in the lab, as well as cross-culturally, but it appears general to intergroup competition rather than specific to intergroup violence. In other words, we are not yet able to interpret these data as evidence of adaptation for collective *violence*, per se, even if the corresponding systems are certainly online during instances of collective violence. This underscores a more general puzzle in research on the evolved psychology of war, which is: to what extent do the psychological processes that are often observed during and associated with warfare (e.g. parochial altruism, xenophobia) represent the operation of adaptations designed for other closely-related phenomena (e.g. hunting, collective action) rather than warfare specifically? This puzzle remains insufficiently addressed. Second, and relatedly, researchers have only recently begun to try to disambiguate an effect of "war" on within-group cooperation from other confounds such as "threshold effects" (Jordan *et al.*, 2017). Third, assuming an adaptive link exists between intergroup conflict and within-group cooperation, we cannot yet conclusively say whether its existence is best explained by group selection or selection operating at lower levels (Gneezy and Fessler, 2011). Warfare is a sufficient, but not necessary, trigger of within-group heuristics and biases.

Coalitional asymmetries facilitate action: defence, offence, punishment and reward

There is growing evidence that offensive and defensive aggression have been two evolutionarily recurrent and reproductively significant challenges in our species' history, and therefore that human psychology may be designed to reason about and behave in these contexts in ways that would have been ancestrally adaptive (Lopez, 2010. 2017; Rusch, 2014; Böhm *et al.* 2016; De Dreu and Gross, in prep). Briefly, in defence, within-group members are powerfully motivated to solve a relatively simple coordination problem, whereas in offence, the initiation of violence must solve relatively more complex problems of target selection and the distribution of risk, in which the benefits are occasionally general to the group but are more often ambiguous and privatised among the initiating sub-group of attackers.

What this means is that, in general, to the extent that warfare can be thought of as collective action, there is a labour recruitment problem that is relatively more challenging in cases of offensive aggression than in defensive aggression (Lopez, 2019). Despite overwhelming evidence that competition between groups tends to enhance cooperation within them, this literature has tended not to distinguish between types of violence, such as offence and defence. When they are distinguished, important asymmetries emerge. For example, De Dreu *et al.* (2016) find that in-group identification is stronger among group members when they are being attacked versus when they are attacking, and Rusch (2013) shows that sacrifice in combat is more common in defence than in offence, which he labels the "asymmetry hypothesis."

Generally, there appears to be a defence bias in human collective violence (Böhm *et al.*, 2016). More concretely, there exists a range of motivational asymmetries between the two types of aggression. For example, within-group punishment of non-participants may be more useful and salient in defence than in offence (Lopez, 2017), particularly owing to defence being more of a "true" public good than offence (Tooby and Cosmides, 1988; Price *et al.*, 2002), while individual prospective rewards such as status and honour seem to be especially useful for incentivising participation in high-risk offensive raids (Glowacki and Wrangham, 2013). The asymmetric game theoretic structure of these two types of aggression also suggests that within-group leader deception plays a larger role in offensive rather than in defensive aggression (Gagnon, 1994; McDermott, 2017; Lopez, 2019). In short, defence unites and offence divides.

Collective violence can bargain or destroy

There is a broad literature on the emotional underpinnings of warfare that includes research on phenomena such as xenophobia (Reynolds *et al.*, 1987), dehumanisation (McDonald *et al.*, 2015), and revenge (Lickel *et al.*, 2006; Michener, 2012). This research tends to situate these attitudes or emotions within a context of intergroup competition generally, or warfare specifically. It is possible that a very simple distinction can cut across and organise many of these dynamics; namely the distinction between anger and hatred.

Anger and hatred represent distinct reasoning and behavioural repertoires, with anger facilitating processes of agonistic bargaining and hatred facilitating relatively unqualified destructive attitudes and action. Sell *et al.* (2009) demonstrate that anger functions uniquely to resolve conflicts of interest in favour of the angry individual, and Halperin *et al.* (2011) show that anger can, relative to hatred, facilitate a degree of compromise in conflict scenarios. Where anger bargains, hate destroys. Applied to domains of intergroup aggression, to the extent that these distinct emotions drive behaviour, we can expect to observe patterned distinctions in the resulting forms of warfare (Sell and Lopez, Chapter 3, this volume). In the case of anger-based aggression, warfare is relatively constrained in terms of the conduct of violence and is sensitive to cues of preference-restructuring in one's adversary in the form of apologies or surrender. In contrast, hate-based aggression in warfare is intrinsically cost-imposing and relatively indifferent to cues of preference-restructuring in the target of one's hate. Therefore, we are more likely to see hatred manifest in situations of enduring and/or intense violence, such as multi-generational intractable conflicts (Staub, 1992), extremist or terrorist violence (Baele *et al.*, 2019; but see also Piazza, 2009) or otherwise irrational commitments of massive retaliation (McDermott *et al.* , 2017). In the case of anger, violence *itself* is bargaining language, while in the case of hatred, violence is meant to cause suffering for its own sake.

Conclusions: the emergence of warfare

Debates on the evolutionary and historical origins of warfare are raucous and divisive, but they are not needlessly so. By accepting that definitions are methodological tools rather than ontological claims, and instead focusing on our best approximations of ancestral socio-ecology, we can develop a sharper image of what adaptations ought to exist given known or probable behavioural patterns, independently of what those patterns are labelled. There is evidence for an evolved psychology in humans that is designed for coalitional aggression (or, collective violence, in the language of this volume). Indeed, this psychology shapes human reasoning and behaviour in *many* instances of political violence, not simply warfare. For example, political scientists sometimes draw a distinction between terrorism and warfare, arguing that the former is not an instance of the latter; however, it is unlikely that adaptations for coalitional aggression are active in warfare but not in acts of terrorism (Thayer and Hudson, 2010; Lopez, 2016b). This is the danger of treating definitions as first principles when they should properly be viewed as placeholders of conceptual convenience.

Research on the evolution of war might usefully distinguish between our evolved psychology of coalitional aggression and the myriad behavioural forms that can be evoked from this universal psychology given changes in social and environmental complexity across time and space. Otterbein (2004), Kelly (2005), and others are right to acknowledge that a significant shift takes places toward the beginning of the Holocene as humans increasingly take advantage of agriculture, become relatively sedentary, accumulate wealth, and develop more elaborate social and political institutions (Levy and Thompson, 2011). Although it is not intrinsically inappropriate to refer to that time period as marking the origin of warfare, it is also just as easily described as an era in which older patterns of intergroup violence took on a new scale and complexity (Keeley, 1996; Gat, 2006). Thus, debates about whether warfare began in this time period or earlier are often less a foundational disagreement about objective reality than a rather trivial dispute about the proper angle at which to view the necker cube of collective violence.

References

Allen, M. (2014) Hunter-gatherer conflict: The last bastion of the pacified past? In *Violence and Warfare Among Hunter-Gatherers*. New York: Routledge, pp. 15–25.

Allen, M. W. and Jones, T. L. (eds) (2014) *Violence and Warfare among Hunter-Gatherers*. New York: Routledge.

Baele, S. J., Bettiza, G., Boyd, K. A., and Coan, T. G. (2019) ISIS's clash of civilizations: constructing the "West" in terrorist propaganda. *Studies in Conflict & Terrorism*, pp. 1–33, www.tandfonline.com/doi/abs/10.1080/1057610X.2019.1599192?journalCode=uter20.

Bauer, M., Blattman, C., Chytilova, J., Henrich, J., Miguel, E., and Mitts, T. (2016) Can war foster cooperation? *Journal of Economic Perspectives*, 30(3), pp. 249–274.

Bird, D. W., Bird, R. B., Codding, B. F., and Zeanah, D. W. (2019) Variability in the organization and size of hunter-gatherer groups: foragers do not live in small-scale societies. *Journal of Human Evolution*, 131, pp. 96–108.

Boehm, C. (2011) Retaliatory violence in human prehistory. *British Journal of Criminology*, 51(3), pp. 518–534.

Böhm, R., Rusch, H. and Gürerk, Ö. (2016) What makes people go to war? Defensive intentions motivate retaliatory and preemptive intergroup aggression. *Evolution and Human Behavior*, 37(1), pp. 29–34.

Bowles, S. (2009) Did warfare among ancestral hunter-gatherers affect the evolution of human social behaviors? *Science*, 324(5932), pp. 1293–1298.

Burton-Chellew, M. N., Ross-Gillespie, A. and West, S. A. (2010) Cooperation in humans: competition between groups and proximate emotions. *Evolution and Human Behavior*, 31(2), pp. 104–108.

De Dreu, C. K. W. and Gross, J. (in prep) Revisiting the form and function of conflict: neurobiological, psychological and cultural mechanisms for attack and defense within and between groups. *Behavioral and Brain Sciences*.

Dreu, C. K. W. D., Gross, J., Meder, Z., Griffin, M., Prochazkova, E., Krikeb, J., and Columbus, S. (2016) In-group defense, out-group aggression, and coordination failures in intergroup conflict. *Proceedings of the National Academy of Sciences*, 113(38), pp. 10524–10529.

Ember, C. R. and Ember, M. (1992) Resource unpredictability, mistrust, and war – a cross-cultural-study. *Journal of Conflict Resolution*, 36(2), pp. 242–262.

Enquist, M. and Leimar, O. (1990) The evolution of fatal fighting. *Animal Behaviour*, 39(1), pp. 1–9.

Ferguson, R. B. (1997) Violence and war in prehistory. In *Troubled Times: Violence and Warfare in the Past*. Amsterdam: Gordon and Breach Publishers, pp. 321–356.

Ferguson, R. B. and Whitehead, N. L. (eds) (1992) *War in the Tribal Zone: Expanding States and Indigenous Warfare*. Santa Fe, NM: Seattle, WA: School of American Research Press.

Fry, D. P. (2007) *Beyond War: The Human Potential for Peace*, 1st ed. New York: Oxford University Press.

Fry, D. P. (2013) *War, Peace, and Human Nature: The Convergence of Evolutionary and Cultural Views*. New York: Oxford University Press.

Fry, D. P. and Söderberg, P. (2013) Lethal aggression in mobile forager bands and implications for the origins of war. *Science*, 341(6143), pp. 270–273.

Gagnon, V. P. (1994) Ethnic nationalism and international conflict: the case of Serbia. *International Security*, 19(3), pp. 130–166.
Gat, A. (2006) *War in Human Civilization*. Oxford: Oxford University Press.
Gleditsch, N. P., Wallensteen, P., Eriksson, M., Sollenberg, M., and Strand, H. (2002) Armed conflict 1946–2001: a new dataset. *Journal of Peace Research*, 39(5), pp. 615–637.
Glowacki, L. and Wrangham, R. W. (2013) The role of rewards in motivating participation in simple warfare. *Human Nature*, 24(4), pp. 444–460.
Glowacki, L. and Wrangham, R. (2015) Warfare and reproductive success in a tribal population. *Proceedings of the National Academy of Sciences*, 112(2), pp. 348–353.
Glowacki, L., Wilson, M. L. and Wrangham, R. W. (2017) The evolutionary anthropology of war. *Journal of Economic Behavior & Organization*.
Gneezy, A. and Fessler, D. M. T. (2011) Conflict, sticks and carrots: war increases prosocial punishments and rewards. *Proceedings of the Royal Society B: Biological Sciences*, 279(1727), 219–223.
Halperin, E., Russell, A. G., Dweck, C. S., and Gross, J. J. (2011) Anger, hatred, and the quest for peace: anger can be constructive in the absence of hatred. *Journal of Conflict Resolution*, 55(2), pp. 274–291.
Hames, R. (2019) Pacifying hunter-gatherers. *Human Nature*. doi: 10.1007/s12110-019-09340-w.
Johnson, D. D. P. and MacKay, N. J. (2015) Fight the power: Lanchester's laws of combat in human evolution. *Evolution and Human Behavior*, 36(2), pp. 152–163.
Jordan, M. R., Jordan, J. J. and Rand, D. G. (2017) No unique effect of intergroup competition on cooperation: non-competitive thresholds are as effective as competitions between groups for increasing human cooperative behavior. *Evolution and Human Behavior*, 38(1), pp. 102–108.
Keeley, L. H. (1996) *War before Civilization: The Myth of the Peaceful Savage*. New York: Oxford University Press.
Kelly, R. C. (2000) *Warless Societies and the Origin of War*. Michigan: University of Michigan Press.
Kelly, R. C. (2005) The evolution of lethal intergroup violence. *Proceedings of the National Academy of Sciences of the United States of America*, 102(43), pp. 15294–15298.
Lahr, M. M., Rivera, F., Power, R.K., Mounier, A., Copsey, B., Crivellaro, F., Edung, J. E., Maillo Fernandez, J. M., Kiarie, C., Lawrence, J., Leakey, A., Mbua, E., Miller, H., Muigai, A., Mukhongo, D.M., Van Baelen, A., Wood, R., Schwenninger, J.-L., Grün, R., Achyuthan, H., Wilshaw, A., and Foley, R.A. (2016) Inter-group violence among early Holocene hunter-gatherers of West Turkana, Kenya. *Nature*, 529(7586), pp. 394–398.
Laustsen, L. and Petersen, M. B. (2017) Perceived conflict and leader dominance: individual and contextual factors behind preferences for dominant Leaders. *Political Psychology*, 38(6), pp. 1083–1101.
LeBlanc, S. A. (2014) Forager warfare and our evolutionary past. In M. W. Allen and T. L. Jones (eds), *Violence and Warfare among Hunter-Gatherers*. New York: Routledge.
LeBlanc, S. A. and Register, K. E. (2003) *Constant Battles: The Myth of the Peaceful, Noble Savage*. New York: St. Martin's Press.
Levy, J. S. and Thompson, W. R. (2011) *The Arc of War: Origins, Escalation, and Transformation*. Chicago, IL: University of Chicago Press.
Lickel, B., Miller, N., Stenstrom, D. M., Denson, T. F., and Schmader, T. (2006) Vicarious retribution: the role of collective blame in intergroup aggression. *Personality and Social Psychology Review: An Official Journal of the Society for Personality and Social Psychology, Inc*, 10(4), pp. 372–390.
Lopez, A. C. (2010) *Evolution, Coalitional Psychology, and War*. I. H-Diplo ISSF Roundtable on 'Biology and Security'.
Lopez, A. C. (2016a) Conditions required for evolution of warfare adaptations. In V. Weekes-Shackelford, T. K. Shackelford and V. A. Weekes-Shackelford (eds), *Encyclopedia of Evolutionary Psychological Science*. Cham: Springer International Publishing, pp. 1–10. doi: 10.1007/978-3-319-16999–6_914–1.
Lopez, A. C. (2016b) The evolution of war: theory and controversy. *International Theory*, 8(01), pp. 97–139.
Lopez, A. C. (2017) The Evolutionary psychology of war: offense and defense in the adapted mind. *Evolutionary Psychology*, 15(4), doi: 10.1177/1474704917742720.
Lopez, A. C. (2019) Making "my" problem "our" problem: warfare as collective action, and the role of leader manipulation. *The Leadership Quarterly*, doi: 10.1016/j.leaqua.2019.05.001.
Lopez, A. C. and Johnson, D. D. P. (2017) The determinants of war in international relations. *Journal of Economic Behavior & Organization*, doi: 10.1016/j.jebo.2017.09.010.
Maoz, Z., Johnson, P. L. Kaplan, J., Ogunkoya, F., and Schreve, A. P. (2019) The dyadic militarized interstate disputes (MIDs) dataset version 3.0: logic, characteristics, and comparisons to alternative datasets. *Journal of Conflict Resolution*, 63(3), pp. 811–835.

McDermott, R., Lopez, A. C. and Hatemi, P. K. (2017) "Blunt Not the Heart, Enrage It": the psychology of revenge and deterrence. *Texas National Security Review*, 1(1), Available at: https://tnsr.org/2017/10/blunt-not-heart-enrage-psychology-revenge-deterrence/.

McDonald, M., Porat, R., Yarkoney, A., Tagar, M. R., Kimel, S., Saguy, T., and Halperin, E. (2015) Intergroup emotional similarity reduces dehumanization and promotes conciliatory attitudes in prolonged conflict. *Group Processes & Intergroup Relations*, p. 1368430215595107. doi: 10.1177/1368430215595107.

McDonald, M. M., Navarrete, C. D. and Van Vugt, M. (2012) Evolution and the psychology of intergroup conflict: the male warrior hypothesis. *Philosophical Transactions of the Royal Society B: Biological Sciences*, 367(1589), pp. 670–679.

Michener, W. (2012) The individual psychology of group hate. *Journal of Hate Studies*, 10(1), p. 15.

Murdock, G. P. and White, D. R. (1969) Standard cross-cultural sample. *Ethnology*, 8(4), pp. 329–369.

Otterbein, K. F. (2004) *How War Began*, 1st ed. TAMU Press.

Piazza, J. A. (2009) Is Islamist terrorism more dangerous? An empirical study of group ideology, organization, and goal structure. *Terrorism and Political Violence*, 21(1), pp. 62–88.

Pietraszewski, D. (2016) How the mind sees coalitional and group conflict: the evolutionary invariances of n-person conflict dynamics. *Evolution and Human Behavior*, 37(6), pp. 470–480.

Pinker, S. (2011) *The Better Angels of Our Nature: Why Violence Has Declined*. Penguin.

Price, M. E., Cosmides, L. and Tooby, J. (2002) Punitive sentiment as an anti-free rider psychological device. *Evolution and Human Behavior*, 23(3), pp. 203–231.

Prosterman, R. (1972) *Surviving to 3000: An Introduction to the Study of Lethal Conflict*, Ex-seminary Library edition. CA: Duxbury.

Reynolds, V., Falger, V. S. E. and Vine, I. (1987) *The Sociobiology of Ethnocentrism: Evolutionary Dimensions of Xenophobia, Discrimination, Racism, and Nationalism*. Athens: University of Georgia Press.

Rusch, H. (2013) Asymmetries in altruistic behavior during violent intergroup conflict. *Evolutionary Psychology: An International Journal of Evolutionary Approaches to Psychology and Behavior*, 11(5), pp. 973–993.

Rusch, H. (2014) The two sides of warfare: an extended model of altruistic behavior in ancestral human intergroup conflict. *Human Nature (Hawthorne, N.Y.)*, 25(3), pp. 359–377.

Sarkees, M. R. and Wayman, F. (2010) *Resort to War: 1816–2007*, 1st ed. Washington, DC: CQ Press.

Sell, A., Tooby, J. and Cosmides, L. (2009) Formidability and the logic of human anger. *Proceedings of the National Academy of Sciences*, 106(35), pp. 15073–15078.

Staub, E. (1992) *The Roots of Evil*, Reprint edition. Cambridge: Cambridge University Press.

Thayer, B. A. and Hudson, V. M. (2010) Sex and the Shaheed: insights from the life sciences on Islamic suicide terrorism. *International Security*, 34(4), pp. 37–62.

Tooby, J. and Cosmides, L. (1988) The evolution of war and its cognitive foundations. *Institute for Evolutionary Studies Technical Report*, 88–1.

Wilson, M. L., Kahlenberg, S. M., Wells, M., and Wrangham, R. (2012) Ecological and social factors affect the occurrence and outcomes of intergroup encounters in chimpanzees. *Animal Behaviour*, 83(1), pp. 277–291.

Wilson, M. L., Boesch, C., Furuichi, T., Gilby, I. C., Hashimoto, C., Hobaiter, C., Hohmann, G., *et al.* (2014) Lethal aggression in Pan is better explained by adaptive strategies than human impacts. *Nature*, 513(7518), pp. 414–417.

Wrangham, R. (1999) Evolution of coalitionary killing. *Yearbook of Physical Anthropology*, 42, pp. 1–30.

Wrangham, R. and Peterson, D. (1996) *Demonic Males: Apes and the Origins of Human Violence*. Boston: Houghton Mifflin.

Wrangham, R. W. and Glowacki, L. (2012) Intergroup aggression in chimpanzees and war in nomadic hunter-gatherers: evaluating the chimpanzee model. *Human Nature*, 23(1): 5–29.

2

WHEN SOCIAL IDENTITY-DEFINING GROUPS BECOME VIOLENT

Collective responses to identity uncertainty, status erosion, and resource threat

Sucharita Belavadi, Mark J. Rinella and Michael A. Hogg

Introduction

Collective violence is characterized by orchestrated, coordinated, and sustained violent acts that are perpetrated by one group of people against another, such as nations, military groups, ethnic and religious groups, terrorist organizations, and even smaller groups such as gangs (e.g. see Tilly, 2003). Division across intergroup lines is a characteristic feature of sustained collective violence (Staub, 1999), and it can take several forms, such as wars, intractable and protracted conflict (e.g. see Bar-Tal, 2000; Coleman, 2006, Staub & Bar-Tal, 2003), genocide and mass killings (e.g. Staub, 1989, 1999; Staub and Bar-Tal, 2003), gang violence (e.g. Goldman *et al.*, 2014), and terrorism (e.g. Moghaddam, 2005). In this chapter, we discuss collective violence as a systematically orchestrated act that is led by influential in-group sources, such as leaders, against clearly defined enemies.

The orchestration and execution of acts of collective violence requires the concerted effort and mobilization of a group of people under guidance. How are groups of people mobilized to commit acts that cause irreparable damage, destruction, and loss of countless lives? In exploring the answer to this question, in this chapter, we argue that the quest for a coherent, distinctive, and positive social identity is at the core of such mobilization efforts. We take a social identity approach to examine how the need to *promote* and *protect* (e.g. Hogg *et al.*, 2013) one's social categories, which have implications for self-definition and the fashioning of clear and distinctive identities, can motivate and mobilize groups of individuals to engage in acts of violence against other groups of people.

We begin by presenting an overview of social identity and self-categorization processes (e.g. Tajfel and Turner, 1986; Turner *et al.*, 1987; Abrams and Hogg, 2010; Hogg, 2018a) and their relevance to explaining collective violence. Of specific focus will be two key social identity motivations that frame intergroup violence – the need for *uncertainty reduction* and *self-enhancement*. We discuss the processes through which these motives shape troubled intergroup relations and, at extremes, drive intergroup violence, especially when threats to in-group resources and status loom large. In our discussion throughout, we emphasize the self within groups and the ways in which individuals come together through a shared sense of *us* versus *them*, such that acts of intergroup violence serve a specific purpose for individuals within groups in their quest for a positive and clear sense of self.

Given that acts of collective violence are coordinated and organized, the role of authority figures that typically emerge as guides from within the group cannot be understated. We discuss the important role that leaders play as mobilizers and catalysts leading the way, shaping in-group narratives and the meaning of intergroup contexts for group members, while helping group members make sense of the situation.

Toward the end of the chapter, we discuss the ideologies and belief systems that drive collective violence. That is, within groups, specific narratives develop that characterize intergroup conflict and violence and shape images of the in-group and the out-group. We discuss the language of *dehumanization* (e.g. Haslam, 2006; Bar-Tal and Hammack, 2012; Haslam and Loughnan, 2014) that is used to portray out-group members as less than human, outside of the realms of human morality, lacking in human essence, and thus as justified in suffering the harm that is directed at them. We also discuss the implications of *collective victimhood* (e.g. Bar-Tal *et al.*, 2009), and how a narrative of viewing the in-group as a victim of the actions of a demonized and evil out-group shapes intergroup conflict and hatred between groups.

Social identity and self-categorization processes

We begin by discussing the basic processes of social identity and self-categorization. Social identity theory began and was conceived as a theory of intergroup relations to explain conflict and cooperation between groups (Tajfel and Turner, 1979). Over the years, the focus of the theory has broadened to include the processes through which identity and a sense of self is derived from group memberships (Turner *et al.*, 1987). The explanatory merit of social identity theory is in illuminating the role that the self plays within broader group processes and intergroup relations.

Social identity theory explicates why people join groups and the meaning of social categories to individuals who identify with them. Tajfel defined social identity as an "individual's knowledge that he belongs to certain social groups together with some emotional and value significance to him of this group membership" (Tajfel, 1972, p. 292). When individuals identify with groups, they derive self-definition from their group memberships. Groups of course never exist in a vacuum and such self-definition through group memberships always occurs in relation to other groups – what one's group is not. Thus, it is through comparison with other groups that we get a sense of who *we* are relative to who *they* are.

Attachment to groups is a means for us to derive a positive sense of self. When a particular social identity is salient in our minds, we compare our group's standing to other groups in an intergroup context. Our quest is to attain a positive and distinctive social identity – one that is better than, and is clearly defined and distinct from, other groups. Shared subjective beliefs within groups determine how group members perceive status relations between their group and other groups (Ellemers, 1993), as well as subsequent intergroup behaviours. For instance, when boundaries between groups are seen as impermeable and status relations are seen as illegitimate, *social competition* between groups can take the form of revolutions and protests with the aim of changing existing status relations – a *social change* strategy. When such status relations are seen as legitimate, group members might engage in *social creativity* strategies, for instance, comparing one's group to a lower status group to gain positive social identity. In other conditions, where boundaries between groups are seen as permeable, group members might seek *intergroup mobility* and move into groups through which they can seek a positive sense of self. Such belief structures within groups can thus determine the nature of intergroup relations.

Strong identification with a group means that the way we think, feel, and behave toward the world around us is framed by the group membership that is cognitively salient in our mind at the time. Through social categorization we make sense of the world around us. When we encounter individuals, we categorize them into social categories that are meaningful to us. We not only categorize others, we also categorize our own selves and other group members into such social categories. Once we have categorized ourselves and others, we cease to view them as unique individuals, rather, we now view them through the lens of group membership. In other words, we *depersonalize* them and view them as embodiments of the attributes of what it means to be a member of a specific group.

According to *self-categorization theory* (Turner *et al.*, 1987), which maps the social-cognitive mechanisms of how groups are represented psychologically, we represent social categories in our minds as *prototypes*. Prototypes are fuzzy sets of attributes that define a group and its associated social identity, and thus what it means to be a member of a group – for instance, in terms of dress, language, attitudes, beliefs, customs, appearance, etc. Prototypes help fashion distinctive identities as they embody those group attributes that minimize in-group differences and maximize intergroup differences.

Prototypes about one's own group and about relevant out-groups are typically shared within a group, such that "we" agree about who "we" are and about who "they are". In this respect prototypes are stereotypes. Thus, it is possible not only to stereotype other group members but also our own selves in line with a shared belief about what it means to be a member of the group. As a result, a sense of *shared reality* that shapes our outlook on the world develops within groups that are clearly defined by a social identity (Hogg and Rinella, 2018). The prototype of the group varies depending on the intergroup context of comparison. Thus, what it means to be a member of a group, depends significantly on the intergroup context of comparison.

Binary distinctions regarding who we are and who they are can impact intergroup relations depending on the nature of the intergroup context. In contexts, where in-group prototypes are defined rigidly and are pulled to extreme positions and away from the out-group, polarized identities can result. This is especially the case when group members feel highly uncertain about who they are and are thus on a quest for a distinctive and clearly defined identity (e.g. Gaffney *et al.*, 2014), as we discuss in detail in the next section. Such intergroup contexts that are characterized by extreme binary distinctions allow for little harmony or cooperation between the two groups; the out-group and the in-group are painted in rigid and contrasting images and it can be difficult to introduce change in such perceptions. In the next section, we discuss two key social identity motives that in specific conditions can drive identities to become polarized. Polarized identities are characteristic of instances of collective violence, hatred, and extremely troubled relations between groups. Identities on both sides become entrenched and each side refuses to view positive attributes in the out-group (Bar-Tal, 2000; Staub and Bar-Tal, 2003)

Social identity motives, status erosion, and resource threats

Key social identity motives: uncertainty reduction and collective self-enhancement

People join groups and seek social identities to construct a coherent and positive sense of self (e.g. Tajfel and Turner, 1986; Hogg, 2018a). Two key motives for why we join and identify with groups are *uncertainty reduction* and *collective self enhancement*. When we identify with groups, we frame our sense of self in line with group attributes and manage uncertainty about the self-concept while also seeking a positive sense of self through comparison with other groups.

The uncertainty reduction motive

Uncertainty about our sense of self – about who we are and our place in the world makes us thirst for guidance and direction. While at times uncertainty can be exciting, we are particularly motivated to reduce uncertainty when it is cognitively demanding and is viewed as a threat (cf. Blascovich and Tomaka, 1996). In such conditions, the groups we identify with act as sense-making frameworks guiding our thoughts, feelings, and actions (Hogg and Mahajan, 2018). This is especially true of *entitative* groups that are distinctive and clearly defined around an unambiguous and consensual central core and thus provide a coherent framework for self-definition (Hogg *et al.*, 2007; Sherman *et al.*, 2009). These are the central premises of *uncertainty-identity theory* (Hogg, 2000, 2007, 2012, 2014, 2018b), which was developed within the broad framework of social identity theory.

Extremely heightened self-uncertainty, which is a characteristic feature of specific contexts that have been termed *difficult life conditions* (e.g. Staub, 1989, 1999, 2012), can drive uncertain individuals to seek groups that are extremely rigidly structured and have closed-off group boundaries (Hogg, 2014; Hogg and Adelman, 2013; Hogg *et al.*, 2010). Difficult life conditions are characterized by conditions such as economic upheaval and tense intergroup relations riddled with persistent and unresolved hatred and extremely negative views of people on the other side of the intergroup division.

Such conditions are characteristic of wars, threats from terrorist organizations, genocide, gang wars, and other extreme intergroup divisions. In these contexts, heightened uncertainty about oneself and one's future, and about the safety and protection of one's people weigh heavily on individuals' minds. A well-knit group with a clearly-defined and distinctive prototype of the in-group and a rigid agenda about who *we* are and who *they* are – invariably the perpetrators responsible for in-group plight – becomes especially attractive to uncertain individuals. Since distinctive in-group prototypes not only define who *we* are but also how we are different from *them*, rigid prototypes, by defining clearly the separateness of one's group from a hated out-group, help delineate intergroup boundaries and construct a distinctive social identity.

Given that social identities are pertinent to self-definition, one of the sources of heightened self-uncertainty is loss of a social identity through threats to intergroup distinctiveness and vitality, that is, uncertainty about in-group existence and the future survival of in-group practices and traditions – a form of extinction threat (Moghaddam and Love, 2012; Dupuis *et al.*, 2015; Wohl *et al.*, 2010; 2011).

In contexts of contentious intergroup relations, groups can become concerned about a dangerous out-group that looms large aiming to usurp members from the group, thereby corroding the distinctiveness between groups and raising concerns of in-group survival. Such threats lead to a sense of *collective angst* about the future of the group and produce in-group strengthening behaviours by in-group members (Wohl *et al.*, 2010). The group itself becomes rigid such that complete conformity to in-group norms is demanded and dissent is squashed as a means of protecting group boundaries from out-group infiltration (e.g. see Moghaddam and Love, 2012). Meanwhile narratives demonizing the out-group as threats to in-group survival also shape extreme hatred toward out-group members (e.g. Giner-Sorolla *et al.*, 2012) Thus, while heightened uncertainty drives group members to embrace rigidly defined and perceptually entitative groups (Sherman *et al.*, 2009), it also drives extreme and radical acts that are aimed at removing threats to the group and protecting and preserving intergroup boundaries (e.g. Hogg and Adelman, 2013).

These collective acts aimed at preserving the group and its boundaries from a perceived enemy can result in extreme acts of violence against out-group members. For instance, such acts of preservation can take the form of *vicarious retribution* (e.g. Stenstrom *et al.*, 2008) to avenge the loss of fellow group members who are tied closely to the self through a shared social identity. Following losses to the out-group, radical acts of collective violence can also act as a means to restore a sense of significance, competence, and control – as a form of *quest for significance* (e.g. Kruglanski *et al.*, 2014). Thus, individuals seek not only a distinctive identity to manage uncertainty, but they also seek to derive positive esteem from their group memberships. The two social identity motives – the need to be superior to and distinct from other groups – can prove detrimental to intergroup relations in the context of threat from another group and can manifest in two in-group behaviours – promoting and protecting the in-group (e.g. Hogg *et al.*, 2013).

The collective self-enhancement motive

The need to compare ourselves with the out-group and the desire to win and be better than them is a pervasive aspect of intergroup relations, even in the most minimal intergroup contexts. This has been demonstrated robustly by numerous studies employing the *minimal group paradigm* (Tajfel, 1970; Tajfel *et al.*, 1971; for a meta-analytic overview see Mullen *et al.*, 1992). In these minimal group studies, participants are randomly categorized into groups ostensibly on the basis of minimal criteria such as artist preference, dot-estimation, meaningless personality constellations, and even explicitly randomly as X-group and Y-group members. When asked to distribute money or points to other participants who are identified by code number and group membership, participants who are categorized as a member of a specific group (as opposed to those not categorized) tend to favour their own group member. Thus, the paradigm demonstrates that even in the most minimal intergroup conditions, intergroup categorization shapes in-group favouritism and ethnocentrism (Hogg, 2016; cf. Kerr *et al.*, 2018).

To be noted here is the point that simply being categorized does not motivate out-group hate or derogation. Minimal intergroup categorization simply motivates in-group favouritism and differentiation, which falls far short of extreme behaviours such as acts of violence or retribution against the out-group (e.g. Brewer, 1999). There is an asymmetry in which people favour their in-group rather than discriminate against the out-group. For out-group discrimination to arise, other conditions need to exist, such as a perceived threat to the in-group (Mummendey and Otten, 1998; Blanz *et al.*, 1995). It appears that when certain "aggravating" conditions (e.g. see Blanz *et al.*, 1995) are added to minimal intergroup contexts, intergroup relations can escalate from intergroup differentiation and ethnocentrism to full-blown out-group derogation and hatred. Threat to the status and position of one's group in an intergroup context is one such condition.

Relative deprivation and resource threat

When a particular group membership is salient, people compare their group to relevant out-groups with the goal of deriving a positive and distinctive social identity. When making an intergroup comparison, in-group members may feel their group is unfairly disadvantaged compared with an out-group, or that their group is unfairly disadvantaged compared with what they deserve and that the out-group is to blame. The result of such a comparison is a feeling of angry resentment by in-group members known as *group relative deprivation* (Smith *et al.*, 2012). These feelings of angry resentment toward the out-group can be conceptualized as a reaction to a group status threat because the group is not perceived to be sufficiently positive and distinct relative to the out-group.

Feelings of group relative deprivation can have important intergroup consequences. For example, research has shown that group relative deprivation is negatively related to warmth towards the out-group (Osborne and Sibley, 2015) and positively related to intergroup prejudice (Pettigrew *et al.*, 2008). Moreover, relative deprivation is a factor that is commonly included in models of radicalization (King and Taylor, 2011). Indeed, research suggests that group relative deprivation is directly and indirectly related to components of radical belief systems, such as perceived in-group superiority and perceived illegitimacy of authorities; in turn, these factors predict attitudes toward violence against out-groups and individuals' violent intentions (Doosje *et al.*, 2012; 2013; van Bergen *et al.*, 2015).

A group's status or position may also come under threat due to real or perceived competition with an out-group. According to realistic group conflict theory (RCT), intergroup conflict is a result of in-groups and out-groups having competing goals over tangible resources (LeVine and Campbell, 1972). The core tenets of this theory were tested in Muzafer Sherif's famous Robber's Cave experiment (Sherif, 1966; Sherif *et al.*, 1988). In this experiment, boys at a summer camp were split into two groups, and the groups engaged in a series of competitions introduced by the experimenters. Researchers found that competition over scarce resources between boys who were categorized into two distinctive groups escalated into severe tensions, even acts of violence directed at the other group. More recent theories of intergroup competition and conflict have built on the principles of RCT. For example, Esses and colleagues' instrumental model of group conflict outlines the antecedents and effects of real or perceived intergroup competition, noting that "perceived competition leads to attempts to remove the source of competition, using a variety of strategies." (Esses *et al.*, 1998, p. 702). In extreme cases, groups may resort to strategies such as collective violence or elimination of the out-group (McPherson and Parks, 2011; Waller, 2003).

In many conflict and collective violence situations, there is a strong narrative of resource threat – for instance immigrants taking away jobs and land from natives (Esses *et al.*, 1998; Rios *et al.*, 2018), while in other instances, the narrative revolves around out-groups usurping in-group territory (e.g. Belavadi and Hogg, 2016). The actual conflict, however, often revolves around identity concerns – protection and promotion of social identity, as well as how the in-group can preserve its resources, win, emerge victorious, and save the day by defeating an unjust and harmful out-group (e.g. Donohue, 2012). The mobilizing potential of narratives of resource threat cannot be tapped unless an in-group source actively articulates talk regarding the deprivation of the in-group and the injustice one's people face relative to the out-group. Leaders are one such in-group source – a source that wields influence on the in-group, which in turn follows their guidance.

Leaders as entrepreneurs of identity and mobilizers of collective action

Leaders are a source of in-group influence and a galvanizing force within groups. As previously mentioned, the groups that people belong to make up an important part of their self-concepts, so people seek to have a clear understanding of these identities. However, some members are more reliable sources of identity-related information than others. Prototypical members are viewed by others as the best source of identity-related information, so they have the most influence over other group members. Correspondingly, leaders who are seen as highly prototypical are more trusted and perceived to be more effective than non-prototypical leaders (Hogg *et al.*, 2012). This is the basic premise of the *social identity theory of leadership* (Hogg and Van Knippenberg, 2003; Hogg *et al.*, 2012). A substantial body of research has supported this theory, showing that as people identify more strongly with groups, prototypical leaders are more trusted, supported, and influential than non-prototypical leaders (Barreto and Hogg, 2017).

There are several processes that additively explain why high prototypicality increases leaders' influence and effectiveness. First, self-categorization and depersonalization based on the group prototype lead group members to conform to a shared group prototype and likewise to the behaviour of group members who are perceived to best embody group-defining attributes. This projects the appearance that highly prototypical group members are disproportionately influential and, as a result, people perceive them to be a reliable source of identity-related information.

Second, highly prototypical members tend to be liked more than their less prototypical counterparts (Hogg, 1993), which increases the likelihood that others will be influenced by them. Finally, because prototypical members embody the group's norms, they tend to be highly identified with the group (Hogg *et al.*, 1998), making them more likely to behave in a group-serving manner. This leads other group members to trust that prototypical members will behave according to the group's interest (Giessner and Van Knippenberg, 2008). This trust that prototypical leaders will behave in a group-serving fashion creates a paradox in which highly prototypical leaders are afforded the most leeway to innovate and take the group in new directions (Abrams *et al.*, 2008). Given prototypical leaders' high investment in the group, the leeway to move the group in new directions should be welcomed by group-serving prototypical leaders.

People rely on leaders to define the identities of the groups they belong to, and prototypical leaders are particularly influential because they tend to be liked and trusted by their followers. In this way, prototypical leaders can be considered "entrepreneurs of identity" (Reicher and Hopkins, 2003). Leaders play a significant role in shaping and managing the content of the group's prototype, and thus what it means to be a group member (Reicher and Hopkins, 2003; Seyranian, 2012; Seyranian and Bligh, 2008). Through strategic rhetoric and behaviour, leaders can effectively convey their image of the group, which is often based on their future goals (Reicher *et al.*, 2005).

Although people generally prefer prototypical over non-prototypical leaders, research has shown that uncertainty can reduce or eliminate this preference (Rast *et al.*, 2012). Under conditions of uncertainty, people have such a strong desire for leadership and direction that they are less concerned with the prototypicality of the leader – they just need identity-defining leadership. Thus, it is not that people prefer prototypical leaders less when uncertain, but the need for guidance when self-uncertain is so strong that even non-prototypical leaders can gain an advantage. This strong need for leadership provides an opening for "dark" or toxic leaders to exert influence over the group. For instance, research has demonstrated that increased self-uncertainty is related to more support of an autocratic compared with a non-autocratic leader (Rast *et al.*, 2013). Another programme of research, by Guillén and colleagues, has shown how self-uncertainty is associated with leaders who possess the dark triad attributes of Machiavellianism, Narcissism and Psychopathy securing and maintaining positions of leadership, and that followers are supportive of this leadership dynamic (e.g. Guillén *et al.*, 2018). Overall, directive and autocratic leaders are more attractive under uncertainty because they communicate a simple, unambiguous prototype for the group that effectively reduces uncertainty.

Not only does uncertainty make extreme and autocratic leaders more attractive, but leaders can provoke uncertainty among their followers to mobilize the group toward the leader's goals or to consolidate power and create a rigid and highly entitative identity for the group. Rhetoric provoking self-uncertainty by a prototypical leader has been shown to increase followers' identification with the group (Hohman *et al.*, 2010). There are a number of ways in which leaders can create uncertainty among their followers, including rhetoric that emphasizes existing instabilities in the social environment, ostracizing or derogating deviants and dissenters, or focusing on failures and shortcomings of the group (Seyranian, 2012). One strategy that leaders can use to create uncertainty among their followers that may be particularly relevant to collective violence is exaggerating out-group threats. It has been suggested that when an out-group is determined to be a substantial threat, people may be more willing to endorse a leader who takes a hard-stance against the out-group and proposes extreme solutions for dealing with the threat (Hogg, 2018b; Seyranian, 2012).

In-group narratives, ideologies and collective violence

In the face of real or perceived threat from an out-group, leaders can play a key and influential role in mobilizing in-group members against the out-group by espousing narratives and ideologies that shape specific images of the in-group relative to the out-group. Thus far, in our discussion of orchestrated violence we have discussed the antecedents or the *why* of collective violence by examining two key social identity motivations. We have also examined *who* orchestrates or mobilizes in-group members in a collective, unifying cause against the out-group. In this section, we examine *how* mobilization of group members occurs in the service of collective violence. We explore the ways in which specific in-group beliefs that paint out-group members as dangerous and threatening to the in-group help justify and make possible violence and extreme behaviours against out-group members. We discuss dehumanizing and delegitimizing speech and narratives of collective victimhood within groups that serve to legitimize violence against out-group members by shaping an image of the out-group as villains and perpetrators.

Dehumanization and delegitimization

Recent research in social psychology – on *dehumanization* and *infrahumanization* – has examined in some detail the ways in which groups of individuals undermine or engage in the denial of human essence or uniquely human characteristics to out-group members (Haslam, 2006; Leyens *et al.*, 2000; Bar-Tal and Hammack, 2012; Haslam and Loughnan, 2014, Kteily and Bruneau, 2017). *Delegitimizing* (e.g. Bar-Tal and Hammack, 2012) the out-group in this manner allows in-group members to justify atrocities against them, while portraying out-group members as violators of basic human values and norms, excluding them from the boundaries of justice, fairness, and the moral community (Opotow, 1990), and viewing them as lacking in secondary human emotions characteristic of humanness (see Leyens *et al.*, 2000).

Dehumanization is especially dangerous as indicated by historical evidence from acts of systematic collective violence against a specific group of people, such as the Holocaust and the Rwandan genocide. In both these contexts, hate speech characterized out-group members as vermin (in the former case) and cockroaches (in the latter). While such dehumanization can also occur outside the context of intergroup violence (e.g. Haslam, 2006), given intergroup conflict, it can be used as an ideology of hate to justify violence against a group of individuals who are likened to animals and as less than human.

In the literature on dehumanization, two types have been discussed – the denial of uniquely human characteristics and the denial of human nature to others. The former has been likened to *animalistic* dehumanization and infrahumanization and involves characterizing the out-group as less civilized, lacking in secondary human emotions, and qualities that distinguish humans from animals. Similar to the examples above, such images of the out-group are seen in colonial narratives characterizing natives as savages and are common in contexts of genocide and ethnic violence. The latter has been likened to *mechanistic* dehumanization, where the out-group is treated as lacking in human essence and thus as similar to automata, machines and robots – as high in competence but low in warmth (Fiske *et al.*, 2002; Li *et al.*, 2014). Mechanistic dehumanization is less likely in contexts of collective violence between groups and is restricted to contexts of competitive relations between groups. Unlike animalistic dehumanization, which encourages downward comparisons and derogation of the out-group, mechanistic dehumanization encourages horizontal comparisons with a competitor (Haslam, 2006).

Placing individuals outside moral consideration and denying a human essence in them is used as a narrative to justify harmful, oppressive, and exploitative acts against them. Once the out-group is delegitimized, in-group members view it as their moral obligation to reform, rid and cleanse the world of such violators, viewing in-group acts as noble and morally required.

In his discussion of the antecedents and possible strategies that could have prevented the Rwandan genocide, Stanton (2004) discusses the eight stages of genocide. The first three stages of *classification*, *symbolization* and *dehumanization* are especially relevant to understanding how the stage is set for orchestrated violence to be justified to in-group members in the later stages. First, the two groups are clearly classified – us versus them; the second is attaching specific identifying symbols to the other group, such as identifying cards, while the third stage is dehumanizing the out-group and likening them to disease or animals. In the later stages, in-group members are trained and organized as a militia against the out-group while polarized identities develop and are encouraged and moderates within the in-group are targeted. Donohue (2012) states that, in such circumstances, groups fall into an *identity trap* such that the language used in intergroup contexts encourages a clash of polarized identities making discussion of moderate points of view or reconciliation impossible. The identity trap enables in-group members to view their acts as justified and, in fact, aiding in the creation of a better society by ridding the world of the out-group.

Collective victimhood

A similar identity trap is the tendency of groups to view themselves as the sole victims in conflict and the other group as the sole perpetrator. Developed within the context of intractable and protracted intergroup conflict, the concept of collective victimhood describes how groups come to define themselves and shape their identities around victimhood experiences (e.g. Bar-Tal *et al.*, 2009; Noor *et al.*, 2017). A shared sense of us as victims and them as perpetrators divides the two groups, resulting in extremely tense, rigid, and entrenched intergroup relations that become difficult to reconcile. The in-group is perceived as the sole sufferer and as the target and victim of unjust and immoral harm; the rival out-group is delegitimized and seen as evil wrong-doers, flouting the norms of human society by causing suffering and harm.

A narrative of collective victimhood intensifies intergroup divisions and hatred as divisions on group lines prevent a group of individuals from seeing any positive qualities in the rival – relations become defined by binary distinctions and zero sum in nature. A shared sense of victimhood thus becomes a prism or lens through which group members view even harmless actions of the out-group as threatening to one's group and its members.

While adopting a sense of victimhood might appear counterintuitive to the quest for a positive identity, a position of victimhood can often be a powerful one in the context of tense intergroup relations. A position of victimhood or claims of being the sole victims in conflict makes the group appear to have moral standing, entitled to sympathy and resources, and protected from criticism. In fact, when groups claim to be the sole victims in the context of intractable conflict, neutral third parties are more likely to legitimize revenge-seeking behaviours by such groups against a villainous out-group, and this relationship is mediated by perceptions of the victim-claiming group as highly uncertain about themselves and the safety of their group (Belavadi and Hogg, 2018).

Thus, a sense of victimhood can have damaging implications for intergroup relations, as groups actively delegitimize out-group members while seeking justification for revenge from third parties and mobilizing fellow in-group members against the out-group. When such a sense of victimhood is present on both sides of the conflict with differing third-party support on either side, relations can truly come to a head. According to Bar-Tal *et al.* (2009), societal beliefs about victimhood are one aspect of what is termed as the *ethos of conflict* – the other two aspects, of belief of justness in one's goals and delegitimization of the rival group, serve as themes that feed into each other to sustain the intergroup conflict. Thus, while such an ethos of conflict helps sustain conflict, a narrative of collective victimhood helps mobilize in-group members against a wrongdoing, evil, and delegitimized out-group.

Our discussion of dehumanization and collective victimhood narratives shows that such ideologies develop within groups and encourage a form of rigid hatred toward out-group members to the extent of demonizing them and placing them outside the norms of human society. In such contexts, all out-group members are painted in one broad stroke and seen as one homogeneous unit capable of irreparable injustice and harm against in-group members. Leadership in such groups is typically totalitarian, and such leaders are especially attractive as guides and torchbearers when group members experience heightened uncertainty and are in special need of direction (e.g. Rast *et al.*, 2013). Thus, while an us-versus-them categorization may not be sufficient to encourage collective violence, intergroup relations escalate to violent and dangerous proportions when such divisions become rigid and polarized, headed by authoritarian leaders who eschew dissent of any kind, the out-group is delegitimized and dehumanized, and the defeat of the evil out-group is seen as a self-protective, just, and noble act by the in-group.

Conclusion

In this chapter, we have discussed some ways in which a sense of us versus them is required for collective violence to be enacted. While arguments regarding resource threat and a sense of being deprived relative to the out-group are used to mobilize a group of individuals, a shared sense of identity – a sense of shared common fate and restoring a positive identity for us relative to them – is at the core of deep and inflexible intergroup divisions. Without a sense of *us* on one side against *them* on the other, orchestrated acts of violence could not occur. Moreover, when differences between groups are seen as immutable, a divide is presumed; this makes intergroup reconciliation and resolution of differences difficult (Miller and Prentice, 1999).

For an escalation of such rigid intergroup divisions into violent and aggressive acts against the out-group, a few more steps or aggravating conditions are required. As discussed above, such aggravating conditions could appear in the form of perceived and real threats to positive social identity or as a result of heightened identity-uncertainty – uncertainty about matters concerning the self-concept. In the quest for a positive, clear, and distinctive identity, groups can be mobilized by leaders who rely on ideologies that paint the out-group and in-group in clear binary distinctions.

In order to explicate the nature of intergroup divisions and in-group mobilization against an enemy, Moghaddam (2005) explains mobilization toward terrorist acts by envisioning a metaphorical staircase that comprises several floors that escalate toward the justification of violence and harmful acts against the out-group. At the lower floors of this staircase, people generally feel discontent and deprived relative to the out-group; there are no violent or aggressive acts carried out at this level. As one progresses toward the higher floors, one's worldview is characterized in terms of increasingly solidified divisions between one's in-group and the out-group.

It is at these higher stages that recruitment into radical organizations takes place. At these higher levels, violent acts are framed as just, noble, and in-group protective, while the enemy is psychologically distanced, for instance, through moral exclusion, dehumanization, or delegitimization. Thus, as one moves higher in this hierarchy of hate, an ideology that justifies destruction of the out-group is seen as valid. Ridding the world of the evil out-group and preserving one's group that is closely attached to the self is seen as a moral and even a noble act.

References

Abrams, D. and Hogg, M. A. (2010) Social identity and self-categorization. In J. F. Dovidio, M. Hewstone, P. Glick and V. M. Esses (eds.), *The SAGE Handbook of Prejudice, Stereotyping and Discrimination.* London: SAGE, pp. 179–193.

Abrams, D., Randsley de Moura, G., Marques, J. M., and Hutchison, P. (2008) Innovation credit: When can leaders oppose their group's norms? *Journal of Personality and Social Psychology*, 95, 662–678.

Barreto, N. B. and Hogg, M. A. (2017) Evaluation of and support for group prototypical leaders: A meta-analysis of twenty years of empirical research. *Social Influence*, 12, 41–55.

Bar-Tal, D. (2000) From intractable conflict through conflict resolution to reconciliation: Psychological analysis. *Political Psychology*, 21, 351–365.

Bar-Tal, D. and Hammack, P. (2012) Conflict, delegitimization, and violence. In L. Tropp (ed.), *The Oxford Handbook of Intergroup Conflict.* New York: Oxford University Press, pp. 29–52.

Bar-Tal, D., Chernyak-Hai, L., Schori, N., and Gundar, A. (2009) A sense of self-perceived collective victimhood in intractable conflicts. *International Review of the Red Cross*, 91, 229–258.

Belavadi, S. and Hogg, M. A. (2016) Conflict between ethno-linguistic groups: Language traitors, language loyalists, and the influence of uncertainty. *Journal of Language and Social Psychology*, 35, 446–457.

Belavadi, S. and Hogg, M. A. (2018) We are victims! How observers evaluate a group's claims of collective victimhood. *Journal of Applied Social Psychology*, 48, 651–660.

Blanz M., Mummendey A., and Otten S. (1995) Positive–negative asymmetry in social discrimination: The impact of stimulus valence and size and status differentials on intergroup evaluations. *British Journal of Social Psychology*, 34, 409–419.

Blascovich, J. and Tomaka, J. (1996) The biopsychosocial model of arousal regulation. *Advances in Experimental Social Psychology*, 28, 1–51.

Brewer, M. B. (1999) The psychology of prejudice: Ingroup love and outgroup hate? *Journal of Social Issues*, 55, 429–444.

Coleman, P. T. (2006) Intractable conflict. In M. Deutsch, P. T. Coleman and E. C. Marcus (eds), *The Handbook of Conflict Resolution: Theory and Practice.* San Francisco: Jossey-Bass, pp. 533–560.

Donohue, W. A. (2012) The identity trap: The language of genocide. *Journal of Language and Social Psychology*, 31, 13–29.

Doosje, B., Loseman, A., and van den Bos, K. (2013) Determinants of the radicalization process of Islamic youth in the Netherlands: Personal uncertainty, perceived injustice and perceived group threat. *Journal of Social Issues*, 69, 586–604.

Doosje, B., van den Bos, K., Loseman, A., Feddes, A. R., and Mann, L. (2012) My in-group is Superior! Susceptibility for radical right-wing attitudes and behaviors in Dutch youth. *Negotiation and Conflict Management Research*, 5, 253–268.

Dupuis, D. R., Porat, R., and Wohl, M. J. A. (2015) Collective angst and intractable conflicts: How concern for the in-group's future vitality shapes adversarial intergroup relations. In K. Sharvit and E. Halperin (eds), *The Social Psychology of Intractable Conflicts: Celebrating the Legacy of Daniel Bar-Tal, Volume I.* New York: Springer, pp. 131–142.

Ellemers, N. (1993) The influence of socio-structural variables on identity management strategies. *European Review of Social Psychology*, 4, 27–57.

Esses, V. M., Jackson, L. M., and Armstrong, T. L. (1998) Intergroup competition and attitudes toward immigrants and immigration: An instrumental model of group conflict. *Journal of Social Issues*, 54, 699–724.

Fiske, S. T., Cuddy, A. J. C, Glick, P., and Xu, J. (2002) A model of (often mixed) stereotype content: competence and warmth respectively follow from perceived status and competition. *Journal of Personality and Social Psychology*, 82, 878–902.

Gaffney, A. M., Rast III, D. E., Hackett, J. D., and Hogg, M. A. (2014) Further to the right: Uncertainty, political polarization and the American "Tea Party" movement. *Social Influence*, 9, 272–288.

Giessner, S. R., and van Knippenberg, D. (2008) "License to fail": Goal definition, leader group prototypicality, and perceptions of leadership effectiveness after leader failure. *Organisational Behaviour and Human Decision Processes*, 105, 14–35.

Giner-Sorolla, R., Leidner, B., and Castano, E. (2012) Dehumanization, demonization, and morality shifting: Paths to moral certainty in extremist violence. In M. A. Hogg and D. L. Blaylock (eds), *Extremism and the Psychology of Uncertainty.* Chichester, UK: Wiley-Blackwell, pp. 165–182.

Goldman, L., Giles, H., and Hogg, M. A. (2014) Going to extremes: Social identity and communication processes associated with gang membership. *Group Processes & Intergroup Relations*, 17, 813–832.

Guillén, L., Jacquart, P., and Hogg, M. A. (2018) *Leadership and the Dark Triad: How Self-uncertainty Helps Malevolent Leaders Rise to the Top*. Academy of Management Best Paper Proceedings.
Haslam, N. (2006) Dehumanization: An integrative Review. *Personality and Social Psychology Review*, 10, 252–264.
Haslam, N. and Loughnan, S. (2014) Dehumanization and infrahumanization. *Annual Review of Psychology*, 65, 399–423.
Hogg, M. A. (1993) Group cohesiveness: A critical review and some new directions. *European Review of Social Psychology*, 4, 85–111.
Hogg, M. A. (2000) Subjective uncertainty reduction through self-categorization: A motivational theory of social identity processes. *European Review of Social Psychology*, 11, 223–255.
Hogg, M. A. (2007) Uncertainty–identity theory. *Advances in Experimental Social Psychology*, 39, 69–126.
Hogg, M. A. (2012) Uncertainty-identity theory. In P. A. M. Van Lange, A. W. Kruglanski, and E. T. Higgins (eds), *Handbook of Theories of Social Psychology Vol. 2*. Thousand Oaks, CA: Sage, pp. 62–80.
Hogg, M. A. (2014) From uncertainty to extremism: Social categorization and identity processes. *Current Directions in Psychological Science*, 23, 338–342.
Hogg, M. A. (2016) Social identity theory. In S. McKeown, R. Haji, and N. Ferguson (eds), *Understanding Peace and Conflict Through Social Identity Theory*. Cham, Switzerland: Springer International, pp. 3–17.
Hogg, M. A. (2018a) Social identity theory. In P. J. Burke (ed.), *Contemporary Social Psychological Theories*, 2nd ed. Stanford, CA: Stanford University Press, pp. 112–138.
Hogg, M. A. (2018b) Self-uncertainty, leadership preference, and communication of social identity. *Atlantic Journal of Communication*, 26, 111–121.
Hogg, M. A. and Adelman, J. (2013) Uncertainty-identity theory: Extreme groups, radical behavior, and authoritarian leadership. *Journal of Social Issues*, 69, 436–454.
Hogg, M. A. and Mahajan, N. (2018) Domains of self-uncertainty and their relationship to group identification. *Journal of Theoretical Social Psychology*, 2, 67–75.
Hogg, M. A. and Rinella, M. J. (2018) Social identities and shared realities. *Current Opinion in Psychology*, 23, 6–10.
Hogg, M. A. and Van Knippenberg, D. (2003) Social identity and leadership processes in groups. *Advances in Experimental Social Psychology*, 35, 1–52.
Hogg, M. A., Hains, S. C., and Mason, I. (1998) Identification and leadership in small groups: Salience, frame of reference, and leader stereotypicality effects on leader evaluations. *Journal of Personality and Social Psychology*, 75, 1248–1263.
Hogg, M. A., Kruglanski, A., and van den Bos, K. (2013) Uncertainty and the roots of extremism. *Journal of Social Issues*, 69, 407–418.
Hogg, M. A., Meehan, C., and Farquharson, J. (2010) The solace of radicalism: Self-uncertainty and group identification in the face of threat. *Journal of Experimental Social Psychology*, 46, 1061–1066.
Hogg, M. A., Van Knippenberg, D., and Rast, D. E. III (2012) The social identity theory of leadership: Theoretical origins, research findings, and conceptual developments. *European Review of Social Psychology*, 23, 258–304.
Hogg, M. A., Sherman, D. K., Dierselhuis, J., Maitner, A. T., and Moffitt, G. (2007) Uncertainty, entitativity, and group identification. *Journal of Experimental Social Psychology*, 43, 135–142.
Hohman, Z. P., Hogg, M. A., and Bligh, M. C. (2010) Identity and intergroup leadership: Asymmetrical political and national identification in response to uncertainty. *Self and Identity*, 9, 113–128.
Kerr, N. L., Ao, X., Hogg, M. A., and Zhang, J. (2018) Addressing replicability concerns via adversarial collaboration: Discovering hidden moderators of the minimal intergroup discrimination effect. *Journal of Experimental Social Psychology*, 78, 66–76.
King, M. and Taylor, D. M. (2011) The radicalization of homegrown jihadists: A review of theoretical models and social psychological evidence. *Terrorism and Political Violence*, 23, 602–622.
Kruglanski, A. W., Gelfand, M. J., Bélanger, J. J., Sheveland, A., Hetiarachchi, M., and Gunaratna, R. (2014) The psychology of radicalization and deradicalization: How significance quest impacts violent extremism. *Political Psychology*, 35, 69–93.
Kteily, N. S. and Bruneau, E. (2017) Darker demons of our nature: The need to (re) focus attention on blatant forms of dehumanization. *Current Directions in Psychological Science*, 26, 487–494.
LeVine, R. A. and Campbell, D. T. (1972) *Ethnocentrism: Theories of Conflict, Ethnic Attitudes, and Group Behavior*. Oxford: John Wiley & Sons.
Leyens, J. P., Paladino, P. M., Rodriguez-Torres, R., Vaes, J., Demoulin, S., Rodriguez-Perez, A., and Gaunt, R. (2000) The emotional side of prejudice: The attribution of secondary emotions to ingroups and outgroups. *Personality and Social Psychology Review*, 4, 186–197.

Li, M., Leidner, B., and Castano, E. (2014) Toward a comprehensive taxonomy of dehumanization: Integrating two senses of humanness, mind perception theory, and stereotype content model. *Testing, Psychometrics, Methodology in Applied Psychology*, 21, 285–300.

McPherson, S. and Parks, C. D. (2011) Intergroup and interindividual resource competition escalating into conflict: The elimination option. *Group Dynamics: Theory, Research, and Practice*, 15, 285–296.

Miller, D. T. and Prentice, D. A. (1999) Some consequences of a belief in group essence: The category divide hypothesis. In D. A. Prentice and D. T. Miller (eds), *Cultural Divides: Understanding and Overcoming Group Conflict*. New York: Russell Sage Foundation.

Moghaddam, F. (2005) The staircase to terrorism: A psychological explanation. *American Psychologist*, 60, 161–169.

Moghaddam, F. and Love, K (2012) Collective uncertainty and extremism: A further discussion on the collective roots of subjective experience. In M. A. Hogg and D. L. Blaylock (eds), *Extremism and the Psychology of Uncertainty*. Chichester, UK: Wiley-Blackwell, pp. 246–262.

Mullen, B., Brown, R., and Smith, C. (1992) Ingroup bias as a function of salience, relevance, and status: An integration. *European Journal of Social Psychology*, 22, 103–122.

Mummendey, A. and Otten, S. (1998) Positive-negative asymmetry in social discrimination. *European Review of Social Psychology*, 9, 107–143.

Noor, M., Vollhardt, J. R., Mari, S., and Nadler, A. (2017) The social psychology of collective victimhood. *European Journal of Social Psychology*, 47, 121–134.

Opotow, S. (1990) Moral Exclusion and Injustice: An Introduction. *Journal of Social Issues*, 46, 1–20.

Osborne, D., and Sibley, C. G. (2015) Opposing paths to ideology: Group-based relative deprivation predicts conservatism through warmth toward ingroup and outgroup members. *Social Justice Research*, 28, 27–51.

Pettigrew, T. F., Christ, O., Wagner, U., Meertens, R. W., van Dick, R., and Zick, A. (2008) Relative deprivation and intergroup prejudice. *Journal of Social Issues*, 64, 385–401.

Rast, D. E. III, Gaffney, A. M., Hogg, M. A., and Crisp, R. J. (2012) Leadership under uncertainty: When leaders who are non-prototypical group members can gain support. *Journal of Experimental Social Psychology*, 48, 646–653.

Rast D. E. III, Hogg, M. A., and Giessner, S. R. (2013) Self-uncertainty and support for autocratic leadership. *Self and Identity*, 12, 635–649.

Reicher, S., and Hopkins, N. (2003) On the science of the art of leadership. In D. van Knippenberg and M. A. Hogg (eds), *Leadership and Power: Identity Processes in Groups and Organizations*. London, UK: Sage, pp. 197–209.

Reicher, S., Haslam, S. A., and Hopkins, N. (2005) Social identity and the dynamics of leadership: Leaders and followers as collaborative agents in the transformation of social reality. *The Leadership Quarterly*, 16, 547–568.

Rios, K., Sosa, N., and Osborn, H. (2018) An experimental approach to Intergroup Threat Theory: Manipulations, moderators, and consequences of realistic vs. symbolic threat. *European Review of Social Psychology*, 29, 212–255.

Seyranian, V. (2012) Constructing extremism: Uncertainty provocation and reduction by extremist leaders. In M. A. Hogg and D. L. Blaylock (Eds.), *Extremism and the Psychology of Uncertainty*. Boston: Wiley-Blackwell, pp. 228–245.

Seyranian, V. and Bligh, M. C. (2008) Presidential charismatic leadership: Exploring the rhetoric of social change. *The Leadership Quarterly*, 19, 54–76.

Sherif, M. (1966) *In Common Predicament: Social Psychology of Intergroup Conflict and Cooperation*. Boston: Houghton Mifflin.

Sherif, M., Harvey, O. J., White, B. J., Hood, W. R., and Sherif, C. W. (1988) *The Robber's Cave Experiment: Intergroup Conflict and Cooperation*. Connecticut: Wesleyan University Press.

Sherman, D. K., Hogg, M. A., and Maitner, A. T. (2009) Perceived polarization: Reconciling ingroup and intergroup perceptions under uncertainty. *Group Processes & Intergroup Relations*, 12, 95–109.

Smith, H. J., Pettigrew, T. F., Pippin, G. M., and Bialosiewicz, S. (2012) Relative deprivation: A theoretical and meta-analytic review. *Personality and Social Psychology Review*, 16, 203–232.

Stanton, G. H. (2004) Could the Rwandan genocide have been prevented? *Journal of Genocide Research*, 6, 211–228.

Staub, E. (1989) *The Roots of Evil: The Origins of Genocide and Other Group Violence*. New York: Cambridge University Press.

Staub, E. (1999) The origins and prevention of genocide, mass killing and other collective violence. *Peace and Conflict: Journal of Peace Psychology*, 5, 303–337.

Staub, E. (2012) Uncertainty, and the roots and prevention of genocide and terrorism. In M. A. Hogg and D. L. Blaylock (eds), *Extremism and the Psychology of Uncertainty*. Chichester, UK: Wiley-Blackwell, pp. 263–280.

Staub, E. and Bar-Tal, D. (2003) Genocide, mass killing and intractable conflict: Roots, evolution, prevention and reconciliation. In D. Sears, L. Huddy, and R. Jervis (eds), *Handbook of Political Psychology*. New York: Oxford University Press, pp. 710–754.

Stenstrom, D. M., Lickel, B., Denson, T. F., and Miller, N. (2008) The roles of ingroup identification and outgroup entitativity in intergroup retribution. *Personality and Social Psychology Bulletin*, 34, 1570–1582.

Tajfel, H. (1970) Experiments in intergroup discrimination. *Scientific American*, 223, 96–102.

Tajfel, H. (1972) Social categorization. English manuscript of 'La catégorisation sociale'. In S. Moscovici (ed.), *Introduction à la psychologie sociale*, Vol. 1. Paris: Larousse, pp. 272–302.

Tajfel, H., and Turner, J. C. (1979) An integrative theory of inter-group conflict. In W. G. Austin and S. Worchel (eds), *The Social Psychology of Intergroup Relations*. Monterey, CA: Brooks/Cole, pp. 33–47.

Tajfel, H., and Turner, J. C. (1986) The social identity theory of intergroup behaviour. In S. Worchel and W. G. Austin (eds), *Psychology of Intergroup Relations*, 2nd ed. Chicago: Nelson-Hall, pp. 7–24.

Tajfel, H., Billig, M., Bundy, R. P., and Flament, C. (1971) Social categorization and intergroup behaviour. *European Journal of Social Psychology*, 1, 149–177.

Tilly, C. (2003) *The Politics of Collective Violence*. Cambridge, UK: Cambridge University Press.

Turner, J. C., Hogg, M. A., Oakes, P. J., Reicher, S. D., and Wetherell, M. S. (1987) *Rediscovering the Social Group: A Self-categorization Theory*. Oxford, UK: Blackwell.

van Bergen, D. D., Feddes, A. F., Doosje, B., and Pels, T. V. M. (2015) Collective identity factors and the attitude toward violence in defense of ethnicity or religion among Muslim youth of Turkish and Moroccan descent. *International Journal of Intercultural Relations*, 47, 89–100.

Waller, J. (2003) *Becoming Evil: How Ordinary People Commit Genocide and Mass Killing*. New York: Oxford University Press.

Wohl, M. J. A., Branscombe, N. R., and Reysen, S. (2010) Perceiving your group's future to be in jeopardy: Extinction threat induces collective angst and the desire to strengthen the ingroup. *Personality and Social Psychology Bulletin*, 36, 898–910.

Wohl, M. J., Giguère, B., Branscombe, N. R., and McVicar, D. N. (2011) One day we might be no more: Collective angst and protective action from potential distinctiveness loss. *European Journal of Social Psychology*, 41, 289–300.

3

EMOTIONAL UNDERPINNINGS OF WAR

An evolutionary analysis of anger and hatred

Aaron N. Sell and Anthony C. Lopez

Introduction

Warfare is an instance of collective action in which members of one group impose physical damage upon one or more members of another group (Pietraszewski, 2016; Glowacki *et al.*, 2017; Lopez, 2019). Although the stated rationales for warfare are myriad and not mutually exclusive, ranging from sex and sorcery, to revenge and resources (Keeley, 1996; Gat, 2006), these goals are often facilitated by one or a combination of emotions that are designed to organise motivation, reasoning, and behaviour in ways that would have been ancestrally adaptive.

Although many emotions likely facilitate political violence generally and warfare specifically, we focus on two in particular: anger and hatred. These two emotions predictably and distinctly shape the character of collective violence at multiple stages of fighting, including: the triggers of aggression, the selection of targets, the pace and character of escalation and brinkmanship, and the possibility of surrender and reconciliation. Since large-scale social phenomena (such as warfare) must rest upon ecologically valid microfoundations of individual psychology, we begin by elaborating the adaptationist approach to understanding the evolved function of anger and hatred. Once the contours of this framework are outlined, we describe some of the ways in which this psychology is manifest in contexts of modern warfare.

Evolution and the adaptationist programme

Life on Earth is the product of natural selection (Darwin, 1859 [2004]; Dawkins, 1996). The differential reproductive success of different genes over long periods of time led to organisms acquiring functional design that aided the replication of their genes in ancestral environments. Put unemotionally, animals are "gene machines" – highly ordered mechanisms composed of chemical matter (mostly carbon and water) that inherited their current form because their ancestors had mutations that increased their probability of reproducing their genetic code (Dawkins, 1976).

Taking evolution seriously led biologists to create a programme for understanding animal design and behaviour – the adaptationist programme (Williams, 1966). This programme involves matching evolved design (e.g. fur) with the way in which it aided reproduction for that animal's ancestors (e.g. conserving body heat). This initial match is treated as a hypothesis and is supported only if multiple independent features of the "adaptation" are improbably well-designed for performing that function. For example, the fur of aquatic mammals is improbably well tailored to underwater thermal regulation – the hairs are shorter, denser, and flatter in ways that enable air to be trapped in the fur and act as a buffer to the colder water (Liwanag *et al.*, 2012). The more features of the adaptation that are consistent with the posited function, the more confident we can be that the adaptation evolved for that function.

Evolutionary psychologists use this adaptationist programme to discover the evolved function of human cognitive systems (Buss, 2005; Cosmides and Tooby, 1994, 1995, 2000; Tooby and Cosmides, 1989). They can then use those functions to "map the mind" – that is, to identify the myriad components of human nature, such as: the way the mind identifies kin (Lieberman *et al.*, 2007), the function of emotions such as pride (Sznycer *et al.*, 2017) and forgiveness (McCullough, 2008), as well as coalitional dynamics such as our attentiveness to and evaluation of leaders (Antonakis and Dalgas, 2009; Garfield *et al.*, 2019).

The recalibrational theory and the evolved function of anger

Anger is a universal human emotion, experienced in a similar fashion across cultures and individuals (Ekman, 1973; Sell, 2011; Sell *et al.*, 2017). It bares the hallmarks of being an evolved adaptation, including early ontogenetic development (Galati *et al.*, 2003), universal design (Ekman, 1973; Scherer and Wallbott, 1994; Sell *et al.*, 2017), and most importantly *functional* design (Sell *et al.*, 2017). To understand what anger is and why it works the way it does, we have to understand why anger evolved, i.e. why did human ancestors who experienced anger the way that we do out-reproduce those who inherited different variants of anger? Framed differently, what was the problem that anger solved for our ancestors?

The recalibrational theory of anger (Sell, 2011; Sell *et al.*, 2009, 2017) posits that the evolved function of anger is to bargain for better treatment. When successful, anger "recalibrates" the target so that they put greater concern on the angry individual's welfare in current and future decisions. For example, a man is rude to his colleague, the colleague becomes angry at him and confronts him about his behaviour. His rudeness is illustrated to him, and he apologises, recalibrates, and treats his colleague better in the future. In this way, angry individuals in our evolutionary past protected their own interests and out-reproduced those who tolerated poor treatment from others.

To understand this recalibration process, we must understand what is actually being recalibrated. What part of the mind is changed when a person concedes a fight and apologises? According to the recalibrational theory, anger has its effects by upregulating the "welfare trade-off ratio" toward the angry individual. Welfare trade-off ratios are hypothetical mental barometers that store the extent to which we will value another individual's welfare compared with our own when making decisions that affect us both (Tooby *et al.*, 2008). For example, a student asks their professor to look over a paper they have due in another class. Whether he helps or not depends on how much he values the student's welfare (i.e. his welfare trade-off ratio (WTR) toward the student). Conflicts of interest thus indicate how much an individual values another's welfare. For example, if a hungry man skips dinner to comfort a friend, it indicates a high value WTR toward that friend. If a wealthy individual refuses a hungry orphan a slice of bread, it indicates a low WTR toward the child (see Sell *et al.*, 2017).

Of course, setting a welfare trade-off ratio above zero (i.e. caring about another's welfare at all) comes at a cost to that individual, by definition. Evolution would – generally – design animals to put no weight on the welfare of others. But there are known exceptions to this wherein an organism can reproduce more by accepting temporary costs (Nowak, 2006). Most relevant to anger, animals will frequently accept costs and forgo benefits when competing with more formidable animals, i.e. animals that can impose greater costs typically via aggression. Because the costs of punishment can be greater than the costs of deferring to the more dominant animal (Clutton-Brock and Parker, 1995) weaker animals will (in general) evolve to cede resources to stronger animals. This is the source of dominance hierarchies (Archer, 1988).

Thus, welfare trade-off ratios appear calibrated by relative formidability such that those with greater fighting ability expect and demand better treatment (Lukaszewski *et al.*, 2016; Sell *et al.*, 2009). The fact that welfare trade-off ratios are calibrated by formidability offers anger an opportunity to fulfil its function – if WTRs respond to estimates of formidability and the willingness to impose costs, then anger can demonstrate formidability and the willingness to impose costs as a means of recalibrating a low WTR in the target of anger (i.e. the person one is angry at). This, as we argue below, typifies anger-based aggression.

In sum, the evolved function of anger is to recalibrate the status-setting mental mechanisms of individuals who indicate that they value your interests insufficiently. Its evolved purpose is to recalibrate the target, and restore acceptable treatment. This is not the function of hatred (see Table 3.1).

The neutralization theory of hatred

An analysis of hatred indicates contrasting design to anger. Rather than attempting to recalibrate a target and restore deference and cooperation, hatred appears designed to limit or eliminate a target whose existence is damaging to the hate-filled person. We will refer to such a person as an "enemy". Our definition deviates somewhat from the dictionary definition of "enemy"

Table 3.1 Functional differences between anger and hatred

	Anger	*Hatred*
Adaptive Problem	People who lack enough concern for your welfare; e.g. disrespect	People whose existence is bad for you
Primary Purpose	Recalibrate target, restoring compliance and/or cooperation	Diminish negative externalities by depowering or eliminating the target
Trigger	Cues of low WTR	Cues of negative association value
Verbal behaviours	Arguments designed to recalibrate the target of anger	Surreptitious recruitment of allies Harm the target's reputation
Signals	Attention gathering displays Formidability-enhancement displays (e.g. anger face/posture)	None
Style of aggression	Bargaining (i.e. low-cost demonstrations, followed by rule-based escalation if necessary)	Predatory. High-damage timed to when the target is vulnerable
Ending conditions	Realize target has high WTR Target recalibration (i.e. apology)	Association value becomes positive Target neutralised
Individual differences	Preferred strategy for those with high relative bargaining power	Preferred strategy for those with low relative bargaining power

which implies mutual hostility between the parties. Our definition of enemy is specifically a person whose existence is damaging to the hate-filled person, and can include someone who is not hostile in return (e.g. a romantic rival who nonetheless like you can still be your enemy).

An enemy can be precisely defined as an individual for whom one has a negative association value. An association value is the net fitness consequences one individual has on another. High association values are typically held by friends and family members who improve your welfare by monitoring social environments, sharing rare resources, dispensing knowledge, combining labour, dispersing risk, and so forth. An enemy is one who has a negative association value: their existence is (on average) bad for you. The existence of enemies in our ancestral past would have selected for a cognitive adaptation, a part of human nature, designed to deal with their existence in ways that increased our ancestors' reproduction. Just as with anger, the design of the emotion hatred should match the nature of the problem it evolved to address. What could our ancestors do to minimise the consequences of their enemies? By hypothesis, we propose that a general solution evolved to deal with enemies, which is to heap costs upon them. These increasing costs could have had up to three beneficial effects for the hate-filled person:

(1) the target can respond to their worsening conditions by removing themselves (physically or socially) from the hate-filled person and thus minimise their interactions and the opportunities to impose costs on the hate-filled person;
(2) the target can be rendered less powerful (via physical, reputational, sexual, or other mediums) and thus less able to impose costs on the hate-filled person; or
(3) the target can die, rendering them incapable of actively imposing costs on the hate-filled person.

How are these cost impositions accomplished? We argue in this chapter that hatred calibrates the hate-filled person's welfare trade-off ratio toward the target to be negative, i.e. costs to the hated person are treated as benefits to the hate-filled person. As discussed with anger, welfare trade-off ratios function to make trade-offs during conflicts of interest. For example, the higher a welfare trade-off ratio Bob has toward Nancy, the more Bob will accept costs to benefit her, and the less Bob will impose costs on Nancy to benefit himself. If Bob hates Nancy (i.e. adopts a negative welfare trade-off ratio) he will treat any benefit to Nancy as a reason *not* to do the action, and will treat a cost to Nancy as a reason to do it. In other words, negative welfare trade-off ratios sanction spiteful acts (e.g. hurting yourself just to hurt the other person, and denying yourself a benefit as long as it hurts the other person). The magnitude of the welfare trade-off ratio indicates the extent to which they will accept costs to hurt the hated other. For example, an extremely negative WTR was exemplified by Captain Ahab at the end of Moby Dick (a classic book detailing an obsessive quest of Captain Ahab for revenge on Moby Dick, the giant white sperm whale that had previously bitten off his leg at the knee). Here Captain Ahab gives all he has (his last breath – a precious thing) to spit at the whale (a trivial cost to the hated other).

Highly negative WTRs presumably have many effects similar to highly positive WTRs, e.g. person-specific memory is probably enhanced such that individuals remember information about both their loved friends and hated enemies. On the other hand, some effects are likely opposite; e.g. while a high positive WTR engages empathy such that the suffering of one's loved child is "felt" as suffering to the parent, a highly negative WTR reverses the polarities such that the suffering of one's hated enemy is felt as enjoyment to the hate-filled person.

In addition to sanctioning actual cost infliction, hatred should be designed to deploy social forces against the target. In short, hatred is predicted to motivate the spread of information detrimental to the well-being and social status of the target of hatred. This serves both to lessen the hated person's status but also recruit allies for group-based aggression. Interestingly, there is no particular need for the hate-filled person to be honest when they spread gossip and rumours about the target of hatred. This is unlike anger-based arguments, which are often rebutted by the target and which function primarily in cooperative relationships, wherein truth-telling between partners is of value to both participants (i.e. lying to win an argument with your spouse will likely have detrimental repercussions later). Furthermore, anger-based arguments even outside of cooperative relationships can risk costly escalation when one party is found to be lying. However, in hatred-based information warfare the target's association value is negative so there is little danger in sacrificing future cooperation, and escalations are less concerning because the target is already an enemy. In short, we should expect a hunger for negative information about a hated target and no substantial concern about the truth of that information. In fact, insistence on the truth of a charge against a hated individual will likely imply a lack of hatred that can be disconcerting (e.g. someone standing up for Hitler against claims that he was an animal-abuser may sound insufficiently anti-Nazi even though he is innocent of those charges). In total, the negative WTR that is adopted under hatred leads the hate-filled individual to damage the welfare of the target by denying them benefits and actively imposing costs. It functions to neutralise the enemy and reduce their power rather than recalibrate them and restore cooperative treatment.

Triggers of anger and hatred

Anger and hatred have distinct functions, and therefore they are predicted to have distinct triggers. Anger should be deployed at individuals who indicate that their WTR toward the angry person is lower than some threshold of acceptability. This threshold is presumably set by factors that relate to bargaining power; e.g. stronger men expect higher WTRs from others (Sell *et al.*, 2009) and deploy anger over a greater range of offences, as do juvenile boys and girls (Sell *et al.*, 2016). While we focus on formidability-based WTRs in this chapter, it is important to note that the cooperative nature of human relationships also means that bargaining power and WTRs can be set by many other factors, e.g. the mutual regard that spouses have for one another is rarely based on their ability to physically harm each other. Another example: more physically attractive women (and to a lesser extent men) have also been shown to demand higher WTRs and deploy anger over a greater range of offences (Sell *et al.*, 2009, 2016).

Indications of one's WTR can come from many channels. In fact, argument analyses suggest at least 12 computationally distinct triggers of anger (Sell, 2014). The most common is a cost infliction; specifically, the target of anger imposes a cost or refuses a benefit to the angry person, e.g. a roommate refuses to pick you up from class in their car, or a colleague takes your headphones without asking (see Sell *et al.*, 2017). Others can be symbolic or material indicators that correlate with less respect (i.e. a lower WTR). For example, insults that imply that one is unworthy of value (e.g. that the target is unattractive or unintelligent or emits foul odours), or failure to remember information about the individual (e.g. forgetting an anniversary), and so on (see Sell *et al.*, 2017). In each case, anger is triggered because of information that implies the target of anger holds a low WTR toward the angry person.

Hatred, on the other hand, responds to cues of a negative association value; i.e. when the totality of another's impact on your life is negative, or, colloquially, your life would be better off without them. Commonly, such a person is hated because they place little value on your welfare and thus anger and hatred can both be active. For example, a bully who treats you disrespectfully at work can be both the subject of your anger – as a bargaining strategy to recalibrate their WTR toward you – and hatred – as a strategy for getting rid of them from your social world. If the anger is successful and the bully apologises and ends their mistreatment, then hatred too may switch off because the bully is not likely to negatively impact your life in the future.

In most cases of anger, however, hatred is not active. This is known because most cases of anger occur within the context of valued relationships –often characterised by love (Averill, 1982). In these cases, anger functions to bargain for better treatment, but the association value with the target of anger is still positive. Hatred is caused by a negative association value, which is an average of another's impact on your welfare, e.g. someone who abuses your child but gets you a great deal on car insurance is still an enemy. This means that hatred can be triggered even by multiple justifiable impositions, while anger may not, e.g. a needy and incompetent colleague who constantly requires help and never seems to improve. Each individual imposition may be justified: after all, you are better able to solve the problem than they are – but taken together your life is made worse for their existence. As noted by Sell (2012), this could explain the abuse of elders in assisted living conditions, some of whom require costly and repeated help to maintain their lives.

Hatred evolved because it increased our ancestors' reproduction by preventing future harms (i.e. there is no logical reason to punish past harms unless it impacts the future). This means that if a person with an innocuous history is likely to produce harms sufficient to turn their association value negative in the future, then hatred will likely be triggered. This is one explanation for some classic work in social psychology showing that individuals will dislike their own victims, i.e. by hurting someone unjustly you have made an enemy because their future behaviour toward you will likely be negative (Schopler and Compere, 1971).

Aggression borne of anger and hatred

Anger-based aggression

The recalibrational theory of anger states that the primary evolved function of anger is to recalibrate the target's WTR. This is because, for some human relationships, the WTR is calibrated by estimates of formidability, the anger system should be designed to deploy demonstrations of fighting ability and willingness to aggress as a low-cost means of winning the conflict and recalibrating the target. There are abundant animal precedents for this kind of aggression, called "ritualized aggression" "conflicts of assessment" or "sequential assessment" (Alcock, 2009; Archer, 1988; Sell, 2011). From an evolutionary biological point of view, ritualized aggression is an interaction wherein two animals attempt to assess each other's fighting ability so as to avoid the costs of a real fight. The early stages of ritualized aggression are typically perceptual evaluations during which animals flex and enhance their cues of fighting ability (e.g. baring fangs, piloerections). For example, a breed of cichlid (a fish) will engage in staring contests and parallel swimming during which they evaluate the fighting ability of their opponent (Enquist and Leimar, 1983). If one of the fish indicates submission, the aggression ends. If not, the fight can escalate to more accurate but dangerous indicators of fighting ability (e.g. the fish can lock jaws with one another and shake, sometimes damaging their mouths, a process called "mouth-wrestling"). Only in the later stages of assessment are these bouts potentially lethal. These contests evolved from mutualism: both contestants benefit by not paying the full costs of aggression, which likely involves injury to both the winner and loser.

Anger-based aggression is strikingly similar to these contests. A typical bout of anger-based aggression involves assessment, posturing, and the deployment of the universal "anger face" (Sell, 2011). The anger face itself is a relatively recent evolutionary adaptation – distinct from chimpanzee aggressive faces and part of evolved human nature (e.g. it is present in blind children, see Sell *et al.*, 2014). It is composed of at least seven distinct facial muscle movements that independently increase the features of the fact that distinguish physically strong from physically weak men (Sell, 2014). For example, stronger men typically have wider nostrils, a lower browridge, and thinner lips, and so the anger face flares the nostrils, pushes flesh over the browridge in ways that make it appear larger, and bends the lips inward to shrink their apparent size (Sell *et al.*, 2014, see also Marsh *et al.*, 2005). This face evolved because those who deployed it were able to intimidate their opponents and achieve recalibration earlier and at lower cost than those who deployed different faces. Similar processes presumably explain the human posturing that takes place in the early stages of anger-based aggression (e.g. chest inflated, legs together to maximise height, head tilted up to give the illusion of height, shoulders out).

When posturing does not resolve a conflict, it can escalate to actual aggression, though typically sub-lethal aggression. Pushing and shoving, for example, is extremely unlikely to incapacitate a target, but can indicate relative strength. These escalating patterns to aggression are extremely common in human fighting (Luckenbill, 1977; Daly and Wilson, 1988) and appear to be a feature particular to bargaining aggression (Sell, 2011). Some cultures have formalised these rituals in ways that remove the ambiguity of when to escalate, e.g. see Chagnon's (1983) descriptions of Yanamamo fighting, or William's (1980) description of Southern duelling. Regardless of these formal examples, there appears to be an instinct for the rules of assessment-based combat such that "cheating" invalidates the outcome (Romero *et al.*, 2014). The concept of "cheating" at aggression is sensible *only* if there are implicit rules to combat. These rules mean that aggression is designed to do something other than simply destroy one's opponent. In the case of anger-based aggression, a "cheap" or "cheating" move is one that reduces the accuracy of the bout such that the putative winner may not be the most formidable (e.g. a "sucker punch", challenging someone when they are already injured, and so on). These escalating fights work, when they work, by demonstrating one's formidability to the target in ways that lead them to upregulate their WTR.

Hatred-based aggression

Aggression deployed by hatred is predicted to be simpler than anger-based aggression. While anger-based aggression is akin to bargaining aggression in other animals, hatred-based aggression should look more like predatory aggression. While a predator hunts, it is not attempting to recalibrate territorial boundaries or change the dominance hierarchies stored in the prey animal: it is efficiently attempting to injure or kill the prey. Hatred-based aggression is similarly functional: it is designed to impose damage in a cost-effective way on the target. This predicts several discrepancies with anger-based aggression. Anger-based aggression is typically "loud" with attention-grabbing vocalizations, facial displays, posturing, yelling and low-cost demonstrations of formidability, such as hitting inanimate objects. Hatred-based aggression is predicted to be relatively quiet, like a predator stalking prey. Signalling the aggressive intent is a crucial part of anger-based bargaining aggression because it allows the target to recalibrate without having to pay the mutual costs of aggression and it sets the stage for a "fair" fight to determine who is more formidable. Signalling is a mistake in hatred-based predatory aggression because it allows the target to prepare to defend themselves.

As hatred is not trying to recalibrate the target, it does not need to gather the attention of the target or signal information to them. Rather, information (true information at least) should be denied the hated person so as to render them less competent. For this reason, there does not appear to be a "hate" face in the same way that there is an anger face.[1] For example, when Leon

Gary Plauche shot the man who was accused of abusing his son – a crime caught on camera – his face appeared plain and unemotional. The function of the anger face is to bargain with the target by exaggerating cues of fighting ability in the face, but hatred does not need to interface with the cognitive mechanisms in the target or bargain for better treatment. It is designed to hurt the target surreptitiously, if possible.

Hatred-based aggression is also predicted to be shorter in duration, much as predatory aggression is in the wild. While anger-based aggression involves prolonged escalating aggression with ample time for either party to recalibrate and concede, hatred-based aggression is not designed to allow recalibration because the problem isn't a lack of WTR calibration but is rather the existence and power of the opponent. For this reason, hatred-based aggression should not escalate in a given bout but be at maximum from the start and rapidly deployed without signal (again, Leon Gary Plaunche's assassination of his enemy is a clear example of this).[2]

Anger and hatred-based aggression respond differently to signs of weakness in the target. Bargaining aggression often conforms to implicit or explicit rules about allowing a defeated opponent to retreat. These limitations, like the ritualised aggression of other animals, allow for accurate estimates of formidability so as to trigger recalibration. Yet, hatred is functioning to inflict damage on the target, not to recalibrate it, and so any temporary weakness or vulnerability in the target is an opportunity to inflict costs with less retaliatory risks. As such, hatred should motivate increased aggression toward an enemy that signals weakness, an unwillingness to fight, or other indicators that cost-infliction will not lead to retaliation. The instinct to crush an enemy when they indicate weakness has been described under the term "forward panic" (Collins, 2008).

Ending conditions of hatred and anger

Emotions are temporary modes of operation (Cosmides and Tooby, 2000). As such, they have endpoint conditions that shut them off. Two such endpoint conditions have been posited for anger: (1) a contradiction of the inputs, i.e. you realise you are angry when you shouldn't be; and (2) anger fulfils its function and the target recalibrates, i.e. the target apologises and you aren't angry anymore (see Sell, 2011). The first can occur during anger-based arguments when individuals present evidence and reframe social conflict in ways that change the angry person's estimate of their WTR. Indeed, research shows that targets of anger will select arguments that indicate that their actions were consistent with a high WTR, e.g. "it didn't hurt you that bad, and I had a good reason…" or that their relative bargaining power is in their favour, "Fine … but who is going to loan you money next week when your rent is due?" If the arguments made by the target of anger are effective in showing that the target's behaviour was consistent with a high WTR, or that the angry person was demanding too much deference from the target, then the episode will be terminated. The other endpoint condition of anger occurs when the target actually recalibrates and anger fulfils its function. Research shows conclusively that anger can, in many circumstances, be switched off by a sincere verbal apology even in the absence of any tangible recompense (Frantz and Bennigson, 2005). This is consistent with its function to recalibrate WTRs, i.e. the point is to change the target's mind.

For hatred, a logical analysis of its function suggests two means of switching off hatred. The first, as with anger, is evidence counteracting its triggers; i.e. discovering that you hate someone who actually has a positive association value. Put colloquially, love can trump hate. If a hate-filled person discovers that their enemy had been responsible for naming them for an award, or donating anonymously to their child's healthcare fund, or merely having said some nice words about the hate-filled person in a conversation that was thought to be private, then the predicted association value can become positive and hatred terminated. Whether this strategy for terminating an incident of hatred works depends, presumably, on the magnitude of the negative association value (i.e. were they hated a lot or a little?). The second way to end an incident of hatred is for it to fulfil its function and weaken, ostracise, or kill the target, at which point further hatred would be a waste of effort. While this prediction can be logically derived from our posited function of hatred, our intuition is that it may not be correct. Humans have a peculiar tendency to experience social emotions toward the dead, e.g. gratitude, anger, hatred, love. Nonetheless, when a hated target is depowered, this can satiate hatred if it removes the negative externalities caused by the hated person; e.g. a boss who is hated by the employees is demoted to a harmless entry-level position and then pitied.

Strategy preferences – who gets angry and who becomes full of hate?

When an individual is the victim of a cost, they have evidence that the offender has a low WTR toward them (i.e. the offender was willing to impose that cost) but also that the offender may have a negative association value (i.e. their life is now worse off because of the cost imposed by the offender). This means that anger and hatred may fire simultaneously, which we suspect is a common occurrence. That said, some individuals may be better able to bargain directly with the target via anger and other individuals may be better able to neutralise negative externalities by surreptitiously imposing costs on the target. If these asymmetries existed in our evolutionary past, then we should expect modern humans to calibrate their retaliatory strategies to the ancestral cues that determined which strategy was best given their circumstances. For example, the efficacy of anger depends primarily on bargaining power. Those with more power, can recalibrate others by demonstrating it. Those with less will find their attempts at bargaining frequently fail. Thus, research shows that individuals with more bargaining power (e.g. coalitional strength, individual fighting ability, and sexual attractiveness) are, on average, more prone to anger and aggressive bargaining than others (Sell *et al.*, 2009; Sell *et al.*, 2016). Hatred may be an emotion more common among the weak and others who cannot directly bargain for better treatment. For example, Mackie *et al.* (2000) find that appraisals of in-group strength (in contrast to weakness) elicited anger (instead of fear), as well as greater willingness to confront and attack a threatening out-group.

Key points and summary

The features of anger indicate its evolved function. Anger is a temporary state activated primarily by cues that indicate that someone holds a low welfare trade-off ratio toward the angry person. Anger then generates behavioural patterns that gather the target's attention and feeds them information relevant for the calibration of WTRs. The early stages of this bargaining are typically verbal (Sell, 2012), and involve information exchange about the events that triggered anger (e.g. "you were being so rude!") and interrogations of the target of anger to determine if the WTR apparent in their actions truly represents their actual concern for the angry person's welfare (e.g. "what were you thinking?" "do you know who I am?" "do you even know how mean you've been?"). If recalibration is not evident, anger can orchestrate bargaining tactics designed to recalibrate the target's WTRs. In the case of aggressive bargaining, this is done by enhancing cues of formidability in the body and face, and then engaging in an escalating pattern of aggression designed to prove to the target that they would be better off recalibrating than continuing to suffer from the aggression.

The primary purpose of anger is to recalibrate the target and restore compliance and/or cooperation. This is why it is most commonly deployed in the context of cooperative, even loving, relationships (Averill 1982). The same is not true of hatred. Hatred is an orientation toward an enemy, defined as an individual with a negative association value. Association value is a summary variable of the average predicted future consequences of that person's existence on one's welfare. If John has a negative association value for Daryl, it means that Daryl's life would be better without John. Such a circumstance would have recurred frequently among our ancestors and, as a result, hatred appears to have evolved to navigate this problem. The primary way hatred does that is to set a negative welfare trade-off ratio toward the hated other; i.e. to positively value costs to that person. Hatred then generates thoughts, fantasies, and plans of hurting that individual, often in ways that prevent detection, and remains vigilant for circumstances that enable cheap, efficient means of damaging the enemy. Any aggression generated by hatred will be akin to predatory aggression in animals: quick, highly damaging, and deployed using every available advantage. The primary purpose of hatred is to neutralise the enemy.

Anger, hate and warfare

Warfare can be defined simply as collective action with the purpose of hurting members of other groups, and its occurrence varies extensively across time and space in terms of motivations, instruments and scale. The application of anger and hatred to warfare relates to questions of motivation specifically, and we leave as an empirical question the issue of whether and how variation in the instruments and scale of war might affect the expression of these emotions. For example, some have argued that democracy relative to autocracy may be unusually susceptible to jingoism and vengeance (Levy, 1988). Others have argued that a capacity for hatred and revenge is what makes possible the irrational commitment to nuclear retaliation upon which stable deterrence depends (McDermott *et al.*, 2017). In the remainder of this chapter, however, we focus on the more general argument that the form of warfare reflects its underlying motivation. In the case of anger and hatred, this generates at least two types of warfare: rule-based bargaining war, and unrestrained total war.

Anger-based bargaining aggression and the limits of war

Many features of animal bargaining aggression appear prominently in human warfare. The key feature of anger-based aggression is that it functions to send bargaining signals that shape preferences, and does not seek the destruction of the target. Thus, generally speaking, warfare in these instances is "lethal but limited". In other words, the delivery of costs should be limited in such a way as to facilitate restructuring of adversary preferences. What are some of these limits? Scholarship on the limits of war is perhaps as old as war itself, as evidenced by ancient philosophical inquiries into "just war" as well as modern investigations of "limited war" (Osgood, 1957; Walzer, 2015). In practice, some limits are specific and codified, such as the Chemical Weapons Convention and the Geneva Accords. Other limits are clearly more ancient, such as the principle of diplomatic immunity, which has clear analogues in rules against killing the messenger or a guest in one's home, and are also common among foraging peoples (Boehm, 1984). Rules such as these that place limits on the methods of warfare are useful in only one context: when it is both possible and desirable to adjust the preferences of others. These limits can be organised in terms of the conduct and termination of war.

Conduct of war

One prominent limit that emerges in bargaining aggression involves the targeting of "innocents"; that is, bargaining aggression should differentially target an out-group's coercive abilities (e.g. combatants, not civilians; weapons, not warehouses). Therefore, modern efforts to limit the targeting of civilians are likely the product of an evolved intuition for bargaining aggression. For this aggression to be effective in restructuring an adversary's preferences, it must be discriminant, at least to a degree, even if it simultaneously carries the promise of greater pain – which it often must for coercive leverage. The point is not that bargaining aggression should *never* target non-combatants. Indeed, under some circumstances, targeting civilians can uniquely convey the costs of war so as to incentivise a restructuring of enemy preferences. This bargaining logic is evident, for example, in the decision of the United States to drop two atomic bombs on Japan in the Second World War, and in General Sherman's infamous March to the Sea during the American Civil War. In each of these cases, the targeting of civilians was not meant to cause pain for its own sake, but rather to compel a revision of relative bargaining power, it being clear that a cessation of aggression (i.e. the further targeting of civilians) was conditional upon it. This is in marked contrast to hate-based aggression, in which the targeting of civilians is intrinsically purposeful, unconditional, and unrestrained. This principle of discriminant violence spawns and explains a host of limits on the conduct of war, including the non-targeting of civilians as well as prohibitions against the use of certain weapons that are by nature non-discriminating, such as nuclear, chemical, and biological weapons. Such weapons are tellingly lumped together under the label of "Weapons of *Mass* Destruction".

The political science literature on "limited war" helps to convey the nature of these restraints in a useful way. For example, McClintock defines limited war as a conflict "short of general war to achieve specific political objectives, using limited forces and limited force" (McClintock, 1967). Stoker (2016), with reference to Clausewitz and Corbett, defines limited war more narrowly in terms of its objectives; that is, it is anything short of the overthrow of an enemy government. We are agnostic on whether the label "limited war" should rest on criteria specific to aims or methods; rather, we argue that the method of violence is likely to be shaped in character by its underlying motivation. In other words, the form of violence mirrors its ultimate function. In the case of anger-based aggression, this function is bargaining. Therefore, we are closer to Schelling, who notes that "[limited] war is always a bargaining process … The critical targets in such a war are in the mind of the enemy…" (Schelling, 1966, p. 142). Furthermore, and to emphasise the limits of force in bargaining aggression, Schelling also observes that "Coercion depends more on the threat of what is yet to come than on damage already done … the object is to make the enemy behave … not to destroy the subject altogether" (Schelling, 1966, p. 173).

Termination of war

To avoid the full costs of unlimited war, bargaining aggression must cease when cues of recalibration are received. This involves at least two steps: one is allowing the target the opportunity to signal recalibration (holding the head of one's adversary under water is a poor method for determining whether preference adjustment has occurred), and the second is cessation of aggression itself. As Schelling (1966, 126) illustrates, "the very idea of 'surrender' brings bargaining and accommodation into warfare". Bargaining aggression should therefore be characterised by restraint at the treatment of prisoners (e.g. inhibition toward trophy taking, torture), and surrender should be meaningful and lead to a cessation of aggression rather than seized upon as an opportunity for ambush and complete rout.

For example, Harkavy explains that part of Kissinger's strategy for a resolution to the 1973 Arab–Israeli war entailed allowing the Arabs a "limited victory, even if largely mythical", which was meant to mitigate the feelings of shame and humiliation that Kissinger expected in the case of a complete routing at the hands of the Israelis (Harkavy, 2000, p. 348). Although such a routing would be useful for eradication, it would be counterproductive as a bargaining strategy. This same principle was similarly at work thousands of years prior, when Archidamus of Sparta offered the following advice:

> ...when they see that our actual strength is in keeping pace with the language that we use, they will be more inclined to give way, since their land will still be untouched and, in making up their minds, they will be thinking of advantages which they still possess and which have not yet been destroyed. For you must think of their land as though it was a hostage in your possession, and all the more valuable the better it is looked after. You should spare it up to the last possible moment, and avoid driving them to a state of desperation in which you will find them much harder to deal with.
> *(Finley, 1972, 82)*

Bargaining aggression between groups should generate a form of aggression that seeks preference restructuring and is limited toward that end in both the conduct of war and war termination, when the treatment of prisoners, respect for enemy leaders and non-exploitation of weakness and surrender can facilitate an end to hostilities consistent with recalibrated preferences. This is similar to Blainey's (1973) classic argument that war is fundamentally a disagreement about relative power, in which peace is more likely after decisive wars, in which relative (bargaining) power is clear than after stalemates. It should come as no surprise, therefore, that bargaining aggression is often preceded by pre-battle displays of coalitional power, or what international relations theorists would classify as "swaggering" (Art, 1980). In contrast, hate-filled adversaries gain nothing and potentially lose much by seeking to advertise offensive capabilities in advance of attacking. Anger is the realm of bluster and bluff, while hatred is quiet and unyielding.

Hate-based aggression and the concept of total war

In contrast to anger, hate-based aggression has no bargaining function, and therefore, wars characterised by this motivation are more likely to be total rather than limited. Whereas restraints on the methods of violence are necessary to facilitate bargaining, hate seeks the extermination of an out-group rather than its preference restructuring. While anger operates to differentiate and discriminate among an out-group population, hate activates heuristics of out-group homogeneity and social substitution. In a discussion of hate, Michener (2012) labels the heuristic simply as 'one did it, they all did it'. In total war there is little incentive to avoid the most damaging attacks because the enemy will likely abandon those rules as well. Similarly, surrender is a meaningless gesture in wars of extermination, as are related overtures of apology and accommodation. Thus, behaviours such as the torture of prisoners, assassination of leaders, and the targeting of civilians are reciprocally likely to send signals that one's adversary seeks extermination rather than preference restructuring.

The cue structure of negative association value combined with perceived intransigence are on dramatic display in the context of forms of violent extremism. For example, in their extensive review of ISIS rhetoric and propaganda, Baele *et al.* (2019) demonstrate that a persistent and foundational theme of stated grievances contains the assertion that anti-Western sentiment is not rooted in policy but identity. It is worth reviewing this language directly:

> ... although some might argue that your foreign policies are the extent of what drives our hatred, this particular reason for hating you is secondary. [...] The fact is, even if

> you were to stop bombing us, imprisoning us, torturing us, vilifying us, and usurping our lands, we would continue to hate you because our primary reason for hating you will not cease to exist until you embrace Islam.
>
> (*Baele et al., 2019, p. 11*)

ISIS does not view itself as bargaining with the West; more to the point, it does not see bargaining itself as possible or desirable. Rather, it views the West as a civilization of humiliation and subjugation. Warfare motivated by such hatred will not be characterised by bargaining aggression, but rather unrestrained aggression, e.g. genocide, torture, civilian targeting, chemical weapons, absence of displays of open war, attempts at assassinations, and so forth.

A leading framework for the causes of war in international relations is the bargaining model of war (Fearon, 1995; Powell, 2006), which views war as the rational outcome of issue incompatibilities between actors. Importantly, however, this model of war begins with the overarching claim that political actors should rationally *always* be motivated to seek negotiated settlements that avoid war. According to the model, this is in part a consequence of two assumptions: states are risk averse and war is costly for the actors. However, when hate motivates warfare, rather than preferring to seek negotiated settlements that avoid the costs of war – as Fearon's (1995) bargaining model assumes – actors will instead be characterised by an inversion of these assumptions; namely, they will view violence as intrinsically beneficial and peace as costly.

Conclusion

Just as interpersonal retaliations can be motivated by two somewhat distinct styles of aggression – anger-based bargaining aggression and a hatred-based predatory aggression – so can warfare be characterised as either rule-based bargaining war or unrestrained total war. As warfare is ultimately the result of many different human minds making many decisions, and because anger and hatred can fire in unison, these types of war will often coincide; e.g. troops abandoning rules of engagement to get revenge on the battlefield. However, the distinctions between these two types of war are extremely important because they are predicted to respond to different strategies in very different ways. In particular, rule-based warfare is likely to respond to concessions and peace talks, because this type of war appears designed to resolve conflicts of interest at relatively minimal cost. However, those engaged in hatred-based unrestrained warfare will likely see attempts to negotiate as indicators of weakness on the opponent's behalf, and this may be a signal that it is a good time to escalate. Similarly, the value of negotiating at all depends on whether one is facing an opponent who is willing to bargain or one who is only interested in getting more information so as to better harm you. While this should make us cautious of negotiating with hate-filled enemies, it does not doom us to unrestrained war. Hatred can, in some circumstances, be counteracted by changing the perceived association value with the enemy, e.g. uniting against a common enemy, benefiting from gains in trade, or more direct acts of charity. Finally, nations are not monolithic, and an army directed by hate-filled rulers can be usurped by moderates willing to bargain.

Notes

1 Combining an anger face with a smile will sometimes produce a sadistic face – as if someone is aggressing against another and is happy about it. We consider this face and its connection to hatred an interesting source of future research.

2 There may be an exception to the rapid deployment of maximum aggression in the form of prolonged torture when the hate-filled person is protected from retaliation. This would presumably be an evolutionary by-product (i.e. a functionless accident of design, like the bellybutton or the fact that humans are flammable), stemming from the fact that hate-filled people experience vicarious enjoyment at their enemy's suffering.

References

Alcock, J. (2009) *Animal Behaviour: An Evolutionary Approach*, 9th ed. Sunderland, MA, US: Sinauer Associates.

Antonakis, J. and Dalgas, O. (2009) Predicting elections: child's play! *Science*, 323(5918), pp. 1183–1183.

Archer, J. (1988) *The Behavioural Biology of Aggression* (Vol. 1). New York: CUP Archive.

Art, R. J. (1980) To what ends military power? *International Security*, 4(4), p. 3.

Averill, J. R. (1982) *Anger and Aggression: An Essay on Emotion*. New York: Springer Science & Business Media.

Baele, S. J., Bettiza, G., Boyd, K. A., and Coan, T. G. (2019) ISIS's Clash of Civilizations: constructing the "West" in terrorist propaganda. *Studies in Conflict & Terrorism*, https://doi.org/10.1080/1057610X.2019.1599192.

Blainey, G. (1973) *The Causes of War*. London: Macmillan.

Boehm, C. (1984) *Blood Revenge: The Anthropology of Feuding in Montenegro and Other Tribal Societies*. Lawrence, KS: University Press of Kansas.

Buss, D. M. (2005) *The Handbook of Evolutionary Psychology*. New Jersey: John Wiley & Sons.

Chagnon, N. A. (1983) *Yanomamö: The Fierce People*. New York: Holt McDougal.

Clutton-Brock, T. H. and Parker, G. A. (1995) Punishment in animal societies. *Nature*, 373(6511): 209.

Collins, R (2008) *Violence: A Micro-Sociological Theory*. Oxford: Princeton University Press.

Cosmides, L. and Tooby, J. (1994) Origins of domain-specificity: the evolution of functional organization. In L. Hirschfeld and S. Gelman (eds), *Mapping the Mind: Domain Specificity in Cognition and Culture*. New York: Cambridge University Press.

Cosmides, L. and Tooby, J. (1995) From evolution to adaptations to behaviour: toward an integrated evolutionary psychology. In R. Wong (ed.), *Biological Perspectives on Motivated Activities*, Norwood, NJ: Ablex.

Cosmides, L. and Tooby, J. (2000) Evolutionary psychology and the emotions. In M. Lewis and J. M. Haviland-Jones (eds), *Handbook of Emotions*, 2nd ed. New York: Guilford, pp. 91–115.

Daly, M. and Wilson, M. (1988) *Homicide*. New Brunswick: Transaction Books.

Darwin, C. (1859 [2004]) *On the Origin of Species*. New York: Routledge.

Dawkins, R. (1976) *The Selfish Gene*. New York: Oxford University Press.

Dawkins, R. (1996) *The Blind Watchmaker: Why the Evidence of Evolution Reveals a Universe Without Design*. New York: W. W. Norton & Company.

Ekman, P. (1973) Cross-cultural studies of facial expression. In P. Ekman (ed.), *Darwin and Facial Expression: A Century of Research in Review*. New York: Academic Press, pp. 169–222.

Enquist, M. and Leimar, O. (1983) Evolution of fighting behaviour: decision rules and assessment of relative strength. *Journal of Theoretical Biology*, 102(3), 387–410.

Fearon, J. D. (1995) Rationalist explanations for war. *International Organization*, 49(3), pp. 379–414.

Finley, M. I. (1972) *History of the Peloponnesian War*. Penguin Classics.

Frantz, C. M. and Bennigson, C. (2005) Better late than early: the influence of timing on apology effectiveness. *Journal of Experimental Social Psychology*, 41(2), pp. 201–207.

Gat, A. (2006) *War in Human Civilization*. Oxford: Oxford University Press.

Galati, D., Sini, B., Schmidt, S. and Tinti, C. (2003) Spontaneous facial expressions in congenitally blind and sighted children aged 8–11. *Journal of Visual Impairment & Blindness*, 97(7), 418–428.

Garfield, Z. H., von Rueden, C., and Hagen, E. H. (2019) The evolutionary anthropology of political leadership. *The Leadership Quarterly*, 30(1), pp. 59–80.

Glowacki, L., Wilson, M. L., and Wrangham, R. W. (2017) The evolutionary anthropology of war. *Journal of Economic Behavior & Organization*, https://doi.org/10.1016/j.jebo.2017.09.014.

Harkavy, R. E. (2000) Defeat, national humiliation, and the revenge motif in international politics. *International Politics*, 37(3), pp. 345–368.

Keeley, L. H. (1996) *War before Civilization: The Myth of the Peaceful Savage*. New York: Oxford University Press.

Levy, J. S. (1988) Domestic politics and war. *The Journal of Interdisciplinary History*, 18(4): 653–673.
Lieberman, D., Tooby, J. & Cosmides, L. (2007) The architecture of human kin detection. *Nature*, 445(7129), 727–731. doi: 10.1038/nature05510
Liwanag, H.E.M., Annalisa, B, Costa, D.P., Masako A., and Terrie M.W. (2012) Morphological and thermal properties of mammalian insulation: the evolution of fur for aquatic living. *Biological Journal of the Linnean Society*, 106(4), 926–939. https://doi.org/10.1111/j.1095-8312.2012.01900.x
Lopez, A. C. (2019) Making "my" problem "our" problem: warfare as collective action, and the role of leader manipulation. *The Leadership Quarterly*, doi: 10.1016/j.leaqua.2019.05.001.
Luckenbill, D. F. (1977) Criminal homicide as a situated transaction. *Social Problems*, *25*(2), 176–186.
Lukaszewski, A. W., Simmons, Z. L., Anderson, C., and Roney, J. R. (2016) The role of physical formidability in human social status allocation. *Journal of Personality and Social Psychology*, 110(3), 385.
Mackie, D. M., Devos, T., and Smith. E. R. (2000) Intergroup emotions: Explaining offensive action tendencies in an intergroup context. *Journal of Personality and Social Psychology*. 79(4), 602–616.
Marsh A. A., Adams R. B., and Kleck R. E. (2005) Why do fear and anger look the way they do? Form and social function in facial expressions. *Personality and Social Psychology Bulletin*, 31(1), 73–86.
McClintock, R. (1967) *The Meaning of Limited War*. Houghton Mifflin.
McCullough, M. (2008) *Beyond Revenge: The Evolution of the Forgiveness Instinct*. San Francisco, CA: John Wiley & Sons.
McDermott, R., Lopez, A., and Hatemi P. (2017) Blunt not the heart, enrage it: the psychology of revenge and deterrence. *Texas National Security Review*, 1(1): http://hdl.handle.net/2152/63934.
Michener, W. (2012) The individual psychology of group hate. *Journal of Hate Studies*, 10(1), 15.
Nowak, M. A. (2006) Five rules for the evolution of cooperation. *Science*, 314(5805), 1560–1563.
Osgood, R. E. (1957) *Limited War: The Challenge to American Strategy*, 5th ed. Chicago: University of Chicago Press.
Pietraszewski, D. (2016) How the mind sees coalitional and group conflict: the evolutionary invariances of n-person conflict dynamics. *Evolution and Human Behavior*, 37(6), 470–480.
Powell, R. (2006) War as a commitment problem. *International Organization*, 60(1), 169–203.
Romero, G. A., Pham, M. N., and Goetz, A. T. (2014) The implicit rules of combat. *Human Nature*, 25(4), 496–516.
Schelling, T. C. (1966) *Arms and Influence*. New Have, CT: Yale University Press.
Scherer, K. R. and Wallbott, H. G. (1994) Evidence for universality and cultural variation of differential emotion response patterning. *Journal of Personality and Social Psychology*, 66, 310–328.
Schopler, J. and Compere, J. S. (1971) Effects of being kind or harsh to another on liking. *Journal of Personality and Social Psychology*, 20(2), 155–159.
Sell, A. (2011) The recalibrational theory and violent anger. *Aggression and Violent Behaviour*, 16, 381–389.
Sell, A. (2012) Revenge can be more fully understood by making distinctions between anger and hatred. Commentary on McCullough, Kurzan & Tabak's 'Cognitive Systems for Revenge and Forgiveness'. *Behavioural and Brain Sciences*, 36(1) 36–37.
Sell, A. (2014) Twelve triggers of anger and how they invalidate all major theories of anger and aggression. *International Society for Research on Aggression*, Georgia State University, 19 July.
Sell, A., Cosmides L. and Tooby, J. (2014) The human anger face evolved to enhance cues of strength. *Evolution and Human Behaviour*, 35(5), 425–429.
Sell, A., Eisner, M. and Ribeaud, D. (2016) Bargaining power and adolescent aggression: the role of fighting ability, coalitional strength, and mate value. *Evolution and Human Behaviour*, 37(2), 105–116.
Sell, A., Sznycer, D., Al-Shawaf, L., Lim, J., Krauss, A., Feldman, A., Rascanu, R., Sugiyama, L., Tooby, J., and L. Cosmides (2017) The grammar of anger: mapping the computational architecture of a recalibrational emotion. *Cognition*, 168, 110–128.
Sell, A., Tooby, J., and Cosmides, L. (2009) Formidability and the logic of human anger. *Proceedings of the National Academy of Science*, 106(35), 15073–15078.
Stoker, Donald. (2016) Everything you think you know about limited war is wrong. *War on the Rocks*, 22 December.
Sznycer, D., Al-Shawaf, L., Bereby-Meyer, Y., Curry, O. S., De Smet, D., Ermer, E., Kim, S., Kim, S., Li, N. P., Lopez Seal, M. F., McClung, J., O, J., Ohtsubo, Y., Quillien, T., Schaub, M., Sell, A., van Leeuwen, F., Cosmides, L., and Tooby, J. (2017) Cross-cultural regularities in the cognitive architecture of pride. *Proceedings of the National Academy of Sciences*, 114(8), 1874–79.
Sznycer, D., Tooby, J., Cosmides, L., Porat, R., Shalvi, S., and Halperin, E. (2016) Shame closely tracks the threat of devaluation by others, even across cultures. *Proceedings of the National Academy of Sciences*, 113(10), 2625–2630. doi: 10.1073/pnas.1514699113

Tooby, J. and Cosmides, L. (1989) Evolutionary psychologists need to distinguish between the evolutionary process, ancestral selection pressures, and psychological mechanisms. *Behavioural and Brain Sciences*, 12(4), 174–175. doi: 10.1017/S0140525X00025577

Tooby, J., Cosmides, L., Sell, A., Lieberman, D., and Sznycer, D. (2008) Internal regulatory variables and the design of human motivation: A computational and evolutionary approach. In Elliot, A. J. (ed.), *Handbook of Approach and Avoidance Motivation*. New York: Psychology Press, pp. 251–271.

Walzer, M. (2015) *Just and Unjust Wars: A Moral Argument with Historical Illustrations*. New York: Basic Books.

Williams, G. C. (1966) *Adaptation and Natural Selection: A Critique of Some Current Evolutionary Thought*. Princeton, NJ: Princeton University Press.

Williams, J. (1980) *Duelling in the Old South. Vignettes of Social History*. College Station, TX: Texas A & M University Press.

4
WOMEN, GOD AND WAR
Analysing an odd triangle

Fernanda Buril

Introduction

Extensive research conducted cross-nationally and across time indicates that women are much more likely than men to disapprove of violence and to seek and support more peaceful paths to addressing conflict. Just as consistent is the finding that women display higher levels of religiosity than do men, both in what concerns belief in god and frequency of religious practices. But some factors that are usually attached to religiosity, such as in-group bias, high levels of moral certainty, and a sense of obedience to god also predict greater support for violent warfare. These findings beg the question of why women, being more religious, are still less likely to support wars in general, and whether this pattern can change when the god factor is more salient in a context of war.

This chapter reviews the literature on the links between religiosity, support for warfare, and gender, and explores the specific aspects of religiosity that might drive women's support for intergroup warfare. It also explores the results of a survey-experiment conducted with college students which suggest that bringing god to the context of wars does make women more likely to accept them – in the experiment, when wars were suggested to be approved by god, the usual gender gap in support for the intervention closed, and women became just as likely as men to support warfare.

Religion, morality and support for warfare

The salience of religious issues in modern conflict and wars is not a mere product of mediatic framing or sensationalism. An empirical survey of civil wars happening from 1940 to 2000 has shown that the frequency of civil wars with a central religious factor has increased over time. Furthermore, religious civil wars were also four times as deadly for non-combatants, and they tended to last longer (Toft, 2007, p. 98). Another study analysing data on religion and conflict worldwide from 1975 to 2015 also revealed that civil armed conflicts fought over religious issues are becoming more common over time. While, in 1975, only 3 per cent of the world's intrastate wars were fought over religious issues, in 2015, more than half of them involved a religious cause (Svensson and Nilsson, 2018). Given this role of religious appeals in political discourses and the rise of religious extremist organizations changing political dynamics around the world, it becomes crucial to understand how religious beliefs shape people's perceptions of the world and motivate them to act politically, including supporting aggressive policies and wars.

A quick review of the evolutionary origins of religion can help understand the role it plays in shaping people's prosocial behaviour towards one's group and potential hostility towards outsiders. In order to hunt, to protect themselves from other predators, or even to attack other tribes for resources, humans have had to learn to cooperate, at least within their specific groups. Both predator-defence and resource-defence hypotheses invariably lead to human bonding (Brereton, 1995) and, therefore, to the consolidation of groups as a more effective configuration in the struggle to survive the environment and its threats. In instances when resources were scarce, however, these small groups would find themselves in competition with each other. Drawing lines to separate the in-group from the out-group became necessary in order to know with whom to cooperate and with whom to fight (Kelly, 2000, 2013; Otterbein, 2004). In order to manage these two needs, humans have evolved a capacity to develop and maintain large coalitions, cooperating with unrelated individuals on the basis of trust, building social networks and interpersonal attachments (Navarette *et al.*, 2004), and organizing themselves to fight. The set of underlying psychological mechanisms that guide the dynamics of this internal coalition, as well as the competitive relations between coalitions, is what is called *coalitional psychology* (Lopez *et al.*, 2011).

As Boyer (2008) explains, this coalitional psychology is a clear feature of public religiosity. When people adhere to a particular faith or religious community, showing commitment to that group and set of ideas even in the absence of evidence, spending time, energy, and efforts on them, they are signalling their willingness to embrace that coalition. Individuals and groups outside such coalition might more easily be seen through an adversarial lens. Religious discourses also generally reinforce dualistic views of the world (e.g. mundane vs. sacred, good vs. evil), and religious individuals tend to have firm views of what is "right" or "wrong" (Graham and Haidt, 2010). This tendency to have more clearly defined moral judgements influences religious individuals' ways of perceiving warfare. As McAlister *et al.* (2006) have found, providing a moral justification for an action that will cause harm makes people more likely to accept such actions and their consequences – noble ends would justify harmful means.

Morality can also influence support for warfare in another way: when individuals perceive their own behaviour as sufficiently moral, they can give themselves a "moral licence" to behave less morally in certain situations. For instance, researchers have shown that, when participants were led to think about themselves as kind, compassionate and generous, they felt comfortable donating less for charity (Sachdeva *et al.*, 2009). Another study has shown that not only does moral certainty relate to greater support for violent conflict, it also plays an even stronger role in warfare that is portrayed as being waged for a religious motivation rather than a geopolitical one. More specifically, Shaw *et al.* (2011, p. 282) found that "the moral certainty that comes along with belonging to a religion [...] down-regulates people's moral reservations about violent warfare".

Fear of god and support for warfare

While not necessarily focused on direct support for warfare, other studies analysing the relationship between god and pro-sociality can also shed light on how religious individuals form their attitudes towards others and on policies that might harm them. In this area, another variable that has been explored as mediating people's positive or negative attitude towards others is their fear of a divine punishment. Both theoretically and experimentally, considerable progress has been made in identifying how human behaviour is influenced by the fear of facing god's fury. Most research in the field points to a significant correlation between fearing divine punishment and a higher likelihood of engaging in "moral" or pro-social behaviour. This fear of divine punishment also appears to motivate cooperation and pro-sociality regardless of self-reported degree of religiosity. Shariff and Norenzayan (2007) have shown, for instance, that priming individuals with god-related concepts was enough to make them allocate more money to strangers in a dictator game. Moreover, the authors defend that their findings can be "better explained by egoistic motives such as seeking praise or avoiding guilt, rather than by higher levels of compassion or by a stronger motivation to benefit other people" (Shariff and Norenzayan, 2007, p. 803). The simple reminder of god might have activated both religious and nonreligious participants' feelings of being observed, judged, and, possibly, punished for bad behaviour. Participants basically avoided allocating more money to themselves, an objective gain, likely to avoid the risk of facing god's response to an undesirable behaviour.

In a previous study, the same authors had also shown how different perceptions of god could change university students' behaviour toward cheating. They found that those who believed in a comforting and forgiving god were more likely to cheat in an academic task than those who viewed god as a punitive being (Shariff and Norenzayan, 2011). Along the same lines, DeBono *et al.* (2012) have also found that priming individuals with the idea of a forgiving god led them to overpay themselves in a task significantly more than individuals who were primed with the thought of a punishing god and a control group.

These findings suggest that both how individuals perceive god and whether they fear being punished by him might influence their attitude towards "morality" (in the sense of doing what one believes is "right"). They also bring the question of whether believers will be inclined to perpetrate or support actions that harm others if they understand these actions as being approved by god or not provoking divine punishment.

If individuals seek to behave in ways that will be seen as moral by god, god's position about a certain war (approval or disapproval) might be, thus, an important factor in their calculation of the worth of supporting them. This adds to the potential causes for religious people's support for warfare. Besides supporting a war because they see it as moral or because their otherwise moral behaviour compensates for that support, people might also support it because (1) god approves of the war, and (2) not supporting it could potentially lead to divine punishment. These ideas will be tested after another piece of the puzzle is discussed: how the god factor might affect men and women differently.

Women, religiosity and warfare

The finding that women are, on average, more religious than men is among the best attested in the field of religious studies (Francis, 1997, p. 81). Across all age ranges, more females attend church than males (Ploch and Hastings, 1994). They are also more likely to participate in church groups or clubs (Thompson, 1991) and to identify themselves with a specific religious denomination (Chatters and Taylor, 1989). Besides what can be considered public social behaviour, religious behaviours and beliefs that are private are also more common among women. Women are, on average, more likely to pray and to read the Bible (Wormald and Wormald, 2017; Thompson, 1991) to believe in life after death (Ferraro and Albrecht-Jensen, 1991), and to attribute more importance to god in their lives (Bouma *et al.*, 1987).

In his extensive review of empirical research in the area, Francis (1997) identified two main categories of theories proposed to account for these gender differences in religious affairs: (1) the role of "social or contextual influences", such as cultural traditions regarding gender roles, and (2) "personal or individual psychological characteristics which differentiate men and women"

(Francis, 1997, p. 81). According to Francis' review, the explanations better supported by current evidence comprise gender-orientation theories. Being male or female would not predict religiousness, but having personality traits associated with one or other sex would. Compatible with this line of explanation, Thompson (1991) has found that submission, passivity, obedience and nurturing characteristics could better predict religiosity not only between sexes, but also within each sex. In other words, men with those traits would be more likely to be religious than other men, and the same would hold true for women.

Just as clear as the gender gap in religiosity was the gap between men's and women's support for warfare. This difference is considered the largest and most consistent gender gap observed in public polling (Conover and Shapiro, 1993). In the United States, this gender difference on support for military interventions averages around 8 per cent across events such as World War II, the Vietnam War, and the Iraq War (Lizotte, 2017). But some recent research has started to show that, in some specific contexts, this gender gap in support of the use of force can disappear. Conducting two controlled experiments, Brooks and Valentino (2011) presented male and female participants with very similar articles about a conflict between two hypothetical countries and then asked them about their likelihood of supporting a US military intervention in those cases. The difference between the two conditions in one of the experiments was that one of the articles framed the intervention as having economic/strategic stakes (access to oil fields), while the other article framed it as a humanitarian intervention (saving civilian lives). In the second experiment, the articles varied regarding whether the war had multilateral support (UN approval vs. UN disapproval). The authors found that the gender gap in support of military interventions depends heavily on the specific contexts of wars, with women being just as likely (or even more likely) than men to support interventions when they were implemented for humanitarian reasons and when they had multilateral approval. But humanitarianism and multilateralism are likely not the only factors that can interfere with the common gender gap in support of wars. As suggested by the literature reviewed in this chapter, certain features of religiosity can make people more accepting of warfare and, as women display on average higher levels of religiosity, these factors might have a stronger effect on women. It might be that making these factors more salient will also make women more prone to supporting wars.

Given women's consistent higher levels of religiosity and sense of obedience to god and the evidence pointing to factors such as religious moral certainty and fear of god's punishment influencing human behaviour, it is worth exploring how these issues might affect women's view of warfare. This study explores, more specifically, whether the suggestion of god's approval of a military intervention can make women more likely to support it. The main hypotheses are thus that:

(1) God's approval of wars will have a stronger effect on women than on men.
(2) Women are more likely to support wars suggested to be approved by god than wars without this divine approval.

Because people's need to align with god's will has been shown to be often driven by the fear of divine punishment, I also hypothesize that:

(3) Women see god as more punishing and less forgiving than men do.

Study

The survey-experiment was based on the above-mentioned Brooks and Valentino's (2011) study, originally designed to test for gender gaps in support of war. To measure the effect of the "god factor", I used two of Brooks and Valentino's fictional news articles as conditions one (humanitarian context, no reference to god's approval) and three (economic context, no reference to god's approval), and added two more conditions to the experiment. Conditions two (humanitarian context, with reference to god's approval) and four (economic context, with reference to god's approval). The suggestions of god's approval of the war were given by slightly modifying a fictional senator's quotes already present in the original fictional articles throughout the text, as shown in Table 4.1.

The experiment was conducted with a sample of college students enrolled in Political Science courses at Washington State University in the Fall of 2017. All students received extra credit for consenting to answer the survey online. From the original sample of 470 respondents, 385 proved to have read the news article to which they were assigned by answering correctly to an attention-check question about the countries involved in the conflict. This final sample consisted of 54.8 per cent males and 76.1 per cent White. The average age of participants was 19.8 years (SD = 1.67).

All participants were asked to answer demographic questions prior to being randomly directed to one of the four articles. Then, respondents were asked to read the text carefully and answer questions regarding their support for military interventions, and the potential risks involved in deploying troops to the region. Participants were finally asked to answer to the Centrality of Religiosity Scale (CRS) Questionnaire (Huber and Huber, 2012), a 15-item measure of level of individual religiosity, and the Views of God Questionnaire (Benson and Spilka, 1973), which measures how believers perceive god in a benevolent/forgiving – malevolent/punishing scale.

Table 4.1 Fictional senator's quotes by condition

Condition	*Motivation*	*God's approval*	*Quotes*
1	Humanitarian	No	"40,000 U.S. ground troops would halt the killing."
			"We cannot sit idly by as thousands upon thousands of innocent civilians are slaughtered. We must send a clear message that this kind of aggression will not be tolerated."
2	Humanitarian	Yes	"40,000 U.S. ground troops protected by god would halt the killing."
			"We cannot sit idly by as thousands upon thousands of innocent civilians are slaughtered. We must send a clear message that this kind of aggression will not be tolerated and that god approves of what we are doing."
3	Economic	No	"40,000 U.S. ground troops would secure the oil fields."
			"We cannot sit idly by and watch this happen. We must send a clear message that this kind of aggression will not be tolerated."
4	Economic	Yes	"40,000 U.S. ground troops protected by god would secure the oil fields."
			"We cannot sit idly by and watch this happen. We must send a clear message that this kind of aggression will not be tolerated and that god approves of what we are doing."

Results and discussion

Religiosity, god's approval, gender, and support for interventions

Consistent with the previous literature in the area, the gender gap in levels of religiosity was shown to be statistically significant. Women (M=2.76) displayed, on average, higher levels of religiosity than did men (M=2.55), $t(344.73)=-1.98$, $p=0.048$). An OLS regression analysis was conducted first to analyse the main effects of religiosity (the final CRS score, calculated as the average of all 15 CRS items) and of god's approval (as a dummy variable) on support for intervention. While the model was significant, only religiosity was a significant predictor of support for intervention. Also consistent with previous studies, the more religious respondents were, the more likely they were to support interventions in general. The quotation by the senator suggesting god's approval of the intervention, however, did not significantly change participants' support for such interventions in general. A second model including an interaction term for religiosity and god's support also showed only religiosity as a significant predictor of support for interventions. Religiosity did not moderate the effect of god's approval on support for intervention. The summary of the regression analyses is shown in Table 4.2.

Just as Brooks and Valentino (2011) found in their tests, the gender patterns in support for war were similar in this replication. Men were more likely than women to support interventions with economic purposes. When the wars were framed as necessary to save civilian lives, however, women were just as likely as men to support the interventions. A regression analysis for the interaction between gender and condition yielded significant results. As the summary of the regression analysis (Table 4.3) and the graph in Figure 4.1 show, the character of the interventions is a good predictor of gender differences in support for them, with the humanitarian frame consistently increasing women's acceptance of interventions. Figure 4.1 also shows that both men and women are more likely to support the humanitarian intervention rather than the intervention motivated by economic reasons, but the difference in acceptance of the two justifications is much larger for women.

Table 4.2 Summary of regression analyses for CRS, god's approval, and interaction of CRS and god's approval on support for interventions

	Dependent variable: support for intervention	
CRS	0.206**	0.273**
	(0.082)	(0.117)
God's approval	–0.077	0.270
	(0.163)	(0.464)
CRS × god's approval		–0.131
		(0.164)
Constant	3.697***	3.527***
	(0.239)	(0.321)
Observations	379	379
R^2	0.017	0.018
Adjusted R^2	0.011	0.011
Residual std. error	1.581 (df=376)	1.582 (df=375)
F statistic	3.198** (df=2; 376) (p=0.042)	2.342* (df=3;375) (p=0.073)

Note
*p<0.1; **p<0.05; ***p<0.01

Table 4.3 Summary of regression of gender, condition, and interaction term of gender and condition on support for intervention

	Dependent variable: support for intervention
Humanitarian/economic	0.305
	(0.496)
Gender	0.264
	(0.236)
Gender × humanitarian/economic	–.581*
	(0.324)
Constant	4.117***
	(0.355)
Observations	380
R^2	0.037
Adjusted R^2	0.029
Residual std. error	1.567 (df=376)
F statistic	4.802 (df=3; 376) (p=0.0003)***

Note
*p<0.1; **p<0.05; ***p<0.01

The first new hypothesis to be tested here assumes that god's approval could have a similar effect as the humanitarian frame:

1. God's approval of war will have a stronger effect on women's support for war than on men's.
2. Women are more likely to support wars suggested to be approved by god than wars without this divine approval.

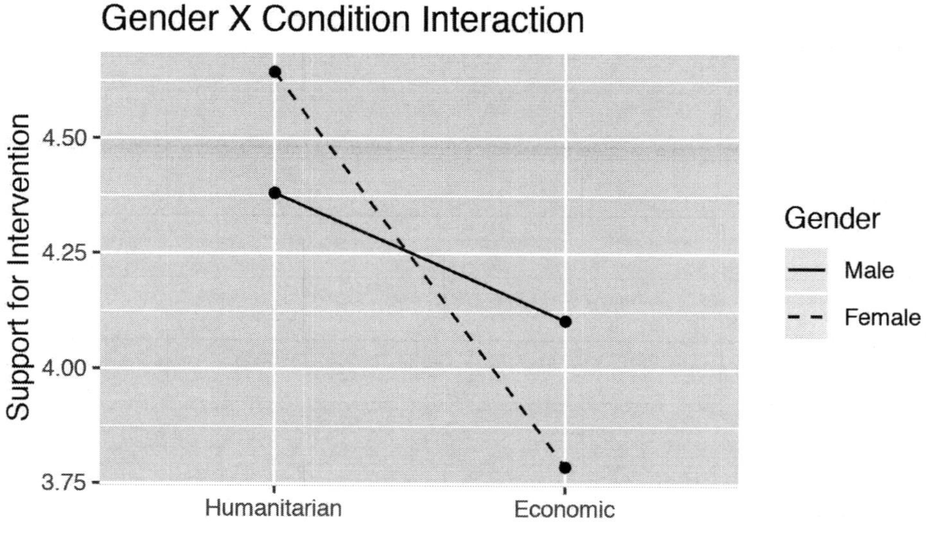

Figure 4.1 Gender × condition interaction.

In order to test the first hypothesis, I ran an OLS regression with gender, god's approval (as a dummy variable), and the interaction term of gender and god's approval as independent variables. As predicted, the interaction term was significant, showing that god's approval has a stronger effect on women's support for the interventions than on men's.

The summary of the regression analysis is shown in Table 4.4.

The interaction term of gender and god's approval shown in Figure 4.2, however, shows that not only does god's approval increase women's support for war, it also appears to decrease men's support for it.

Figure 4.3 shows the details of this interaction between gender and god's approval per condition. The graph shows that god's approval increased the gender gap in support of interventions with humanitarian motivations (women much more likely than men to support them) and almost closed the gender gap in support for interventions with economic motivations.

While these results corroborate the second hypothesis, as women did become more willing to support the military interventions when it was suggested that god backed these interventions up, they also bring a new question as to why god's approval appeared to *decrease* men's support for war. While not conclusive, men's lower levels of religiosity and more negative views of god could help explain why men became less likely to support wars after they were suggested to be approved by god. Being less religious, men might fear divine punishment less; and by seeing god through a more negative lens, men might also refrain more from accepting what is approved by god as moral.

Images of god and fear of divine punishment

Using the Views of God Questionnaire (Benson and Spilka, 1973), it was possible to analyse further whether gender differences in images of god (whether they see god as more forgiving or punishing) have anything to do with how religious people see interventions that are "approved

Table 4.4 Summary of regression of god's approval, gender, and interaction term of god's approval and gender on support for interventions

	Dependent variable: support for intervention
God's approval	–0.277 (0.22)
Gender	–0.341 (0.23)
God's approval × gender	0.548* (0.328)
Constant	4.376*** (0.152)
Observations	380
R^2	0.008
Adjusted R^2	0.00004
Residual std. error	1.591 (df=376)
F statistic	1.005 (df=3; 376) (p=0.391)

Note
*p<0.1; **p<0.05; ***p<0.01

by god." Belson's and Spilka's (1973) six-point scale can be divided into two main categories: god as loving/hating and god as controlling/lenient. In the first category, women ($M=4.81$) scored higher than men ($M=4.55$), displaying a warmer view of god as loving and forgiving. This difference was statistically significant, $t(376)=-2.58$, $p=0.01$. In the second category, although only marginally significant, men ($M=3.41$) scored higher than women ($M=3.21$), showing that men tend to hold an image of god as more controlling and repressive than women do, $t(376)=1.90$, $p=0.06$. It is also clear from the sample that the group of less religious people

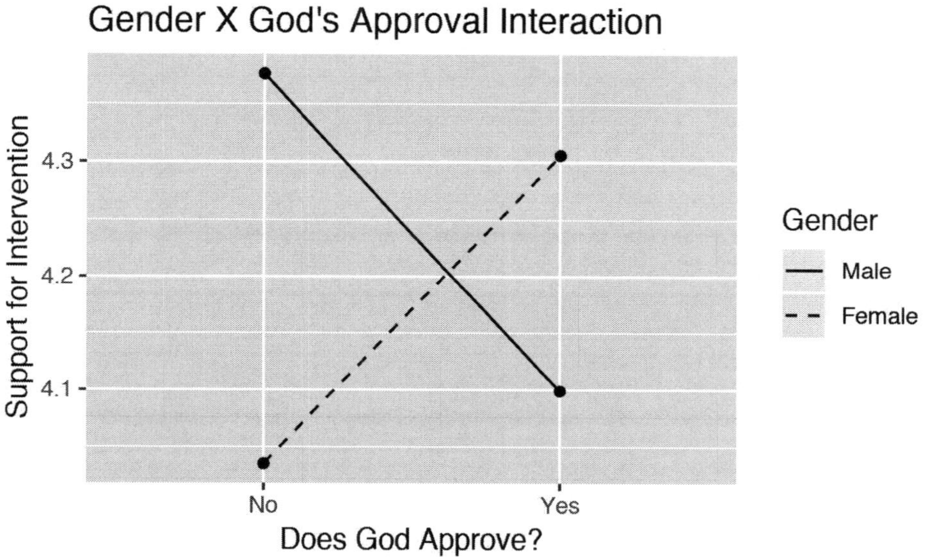

Figure 4.2 Gender × god's approval interaction.

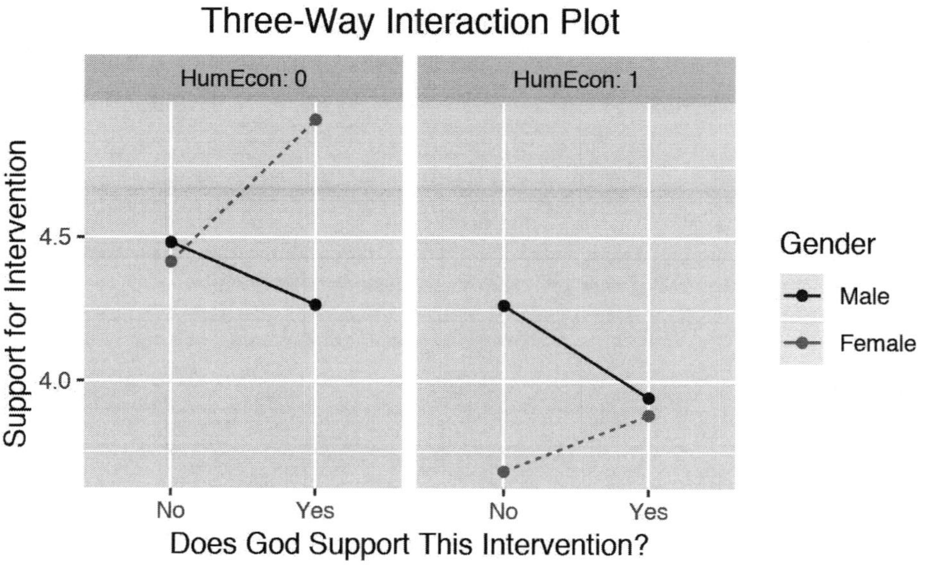

Figure 4.3 Three-way interaction plot.

significantly differed from the group of more religious people regarding these images. Independent-samples t-tests showed that people who scored lower on the Centrality of Religiosity Scale also scored lower in the "Loving God" scale, $t(346.59) = -11.26$, $p < 0.001$, and scored higher in the "Controlling God" scale, $t(376) = 7.29$, $p < 0.001$.

Scores on the "Loving God" scale and "Controlling God" scale did not significantly account for the general variation in support for military intervention, but it is still important to highlight how women seem to be more affected by god's expectations (being more likely to follow such expectations) even though they report holding images of god as less controlling or punishing than do men. These results are inconsistent with hypothesis 3 and challenge the claim that women's alignment with god's expectations would be mainly driven by a fear of divine punishment.

Conclusions

The results shown here are important in at least two different ways. First, they corroborate Brooks and Valentino's finding that, although men are more likely than women to support interventions to secure economic interests, framing military interventions as motivated by humanitarian reasons makes women at least just as likely as men to support them. Second, they expose the power of another factor influencing especially women's attitudes towards wars: whether god approves of them. In humanitarian interventions approved by god, female respondents indicated much higher rates of support than did male respondents. In the scenario of intervention framed as guided by the need to secure oil fields (economic interests), which usually receives more support from men, god's approval virtually closed the gender gap. Such results are even more surprising given the fact that women reported to hold images of god as more loving and less controlling than did men, which could indicate that the fear of god's punishment is not a main driver of women's obedience.

One of the main limitations of this study is that using a fictional senator's quotation to convey god's approval can have drawbacks, as participants do not know how trustworthy the senator is or if he or she has the authority to talk about god's opinion on the intervention. In the real world, however, political leaders do appeal to religious frames to justify decisions and policies quite often, and it is important to investigate to what extent, and among what audiences, their framings can be more effective, regardless of their authority to voice god's will. As well as that specific issue, this study is also subject to general limitations of survey experiments. It is important to keep in mind that survey experiments are, in Sniderman's (2018) words, "modest" by nature, as they usually limit themselves to a specific group or a few groups (limiting generalization), lack duration (failing to grasp changes over time), and rely on only one or a few indicators to measure the dependent variable. The results of this study, while "modest", bring attention to an overlooked correlation between gender, perception of god's opinions, and support for war, and invite others to investigate this link further.

While women's higher sense of nurturing and care for others might be pushing them away from supporting warfare and its harmful consequences, other characteristics that are also stronger among women can be manipulated to make them embrace wars. Women's higher levels of obedience to god might make them more devoted and more willing to accept what comes from a divine authority – including when these commandments can harm others. While women's views of god as predominantly good and loving might count against the hypothesis that women obey him for fear of punishment, these positive views might indicate that they are more likely to give god a moral licence to harm.

References

Benson, P. and Spilka, B. (1973) God image as a function of self-esteem and locus of control. *Journal for the Scientific Study of Religion*, 12(3), p. 297.
Bouma, G. D., Dixon, B. R., and Bardin, N. (1987) *The Religious Factor in Australian Life*. Tertiary Resource Service, Royal Victorian Institute for the Blind.
Boyer, P. (2008) Religion: bound to believe? *Nature*, 455(7216), pp. 1038–1039.
Brereton, A. R. (1995) Coercion-defence hypothesis: the evolution of primate sociality. *Folia Primatologica*, 64(4), pp. 207–214.
Brooks, D. J. and Valentino, B. A. (2011) A war of one's own: understanding the gender gap in support for war. *Public Opinion Quarterly*, 75(2), pp. 270–286.
Chatters, L. M. and Taylor, R. J. (1989) Age differences in religious participation among black adults. *Journal of Gerontology*, 44(5), pp. S183–S189.
Conover, P. J. and Sapiro, V. (1993) Gender, feminist consciousness, and war. *American Journal of Political Science*, 37(4), p. 1079.
DeBono, A., Shariff, A. F., Poole, S., and Muraven, M. (2017) Forgive us our trespasses: priming a forgiving (but not a punishing) god increases unethical behavior. *Psychology of Religion and Spirituality*, 9(Suppl 1).
Ferraro, K. F. and Albrecht-Jensen, C. M. (1991) Does religion influence adult health? *Journal for the Scientific Study of Religion*, 30(2), p. 193.
Francis, L.J. (1997) The psychology of gender differences in religion: a review of empirical research. *Religion*, 27(1), pp. 81–96.
Graham, J. and Haidt, J. (2010) Beyond beliefs: religions bind individuals into moral communities. *Personality and Social Psychology Review*, 14(1), pp. 140–150.
Huber, S. and Huber, O. W. (2012) The centrality of religiosity scale (CRS). *Religions*, 3(3), pp. 710–724.
Kelly, R. C. (2000) *Warless Societies and the Origin of War*. Ann Arbor, MI: University of Michigan Press.
Kelly, R. L. (2013) From the peaceful to the warlike: ethnographic and archaeological insights into hunter-gatherer warfare and homicide. In Fry, D. P. (ed.), *War, Peace, and Human Nature: The Convergence of Evolutionary and Cultural Views*. Oxford: Oxford University Press, pp. 151–167.
Lizotte, M.-K. (2017) Investigating the origins of the gender gap in support for war. *Political Studies Review*, 17(2), pp. 124–135.
Lopez, A. C., McDermott, R., and Petersen, M. B. (2011) States in mind: evolution, coalitional psychology, and international politics. *International Security*, 36(2), pp. 48–83.
McAlister, A. L., Bandura, A., and Owen, S. V. (2006) Mechanisms of moral disengagement in support of military force: the impact of Sept. 11. *Journal of Social and Clinical Psychology*, 25(2), pp. 141–165.
Navarrete, C. D., Kurzban, R., Fessler, D. M., and Kirkpatrick, L. A. (2004) Anxiety and intergroup bias: terror management or coalitional psychology? *Group Processes & Intergroup Relations*, 7(4), pp. 370–397.
Otterbein, K. F. (2004) *How War Began* (Vol. 10). College Station, TX: Texas A&M University Press.
Ploch, D. R. and Hastings, D. W. (1994) Graphic presentations of church attendance using General Social Survey data. *Journal for the Scientific Study of Religion*, 33(1) pp. 16–33.
Sachdeva, S., Iliev, R., and Medin, D. L. (2009) Sinning saints and saintly sinners: The paradox of moral self-regulation. *Psychological Science*, 20(4), pp. 523–528.
Shariff, A. F. and Norenzayan, A. (2007) God is watching you: priming God concepts increases prosocial behavior in an anonymous economic game. *Psychological Science*, 18(9), pp. 803–809.
Shariff, A. F. and Norenzayan, A. (2011) Mean gods make good people: different views of God predict cheating behavior. *The International Journal for the Psychology of Religion*, 21(2), pp. 85–96.
Shaw, M., Quezada, S. A., and Zárate, M. A. (2011) Violence with a conscience: religiosity and moral certainty as predictors of support for violent warfare. *Psychology of Violence*, 1(4), p. 275.
Sniderman, P.M. (2018) Some advances in the design of survey experiments. *Annual Review of Political Science*, 21(1), 259–275.
Svensson, I. and Nilsson, D. (2018) Disputes over the divine: introducing the religion and armed conflict (RELAC) data, 1975 to 2015. *Journal of Conflict Resolution*, 62(5), 1127–1148.
Thompson Jr, E. H. (1991) Beneath the status characteristic: gender variations in religiousness. *Journal for the Scientific Study of Religion*, 30(4), 381–394.
Toft, M. D. (2007). Getting religion? The puzzling case of Islam and civil war. *International Security*, 31(4), pp. 97–131.
Wormald, B. and Wormald, B. (2017). America's changing religious landscape. *Pew Research Center's Religion & Public Life Project*. Available at: www.pewforum.org/2015/05/12/americas-changing-religious-landscape/ (accessed 4 June 2019).

5

ETHNIC CLEANSING

Reversing the effects

Neophytos Loizides and Djordje Stefanovic

Introduction

"Worldwide forced displacement is at the highest level ever recorded, exceeding 65 million in 2018 (UNHCR, 2019)". Although return is the preferred solution and is generally seen as the most durable and socially appropriate, the factors and processes that enable peaceful voluntary returns are sparsely examined in the academic literature.[1] This chapter focuses on and enumerates some of the factors enabling return after prolonged displacement by looking at a number of counter-intuitive cases. Whilst many scholars have focused on displacement (e.g. McGarry, 1998; Mann, 2005), only a handful of academic or policy-related studies have systematically studied and compared voluntary return following negotiated peace settlements. To cover this gap, in this chapter, we discuss the broader literature and key findings in recent studies of durable returns. We look more closely at the cases from Southeast Europe and the Middle East, highlighting the role of established explanations in the literature (i.e. economic, psychological and security related factors), as well as some more novel ones, such as social capital and institutional design. We point out the strengths and weaknesses of the existing solutions and propose ways to facilitate successful returns in post-conflict societies. We conclude with a discussion of the meaning and operationalization of "right to return".

Common wisdom?

UNHCR (2013) defines protracted displacements as those involving 25,000 or more refugees for more than five years and generally recommends the reversal of those situations as quickly, voluntary and as peacefully as possible. Yet evidence on whether return is feasible or even desirable following protracted displacement is mixed and contradictory (Zetter, 1999; Adelman and Barkan, 2011). Conventional wisdom says displaced persons are unlikely to return to their former homes with the passage of time. As studies on durable solutions have demonstrated, the broader context matters (Black, 2001; Dahlman and Ó Tuathail, 2010; Başer and Çelik, 2014). Victims of displacement could be accommodated (or more frequently forced to stay) in designated refugee camps and face unbearable restrictions, or they could be integrated into a new environment in mixed neighbourhoods in major metropolitan centres; each situation will differently influence intentions to return home; therefore, generalizations are often problematic.

Furthermore, return is conditioned by domestic legal frameworks often established against the rights of IDPs and refugees. Some forced migrants cannot possibly return because of nationalist opposition or legal restrictions, as in the case of Palestinians in Israel, ethnic Georgians in Abkhazia and South Ossetia or Greek Cypriots forced out of Northern Cyprus. In other cases, migrants are forced to return, as in the case of the mass return of Bosnian refugees from Germany after the Bosnian War or, more recently, the Rohingyas repatriated from Bangladesh to Myanmar despite UN genocide warnings. In still other cases, displaced persons might have developed a sense of belonging in their place of exile and have no desire to go 'home'. Sometimes, however, returning to pre-displacement homes is a real possibility and a meaningful voluntary choice. In those cases, asking what drives voluntary return makes sense, and systematic research on the views of refugees themselves becomes a priority, not least because it facilitates the development of effective policies.

Scholars have already formulated several hypotheses about why people return. These often come from the social capital literature, institutional design and intergroup contact. Inspired by the social capital theory (Putnam, 1993, p. 167; Varshney, 2001; Castles, 2003; Çelik, 2005b) one could emphasize the efficacy of trust, norms and networks in facilitating return. The institutional design theory focuses on constitutional provisions for refugees and the broader design of institutions in peace processes (Loizides, 2016; Psaltis *et al.* 2020), including property restitution and compensation, policing arrangements and specific provisions in the electoral system that encourage participation and enable displaced persons to vote (see also Leckie, 2007). Finally, the contact theory examines the direct and indirect contact of displaced persons with the historical out-group and shows how it may affect their desire to return under that group's administration (Brown and Hewstone, 2005; Psaltis *et al.*, 2019).

Despite the development of novel theoretical foundations in the refugee literature, few studies have specifically asked why displaced persons choose to return or to stay in a new environment. Nor can the sparse findings be generalized, as existing research tends to focus on single cases, such as Bosnia (Dahlman and Ó Tuathail 2005; Stefanovic and Loizides, 2017), the South Caucasus (Toal and Grono, 2011), Kazakhstan (Kuşçu, 2014), Colombia (Ibánez Moya, 2010), Turkey (Çelik, 2005a) and Northern Uganda (Joireman *et al.*, 2012). Although studies are country and case-specific and, as such, not entirely generalizable, most indicate the importance of a general set of push and pull factors (Ozaltin *et al.*, 2019; Stefanovic *et al.* 2014). As noted above, displaced persons are less likely to return to their former homes if they successfully settle in a new environment (see Zolberg, 1989, p. 406; Zetter, 1999; Ibánez and Moya, 2010). If they have found permanent jobs, acquired property and developed their language skills (Wahlbeck, 1999; Annan *et al.*, 2011; Toal and Grono, 2011), they may have less inclination to leave. Another factor is accommodation in the place of exile: looking at the case of Northern Uganda, Joireman *et al.* (2012) point to the relocation of displaced persons in close proximity to roads, suggesting the centrality of access to social aid and provisions. Also relevant is the ethno-political make-up of the neighbourhood of pre-conflict residence and the extent of community support in exile. Here, researchers note the salience of majority/minority patterns and the limitations minority returnees face when they choose to relocate in areas controlled by potentially hostile local or national majorities (Toal and Dahlman, 2005; Çelik, 2005a; Belloni, 2006).

The way home project

By studying cases of successful voluntary return, we might be able to determine which institutional arrangements and policies could help people decide to return and then support them once they're back. With this possibility in mind, in 'The Way Home Project', funded by EU,

Canadian, Cypriot and UK grants,[2] we analysed three cases of forced displacement: Bosnians, ethnic Kurds in Turkey, and Greek Cypriots. By minority returnees, we are referring to displaced persons returning (or aiming, in the case of Greek Cypriots, to return) to an area now under the political control of another ethnic group. As nationalisms in the region have often sought to end ethnic and religious diversity through assimilation, ethnic cleansing and genocide, our research is driven by an attempt to understand how communities and individuals, often in opposition to state policies, struggle to defend their rights of return. We also examine the interrelated objectives of international organizations and peacekeeping missions such as restoring a multi-ethnic environment and re-introducing positive and mutually respectful relations among conflicted communities.

Our findings point to gender, age and education as main individual-level predictors of return. In both Bosnia (Stefanovic and Loizides, 2017) and Turkey's Kurdish region (Stefanovic *et al.*, 2014), for example, those who are highly educated and have found permanent employment in the place of displacement are less likely to return. In the various models we present in these two studies, young and educated women are very unlikely to return while elderly men with low education are very likely to do so. To be more specific, our statistical model for Bosnia, which correctly predicted return in 89.29 per cent of the cases we analysed, gives the probability of return for a 30-year old woman with a permanent job as 11.54 per cent; in stark contrast, a 63-year-old man without a permanent job has a 93.92 per cent probability of return. The model is based on the survey evidence, and we offer some possible explanations for age and gender differences below. However, our ability to fully explain the differences is constrained by the questionnaire used. Future research focusing, for instance, on integration opportunities and family dynamics could explain why elderly men are most pro-return whilst young women are the most opposed, while public policy could adjust to those findings. As Jansen (2009) summarizes the situation in Bosnia, "the elderly are dying to return and returning to die." Our research indicates the pattern is repeated among Kurdish forced migrants in Turkey and Greek Cypriot potential returnees (Loizides and Stefanovic, under review).

Many factors driving return are emotional/ideological rather than pragmatic (i.e. job availability in the new place). Forced migrants are more likely to return if they have positive memories of pre-conflict inter-ethnic relations, and they still see the pre-conflict residence as "home". Data from Bosnia and Cyprus also demonstrate how less nationalistic persons are more likely to return and accept life as a minority in their old place of residence than more nationalistic ones. A possible explanation of this finding is that nationalists tend to subscribe to dominant narratives emphasizing ethnic homogeneity as well, as they might be more prejudiced or fearful of other communities. Another commonality across cases is that informal associations of neighbours in exile play a role in facilitating return, at least in rural areas. A related finding is that forced migrants from areas of high return are more likely to return themselves (Metivier *et al.*, 2017).

Co-ethnicity is another issue driving decisions to return. In protracted displacements, return is not always desirable as people have re-established their lives but even after decades, a significant percentage aspires to return, especially to areas with a high concentration of co-ethnics. In Cyprus, the percentage of those Greek Cypriots aspiring to return under Greek Cypriot administration is almost triple of that of those aspiring to return under Turkish Cypriot administration. In the 2016 University of Cyprus/Centre of Field Studies survey about a third claimed they never thought of returning even following a negotiated peace settlement, another third said they rarely or sometimes thought about it, and the final third said they were always thinking about it (Psaltis *et al.*, 2020). Taking into consideration that a reunited Cyprus will be a federation with Greek and Turkish Cypriot constituent states, we presented alternative scenarios and options to potential returnees. When they were asked "How likely it is for you to return and live in your pre-1974 home under a Greek Cypriot administration in the next 3 years?", 59.5 per cent said they would likely or very likely return. When the same question was asked in the same way but "under a Turkish Cypriot administration", numbers dropped to 22.5 per cent (Psaltis *et al.*, 2020).

While the above findings are significant, current studies have failed to systematically collect data on decision-making processes within forced migrant families. The return decisions often seem to be made by families – not individuals. We know that elderly men are most pro-return whilst young women are most opposed. However, to the best of our knowledge, existing studies do not include the necessary evidence to help us understand how and why families arrive at a certain return decision, hopefully without a painful split if, for example, there are both elderly men and young women in the family unit. And while we know young women, particularly educated women, are the least likely to return, we are unable to tell whether this preference is the result of greater educational and paid employment opportunities in their new surroundings. Perhaps they simply want to avoid returning to a patriarchal rural community. This gap in the refugee and gender studies literature requires more investigation especially for NGOs and international organizations attempting to tailor their policy to attract and keep returnees.

In addition, we know the majority of successful mass return cases have been to mono-ethnic rural communities, but we would like to know what kind of policies are needed to facilitate mass minority returns to urban areas, especially to re-create multi-cultural cities. As Joireman (2017) observes, Kosovo Serb returns have been into minority ghettos or ethnic enclaves, as these likely provide a sense of security and community. By way of contrast, the small number of urban minority returns suggests the limits in restoring pre-war communities and the need for alternative policies to support urban returnees such as the creation of economic and employment opportunities and a multi-ethnic police force. Urban returnees may also depend on the willingness of others (i.e. the majority) to hire them, therefore enforcing non-discriminatory hiring practices should be an important priority in the legal frameworks of post-conflict societies.

How to engage and support returnees

Despite these gaps, we have some suggestions about the kind of policies and institutional arrangements that may facilitate return, especially among those who are less inclined to do so. Obviously, preventing ethnic cleansing in the first place should be the most critical priority given the rising numbers of forced migrants worldwide. Yet this may not be always possible given global environmental challenges and political violence, the reluctance of the international community to enforce norms on ethnic cleansing, and new technologies enabling an easier escape of forced migrants from deadly violence. For these reasons, research on ethnic cleansing and possible options in reversing its effects is extremely important. In this section, to lay the foundation for our suggestions, we take a closer look at several cases, particularly Bosnia, arguably a counter-intuitive case of relatively successful returns. For the most part, the experience of Bosnia has the potential to shed useful light on what triggers return and what keeps people "home" once they're back.

In Bosnia, the presence of international security forces and the removal of war criminals from a position of power have certainly been helpful, convincing many to return. In addition, in Bosnia and also in Turkey's Kurdish region, the return of property (houses and land) or compensation for lost or destroyed property definitely facilitated returns. In the Kurdish case, during the country's brief democratic opening in 2009–2012 there has been a degree of reconciliation.

Specifically, returnees receiving state compensation were three times more likely to return, net of other factors (Stefanovic *et al.*, 2014), however the return of violence in the Kurdish case also suggests the limits of durable returns in the absence of a completed peace settlement. By way of contrast and despite its limitations, the peace process in Bosnia provided the full range of support mechanisms for the displaced, including full property restitution, civilian protection mechanisms, and electoral rights for the IDPs in their pre-conflict residences.

In particular, the latter tend to receive little attention among scholars of forced migration. Importantly, enabling forced migrants to vote in the local elections in their pre-war place of residence (distant voting) was a very important facilitator of the re-capture of local political power in several Bosnian cases of successful mass return (e.g. Kozarac and Drvar). Annex 3 Article IV of the Dayton Peace Agreement should be a template for peace processes around the world. The annex stipulates that "a citizen who no longer lives in the municipality in which he or she resided in 1991 shall, as a general rule, be expected to vote, in person or by absentee ballot, in that municipality" (Stefanovic and Loizides, 2017. This electoral provision permitted refugees and internally displaced persons (IDPs) to cast absentee ballots in their pre-war home cities; in 1997, for example, the exiled Mile Marčeta was elected mayor of Drvar on the strength of the absentee ballot. Described by the international media as a "symbol of hope in a land of hate", the mayor convinced 1600 to 2000 displaced persons to accompany him back to the municipality. Despite Croat ultra-nationalists' resistance, the murder of two elderly returnees and an assassination attempt against Marčeta himself, forced migrants managed to re-establish themselves on their land. The Coalition for Drvar not only helped reverse ethnic cleansing but also played a leading role in mobilizing support from the international community and at home among the multi-ethnic country-wide Coalition for the Return of the Expelled.

The Drvar experience highlights the importance of remote voting for successful returns. Many continued to vote in their pre-conflict municipalities while in exile. As per Article 20.8 of the Bosnian Election Law, distant voting for displaced persons will remain in place until decided otherwise by the UN High Representative or the Parliamentary Assembly of BiH. Voting rights was a key element of the Dayton architecture – in contrast to other UN-led peace mediations such as the Annan Plan for Cyprus, which included significant restrictions on the political rights of displaced persons, or national laws such as the ones in Georgia restricting IDPs from Abkhazia and South Ossetia voting in national elections (even though the latter are ethnic Georgians). As Mooney and Jarrah (2005) argue, in Georgia the Soviet legacy of *propiska* (i.e. restricting freedom of movement by tying the exercise of rights to an individual's approved place of residence), was reinforced by the political goal of promoting return, and resulted in legal restrictions denying IDPs (until 2001) the right to vote for representatives in the areas where they were "temporarily" residing.

How should post-conflict societies balance the electoral rights of new and old residents? It is imaginable that under any electoral system problems might arise, especially if one of the groups comes to dominate the political system on a permanent basis. To prevent situations where municipal authorities represent either new or old inhabitants but not both, we suggest that peace settlements should combine remote voting with power-sharing systems at the local level. Such institutional mechanisms could allow displaced persons to maintain financial, institutional and political ties with their home region while rebuilding majority–minority relations at the local level.

Despite its many successes, the Bosnian return experience points to several limitations of internationally sponsored peacekeeping. In outlining these limitations and proposing solutions, we are seeing return not as a single act, but as a process with several key phases – intention to return, return attempts, and sustainable return – in which factors crucial for success in some phases might be less significant in others. Even in the townships where the intention to return was strong, with community effort leading to successful returns, the mass return was generally not followed by well-designed and well-funded economic development programmes. Consequently, many returnees left again, this time for economic reasons – to find jobs. To ensure sustainability, local economic development and economic opportunities need to be planned well in advance, and returnees will need support once they arrive.

Safeguarding rights of return

Could successful returns in Bosnia be replicated in other post-conflict societies? Whilst some conditions appear to be unique to Bosnia and hard to replicate – such as the massive presence of the international agencies in a de facto protectorate – others might work elsewhere. In Bosnia, the Dayton Peace Agreement (DPA) guaranteed the victims of ethnic cleansing the right to return. While the exercise of that right was fiercely resisted by ultra-nationalists, there was clarity as to its implementation and commitment of the international community.

In contrast to the provisions of Dayton, many of the conflicts around the world feature conflicting legal, political and normative interpretations of the "right of return". This largely depends on its definition of the "right of return" which could, in theory, involve not only the right of mobility/movement (i.e. a person's right to return to a pre-conflict village or city) but also three other necessary components: first, the right to restitution for property, including financial support for the loss of income and for the reconstruction of destroyed properties; second, individual and communal rights, such as non-discrimination, electoral rights, participation in local decision-making processes and representation in policing and security mechanisms; and third, the transferability of those rights to one's immediate family, for instance, descendants and spouses. Even though each is necessary for the restoration of a multicultural community, no comprehensive legal framework currently includes all three, let alone credible enforcement mechanisms.

There is also a key differentiation between international and EU/Council of Europe decisions. Within the EU legal system, it is possible for the right of movement and re-acquisition of properties to be seen as facilitating potential returnees. While the right of mobility for European citizens de facto mitigates part of the older displacement disputes among EU members (e.g. post-Second World War Germans fleeing Poland), it has several major weaknesses and cannot be seen as a resolution for historical cases of ethnic cleansing. To begin with, it lacks all other aforementioned elements that constitute the right of return. Second, it has led to no practical returns among the many cases occurring within European nations for centuries and, finally, it downgrades displaced persons and their rights to the level of migrants/citizens of third states covered by EU treaties that might or might not be preserved in the future.

Displaced persons are more likely to return if they have the right to do so under international law. Our own interpretation is that following the wars in the former Yugoslavia, international law is in the process of integrating the right of return but, at the time of writing, this right has not been secured in relevant international legal provisions, practices and norms. The UN's Pinheiro Principles on housing and property restitution come close to integrating the right of return into international legal practices (ECOSOC 2005). The Principles include detailed provisions on the rights of dispossessed owners, emphasizing their right to have their properties restituted, if they so wish and without stipulating time limitations. They require adequate consultation and participation of displaced persons in decision-making (principle 14) during the process of return. Pinheiro, however, proposes non-binding principles (soft law), which are up to the discretion of individual member states to accept or reject. The Principles also fail to include the need for electoral decision-making mechanisms, such as distant voting (a key finding for the Bosnian case) and the role of community rights and organizations.

Beyond the 'universal' Pinheiro Principles, standards on the right of return are documented in resolutions of international organizations such as the UN (Leckie, 2007, p. 12) but with relevance only to specific country cases. Leckie cites two types of UN resolutions: binding ones from the Security Council and non-binding from the General Assembly. Security Council resolutions have emphasized the right of return in the former Yugoslavia (Kosovo), Georgia, (Abkhazia), Croatia, Iraq (Kuwait) and Cyprus; General Assembly resolutions have focused on Palestine/Israel. To give an example, Cyprus SC RES. 361, August 30, 1974 calls on parties to "permit persons who wish to do so to return to their homes" (Leckie, 2007, p. 12). Critics of the resolution might argue that the conditions 40 days after the Turkish invasion were far different from the conditions now, after 50 or so years. ECHR decisions already point in this direction, with decisions restricting property restitution to second-generation displaced persons (Skoutaris, 2010). Countering this point, Barkan argues that no matter how long ago an injustice occurred, its legitimization or a concomitant failure to defend displaced persons encourages other wrongdoing (Barkan, 2000, p. xxxiii).

Another concern is that the right of return cannot be established without family reunification and community rebuilding. As this chapter demonstrates, displaced persons particularly minority groups are very unlikely to return in significant numbers unless there is significant community involvement and mobilization for return. Likewise, the right of return could be interpreted as covering descendants and non-displaced partners. On many occasions, displaced persons might not have been displaced directly at the time of the conflict; some might have left earlier for financial reasons but found the right of return to an ancestral land restricted as a result of a conflict.

A key challenge for human rights activists is that the right of return is not universally defined or even welcomed in legal or political terms. Characterizing a population en masse, rather than making the effort to break down various demographic and attitudinal characteristics is highly problematic. An often-unchallenged view is that protracted refugee situations produce radicalized populations who will cause renewed conflict if allowed to return (Adelman, 1998; Lischer, 2015). Following the signing of the Dayton Accords, for instance, Chaim Kaufmann argued that refugee return provisions were undesirable and unenforceable, suggesting compensation for lost property instead (Kaufmann, 1996, p. 168). Others have emphasized the security dimension and even coined the term "refugee warriors" (Zolberg *et al.*. 1986), thus introducing a language that explicitly uses security concerns to limit the rights of displaced persons. Adelman and Barkan have probably been the strongest proponents of the "irreversibility thesis"; they specifically argue that "the ideology and commitment to return, conveys the notion of repatriation as a distant, impractical solution in the face of real desperation" (Adelman and Barkan, 2011, p. xvii). Even though its advocates offer many well-reasoned qualifications, their general assumption is that forced displacements are irreversible once new demographic facts are established on the ground (e.g. Kaufmann, 1996; Adelman and Barkan, 2011).

Our own research challenges the irreversibility thesis and acknowledges more opportunities for returnees than conventionally assumed. Beyond the case of Bosnia, our database of peace processes and durable returns demonstrates how in comprehensive peace settlements, displaced persons are supported by various mechanisms. The rates of return in 25 settlements we examined using the Peace Accords matrix of the Kroc Institute suggest a range of outcomes from almost full return (e.g. El Salvador) to 10 per cent return (Angola); the remaining cases lie within this range. Second, as noted above, public opinion data outside Bosnia do not support claims that displaced persons tend to be more radicalized (see Psaltis *et al.*, 2020, on Cyprus) whilst, in Bosnia, returnees were more open to reconciliation (Hall *et al.*, 2018).

Conclusion

To this point, seeing displaced persons as potentially radicalized populations constitutes a view that needs to be challenged by broader comparative evidence. As mentioned earlier, in Cyprus we discovered – much to our surprise – stronger pro-settlement attitudes among Greek Cypriot displaced persons. Specifically, the percentage of non-displaced persons determined to reject a future peace plan was almost double that of the displaced,[3] whilst comparable research by Khalil Shikaki and Dahlia Scheindlin among Palestinians suggests refugees are slightly more likely to accept a peace plan than never-displaced Palestinians (39 per cent compared with 35 per cent for non-refugees) indicating similar trends even in more polarized environments (see also Hall, 2016, on Bosnians).[4] Giving a voice to those affected most by conflict and, in the case of forced migrants, who have lost properties is not only a normative necessity in shaping future humanitarian missions but also a practical step in establishing durable peace settlements.

A second important conclusion, relates to the role of social and political capital among forced migrants. Well-organized associations of neighbours in exile also provided coordination in the Bosnian return, enhanced a sense of security and recreated some sense of community after return in Drvar and Kozarac, as shown by Sivac-Bryant's (2016) ethnography. In the absence of political institutions and organized associations, new technological improvements might potentially assist peace mediations and the right of return. This could include, for instance, new software/apps popularizing public consultation in peace processes and census platforms aiming to collate and verify property data across dispossessed owners and to assist them in reaching amicable compromises with the new occupants of disputed homes and properties (Andrade and Doolin 2016; Psaltis *et al.* 2020; Loizides and Stefanovic, forthcoming).

These potential solutions could facilitate but not substitute political leadership. As the differences in the experiences and the minority return rates of Bosniacs and Bosnian Serbs imply, if the political leaders of an ethnic/religious community openly and consistently support the return as 'patriotic', forced migrants are more likely to be successful. The case of Bulgaria is also particularly instructive here in terms of involving each community's political leadership. Following the voluntary return of approximately 40 per cent of forcibly expelled Turks in the post-Zhivkov era, an ambitious process of improving minority–majority relations and integrating Bulgaria to the EU was initiated. The return of the displaced was not only supported by EU institutions during the accession talks but also by Bulgaria's own inclusive political institutions (i.e. the use of proportional representation) which incentivised coalitions and allowed the Movement for Rights and Freedoms (MRF), the political party formed by the Turkish community following Bulgaria's transition to democracy, to become the "king-maker" in elections and to play an active role in all critical legislative processes in Parliament (Loizides and Kutlay, 2019). The return of the displaced in the case of Bulgaria provides additional evidence of the positive role of electoral institutions and (informal) power-sharing in enhancing durable solutions to displacement (Koinova, 2013; Kutlay, 2017).

Finally, this chapter highlights the demographic profile of returnees (i.e. age, education and gender), their immediate and long-term needs, as well as other support mechanisms. As the majority of the early returnees are likely to be older persons, the provision of good healthcare services might be a crucial factor. Moreover, the finding that displaced persons from rural areas are more likely to return, because coordination, social organization and economic sustainability are easier to achieve in such settings, suggests that dedicated community lands for returnees might increase return. Co-ethnic neighbours could provide a sense of community, solidarity and security in line with emerging normative practices in most liberal democracies (Kymlicka, 1995, p. 43; see Joireman, 2017, for post-conflict settings). Finally, our survey findings on demographics (e.g. age, rural/urban split) could help international agencies to better target the scarce funds for the support of the return process. For the reasons we provide, a voluntary, sustainable and successful return process, requires forced migrants in question – from Syria, Columbia, Myanmar or any other country – to voice their concerns, trade-offs, priorities and intentions. They are the ones who must find the strength and the courage to face hardships and dangers – but hopefully also joys and victories – as they take the difficult path home.

Notes

1 For exceptions see Black and Koser (1999); Belloni (2008); O'Loughlin *et al.* (2011).

2 Our research and surveys were funded by EURIAS, SSHRC, Leverhulme and British Academy grants

3 All participants (IDPs and non-IDPs) with voting rights in the Greek Cypriot community were asked about their stance if there was a referendum and their political party supported a Yes vote. About 40 per cent said they tended towards voting Yes or were sure to vote Yes, about 26 per cent tended towards or were sure to vote No, and about 34 per cent were equally likely to vote Yes or No. Twenty-one per cent of non-IDPs were sure to vote No, compared with 12.5 per cent of IDPs (Psaltis *et al.*, 2020).

4 For the Israeli/Palestinian data, see panel discussion at Mitvim Institute at https://p-upload.facebook.com/Mitvim/posts/2116956235028539 and Khalil Shikaki's Palestinian Center for Policy and Survey Research at www.pcpsr.org/en/node/154

References

Adelman, H. (1998) Why refugee warriors are threats. *Journal of Conflict Studies*, 18(1), 49–69.

Adelman, H. and Barkan E. (2011). *No Return, No Refuge: Rites and Rights in Minority Repatriation*. New York: Columbia University Press.

Andrade, A. D. and Doolin, B. (2016) Information and communication technology and the social inclusion of refugees. *MIS Quarterly*, 40(2), 405–416.

Annan, J. *et al.* (2011) Civil war, reintegration, and gender in northern Uganda. *Journal of Conflict Resolution*, 55(6), 877–908.

Barkan, E. (2000) *The Guilt of Nations: Restitution and Negotiating Historical Injustices*. London: W. W. Norton & Company.

Başer, Z., and Çelik, B. (2014) Imagining peace in a conflict environment: Kurdish youths' framing of the Kurdish issue in Turkey. *Patterns of Prejudice*, 48(3), 265–285.

Belloni, R. (2006) Peacebuilding at the local level: refugee return to Prijedor. In Chandler D. (ed.), *Peace without Politics? Ten Years of International State-building in Bosnia*. London: Routledge, 28–141.

Belloni, R. (2008) *State Building and International Intervention in Bosnia*. London: Routledge.

Black, R. (2001) Return and reconstruction in Bosnia-Herzegovina: missing link, or mistaken priority? *SAIS Review*, 21(2), 177–199.

Black, R. and Koser, K. (1999) *The End of the Refugee Cycle?: Refugee Repatriation and Reconstruction*. New York: Berghahn Books.

Brown, R. and Hewstone, M. (2005) An integrative theory of intergroup contact. *Advances in Experimental Social Psychology*, 37(37), 255–343.

Castles, S. (2003) Towards a sociology of forced migration and social transformation. *Sociology*, 37(1), 13–34.

Çelik, A. B. (2005a) Transnationalization of human rights norms and its impact on internally displaced Kurds. *Human Rights Quarterly*, 27(3) 969–997.

Çelik, A. B. (2005b) 'I miss my village': forced Kurdish migrants in Istanbul and their representation in associations. *New Perspectives on Turkey*, 32(1). 137–163.

Dahlman, C. and Ó Tuathail, G. (2005) The legacy of ethnic cleansing: the international community and the returns process in post-Dayton Bosnia–Herzegovina. *Political Geography*, 24(5), 569–599.

ECOSOC (2005) Housing and property restitution in the context of the return of refugees and internally displaced persons. Final report of the Special Rapporteur, Paulo Sérgio Pinheiro for the United Nations Economic and Social Council available at http://unispal.un.org/unispal.nsf/0/577d69b243fd3c048525 7075006698e6?OpenDocument (accessed 16 August 2013).

Hall, J. (2016) Are migrants more extreme than locals after war? Evidence from a simultaneous survey of migrants in Sweden and locals in Bosnia. *Journal of Conflict Resolution*, 60(1), 89–117.

Hall, J., Kovras, I., Stefanovic, D., and Loizides, N. (2018) Exposure to violence and attitudes towards transitional justice. *Political Psychology*, 39(2), 345–363.

Ibánez, A. M. and Moya, A. (2010) Vulnerability of victims of civil conflicts: empirical evidence for the displaced population in Colombia. *World Development,* 38, 647–663.

Jansen, S. (2009) Troubled locations. In S. Jansen and S. Lofving (eds), *Struggles for Home: Hope and the Movement of People.* New York: Berghahn Books.

Joireman, S. (2017) Ethnic violence, local security and return migration: enclave communities in Kosovo. *International Migration*, 55(5), 122–135.

Joireman, S. F., Sawyer, A., and Wilhoit, J. (2012) A different way home: resettlement patterns in Northern Uganda. *Political Geography*, 31, 197–204.

Kaufmann, C. (1996) Possible and impossible solutions to ethnic civil wars. *International Security*, 20(4), 136–175.

Koinova, M. (2013) *Ethnonationalist Conflict in Postcommunist States: Varieties of Governance in Bulgaria, Macedonia, and Kosovo.* Philadelphia, PA: University of Pennsylvania Press.

Kuşçu, I. (2014) Ethnic return migration and public debate: the case of Kazakhstan. *International Migration*, 52(2), 178–197.

Kutlay, M. (2017) The Turks of Bulgaria: an outlier case of forced migration and voluntary return. *International Migration*, 55(5), 162–179.

Kymlicka, W. (1995) *Multicultural Citizenship: A Liberal Theory of Minority Rights.* Oxford: Clarendon Press.

Leckie, S. (ed.) (2007) *Housing and Property Restitution Rights of Refugees and Displaced Persons: Laws, Cases, and Materials.* Cambridge, UK: Cambridge University Press.

Lischer, S. K. (2015) *Dangerous Sanctuaries: Refugee Camps, Civil War, and the Dilemmas of Humanitarian Aid.* Ithaca: Cornell University Press.

Loizides N. (2016) *Designing Peace: Cyprus and Institutional Innovations in Divided Societies.* Philadelphia, PA: University of Pennsylvania Press

Loizides, N. and Kutlay M. (2019) The Cyprus stalemate: opportunities for peace and lessons from Turkish-Bulgarian ethnic relations. In A. Heraclides and G. Cakmak, (eds), *Greece and Turkey in Conflict and Cooperation.* New York: Routledge

Loizides, N. and Stefanovic D. (2013) Displacement and return: public policy and practice in Cyprus. CARC Thematic Program on *Diasporas and Securitization* available at www.kent.ac.uk/politics/carc/diasporas-and-securitisation/documents/policy-manual.pdf

Loizides, N and Stefanovic D. (In preparation) *The Way Home: Peaceful Return of Victims of Forced Displacement.* Book manuscript in preparation.

Loizides N. and Stefanovic D. (Under review) Successfully integrated but determined to return: surveying attitudes on forced displacement in Cyprus.

Mann, M. (2005) *The Dark Side of Democracy (Explaining Ethnic Cleansing).* Cambridge, UK: Cambridge University Press.

McGarry, J. (1998) 'Demographic engineering': the state-directed movement of ethnic groups as a technique of conflict regulation. *Ethnic and Racial Studies*, 21(4), 613–638.

Metivier S., Stefanovic D., and Loizides N. (2017) Struggling for and within the community: what leads Bosnian forced migrants to desire community return? *Ethnopolitics*, 17(2), 147–164.

Metivier, S., Stefanovic, D., and Loizides, N. (2017) Struggling for and within the community: what leads Bosnian forced migrants to desire community return? *Ethnopolitics*, 17(2), 147–164.

Mooney, E. and Jarrah, B. (2005) Safeguarding IDP voting rights. *Forced Migration Review*, 23, 55.

O'Loughlin, J., Kolossov, V., Toal, G., and Tuathail, G. (2011) Inside Abkhazia: survey of attitudes in a de facto state. *Post-Soviet Affairs*, 27(1), 1–36.

Ozaltin, D., Shakir, F., & Loizides, N. (2019) Why do people flee? Revisiting forced migration in post-Saddam Baghdad. *International Migration & Integration*, https://doi.org/10.1007/s12134-019-00674-z

Psaltis C., Loizides N., LaPierre A., and Stefanovic, D. (2019) Transitional justice and acceptance of cohabitation in Cyprus. *Ethnic and Racial Studies*, 42(11), 1850–1869. DOI: 10.1080/01419870.2019.1574508 20

Psaltis, C., Cakal, H., Loizides, N., and Kuscu, I. (2020) Internally displaced persons and the exclusion amid inclusion dilemma in the Cyprus peace process. *International Political Science Review* (forthcoming).

Putnam, R. (1993) *Making Democracy Work: Civic Traditions in Modern Italy.* Princeton, NJ: Princeton University Press.

Sivac-Bryant S. (2016) *Re-Making Kozarac*. London: Palgrave Macmillan.
Skoutaris, N. (2010) Building transitional justice mechanisms without a peace settlement: a critical appraisal of recent case law of the Strasbourg Court on the Cyprus issue. *European Law Review*, 35(5), 720–734.
Stefanovic, D. and Loizides, N. (2011) The way home: peaceful return of victims of ethnic cleansing. *Human Rights Quarterly*, 33(3), 408–430.
Stefanovic, D. and Loizides, N. (2017) Peaceful returns: reversing ethnic cleansing after the Bosnian War. *International Migration*, 55, 217–234.
Stefanovic, D., Loizides, N., and Parsons, S. (2014) Home is where the heart is? Forced migration and voluntary return in Turkey's Kurdish regions. *Journal of Refugee Studies*, 28, 276–296.
Toal, G. and Dahlman C. (2005) Has ethnic cleansing succeeded? Geographies of minority return and its meaning in Bosnia-Herzegovina. In A. Gosar (ed.), *Dayton Ten Years After: Conflict Resolution, Co-operation Perspectives*. Slovenia: Primorska.
Toal, G. and Grono M. F. (2011) After ethnic violence in the Caucasus: attitudes of local Abkhazians and displaced Georgians in 2010. *Eurasian Geography and Economics*, 52(5), 655–678.
UNHCR (2013) *Displacement: The New 21st Century Challenge (UNHCR Global Trends 2011)*.
UNHCR (2019) *UNHCR Statistics the World in Numbers*. http://popstats.unhcr.org/en/overview#_ga=2.89497883.1226693269.1563901391-1809765446.1563901391 (accessed July 16, 2019).
Varshney, A. (2001) Ethnic conflict and civil society: India and beyond. *World Politics* 53 (3): 362–398.
Wahlbeck Ö. (1999) *Kurdish Diasporas: A Comparative Study of Kurdish Refugee Communities*. London: Macmillan.
Zetter, R. (1999) Reconceptualizing the myth of return: continuity and transition amongst the Greek-Cypriot refugees of 1974. *Journal of Refugee Studies*, 12(1), 1–22.
Zolberg, A. R. (1989) The next waves: migration theory for a changing world. *International Migration Review*, 23(3), 403–430.
Zolberg, A. R., Suhrke, A., and Aguayo, S. (1986) International factors in the formation of refugee movements. *International Migration Review*, 20(2), 151–169.

6

HOW MODERN IS THE HOLOCAUST?[1]

Amos Goldberg

In his *Modernity and the Holocaust* (Bauman, 1989), the eminent sociologist Zygmunt Bauman argued that instead of signifying a retreat from modernity, the Holocaust was actually a distinct expression of it, emerging directly from modern worldviews and the structures of modern existence.[2] Bauman's book sparked an ongoing debate in a way that very few other books have done (Stone, 2010, p. 121). It touched on a question that remains central to our understanding of the Holocaust: to what extent were the Nazi regime and the Holocaust fundamentally related to the major aspects of modernity as an era emerging from the ideas of European rationalism and enlightenment? Popular imagination and representations tend to view the Holocaust as unique and transgressive to the extent that it is very much remote from our own modern life. However within scholarly literature which is of course not disconnected from popular representations but nonetheless not identical to it, this question steered huge debates and controversies. This chapter, which in its very nature is highly partial in terms of content and works cited, will explore a number of the different incarnations of the concept of modernity as it pertains to historical works on the Holocaust, and will argue that although some of its elements have been rejected as reductionist, modernity nonetheless continues to serve as an extremely important analytic framework for understanding the Holocaust and its relationship to other events.

Bauman's (1989) book is undoubtedly the most comprehensive conceptual formulation of the relationship between modernity and the Holocaust written thus far and will serve as a main trajectory for the discussion. However, before discussing Bauman, and in order to better understand the arguments he makes, we must first turn to the historiography of the Holocaust written since the 1960s.

It is customary to speak of the emergence of two major historiographical schools in the study of the "Final Solution" since the 1960s, and during the 1980s and 1990s in particular: the intentionalist school, which places a major emphasis on the dominance of Hitler as a primary force in leading the evolution of the Final Solution, and the structuralist or functionalist school, which stresses the role of the bureaucratic echelons. Scholars associated with the former have emphasized the role of anti-Semitic ideology, whereas scholars associated with the latter have highlighted the role of local circumstances and relatively "rational" considerations (Burrin, 1994; Kershaw, 2000, pp. 69–92; Evans, 1989). Though not a historian, Bauman's understanding of the Holocaust is based on the functionalist school, whose approach he espouses and bolsters from the perspective of sociological theory. Raul Hilberg is considered to be the forefather of this school. His monumental work *The Destruction of the European Jews*, published in 1961, was the first book to draw a complete, detailed and comprehensive picture of the extermination of European Jewry based on rich German documentation. Hilberg's book was preceded by a number of studies, the best known of which are Poliakov (1954) and Reitlinger (1953). These works, however, failed to present a picture that was as full and well based as that presented by Hilberg. In *The Destruction of the European Jews*, Hilberg focuses his research on the bureaucratic structure, which emerges as the protagonist of the story. According to Hilberg, the key to understanding the Holocaust and the Final Solution is found not in the question "why did the Germans murder the Jews?" but rather "how did this full-blown genocide evolve?"

Largely influenced by his teacher Franz Neumann's book *Behemoth* (Hilberg, 1996, pp. 61–65), Hilberg's work paints a picture of a well-oiled modern bureaucratic machine operating based on its own internal dynamics. This synchronized, though not necessarily coordinated machine, was powered not by ideology but rather by bureaucratic logic. Understanding the Final Solution then requires in-depth exploration of this system and the manner in which it operated. Bauman's book in many ways constitutes a direct continuation of *The Destruction of the European Jews* (Stone, 2010, pp. 121; Matthäus, 2019).

Bauman's fundamental argument in this context is that the Holocaust cannot be understood as a return to barbarism that released primeval murderous instincts which modern society had learned to restrain. It must, rather, be understood as a structural product of modernity itself, indicative of its shrouded catastrophic potential. "Modern civilization was not the Holocaust's sufficient condition," Bauman (1989, p. 13) asserts. "It was, however, most certainly its necessary condition," as "without it, the Holocaust would be unthinkable" (Bauman, 1989, p. 13). Contrary to the conception of modernity as a historical and political product of the enlightenment and, as such, an advanced, progressive and, on the whole, more moral phase of history, Bauman builds on Horkheimer and Adorno's argument regarding the instrumental rationality of modernity, particularly in its capitalist form. It is a rationality devoid of ethical restraints that objectifies the world (the human world included) for the sake of its needs – a rationality by which humans have become objects of research, planning, exploitation, and organization that constantly strive toward maximum efficiency. In such a conceptual system, the human being as a creature toward which others have an ethical obligation vanishes along with ethical subject himself. When this happens, the path is clear for the large-scale perpetration of crimes (Horkheimer and Adorno, 1972).

Bauman returns to the bureaucrat as a characteristic figure of the modern era. This portrait and importance of the bureaucrat within the structure and leadership of the modern state was outlined by Max Weber, whose influence on Bauman's book was decisive. In the context of the Nazi era, the bureaucrat is characterized as someone who murders while seated at his desk – someone who is not overwhelmed by unfathomable hatred of his victims but is merely fulfilling his or her role in the hierarchical system in which they is situated while sending thousands to the gas chambers. This is the grey bureaucrat (the image of Eichmann rendered by Arendt, 1963, in *Eichmann in Jerusalem*) motivated primarily by their own desire to excel and to complete their task as well as possible, and whose main aspiration is to climb the hierarchical ladder of the bureaucratic system. This type of person employs no ethical considerations in their work, and is not necessarily driven by ideology, even when they recite the hegemonic ideology like a parrot or out of self-persuasion, but rather by strictly rational considerations of efficiency. In this way, the bureaucracy, which is perhaps the best manifestation of the Weberian iron cage, produces modern types of people who are necessarily estranged from the suffering of others who, according to Bauman (following Helen Fein's conceptualization), are remote from the bureaucrat's ethical "universe of obligations." Thus, concludes Bauman: "The light shed by the Holocaust on our knowledge of bureaucratic rationality is at its most dazzling once we realize the extent to which the very idea of the Endlösung [Final Solution] was an outcome of the bureaucratic culture" (Bauman, 1989, p. 15).

This, however, is only one dimension of Bauman's argument. Employing the same critical approach to modernity, Bauman also contends with the ideological aspects of the extermination and the consciousness that led to and justified these crimes. The Jews had been Europe's "other" for many centuries, Bauman explains, and were the focus of considerable popular bitterness as alleged god killers, usurers, poisoners of wells, and the like. However, as long as Jews were conspicuous and identifiable, they were also tolerable, albeit as an inferior subject within a hierarchical political and religious system. However, in the modern era Jews lost their visibility as a result of emancipation and became members of the bourgeoisie, primarily in Central and Western Europe but to a large extent also in Eastern Europe. They were no longer conspicuously Jewish in their appearance, their professions, their language, or even their lifestyle. The result of the blurring of these distinctions was a phobia that was much worse than it had been in the past. As Jews now preserved their differentness in a manner that was no longer visible to the eye, they could appear anywhere without being identified: in industry, in the media, in the arts, in the street, at work, and in the family. In this capacity, they became in the popular imagination much more demonic and were transformed into a ghost that exists everywhere but without being identified. In this way, and quite paradoxically, the modern era, which was expected to emancipate the Jews, transformed the "Jew" into an intolerable "other" (Žižek, 1995, pp. 125–129). From this perspective, the "Jew" was, in many respects, the Freudian "uncanny" (Freud, 2003).

This state of affairs must be considered, according to Bauman, in conjunction with modernity's primary sin: its aesthetic conception of the identity politics it manages. After all, a rational approach to the world always desires to engineer it in an ordered and perfect manner. To this end, it sorts and classifies according to rigid categories and has natural difficulty dealing with "others" who disrupt this order by not completely fitting into these rigid categories. According to this worldview, such hybrid phenomena are intolerable and those who bear them are perceived as weeds polluting the social garden and are destined to be uprooted and eliminated. From this vantage point, Bauman, concludes,

> Modern genocide, like modern culture in general, is a gardener's job. [...] If garden design defines its weeds, there are weeds wherever there is a garden. And weeds are to be exterminated. Weeding out is a creative, not a destructive activity.
>
> *(Bauman, 1989, p. 92)*

The concept by which hatred of the Jews became "a gardener's job" of weed and pest extermination, as part of the project of population engineering, was a clear modern scientific concept – racism. The violent socio-political discourse of racism was based on the scientific racial discourse that characterized significant fields of the humanities and the social and natural sciences during the final third of the nineteenth century and the beginning of the twentieth century. Although this discourse did not initially emerge in the Jewish context, in Nazi thought it contended anew with the "Jewish problem" in its association of the Jew with permanent, unalterable attributes. It did not matter if they dressed like others, spoke like others, or lived a lifestyle exactly like that of others; because of the assemblage of genetic and racial characteristics that were inherent in them, they remained Jews and needed to be identified and separated from the rest of the population.

Hence, according to Bauman, the Holocaust is neither merely the specific story of the Jews in Europe nor an account of insane anti-Semitic hatred that released primeval instincts and ended in tragedy. Rather, it is first and foremost the most extreme and catastrophic realization of a fundamental element that has always been present in modern social and political thought: the desire to impose complete rational order within a political reality in which the "exception" has no place and ultimately becomes waste. The intolerance toward the "other" has radically intensified in modern times – hence the unprecedented amount of violence that it liberated and hence the radical and unprecedented form of outcasting the Jews. Modern anti-Semitism, holds Bauman, which the Nazis radicalized into its most racist form, is an expression of this desire.

Bauman's book was first published in 1989, in the heyday of the functionalist school which then dominated the field of Holocaust research. Since then, the study of the history of the Third Reich and the Holocaust has made great strides, enabling us to consider Bauman's claims in a different light. On the one hand, the exemplary clean and rational order (reflected in the garden metaphor) that Bauman imposes – largely following Hilberg – on the Nazis' policies toward the Jews that ended in their extermination is somewhat reductive and misleading. For example, Ulrich Herbert, a prominent German historian of the Final Solution, sums up this point as follows:

> ...the widespread conception of mass murder as a quasi-anonymous process, or as "factory-like" killing, is misleading. The number of Jews gassed in the large killing centers account for about 60 percent of the six million Jews murdered [Desbois, 2008]. [...] The image of a "clean" death by gassing does not apply to much of the genocide. On the contrary, the Holocaust meant, to a considerable degree, exterminating human beings in very traditional, even archaic, ways [e.g. Westermann, 2018], with a correspondingly high number of direct perpetrators. The notion of a modern "industrial" genocide, in which the victim-perpetrator structure is replaced by anonymous relationships, is clearly an attempt to represent the mass murder as an abstract, even metaphysical, mass death of nameless victims.
>
> *(Herbert, 2000, p. 37; Roseman, 2011. p. 696)*

Therefore, pushing the Holocaust in its entirety into the one all-explaining category of modernity, as a form of organization and rational order, is oversimplifying matters somewhat, and for this reason Bauman's thesis has been subject to harsh criticism from various quarters (Bauer, 2001, pp. 68–66; Aschheim, 1996, p. 131; Stone, 2003, pp. 246–252; Hayes, 2017, pp. 329–330).

As a matter of fact, even Bauman's concept of the "modern" and its relation to mass atrocities was far from being consensual and uncontested. Already in 1984, historian Jeffrey Herf published an influential book named *Reactionary Modernism* in which he examined the "paradox of German modernity namely the embrace of modern technology by German thinkers who rejected Enlightenment reason" (Herf, 1984, p. 1). According to him and contrary to Bauman (and Adorno and Horkheimer) the Holocaust was not a child of enlightened moral values but rather a reactionary (yet still modern) response to it. However, the Nazis did take advantage of modern technology that enabled them to pursue their reactionary goals on a new scale of violence.

Moreover, over the past three decades, Holocaust historiography has changed, and as a result of the above-mentioned developments and heated historiographical discussions and debates, intentionalists and functionalists have moved closer to one another's positions and have recognized both the evidence for the claims of the other and the importance of these claims themselves. As a result, the explanations for the Holocaust and the Final Solution have become much more complex and much less one-dimensional.

However, these historiographical tendencies do not detract from the importance of the context of modernity in understanding the Holocaust. On the contrary, we are nonetheless left with the understanding that the Holocaust was primarily an event of modern history constructed out of building blocks that were alarmingly modern in nature. This means that the Holocaust is part of a continuum containing other modern events, and that these modern building blocks also exist in our world today and can (as they have in the past and continue to do in the present) bring about major tragedies for entire populations.

This is not to say of course that genocide did not occur in pre-modern times. On the contrary, some ancient and Middle-Ages genocides are well documented (Kiernan, 2007). However, modern genocides do bear their own characteristics and are much more frequent than in previous times. There is something in modernity that seems to encourage genocidal tendencies. Rudolph Rummel found that from the beginning of the twentieth-century until 1989 (the year of the end of the Cold War), some 170 million people uninvolved in fighting (including surrendered troops) were killed all over the world – 38 million of these deaths would fall under the UN definition of "genocide" (Rummel, 1997).

For this reason, the modernity of the Holocaust is a subject that refuses to budge from the historical and philosophical agenda. In what follows I will briefly sketch a number of trajectories of research that continue to develop, in a fascinating and challenging manner, different ways of understanding the relationship between the Holocaust and the attributes of the modern era.

In 1991, the German scholars Götz Aly and Susanne Heim published the book *Vordenker der Vernichtung*, which came out in English a decade later under the title *Architects of Annihilation* (Aly and Heim, 2002). This book astounded the historical community and elicited extremely enthusiastic reviews alongside harsh criticism (Aly and Heim, 1994; Bankier, 1994; Diner, 1994; Herbert, 1994). Aly and Heim's study focused on a group of academic experts – technicians, economists, population engineers, demographers, agricultural experts, nutrition experts, and the like – who played an exceedingly important role in the development of a policy of Jewish persecution and extermination. This stratum of academic "professionals" – some of whom worked in academic institutions and research institutes and others who worked in official agencies of the Nazi state, the party, and the SS, writing position papers and lending professional direction to exceedingly important organizations – had until then been left out of the historical picture.

Aly and Heim's study, and a number of follow-up studies by other scholars, have revealed the central role played by this echelon in the drama of the catastrophe of the Jews (Gerlach 1999a and b). The work of these professionals were motivated not by hatred, ideology, or bureaucratic blindness, but rather first and foremost by completely rational considerations of an economy of profit, of modern agricultural development, and of a demographic organization of Eastern Europe which they regarded as more rational and, therefore, as better serving the interests of the Third Reich. Racial considerations were interwoven into concerns that were economic, industrial, agricultural, and settlement-oriented in character, primarily within the determination of a hierarchy of priorities relating to the different population groups. The murder of the Jews, according to these scholars, was only one component of an overall reorganization of Eastern Europe as a whole, which was part of a broader programme of economic and demographic modernization aimed at benefiting the empire of the Third Reich. Ukraine, for example, was meant to become the Reich's cereal granary, based on a plan that required killing millions of hungry mouths and saving the food they would have consumed. During the first stage of this move, some 30 million people were supposed to be murdered, die of hunger, or be deported as part of the "Hunger Plan" (*der Hungerplan*), followed by tens of millions of others during its second phase. These plans, which were formulated and stimulated primarily by this echelon of technicians and academics, were ultimately assembled into one plan known as the "General Plan for the East" (*Generalplan Ost*), which in practice was a plan for the Reich's colonization of Eastern Europe. The murder of the Jews also stemmed first and foremost from economic considerations. Racial considerations determined only the hierarchy of populations within the new economic-demographic order imposed by the Nazis, and the lowest on the list, the Jews, were the first to pay the price of the project for the economic, agricultural, and demographic modernization of Eastern Europe.

These works, influenced by post-Marxist trends, drew attention to material and economic aspects, which played a major role in the persecution, deportation, and murder of the Jews, as this enterprise was ultimately profitable (or ostensibly profitable) for parts of German society and elements within the party and the state. In short, the persecution and murder of the Jews reflected a distinct dimension of rational material/economic interest.

Recently, the highly celebrated historian Timothy Snyder continued this line of thought with an ecological twist in his book *Black Earth*, claiming that the Nazi assault on the East in search for living space (*Lebensraum*), which also included the annihilation of the Jews, was driven to a large extent by what was perceived as a need to restore ecological balance to the world and to win the resources Germany needed so badly. He also warns that in a climate-changed world, drought and the search for basic resources will in the near future draw large sections of the world into genocidal wars (Snyder, 2015).

Another direction of research situating the Holocaust in extremely modern contexts has been "genocide studies", a field in which a number of relatively recent publications have proven especially fascinating. Historian Mark Levene has provided a most comprehensive history of modern genocide. In his seminal two volumes, *The Crisis of Genocide*, he describes the weakening and breakdown of the big nineteenth-century empires – the Ottoman, Russian Habsburgian and German – before, during and following the Great War and how this resulted in a series of genocides and genocidal ethnic cleansings (Levene, 2013). These processes, inherent in the establishment of new nation states on the ruins of the former empires, were most intensive in the south-eastern part of the continent:

> [T]hese historically plural borderlands or, as I would prefer, "rimlands" (that is, countries at the geographical conjuncture between the metropolitan, avant-garde, already heavily homogenized nation-states of the West and the retreating world empires of what in Wallersteinian terms were now a semiperiphery) became not just in the course of Hitler's conquests but in a period spanning 1912 to 1948 the primary locus of a repeated sequence of genocides, or genocidal ethnic cleansings. This process, in what amounted to the state-authorized expurgation of ethnoreligious difference, thus fated not only Jews but many other internally complex and heterogeneous communities to compulsory deportation and/or overt elimination across a geographical range spanning the lands between Danzig to Trieste in the west and the Caucasus to Mosul in the east and southeast.
>
> *(Levene, 2018, p. 46)*

Like him, Donald Bloxham also perceives the Final Solution as part of the process of ethnic homogenization experienced by modern Europe beginning in the nineteenth century. At their very core, these violent processes gave birth to "ethnic cleansing", which Bloxham refers to as "a very modern form of violence" that became an accepted form of action (Bloxham, 2009, p. 59; Ther, 2014).

The victims of this violence included Muslim groups within the Christian empires and Christian peoples within the Ottoman Empire. These processes sometimes evolved into actual genocide, the best known of which in these regions was the genocide perpetrated by the Turks against the Armenians in 1915. During this event (which constituted the high point of a bloody process that had already begun during the final decade of the nineteenth century and that involved the murder of between 150,000–300,000 Armenians), approximately one-third of the Armenian people were killed. The Final Solution, argues Bloxham, must be understood against the background of the processes experienced by modern Europe, among other things, and as the pinnacle of these processes. Bloxham's thesis steered a harsh historiographical controversy, (Matthäus *et al.*, 2011, pp. 107–152), but seems to me to be very convincing.

This connects to another historiographical approach that has become more and more convincing in the past two decades; the approach that, in understanding Nazi Germany, focuses on one dominant aspect of the modern period – nationalism and the nation state. Whereas the Nazi state was once understood as a unique racial state that differed from all other nation states and if, as a result, its brutal policies were once seen as being derived from its racially-based political character (Burleigh and Wippermann, 1991), today many scholars of Nazism, racism, genocide, and nation states today tend to disagree with this assessment for convincing reasons.

In this context, Mark Mazower's book *Hitler's Empire* is critical of the approach of many historians who regard the Nazi state not as an extreme expression of the modern, all-European national phenomenon but rather as a kind of political pathology reflecting a unique desire for violence and murder (Mazower, 2008, p. 9). Yet the Nazis' uniqueness, argues Mazower in this context, lay not in their imperial aspirations based on the geographical expansion of the territories controlled by the nation state, but in the extremely limiting Nazi definition of German nationalism, which allowed almost no partnership with conquered peoples, not to mention the Jews (Mazower, 2008, p. 7). Contrary to other scholars (whom we will discuss below) who regarded Nazi racial concepts as a metaphor for national ethnic concepts, Mazower maintains that Nazi nationalism was based on an extreme conception of the science of race. German nationalism as the Nazis sought to construct it, he holds, was characterized by two quite modern phenomena: romantic nostalgia for the Middle Ages (represented by Himmler) and a total commitment to the science of race (Mazower, 2008, p. 181). And still, a large portion of the national-imperial Nazi political lexicon was not new but rather based on German and European concepts that crystallized in the course of the nineteenth century and the beginning of the twentieth century. One example was the concept of "living space" (*Lebensraum*) that was so central to the violence that Nazi Germany unleashed against the occupied populations, including the Jews (Mazower, 2008, pp. 15–52).

Mazower also maintains that the plan to deport European Jewry to the island of Madagascar proposed after the fall of France in the summer of 1940 was not an original Nazi idea but rather had a long European history (Mazower, 2008, p. 118; Baranowski, 2011; "Forum", 2013).

This extreme nationalism found condensed expression in the concept of "the people's community" (*Volksgemeinschaft*), which more and more scholars (though not all, see Eley, 2013, pp. 59–130) are coming to regard as a key concept for understanding Nazism and the brutal violence with which it operated. "The enduring popularity of the Nazis," posits Peter Fritzsche, "rested on the idea of *Volksgemeinschaft*, or people's community. It was not a Nazi idea and it was not perceived as something imposed or strange" (Fritzsche, 2008, p. 38). It is also important to remember, argues Mark Roseman in a similar spirit, that German nationalism under Nazi rule was referred to not as a racial community but rather as a people's community in the Volkist sense. "It was the language of Volk, rather than race, which served a primary mobilizing function in the Third Reich" (Pendas *et al.*, 2017, p. 9; Roseman, 2017, pp. 31–57). Further, the language of Volk is a variation of the extremist nationalist language that is constantly attempting to establish ethno-national homogeneity, which is also perceived as guaranteeing collective security.

This tendency, continues Roseman following Bloxham, Mazower, and many others, is directly linked to European colonialism and imperialism. These, in turn, were born hand in hand with the evolution of modern nation states, which competed with one another other for new spaces and markets, political and military power, and prestige. In doing so, they brutally and murderously trampled the rights of indigenous peoples, which were almost always perceived as inferior (Mann, 2005; Weitz, 2005). Imperial and colonial experiments generated and shaped the language of European nationalism in general, and had a decisive impact on the language of German nationalism in particular.

Indeed, by 1942, the Marxist German philosopher Karl Korsch, who fled to the United States in 1933, had already asserted: "The novelty of totalitarian politics in this respect is simply that the Nazis have extended to 'civilized' European peoples the methods hitherto reserved for the 'natives' or 'savages' living outside so-called civilization" (Traverso, 2003, p. 50).

Just over a decade later, in 1955, a similar assessment was offered by early anti-colonialist thinker Aimé Césaire (1972). In her 1951 book, *The Origins of Totalitarianism*, Hannah Arendt formulated a fundamental link between colonial-imperial violence and the violence of the Final Solution (Arendt, 1951). This line of inquiry was largely neglected until the end of the 1990s when it returned to centre stage. Indeed, it is difficult to overlook the direct relationship between the manner in which racially-based violence evolved in colonial contexts and the evolution of murderous ideology and practices during the Holocaust, even if this relationship, too, is not all-explanatory but rather constitutes one of many critical contextual layers of the historical palimpsest outside of which it is impossible to understand the Holocaust.

In this context, a number of scholars have highlighted the connection (which is not necessarily causal but rather more contextual) between the Holocaust and the first genocide of the twentieth century, which was also perpetrated by the Germans, between 1904 and 1908, against the Herero and Nama tribes in South West Africa (modern-day Namibia) during their rebellion against German colonial rule (Zimmerer, 2011; also Ehmann, 1998; Schaller, 2010, pp. 354–355; Zimmerer and Zeller 2008). This genocide, which also involved the use of racial ideology and may have actually been caused by it (some maintain against rational economic logic and interests), resulted in the premeditated extermination of almost the entire Herero and Nama population. Some were murdered and others were expelled to the desert where the wells were poisoned. In the course of the genocide, the German authorities set up a concentration camp on Shark Island, which implemented the principle of "extermination through labour" that would become a familiar component of the Nazi concentration camps.

Scholars who have explored the connections between different acts of colonial genocide and the Final Solution have pointed out these important contexts, as well as the attributes unique to each instance (Lower and Furber, 2008; Stone, 2010, pp. 203–244; Moses, 2008; Conrad, 2012, pp. 159–165). As in all such historical cases, while the colonial context is undoubtedly of great importance, it is not, in itself, a sufficient explanation for the historical phenomenon in question but must rather be considered in conjunction with additional contexts, each of which is critical for understanding of the evolution of the Final Solution.

These historiographical tendencies were developed in an interesting way by the Israeli historian Raz Segal. Segal, who has undertaken in-depth research on the Subcarpathian Rus region, has recently advanced a new understanding of certain aspects of the Holocaust using a paradigm that examines the persecution and extermination of the Jews within the context of the nation state's desire for homogenization, chiefly in colonial frontier regions. Segal's study reflects a recent trend in Holocaust research that seeks to examine the history of the Jews, primarily in Eastern Europe, in the multi-ethnic context of each individual region. Another example of this approach is the work of Omer Bartov, who has recently been conducting research on the

Holocaust in Buczacz, Galicia, in the context of the tension-fraught multi-ethnic relations and contradictions that have existed in this region over the years. Bartov's studies offer an interesting multi-dimensional picture in which each side has its own story and its own truth. The result provides us with minute details (provided primarily by the different witnesses) regarding the murder and the dynamics that emerge during such periods between neighbours (Bartov, 2018). In the Polish context see Gross (2001); on Croatia see Korb (2013). Segal's work is also part of this trend but goes a step further by drawing much broader conclusions.

Like Germany, which dreamed of a "greater German empire", nationalist Hungary (like other countries) dreamed of a "greater Hungary", albeit on a more modest scale. As part of these imperial aspirations, Hungary seized control of the Subcarpathian Rus region, which was then part of Czechoslovakia, in two stages, at the end of 1938 and the beginning of 1939, as the latter collapsed under the pressure of Nazi Germany. It was an annexed frontier region in which Hungarians constituted a minority, and the state therefore implemented a policy of discrimination, persecution, deportation, and even murder against all other minorities in the region, including the Jews, who were frequently mentioned as a threat in the same breath as the Roma, for example. The Hungarian state sought to oppress the minorities in the region and to change the demographic balance in order to achieve a Hungarian majority. For many reasons, this policy was only partially successful. However, when Nazi Germany invaded Hungary in March 1944 and demanded the deportation of all its Jews to Auschwitz, Hungary was presented with a "golden opportunity" to rid itself of its Jews, which, as noted, were perceived as a problem within the homogenization-oriented thinking of the Hungarian state, especially in its frontier regions. The Hungarians agreed willingly, not as a result of German pressure but due to what they regarded as their national interest. As a result, the Hungarians conducted the assembly and deportation of Jews on a completely independent basis up to the Kassa border crossing, where the Germans assumed responsibility for the trains that continued on from there to Auschwitz. Indeed, the majority of the deportees were from frontier regions.

This pattern of shared interests between Nazi Germany and other countries re-emerged repeatedly during the war in other places as well. On this basis, Segal concludes that without understanding these nation-states' aspiration for ethnic homogenization, especially in the annexed frontier regions, significant parts of the story of the extermination of the Jews remain undecipherable. In this way, contexts of extremist imperialist nationalism also had an impact on the extermination of the Jewish people outside the immediate Nazi context (Segal, 2016, 2014). Segal's proposal is actually even more radical in his deconstruction of the event referred to as the "Holocaust" into different events that took place in different, historically non-identical arenas. This approach of "deconstructing" the Holocaust into separate secondary events that do not necessarily add up to one event is also reflected in Blatman (2011), which persuasively proposes understanding the death marches as a genocide in their own right, directed against the camp inmates in the context of the twilight of the Third Reich, and not against the Jews as part of the Final Solution.

As we can see, modern trends of ethnocentric nationalism that were not necessarily racial in the strict scientific sense of the word had a decisive influence on the fate of the Jews during the Holocaust.

Still, however, racializing the state in Nazi Germany did mark a transition, at least in German political and intellectual history – even if not as dramatic as earlier historians had thought it to be. I wish to conclude this chapter by reflecting on the meaning of this transition.

Some, for example, point to the transition from the authority of ethics and religion to the authority of modern science – a transition that became extremely significant in the current context. This, at least, is the claim of some scholars. One example is Richard Weikart, whose book *From Darwin to Hitler* (Weikart 2004) considers the evolution of the modern scientific discourse of race, primarily in Germany. Weikart claims that the racial obsession of Hitler and the Nazi elite, which reached its height during the murder of the Jews, must be understood in the broader context of the evolution of the discourse of race in Europe and the political practices with which it was linked. Original sin, according to Weikart, lay with Darwin who, although he was a liberal Englishman who supported the abolition of slavery, conducted scientific work that laid the foundations not only for a new biology but also for a new moral doctrine, or, to be more precise, for the biologization of morality.

Weikart maintains that one of the most serious impacts of Darwin's Copernican revolution was the fact that it grounded morality in nature and explained the role of conscience and morality as part of the doctrine of biological evolution. In this way he made morality relative, introduced the concept of "natural selection" into the ethical realm, and changed the concepts of human nature and the value of human life. Death was no longer perceived to be only negative but was also regarded as an important, essential, and productive process. Darwin's theories, therefore, dealt not only with biological matters but also with life and death. As a result, for many people at the end of the nineteenth century, science replaced religion as the source of the mythology that articulated meaning. Darwinism was understood as the final word in science, and in the mythology it articulated, ethics were grounded in biology and not in any transcendental dimension, as in the monotheistic religions in general and Christianity in particular. Contrary to Weikart, others have drawn more continuous lines from Christian anti-Semitism to Nazi anti-Semitism (Confino, 2014; Heschel, 2008; Bergen, 1996).

The conception that all men are equal before God began to crumble. According to the theories of Darwinism and social Darwinism, the value of people derived not from their being God's creations but rather from nature. Of particular significance within the thinking on development and progress, to which nature was party, was the notion that whereas certain human beings and groups advance and develop nature, others cause its degeneration. As nature was the standard for moral assessment, those who caused degeneration were not worthy of life. In this way, the morality that emerged from nature was also imbued with the absolute validity of a law of nature. When the category of race was established within the scientific field as central to the understanding of the evolution of nature in general and of humans in particular, the struggle between human societies was reformulated as a struggle between races, that is, a struggle that is subject to the laws of nature. According to the law of nature, which was also the law of morality, the strong race would be victorious and the weak race was destined to die. Within this conceptual world, Weikart demarcates a path of development – which may not have been deterministic or inevitable, but was nonetheless disastrous – from Darwinism, to social Darwinism, to eugenics and racial improvement, to colonial and continental racism, and to the most horrifying actualization of these ideas possible, as reflected in the Nazis' attitude toward the Jews, and, ultimately, in the Final Solution.

Weikart argues that at the very beginning of this disastrous path of development, meaning as early as Darwin, the potential notion of the annihilation of entire population groups already exists implicitly as part of a perhaps inevitable process of nature. After Darwin, important race scientists added significant detail to this idea, which was regarded as a welcome and necessary initiative that humanity (that is, white humanity of European origin) must employ if it does not wish to degenerate or be destroyed. This notion of the extermination of peoples was therefore present in Darwinism from the outset and quickly spread, to the extent that some pacifists in Europe were virulently opposed to all wars between European peoples, which would deplete the European racial pool, but were indifferent to, and frequently supported and even encouraged boundless violence in colonies in Africa and Asia.

There are a number of additional modern historical contexts that can assist us in better understanding the Holocaust as a historical event and in locating it, despite its horrifying and extreme nature, within the state-focused historical processes of the twentieth century. Especially noteworthy in this context is Tim Snyder's (2010) controversial and eye-opening book *Bloodlands: Europe between Hitler and Stalin*. In this book, Snyder argues that the two totalitarian regimes of Nazism and Stalinism must be understood using one conceptual framework as operating in one colonial area (more or less between Poznan in the west and Smolensk in the East, and between the Baltic states in the north and Ukraine in the south) using political methods of mass extermination. It should be stressed though, that all those modern contexts – including the ones I briefly sketched here – were, and still are, hotly debated by historians and none are completely consensual. However, I wish to conclude this brief survey by quoting the historian Saul Friedländer's precise summary of the critique versed by one of the doyens of postmodernism, the French philosopher Jean-François Lyotard, of modernity and its totalizing tendencies in regards to the Holocaust:

> It is precisely the "Final Solution" which allows postmodernist thinking to question the validity of any totalizing view of history, of any reference to a definable meta discourse ... The striving for totality and consensus is, in Lyotard's view, the very basis of the fascist enterprise.
>
> *(Friedländer, 1992, p. 5)*

I find these words to be as true today as they ever were.

Notes

1 I wish to thank Anthony Lopez, Jürgen Matthäus and Jan Lambertz for their extremely helpful comments. Obviously I am solely responsible for any errors or inaccuracies in this chapter. This chapter is an abridged, updated and revised version of the author's introduction to the Hebrew edition of Zygmunt Bauman, *Modernity and the Holocaust* (Tel Aviv: Resling, 2013). A slightly revised version of that introduction was reprinted in Hebrew and English in *Moreshet: Journal for the Study of the Holocaust and Antisemitism*, 12 (2015), 190–238.

2 I make imprecise and almost random use of concepts that bear different meanings in different contexts, such as "modernity", "modernism", "modern" and other such terms. As we will see, however, this survey does not require us to define each one of these terms separately. For a closer examination of these concepts and their relevance to the discussion of the Holocaust, see Roseman (2011).

References

Aly, G. and Heim, S. (1994) The Holocaust and population policy: remarks on the decision on the 'Final Solution'. *Yad Vashem Studies* 24, 45–70.

Aly, G. and Heim, S. (2002) *Architects of Annihilation: Auschwitz and the Logic of Destruction*. London: Weidenfeld & Nicolson.

Arendt, Hannah (1951) *The Origins of Totalitarianism*. New York: Meridian Books.

Arendt, Hannah (1963) *Eichmann in Jerusalem: A Report on the Banality of Evil*. New York: Penguin Adult.

Aschheim, Steven (1996) *Culture and Catastrophe: German and Jewish Confrontations with National Socialism and Other Crises*. New York: New York University Press.

Bankier, David (1994) Response to Götz and Heim. *Yad Vashem Studies*, 24, 71–146.

Baranowski, Shelley (2011) *Nazi Empire: German Colonialism and Imperialism from Bismark to Hitler*. Cambridge: Cambridge University Press.

Bartov, Omer (2018) *Anatomy of a Genocide: The Life and Death of a Town Called Buczacz*. New York: Simon & Schuster.

Bauer, Yehuda (2001) *Rethinking the Holocaust*. New Haven: Yale University Press.

Bauman, Zygmunt (1989) *Modernity and the Holocaust*. Cambridge: Polity Press.
Bergen, Doris (1996) *Twisted Cross: The German Christian Movement in the Third Reich*. Chapel Hill and London: The University of North Carolina Press.
Blatman, Daniel (2011) *The Death Marches: The Final Phase of Nazi Genocide*. Cambridge, MA: Harvard University Press.
Bloxham, Donald (2009) *The Final Solution: A Genocide*. Oxford: Oxford University Press.
Burleigh, M. and Wippermann, W. (1991) *The Racial State: Germany, 1933–1945*. Cambridge, UK; New York: Cambridge University Press.
Burrin, Philip (1994) *Hitler and the Jews: The Genesis of the Holocaust*. London: Edward Arnold.
Césaire, Aimé (1972) *Discourse on Colonialism*. New York: Monthly Review Press.
Confino, Alon (2014) *A World without Jews*. New Haven: Yale University Press.
Conrad, Sebastian (2012) *German Colonialism: A Short History*. Cambridge, UK: Cambridge University Press.
Desbois, Patrick (2008) *The Holocaust by Bullets*. New York: Palgrave Macmillan.
Diner, Dan (1994) Response to Götz and Heim. *Yad Vashem Studies*, 24, 71–146.
Ehmann, Annegret (1998) From colonial racism to Nazi population policy: the role of the so-called mischlinge. In M. Berenbaum and A. J. Peck (eds), *The Holocaust and History: The Known, the Unknown, the Disputed, and the Reexamined*. Bloomington, IN: Indiana University Press, pp. 115–133.
Eley, Geoff (2013) *Nazism as Fascism: Violence, Ideology and the Ground of Consent in Germany 1930–1945*. London and New York, Routledge.
Evans, Richard (1989) *In Hitler's Shadow: West German Historians and the Attempt to Escape from the Nazi Past*. New York: Pantheon Books.
"Forum: The Holocaust: An Imperial Genocide?" (2013) *Dapim: Studies on the Holocaust*, 27(1), 40–73.
Freud, Sigmund (2003) *The Uncanny*. London: Penguin Books.
Friedländer, Saul (1992) Introduction to S. Friedländer (ed.), *Probing the Limits of Representation: Nazism and the "Final Solution"*. Cambridge, MA: Harvard University Press.
Fritzsche, Peter (2008) *Life and Death in the Third Reich*. Cambridge, MA: Belknap Press of Harvard University Press.
Gerlach, Christian (1999a) German economic interests, occupation policy, and the murder of the Jews in Belorussia, 1941–1943. In Ulrich Herbert (ed.), *National Socialist Extermination Policies*. New York: Berghahn Books, pp. 210–239.
Gerlach, Christian (1999b) *Kalkulierte Morde: die deutsche Wirtschafts- und Vernichtungspolitik in Weissrussland 1941 bis 1944*. Hamburg: Hamburger Edition.
Gross, Jan Tomasz (2001) *Neighbors: The Destruction of the Jewish Community in Jedwabne, Poland*. Princeton, NJ: Princeton University Press.
Hayes, Peter (2017) *Why?: Explaining the Holocaust*. New York and London: W. W. Norton.
Herbert, Ulrich (1994) Response to Götz and Heim. *Yad Vashem Studies*, 24, 71–146.
Herbert, Ulrich (2000) Extermination policy: new answers and questions about the history of the Holocaust in German Historiography. In Ulrich Herbert (ed.), *National Socialist Extermination Policies*. New York: Berghahn Books, p. 37.
Herf, Jeffrey (1984) *Reactionary Modernism: Technology, Culture and Politics in Weimar*. Cambridge, UK: Cambridge University Press.
Heschel, Susannah (2008) *The Aryan Jesus: Christian theologians and the Bible in Nazi Germany*. Princeton, NJ: Princeton University Press.
Hilberg, Raul (1996) *The Politics of Memory*. Chicago: Ivan R. Dee.
Hilberg, Raul (2003) *The Destruction of the European Jews*. New Haven: Yale University Press.
Horkheimer, M. and Adorno, T. W. (1972) *Dialectic of Enlightenment*. New York: Seabury Press.
Kershaw, Ian (2000) *The Nazi Dictatorship: Problems and Perspectives*. London: Arnold.
Kiernan, Ben (2007) *Blood and Soil: A World History of Genocide and Extermination from Sparta to Darfur*. New Haven: Yale University Press.
Korb, Alexander Martin (2013) *Im Schatten des Weltkriegs: Massengewalt der Ustaša gegen Serben, Juden und Roma in Kroatien 1941–1945*. Hamburg: Hamburger Edition.
Levene, Mark (2013) *The Crisis of Genocide: The European Rimlands, 1912–1953*, 2 vols. Oxford: Oxford University Press.
Levene, Mark (2018) Harbingers of Jewish and Palestinian disasters: European nation-state building and its toxic legacies, 1912–1948. In Bashir Bashir and Amos Goldberg (eds), *The Holocaust and the Nakba: A New Grammar of Trauma and History*. New York: Columbia University Press, p. 46.

Lower, W. and Furber, D. (2008) Colonialism and genocide in Nazi occupied Poland and Ukraine. In D. Moses (ed.), *Empire, Colony, Genocide: Conquest, Occupation, and Subaltern Resistance in World History*. New York: Berghahn Books, pp. 372–399.

Mann, Michael (2005) *The Dark Side of Democracy: Explaining Ethnic Cleansing*. New York: Cambridge University Press.

Matthäus, Jürgen (2019, forthcoming) Raul Hilberg und der Führerbefehl. In René Schlott (ed.), *Raul Hilberg und die Holocaust-Historiographie* (Beiträge zur Geschichte des Nationalsozialismus, vol. 35). Göttingen: Wallstein, pp. 131–142.

Matthäus, J., Shaw, M., Bartov, O., Bergen, D., and Bloxham, D. (2011) Review forum: Donald Bloxham, The Final Solution: a genocide. *Journal of Genocide Research*, 13(1–2) (March-June), 107–152.

Mazower, Mark (2008) *Hitler's Empire: Nazi Rule in Occupied Europe*. New York: Penguin Press.

Moses, A. Dirk (2008) Empire, colony, genocide: keywords and the philosophy of history. In A. D. Moses (ed.), *Empire, Colony, Genocide: Conquest, Occupation, and Subaltern Resistance in World History*. New York: Berghahn Books, pp. 3–54.

Pendas, D. O., Roseman, M. and Wetzell, R. F. (2017) Introduction. In D. O. Pendas, M. Roseman, and R. F. Wetzell (eds), *Beyond the Racial State: Rethinking Nazi Germany*. Cambridge, UK: Cambridge University Press, p. 9.

Poliakov, Léon (1954) *Harvest of Hate: The Nazi Program for the Destruction of the Jews of Europe*. Philadelphia: The Jewish Publication Society of America.

Reitlinger, Gerald (1953) *The Final Solution*. New York: Beechhurst Press.

Roseman, Mark (2011) National Socialism and the end of modernity. *American Historical Review*, 116(3) (June), 688–701.

Roseman, Mark (2017) Racial discourse, Nazi violence and the limits of the racial state model. In D. O. Pendas, M. Roseman, and R. F. Wetzell (eds), *Beyond the Racial State: Rethinking Nazi Germany*. Cambridge, UK: Cambridge University Press, pp. 31–57.

Rummel, Rudolph J. (1997) *Statistics of Democide: Genocide and Mass Murder since 1900*. Charlottesville, VA: Center for National Security Law, School of Law, University of Virginia.

Schaller, D. J. (2010) Genocide and mass violence in the 'Heart of Darkness': Africa in the colonial period. In D. Bloxham and A. D. Moses (eds), *The Oxford Handbook for Genocide Studies*. New York: Oxford University Press, pp. 345–364.

Segal, Raz (2014) Beyond Holocaust studies: rethinking the Holocaust in Hungary. *Journal of Genocide Research*, 16(1), 1–23.

Segal, Raz (2016) *Genocide in the Carpathians: War, Social Breakdown, and Mass Violence, 1914–1945*. Stanford, CA: Stanford University Press.

Snyder, Timothy (2010) *Bloodlands: Europe between Hitler and Stalin*. New York: Basic Books.

Snyder, Timothy (2015) *Black Earth: The Holocaust as History and Warning*. New York: Crown.

Stone, Dan (2003) *Constructing the Holocaust: A Study in Historiography*. London; Portland.

Stone, Dan (2010) *Histories of the Holocaust*. Oxford: Oxford University Press.

Ther, Philipp (2014) *The Dark Side of Nation States: Ethnic Cleansing in Modern Europe*. New York and Oxford: Berghahn.

Traverso, Enzo (2003) *The Origins of Nazi Violence*. New York: New Press.

Weikart, Richard (2004) *From Darwin to Hitler: Evolutionary Ethics, Eugenics, and Racism in Germany*. New York: Palgrave Macmillan.

Weitz, Erik (2005) *A Century of Genocide: Utopias of Race and Nation*. Princeton, NJ: Princeton University Press.

Westermann, Edward B. (2018) Drinking rituals, masculinity, and mass murder in Nazi Germany. *Central European History*, 51, 367–389.

Zimmerer, Jürgen (2011) *Von Windhuk nach Auschwitz?* Berlin: Lit.

Zimmerer, J. and Zeller J. (eds) (2008) *Genocide in German South-West- Africa: The Colonial War of 1904–1910 and its Aftermath*. Monmouth: Merlin Press.

Žižek, Slavoj (1995) *The Sublime Object of Ideology*. London and New York: Verso.

PART II

Terrorism

7

THE EVOLUTION OF TERRORISM

Historical underpinnings and the development of group terrorism

Randall D. Law

It has become a truism to declare that terrorism is undefinable, and there is some truth in that, at least historically. Academics, government agencies, and the public have never fully agreed what constitutes terrorism. Nonetheless, in recent decades, scholars of terrorism studies as well as policymakers charged with countering terrorism have largely reached a consensus on the core features of terrorism. In short, they agree that terrorism is symbolic violence used against the few to influence the behaviour of the many. The terrorism studies pioneer Alex Schmid (2011, pp. 86–87) has developed a "revised academic consensus definition of terrorism", the core of which is clear: terrorism is communicative violence used in indirect pursuit of ideological goals. It is worth noting that his continually "revised" definition now includes a lengthy list of caveats, explanations, and applications. Nonetheless, the frequency with which policy makers and academics refer to Schmid's definition suggests that the field has indeed found agreement on what constitutes terrorism.

It is valuable to note the ways in which terrorism is conceptually distinct from, yet in practice often similar to, other forms of violence. Terrorism can be understood as altruistic violence in that it serves an ideology, which is to say a set of political, social, economic, or religious goals. On this basis, terrorism can be distinguished from crime, which is principally pursued for selfish gain. Terrorism is also different from conventional war and guerrilla war. As described above, terrorism is a strategy used to achieve results indirectly by communicating with various audiences through the symbolism of target, place, violent means, and context. Conversely, conventional war is a strategy primarily meant to achieve results through the direct use of violence. States deploy their militaries against their enemies in order to seize or defend territory or render them incapable of fighting. And while terrorism has many tactical similarities to guerrilla war, the latter is usually waged by semi-uniformed, organized units with the visceral goal of degrading the enemy's ability to continue fighting. It is important to note that terrorism, guerrilla fighting, and conventional war can be used by a combatant within the same conflict, as was done, for instance, by the Algerians against France, and the Vietnamese against the United States, in those people's anti-colonial wars (Laqueur, 1977; Law, 2015; Law, 2016; Miller, 2012).

Like guerrilla war and conventional war, terrorism has evolved in response to broader historical changes, such as developments in weapons and explosives, organizational behaviour, and logistics. Given that it functions primarily as *symbolic* violence, terrorism has been especially sensitive to transformations in media, communications, political and social identity, and rhetoric

(Law, 2016). Here we come to the crux of this chapter: while scholars of the phenomenon can see great continuity in the fundamental nature of terrorism since the late eighteenth century, there is dynamic change and growth in how groups have organized and executed campaigns and acts of terrorism. In turn, the evolution of the organization and use of terrorism has refined and clarified but not substantially changed the core nature of terrorism. In this, terrorism has shown itself to be easily adapted to an encyclopaedic range of ideologies and motives.

Successful terrorism?

Does terrorism lead to success? To answer that question we need to understand what is meant by success; here, it is helpful to think about what those who use terrorism expect in the short, medium, and long terms. In the short term, this means successfully completing an attack against a particular target. Success in the medium term means reaching an intended audience and subsequently generating media attention, provoking the desired responses (such as a military intervention or political crackdown), and/or growing a movement. Long-term success can be judged in terms of achieving stated ideological objectives, such as national independence, the recognition of a minority's rights, or changes in the government's political, economic, or social practices (Law, 2016).

Terrorist groups often achieve short- or medium-term success of the sort that can produce notoriety. Examples include the assassination of Tsar Alexander II by the People's Will; the spate of anarchist assassinations and bombings in the United States and Europe at the turn of the nineteenth century; bombings carried out by 1970s revolutionary organizations such as Weatherman in the US and the Red Army Faction in West Germany; and, most recently, the spectacular violence of al-Qaeda. But groups that use terrorism rarely meet their intended goals in the grand scheme of things. A few groups, such as the Provisional Irish Republican Army and the Palestine Liberation Organization (specifically Yasser Arafat's faction, Fatah), have seen some of their goals met through diplomatic efforts that were partially made possible through terrorism and political violence. The Islamic State in Iraq and Syria (ISIS) established a state in the Middle East, although it was primarily the result of guerrilla operations not terrorism, and in any case lost its territory in less than five years. Groups that have used terrorism have rarely achieved success in the long term. The Ku Klux Klan and related white supremacist organizations used terrorism to defeat Reconstruction and establish a system of racial apartheid in the US that lasted for over 80 years. The Zionist terror groups Irgun and LEHI contributed to the defeat of the British and the establishment of the state of Israel in 1948; and the National Liberation Front (the FLN) used terrorism and led the struggle to achieve Algerian independence from France in 1962. All three campaigns are described in greater detail below.

Organizational factors have typically been the most important ones in determining short and medium-term success. Given that most groups described herein have had relatively few resources, success in launching attacks and provoking the intended responses has largely hinged on their ability to use those resources efficiently and to conserve and protect their strength. Conversely, long term success – i.e. the actual achievement of stated goals – has been attributable to a broader range of factors beyond the ability to organize and operate effectively, such as the effectiveness of broader propaganda efforts and the size of the population that the group is able to appeal to.

The French Revolution

There are few instances of terrorism before the eighteenth century. In fact, nearly all premodern political violence that bears some similarity to modern terrorism does so in terms of the tactics used, such as assassination and conspiratorial organization (Ford, 1985), but little in the use of symbolic targets chosen for their ability to sway various audiences. Therefore, most historians (e.g. Laqueur, 1977; Law, 2016; Rapport, 2015) consider the French Revolution as the moment when modern terrorism first emerged. It is important to recognize that revolutionaries used terrorism both from above and from below and largely *after* King Louis XVI was deposed, the estate system abolished, and a republic declared. Terrorism was only adopted after a vast array of counter-revolutionary enemies began to mount a civil war and war erupted between France and most of its neighbours. In September 1793, radical Jacobins, known as the Mountain and led by Maximilien Robespierre, suspended a newly minted constitution and declared a policy of "terror" against any and all opponents of the new regime. Authorities in Paris and throughout the country arrested suspects on the flimsiest of evidence; hundreds of thousands were interred and as many as 40,000 were executed. While the Mountain was indeed fixated on eliminating as many people as possible who could challenge the new revolutionary order, Robespierre and his colleagues understood that they could not kill them all. Hence this policy of terror was intended to destroy those enemies who fell into the government's clutches and intimidate the rest, even – or especially – if they had not yet committed an overt act of counter-revolution (Andress, 2005; Law, 2016; Rapport, 2015). Jean-Lambert Tallien (1999, p. 266), a moderate Jacobin who was involved in the plot to overthrow Robespierre, captured the essence of the Reign of Terror and the new phenomenon of terrorism when he said in 1794, "if the government of terror pursues a few citizens for their presumed intentions, it will frighten all citizens." Tallien, Robespierre, and the Jacobins grasped that the fundamental point of terror was to sway the behaviour of the entire citizenry by targeting a relatively small number of representative and symbolic targets.

This became even clearer in the spring and summer of 1794. By then, most counter-revolutionaries who had taken up arms or made explicit calls to oppose the state had been killed, arrested, or driven into hiding. And yet the Terror continued. Its new victims were targeted for their former social standing, their resistance to the regime's programme, or, increasingly, commitment to slightly different shades of grey within the revolutionary agenda. In essence, the violence of the Terror was increasingly used to educate France's citizenry about how to behave in the new revolutionary state – terror(ism) in pursuit of social engineering. It was the use of arrest and execution to destroy rivals within the Jacobins that eventually led to Robespierre's fall from power in July 1794 (Andress, 2005; Rapport, 2015).

Even as France's revolutionary government carried out a programme of state terror from above against its enemies (real and imagined), terror was carried out from below, primarily by the so-called sans-culottes. These were day labourers and urban poor who were the most radical "common" supporters of the Revolution. Often denounced as the mob by their opponents, they actually achieved a high level of organization, particularly in Paris, through neighbourhood watch committees, tribunals, and highly democratic and regular "sectional" meetings. These "street" revolutionaries targeted hoarders and speculators, sought out nobles, clerics, and out-of-favour journalists, and generally policed behaviour. As was the case with terror from above, the sans-culottes went after symbolic targets not just to settle accounts and eliminate specific threats but to enforce new cultural and political norms. But with the Mountain firmly in power, the authorities came to see street terror as a threat to order and the government's hold on power. By the spring of 1794, the state clamped down on sectional meetings, local tribunals, and watch committees and thus on terror from below (Andress, 2005; Rapport, 2015).

The end of revolutionary terror was not the end of revolutionary France or the ideals that it represented, namely democracy, civil liberties, and a collective identity primarily based on nationalism. Despite the fact that many of these elements were honoured more in theory than in practice, these were powerful ideas that energized millions of French women and men, and millions more beyond the new republic's borders. In time, France found stability through the new dictatorship of Napoleon Bonaparte. When he was finally defeated and replaced by a restored Bourbon dynasty in 1815, the Revolution's ideals went underground where they motivated the opponents of conservative regimes across Europe throughout the rest of the century. Thus, for much of the nineteenth century the French Revolution provided the agenda for progressives and the various opponents of conservatism, both in terms of means (terror and terrorism) and ends (democracy, secularism, and nationalism).

While terrorism as a strategy and a world view went underground after the French Revolution, there was little of it in practice. Nonetheless, this was an important chapter in the organizational history of terrorism since groups were forced to develop the means to survive in secret. Opposition to Europe's conservative governments was mostly scattered and disorganized in the years after the Congress of Vienna, but some opponents organized in a loose network of cells under the name Carbonari, primarily in France and Italy. Adherents possibly numbered into the tens of thousands, and their agenda was broadly democratic, liberal, secular, and nationalist. Some cells devised plans to use assassinations, prison breaks, and arson to intimidate governments and create revolutionary moments for the seizure of power. The plans were often quite bloodthirsty in their conception, but few of these efforts progressed beyond the planning stage. Not surprisingly they caught the attention of governments across Europe who denounced the Carbonari as dangerous threats to law, order, and civilization. Before long Carbonari cells developed the conspiratorial means to function in secret; in fact, their existence came to be dominated by the need to resist the growing legions of governmental infiltrators, spies, detectives, and censors. Cells developed extensive ceremonies complete with scripts, props, and oaths intended to bind recruits to their new revolutionary families (Bartholdy, 1821; Hodde, 1856; Roberts 1972). These rituals and practices, in turn, heightened the authorities' fear about both the extent and the real threat of revolutionary organizations. According to Adam Zamoyski (2015), it was this interplay between paranoid governments and toothless revolutionaries that created both terrorism and the modern police state. It is therefore important to note that – contra the modern conception of terrorism – the phenomenon's first incarnation was carried out by the state and its second mostly existed in the imagination of the state.

Russian revolutionary terrorism

It was not until the 1860s and 1870s that well-developed sub-state group terrorism really developed and achieved the organizational contours that we recognize in the twenty-first century. Terrorism was used in pursuit of three different ideologies – socialism (or populism, as it was known) in Russia; anarchism in Europe, Russia, and the United States; and white supremacy in the US – and assumed three different organizational profiles, each of which remain important models today.

The first tentative foray into Russian revolutionary terrorism was Dmitri Karakozov's failed attempt to assassinate Tsar Alexander II in 1866 (Verhoeven, 2009). Most revolutionaries hoped that education and propaganda could eventually defeat tsarism, but the meagre results led fanatics to fully embrace terrorism. This belief crystallized in 1879 with the formation of the People's Will (Venturi, 1960). One-time member and assassin-turned-propagandist Sergei Kravchinsky described terrorism as a programme of targeted assassination of generals, leading bureaucrats, and eventually the tsar. Terrorism, he said, couldn't directly topple the regime; rather, it was a "flank movement" that could produce heroic opponents to the regime, around whom would slowly build a mass movement (Stepniak-Kravchinsky, 1883, p. 38). He was also one of the first to articulate what later became a key component of the strategy of terrorism: the notion that terrorist strikes could force an undemocratic regime to engage in more naked and more brutal acts of repression, thus radicalizing the heretofore passive bulk of the population.

The People's Will consisted of at most 500 members. What was new was its method of organizing its members into cells, each of which was devoted to one task: propaganda, target surveillance, smuggling chemicals and building bombs, running safe houses, and the actual terrorist attacks. This was a logical solution to the problem of how to carry out revolutionary activities against a state committed to using all means to infiltrate and destroy its opposition. But the assassination of Tsar Alexander II in March 1881 produced little reaction from the populace, and the authorities quickly rounded up revolutionaries, executed their leaders, and rolled back the limited reforms that had allowed for more agitation and propaganda (Venturi, 1960). In other words, the People's Will had shown how a small group could use terrorism to achieve impressive short and mid-term successes through careful and innovative organization. But they had utterly failed to translate these achievements into the long-term success that they ultimately sought. Nonetheless, this strategy of carefully orchestrated conspiratorial organization and targeted assassination became known as the Russian Method and influenced generations of revolutionaries around the world.

International anarchist terrorism

Meanwhile, terrorism was also adopted by anarchists around the world, but particularly in France, Spain, Russia, and the United States. Anarchists denounced the inequities of industrial capitalism and rejected government itself as a repressive institution. Most were pacifists or channelled their activism into labour unions, but a radical fringe embraced violence as the only way to achieve justice. The main concept behind anarcho-terrorism was "propaganda of the deed", which was first espoused by the Italian Carlo Pisacane in the 1850s but widely popularized in the 1870s by Peter Kropotkin, a Russian nobleman and key theoretician of anarchism (Miller, 1976). Kropotkin (1975, pp. 7–9) believed that the main obstacle to the emergence of a mass revolutionary movement was the workers' internalized sense of inferiority. Kropotkin called for activists to use strikes, demonstrations, and acts of disobedience to awaken in workers the ability to organize and shake off their oppression. Others, such as Johann Most, Europe's most notorious bomb-maker and radical anarchist, explicitly endorsed terrorist violence (Trautmann, 1980).

Anarchists engaged in sporadic assassination attempts against kings, politicians, judges, and other leading figures of upper-class society in the 1870s and 1880s. By the 1890s, anarcho-terrorists in France, Italy, and Spain added a new tactic to their strategy of terrorist violence: mass-casualty bombings of cafes, parades, religious celebrations, stock exchanges, and other symbolic bourgeois locations. These attacks were conceptualized as classic acts of propaganda of the deed but were also intended to intimidate middle- and upper-class society and to draw stark dividing lines between the exploiters and the exploited. The most notorious spate of violence took place in Paris in 1891–1894, culminating with the assassination of the president of the French Third Republic, Sadi Carnot. Most of the attacks were carried out by individuals – often described as the forerunners of today's "lone wolf" terrorists – but they fed a vivid (and fanciful) picture of a vast underground conspiracy bent on nothing less than the destruction of industrial society, Western Christianity, and civilization itself. The truth was somewhere in between: these anarchists rarely knew each other personally but nonetheless formed a network through illegal newspapers and manifestos, speaking tours and demonstrations, tangential relationships to labour movements and political parties, and speeches delivered at jury trials by defendants who used the opportunities to give lectures on anarchism (Jensen, 2014; Joll, 1980; Merriman, 2009).

Small anarchist cells carried out terrorist attacks in the United States in 1917–1920 and in Russia during the 1905 Revolution, but even then the highest-casualty attacks (such as the Wall Street bombing of September 1920 that killed 38) were carried out by individuals (Gage, 2009; Geifman, 1993).

White supremacist terrorism in the United States

The most shocking display of terrorist violence during this era was white supremacist violence during and after Reconstruction in the American South, which was the product of a different context and produced a different set of organizational models which evolved in response to changing circumstances. It was also different from other terrorist campaigns of the era in that it was successful.

The Confederacy fought the American Civil War to preserve slavery and white supremacy as the cornerstones of the Southern states' economic and social system. As it turned out, defeat at the hands of Union troops via conventional war in 1865 simply meant a shift in tactics and strategy. Southern state governments found pseudo-legal ways to limit black emancipation, but some diehards turned to terrorism (Foner, 2014). The targets were former enslaved persons and the whites – mostly in the Republican Party, the party of Abraham Lincoln – who supported them in their bid to achieve some measure of education, economic opportunity, and political involvement. Confederate veterans and other white supremacists operated at first in both loosely organized local gangs and more formalized groups. The most (in)famous was the Ku Klux Klan, which came together in 1865 or 1866 in Pulaski, Tennessee, and briefly existed as a national organization with a formal structure. A steady increase in violence and the refusal of Southern states to grant blacks citizenship and voting rights led the US Congress in 1867 to reintroduce Union military occupation, systematically enforce black suffrage, disenfranchise former Confederates, and pursue what came to be known as Radical Reconstruction. The Klan and other groups went underground to evade Federal efforts to crack down on them, but they could often achieve local numerical superiority to carry out acts of violence. Just as importantly, they operated with the support of much of the white citizenry, who often refused to cooperate with Republican authorities (Gates, 2019; Rable, 1984; Trelease, 1995 [1971]).

The result was a terrorist campaign that differed from the revolutionary violence of the era – whether socialist or anarchist – in fundamental ways. While leftist terror was essentially ideological and thus limited in the number of people to whom it could appeal, white supremacist terror (while certainly ideological in its construction) was principally ethnic or racial and therefore appealed to a majority of the population of the American South. The scale of the violence, in terms of perpetrators, popular support, and victims, was a function of this. In fact, it even had a nationalist component, since white supremacy was the raison d'être of the Confederacy – which fashioned itself an independent nation – and thus the Lost Cause mythology that motivated resistance to Reconstruction. Indeed, white supremacist violence during Reconstruction constitutes the first modern example of ethno-nationalist terrorism.

Night riders, consciously modelling themselves on antebellum slave patrols, acted under the cover of darkness to beat, shoot, and rape African-Americans who tried to get educated, establish businesses, buy property, vote in elections, organize self-defence, or, in general, lay claim to the rights guaranteed to all Americans in the US Constitution. This was symbolic violence intended to intimidate all Southern blacks and to coerce them into being more compliant, but sometimes the violence was purely random. An official tally of the number of victims at the national level does not exist, but local totals and anecdotal evidence suggest that it reached into the tens of thousands (Rable, 1984; Trelease, 1995 [1971]).

When local Republican authorities were backed by Union troops and well-financed courts, they could temporarily suppress the Klan and other terrorist cells, as they did in York County, South Carolina, in 1871 (Trelease, 1995 [1971]). But across most of the South, white supremacist violence combined with both active and passive local white support to grind down Republican governments at the local, county, and finally state levels. Already by 1871, black and Republican voters had been so intimidated that in four of the 11 former Confederate states, all-white Democratic governments had returned to power and effectively disenfranchised blacks (Foner, 2014). A new organizational development further aided this. In Mississippi in 1874, white supremacists felt sufficiently empowered to operate open militias, which kept blacks and Republicans away from polling places during elections. The so-called Mississippi Plan was adopted in other locales; this campaign of terroristic voter intimidation turned four more states Democratic by 1876 (Lemann, 2007 [2006]). By this point Northerners – among whom support for racial equality was not much stronger than in the South – had tired of spending the blood and treasure necessary to see Radical Reconstruction through to the end. After Southern Democrats helped elect Republican Rutherford Hayes in the disputed presidential election of 1876, Reconstruction was officially declared over, the last Union troops were withdrawn from the South, the former Confederate states were fully integrated into the US, and Southern blacks lost most of what they had gained beyond emancipation (Foner, 2014; Gates, 2019). While the North had won the Civil War, white supremacists had won Reconstruction, greatly aided by their systematic use of terrorism.

And yet another transition in the history of white supremacist terrorism was in store. In the 1880s and 1890s, Southern states put in place new Black Codes that formalized virtually total Black disenfranchisement and segregation between the races, a system that came to be known as Jim Crow. Night-riding terrorism was gone, since conspiratorial violence was no longer needed to enforce legal American apartheid. What emerged to take its place was lynching. These were extrajudicial killings carried out by mobs, usually against African-American men who had been accused – but not convicted in a court of law – of crimes against whites, sexual advances or interactions with white women, or minor efforts to live outside the constraints of Jim Crow (Gates, 2019). The Equal Justice Initiative (2017) of Montgomery, Alabama, has determined that over 4000 of these racial killings took place between 1877 and 1950 in the 11 former states of the Confederacy plus Kentucky. These killings were usually carried out in the open by people whose identities were known to all. In fact, lynchings were often advertised in advance, memorialized on postcards, and attended by festive crowds. Very few perpetrators were ever held responsible since the killings were condoned by white society and often organized and carried out by prominent members of the community (Allen, 2000; Dray, 2002). Since lynchings were acts of symbolic violence intended to intimidate all Blacks by targeting a relatively small number of them, they functioned as terrorism or, more accurately, quasi-state terror. In his autobiography *Black Boy*, the author Richard Wright (2007 [1944], p. 172) wrote,

> The things that influenced my conduct as a Negro did not have to happen to me directly; I needed but to hear of them to feel their full effects in the deepest layers of my consciousness. Indeed, the white brutality that I had not seen was a more effective control of my behavior than that which I knew.

This sort of racial terrorism only began to decline in the 1950s and 1960s with the success of the African-American Civil Rights Movement (Dray, 2002), although racially-based lynchings have occurred well into the twenty-first century.

State terror

This transition in the nature of white supremacist violence in the late nineteenth century presaged a general global shift from sub-state to state terrorism in the 1920s triggered by the growth of mass politics, the rise of new forms of authoritarianism, and the failures of left-wing revolutionary terrorism. In Russia, despite decades of revolutionary unrest and political violence, the triumph of the Bolsheviks owed little to terrorism, although Vladimir Lenin's party borrowed extensively from the People's Will and other revolutionaries in terms of conspiratorial organization. What is beyond question is that the Bolsheviks – like the French revolutionaries of 1793–1794 whom they idolized – relied on systematic and pervasive terror *after* they seized power in October 1917 (Figes, 1997). One of the first decrees of the new Soviet government was the creation of the Extraordinary Commission, which was granted virtually unfettered authority to operate outside of the law to root out political, social, and economic enemies of the new regime. But the organization – known as the Cheka from its Russian abbreviation – went well beyond destroying armed and organized counterrevolutionaries. As the Soviet minister of justice put it, "We must execute not only the guilty. Execution of the innocent will impress the masses even more" (Pipes, 1990, p. 822). The Bolsheviks were committed to ruling alone and enacting their radical quasi-Marxist agenda, so they came to rely on this combination of literal and symbolic violence to eliminate their overt enemies and intimidate the rest of the population. The Cheka executed as many as 200,000 people from 1918 to the early 1920s (Leggett, 1981, pp. 466–467), but this death toll pales in comparison with the millions of lives destroyed in the 1930s and 1940s. Under Joseph Stalin, the terror – particularly in what became known as the Great Terror of 1936–1938 – continued to function as a way to cow the state's dwindling enemies and as social engineering (à la the French Revolution) (Conquest, 2007; Getty and Naumov, 1999). But it also grew beyond terrorism because it became institutionalized as a means to create an immense prison population that was used for slave labour, which became a pillar of the Soviet economy (Applebaum, 2003).

Whereas the Bolsheviks only really became terrorists after their revolution, the fascists of Italy and Germany used terrorism to lay the groundwork to seize power and then institutionalized it to help them remain. In Italy after the Great War, Benito Mussolini's Fascist Party formed a paramilitary group whose members were known as *squadristi* or Blackshirts. They terrorized their rivals on the left – socialists, anarchists, and trade unionists – through beatings, arson, kidnappings, and murders, and used marches and street violence to contribute to a general sense of disorder. In 1922, 30,000 Blackshirts staged the "march on Rome" as a show of force that convinced the Italian king, Victor Emmanuel III, that the fascists were the only group strong enough to protect the state and the Italian people from lawlessness and a communist revolution (Petersen, 1982).

In Germany, the Sturmabteilung (the SA – but also known as the Brownshirts) played a similar role. Brownshirt terrorism, street fighting, and the romance of defending the homeland against home-grown Bolsheviks was designed not just to intimidate opponents but also to attract recruits to Adolf Hitler's Nazi Party, a kind of right-wing propaganda of the deed. With the beginning of the Great Depression and the collapse of the political centre, near daily street brawls between the SA and communist paramilitaries heightened the sense that liberal democracy had failed, that the police could not preserve order, and that economic desperation called for the radical political solution proffered by the Nazis. With Hitler's appointment as chancellor in 1933, many Brownshirts immediately entered the ranks of Germany's police, becoming part of the state apparatus (Merkl, 1982). After Hitler's purge of the SA in the Night of the Long Knives in 1934, the SS and Gestapo took on the principal roles as the regime's thuggish enforcers against its political and racial enemies. Throughout the 1930s, the Nazi state continued to use symbolic violence to intimidate enemies – and to encourage the emigration of Jews and other ethnic minorities – as well as to promote a new social and cultural identity. But as in the Soviet Union, at some point state terror passed over into something new. In the case of Nazi Germany, slave labour and the Holocaust were not "merely" symbolic but were quite literal expressions of the Nazi desire to enslave or eliminate all racial enemies (Johnson, 2000). The sheer scale of the casualties caused by state terror – in China, Cambodia and a host of other countries besides the USSR, Italy and Germany – serves as a stark reminder that, in the modern era, states have always been responsible for far more than deaths than have sub-state groups. And this is true even when we draw a line between the symbolic violence of state terror thuggery and the exterminationist violence of Auschwitz or the Gulag (Courtois, 1999).

Terrorism, ethno-nationalism and de-colonization

But even during the heyday of state terror, sub-state terrorism began to return, primarily as a tool of ethno-nationalist struggles, which picked up speed after the Second World War and the beginning of global decolonization. The factors that spurred on revolts against European imperialism in Africa and Asia also encouraged the use of terrorism and enabled its increasingly frequent success. The first factor was ideological. During the Second World War, the United States and its allies rallied their populations with the idea that this was a just war fought to promote democracy. The Atlantic Charter of 1941 explicitly denounced imperialism, and the United Nations charter of 1945 promoted national self-determination as the foundation of the modern state and the international order. This provided a ready-made agenda for groups determined to liberate colonized peoples from imperial domination. And, as we have already seen in the case of the Ku Klux Klan and white supremacist violence, ethno-nationalist causes can appeal to large populations and thus significant popular support, both active and passive.

A second factor was new technologies. The cheap production of fully automatic small arms, especially the submachine gun, enabled small bands of fighters to deploy an extraordinary amount of firepower, even against larger, better trained units, particularly when paired with hit-and-run tactics or terrorism. The proliferation of radio, television, and the international news organizations that used them to feed increasingly literate and information-hungry populations provided groups that were willing to use terrorism with the means to have their acts of symbolic violence reach global populations. And the creation of the United Nations meant that there was a forum in which colonized peoples could aspire to have their grievances aired (Law, 2016).

Another important element in the evolution of anti-colonial and ethno-nationalist terrorism in the mid-twentieth century was strategic fluidity. The idea – that revolutionaries used terrorism as a means of developing a mass movement and graduating from limited, symbolic contact with "the enemy" to a full, militaristic assault – had its origins in the nineteenth century, particularly in American Reconstruction. It was more fully exploited in Michael Collins' use of "flying columns" in the Irish War of Independence (1919–1921) (Dwyer, 2005; Hart, 2005). But it gained its modern expression in the insurgencies of the 1940s and 1950s. First, a note on terminology. In this context, an insurgency is an internal conflict waged by a sub-state entity, one typically not recognized internationally as legitimate or sovereign, against a sovereign state. The goal of an insurgency is to replace a state's government with a new sovereign government or to establish on part of its territory an entirely new sovereign state. As described earlier, terrorism is but one of the strategies that could be deployed toward this end and has typically been used early in the struggle, with the hope that the insurgents would later attract enough resources – in recruits, arms, money, popular support, and/or international attention – to graduate to guerrilla or conventional war and, eventually, the creation of a new sovereign state.

Many of these factors – particularly striking levels of popular support, the availability of new weaponry, and accessibility to an international audience – contributed to Zionist success in Palestine against the British Empire in the late 1930s and 1940s. While the two principal insurgent groups, Irgun and LEHI, emphasized guerrilla operations in their campaign against the British, they also used targeted assassination and terrorist attacks, the most famous of which was the bombing of the British headquarters in Palestine, the King David Hotel in Jerusalem, which killed 91 people. With the declaration of Israeli independence in 1948, most members of Irgun and LEHI joined Israeli's new army, the Israel Defense Forces, and two of their most prominent leaders – Menachem Begin and Yitzhak Shamir – went on to become prime ministers of the new country (Begin, 1977 [1948]; Bell, 1996 [1977]; Hoffman, 2015).

Terrorism was used to particularly striking effect in the Algerian War of Independence. The National Liberation Front (FLN) began its war of independence against France in 1954 with a semi-conventional military campaign in the Algerian hinterland. While the FLN held its own against French troops, the insurgents were unable to gain enough support to force the French to negotiate. Therefore the FLN ramped up violence against Algerian moderates and initiated a campaign of terrorism in the colonial capital of Algiers in an effort to polarize the conflict and to attract international attention. The FLN's terrorist operations in Algiers were carried out by a large network of cells that refined techniques first adopted by the People's Will in the 1870s. The cells were linked together in a chain of command that limited the insurgents' knowledge of other cells. They carried out bombings and shootings against a range of symbolic targets, including police, French citizens, and Algerian proxies. Their ability to hide amongst Algerian civilians and resist all but the most determined counter-terrorism provoked the French military and settlers into using disproportionate, reactive violence. The French came to rely on massive cordon and arrest operations, the suspension of habeas corpus, widespread torture (Aussaresses, 2002), and thousands of extrajudicial executions. These tactics eventually destroyed the FLN's terror cells in Algiers but turned most of the Algerian population against the French and brought the Algerian struggle to an international audience. By 1960, the FLN led a mass movement in the cities and fielded a semi-conventional army in the countryside. French settlers kept demanding a harder and harder line against the insurgency, which precipitated a constitutional crisis in metropolitan France and France's eventual departure from Algeria in 1962 (Evans, 2012; Horne, 2006 [1977]; Thomas, 2015). The example could not have been clearer to other anti-colonial insurgencies around the globe: terrorism could be instrumental in building a mass movement, particularly if the great powers could be provoked into using their disproportionate resources and firepower in ways that radicalized the undecided and undercut an empire's claims to moral superiority.

Other movements sought to follow the FLN's example, but the results proved difficult to duplicate. In Palestine, Arabs displaced by the creation of Israel formed a dizzying array of violent factions. Their goal was to use terrorism and then guerrilla operations to trigger a broader war between Israel and its Arab neighbours that would lead to Israel's destruction. Despite the creation of the quasi-government known as the Palestinian Authority, the strategy has failed for a number of reasons. On the one hand, the Palestinian factions, nominally allied under the umbrella of the Palestine Liberation Organization, have often fought against each other as much as against Israel. Likewise, the Arab states have been keener on sponsoring the squabbling factions than on capitalizing on the disruption created by terrorism and guerrilla fighting. On the other hand, Israeli counter-terrorism has been very successful at degrading the PLO's militias and terror cells, although the severity of the Israeli response has sometimes handed propaganda victories to the Palestinians. The Palestinian factions, however, have often handed the advantage right back, particularly through radically violent terrorist actions – such as the seizure and killing of Israeli athletes at the Munich Olympics in 1972 – that galvanized international opposition to the Palestinian cause (Aburish, 2004; Becker, 1984; Reeve, 2000; Rubin and Rubin, 2003).

Urban guerrillas and terrorism

Meanwhile some of the same factors that spurred violent anti-colonial movements produced, under the influence of Cold War Marxism, a return of leftist revolutionary terrorism. The key early figure was the Brazilian revolutionary Carlos Marighella who developed a revolutionary model based on the use of so-called urban guerrillas (Marighella, 2002 [1969]). This was the furthest thing from the Russian Method of tightly orchestrated targeted assassinations. Instead, widely dispersed, largely independent cells would be given carte blanche to target anything associated with the economic and political powers-that-be in an effort to harden battle lines, spread chaos, and trigger a crackdown from the authorities. In short, the goal was propaganda of the deed on such a massive scale that it would provoke the state into revealing itself to be a fascist dictatorship. This – it was hoped – would spur the growth of a mass movement, with revolution to soon follow. While Marighella's model has not produced a single successful revolution – that is, successful in the long term – it has proven to be the signature terrorism strategy of the last 50 years.

The Tupamaros of Uruguay implemented the purest version of Marighella's plan but succeeded only in triggering a devastating decade-long police state crackdown (Brum, 2014). In Italy, the Red Brigades had a highly centralized cell structure that closely coordinated its attacks – much like the FLN of Algeria – but also inspired a secondary tier of loosely coordinated urban guerrillas (Della Porta, 2001 [1995]). West Germany's Red Army Faction (originally known as the Baader-Meinhof Gang) never succeeded in developing a wide-scale terrorist movement, although they did attract considerable support from the country's youth (Aust, 2009). In the United States, a wide range of colourful, bizarrely violent groups – including Weatherman/Weather Underground and the Symbionese Liberation Army – independently organized but collectively constituted a classic urban guerrilla terrorist campaign (Burrough, 2015). These US and European terrorists attracted a great deal of media and government attention and garnered some sympathy, primarily from middle-class students, but in the end terrorism failed to help them produce a revolutionary movement.

Radical Islamist and jihadist terrorism

With the end of the Cold War, left-wing revolutionary terrorism largely dried up. Meanwhile there has been a resurgence in white supremacist and radical right violence in the United States and Europe. But in the last several decades, the most significant ideological motivator behind terrorism globally has been jihadism and radical Islamism. Both trace their modern origins back to the creation of the Muslim Brotherhood in Egypt in 1928. They share the goal of ridding Islamic societies of corrupting, external influences so that devout Muslims can seek spiritual, social, and cultural rejuvenation, and often according to puritanical norms imputed to the early Muslim communities of the seventh and eighth centuries (Bell, 2002; Kepel, 2002).

Scholars differ in their analyses of these movements, but there are a few generally agreed upon differences between them. On the one hand, radical Islamist groups have nominally eschewed modern political forms but tend to organize along familiar lines. Most seek to infiltrate or replace their governments while retaining the form of the nation-state; thus many of them have an ethno-nationalist component to their programme. When radical Islamist groups use terrorism, it is usually tactically purposeful and deployed against their own governments or against what are decried as colonial powers (Habeck, 2007; Kepel, 2002). Radical Sunni Islamist groups staged uprisings and mounted terrorist campaigns in Syria, Egypt and Saudi Arabia in 1979–1981, but these failed to produce larger revolutionary movements and instead led to violent state repression. In Iran, a Shiite version of radical Islam came to power after the overthrow of the Shah in 1978 and remains there today. Young members of the movement helped to radicalize the revolution with the seizure of American embassy personnel in Tehran in 1979, and Iran has exported revolution and sponsored terrorism throughout the Middle East, most notably through its Revolutionary Guard and the Lebanese group Hezbollah (Lesch, 2001; Norton, 2014). The most successful radical Sunni Islamist group has been Hamas, which began as a branch of the Muslim Brotherhood in Palestine in the early 1980s. It used terrorist attacks against civilians – particularly suicide bombings – to help build a larger movement, going so far as to emerge as the recognized government of the Gaza Strip in the Palestine Authority (Bloom, 2005; Milton-Edwards and Farrell, 2010; Pape, 2006).

On the other hand, jihadist groups have looked beyond their own governments in Egypt, Saudi Arabia, and elsewhere (which they identify as the "near enemy") and typically engage in broader campaigns of violence against foreigners and foreign governments (described as the "far enemy" responsible for propping up local puppets) as well as against those Muslims identified as insufficiently Islamic or even apostate. Jihadists generally seek to erase modern political borders and states; they are usually trans-national and intentionally multi-ethnic. Many seek to recreate the Caliphate, which secular Turkish leaders abolished in 1924. Jihadist groups have made widespread use of terrorism and, with notable exceptions, have not succeeded in transitioning to guerrilla warfare or broader insurgent campaigns. Moreover, jihadist terrorism tends to have an apocalyptic element; suicide missions can have tactical or strategic value but for those involved this element takes a backseat to the desire for a liberating, sanctifying death (Bell, 2002; Habeck, 2007; Kepel, 2002).

Al-Qaeda is the most notorious of modern terrorist groups but it also provides a fascinating study of how groups that use terrorism can rapidly evolve. Al-Qaeda was founded by Osama bin Laden in the mid-1980s to fight in Afghanistan against the Soviets and their puppets. At this time, al-Qaeda was essentially a private jihadist militia that used guerrilla tactics (Coll, 2004; Wright, 2006). After the withdrawal and later collapse of the Soviet Union, al-Qaeda began to disintegrate without an enemy to focus its energy and overcome its internal ethnic rivalries. By 1996, bin Laden re-oriented al-Qaeda against the United States, which he decried for its presence near the Saudi holy cities of Mecca and Medina and as the "far enemy" responsible for Muslim suffering and humiliation in Palestine and Iraq (Bergen, 2001; Ibrahim, 2007; Wright, 2006). He also redesigned al-Qaeda as a centralized, conspiratorial organization dedicated to the use of terrorism. After terrorist attacks against a US ship in Yemen and US embassies in Kenya and Tanzania, bin Laden and al-Qaeda pulled off the deadliest terrorist attack in history on September 11, 2001. The simultaneous airplane hijackings/suicide attacks against the World Trade Center and the Pentagon (plus one plane that came down in a field in Pennsylvania) killed nearly 3000 civilians. The attacks were carried out with multiple audiences in mind. Bin Laden hoped to provoke the US into lashing out and creating new confrontations between the West and the Muslim world, which would bind together al-Qaeda, radicalize Muslims, and create a global jihad – in the words of Reza Aslan, a "cosmic war" – that would lead to the final jihadist victory (*The 9/11 Commission Report*, 2004; Aslan, 2009; Wright, 2006). The United States and its allies did indeed invade Afghanistan, which had been sheltering al-Qaeda, but the swift operation drove al-Qaeda underground and destroyed much of its leadership. Two years later, the US invasion of Iraq toppled the dictator Saddam Hussein, but it diverted allied attention from the stabilization operation in Afghanistan and – much worse – created exactly the jihadist cause that bin Laden had hoped for (Burke, 2011; Coll, 2018).

And al-Qaeda evolved once more, this time essentially into a board of directors that sought to direct global jihad at a distance by promoting a brand and backing what some have identified as franchises (Farrall, 2011). Al-Qaeda eventually endorsed local insurgent and/or terrorist operations from Northern Africa to the Philippines. The most destructive franchise – al-Qaeda in Iraq (AQI) – killed thousands in Iraq and helped foment a brutal civil war that lasted for several years. After an uneasy peace was re-established in Iraq in 2011, AQI metastasized into the Islamic State in Iraq and Syria (ISIS), which took advantage of the chaos of the Syrian Civil War to briefly establish a new self-proclaimed Caliphate. In fact, ISIS emerged as a rival to al-Qaeda and itself attracted affiliates in West Africa, Somalia, Afghanistan, and the Philippines (Byman, 2015; McCants, 2015). After ISIS went on the defensive in Syria and Iraq, it unleashed terrorist attacks against targets in Europe (such as the November 2015 attacks in Paris that killed 130 people) and used slick online promotional videos – including grisly videos of executions – to radicalize "lone wolves", who carried out attacks in several global locations, including San Bernardino, California (December 2015); Nice, France (July 2016); and London (June 2017). While these latter attacks have been carried out by individuals, they follow the pattern of anarcho-terrorism from the turn of the previous century when individuals or small cells that were personally unaware of each other operated on separate fronts in a widely-dispersed movement brought together by propaganda.

Conclusion

This cross-century comparison is a strong reminder that the history of group terrorism is a set of variations on a theme. The core of what we would today recognize as terrorism emerged in the French Revolution and developed most of its critically important features in the nineteenth century. Then, as now, terrorism has been used by both states and sub-state groups and can be identified as the use of symbolic violence to achieve political goals. Even as the scale of terrorist violence and the range of ideological motivations expanded across the twentieth century, the core features of terrorism remained. What has changed most dramatically in the two-plus centuries since the dawn of modern terrorism during the French Revolution is the organizational basis, the technological capabilities, and the use of tactical innovations, as described above. Given the expanding use of terrorism and the stability within its core features, it should be assumed that terrorism will continue to be with us for the foreseeable future.

References

Aburish, S. (2004) *Arafat: From Defender to Dictator*, updated edition. New York: Bloomsbury.

Allen, J. (ed.) (2000) *Without sanctuary: Lynching Photography in America*. Santa Fe, NM: Twin Palms.

Andress, D. (2005) *The Terror: The Merciless War for Freedom in Revolutionary France*. New York: Farrar, Straus & Giroux

Applebaum, A. (2003) *Gulag: A History*. New York: Doubleday.

Aslan, Reza. (2009) *How to Win a Cosmic War: God, Globalization, and the End of the War on Terror*. New York: Random House.

Aussaresses, P. (2002) *The Battle of the Casbah: Terrorism and Counterterrorism in Algeria 1955–1957*. New York: Enigma.

Aust, S. (2009) *Baader-Meinhof: The Inside Story of the R.A.F.* Oxford: Oxford University Press.

Bartholdy, J. (1821) *Memoirs of the Secret Societies of the South of Italy*. London: Murray.

Becker, J. (1984) *The PLO: The Rise and Fall of the Palestine Liberation Organization*. London: St. Martin's.

Begin, M. (1977 [1948]) *The Revolt*. Los Angeles: Nash.

Bell, J.B. (1996 [1977]) *Terror out of Zion: The Fight for Israeli Independence*. New Brunswick, NJ: Transaction.

Bell, J.B. (2002) *Murders on the Nile: The World Trade Center and Global Terror*. San Francisco: Encounter.

Bergen, P. (2001) *Holy War Inc.: Inside the Secret World of Osama bin Laden.* London: Weidenfeld & Nicolson.
Bloom, M. (2005) *Dying to Kill: The Allure of Suicide Terrorism.* New York: Columbia University Press.
Brum, P. (2014) *The Robin Hood Guerrillas: The Epic Journey of Uruguay's Tupamaros.* USA: CreateSpace.
Burke, J. (2011) *The 9/11 Wars.* New York: Allen Lane/Penguin
Burrough, B. (2015) *Days of Rage: America's Radical Underground, the FBI, and the Forgotten Age of Revolutionary Violence.* New York: Penguin
Byman, D. (2015) *Al Qaeda, the Islamic State, and the Global Jihadist Movement.* Oxford: Oxford University Press
Coll, S. (2004) *Ghost Wars: The Secret History of the CIA, Afghanistan, and bin Laden.* New York: Penguin.
Coll, S. (2018) *Directorate S: The C.I.A. and America's Secret Wars in Afghanistan and Pakistan.* New York: Penguin.
Conquest, R. (2007) *The Great Terror: A Reassessment.* Oxford: Oxford University Press.
Courtois, S. (ed.) (1999) *The Black Book of Communism: Crimes, Terror, Repression.* Cambridge, MA: Harvard University Press.
Della Porta, D. (2001 [1995]) Left-wing terrorism in Italy. In M. Crenshaw (ed.), *Terrorism in Context.* University Park: Pennsylvania State University Press.
Dray, P. (2002) *At the Hands of Persons Unknown: The Lynching of Black America.* New York: Random House.
Dwyer, T.R. (2005) *The Squad and the Intelligence Operations of Michael Collins.* Cork, Ireland: Mercier.
Equal Justice Initiative. (2017) *Lynching in America: Confronting the Legacy of Racial Terror* (3rd edn). Montgomery, AL: EJI. Available online at https://eji.org/reports/lynching-in-america. Accessed June 19, 2019.
Evans, M. (2012) *Algeria: France's Undeclared War.* Oxford: Oxford University Press.
Farrall, L. (2011) How al-Qaeda works. *Foreign Affairs*, 90(2), 128–138.
Figes, O. (1997) *A People's Tragedy: The Russian Revolution: 1891–1924.* New York: Viking.
Foner, E. (2014) *Reconstruction: America's Unfinished Revolution, 1863–1877*, updated edition. New York: Harper Perennial Modern Classics.
Ford, F.L. (1985) *Political Murder: From Tyrannicide to Terrorism.* Harvard: Harvard University Press.
Gage, B. (2009) *The Day Wall Street Exploded: A Story of America in its First Age of Terror.* Oxford: Oxford University Press.
Gates, H.L. Jr. (2019) *Stony the Road: Reconstruction, White Supremacy, and the Rise of Jim Crow.* New York: Penguin.
Geifman, A. (1993) *Thou Shalt Kill: Revolutionary Terrorism in Russia, 1894–1917.* Princeton: Princeton University Press.
Getty, J.A. and Naumov, O.V. (eds) (1999) *The Road to Terror: Stalin and the Self-destruction of the Bolsheviks, 1932–1939.* New Haven: Yale University Press.
Habeck, M. (2007) *Knowing the Enemy: Jihadist Ideology and the War on Terror.* New Haven: Yale University Press.
Hart, P. (2005) *The I.R.A. at War 1916–1923.* Oxford: Oxford University Press.
Hodde, L. (1856) *History of Secret Societies and of the Republican Party of France from 1830 to 1848.* Philadelphia: Lippincott.
Hoffman, B. (2015) *Anonymous Soldiers: The Struggle for Israel, 1917–1947.* New York: Knopf.
Horne, A. (2006 [1977]) *A Savage War of Peace: Algeria 1954–1962.* New York: NYRB.
Ibrahim, R. (ed.) (2007) *The Al Qaeda Reader.* New York: Doubleday.
Jensen, R.B. (2014) *The Battle against Anarchist Terrorism, 1878–1934: An International History.* Cambridge: Cambridge University Press.
Johnson, E.A. (2000) *Nazi Terror: The Gestapo, Jews and Ordinary Germans.* New York: Basic Books.
Joll, J. (1980) *The Anarchists* (2nd edn). Cambridge, MA: Harvard University Press.
Kepel, G. (2002) *Jihad: The Trail of Political Islam.* Cambridge, MA: Harvard University Press.
Kropotkin, P.A. (1975) The spirit of revolt. In E. Capouya and K. Tompkins (eds), *The Essential Kropotkin.* New York: Liveright, pp. 7–9.
Laqueur, W. (1977) *A History of Terrorism.* Boston: Little, Brown.
Law, R.D. (ed.) (2015) *The Routledge History of Terrorism.* Abingdon: Routledge.
Law, R.D. (2016) *Terrorism: A History* (2nd edn). Malden, MA: Polity.
Leggett, G. (1981) *The Cheka: Lenin's Political Police.* Oxford: Clarendon Press.
Lemann, N. (2007 [2006]) *Redemption: The Last Battle of the Civil War.* New York: Farrar, Straus and Giroux.
Merriman, J. (2009) *The Dynamite Club: How a Bombing in Fin-de-Siècle Paris Ignited the Age of Modern Terror.* Boston: Houghton Mifflin Harcourt.

Lesch, D.W. (2001) *1979: The Year that Shaped the Modern Middle East.* Boulder, CO: Westview.
Marighella, C. (2002 [1969]) *Mini-manual of the Urban Guerrilla.* Montreal: Abraham Guillen Press.
McCants, W. (2015) *The ISIS Apocalypse: The History, Strategy, and Doomsday Vision of the Islamic State.* New York: St. Martin's Press.
Merkl, P.H. (1982) Approaches to political violence: the stormtroopers, 1925–33. In W.J. Mommsen and G. Hirschfeld (eds), *Social Protest, Violence and Terror in Nineteenth- and Twentieth-century Europe.* London: St. Martin's Press.
Miller, M.A. (1976) *Kropotkin.* Chicago: University of Chicago Press.
Miller, M.A. (2012) *The Foundations of Modern Terrorism: State, Society and the Dynamics of Political Violence.* Cambridge, UK: Cambridge University Press.
Milton-Edwards, B. and Farrell, S. (2010) *Hamas: The Islamic Resistance Movement.* Malden, MA: Polity.
Norton, A.R. (2014) *Hezbollah: A Short History*, updated edition. Princeton, NJ: Princeton University Press
Pape, R.A. (2006) *Dying to Win: The Strategic Logic of Suicide Terrorism.* New York: Random House.
Petersen, J. (1982) Violence in Italian fascism, 1919–25. In W.J. Mommsen and G. Hirschfeld (eds), *Social Protest, Violence and Terror in Nineteenth- and Twentieth-century Europe.* London: St. Martin's Press.
Pipes, R. (1990) *The Russian Revolution.* New York: Knopf.
Rable, G.C. (1984) *But There was No Peace: The Role of Violence in the Politics of Reconstruction.* Athens, GA: University of Georgia Press.
Rapport, M. (2015) The French Revolution and early European revolutionary terrorism. In R.D. Law (ed.), *The Routledge History of Terrorism.* Abingdon: Routledge, pp. 63–76.
Reeve, S. (2000) *One Day in September: The Full Story of the 1972 Munich Olympics Massacre and the Israeli Revenge Operation "Wrath of God".* New York: Arcade.
Roberts, J.M. (1972) *The Mythology of the Secret Societies.* New York: Scribner.
Rubin, B. and Rubin, J.C. (2003) *Yasir Arafat: A Political Biography.* Oxford: Oxford University Press.
Schmid, A.P. (2011) The definition of terrorism. In A.P. Schmid (ed.), *The Routledge Handbook of Terrorism Research.* Abingdon: Routledge, pp. 39–98.
Stepniak-Kravchinsky, S. (1883) *Underground Russia.* New York: Scribner.
Tallien, J.L. (1999) J.-L. Tallien on the Terror. In L. Mason and T. Rizzo (eds), *The French Revolution: A Document Collection.* Boston: Houghton Mifflin, pp. 263–267.
The 9/11 Commission Report. (2004) New York: Norton.
Thomas, M.C. (2015) Violence in the Algerian War of Independence. In R.D. Law (ed.), *The Routledge History of Terrorism.* Abingdon: Routledge.
Trautmann, F. (1980) *The Voice of Terror: A Biography of Johann Most.* Westport, CT: Greenwood.
Trelease, A.W. (1995 [1971]) *White Terror: The Ku Klux Klan Conspiracy and Southern Reconstruction.* Baton Rouge: Louisiana State University Press.
Venturi, F. (1960) *The Roots of Revolution: A History of the Populist and Socialist Movements in Nineteenth-century Russia.* Chicago, IL: University of Chicago Press.
Verhoeven, C. (2009) *The Odd Man Karakozov: Imperial Russia, Modernity, and the Birth of Terrorism.* Ithaca: Cornell University Press.
Wright, L. (2006) *The Looming Tower.* New York: Knopf
Wright, R. (2007 [1944]) *Black Boy.* New York: Harper Perennial.
Zamoyski, A. (2015) *Phantom Terror: Political Paranoia and the Creation of the Modern State, 1789–1848.* New York: Basic Books.

8

PSYCHOLOGICAL AND CRIMINOLOGICAL UNDERSTANDING OF TERRORISM

Theories and models[1]

Zoe Marchment and Paul Gill

Introduction

Terrorism studies began as a niche area of enquiry in the early 1970s within history, political science and sociology. Such approaches explain the emergence of, and motivation for, politically violent campaigns within their socio-political context. From the outset, the field of terrorism studies was not so interested in the terrorist event itself. Instead, studies focused upon two almost incompatible approaches, each with varying, and often dubious, levels of scientific rigour. First, analyses sought to discover the dispositional traits of terrorist group members (Cooper, 1978). Such approaches initially offered anecdotal glimpses into the supposed 'irrationality' of the individual perpetrator by emphasizing psychopathy and other particular personality traits. Second, analyses focused on the 'root causes' of terrorist grievances (Alexander, 1976), offering empirical descriptions of the 'rationality' of terrorist groups turning toward violence. The emphasis was on individual and group 'agency' in strategic decision-making. For example, various studies examine how terrorism can be an effective political strategy that is more optimal than other forms of military engagement, can produce effective gains, and can undermine confidence in the functioning and authority of the state.

The initial dominance of history and political science had a major path-dependent effect upon the study of terrorism. Instead of viewing a terrorist attack as a single crime, the tendency within the literature has been to explain the attack in terms of a group's ideological position (Drake, 1988) or strategic orientation (Abrahms, 2008). Such depictions emphasize terrorism as a political, rather than a criminal, problem. Correspondingly, whereas these studies traditionally focused upon the rational adoption of terrorism as a strategy or a tactic, they typically do not look at the 'rationality' underpinning the actual commission of a terrorist offence.

In the past few years however, there has been a major shift within terrorism studies. A greater variety of disciplines now bring their methodological expertise to the domain. Insight from the humanities now extends beyond the discipline of history and includes linguistics, the visual arts and theology (Maher, 2016). The social sciences have increased their problem-oriented approaches, bringing in a diverse range of disciplines, including geography (Bahgat and Medina, 2013) and psychology (Horgan, 2015). The natural sciences have also applied their methodological tools and paradigms to understand terrorist behaviour (Johnson et al., 2013; Manrique et al., 2016). The growth of importance in the internet for radicalization and terrorist engagement (Gill et al., 2017) has also witnessed more input from computer science (Brynielsson et al., 2013). Terrorism studies, as a whole, is becoming increasingly more empirically and quantitatively oriented after years of questionable data and science (Schuurman, 2018).

Psychopathology, personality and pathways

As with the study of more traditional crimes, early psychological approaches to understanding terrorism were based on the assumption that something in the makeup of terrorists differed to the "normal" population (Mullins and Dolnik, 2009). Silke (2003, p. 30) commented that "in the early 1970s … it was widely believed that terrorists suffered from personality disorders and that there would be an exceptionally high number of clinical psychopaths, narcissists and paranoids in the ranks of the average terrorist group." Walter Laqueur wrote that "all terrorists believe in conspiracies by the powerful, hostile forces and suffer from some form of delusion and persecution mania … The element of … madness plays an important role in terrorism" (as quoted in Silke, 2003, p. 30).

The quest for a terrorist psychopathology or for a unique terrorist personality profile has borne disappointing results, with the majority of such research pointing to the 'normality' of individuals involved in terrorist organizations. Horgan (2003, p. 114) commented that "despite their attractiveness, personality traits are useless as predictors for understanding why people become terrorists". "The concepts of abnormality and psychopathology are not useful in understanding terrorist psychology or behaviour" (Post, 2007).

Multiple papers have attempted to use psychoanalytical theories to explain the cause of terrorist behaviour. Kaplan (1978, p. 247) wrote that terrorism is a response to poor self-esteem, used by an individual to counter impulses of self-contempt. By carrying out terrorist acts, it can "not only shore up a weakened ego; it can also shatter its walls altogether, freeing the self from what has come to be felt as a prison". Friedland (1992) proposes that terrorism is a result of interactions between social processes and individual character. An individual's quest for significance may increase their readiness to be recruited. Terrorists groups may also (a) seek out individuals who want to increase their social significance and (b) highlight how group membership may facilitate the attainment of supreme significance (Kruglanski and Fishman, 2009). Motivations for becoming a member of an organization vary across individuals, and personal desires facilitating radicalization and entry are not necessarily due to social factors.

Bartlett and Miller (2012) suggest that those who engage in violence have the following characteristics: they have a strong emotional pull to act in the face of injustice; they have a strong sense of thrill and excitement associated with action; they have a sense of status; and have been affected by peer pressure. Moghaddam (2005) distinguishes terrorists from other individuals as those that "believe they have no effective voice in society, are encouraged by leaders to displace aggression onto out-groups, and become socialized to see terrorist organizations as legitimate and out-group members as evil".

Empirical lessons about group dynamics from social psychology help to clarify some of the behaviour of terrorist collectives. Group contexts promote extreme attitudes. Group opinions and attitudes tend to be more extreme than those held by its individual members, and individual opinions and attitudes tend to become more extreme in a group context. Groups have internal norms and rules that control member behaviour; there are implicit and explicit expectations for how individual members behave (McCauley and Segal, 1987).

Early group theories of terrorism focused on psychological heterogeneity and group-induced homogenization. Although each individual has a different personal justification for entering into an organization, the collective moderates their behaviour when they become part of a group. This sense of collective is said to overwhelm an individual and provide validation for actions carried out whilst part of the group (Post *et al.*, 2003). Sageman draws attention to the fact that terrorists are not always aware of the main reasons for their actions, "Consciousness, like solidarity and collective identity, does not always precede action, but may arise in the process of carrying out an action" (Sageman, 2004, p. 7). Horgan (2015, p. 138) contends that "for the individual terrorist increasing psychological investment, or the process of becoming a more committed member, is shaped most remarkably through engagement in terrorist activities" (p. 138).

At the collective level, identification with a given ethnicity or religion promotes empathy and a desire to pursue justice in the name of "the people". This also encourages a dualistic categorization of the world into "us" and "them", thus stereotyping social groups and dehumanizing the enemy. This "us vs them" dichotomy between members and non-members of an organization effectively weakens psychological barriers against violence (Grossman, 2014) and eases the process of viewing civilians as legitimate targets (Tilly, 2003). Likewise, identification with others may promote diffusion of responsibility, and individuals may feel less personally responsible for the actions of the group. Post (2007, p. 7) explained that collective identity may provide justification for actions: "terrorists have subordinated their individual identity to the collective identity, so that what serves the group, organisation or network is of primary importance."

While psychopathy and personality approaches focus on 'why' individuals become members of terrorist groups, pathway approaches primarily focus on 'how' individuals become members. Shaw (1986) published the first 'pathway model', consisting of four elements: socialization processes, narcissistic injuries, escalatory events, and personal connections with militant group members. The dominant explanation, narcissism, profoundly influenced the model. Taylor and Horgan (2006) suggest that, rather than a psychological state, researchers should view terrorism as highly complicated process. They suggested that a pathway involves the interaction between three critical elements: setting events (relating to contextual influence); personal factors (relating to psychological and environmental experiences); and social/political/organizational contexts. During terrorist involvement, the influence of setting events and personal factors weaken. Social, political and organizational factors grow in their influence on an individual and merge with personal factors. Horgan (2008) expresses the importance of focusing on contexts and relationships, as opposed to psychological or moral qualities, and advocates that terrorism should be viewed as a pathway process. This process involves three phases: becoming involved in terrorism, engaging in terrorist activity, and disengaging from terrorism.

Interpersonal connections shape individual behaviour. In a review of case studies from the Weatherman organization. Sageman (2004) suggests that social bonds are vital in understanding terrorist behaviour and of greater importance than ideology: "it's a group phenomenon. To search for individual characteristics in order to understand them is totally misleading. It will lead you to a dead end". The process of becoming involved in terrorism may develop through natural group interactions. These connections strengthen their identity, facilitate radicalization, and encourage action (Leistedt, 2013). Mullins (2009) hypothesized that dynamic variations in group structure correlate with changes in group and individual psychology. When modelling the development of two Islamic terrorist organizations using social network analysis, Mullins (2009) concluded that individuals strengthen their commitment to the group through assimilation of the ideas put out by influential figures.

In his book, *Understanding Terror Networks*, Sageman discusses the origins, evolution and nature of the "global Salafi jihad". He found that "78 percent [of 172 Al Qaeda members] were cut off from their cultural and social origins" (Sageman, 2994, p. 92). He found that there was a common experience of displacement – of separation, loneliness and cultural disorientation, with individuals often seeking companionship and solidarity with others similarly perturbed. As these relationships intensified so did their resentment of society, which they perceived as excluding them. A common religious collective identity followed, which may have been a driving force on to greater extremism.

A theoretical framework often applied to understanding radicalization processes and violent extremism is Social Movement Theory (SMT), where movements arise from collective behaviour occurring under strained environmental conditions. SMT is useful in the study of terrorism as it focuses on processes, not sociodemographics (Dalgaard-Nielsen, 2010). Della Porta (1995) connected SMT concepts to violent extremism in her studies of Italian and German militants. Wiktorowicz conducted an in-depth study of how people came to join Al-Muhajiroun and presented a four-component developmental model for radicalization using SMT as a framework. Those who came to be radicalized first revealed an openness to new worldviews (cognitive opening), then came to view religion as a path to find meaning (religious seeking), eventually found the group's narrative and ethos to "make sense" (frame alignment), and, ultimately, through a process of socialization, became fully indoctrinated into the movement. Similarly, concluding their study of a millenarian cult, Lofland and Stark (1965) commented,

> For conversion, a person must experience, within a religious problem-solving perspective, enduring, acutely-felt tensions that lead him to define himself as a religious seeker; he must encounter the cult [deviant perspective] at a turning point in his life; within the cult an affective bond must be formed (or pre-exist) and any extra-cult attachments neutralized; and there he must be exposed to intensive interaction if he is to become a 'deployable agent'.

Traditional criminology

Few studies have empirically tested traditional criminological theories such as anomie, strain, disorganization, or control approaches in a terrorism context (Agnew, 2010; Akyuz and Armstrong, 2011; LaFree and Dugan, 2009; Shechory and Laufer, 2008). Pisoiu (2015) tested elements of strain and subcultural perspectives, focusing on the individual situation and motivation for involvement in terrorism, in a qualitative study of seven jihadi and far-right case studies in Germany. The findings showed little support for the appraisal of subcultural capital drawing on socially deprived groups or status frustration. Her findings supported the illegitimate opportunity structure thesis and sub-cultural claims such as resistance, bricolage, homology, agency, and cultural cross-fertilization. Pisoiu concluded that the extremists in her study were assertive and purposive agents who were not directed by situational circumstances.

Chermak and Gruenewald (2015) highlight the importance of considering the macro contexts in which terrorists choose to act. They compared individual and contextual sociodemographic characteristics across far-right, far-left, and jihadi extremists who committed violent crimes. They considered whether these violent extremists, which are similar to more typical non-extremist offenders, experience an identity crisis caused by the strain of wanting to achieve the goals of society but having inadequate means to achieve them. Those with an extreme right-wing ideology were less educated and less successful when it came to employment, Jihadists were unable to integrate fully into American communities, and members of far-left groups believed the "American Dream" to be uncertain and harmful, especially to the environment.

The classic social disorganization perspective posits that individuals experiencing rapid social changes such as revolutionary and ethnic war, adverse regime change, and genocide will stop conforming to social norms and laws. Fahey and LaFree (2015) examined the effects of a measure of country-level social disorganization on levels of terrorist attacks and fatalities in 101 countries from 1981 to 2010. They found that social disorganization is consistently associated with increases in terrorist attacks and fatalities (even when controlling for variables such as state capacity).

Understanding relationships is critical to understanding involvement in terrorism. The importance of friends, family and social ties for recruitment into terrorist groups is long established across multiple terrorist groups, including al-Qaeda (Sageman, 2004), the Hofstad Group (Schuurman, 2017), al-Shabaab (Botha, 2014), German foreign fighters (Reynolds and Hafez, 2019), Italian left-wing groups (Della Porta, 1988), the PKK (Columbian terrorist groups. Florez-Morris, 2010), Palestinian terrorists (Post *et al.*, 2003), and the extreme right in the US (Schafer *et al.*, 2014). Such social ties expose individuals to radicalizing agents and settings (Bouhana and Wikström, 2011), builds peer pressure (Botha, 2014), develops trust between potential co-offenders (Morrison, 2016), and reinforces extremist beliefs and commitment to the group (Gill, 2012).

The formation of social relationships is constrained by geography, and people who live within close proximity to one another are more likely to know each other than other individuals who live further away (Onnela *et al.*, 2011). Owing to this elevated chance of meeting one another, those who are spatially close also tend to be socially close (Tayebi, 2012). Indeed, criminals are more likely to commit offences with the people they spend the most time with socially (Olofsson, 1967, 1971; Dunér and Haglund 1974; Ward 1998). Correspondingly, one of the strongest predictors of criminal behaviour is the number of criminal friends an individual has (Matsueda, 1988; Warr, 1996; Matsueda and Anderson, 1998; Loeber *et al.*, 1998), and the importance of the role of family members in the recruitment to co-offending has also been emphasized (Jones *et al.*, 1980). There is a temporal relationship between criminal behaviour and exposure to delinquent peers, finding a new relationship with a delinquent peer to be an antecedent for involvement in criminal behaviour. In other words, co-offending is spatially situated, and such collaborations play a role in the recruitment of others into criminal behaviour who may not have participated in crime otherwise (Cohen and Felson, 2003; Reiss, 1988; Warr 1996).

Qualitative autobiographical accounts and interviews conducted with members of Provisional Irish Republican Army (PIRA) highlight the importance of local connections in the recruitment process. One former member, Eamon Collins, explained that "He suggested another possible recruit… I had been at junior school with him" (Collins, 1998, p. 92) and "I asked him if he knew any other people who would be suitable. He gave me eight names" (Collins, 1998, p. 88). Other academics emphasize the importance of "local and family connections" (English, 2003, p. 113) for PIRA recruitment and discuss how "family connections, and the immediate concerns of his northern setting, helped lead [Gerry] Adams towards the Provisionals…" (English, 2003, pp. 109–110). Many members of PIRA were not motivated by ideology or considered themselves as national-ists when they entered the organization (Alonso, 2006): "[I was] not politically motivated at that time… the whole thing permeated right through into our lives, into our local communities" (Alonso, 2006). Bosi (2012) and Bosi and Ó Dochartaigh (2018) systematically examined the pathways of individuals who joined Republican groups in Northern Ireland between 1969 and 1972. They found local connections to be a facilitating factor in this process and that individuals often joined alongside people they knew: "I think that they made decisions because of who they knew, or which street they lived on..." (cited in Bosi, 2012, p. 369); "When I first joined the Republican movement, I first joined the Officials with a group of friends from the same street where I was living" (cited in Bosi and Ó Dochartaigh, 2018, p. 42). This facilitated the recruitment process as new volunteers could be personally introduced by their friends, families and colleagues. This, in turn, reduced the risk of informers and ensured operational security. Finally, Gill *et al.* (2014) found that residing in the same county was a consistently stronger predictor of co-offending within PIRA than other homophily-related characteristics (e.g. age, gender, etc.)

Anecdotal evidence further suggests that when individuals join terrorist organizations, either (a) recruiters assign roles and tasks based on an assessment of organizational needs and the individuals' ability, or (b) the new recruit has a sense of what roles they are willing or eager to adopt. For example, when US troops raided an al-Qaeda safe house in the Iraqi town of Sinjar in October 2007, they found a wealth of data on the biographies of individuals who had signed up for the insurgency. Of those who joined, most requested assignment as a fighter, combatant or martyr. However, others asked to be doctors, journalists and to occupy other media roles. Furthermore, in an interview with Horgan (2009, p. 80), a former member of the Provisional Irish Republican Army stated:

> There have always been very astute people involved in recruiting to the IRA ... There is a sense in which people were evaluated and put into certain roles ... Every large organization is going to have that challenge – how do you fit people into things?

This suggests that (at least in the case of the Provisional IRA) there is often a purposeful relationship between individuals and the roles into which they are initially guided. In addition, there may be a natural logic to how actual and subsequent involvement unfolds and diversifies for the individual. Taylor and Horgan (2006, p. 595) argue that some roles and activities might "tend to cluster together more naturally than others" (they give the example of financing, political and community activism), but to date there is no empirical evidence to support this claim.

Understanding the nature and function of terrorist roles is important for many reasons. From a disruption perspective, policies need to be tailored for role-specific interventions. Because their behaviours, routines and proximity to violent plots differ substantially, what works in the effective disruption of tasks conducted by a bomb-maker may not necessarily be applicable to those of a financier of a terrorist organization. From a justice perspective, a greater understanding of roles may help with targeted treatment policies and risk assessments (Tracy and Kempf-Leonard, 1996). From a research perspective, it will ultimately help with our understanding of who joins terrorist organizations, the nature of their involvement with the terrorist organization, how individuals migrate from one kind of role to another over time, and ultimately how they desist or disengage from terrorist activities (Horgan, 2009; Taylor & Horgan, 2006). Investigating whether particular variables more closely correlate with particular terrorist roles also concerns the very nature of how we theorize about terrorist involvement and whether general models of 'radicalization' or 'pathways' into terrorism are appropriate or whether they should be tailored for particular manifestations of terrorist activity.

Environmental criminology

Traditional criminology seeks to identify and explain *why* individuals engage in criminal activity, with a focus on sociological, psychological and developmental perspectives. There is a focus on criminality and the criminal disposition, and the factors underlying why an individual would engage in crime. However, this emphasis on the distal causes of crime offers little insight to the proximal determinants of criminal activity (Brantingham and Brantingham, 1981; Clarke, 2004). To address these limitations an alternative framework, *environmental criminology*, was introduced (Brantingham and Brantingham, 1981). Environmental criminology emphasizes the importance of the crime setting and the role of person–situation interactions. It posits situational factors and the environment as key in determining spatial and temporal distributions of crime. Environmental criminology is focused on *where*, *when* and *how* crime events occur, rather than *why* they occur.

The modern rational choice perspective of crime, as proposed by Cornish and Clarke in 1986,[2] assumes that offenders are rational and purposeful in their decision-making. The perspective denotes that an offender acts in their own self-interest while calculating the costs and benefits of each possible alternative, before making a choice that offers the greatest benefit and lowest cost (Cornish and Clarke, 1986). This decision-making process can then be subdivided into: (a) decisions regarding criminal *involvement*, and (b) decisions regarding criminal *events*. When a rational actor makes a choice, there is the assumption that they will be utility maximizing (making a decision that offers the best perceived utility) based on expected rewards, effort and risk (Phillips, 2011; Phillips and Pohl, 2012). Rationality is subject to limits and is guided by time, effort, experience and knowledge (Clarke and Felson, 1993). This led Cornish and Clarke[3] to posit that offenders act with *bounded rationality*. This concept, relating to the criminal event, posits that crime is influenced by opportunities, and that the opportunities are dependent on the individual's environment. Although their knowledge of the associated effort, rewards and risks is imperfect, an offender will still maximize utility based on what they do know.

Treating the terrorist as a rational actor is not a new approach. Although the goals of a terrorist may be irrational, their actions will be guided by rationality. Much like 'ordinary' criminals, terrorists make a series of cost–benefit analyses to judge whether an act is worth committing (Gill *et al.*, 2020). They make carefully calculated decisions that are utility-maximizing (Asal et al., 2009) and are likely to increase their probability of success (Clarke and Newman, 2006; Hoffman, 2006). A terrorist's rationality is bounded by a number of individual factors such as risk sensitivity, group guidance, prior experience, and personality. Rationality, in this sense, is bounded by time, effort, experience, and knowledge, which in turn feeds into the weighting of rewards, costs, and alternative action plans. Such rational calculations may include having to choose between terrorism and opting for the strategically most advantageous tactics. Pape's (2005) work on suicide terrorism is probably the most oft-cited example of such an approach. Rational calculations are also framed by the group's ideological content and therefore targeting practices may differ across the ideological spectrum. For example, Drake (1998) notes that a terrorist organization's ideology relates to targeting practices because "it sets out the moral framework within which they operate."

The rational choice perspective has been useful in understanding political violence including terrorism (Pape, 2005; Clarke and Newman 2006) and literature consistently supports the presumption that terrorists are rational actors (Sandler *et al.*, 1983; Enders *et al.*, 1990; Enders and Sandler, 1999; Crenshaw, 2000; Silke, 2001; Pape, 2005; Taylor and Horgan, 2006; Caplan, 2006). Perry and Hasisi (2015) used rational choice theory to analyse the motivations of jihadist suicide attackers and concluded that there is no fundamental difference between terrorist perpetrators' motivations and those of more ordinary criminals. They argue that suicide attackers are mostly driven by the anticipation of future self-gratifying benefits, not by altruistic motivation. Dugan *et al.* (2005) examined trends in 1101 attempted aerial hijackings that occurred around the world from 1931 to 2003. Using survival analysis, they estimated the impact of major counter-hijacking interventions on the hazard of differently motivated hijacking attempts. New hijacking attempts were less likely to be undertaken when the likelihood of apprehension was increased through metal detectors and law enforcement at passenger checkpoints.

Insights from environmental criminology into why people engage in terrorist acts have been limited, to date, for a number of reasons. First, the overwhelming emphasis within the field has been to explain the "terrorist" as opposed to explaining the "terrorist act". Second, existing studies have tended to focus on entirely different units of analysis than is traditionally the case within crime science. For example, Desmarais *et al.* (2017) conducted a systematic review of the scientific knowledge regarding risk factors for terrorist involvement. The review demonstrates the existing literature has tended toward 'distal' explanations rooted in factors associated with sociodemographic characteristics, criminal history, religiosity, attitudes and beliefs, employment status, education, poverty, relationship status and mental health. On the other hand, studies looking at the association between personal experiences (e.g. proximal factors) and terrorist engagement were depicted as 'rare' and 'infrequently examined' (Desmarais *et al.*, 2017, p. 190). Second, there has also been a lack of rigorous attention to causal *mechanisms* behind radicalization and engagement in terrorism. Gøtzsche-Astrup (2018) evaluated several common approaches to understanding such mechanisms. These approaches leant on aspects of social-identity theory, ideology and values, and various motivational frameworks. The study concluded that research designs insufficiently demonstrated causality and could only offer simple correlations.

Finally, perhaps the biggest problem has been the field's lack of specificity in terms of the dependent variable being considered. To date, academic approaches to understanding who becomes a 'terrorist' have largely tended toward generalist explanations. Such explanations, be they psychopathological, psychoanalytical, theoretical models or descriptive analyses of large-*N* datasets, tend to treat each individual group member equally. That is, they fail to effectively distinguish different member types, not just across terrorist groups, but also within them. Analyses of "the terrorist" frequently treat actors as monolithic in nature, differing merely in presumed personality traits and little else. Terrorist organizations, however, tend to possess some form of command and functional structure, be it hierarchical or linear. Within this structure, a wide variety of roles, responsibilities and behaviours are delegated to individual members and sub-units. Such responsibilities may range from storing weapons to engaging in shooting attacks; from procuring vehicles for car-bombing attacks to being a bomb-maker; from being a suicide bomber to being a recruiter of suicide bombers; from being a foot soldier to being an executive leader. Because of this differentiation of focus and task, there are some important differences in both the nature and level of involvement by different members of terrorist groups. An individual may hold one or several distinct roles over time in their "terrorist career". These roles may be distinctive in the nature of the social, psychological and organizational demands required of the person in that role. The differences range from the level of violence the individual either directly engages in or merely facilitates; in expertise levels; individual risk to personal liberty and harm; and responsibility for overall strategy (Taylor and Horgan, 2006, p. 595).

Terrorists make cost–benefit decisions in much the same way as ordinary criminals (Gill *et al.*, 2020; Marchment *et al.*, 2019). The field of crime prevention is testament to the vast potential for situationally focused crime-prevention approaches. Situational prevention means focusing on the settings in which offences take place, rather than the underlying motivation or criminal disposition of the individual. Reducing the opportunities for terrorism via environmental design broadly construed is, therefore, a valid and worthwhile pursuit. Each type of terrorist attack, be it a vehicular assault or a bombing, depends on a crystallization of multiple opportunities. Marchment *et al.* (2019) found differences in risk factors for bombings and bomb hoaxes by dissident Republicans in Northern Ireland. Police stations were found to be risky for bomb hoaxes but not significantly correlated with bombings. The targeting of police services naturally comes with a higher risk of arrest and the level of security at these premises may have affected the offender's perceived risk of detection. This suggests that there is some assessment of risk by the offenders, and that they are selecting targets rationally.

In turn, each specific attack type offers its own set of environmental opportunities that can be manipulated with the intention of impacting the terrorist cost–benefit calculus. Such endeavours increase the effort via target hardening, controlling access to facilities, deflecting offenders, and controlling access to the necessary weapons. They also increase the risks by extending guardianship, assisting with natural surveillance, and increasing surveillance. They may also reduce the rewards of an attack by concealing or removing potential targets. Such approaches focus on the situational qualities of terrorist behaviour (e.g. what terrorists do and how they do it) and are largely informed by developments in the area of environmental criminology and situational crime prevention.

Although it still may be true that the "criminological study of terrorism [lags] far behind many other specialized branches of criminology" (LaFree, 2009, p. 434), there have been major advances recently in a variety of areas. Research increasingly covers issues such as target choice, weapon choice, the spatio-temporal clustering of offences, the distances travelled to commit a terrorist attack, victimology, and the displacement of incidents. Findings show great promise, and reinforce the argument that when we focus on terrorism from a preventative angle, we should focus on terrorist behaviours – *what they do* – rather than remain preoccupied with concerns about *who they are* or *why they have become terrorists*.

Notes

1 This project has received funding from the European Research Council (ERC) under the European Union's Horizon 2020 research and innovation programme (Grant Agreement No. 758834).
2 This work stemmed from economist Gary Becker's 1968 paper, in which he argued that choices regarding crime are not dissimilar to other non-crime related decisions. Cornish and Clarke's model differs from Becker's economic model as it emphasizes that utility is not always dictated by monetary gain.
3 As well as Simon (1957; 1986).

References

Abrahms, M. (2008) What terrorists really want: Terrorist motives and counterterrorism strategy. *International Security*, 32(4), 78–105.

Agnew, R. (2010) A general strain theory of terrorism. *Theoretical Criminology*, 14(2), 131–153.

Akyuz, K. and Armstrong, T. (2011) Understanding the sociostructural correlates of terrorism in Turkey. *International Criminal Justice Review*, 21(2), 134–155.

Alexander, Y. (ed.) (1976) *International Terrorism: National, Regional, and Global Perspectives*. New York: Praeger.

Alonso, R. (2006) *The IRA and Armed Struggle*. London: Routledge (Cass Series on Political Violence).

Asal, V. H., Rethemeyer, K., Anderson, I., Stein, A. Rizzo, J., and Rozea, M. (2009) The softest of targets: a study on terrorist target selection. *Journal of Applied Security Research*, 4(3), 258–278.

Bahgat, K. and Medina, R. M. (2013) An overview of geographical perspectives and approaches in terrorism research. *Perspectives on Terrorism*, 7(1).

Bartlett, J. and Miller, C. (2012) The edge of violence: Towards telling the difference between violent and non-violent radicalization. *Terrorism and Political Violence*, 24(1), 1–21.

Bosi, L. (2012) Explaining pathways to armed activism in the Provisional Irish Republican Army, 1969–1972. *Social Science History*, 36(3), 347–390.

Bosi, L. and Ó Dochartaigh, N. (2018) Armed activism as the enactment of a collective identity: the case of the Provisional IRA between 1969 and 1972. *Social Movement Studies*, 17(1), 35–47.

Botha, A. (2014) Political socialization and terrorist radicalization among individuals who joined al-Shabaab in Kenya. *Studies in Conflict & Terrorism*, 37(11), 895–919.
Bouhana, N. and Wikström, P. O. (2011) Al Qai'da-Influenced Radicalisation: A Rapid Evidence Assessment Guided by Situational Action Theory. Home Office Occasional Paper No. 97. www.gov.uk/government/publications/al-qaida-influenced-radicalisation-a-rapid-evidence-assessment
Brantingham, P. L. and Brantingham, P. J. (1981) Notes on the geometry of crime. In *Environmental Criminology*. Beverly Hills, CA: Sage, pp. 27–54.
Brynielsson, J., Horndahl, A., Johansson, F., Kaati, L., Mårtenson, C., and Svenson, P. (2013) Harvesting and analysis of weak signals for detecting lone wolf terrorists. *Security Informatics*, 2(1), 11.
Caplan, B. (2006) Terrorism: The relevance of the rational choice model. *Public Choice*, 128(1), 91–107.
Chermak, S. and Gruenewald, J. A. (2015) Laying a foundation for the criminological examination of right-wing, left-wing, and Al Qaeda-inspired extremism in the United States. *Terrorism and Political Violence*, 27(1), 133–159.
Clarke, R.V. and Felson, M. (eds) (1993) *Routine Activity and Rational Choice*. New Brunswick: Transaction Publishers.
Clarke, R. V. and Newman, G. R. (2006) *Outsmarting the Terrorists*. New York: Praeger.
Clarke, R. V. (2004) Technology, criminology and crime science. *European Journal on Criminal Policy and Research*, 10(1), 55–63.
Cohen, L. E. and Felson, M. (2003) Routine activity theory. *Criminological Theory: Past to Present (Essential Readings)*. Edited by F. Cullen and R. Agnew. Los Angeles, CA: Transaction Publishers, pp. 284–294.
Collins, E. (1998) *Killing Rage*. London: Granta Books.
Cooper, H. H. A. (1978) What is a terrorist: A psychological perspective. *Legal Medicine Quarterly*, 1, 16.
Cornish, D. B. & Clarke, R. V. (1986) *The Reasoning Criminal: Rational Choice Perspectives on Offending*. New York: Springer-Verlag.
Crenshaw, M. (2000) The psychology of terrorism: An agenda for the 21st century. *Political Psychology*, 21(2), 405–420.
Dalgaard-Nielsen, A. (2010) Violent radicalization in Europe: What we know and what we do not know. *Studies in Conflict & Terrorism*, 33(9), 797–814.
Della Porta, D. (1988) Recruitment processes in clandestine political organizations. *International Social Movement Research*, 1, 155–169.
Della Porta, D. (1995) Social movements and the state: Thoughts on the policing of protest. Working Paper, EUI RSC, 1995/13.
Desmarais, S. L., Simons-Rudolph, J., Brugh, C. S., Schilling, E., and Hoggan, C. (2017) The state of scientific knowledge regarding factors associated with terrorism. *Journal of Threat Assessment and Management*, 4(4), 180.
Drake, C. J. (1998) The role of ideology in terrorists' target selection. *Terrorism and Political Violence*, 10(2), 53–85.
Dugan, L., LaFree, G., & Piquero, A. R. (2005) Testing a rational choice model of airline hijackings. *Criminology*, 43(4), 1031–1066.
Dunér, A. and Haglund, B. (1974) Tonårspojkar och brott (Teenage boys and crime.) Utbildningsforskning. SÖ rapport 8. Stockholm: Skolstyrelsen.
Enders, W. and Sandler. T. (1999) Transnational terrorism in the post-Cold War era. *International Studies Quarterly*, 43(1), 145–167.
Enders, W., Sandler, T. and Cauley, J. (1990) Assessing the impact of terrorist- thwarting policies: An intervention time series approach. *Defence Economics*, 2(1), 1–18.
English, R. (2003) *Armed Struggle*. London: Pan.
Fahey, S. and LaFree, G. (2015) Does country-level social disorganization increase terrorist attacks? *Terrorism and Political Violence, 27*(1), 81–111.
Florez-Morris, M. (2010) Why some Colombian guerrilla members stayed in the movement until demobilization: A micro-sociological case study of factors that influenced members' commitment to three former rebel organizations: M-19, EPL, and CRS. *Terrorism and Political Violence*, 22(2), 216–241.
Friedland, N. (1992) *Becoming a Terrorist: Social and Individual Antecedents*. New York: Praeger.
Gill, P., Horgan, J., and Deckert, P. (2014) Bombing alone: Tracing the motivations and antecedent behaviors of lone-actor terrorists. *Journal of Forensic Sciences*, 59(2), 425–435.
Gill, P., Corner, E., Conway, M., Thornton, A., Bloom, M., and Horgan, J. (2017) Terrorist use of the internet by the numbers. *Criminology & Public Policy*, 16(1), 99–117.

Gill, P., Marchment, Z., Corner, E., and Bouhana, N. (2020) Terrorist decision-making in the context of risk, attack planning and attack commission. *Studies in Conflict & Terrorism*, 43(2), 145–170.

Gøtzsche-Astrup, O. (2018) The time for causal designs: Review and evaluation of empirical support for mechanisms of political radicalisation. *Aggression and Violent Behavior*, 39(1), 90–99.

Grossman, D. (2014) *On Killing: The Psychological Cost of Learning to Kill in War and Society*. New York: Open Road Media.

Hoffman, B. (2006) *Inside Terrorism*. New York: Columbia University Press.

Horgan, J. (2003) The search for the terrorist personality. In A. Silke (ed.), *Terrorists, Victims and Society: Psychological Perspectives on Terrorism and its Consequences*. Chichester, West Sussex, UK: John Wiley & Sons, pp. 3–27.

Horgan, J. (2008) From profiles to pathways and roots to routes: Perspectives from psychology on radicalization into terrorism. *The ANNALS of the American Academy of Political and Social Science*, 618(1), 80–94.

Horgan, J. G. (2009) *Walking Away from Terrorism: Accounts of Disengagement from Radical and Extremist Movements*. London: Routledge.

Horgan, J. G. (2015) *The Psychology of Terrorism*. London: Routledge.

Johnson, N. F., Medina, P., Zhao, G., Messinger, D. S., Horgan, J., Gill, P., ... and Manrique, P. (2013) Simple mathematical law benchmarks human confrontations. *Scientific Reports*, 3, 3463.

Jones, M. B., Offord, D. R., and Abrams, N. (1980) Brothers, sisters and antisocial behaviour. *The British Journal of Psychiatry*, 136(2), 139–145.

Kaplan, A. (1978) The psychodynamics of terrorism. *Studies in Conflict & Terrorism*, 1(3–4), 237–254.

Kruglanski, A. W. and Fishman, S. (2009) Psychological factors in terrorism and counterterrorism: Individual, group, and organizational levels of analysis. *Social Issues and Policy Review*, 3(1), 1–44.

LaFree, G., and Dugan, L. (2009) Research on terrorism and countering terrorism. *Crime and Justice*, 38(1), 413–477.

LaFree, G. (2009) Criminology third war-special issue on terrorism and responses to terrorism. *Criminology & Public Policy*, 8, 431.

Leistedt, S. J. (2013) Behavioural aspects of terrorism. *Forensic Science International*, 228(1–3), 21–27.

Loeber, R., Farrington, D. P., Stouthamer-Loeber, M., Moffitt, T. E., and Caspi, A. (1998) The development of male offending: Key findings from the first decade of the Pittsburgh Youth Study. *Studies on Crime & Crime Prevention*, 7(2), 141–171.

Lofland, J., & Stark, R. (1965) Becoming a world-saver: A theory of conversion to a deviant perspective. *American Sociological Review*, 30(6), 862–875.

Maher, S. (2016) *Salafi-Jihadism: The History of an Idea*. Oxford: Oxford University Press.

Manrique, P., Cao, Z., Gabriel, A., Horgan, J., Gill, P., Qi, H., ... and Johnson, N. (2016) Women's connectivity in extreme networks. *Science Advances*, 2(6), e1501742.

Marchment, Z., Gill, P., and Morrison, J. (2019) Risk factors for violent dissident republican incidents in Belfast: A comparison of bombings and bomb hoaxes. *Journal of Quantitative Criminology*, 1–20.

Matsueda, R. L. and Anderson, K. (1998) The dynamics of delinquent peers and delinquent behavior. *Criminology*, 36(2), 269–308.

Matsueda, R. L. (1988) The current state of differential association theory. *Crime & Delinquency*, 34(3), 277–306.

McCauley, C. R. and Segal, M. E. (1987) Social psychology of terrorist groups. *Annual Review of Social and Personality Psychology*.

Moghaddam, F. M. (2005) The staircase to terrorism: A psychological exploration. *American Psychologist*, 60(2), 161.

Morrison, J. F. (2016) Trust in me: Allegiance choices in a post-split terrorist movement. *Aggression and Violent Behavior*, 28, 47–56.

Mullins, S. (2009) Parallels between crime and terrorism: A social psychological perspective. *Studies in Conflict & Terrorism, 32(9*), 811–830.

Mullins, S., and Dolnik, A. (2009) Terrorist networks and small group psychology. *The Faces of Terrorism–Multidisciplinary Perspectives*. Chichester, West Sussex: John Wiley & Sons, pp. 137–150.

Olofsson, B. (1967) *Brottslighet bland skolbarn i Örebro* (*Criminality among School-children in Örebro*). Stockholm: Örebroprojektet.

Olofsson, B. (1971) *Vad var det vi sa! Om kriminellt och konformt beteende bland skolpojkar* (*What Did We Tell You! On Criminal and Conformist Behavior among Schoolboys*). Stockholm: Utbildningsförlaget.

Onnela, J. P., Arbesman, S., González, M. C., Barabási, A. L., and Christakis, N. A. (2011) Geographic constraints on social network groups. *PLoS one*, 6(4), e16939.

Pape, R. (2005) *Dying to Win. The Strategic Logic of Suicide Terrorism*. New York. Random House.

Perry, S., and Hasisi, B. (2015) Rational choice rewards and the jihadist suicide bomber. *Terrorism and Political Violence*, 27(1), 53–80.

Phillips, P. J. and Pohl, G. (2012) Economic profiling of the lone wolf terrorist: Can economics provide behavioral investigative advice? *Journal of Applied Security Research*, 7(2), 151–77.

Phillips, P. J. (2011) Lone wolf terrorism. *Peace Economics, Peace Science and Public Policy*, 17(1), 1–29.

Pisoiu, D. (2015) Subcultural theory applied to jihadi and right-wing radicalization in Germany. *Terrorism and Political Violence*, 27(1), 9–28.

Post, J. M. (2007) Countering Islamist militancy. An epidemiologic approach. *Faith-based Radicalism. Christianity, Islam and Judaism: Between Constructive Activism and Destructive Fanaticism*. Brussel: PIE Peter Lang, pp. 191–206.

Post, J., Sprinzak, E., and Denny, L. (2003) The terrorists in their own words: Interviews with 35 incarcerated Middle Eastern terrorists. *Terrorism and Political Violence*, 15(1), 171–184.

Reiss Jr, A. J. (1988) Co-offending and criminal careers. *Crime and Justice*, 10, 117–170.

Reynolds, S. C. and Hafez, M. M. (2019) Social network analysis of German foreign fighters in Syria and Iraq. *Terrorism and Political Violence*, 31(4), 661–686.

Sageman, M. (2004) *Understanding Terror Networks*. University of Pennsylvania Press.

Sandler, T., Tschirhart, J., and Cauley, J. (1983) A theoretical analysis of transnational terrorism. *American Political Science Review*, 77, 36–54.

Schafer, J. A., Mullins, C. W., and Box, S. (2014) Awakenings: The emergence of white supremacist ideologies. *Deviant Behavior*, 35(3), 173–196.

Schuurman, B. W. (2017) Becoming a European homegrown jihadist: A multilevel analysis of involvement in the Dutch Hofstadgroup, 2002–2005 (Doctoral dissertation).

Schuurman, B. (2018) Research on terrorism, 2007–2016: A review of data, methods, and authorship. *Terrorism and Political Violence*, 1–16.

Shaw, E. D. (1986) Political terrorists: Dangers of diagnosis and an alternative to the psychopathology model. *International Journal of Law and Psychiatry*, 8(3), 359–368.

Shechory, M., and Laufer, A. (2011) Ideological delinquency: Gender differences among Israeli youth during the withdrawal from the Gaza Strip. *International Journal of Offender Therapy and Comparative Criminology*, 55(2), 326–343.

Silke, A. (2001) The devil you know: continuing problems with research on terrorism. *Terrorism and Political Violence*, 13, 1–14.

Silke, A. (2003) Terrorists, victims and society. *Psychological Perspectives on Terrorism and its Consequences*. London: Wiley.

Simon, H. A. (1957) *Models of Man, Social and Rational: Mathematical Essays on Rational Human Behavior in a Social Setting*. New York: John Wiley and Sons.

Simon, H. A. (1986) Rationality in psychology and economics. *Journal of Business*, 59(4), 209–224.

Tayebi, M. A., Frank, R., and Glässer, U. (2012) Understanding the link between social and spatial distance in the crime world. In *Proceedings of the 20th International Conference on Advances in Geographic Information Systems*. ACM, pp. 550–553.

Taylor, M., and Horgan, J. (2006) A conceptual framework for addressing psychological process in the development of the terrorist. *Terrorism and Political Violence*, 18(4), 585–601.

Tilly, C. (2003) *The Politics of Collective Violence*. Cambridge, UK: Cambridge University Press.

Tracy, P. E., and Kempf-Leonard, K. (1996) *Continuity and Discontinuity in Criminal Careers*. London: Springer Science & Business Media.

Ward, M. (1998) *Barn och Brott av vår tid?* Självdeklarerad Ungdomsbrottslighet

Warr, M. (1996) Organization and instigation in delinquent groups. *Criminology*, 34(1), 11–37.

9

LEGAL AND SECURITY FRAMEWORKS FOR RESPONDING TO ONLINE VIOLENT EXTREMISM

A comparison of far-right and jihadist contexts

Imogen Richards and Mark Wood

Introduction

In recent years, there has been an intensification of international extremist violence linked in varying degrees to internet-facilitated radicalization. This has related to, among other things, a growth in prevalence of politically violent actors, including "far-right" and "jihadist" collectives, societal responses to deleterious political-economic conditions in the aftermath of the 2008 Global Financial Crisis (GFC), and a mass displacement of people from North Africa and the Middle East, often termed, pejoratively, a "migrant crisis". Extreme political polarization, sometimes termed the "hyper-tribalism" of those with extreme views, has also been reinforced by these entities' participation in social media. While some argue that this is facilitated by the architectures of social media platforms, which comprise "bubble bias" algorithms, and the re-mediating functions of "likes", "shares" and "re-tweets" (Sunstein, 2007; Pariser, 2011), others assert that hate speech and violence online is overwhelming correlated with and caused by offline political and economic conditions.

Drawing from examples of theory and data related to online and offline activity, this chapter reflects, first, on characteristics of social media that can be perceived to support violent extremism, and, second, on legislation and technology that has been developed to prevent and counter online violent extremist expression. It combines a discussion of hate speech laws and broader counter-violent extremist (CVE) measures with insights from media and criminological theory to identify matters in relation to contemporary violent extremism that have, to this point, been under-explored and under-addressed. With a synoptic perspective on international measures that have been adopted to counter violent extremist expression, this chapter proposes a comparative legal, technological, and policy-oriented approach for addressing different forms of extremism in far-right and jihadist contexts.

Our discussion initially reflects on trends in contemporary violent extremism, concentrating on jihadist and far-right examples. Drawing on Goldsmith and Brewer (2015) and Wood (2017a), it then outlines a brief theoretical framework for understanding the role that technology may play in amplifying collective extremist sentiments that can lead to discrimination, violence, and acts of terrorism. Following this, we elaborate a critique of current CVE policies and debates, arguing that certain measures not only have been counterproductive in their efficacy, but also have the potential to perpetuate political violence by promoting civil disunity in targeting 'suspect communities'. Finally, we review select national legislation designed to address hate speech, highlighting the disparity between laws that might be applied to target far-right activity, relative to CVE measures that often target jihadism.

Trends in jihadism and far-right extremism: the role of the internet

Two major trends relevant to this discussion are a rise in prevalence of far-right extremism leading to violence in Western countries, and the enduring importance of the internet for certain perpetrators of this violence. To understand the historical background of far-right extremism in comparison with jihadism, it is first necessary to briefly account for developments in jihadism since the commencement of the "Global War on Terrorism" in 2001.

The entity known as Al-Qaeda altered the landscape of global jihadism on 11 September 2001 (9/11) when its followers flew three planes into the Pentagon, in Washington, and the World Trade Center, in New York, killing 2996 people including the 19 hijackers. Following this event, Al-Qaeda then committed attacks under its newly decentralized governance, including bombing: the Sari Nightclub in Bali in 2002, killing 204 people, a Madrid commuter train system in 2004, killing 193 people, and the London Underground in 2005 killing 56 people (Byman, 2015).

The organization Islamic State (IS) descended from Al-Qaeda, and it has perhaps predominated jihadist attacks in Western states over the course of the past decade. Attacks attributed to IS include the bombing of an Ariana Grande music concert in Manchester in 2016, in which 23 people were killed, and a series of bombings and firearm attacks on restaurants and a concert theatre in Paris in which 137 people were killed. The organization also claimed responsibility for attacks on an airport and metro in Brussels in 2015 that caused 35 deaths, as well as a variety of individual firearm, knife, and vehicular attacks in Australia, Germany, Canada, and the United States (US) (Raja, 2019). Most recently, on 21 April 2019, in the aftermath of the events at Christchurch discussed below, IS claimed responsibility for murdering 253 people in Sri Lanka.

The impact of online propaganda and practical advice for the jihadist organizations Al-Qaeda and IS is well recognized, extending to the latter's former control of more than 30 media departments at its height in 2015 (Zelin, 2015), and both organizations' extensive propaganda output via closed websites, and through the social media platforms Twitter, Facebook, Telegram and YouTube. As experts such as Klausen (2015) highlight, online extremist magazines including *Inspire*, *Dabiq* and *Resurgence* also play a particularly important role in cases where individuals are radicalized to jihadist violence primarily through the internet.

While jihadism has therefore received significant international attention since 9/11, researchers at the University of Maryland recently demonstrated that "White extremism" accounted for approximately 8 percent of terrorist attacks in Europe, Australia and North America, and almost a third of those that occurred in the United States between 2011 and 2017 (Cai and Landon, 2019). In 2018, German authorities also revealed that in 2017 there were 950 attacks on mosques and Muslims in Germany (Shalal and Lawson, 2018), while in the US, the Anti-Defamation League (ADL) estimated that 50 people had been killed by far-right terrorists there in 2018 (ADL, 2019). This represents three times the number of people murdered in the US by jihadists during that year, and a 35 percent increase from the number of deaths caused by far-right extremism in 2017.

An international spotlight was cast on a growth of far-right extremism in the West, and the Asia-Pacific region in particular, following the murder of 51 worshippers at two mosques in Christchurch, New Zealand, on 10 March 2019. While the targeting of places of worship in a relatively prosperous, progressive, and peaceable nation by a far-right extremist was deemed significant in this case, so too was the role of internet. The suspect, Australian Brenton Tarrant, "livestreamed" the attack on Facebook, announced his plan on the US-based far-right imageboard 8chan, and published his post-massacre "Great Replacement" manifesto on Twitter. Digital analysis following the attack revealed that Facebook did not censor or flag Tarrant's footage of the shootings as the platform's anti-violence algorithms mistakenly identified his actions for a "first-person shooter" videogame (Roose 2019). Social media analysis of Tarrant's historical activity also revealed that he was formerly involved in the Australian amateur far-right political scene, participating in intergroup rivalry among far-right groups via online discussions and praising the well-known Australian neo-Nazi Blair Cottrell as his 'Emperor' (Mann *et al.*, 2019).

Earlier, on 27 October 2018, a man named Robert Bowers was charged with 63 federal crimes related to a shooting at a Pittsburgh mosque in which 11 people were killed and seven people were injured. In the lead-up to the attack Bowers had first used the online social network platform Gab to post anti-Semitic messages; stating of the Hebrew Immigrant Aid Society (HIAS) just before the attack: "HIAS likes to bring invaders in that kill our people. I can't sit by and watch my people get slaughtered. Screw your optics, I'm going in" (Jones, 2018). Other recent acts of violence perpetrated by individuals promoting far-right ideologies in Western countries have included the murder of UK Labour Party Member of Parliament Jo Cox in 2016 by a white supremacist, a vehicular attack on London's Finsbury Mosque in 2017 in which one person was killed and nine were injured, and a shooting at a Synagogue near San Diego that caused one fatality and three injuries on 27 April 2019. The latter was alleged perpetrated by an 8Chan user known as "JohnTEarnest", who posted a manifesto similar in style and rhetoric to Tarrant's.

In several cases of far-right violence in the West, including explicitly at Christchurch, perpetrators claimed to have been inspired by historical terrorist actors such as Anders Breivik; a Norwegian man who murdered eight people by detonating a bomb in Oslo and shot to death 69 attendants at a youth summer camp on the island on Utoya in 2011. As was the case with recent far-right activity discussed above, Breivik published an online manifesto that explained how he prepared for the attack by playing *World of Warcraft* and *Call of Duty: Modern Warfare*, as "training simulation[s]". Six hours prior to the attack, Breivik also posted a video to YouTube depicting himself as a "Knights Templar" officer, inciting violence toward Muslims, left-wing people, and migrants (Bangstad, 2014).

While Breivik and other far-right actors discussed here were active in and via the internet in the lead-up to their attacks, often communicating with others who endorsed and promoted violent far-right ideologies, little evidence connects these actors to organized "terrorist" networks. For this reason they are often referred to as "lone wolves" who may be deemed "terrorists" but derive no tangible practical support from international politically violent organizations. Like the individual incidences of jihadism mentioned above, they are often analysed in "radicalization" literature that directs attention toward the psychological processes of radicalization rather than the influence of broader, structural and environmental factors (see McCauley and Moskalenko, 2008; Monaghan and Molnar, 2016).

In the context of far-right extremism and jihadism, a growing body of research has thus analysed the role of the internet in contributing to individual radicalization to terrorism, particularly in the context of the contentious "lone-wolf" phenomenon (Weimann, 2012; Koehler, 2014;

Mills *et al.*, 2019). Discussing how the internet and social media may provide a focus for terrorist groups to radicalize, recruit, and train new followers, Weimann (2012, pp. 78–79) notes that the "lone-wolf" moniker is something of a misnomer, arguing: "In nature, wolves do not hunt alone: they hunt in packs. So, too, with the lone-wolf terrorists: there is a virtual pack, a social network, behind them". In line with this reasoning, studies of "lone wolf" terrorism must by necessity entail a reflection on technological and social factors that contribute to an individual's radicalization to violence, aside from their personal or psychological motivations (Ashour, 2010; Halverson and Way, 2012).

Although the internet is often implicated in contemporary cases of violent extremist radicalization, as Holt *et al.* (2015, p. 107) note, "the role of the Internet in radicalising individuals to violent extremist action is much discussed but remains conceptually and empirically unclear". While traditional sociological crime causation theories, such as subcultural and social learning theories, can be useful in explaining contemporary forms of radicalization (see Holt *et al.*, 2017), they are often limited when it comes to explaining the potentially radicalizing impact of networked computational technologies. They are, in this sense, comparatively *technology-blind theories*. While social learning theory in particular acknowledges that radicalization to terrorism can occur through a variety of media, neither social learning nor subcultural approaches can explain how different media itself might shape the formation of commitments to particular attitudes and practices in the radicalization process.

One such theory that has the potential to address the criminogenic impact of online technologies themselves is Wood's (2017a; 2017b) theory of algorithmic deviancy amplification. This theory attempts to explain the role of personalization algorithms in sustaining and potentially reinforcing attitudes and beliefs that are conducive to crime. In its original conceptualization, Wood's theory focused on how the personalization of News Feeds as adaptive informational environments may promote criminogenic positive feedback loops of information consumption. The original formulation of algorithmic deviancy amplification, in other words, did not attend to the process by which individuals may drift into crime through internet encounters. Rather, the theory presupposed a human actor who was already linked into criminalized networks and content.

Wood's (2017a) theory of algorithmic deviancy amplification might, in this context, be amended to account for the possibility that what we term "algorithmic drift" operates coterminously with criminogenic filter bubbles to meaningfully influence individuals' radicalization into acts of violence; supported online via collective communities such as that which exists on 8Chan. Where criminogenic filter bubbles denote the process by which a human actor comes to *increasingly* occupy an information environment that promotes violence or terrorism, we might also think of "algorithmic drift" as the process through which an internet user *begins* to view more radical material as a result of a site's algorithmic recommendations. Algorithmic drift, in other words, represents one of the potential processes underpinning what Goldsmith and Brewer (2015) have termed digital drift: the process by which individuals "drift" into deviance and criminality online, in part as a result of the specific affordances and architecture of the internet (Goldsmith and Wall, 2019). Herein, the concept may be deployed to understand, for instance, the now often recognized right-wing YouTube "conspiracy train". More broadly it can account for personalization algorithms, closed social systems, and filter bubbles, collectively creating positive feedback loops that reinforce violent extremist messages.

Unlike technology-blind theories of radicalization, Wood's and Goldsmith and Brewer's theories emphasize what Castells (2009) refers to as programming power: the ability to not only direct ideas through existing networks, but also to engineer new networks entirely. While the role of the internet in jihadist networking and radicalization has long been noted, this aspect of the theory is particularly salient in contemporary far-right contexts given evidence of extensive cross-fertilization of the contemporary far-right on a cross-national scale. Further to the aforementioned cases, for example, through a large scale Twitter analysis, Davey and Ebner (2017) highlight extensive reciprocal support, through "likes", "shares" and "retweets", between members of the far-right European organization Generation Identity, and participants in the notorious white supremacist protest in Charlottesville, for their respective offline violent activities in 2016 and 2017.

International counter-violent extremism policies and debates

As with theories to explain radicalization, certain CVE measures, potentially informed by these theories, often foreground human factors over the technological, while they also disproportionately target "lone wolf" individuals suspected of involvement in jihadism over other types of extremism. A review of existing research and commentary on contemporary CVE measures reveals various characteristics of these measures that have the potential to undermine civil and human rights, and potentially reinforce the social divides and criminogenic conditions that fuel individuals' engagement in violence.

There have been a number of different measures applied at both the transnational and local level to counter violent extremism, sometimes extending to hate speech online. As Conway and Walker (2015) highlight, CVE activities prosecuted at a local level by state actors, and also sometimes by transnational organizations, may be conceptualized as "positive and negative" measures. Where "positive" here denotes digital engagement, education, and counter-narratives, negative measures are "the deletion or restriction of violent extremist" content online or "the legal sanctioning of its online purveyors or users" (Conway and Walker, 2015, p. 156).

Notwithstanding freedom of speech arguments, non-state negative measures such as the widespread takedown of terrorism-related material in Twitter's mass censorship of IS content in 2014 (Conway *et al.*, 2018), have been relatively politically uncontentious. State-based negative measures, however, often draw significant international criticism for their sometimes erroneous targeting of innocent individuals rather than politically violent networks or collectives. One recent controversial development was the passage of a 2019 UK Counter-terrorism and Border Security Act, which criminalizes expressing views favourable to terrorist organizations and viewing terrorist material online, creating what has been described as a "click offence". As the outgoing independent reviewer of terrorism legislation, Max Hill QC, who has previously been conservative in his views on the issue asserted in opposition to the bill, "a principled boundary line as to the legitimate usage of criminal law is being crossed" (Edwards, 2018).

Prior to the 2019 Act, UK laws pertaining to the possession of violent extremist online material within the context of the "Prevent" policy agenda had in fact long been criticized for their potential to target reporters and researchers; including as occurred in the case of a Nottingham University student, Rizwaan Sabir (Conway and Walker, 2015), who is now a lecturer at Liverpool John Moores University. Moreover, as Philip Edwards (2018) revealed, between 2006 and 2016, 155 counter-terrorist prosecutions in the UK were successfully brought, involving 391 separate charges, while every one of the offences for which the accused were found guilty were precursor offences. Further demonstrating the country's historical targeting of suspected jihadists over other violent extremists, Edwards provides the example of Hassan Tabbakh, who received a seven-year prison sentence for preparing acts of terrorism on the grounds of possessing chemicals with the intention of making bombs, though he did not have a detonator, while Ryan McGee, a then serving soldier and English Defence League supporter, who kept a home-made bomb with a detonator in his bedroom, received a two-year sentence.

In fact, between 2014 and 2016, in the context and aftermath of IS-inspired and directed attacks, 14 of 28 European Union (EU) member states introduced extensive and expansive new counterterrorist legislation. As noted in an Amnesty International (2017) report, a third of the more than 385 people prosecuted and sentenced for "apologizing for terrorism" in France in 2015, typically for their online activity, were under the age of 18.

Given the often contentious nature of negative measures such as sanctions, positive measures including counternarratives have also been trialled by governments and civil organizations for CVE. On the part of governments, however, these too were often met with criticism. Perhaps the most notorious and contentious counternarrative example was the Center for Strategic Communication's "Think Again Turn Away" campaign, run by the US Department of State (Brown, 2014). While the campaign sought to target individual viewers of extremist material rather than collective violent networks, it was criticized for legitimizing terrorist acts and actors by drawing attention to them, making gross mistakes in the propagandized conflation of actors and organizations as disparate as the Al-Qaeda leaders and the leader of the IS, and for engaging in embarrassing 'tit-for-tat' arguments (Edelman, 2014). Elsewhere the campaign was opposed given its exclusive targeting of violent jihadism despite extensive extreme far-right online activity and gun violence in the US. Related arguments have also recently addressed the US Donald Trump administration after its 2016 defunding of all national CVE programmes except those that target "Islamic extremism" (Hughes and Ingram, 2019).

Indicating the similar orientation of recent historical Australian CVE measures, of the 41 community organizations in Australia funded in 2014–2015 with approximately $2 million dollars from the government as a part of its "one-off" CVE grants programme, only 15 were named. Of these, seven were generalist in nature, while eight were related to migrants, refugees, and culturally and linguistically diverse populations, including Arabic schools and community centres in majority-Muslim residential areas (Australian Government, 2017). Although following the attacks in Christchurch in April 2019, a spokesperson for Australia's Department of Home Affairs told reporters that the federal government had allocated more than $53 million to countering violent extremism (CVE) programmes since 2013–2014, including more than $13 million for intervention programmes, these efforts significantly focused on jihadism. Moreover, as Hardy (2018) highlights, overall funding for *community-based* CVE in Australia has in the last five years been significantly reduced by successive governments in the lead-up to the establishment of the Home Affairs Department in 2017, at which time all funding for these programmes appeared to come to an end. In the 2018/2019 federal budget, although AUD$158 million was allocated for the "National Security and Criminal Justice" programme, the budget line dedicated to CVE was removed; potentially indicating that the majority of future funding would go toward counter-terrorism intelligence and policing rather than prevention (Hardy, 2018).

Despite efforts in the US and Australia to reduce funding for community-led CVE initiatives, and existing measures internationally to target primarily jihadism, as Davies *et al.* (2016) observed, counternarratives run by non-government organizations (NGOs) and other civil organizations that target both far-right extremism and jihadism have been relatively successful. According to Davies and his co-authors' analysis, this is due to their integration of clear, realistic and compelling missions, cultural and public legitimacy, the prospect of success and progress, consistency, and contextualization within broader communication plans that take account of social psychological factors, including collective notions of "identity". Examples they highlight include CVE programmes run by Cases Against Violent Extremism, Against Violent Extremism, Exit White Power, Muflehan, and the Southern Poverty Law Center. One particularly illustrative case was the collective initiative run out of the UK and Western Europe, "Open Letter to Our Sons and Daughters in Syria and Iraq", in which parents of potential foreign fighters for the IS organization were encouraged through family discussion of religious scripture to desist from travelling abroad and participating in violence.

While these and other such messaging efforts may be effective in addressing individual behaviour in a national context, they perhaps have limited utility in dealing with online, transnational far-right collectives. This is, in part, because far-right political agendas often reflect and are protected by cultural biases of the socio-cultural context in which they emerge. Furthermore, as Banks (2010) highlights, national campaigns and legislation to counter cross-border hate speech are often limited, given that US First Amendment commitments to free speech have undermined European and other multilateral efforts to regulate the internet. This occurs due to the peripatetic nature of hate sites, whereby platforms regularly shift from one location to another, while administrators can move the hosting server of their site to locations such as the US with lenient policies governing online extremist expression.

Highlighting the shortcomings of CVE and counter-hate speech laws applied in isolation, Blaya (2018) promotes holistic and integrated legal, technological, and educational intervention programmes to counter violent extremism and hate speech online. Reflecting an awareness of the algorithmic factors we highlight, Blaya argues that a centripetal EU framework, national compliance with this framework, and integrated 'automated' approaches that use the capacities of the internet for preventing as well as facilitating extremism, are all necessary for preventative CVE measures to be effective. From a holistic perspective, Bliuc *et al.*'s (2018) research is also relevant. Drawing from the work of critical media theorists, these researchers argue that along with technology-centred CVE approaches, it is necessary to consider first that race and racism may in fact be embedded in the structure of the internet, while certain types of "psychosocial conditioning" that occur online via engagement with this architecture facilitate the dehumanization and psychological essentialism that is often precursory to violence (see also Haslam *et al.*, 2000; Holtz and Wagner, 2009).

With regard to our argument that hate speech might be conceptualized more often and more consistently as precursory to violence, others have emphasized that new legislation, introduced under the aegis of preventing hate speech online, may be ineffectual given its targeting for surveillance and securitization of suspected terrorist organizations, rather than entailing a broad-based aim of protecting the rights of individuals. In one example, Jubany and Roiha (2015) highlight that legislation to render companies such as Google and Facebook "accomplices" in the crime of hate speech, introduced in France after 2015 by the Francois Hollande government, often targeted "suspect communities" rather than seeking to protect the individual rights of potential hate speech victims. We further stress in this context that, by historically focusing largely on jihadism, these measures potentially create and reinforce discriminatory political environments in which violent extremism thrives.

While there are therefore limits to the utility of national frameworks that seek to counter hate speech in the context of broader CVE campaigns, and America's record of non-compliance often hinders cross-national efforts, there have been a number of relatively successful international CVE cases led by technology corporations. Further to the above-mentioned takedown of IS media on Twitter in 2014, another relatively impactful measure in which hate speech and other terrorism-related content were addressed within the same policy framework was an agreement between Facebook, Microsoft, Twitter and YouTube and the European Commission to remove speech that contravened the platforms' terms of service agreement within 24 hours of its publication. The Commission found in 2019 for instance that 72 per cent of content deemed "illegal hate speech" is removed from these platforms within 24 hours, while 89 per cent of flagged content is reviewed (European Commission, 2019). The agreement was created in the aftermath of the IS attacks in Brussels and Paris in 2015, following which EU watchdogs chastised multinationals for failing to challenge and remove violent extremist content on their platforms, and threatened to impose blanket censorship. A UK Home Affairs Committee report in 2016 stated: "social media companies are consciously failing to combat the use of their sites to promote terrorism and killings" (Price, 2016). Proponents of the measure argue that it provides for cross-border enforcement, that technological expertise to address internet-facilitated radicalization in the national sector is lacking, and that there are otherwise discrepancies in levels of scrutiny viewing extremist content across different national governments.

In a counter-argument, Gan (2017) provided a detailed account of "the Code", synthesizing a number of key concerns for users. These include that it delegates responsibility to private corporations to act as policy-makers, law enforcement, and judicial officers in countering violent extremism and hate speech, whereas these roles should rather be reserved for democratically elected and accountable officials. According to Gan (2017), the Code also reflects a trend in the ongoing empowerment of private multinational and transnational corporations to lead governance initiatives, including growing influence in EU policy-making, and enhanced responsibility for their own regulation. As a soft law instrument, the Commission stated that the Code is intended to serve as a set of guidelines to assist technology companies in enforcing existing laws. As Gan shows, however, interpretations of the Code by these companies take precedence over legal frameworks. The companies thus act as law enforcement, while users increasingly report to Facebook as they would formerly report to police. In this context a company's terms of service agreement would determine the basis on which they would choose to censor suspected hate-filled or extremist material. Unlike a traditional system of law, however, the Code does not allow for a formal appeals process wherein censorship decisions might be reviewed by an autonomous third party. Other concerns cited by Gan include that the corporations cannot effectively act "as both the regulated and the regulator", that corporations are typically motivated by profit, and that they are therefore likely to undertake pre-emptive and overly prohibitive censorship in order to stave off regulation and gain favour with prospective advertisers. Similarly, Coyer (2017) cites a risk that the Code might constitute a form of "state interference by proxy" under the European Charter on Fundamental Rights (see also Citron, 2017; Huszti-Orban, 2018).

Conversely, endorsing the potential utility of transnational soft law approaches such as the Code, techno-optimists including Cohen-Almagor (2017) highlight the potential for these measures to be effectively combined in CVE efforts with software functions. Similarly, Greenberg (2016) argues that logistical issues with counternarratives and counter-messages, including their targeting of individuals over networks and unclear metrics of success, may be offset by blended human–machine approaches, such as the removal of hate-filled content combined with Google's diversion of search terms. As with other CVE measures though, these efforts have historically targeted jihadism over far-right extremism, while they are often orchestrated by governments with guidance from organizations such as the Council on American and Islamic Relations. Moreover, as Pasquale (2010) emphasized regarding search term diversions, Google's long-held secrecy about its algorithms under the justification of trade secrecy protection carries the potential to interfere with network neutrality regulation in undesirable ways.

National hate speech laws

Relative to international CVE measures that primarily target individuals suspected of involvement in jihadism, Australian and international legislation preventing other examples of online hate speech has been less extensive and aggressive. In the context and aftermath of Christchurch, it is relevant that, within an international scopus of online hate speech prevention, Australia has been recognized as among the least proactive of developed Western nations (Gelber and McNamara, 2016). Although signatory to the International Convention on All Forms of Racial Discrimination, and International Covenant on Civil and Political Rights (ICCPR), for instance, the Australian government sought exemptions to Articles 4 and 20 of the relevant statutes, which collectively require states to criminalize the "dissemination of ideas based on racial superiority or hatred" (UNHCR, 2019). In doing so it cited a perceived disproportionality of criminal penalties relative to the injury produced by hate speech, and the potential for criminalization of hate speech to undermine "freedom of expression" (Gelber and McNamara, 2015).

As yet there are no federal statutes in Australia that criminalize online racial, religious, or other discrimination. Rather, in line with the 1975 Australian Racial Discrimination Act, it is

> unlawful for a person to do an act, otherwise than in private, if the act is reasonably likely, in all the circumstances, to offend, insult, humiliate or intimidate another person or a group of people; and the act is done because of the race, colour or national or ethnic origin of the other person, or of some or all of the people in the group.

While Section 474.17 of the Criminal Code Act of 1995 criminalizes using a carriage service such as the internet to communicate hate speech, in this provision, hate speech is only a criminally indictable offence in Australia if the speech also entails an element of threat or harassment. If this criterion is met, the person with the complaint, typically those subject to the abuse, must bring the case to the Human Rights Commission, who would then try to arbitrate the matter. If it remains unresolved, the complainant has recourse to take the matter to the Federal Court or the Federal Magistrates Service. In this context it is also relevant that, before his election to office in 2013, and then again from 2014 to 2016, former Prime Minister Tony Abbott campaigned with Liberal Party members to repeal the words 'offend' and 'insult' from Australia's 1975 Racial Discrimination Act; changes that, had they come into effect, would have made existing hate speech laws effectively unenforceable (see Gelber, 2018).

While discriminatory political expression in the US has various defences related to the country's "free speech" constitutional protections, relative to Australia, the UK and Canada have created federal criminal offences to address serious cases of hate speech. It should also be noted, on the other hand, that "incitement" provisions of Article 20(2) of the ICCPR for prosecuting racial or religious hatred to which the UK is signatory have been recognized as restrictive; particular in their national contexts. Furthermore, as Collingwood and Broadbent (2015) highlight, the gap between the criminal threshold and (what is otherwise) virtually no regulation is significant, and as such, it may be appropriate to establish a civil offence underpinned by statute to deal specifically with incidents of hate speech on social media. As Brown (2018) also revealed, existing laws governing hate speech are out of date in the UK given new discursive expressions of hate, and, in line with our recommendations, they inadequately reflect new affordances for communication provided by the contemporary internet. While Canada's legal regulation of online hate speech is also beset by these same issues, the country's Criminal Code Act of 1985 furthermore prohibitively requires that the prosecution prove that the offender "[incited] hatred against any identifiable group where such incitement is likely to lead to a breach of the peace" (see Coyne, 2012).

Despite the often contentious nature of laws regulating hate speech in light of potential threats to free speech, there is evidence to support their use in reducing the prevalence and reception of offensive and abusive material that may be precursory to extremist violence. Hawdon *et al.* (2017) found, for example, that rates of exposure to online hate speech shared a negative correlation with the restrictiveness of online hate speech laws in the US, relative to

Finland, the UK, and Germany. Through reference to the range of hate speech laws in these countries, and drawing on large cross-national survey data, Hawdon and his co-authors argue that more restrictive laws in effect "serve as a source of guardianship that protects people from such material" (Hawdon *et al.*, 2017, 9).

Concluding comments

When reflecting on CVE policies and frameworks in relation to laws that prevent hate speech online, and prominent global developments in contemporary political violence, this chapter has put forward a series of interrelated suggestions. It has argued that while far-right violence internationally is on the rise, a theory of collective violence such as "algorithmic drift" may be useful in explaining one part of the enduring importance of the internet for such violence, and connective threads between online expressions of hate speech and offline incidence of terrorism or violence. Given far-right and jihadist extremists' mutual engagement with contemporary online environments, as well as their shared experience of certain online and offline political conditions, we further make the case that these different forms of political violence should be examined from a comparative perspective.

Our review and discussion revealed that, not only are the technologized aspects of online radicalization to violence often overlooked by the theories and frameworks that inform CVE measures, these measures often target jihadism, while they are significantly more restrictive than legal counter-hate speech measures that might be used to address far-right extremist expression. Indeed a policy trend of casting violent far-right speech not as precursory to terrorism or sometimes even as political has been historically persistent. In the West this has perhaps been in part because the political ideologies in question derive from historically (neo-)colonial or imperialist host societies. In a notorious example of such "white washing", there was a concerted effort on the part of political and news media to retrospectively depict the infamous mass shooting at Colombine High School in Colorado in 1999 as unrelated to far-right extremism, despite the fact that diary entries by the shooters indicate their inspiration from Timothy McVeigh and the Oklahoma City bombings in 1995, and the fact that they deliberately staged the shooting on the anniversary of Adolf Hitler's birthday. Also similar to Breivik, Tarrant, and Bowers, prior to their massacre, the perpetrators of Colombine played first-person shooter games in a closed online network and here joked with a social network about murdering their parents and friends.

Where ADL research in 2019 revealed that 71 per cent of the 387 "extremist related" fatalities in the US from 2008 to 2017 were committed by far-right and white supremacist groups, and "Islamic extremists" were responsible for a significantly lesser 26 per cent (Cullen, 2019), those living in Western societies may become less tolerant of far-right hate speech. From our perspective, it is necessary in this context to critically reflect on the shared technological environments that facilitate politically violent collectives, while also considering the impact of disparate policy approaches to counter online far-right hate speech, relative to CVE measures that primarily target jihadism.

References

ADL (2019) Right-wing extremism linked to every 2018 extremist murder in the U.S., ADL finds. *ADL: Fighting Hate for Good*, www.adl.org/news/press-releases/right-wing-extremism-linked-to-every-2018-extremist-murder-in-the-us-adl-finds

Amnesty International (2017) EU: Orwellian counter-terrorism laws stripping rights under guise of defending them. *Amnesty*, www.amnesty.org/en/latest/news/2017/01/eu-orwellian-counter-terrorism-laws-stripping-rights-under-guise-of-defending-them/

Ashour, O. (2010) Online de-radicalization? Countering violent extremist narratives: Message, messenger and media strategy. *Perspectives on Terrorism*, 4(6), 15–19.
Australian Criminal Code Act 1995, www.legislation.gov.au/Details/C2017C00235
Australian Government (2017) Update on Australian Government measures counter violent extremism: A quick guide. *Parliament of Australia*, www.aph.gov.au/About_Parliament/Parliamentary_Departments/Parliamentaryto_Library/pubs/rp/rp1718/Quick_Guides/CounterViolentExtremism
Bangstad, S. (2014) *Anders Breivik and the Rise of Islamophobia*. New York: Zed Books.
Banks, J. (2010) Regulating hate speech online. *International Review of Law, Computers and Technology*, 24(3), 233–239.
Blaya, C. (2018) Cyberhate: A review and content analysis of intervention strategies. *Aggression and Violent Behavior*, https://doi.org/10.1016/j.avb.2018.05.006
Bliuc, A, Faulkner, N., Jakubowicz, A., and McGarty, C. (2018) Online networks of racial hate: A systematic review of 10 years of research on cyber-racism. *Computers in Human Behavior*, 87, 75–86.
Brown, A. (2018) What is so special about online (as compared to offline) hate speech? *Ethnicities*, 18(3), 297–326.
Brown, H. (2014) Meet the State Department team trying to troll ISIS into oblivion. *Think Progress*, 18 September, http://thinkprogress.org/world/2014/09/18/3568366/think-again-turn-away/
Byman, D. (2015) *Al Qaeda, the Islamic State, and the Global Jihadist Movement: What Everyone Needs to Know*. New York: Oxford University Press.
Cai, W. and Landon, S. (2019) Attacks by white extremists are growing. So are their connections. *The New York Times*, 3 April, www.nytimes.com/interactive/2019/04/03/world/white-extremist-terrorism-christchurch.html?fbclid=IwAR1tDZdL4FeO1gqonH1njT7HKlMiIRDDrrdgFtcsIUhPbhGxnTAQMlIoI4E
Castells, M. (2009) *Communication Power*. New York: Oxford University Press.
Citron, D. (2017) Extremist speech, compelled conformity, and censorship creep. *Notre Dame Law Review*, 93(3), 1035–1071.
Cobain, I., Parveen, N., and Taylor, M. (2016) The slow burning hatred that led Thomas Mair to murder Jo Cox. *Guardian*, 23 November, www.theguardian.com/uk-news/2016/nov/23/thomas-mair-slow-burning-hatred-led-to-jo-cox-murder
Cohen-Almagor, R. (2017) The role of internet intermediaries in tackling terrorism online. *Fordham Law Review*, 86, 425–453.
Collingwood, L. and Broadbent, G. (2015) Offending and being offended online: Vile messages, jokes and the law. *Computer Law & Security Review*, 31(6), 763–772.
Conway, M. and Walker, C. (2015) Online terrorism and online laws. *Dynamics of Asymmetric Conflict*, 8(2), 156–175.
Conway, M., Khawaja, M., Lakhani, S., Reffin, J., Robertson, A., and Weir, D. (2018) Disrupting Daesh: Measuring takedown of online terrorist material and its impacts. *Studies in Conflict & Terrorism*, 1–20.
Coyer, K. (2017) State power and extremism in Europe: The uneasy relationship between governments and social media companies. In *Perspectives on Harmful Speech Online*, 24–27, https://dangerousspeech.org/wp-content/uploads/2017/08/2017-08_harmfulspeech.pdf#page=24
Coyne, A. (2012) Why does Canada still have a hate speech law? Canada.com, 9 July, https://o.canada.com/news/coyne-why-does-canada-still-have-a-hate-speech-law
Cullen, T. (2019) The grave threats of white supremacy and far-right extremism. *The New York Times*, 22 February, www.nytimes.com/2019/02/22/opinion/christopher-hasson-extremism.html
Davey, J. and Ebner, J. (2017) *The Fringe Insurgency: Connectivity, Convergence and Mainstreaming of the Extreme Right*. London: Institute for Strategic Dialogue.
Davey, J., Saltman, E., and Birdwell, J. (2018) The mainstreaming of far-right extremism online and how to counter it: A case study on UK, US and French elections. In L. Herman and J. Muldoon (eds), *Trumping the Mainstream: The Conquest of Democratic Politics by the Populist Radical Right*. London: Routledge, pp. 37–67.
Davies, G., Neudecker, C., Oullet, M., Bouchard, M., and Ducol, B. (2016) Toward a framework understanding of online programs for countering violent extremism. *Journal for Deradalization*, 6, 51–86.
Edelman, A. (2014) State Department's "embarrassing" "Think Again Turn Away" Twitter campaign could actually legitimize terrorists: expert. *Daily News*, 16 September, www.nydailynews.com/news/politics/state-department-embarrassing-turn-twitter-campaign-legitimizes-terrorists-expert-article-1.1941990
Edwards, P. (2018) Britain's new counter-terrorism legislation will undermine the rule of law even further. *The Conversation*, 29 October, https://theconversation.com/britains-new-counter-terrorism-legislation-will-undermine-the-rule-of-law-even-further-102871

European Commission (2019) Countering illegal hate speech online. 5 February, *European Commission*, https://ec.europa.eu/commission/news/countering-illegal-hate-speech-online-2019-feb-04_en

Gan, H. (2017) Corporations: The regulated or the regulators – the role of IT companies in tackling online hate speech in the EU. *Columbia Journal of European Law*, 24. 111–155.

Gelber, K. (2018) Free speech is under attack, and not in the way racists and bigots claim. *Green Left Weekly*, https://search.informit.com.au/documentSummary;dn=853587803879201;res=IELHSS

Gelber, K. and McNamara, L. (2015) The effects of civil hate speech laws: Lessons from Australia. *Law & Society Review*, 49(3), 631–664.

Gelber, K. and McNamara, L. (2016) Evidencing the harms of hate speech. *Social Identities*, 22(3), 324–341.

Goldsmith, A. and Brewer, R. (2015) Digital drift and the criminal interaction order. *Theoretical Criminology*, 19(1), 112–130.

Goldsmith, A. and Wall, D. S. (2019) The seductions of cybercrime: Adolescence and the thrills of digital transgression. *European Journal of Criminology*, DOI: 1477370819887305.

Greenberg, K. (2016) Counter-radicalization via the Internet. *The ANNALS of the American Academy of Political and Social Science*, 668(1), 165–179.

Halverson, J. and Way, A. (2012) The curious case of Colleen LaRose: Social margins, new media, and online radicalization. *Media, War & Conflict*, 5(2), 139–153.

Hardy, K. (2018) How the Australian government is failing on countering violent extremism. *The Conversation*, 16 October, https://theconversation.com/how-the-australian-government-is-failing-on-countering-violent-extremism-104565

Haslam, N., Rothschild, L., and Ernst, D. (2000) Essentialist beliefs about social categories. *British Journal of Social Psychology*, 39, 113–127.

Hawdon, J., Oksanen, A., and Räsänen, P. (2017) Exposure to online hate in four nations: A cross-national consideration. *Deviant Behavior*, 38(3), 254–266.

Holt, T., Freilich, J., and Chermak, S. (2017) Internet-based radicalization as enculturation to violent deviant subcultures. *Deviant Behavior*, 38(8), 855–869.

Holt, T., Freilich, J., Chermak, S., and McCauley, C. (2015) Political radicalization on the internet: Extremist content, government control, and the power of victim and jihad videos. *Dynamics of Asymmetric Conflict*, 8(2), 107–120.

Holtz, P. and Wagner, P. (2009) Essentialism and attribution of monstrosity in racist discourse: Right-wing Internet postings about Africans and Jews. *Journal of Community & Applied Social Psychology*, 19, 411–425.

Hughes, S. and Ingram, H. (2019) Trump's domestic countering violent extremism policies look a lot like Obama's, *Lawfare*, www.lawfareblog.com/trumps-domestic-countering-violent-extremism-policies-look-lot-obamas

Huszti-Orban, K. (2018) Internet intermediaries and counter-terrorism: Between self-regulation and outsourcing law enforcement. In *2018 10th International Conference on Cyber Conflict (CyCon)*, IEEE, pp. 227–244.

Jones, S. (2018) The rise of far-right extremism in the United States. *Center for Strategic & International Studies*, 7 November, www.csis.org/analysis/rise-far-right-extremism-united-states

Jubany, O. and Roiha, M. (2015) Backgrounds, experiences and responses to online hate speech: A comparative cross-country analysis. *Prism Clic Bang! Words Are Weapons. Preventing, Redressing & Inhibiting Hate Speech in New Media*, Universitat de Barcelona.

Klausen, J. (2015) Tweeting the Jihad: Social media networks of Western foreign fighters in Syria and Iraq. *Studies in Conflict and Terrorism*, 38(1), 1–22.

Koehler, D. (2014) The radical online: Individual radicalization processes and the role of the Internet. *Journal for Deradicalization*, 1, 116–134.

Mann, A., Nguyen, K., and Gregory, K. (2019) Christchurch shooting accused Brenton Tarrant supports Australian far-right figure Blair Cottrell. *ABC*, 23 March, www.abc.net.au/news/2019-03-23/christchurch-shooting-accused-praised-blair-cottrell/10930632

McCauley, C. and Moskalenko, S. (2008) Mechanisms of political radicalization: pathways toward terrorism. *Terrorism and Political Violence*, 20(3), 415–433.

Mills, C., Freilich, J., Chermak, S., Holt, T., and LaFree, G. (2019) Social learning and social control in the off-and online pathways to hate crime and terrorist violence. *Studies in Conflict and Terrorism*, DOI: 10.1080/1057610X.2019.1585628. pp. 1–29.

Monaghan, J. and Molnar, A. (2016) Radicalisation theories, policing practices, and 'the future of terrorism'? *Critical Studies on Terrorism*, 9(3), 393–413.

Pariser, E. (2011) *The Filter Bubble: What the Internet is Hiding from You*. London: Penguin.
Pasquale, F. (2010) Beyond innovation and competition: The need for qualified transparency in internet intermediaries. *Northwestern University School of Law Review*, 104(1), 105–174.
Price, R. (2016) Politicians are accusing Facebook and Twitter of "consciously failing" to tackle terrorism. *Pedestrian*, 25 August, www.businessinsider.com.au/mps-facebook-twitter-youtube-consciously-failing-extremism-terrorism-2016-8?r=US&IR=T
Racial Discrimination Act 1975, www.legislation.gov.au/Details/C2016C00089
Raja, M. (2019) *ISIS: Ideology, Symbolics, and Counter Narratives*. London: Routledge.
Roose, K. (2019) A mass murder of, and for, the Internet. *The New York Times*, 15 March, www.nytimes.com/2019/03/15/technology/facebook-youtube-christchurch-shooting.html
Shalal, A. and Lawson, H. (2018) At least 950 attacks on Muslims reported in Germany in 2017: Report. *Reuters*, 3 March, www.reuters.com/article/us-germany-crime-islam/at-least-950-attacks-on-muslims-reported-in-germany-in-2017-report-idUSKCN1GE2V3
Sunstein, C. (2009) *Going to Extremes: How Like Minds Unite and Divide*. Oxford: Oxford University Press.
UNHCR (2019) *International Convention on the Elimination of All Forms of Racial Discrimination*. www.ohchr.org/en/professionalinterest/pages/cerd.aspx
Weimann, G. (2012) Lone wolves in cyberspace. *Journal of Terrorism Research*, 3(2), 75–90.
Wood, M. A. (2017a) Antisocial media and algorithmic deviancy amplification: Analysing the id of Facebook's technological unconscious. *Theoretical Criminology*, 21(2), 168–185.
Wood, M. A. (2017b) *Antisocial Media: Crime-watching in the Internet Age*. London: Palgrave Macmillan.
Zelin, A. (2015) Picture or it didn't happen: A snapshot of the Islamic State's official media output. *Perspectives on Terrorism*, 9(4), 85–97.

10

CONTINUITIES AND DISCONTINUITIES IN RADICALIZATION TRENDS

The case of Kenya

John Mwangi Githigaro

Introduction

This chapter is concerned with the central puzzle of unravelling the radicalization trends that may lead to violent extremism, with a case of Kenya. In doing so, this chapter probes a variety of agencies and processes that together help to unravel the radicalization trends in Kenya. This chapter uses the case studies of Mombasa and Nairobi counties, examining the trajectory of radicalization into violent extremism. Using a variety of variables, the chapter moves beyond religious agency to examine how radicalization is proceeding in the Kenyan context. The chapter demonstrates that radicalization leading to violent extremism is ever changing and, as such, unravelling the process can be problematic. This chapter argues that, in part, while religious spaces have been important in this trajectory, other variables have been shaping the trends. Key among them have been shifts to online spaces and peer networks. This chapter will first examine the radicalization process in Kenya, followed by examining the radicalization trends.

Radicalization "process" in Kenya

While this chapter is focused on Kenya, there is yet to be global consensus on the process that individuals take on the path towards radicalization globally. Radicalization remains a fluid and a disputed concept globally. It is applied in reference to the adoption of particular belief systems or values that may lead to violent extremism. Radicalization thus ought to be conceptualized as a set of intricate pathways that may lead to multiple outcomes. Its use is dependent on the context and the purpose for which it is applied (Jensen *et al.*, 2018; Mkutu and Opondo, 2019). The word "process" while disputed in scholarship, is used to denote the route that individuals take on the path to being radicalized. Radicalization has possibilities to lead to violent extremism. The "process" approach in unravelling the path towards radicalization is disputed on the basis that it is impossible to unravel a linear path. In other words, individuals' motivations differ. As part of overcoming these conceptual difficulties, a puzzle metaphor is adopted in an effort to unravel the radicalization process. This metaphor is composed of: grievances, networks, ideologies, enabling environments and support structures (Hafez and Mullins, 2015). It is this metaphor framework that shall be explored in unravelling the radicalization process that has so far remained nonlinear.

Grievances

Fieldwork interviews in both Nairobi and Mombasa Counties with community members, grassroot community workers, security officials and counter-terrorism experts, suggests that the radicalization process is broadly mediated by the construction of grievances, and which would then be woven together to motivate recruitment. These grievances relied upon have either been directed at the Kenyan state or the western world, perceived to be in cooperation with the Kenyan state. These grievances were mainly framed around claims of persecution of an Islamic identity; Muslims expressed various forms of persecutions, such as arbitrary arrests and including negative labelling as terrorist sympathizers, largely from state officials.

One of the grievances cited by radicalization networks relates to how the Muslim constituency post 9/11, and arguably post 1998 following the US Embassy bombings in Nairobi, have been treated. Participants argued that, over time, there has been the rise of Islamophobia. Islamophobia relates broadly to the discrimination of Muslims. This could be expressed through a hate ideology including labelling as terrorist threats. Individuals of a Muslim faith have continuously experienced negative labelling as terrorist supporters or sympathizers. This has in part been made possible by the securitization of the Muslim identity by Kenyan state officials over time (Prestholdt, 2011). Securitization in this context is used to mean the speech acts of influential Kenyan state officials that have constructed existential security threats with a link to the Muslim identity. It is this negative discourse that has made possible extra-legal responses to counter terrorist threats. It was this negative labelling and its attendance responses which evoked a sense of collective punishment. This sense of collective punishment was read in the participants' perspectives as making it possible to render the whole Islamic identity as responsible for terror threats in Kenya. The negative labelling of the Muslim identity in Kenya as responsible for terror threats has been sustained by state officials since the late 1990s. Several state interventions, in the participants' accounts, interfered with their human rights and were read as forms of punishment. This then had provided an entry point for radicalizers keen to use negative experiences such as arbitrary arrests and negative labelling as opportunities for redress.

Research participants that included community leaders and religious leaders qualified this collective punishment on several grounds. One related to the discrimination in accessing vital documents such as identity cards and passports. Participants argued that they had to undergo extra vetting processes to prove in the first instance that they belonged to the Kenyan nation. This mainly affected the Somali and Muslim identities. Kenya has, since independence, existed in an uneasy relationship with the Somali identity in Kenya (Mwakimako and Willis, 2014). A section of the participants observed that Kenyan Somalis have always felt marginalized since independence. This marginalization is borne out of the Somali secessionist attempts from Kenya in 1963 after independence. The *Shifta* war (1963–1967) was an attempt by the Kenyan Somalis to secede from Kenya. Their intention was to annex the former Northern Frontier District in pursuit of a greater Somalia (Lochery, 2012). Kenyan Somalis expressed narratives of successive marginalization by the central government post Kenya's independence. The marginalization narrative was then used to lure Somali youth to radicalization. They then hoped that they would rectify the perceived injustices with the formation of an Islamic state that would be distinct from a secular government.

Similarly, previous researchers studying other groups such as the PKK (Kurdistan Workers Party), which mainly operates in Turkey, have reached similar conclusions on the place of belonging, injustices and inequalities. These themes being used by the movement to recruit (Ozeren *et al.*, 2014).

Additionally, participants from a focus group discussion, in Likoni, Mombasa, which comprised of community residents (youth, men and women), when discussing the frames of grievances, spoke of alleged disappearances of Muslim terror suspects in the hands of the Kenya Anti-Terrorism Police Unit (ATPU). Participants noted that in Muslim-inhabited areas, the numerous counter-terrorism raids often led to arbitrary arrests, detention and, in certain instances, gender-based violence such as rape (Mixed focus group discussion, Likoni, Mombasa, 29 September 2017). The Operation *Usalama* Watch (Usalama is security in Kiswahili) conducted in Eastleigh, Nairobi in early 2014 was cited as an example (Balakian, 2016; Botha, 2014). This security operation in Kenya's capital city Nairobi was a counter-terrorism response in the aftermath of the Westgate terrorist attack in September 2013 that claimed 67 lives. This security operation in parts of Nairobi in 2014 evoked the construction of "second-class citizens" and who felt they needed to defend their faith as pointed out by recruitment narratives. External events would also be classified within the frame of a western assault on Islam and which required a defensive response. The next section examines the place of ideology in the radicalization process.

Ideology

Interviews with research participants in Nairobi and Mombasa, and who ranged from security officials to religious leaders, indicated that religious ideology had also been influencing the radicalization process through a section of radical preachers that radicalized youth for violence. These views were collected through individual semi-structured interviews and in focus group discussions. Interviewed participants posited that, while Islam was a peaceful religion, a few individuals were misusing religion to justify political violence. Field accounts remained critical of such concepts as Islamic radicalization or what some scholars call political Islam. The narratives shared in the field generated an unsettled discourse on the place of Islam and violence. Rather, the overriding account was that those who propagated political Islam were misusing the agency of religion to justify political violence. These accounts also remained critical of the use of such terminologies as they tended to place a collective blame on Islam for violence. A section of interviewed participants expressed reservations with the use of such terms for the negative labelling of religion that they carried.

Radical and strategic sermons were being used to radicalize even while possessing little or no doctrinal content. Terrorist attacks, such as the one on 14 June 2014, claiming 50 lives in Mpeketoni Lamu in Kenya's coastal region, were interpreted as part of the land injustices at the Coast and which opened fissures of Christian–Muslim tensions given the predominant Kikuyu population (majority Christians) that has inhabited the area since the 1970s. Al-Shabaab did claim responsibility for this attack, even though the lenses of local politics were offered as part of the causation (Mwakimako and Willis, 2014). Radicalization narratives were essentially attractive if they resonated with a claim of siege. The land question was appropriated as a form of injustice to Muslims and hence the need for violence linked to a marginalization thesis. As part of the radicalization process, the notion of collective punishment was evoked through reminders of Muslim mistreatment not only locally but also globally. This messaging was attractive, especially to new Muslim convertees who hardly understood concepts such as *Jihad*. The concept of *Jihad* has multiple meanings, even though two explanations are more prevalent. One explanation termed as lesser *Jihad* invokes the use of violence or militarized struggles by non-state actors. The second meaning of *Jihad* is what is known as the higher *Jihad*. It means a personal struggle for piety and knowledge and which is non-violent (Cherney and Murphy, 2017). In linking religious ideology to violence, charismatic figures or ideologues in religion were influencing the process (Amble and Meleagrou-Hitchens, 2014).

In Mombasa, a section of interviewed participants claimed that the late Sheikh Aboud Rogo had indoctrinated hundreds of youths to join the Al-Shabaab – a terrorist organization based in

Somalia. A section of research participants went further back in claiming the agency of Abdulaziz Rimo (1949–2015), who influenced a series of Islamic preachers including Aboud Rogo. Rimo was credited with founding the *Answar* sect in Kwale Kenya in the 1990s and which was linked with violent extremism. In Majengo, Nairobi, a former student of Rogo, Iman Ali, is claimed to have been a recruiter for the Al-Shabaab. Iman Ali left for Somalia in 2009 and facilitated hundreds of Kenyan youth to join Al- Shabaab (Key informant interview with a male senior police officer in Nairobi, 2 February 2017). Interviews in Majengo, Nairobi, indicated that Ali left intact a radicalization and recruitment network. This network is in part supported by business spaces that his then Muslim Youth Centre (MYC) controlled around Nairobi's Pumwani area since the mid-2000s. This had become possible when, together with a couple of supporters, he ousted the Pumwani *Riyadha* Mosque committee and took charge (Interview with a male Majengo resident, Nairobi, 17 February 2017). An interviewed religious leader in Mombasa spoke of links between radical preachers and radicalization that could lead to violent extremism. He remarked as follows:

> The late Aboud Rogo at *Msikiti Musa* [*Msikiti* is mosque in Kiswahili], and in tandem with Fazul a Comoran national were allowed to speak hate, including their distribution of free CDs meant to recruit youth to join the Al-Shabaab. He used and broadcast widely, the need for '*Chukua Kisu, Kinoe, Kisu Si Cha Mboga*'... [Metaphorically in Kiswahili, take a knife and sharpen it, a knife is not meant to chop vegetables].
>
> *(Interview with a male religious leader, Mombasa, 25 August 2016)*

Both Rogo and Ali succeeded in framing the Kenya's military intervention in Somalia in 2011 as an assault on a globalized Islam and hence the need for defendants in Somalia. In packaging this narrative, the western-led so-called "War on Terror", which Kenya is part of, was introduced to strengthen the persuasive appeal. It is important to reiterate that, while ideology was considered influential in the radicalization process, it was not a collective process.

Interviews with key informants such as religious leaders noted that indoctrination to a radical movement was a highly individualized process. Research participants also gave conflicting perspectives about whether Wahhabism, a variant of Islam, was responsible for the ideological process. Wahhabism as a variant of Islam calls for a return to puritanical forms of Islam and can justify political violence. It calls for Muslims to return to the times of the teachings of Prophet Muhammed (PBUH). Reference thus is to the Sunnah and the Koran as applied in ancient teachings. This variant of radical Islam calls for *Jihad* (holy war) in efforts to persuade those who do not subscribe to Wahhabism doctrine. This perspective is unsettled at the Kenyan Coast given the global contestations between moderate and radical Islam (Solomon, 2015; Mwakimako and Willis, 2014). It is the latter version that was influential for radicalization and acts of violent extremism. The late Aboud Rogo and his former student Iman Ali were claimed by participants to have been influenced by Wahhabism. While Wahhabism originates from Saudi Arabia, it justifies an intolerant variant of Islam and has been adopted by groups such as Boko Haram in Nigeria (Mutanda, 2017). The next section examines the place of the internet in the radicalization process.

The internet as the mediator of the process

Research participants in Kenya's Mombasa and Nairobi Counties averred that the internet had also been aiding the radicalization process. The internet had facilitated several online radicalization platforms. These social network platforms included Facebook and WhatsApp. A platform such as WhatsApp was said to be regularly relied upon owing to perceptions that it was encrypted. This meant that third parties could not intercept the messaging, thus offering privacy. Both closed groups such as WhatsApp groups and open online content contained carefully prepared narratives that justified violence. Fieldwork findings indicated that the messaging revolved around themes such as an assault on Islam, claims of Christian and/or Western invasions in places such as Iraq, Somalia and Syria. A research participant opined that on the successful execution of attacks by Al-Shabaab at least since the 2013 Westgate attack, a propagandist online video is always developed. The propaganda material is geared towards recruitment. In 2016, following the attack at *El-Adde*, Kenya's Defence forces camp in Southern Somalia, the leader of the Al-Hijra wing of the Al-Shabaab in Kenya posted a video praising the attack but also using the platform to recruit. As this participant noted:

> When Al-Shabaab attacked the KDF camp in *El-Adde*, Somalia in 2016, they developed a propagandist version of the attack … Iman Ali spoke about Jihad and why they were in Somalia. He mentioned that they were in Somalia to fight on behalf of their Muslim brothers … This man – Iman Ali – I believe has never gone to war, but he remains 'inspiring' in his sermons as way to recruit new entrants…
>
> *(Interview with a male security official in Nairobi, 2 February 2017)*

The Al-Shabaab media wing, the *Al-Khataib*, is known to produce high quality Jihadist videos which feature foreign fighters such as American and British citizens as part of an effort to conscript new converts, a tactic that has worked for the group (Mutanda, 2017). The use of videos, online platforms, new media outlets such as Twitter (and which Al-Shabaab has perfected) is not unique to *Al-Khataib* . While Al-Shabaab has been using Twitter to shape public opinion, in the countries in which it is operating, other groups such as the Lord Resistance Army (LRA), and branches of the Islamic State, have relied on such social media. The advantage is that they are relatively inexpensive and reach larger audiences. There is a global presence of these platforms, which can be specifically tailored to reach multiple audiences. These new media thus do not only allow propaganda but also online recruitment, for instance through high quality videos on platforms such as YouTube, which are appealing to youth (Mutanda, 2017). The next section examines the place of weak state capacities and poor governance as variables in the radicalization process.

Weak state capacities and poor governance

Interviews with community residents and security officials in both study locations (Nairobi and Mombasa) pointed to the role of weak state capacities in aiding the radicalization process that could lead to violent extremism. The terminology of weak states, while contested in the literature denotes the general inabilities of states to provide public goods such as security, essential services such as health, and essential freedoms (Eizenstat *et al.*, 2005). A "weak state" in this context refers to the inability of the state to perform essential security functions. Weak states' capacities were evident in poor border controls, mainly along the Kenyan border with Somalia. This was more prevalent at the Coast and in the Northeast of the country. Poor manning of Kenya's porous borders and the perception that police could be bribed to allow terror suspects to move easily was deemed to aid the process. A police officer based in Nairobi and experienced in counter-terrorism, including in the northeast of Kenya, argued that a bribe-taking culture had been influenced by the need to fill financial gaps owing to poor pay. He recounted how corruption could be aiding the radicalization process and could lead to terror acts:

> Porous borders are a challenge in the northeast of Kenya and therefore difficult to police who gets in and out of the country. This is again compromised by corruption within the security agencies. Security officers, especially the police in the border/hardship areas, are easily compromised by bribes... I would link corruption to the overall remuneration of police officers that is inadequate... The police could be tempted to take up bribes and allow suspicious fellows to cross over check points...
>
> *(Interview with a male police officer in Nairobi, 9 November 2016)*

Al-Shabaab members are said to cross the Kenya-Somalia border for bribes of less than US$200 (Cannon and Pkalya, 2017, 10). Bribery then becomes a strategy for Al-Shabaab members to navigate their exit and entry into the country. The next section examines the place of peer networks in the radicalization process.

Peer networks as mediators of the process

Multiple interviews with police officers, religious leaders, youths, civil society officials, including individuals that had relatives in the Al-Shabaab, considered peer networks influential in the radicalization process. It was noted that, relying on peer pressure, friends can easily influence each other, especially with adopting radical beliefs. In addition to conforming to peer pressure, there is the added dynamic of "group think" (conforming to a group's ideals and or persuasion) and which reduces rationality if the decision to join was simply an individual decision to make. Given that friends also spend extended time together, they can, over time, in their various social spaces in their neighbourhoods, begin to discuss their life experiences and aspirations. If part of the aspiration is to address perceived social injustices, this could create opportunities for the rapid uptake of ideas including violent extremism. Furthermore, friends could easily be persuaded to join in the movement if they observed evidence of material gains in their enlisted friends. Given the financial motivation element of joining some of these radical groups, participants found it not so far-fetched for an individual to desire material gains. Previous research, such as Botha's 2014 research on individuals who had joined the Al-Shabaab in Kenya, has similarly found that friendship was a key motivating factor to join. Additionally, a quantitative study by Rink and Sharma (2016) conducted in Nairobi's Eastleigh area on the broad theme of radicalization observed that exposure to radical networks through peer networks remained a principal predictor of religious radicalization. These ideas could be pushed in particular religious institutions and cafes (Rink and Sharma, 2016). Having examined some of the variables influencing the radicalization process, this chapter then looks at the radicalization trends in Kenya.

Radicalization trends in Kenya's Mombasa and Nairobi counties

Individual semi-structured interviews and focus group discussions with religious leaders, community members and leaders, and individual leaders in Mombasa and Nairobi Counties identified a number of radicalization trends. There have been continuities and discontinuities of the trends owing in part to Kenya's counter-terrorism stances. Several trends are discussed below.

Gender trends

Field interviews with a section of community residents, religious leaders, including security officials in both locations noted changing radicalization trends in terms of gender dynamics. Traditionally, the male youth had been the target of recruitment. This has now been changing with young women also being recruited for varied roles. One participant mentioned that, "women were playing a lesser form of Jihad by performing various roles. These roles have included domestic chores such as cooking, but also other functions such as arms trafficking from Somalia to Kenya" (interview with a female civil society official, Nairobi, 12 July 2017).

These young women had joined both the Al-Shabaab and Islamic State (IS) since 2014. These women were not simply performing domestic tasks but could also execute attacks. In Mombasa, an account was raised of at least 200 women returnees who had fled from Al-Shabaab camps in Somalia in 2016 (interview with a female civil society official, Nairobi, 23 June 2017). A section of these women were featured in a BBC investigative documentary that premiered in late May 2017 under the title: *Sex Slaves of Al-Shabaab*. This television documentary claims that these women, in addition to performing domestic chores such as cooking, had been sexually abused. Some had been sexually abused ("sex slaves") for over five years in Somalia. While some of the women had joined the Al-Shabaab on their own volition, some had been falsely lured to join. Participants with access to these women returnees discussed the presence of recruitment cartels especially in the Coastal City of Mombasa that were recruiting young women under the cover of jobs openings, mainly in the Middle East. The recruitment process came complete with interviews and job contracts. An account was given of how they would be drugged through drinks. On regaining consciousness, they would find themselves in Somalia. As this participant observed:

> The trick has to be lure unsuspecting women to take up jobs in Saudi Arabia and other parts of the Middle East. They are then drugged and then find themselves in Al-Shabaab camps in Somalia. In Mombasa, they will be taken through Malindi, through Boni forest and eventually to Somalia. They will then become sex slaves to the fighters in the camps...
>
> *(Interview with a female civil society official, Nairobi, 23 June 2017)*

The above account begs for explanations about how this 'trafficking' would be possible. One explanation claimed the complicity of government officials who took bribes to allow persons to cross roadblocks and border towns without any scrutiny. Most of the women returnees remained underground for fear of reprisals from both the state and active sleeper cells, given that some were deserters. An attack at a police station in mainland Mombasa in late September 2016 was attributed to three women returnees from Somalia. The three women were killed in the raid (interview with a male senior police officer, Mombasa, 23 November 2016). Drawing on field interviews, there existed two motivations for young women to join groups such the Al-Shabaab and Islamic State. A section of them sought to be *Jihadi* brides. The *Jihadi* brides chose to marry combatants, some of whom they had only met online. The other category chose to join their spouses (interview with a female civil society official, Nairobi, 23 June 2017). The next section focuses on social class trends.

Social class trends

Field interviews with religious leaders, and community residents including security officials in both Nairobi and Mombasa, pointed to changing social class trends and disputed the often-cited nexus between poverty and radicalization. Participants argued that, while past trends had been to recruit from the lower social classes, the trend had been changing to include middle class and high achievers in society. Participants mentioned that doctors, lawyers and high-performing university students had become targets of recruitment. This implied that the ideology or persuasion had gradually become more important than one's social class. As a local administrator in Mombasa noted:

> Previously, radicalizers were targeting vulnerable individuals engaged in hard labour such as handcart pushers, touts and so on as their targets ... the trend is changing now ... High school students, and graduate professionals are now targeted for recruitment ... As an example, one of the attackers at the Garissa University College in April of 2015 was a well accomplished lawyer.
>
> *(Interview with a local administrator in Mombasa, 7 June 2017)*

While a majority of interviewed security officials in both Mombasa and Nairobi attributed the vulnerabilities of radicalization to individuals at the margins of society, a section agreed with the views of the local administrator cited above. Groups such as the Al-Shabaab and Islamic State in Iraq and Syria (ISIS), while also recruiting from Kenya, are further strategic with the skill sets they require. ISIS at its formation had the goal of establishing an Islamic State devoid of borders. As an interviewed security official in Nairobi noted:

> We have had cases of educated people joining the Shabaab... We recently arrested two medical doctors at a government hospital in Nairobi. They had plans to carry out an anthrax attack in Kenya. They had been recruited into the Al-Shabaab. Even in Islamic State, they have recruited medical doctors to treat them in battles... we have a Kenyan doctor treating Al-Shabaab in Somalia.
>
> *(Interview with a male senior police officer, Nairobi, 2 February 2017)*

The above discussion highlights the perspective that groups such as the Al-Shabaab and ISIS can recruit from any cadre in society and therefore weakens the overriding perspective that has existed in the radicalization literature about the poverty–radicalization nexus. This perspective is supported by the account of the (in)famous American tweeting *Jihadi*, Omar Al-Hammami, killed in 2014 in Somalia. He was executed by the Al-Shabaab for his criticism of the movement. The Jihadist was recruited while a university student in Alabama, in the USA. He was from a privileged background but chose to join the group. His individual radicalization process was not driven by financial gains but was influenced by a *Jihadi* ideology premised on a claim to defend Islam (Mastors and Siers, 2014).

The links between social class trends and youth radicalization is a mixed perspective. It was applicable in certain instances for terrorist recruiters to target those at the margins of society. Individuals that are desperate for a livelihood can join such groups for financial reasons. This is a view supported by the works of Botha (2014), and Amble and Meleagrou-Hitchens (2014) who have studied radicalization dynamics in the Kenyan context. Individuals of a higher socio-economic status were rather driven by ideology. These mixed perspectives on the individual motivations to radicalize and adopt violent extremist stances demonstrate the complexities of the process. The following section looks at recruitment spaces in Nairobi and Mombasa Counties in Kenya.

Recruitment spaces

Interviews in both Nairobi and Mombasa across a range of participants such as security officials, security analysts, residents, and civil society officials pointed to a change of tactics in recruitment spaces. Radicalization has been intensifying in the last decade at least since the ousting of the

Islamic Courts Union (ICU) in Somalia in 2006, which was considered to have been a subsidiary of the current Al-Shabaab. Kenyans mainly in the capital Nairobi, parts of the northeast and the coastal areas, have had the highest levels of recruitment even though other parts of the country are also becoming sites of recruitment (Hansen, 2016). Parts of Nairobi and Mombasa have been particularly vulnerable to recruitment on at least two grounds. One has been the presence of charismatic preachers in the post 2006 period. These charismatic preachers included Sheikhs Makaburi, Rogo and Iman Ali. Some of these preachers had connections with radical movements in Mainland Tanzania, which created opportunities for cross-border indoctrination (LeSage, 2014; Anderson and McKnight, 2015). Second, some localities in the two counties had high levels of social and economic exclusions prior to the devolution process in 2013. Kenya has, since 2013, had a decentralized form of government, which marked a shift from a centralized form of government since 1964. There are now 47 county/devolved governance units. The recruitment spots have, however, been shifting to other parts of the country.

Drawing on the field interviews, the recruitment spaces have continued shifting, in part due to increased state surveillance. Interviews in both Mombasa and Nairobi with security officials, community residents and religious leaders located various spaces as sites of youth radicalization. Beginning around 2007, several mosques in both Nairobi and Mombasa areas were considered predominant spaces of youth radicalization and recruitment. The Riyadha mosque in Nairobi's Majengo area and Masjid Musa in Majengo, Mombasa were claimed to harbour recruiters. The recruitment was aided in part by religious ideologues. In Majengo area, Nairobi, the recruitment was said to be facilitated by the then Muslim Youth Centre (MYC) that was housed by the Riyadha mosque from 2006. While this view was discounted by a section of interviewed residents in Majengo, Nairobi, a UN Monitoring Group Report in Somalia released in 2013 confirms the mainly statist perspective.

When the state conducted a security swoop in Masjid Musa, Majengo, Mombasa, in early 2014, the recruitment spaces began to shift. The 2014 security raid in Mombasa had been informed in part by social media messaging that had called for a Jihadist youth convention at the mosque (Mwakimako and Willis, 2014). Mosque recruitment was then said to move concurrently with the Madaris (religious schools). Some Madaris are claimed to initiate the long-term process through the instilling of radical ideologies in their young pupils. Field interviews indicate that the radicalization process is long term, and, as such, the groundwork could be laid in Madaris. As a participant in the Majengo area of Nairobi observed:

> The whole process in my opinion starts at the Madaris [Religious Schools]. There are possibilities that Madaris instructors are already radicalized. Most of instructors are not even locals and are mainly from Somalia. The process will begin at an early age, and it will be an innocent 'instilling of virtues' while in the long term the brainwashing will proceed. This is happening in some Mosques around us. This brainwashing then creates justification to kill one's enemy in the name of Allah...
>
> *(Interview with a male police officer, Nairobi, 12 November 2016)*

Owing to increased state surveillance and community agency countering the negative ideologies, the recruitment spaces have been gradually shifting. The radicalization and recruitment spaces are moving to private residences where they attract less scrutiny. Field findings indicated that in physical recruitment sites, the recruitment process was both gradual and targeted. It was targeted in the sense that recruiters were also interested in specific skills sets. An interviewed security official recounted his agency intercepting two doctors that were interning at a hospital in Western Kenya in early 2017. The two doctors were claimed to have the intention of launching a chemical attack (interview with a male senior police officer, Nairobi, 2 February 2017). Recruitment spaces had also moved to football playgrounds. Young men are recruited on the accounts of football tournaments in places such as Somalia or parts of northeastern Kenya only for them to end up in Somalia against their will (interview with a male police officer, Nairobi, 9 November 2016). Recruitment had shifted further to the virtual space, owing to the rapid uptake of the internet in Kenya. Interviewed participants observed that this enabled message sharing, video posts, and propaganda conversations. Participants noted that radicalizing networks were using virtual spaces for several reasons. One is that the messages could reach a global audience given the penetration of the internet globally. Second, there is a level of anonymity that can be found online through the use of pseudo and fake names. There was also a claim that the cyberspace in Kenya was not properly policed and, as such, propagandist materials would be disseminated with ease (mixed focus group discussion, Majengo, Nairobi, 9 June 2016).

Interviews with security officials in both Nairobi and Mombasa also pointed to recruitment networks spreading to Kenya's northeast refugee camp in Dadaab. Prior to the securitization of the Dadaab refugee camp as a new hub for youth radicalization, it had previously been linked with the planning of the 2013 Westgate terror attack. This attack in Nairobi Westlands' area in September 2013 claimed at least 67 lives, with the Al-Shabaab claiming responsibility. It was claimed to be a retaliatory attack for Kenya's military intervention in Somalia since 2011 that had the intention of, among other things, neutralizing the Al-Shabaab security threats. It is some of these security threats that informed the Kenyan government's intention to close the Dadaab refugee camp by May 2017 (multiple interviews with security officials in Nairobi and Mombasa in November 2016 and February 2017). In addition, the planning of the Dusit attack in Nairobi in January 2019 was in part linked to the Dabaab Refugee camp in Kenya's northeast. Prior to the announced closure of the Dadaab camp, principally occupied by Somalis, the government had announced a voluntary repatriation process for the Somali refugees. It suffices to note that recruitment networks have, over time, remained discreet. The next section examines the phenomenon of returning foreign fighters.

The entry of returning foreign fighters

An emerging trend that complicates the recruitment spaces is the returnees or simply the returning foreign fighters. These foreign fighters had previously been in Al-Shabaab or the Islamic State. While some had taken the amnesty, an offer announced by the Kenyan government in 2015 for reintegration and de-radicalization, most have been reluctant. The amnesty programme entailed the rehabilitation of former foreign fighters who had left such groups such as Al-Shabaab. The plan involved providing seed capital to set up businesses, including the returnees' re-integration into the community. There was the lack of a clear and coherent policy on the part of the Kenyan government on how to proceed (Mkutu and Opondo, 2019). There are accounts of at least 1000 returnees at the Kenyan Coast yet to take up the government amnesty. Returnees are reluctant to take up the amnesty for fear of government reprisals given that some returnees have either disappeared or been killed, especially in the Coastal Counties of Mombasa and Kwale. Some participants claimed government complicity in the process, but also acknowledged that terror cells could be punishing deserters. What remains problematic is whether some of the returnees were on a recruitment mission or to launch terror attacks.

Parental involvement in recruitment

A puzzling trend was shared in Mombasa, Kenya, of recruitment into violent extremism through parental agency. This was motivated by promises of financial gain when a family agreed to send their sons or daughters to a group such as the Al-Shabaab. Interviewed research participants interpreted this trend from two perspectives. One, it offered financial support in cases of poor economic prospects. Second, this could be interpreted from the point of support/sympathy of the terrorist networks. As this participant noted:

> You are told that your son or daughter is going to fight a holy war ... As a parent you are given a down-payment of fifty thousand Kenya shillings [equivalent to US$500] with promises of monthly support ... If the individual concerned is the family's bread winner ... they can be persuaded to join these groups [violent extremist groups] for the financial gain.
>
> *(Interview with a local administrator, Mombasa, 25 August 2016)*

While the above account is indicative of parental support, it was not always the case that it was a voluntary process for financial gain. In some instances, the parental consent was coerced through threats or consequences from the violent extremist groups. This worked through death threats mainly if parents did not heed to the forcible recruitment of their children into the violent extremist groups.

Conclusion

This chapter has been concerned with unravelling the radicalization trends in Kenya. It finds multiple trends ranging from ideology, social class, to parental influences among others. The chapter contributes to broadening the discourses on radicalization from a Kenyan case study. These findings are useful in illuminating the ever-unsettled debates on the nonlinearity debates on radicalization into violent extremism (Jensen *et al.*, 2018). The chapter thus sheds light on the multiple contributing yet contextual variables in the radicalization 'process' with the case of Kenya. The chapter accounts for the changing radicalization trends through the case studies of Nairobi and Mombasa counties. The changing radicalization dynamics are in part a response to increased government scrutiny and the attendant counter-terrorism responses. In addition, the utilization of the new media (online platforms, social media networking sites, blogs, online videos) are changing the radicalization trends in multiple ways. The chapter observes that while radicalization is an individualized process, it is moving from the essential human contact to online platforms. New media is thus altering the radicalization landscape with its adaptability of messaging and audiences. Complicating the radicalization landscape is the return of foreign fighters, some of whom are keen to recruit and to mobilize political violence.

Acknowledgements

I am indebted to the Next Generation Social Sciences in Africa (Next-Gen) fellowships under the Social Sciences Research Council, New York (SSRC) with funds provided by the Carnegie Corporation of New York for fieldwork support.

References

Amble, J. C. and Meleagrou-Hitchens, A. (2014) Jihadist radicalization in East Africa: Two case studies. *Studies in Conflict and Terrorism*, 37(6), 523–540.

Anderson, M. and McKnight, J. (2015) Understanding al-Shabaab: Clan, Islam and insurgency in Kenya. *Journal of Eastern African Studies*, 9(3), 536–557.

Balakian, S. (2016) Money is your government: Refugees, mobility, and unstable documents in Kenya's Operation Usalama watch. *African Studies Review*, 59(2), 87–111.

Botha, A. (2014) Political socialization and terrorist radicalization among individuals who joined al-Shabaab in Kenya. *Studies in Conflict & Terrorism*, 37(11), 895–919.

Cannon, B. J. and Pkalya, D. R (2017) Why al-Shabaab attacks Kenya: Questioning the narrative paradigm. *Terrorism and Political Violence*, DOI: 10.1080/09546553.2017.1290607

Cherney, A., and Murphy, K. (2017) Support for terrorism: The role of beliefs in Jihad and institutional responses to terrorism. *Terrorism and Political Violence*, DOI:10.1080/09546553.2017.1313735

Eizenstat, E., Porter, J., and Weinstein, J. (2005) Rebuilding weak states. *Foreign Affairs*, 84(1), 134–146.

Hafez, M. and Mullins, C. (2015) The radicalization puzzle: A theoretical synthesis of empirical approaches to homegrown extremism. *Studies in Conflict & Terrorism*, 38(11), 958–975.

Hansen, S. H. (2016) *Al-Shabaab in Somalia: The History and Ideology of a Militant Islamist Group*. London: C. Hurst & Co. Publishers.

Jensen, M. A., Seate, A. A., and James, P. A. (2018) Radicalization to violence: A pathway approach to studying extremism. *Terrorism and Political Violence*, DOI: 10.1080/09546553.2018.1442330

LeSage, A. (2014) The rising terrorist threat in Tanzania: Domestic Islamist militancy and regional threats. *Strategic Forum*, 288, 1–16.

Lochery, E. (2012) Rendering difference visible: The Kenyan state and its Somali citizens. *African Affairs*, 111(445), 615–639.

Mastors, E., and Siers, R. (2014) Omar al-Hammami: A case study in radicalization. *Behaviour Sciences and the Law*, 32, 377–388.

Mkutu, K. and Opondo, V. (2019) The complexity of radicalization and recruitment in Kwale, Kenya. *Terrorism and Political Violence*, DOI:10.1080/09546553.2018.1520700

Mutanda, D. (2017) What makes terrorism tick in Africa: Evidence from Al-Shabaab and Boko Haram. *Jadavpur Journal of International Relations*, 21(1), 1–21.

Mwakimako, H. and Willis, J. (2014) *Islam, Politics, and Violence on the Kenyan Coast*. Nairobi: French Institute in Eastern Africa.

Ozeren, S., Sever, M., Yilmaz, K., and Sozer, A. (2014) Whom do they recruit? Profiling and recruitment in the PKK/KCK. *Studies in Conflict & Terrorism*, 37(4), 322–347.

Prestholdt, J. (2011) Kenya, the United States and counterterrorism. *Africa Today*, 57(4), 2–27.

Rink, A. and Sharma, K. (2016) The determinants of religious radicalization: Evidence from Kenya. *Journal of Conflict Resolution*, 62(6), 1229–1261.

Solomon, H. (2015) Islam in Africa: From Sufi moderation to Islamist radicalization. *Journal for Contemporary History*, 40(2), 176–196.

United Nations Security Council (2013) *Report on Somalia of the Monitoring Group on Somalia and Eritrea*. New York: United Nations Security Council.

11
RESPONSES TO TERROR
Policing and countering terrorism in the modern age

Mathieu Deflem

Introduction

In recent years, social scientists interested in the study of violence and its control have been challenged by a host of contemporary issues surrounding the persistence and development of collective violence. Our age has modernized in many ways, not least of all economically but also in terms of the spread of democracy and the globalization of human rights. But it is also undeniable and intrinsically paradoxical that various forms of collective violence have not only endured but flared up anew as well. Besides inter-ethnic violence and war, special attention must go to the contemporary conditions of terrorism, especially, though not exclusively, at the international level. While not a completely unprecedented moment in historical time, the events of September 11, 2001 have drastically altered and renewed efforts to combat terrorism at multiple institutional levels, including politics, military, law and policing or law enforcement.

In this chapter, I will discuss the most important dimensions and components of the police aspects involved in counter-terrorism, with special emphasis on international developments and the involvement of US agencies and international cooperation. These policing practices will be discussed in the context of relevant governmental policies and their military and legal components. The perspective applied in this chapter is rooted in the sociology of terrorism and counter-terrorism as crime and social control, respectively. This scholarly orientation has the advantage of being theoretically grounded and empirically focused, rather than normatively based or technocratically involved in seeking to either morally critique or practically develop counter-terrorism programmes. Adopting a social-science approach to the institutions involved in policing and countering terrorism, conceptualization and analysis are argued to be important dimensions to build our understanding of terrorism and counter-terrorism, especially in view of the, at times, very problematic normative implications that are involved.

Terrorism and counter-terrorism: a sociological perspective

It was true on September 11, 2001, and it remains largely true today, that the study of terrorism and counter-terrorism is mostly dominated by political and legal perspectives. A more developed tradition among sociologists and criminologists interested in the analysis of various forms and responses to collective violence, including terrorism, is yet to be formed. The literature on the political dimensions of terrorism and counter-terrorism is arguably the most extensive, but many of these writings tend to be of a normative nature, speculating on the proper role of governments in counter-terrorism and the (largely negative) impact of counter-terrorism policies in modern states (Donohue, 2008; Hamilton, 2006). Works on the legal dimensions of terrorism and counter-terrorism have been written from the viewpoint of constitutional, criminal, and international law (Heymann and Kayyem, 2005; Posner, 2006). Legal scholarship is particularly oriented at untangling the various legislative efforts of counter-terrorism and making suggestions on the best possible legislative models within certain legal parameters.

Turning to the role of law enforcement, most existing works on the policing dimensions of counter-terrorism are of a technical nature, written from a management viewpoint to increase the efficiency of relevant police methods (Lowe, 2016). However, the policing of terrorism has recently also begun to be a subject of scholarly reflection in sociology and criminology (Deflem, 2010). More broadly, the events of September 11 have brought about a distinct upswing in social-scientific studies on the police or law enforcement aspects of counter-terrorism, although much more work still needs to be done. A certain fatigue that may have affected the study of terrorism and counter-terrorism as the tragedy of 9/11 fades from memory needs to be guarded against with all due scholarly attentiveness.

Sociologically, terrorism and counter-terrorism can be approached in terms of the longstanding intellectual traditions of crime and/or deviance and the control thereof (Deflem, 2015; Samimian-Darash and Stalcup, 2017; Shelley, 2014). As such, terrorism is conceptualized as a kind of collective violence and related forms of organized illegal activity that are guided in their motivation by political, religious, or otherwise ideological considerations. Theoretically, such conduct is conceived as a criminal act, as defined by law, or conceptualized as socially deviant on the basis of a broader normative framework (Deflem, 2009). Crime-causation theories will consequently focus on terrorism, in a depoliticized manner, as a form of criminal behaviour, the causal developments of which need to be uncovered at an individual or structural level. Crime-construction perspectives, by contrast, will focus on terrorism as a form of deviance that is motivated by its actors, but that is also responded to and framed (or labelled) as criminal within a particular authoritative structure. From the viewpoint of the latter perspective, therefore, the emphasis shifts from terrorism alone to terrorism in connection with counter-terrorism, specifically applicable national and international governance regimes and their respective legal frameworks to combat terrorism.

Turning from these sociological perspectives of terrorism to the study of corresponding notions of counter-terrorism, responses to terrorism can sociologically either be conceived of as attempts at functional reintegration or as powerful definitions with varying degrees of formality and enforcement that can be contested. As such, the policing of terrorism by law enforcement agencies is arguably among the most formal means of counter-terrorism. The reason for the centrality of policing is that the police function has historically developed to be subjected to governmental control, i.e. policing today is mostly conducted by public police institutions that are legitimated in national states. At the same time, in order to avoid a technical criminal justice approach, a meaningful sociological analysis of counter-terrorism policing can only be developed in a broader context of other mechanisms and institutions designed to fight terrorism, especially at the levels of politics, military, and law.

The patterns and dynamics of counter-terrorism and related cooperation practices among police and other relevant institutions can specifically be examined on the basis of their relative degree of bureaucratization (Deflem, 2002, 2010). The general trend, especially in democratic capitalist societies, has been such that police institutions have in the course of their development acquired a high degree of bureaucratic autonomy from their political centres. Because of this independence, police can independently develop the means as well as the objectives of their activities on the basis of professional standards of knowledge and expertise.

From the viewpoint of police institutions in the modern age, therefore, terrorism is treated as a crime irrespective of any political or ideological underpinnings. Simply put, from a law enforcement perspective, terrorists are criminals, and they should be treated as such regardless of their motivations. In democratic governments, modern police agencies accordingly conduct terrorist investigations with all available technical know-how, including cooperation arrangements with other institutions such as police from other nations or jurisdictions, as deemed necessary in pursuit of an efficient handling of the case. The overriding consideration to use the most efficient means in counter-terrorism policing will be pursued to the point of being conducted irrespective of politics and outside law.

Among the most notable implications of the bureaucratic development of policing in matters of terrorism, which I will clarify in various empirical cases in the coming sections, is that the policing of terrorism coexists, in variably harmonizing and conflicting ways, with other responses to terror. Among these are the policies that governments enact to deal with terrorism (politics), the so-called "war on terrorism" (military), and the formal legal frameworks and mechanisms that are designed to combat terrorism (law). Additionally, these various aspects of counter-terrorism are designed at local, national, international and supranational levels, revealing the whole of counter-terrorism as an essentially multi-dimensional and complex puzzle, which is in need of careful empirical analysis before any justified conclusions can be reached. In what follows, I will apply the bureaucratization theory to uncover the most important contours of these issues in various national and international settings. Necessarily selective, I will especially seek to bring out the relatively neglected role of policing, but I will place it in the context of counter-terrorism at the level of politics, including the military, and law.

Politics: the (global) war on terror

The governments of national states rely on a wide assortment of tools to counter the threat of terrorism as a matter of national security. These efforts range from a domestically organized coordination of counter-terrorism activities and the organization of intelligence operations to diplomatic initiatives and military interventions (Deflem, 2010, pp. 29–44; Zimmermann and Wenger, 2007). National governments have implemented various measures and established specialized institutions that seek to coordinate multiple counter-terrorism functions. In the US Department of State, for example, a specialized Office of the Coordinator for Counter-terrorism provides policy oversight and guidance to the international counter-terrorism activities of various US departments. Nations have at times also developed specialized branches of government, such as the Department of Homeland Security in the USA and Public Safety Canada in the United States' northern neighbour. Other nations have, especially after 9/11 or in view of local terrorism concerns, not developed a dedicated government branch but instead worked to streamline their various counter-terrorism activities through existing departments. As an example, the Counter-terrorism Strategy (CONTEST) in the British Home Office involves a fourfold approach to terrorism in terms of prevent, pursue, protect, and prepare (Hardy, 2015).

Intelligence activities against terrorism are enacted by national governments both at home and abroad (Deflem, 2010, pp. 41–42; Guiora, 2011). In some nations (such as in the United Kingdom, Australia, and France), domestic intelligence services exist next to foreign intelligence agencies. In other nations (such as in the United States), domestic intelligence functions are not assigned to a specialized agency but are part of broader law enforcement responsibilities. In the United States, for example, domestic intelligence activities in terrorism matters are overseen by the Federal Bureau of Investigation (FBI), whereas the Central Intelligence Agency (CIA) is only authorized to work abroad or in cases involving foreign citizens. Foreign intelligence functions may be directed inward, most notably such as when a domestic surveillance programme was authorized in 2002 by then US President George W. Bush and subsequently continued by President Barack Obama (Deflem *et al.*, 2018). Known as the Terrorist Surveillance Program, the National Security Agency was then authorized to engage in the interception of communications within the United States when they involved at least an overseas and a domestic party or at least one party suspected of holding ties to al-Qaeda or an affiliated group. Once discovered, the programme was severely criticized in view of its assumed violations of civil liberties.

At the military level, states engage unilaterally in armed interventions against terrorist targets. One method is to conduct direct strikes against certain terrorist groups and their facilities. Another approach is to undertake subversive activities, such as by means of espionage and sabotage, to undermine the potential or reality of terrorism taking hold in certain areas of the world or among certain groups. In 1986, for instance, the US military undertook a bombing on Tripoli, the capital city of Libya, in retaliation for the role attributed to the Libyan government in the terrorist bombing of a discotheque in Berlin, Germany, earlier that year. Similar retaliatory strikes by US forces took place against terrorist camps in Afghanistan and Sudan in August 1998 and against the Afghan Taliban regime in October 2001.

A few days after September 11, President G.W. Bush explicitly introduced the expression "war on terror" to denote the centrality of the military component in the fight against terrorism (Deflem and Chicoine, 2013). Shortly after 9/11, in a speech on September 20, 2001, Bush referred to the terrorist incidents of September 11 as "an act of war" against the United States that had to be responded to by a "war on terror" that begins with al-Qaeda, but that should also be extended, when deemed necessary, to other groups (Bush, 2001). The term "global war on terror" (GWOT), which has since come into vogue, indicates the essentially international dimension of the terrorist problem from this viewpoint and the need to foster collaboration among nations joined in the fight against a common enemy. Within this framework, it is possible for the military forces of politically aligned national states to engage in cooperation efforts to jointly undertake military missions. Most (in)famously, such coalitions have taken place following the events of September 11 during the invasions of Afghanistan in October 2001 and Iraq in March 2003.

On the basis of the mechanisms of international diplomacy, finally, governments seek to attain counter-terrorism objectives through the peaceful means of negotiation. These efforts can be coordinated among various government representatives of individual national states (ambassadors, ministers of foreign affairs). Similar attempts also take place at meetings organized by international governing bodies, such as the European Union, the Organization of American States, and the United Nations, in order to develop appropriate policies in the context of international law.

Law: counter-terrorism prohibition regimes

Modern legal systems have responded to terrorism in terms of various aspects of law, especially criminal and constitutional law. Within nations and other relatively delineated jurisdictions, laws have been passed that seek to prevent and respond to terrorism. Legally, terrorism is then defined in some, though not always very specific way, so as to allow for a range of concerns to be addressed without giving up on the protection of constitutional rights. In democracies, most typically, such civil-liberties restrictions are more precise than in non-democratic states where law is more politicized. Many of the implications of antiterrorism laws extend their reach across the boundaries of the jurisdictions in which they are passed to also affect cross-national issues. Among the examples are laws concerning migration, asylum, border control, and transnational financial crimes.

Counter-terrorism legislation within nations has typically developed in piecemeal fashion, from the development of laws on specific issues associated with acts of terrorism towards a more global strategy that focuses on terrorism as such (Beckman, 2007; Deflem, 2010, pp. 29–32; Guiora, 2011). In the United States, by example, legislation against terrorism-related activities developed slowly, but steadily, from the 1970s and 1980s onwards. In the 1970s, US laws were passed on terrorism-related issues, such as air transportation security and airplane hijackings. In the 1980s, more comprehensive laws were passed, though typically focusing on terrorism as a foreign problem. In 1984, by example, a federal Act to Combat International Terrorism was passed to provide monetary awards to people assisting in investigations in terrorism against the United States or US properties on foreign soil. Similarly focusing on terrorism abroad, the 1986 Omnibus Diplomatic Security and Antiterrorism Act made terrorism against American citizens abroad subject to federal law enforcement.

In the 1990s, following the World Trade Center Bombing in 1993 and, especially, after the Oklahoma City Bombing on 19 April 1995, the US legal response to terrorism became much broader. In 1996, a comprehensive Antiterrorism and Effective Death Penalty Act was passed that brought counter-terrorism functions under federal control, particularly in cases involving international terrorist groups. Additionally accelerating the US focus on terrorism were the US embassy bombings in Tanzania and Kenya in 1998 and the al-Qaeda attack against the USS Cole navy ship in Yemen. As no other prior incident, the terrorist attacks of September 11, 2011 completed the broadening of antiterrorism legislation in the United States with the passage of the USA PATRIOT Act (the Uniting and Strengthening America by Providing Appropriate Tools Required to Intercept and Obstruct Terrorism Act), which was signed into law on 26 October 2001.

Although there are variations across national legal cultures (Hamilton, 2018), other countries have over the course of their histories developed similar antiterrorism legislation, a process that in many countries has been strengthened and expanded following 9/11. The British Parliament, for example, passed a new Anti-Terrorism, Crime and Security Act in November 2001. The act expanded the provisions of the Terrorism Act of 2000, even though the country had little, if any, direct connection to the al-Qaeda attacks in the United States.

National counter-terrorism laws typically focus on both domestic and international components of terrorist activities and organizations. Comparative legal differences exist in terms of the speed and ease with which counter-terrorism laws in nations became comprehensive, rather than remained narrowly focused (Deflem, 2010, pp. 89–109). Mostly related to a combination of local historical conditions of terrorism as well as the centralized and more or less democratic nature of political regimes, some nations (such as Turkey, Spain, and Israel) have a long history of broadly defined counter-terrorism laws. Other nations (such as the Netherlands and Canada) have instituted laws against terrorism much more recently. Recent changes typically happened after 9/11 to show a political will to collaborate internationally as well as to take advantage of expanded powers nationally should the need arise.

Further differentiating the nations of the world in legal matters of counter-terrorism is the manner in which a balance is struck between the need for security, on the one hand, and the protection of rights and freedoms, on the other. In liberal democracies, civil liberties and constitutional protections can restrict the scope of counter-terrorism activities, or at least subject them to criticisms when they are thought to threaten basic rights (Cherney and Hartley, 2017; Innes *et al.*, 2017). In nations that are politically more autocratic, by contrast, counter-terrorism strategies can be highly repressive and ruthlessly enacted.

Extradition treaties between nations and agreements concerning the international rendition of fugitives from justice in cases of terrorism and other international crimes are among the most important cooperative instruments that nations have developed at a bilateral level (Mitsilegas, 2003). More broadly, multilateral legal efforts against terrorism engage a larger number of nations. Such initiatives can be regionally confined to certain conglomerates of neighbouring or otherwise aligned nations and supranational entities, such as the Organization of American States, the League of Arab States, and the European Union. Among the examples of such international counter-terrorism laws at the regional level, an Arab Convention on the Suppression of Terrorism was adopted by the members of the Arab League in 1998 (Deflem, 2010, p. 101). This convention confirmed and enhanced national legal provisions against terrorism that already existed within Arab nations. On the American continent, a similar approach has been taken by the Organization of American States, which passed an Inter-American Convention Against Terrorism in June 2002.

At the global level, finally, important counter-terrorism efforts have been undertaken by the United Nations. Similar to national counter-terrorism legislation, international conventions against terrorism have developed in a piecemeal fashion (Deflem, 2010, pp. 13–14; Romaniuk, 2010). The League of Nations had already adopted a convention on the Prevention and Punishment of Terrorism as early as 1937, but the convention was not ratified by national governments, except by India. In the 1970s, with various terrorist incidents taking place across the world, the United Nations General Assembly initially adopted specific conventions on terrorism-related activities, such as the International Convention against the Taking of Hostages in 1979. A more comprehensive supranational framework gradually developed during the 1990s and was resolutely pursued following the events of 9/11. In 2006, the United Nations adopted a Global Counter-terrorism Strategy that sought nations across the world to unify their counter-terrorism measures. Despite such multi-nation supranational efforts, however, international terrorism nonetheless often remains a contested issue in international relations.

Policing terrorism: counter-terrorism as crime control

The world of policing and related security functions has developed an ever-expanding role among the modern institutions of counter-terrorism. This increasingly important role of the police still needs special mention to become more publicly recognized, even among scholars, as most discussions and analyses on counter-terrorism remain concerned with political, military and legal issues. In most nation-states and on an international level as well, however, terrorism is treated as a matter of criminal law and crime control and is consequently subject to a host of public police activities.

Historically, the policing of terrorism can be traced back to developments in nineteenth-century Europe when the governments of autocratic states directed police institutions to track down the international movement of political opponents (Deflem, 2002). The policing of terrorism developed out of such political efforts, from which it gradually would become more independent. Specifically, autocratic European states were, during the nineteenth century, involved in seeking to disrupt what were considered extremist political ideas, such as social democracy and anarchism, and directed their police accordingly.

As policing activities became more professionally defined in terms of crime control, police institutions would gradually abandon political goals in favour of criminal enforcement objectives and, on the basis thereof, find common ground across national states. In 1898, for instance, the International Conference of Rome for the Social Defence Against Anarchists led to the signing of an intergovernmental agreement that failed to be ratified at the level of the participating national states. A separate meeting of police professionals at the conference, however, did bring about effective cooperation on related criminal enforcement concerns. In other words, from political efforts against ideologically motivated actions developed enforcement efforts to police the criminal aspects of collective violence as well as other non-political criminal violations. These professionally defined policing practices have remained in existence, in considerably expanded form, until this day.

In some nations, developments in the policing of terrorism especially accelerated from the 1970s and 1980s onwards, mostly depending on local conditions concerning the evolving terrorist threat (Deflem and Chicoine, 2019). In many European countries, for example, terrorism functions have been taken up by specialized divisions in police forces since the 1970s, in the wake of several high-profile terrorist attacks by separatist and radical groups. In other nations, the police functions of counter-terrorism similarly expanded as the terrorism threat grew. In the United States, the Federal Bureau of Investigation has been involved in counter-terrorism investigations since the 1980s, when terrorism became a US concern. Not surprisingly, the Bureau expanded its activities during the 1990s and, especially, following the events of September 11.

The events of 9/11 served as a catalyst for the expansion of the police powers in counter-terrorism matters in many countries across the globe. In some countries, this development was closely related to the terrorist threat coming from al-Qaeda and related groups. In other countries, however, September 11 served a symbolic function to step up criminal law enforcement and other counter-terrorism functions.

Despite variations, several shared characteristics in the contemporary dynamics of counter-terrorism policing can be noted (Deflem and Chicoine, 2019). Most striking is that police institutions focus on terrorism as a crime that needs to be addressed in terms of professional considerations of efficient law enforcement. For that reason, specialized counter-terrorism units are established within police agencies. For example, in the United Kingdom, the Metropolitan Police Service oversees a specialized Counter Terrorism Command that is part of a Specialist Operations division. In the case of the FBI, the lead federal agency on terrorism in the United States, the Bureau operates a Terrorist Screening Center, a Counterterrorism Division, a Weapons of Mass Destruction (WMD) Directorate, and a Terrorism Financing Operations Section (Deflem, 2010, pp. 45–48). As its most important investigative tool, the FBI oversees some 100 Joint Terrorism Task Forces, each of them made up of Bureau agents along with personnel from other security and police agencies at the local and federal level. Intelligence capacities by the FBI, including most contentiously those focused on Muslims in the United States, have been developed as well (Kamali, 2017).

A likewise characteristic development since 9/11 is the expansion of counter-terrorism policing and security in functional terms, specifically the establishment of specialized agencies involved with border control, illegal immigration, and financial crimes. The multifarious nature of counter-terrorism security at multiple levels exists in many nations, sometimes with additional activities against terrorism undertaken by domestic intelligence agencies as well as various civilian and, at times even, military institutions. As a result, the need for inter-agency cooperation becomes an important consideration.

In the United States, the Department of Homeland Security (DHS) was set up in 2003 specifically in view of a coordination of a range of counter-terrorism activities. DHS presently oversees some two dozen offices and agencies involved with a host of activities, ranging from security (e.g. Customs and Border Protection; Immigration and Customs Enforcement) to safety (e.g. Federal Emergency Management Agency) and administration (e.g. U.S. Citizenship and

Immigration Services). Despite the attempt at coordination in DHS, other major players in US counter-terrorism are under the supervision of other branches of the government. Most importantly, the Justice Department oversees the FBI, the lead agency in US counter-terrorism. Additional counter-terrorism policing functions exist at the level of cities and other smaller localities within nations (Nussbaum, 2007), where cooperation among police from adjacent jurisdictions is relatively routinely applied (Sedgwick and Hawdon, 2019).

The many cooperative efforts police agencies have developed, both among themselves as well as with other counter-terrorism agencies in the world of intelligence and security, tend to be functionally defined and based on investigative needs. Within nations and other delineated jurisdictions, for instance, police will cooperate with emergency responders specialized in health and safety in the case of a terrorist incident.

Looking at the international aspects of counter-terrorism policing, international practices comprise unilateral, bilateral, and multilateral forms. Unilaterally, police agencies station officers abroad, while bilateral cooperation between the police of two nations is based on specific needs in concrete cases, such as to ensure the rendition of a fugitive from justice or a particular terrorism investigation involving two countries (e.g. McKenzie, 2018). Multilateral police cooperation takes on a more structured form with the establishment of a permanent organization with wide international representation. Such multilateral police organizations are established at a regional level, as in the case of Europol, or take on global proportions, most specifically in the case of Interpol. Globally, since September 11, important changes in the policing of terrorism have occurred, not only in the United States and other countries more or less directly affected, but on a much wider scale as well. These developments have accelerated the expansion of counter-terrorist policing efforts that are distinctly oriented across the boundaries of national states and have additionally shaped the organization and functions of international police organizations.

Europol and Interpol serve as interesting case-studies in the organization of counter-terrorism by international police organizations (Deflem, 2010, pp. 111–140; Deflem and Chicoine, 2019; Jansson, 2018). The establishment of the European Police Office (Europol) was agreed upon in 1992 in the Treaty on European Union. Europol first took on its activities in 1999 as an international cooperative network to coordinate international policing activities in the various European Union states through a central headquarters in The Hague, the Netherlands. Following the events of 9/11, a specialized unit, the Counterterrorism Task Force, was established at the Europol headquarters. Initially integrated into a more general serious crime unit, the Task Force was revived after the terrorist train bombings in Madrid in March 2004. In addition to analysing relevant information and assisting national police in the various EU states, Europol also cooperates in terrorism matters with other international police organizations, such as the Counter Terrorism Group (CTG) and Interpol, thereby effectively broadening the scope of its activities beyond its otherwise strictly defined jurisdictional boundaries.

Originally formed in 1923, the International Criminal Police Organization (Interpol) is a non-governmental international network of police that currently comprises agencies from 194 nations. Interpol facilitates international police cooperation among its member agencies through a central headquarters that is located in Lyon, France. Since the 1970s, Interpol has focused on international terrorism by passing various resolutions aimed at enhancing cooperation in terrorism-related crimes, such as the taking of hostages. Since the 1990s, the organization broadened its scope to more comprehensively focus on terrorism as an international crime. Since the events of September 11, the Interpol headquarters have additionally set up various new counter-terrorism instruments, specifically an Interpol Terrorism Watch List and an internet-based Global Communications System.

The dynamics of counter-terrorism

It is clear that terrorism has been, and will continue to be, an important concern for many nations across the world as well as the responsible institutions that approach this often contentious, but always problematic, form of collective violence from different angles. Governments and their military, legal policies, and police agencies are among the most important counter-terrorism instruments to form an essentially multi-dimensional constellation. Other components are relevant as well, such as private business involvement related to the financing of terrorist groups, the activities of civil liberties and human rights groups to preserve rights and democratic ideals in view of expanded security measures, and the preventive measures that are undertaken at political and economic levels to thwart the development of social conditions where terrorism is more likely. The complexity of counter-terrorism is additionally exacerbated by its local, national, and international dimensions.

Focused on the policing of terrorism in the context of politics and law, the need to develop efficient cooperation strategies stands out as one of the most challenging aspects of counter-terrorism. The need for inter-agency cooperation is high, but the prospects thereof are not always favourable as agencies tend to guard their respective activities. Even within one country, police and security institutions are not always keen on sharing information and, instead, seek to shield their work from that of other, rival organizations. In the United States, by example, the FBI in the Justice Department is not only notoriously an uneasy partner with the CIA, it is increasingly also placed in a position of competition with the rapidly expanding powers of Immigration and Customs Enforcement (ICE) in the Department of Homeland Security.

Within the world of counter-terrorism institutions, frictions can exist, even within nations and among allies. Policing and intelligence activities in terrorism matters may be at odds with one another, because the law enforcement orientation of police agencies, which focuses on the investigation of terrorism as a depoliticized criminal matter, clashes with the activities of intelligence agencies, which more routinely collect information based on given political and social conditions, even in the absence of a criminal case. Arguably most problematic in terms of an efficient cooperation in counter-terrorism is the coexistence of police and military functions. By and large, police and military functions in the modern age are separated. Yet, the nature of terrorism as a form of collective violence that is positioned in between crime and war brings the law enforcement aspects of counter-terrorism sometimes closer to what is literally, not just metaphorically, a war on terror. This development is remarkable because police institutions historically moved away from the powers of the military, at least in modern democracies, while an unproblematic coexistence of military and police functions is typical of autocratic regimes. However, the terrorist threat, especially since 9/11, is politically often phrased in terms of national security interests that would seek to (re-)align police with military and intelligence.

Among other problems associated with the war on terror, a militarization of counter-terrorism operates on a relatively antiquated model that originated during the days of the Cold War, when external threats came from nations rather than non-state actors that operate transnationally. Moreover, what attempts at a militarization of counter-terrorism overlook is that military professionals are simply not trained nor equipped to deal with law enforcement problems. A striking example in this respect was the failure to establish a peace in Iraq after the invasion and the overthrow of the Ba'athist regime of Saddam Hussein. The tragic consequences of this failure, most notably the development of ISIS and the spread of other jihadist groups, last until today (Kaiser and Hagan, 2018).

Conversely, police institutions have several key advantages in terms of counter-terrorism objectives, such as the investigative capabilities related to local knowledge and their higher degree of international cooperation on the basis of a common "culture of the badge" (Bayer, 2010). Cooperation at the level of police, can and does often take place, even when nations are politically hostile towards one another. By example, police of Western democracies cooperate on terrorism matters with police of autocratic regimes in the Arab world. Cooperation, for instance, has been established between US law enforcement and Syrian security forces, despite the fact that Syria is designated as a state sponsor of terrorism by the US Department of State (Deflem and Chicoine, 2019, p. 241).

It is almost trivial to acknowledge that terrorism is a world problem in which many nations of the world are involved and on which they need to cooperate. But it is still far from trivial to find appropriate methods by which the required international cooperation can be effectively accomplished. An international police organization such as Interpol may pride itself on its wide representation of police from almost all nations of the world, but the organization's infrastructure is severely under-used, especially by police from the world's leading powers. Much like it has been argued that the global counter-terrorism role of the United Nations might undermine the organization's legitimacy precisely when its role in such matters is effective (Karlsrud, 2017), Interpol's activities on terrorism and other international crimes are of secondary importance at best and rendered rather insignificant in scope and impact by the unilaterally conducted international police work that is done by police agencies from various states.

Finally, the many cooperative arrangements that exist on counter-terrorism are relatively independent of each other, even though they are linked (Bensahel, 2006). Ideological differences among different political regimes as well as internal organizational dynamics tend to prevent counter-terrorism developing on the unified global scale it might ideally require. Despite the lip service that is often voiced in support of international cooperation, local and national interests are often seen to direct counter-terrorism work in terms of regionally confined dimensions of various terrorist threats.

Conclusion

This chapter has shown that the institutions engaged in policing and countering terrorism include political bodies and their intelligence and military means, legal institutions at various jurisdictional levels, and law enforcement agencies in the world of professional policing. The forms of counter-terrorism cooperation range from unilaterally enacted international initiatives to bilateral and broader multilateral collaborative efforts. Most forms of both local as well as international counter-terrorism have expanded at various institutional levels. Importantly, however, there is no harmonization or standardization of structures and practices across the various institutional domains and the many forms that are involved.

From a scholarly perspective focused on an analysis of the patterns and dynamics of counter-terrorism, it is striking to observe the relative independence of the many involved institutional components. Indeed, while the developments in politics, military, law, and police are related, they are nonetheless seen to be distinct in terms of their focus and direction. Under special circumstances, such as the events of September 11, there can be attempts to re-politicize police work against terrorism and other concerns that are reframed as national security interests. As police institutions have developed to an unprecedented level of professionalization and bureaucratic independence, however, they can today also better resist such attempts to remain involved in the fight against terrorism on the basis of their acquired standards of efficiency and expertise.

This overview may contribute to developing a proper understanding of the complex constellation of counter-terrorism in all of its manifold dimensions, which may also be useful for the future as problems of terrorism will likely remain of great concern. The multifaceted nature of counter-terrorism begs for precise and relatively modest analyses of the role played by each of its participating institutions. From such careful studies, a more comprehensive perspective can later be developed. Only then will any well-founded, rather than just a well-meaning, reflection informing counter-terrorism policy become possible.

References

Bayer, M.D. (2010) *The Blue Planet: Informal International Police Networks and National Intelligence*. Washington, DC: NDIC Press.

Beckman, J. (2007) *Comparative Legal Approaches to Homeland Security and Anti-Terrorism*. Aldershot, UK: Ashgate.

Bensahel, N. (2006) A coalition of coalitions: international cooperation against terrorism. *Studies in Conflict & Terrorism*, 29, 35–49.

Bush, George W. (2001) Address to a Joint Session of Congress and the American People. 20 September 2001. Available https://georgewbush-whitehouse.archives.gov/news/releases/2001/09/20010920-8.html (accessed 22 March 2019).

Cherney, A., and Hartley, J. (2017) Community engagement to tackle terrorism and violent extremism: Challenges, tensions and pitfalls. *Policing & Society*, 27, 750–63.

Deflem, M. (2002) *Policing World Society: Historical Foundations of International Police Cooperation*. Oxford, UK: Oxford University Press.

Deflem, M. (2009) Terrorism. In J.M. Miller (ed.), *21st Century Criminology: A Reference Handbook*. Thousand Oaks, CA: Sage Publications, pp. 533–540.

Deflem, M. (2010) *The Policing of Terrorism: Organizational and Global Perspectives*. New York: Routledge.

Deflem, M. (ed.) (2015) *Terrorism and Counterterrorism Today*. Bingley, UK: Emerald.

Deflem, M, Silva, D. M. D., and Rogers, A. S. (2018) Domestic spying: A historical-comparative perspective. In A. J. Treviño (ed.), *The Cambridge Handbook of Social Problems*, Volume 2. New York: Cambridge University Press, pp. 109–125.

Deflem, M. and Chicoine, S. (2013) War on terror. In L. M. Salinger (ed.), *Encyclopedia of White-Collar and Corporate Crime* (2nd edn). Thousand Oaks, CA: Sage Publications, pp. 987–990.

Deflem, M., and Chicoine, S. (2019) Policing terrorism. In M. Deflem (ed.), *The Handbook of Social Control*. Hoboken, NJ: Wiley-Blackwell, pp. 235–248.

Donohue, L. K. (2008) *The Cost of Counterterrorism: Power, Politics, and Liberty*. Cambridge, UK: Cambridge University Press.

Guiora, A. N. (2011) *Global Perspectives on Counterterrorism* (2nd edn). New York: Aspen Publishers.

Hamilton, C. (2018) The European Union: Sword or shield? Comparing counterterrorism law in the EU and the USA after 9/11. *Theoretical Criminology*, 22, 206–225.

Hamilton, D.S. (ed.) (2006) *Terrorism and International Relations*. Washington, DC: Center for Transatlantic Relations.

Hardy, K. (2015) Resilience in UK counter-terrorism. *Theoretical Criminology*, 19, 77–94.

Heymann, P. B., and Kayyem, J. N. (2005) *Protecting Liberty in an Age of Terror*. Cambridge, MA: The MIT Press.

Innes, M., Roberts, C., and Lowe, T. (2017) A disruptive influence? "Preventing" problems and countering violent extremism policy in practice. *Law & Society Review*, 51, 252–281.

Jansson, J. (2018) Building resilience, demolishing accountability? The role of Europol in counter-terrorism. *Policing & Society*, 28, 432–447.

Kaiser, J. and Hagan, J. (2018) Crimes of terror, counter-terrorism, and the unanticipated consequences of a militarized incapacitation strategy in Iraq. *Social Forces*, 91, 309–346.

Kamali, S. (2017) Informants, provocateurs, and entrapment: Examining the histories of the FBI's PATCON and the NYPD's Muslim surveillance program. *Surveillance & Society*, 1, 68–78.

Karlsrud, J. (2017) Towards UN counter-terrorism operations? *Third World Quarterly*, 38, 1215–1231.

Lowe, D. (2016) *Policing Terrorism: Research Studies into Police Counterterrorism Investigations*. Boca Raton, FL: CRC Press.

McKenzie, M. (2018) *Common Enemies: Crime, Policy, and Politics in Australia-Indonesian Relations*. Oxford: Oxford University Press.

Mitsilegas, V. (2003) The new EU–USA cooperation on extradition, mutual legal assistance and the exchange of police data. *European Foreign Affairs Review*, 8, 515–536.
Nussbaum, B. (2007) Protecting global cities: New York, London and the internationalization of municipal policing for counter terrorism. *Global Crime*, 8, 213–232.
Posner, R. A. (2006) *Not a Suicide Pact: The Constitution in a Time of National Emergency*. New York: Oxford University Press.
Romaniuk, P. (2010) *Multilateral Counter-Terrorism*. New York: Routledge.
Samimian-Darash, L., and Stalcup, M. (2017) Anthropology of security and security in anthropology: Cases of counterterrorism in the United States. *Anthropological Theory*, 17, pp. 60–87.
Sedgwick, D. and Hawdon, J. (2019) Interagency cooperation in the era of homeland policing: Are agencies answering the call? *American Journal of Criminal Justice*, 44, 167–190.
Shelley, L. I. (2014) *Dirty Entanglements: Corruption, Crime, and Terrorism*. New York: Cambridge University Press.
Zimmermann, D. and Wenger, A. (eds) (2007) *How States Fight Terrorism: Policy Dynamics in the West*. Boulder, CO: Lynne Rienner.

12
HOLY TERROR
How scriptures legitimized group violence in the Middle East

Mark Tomass and Clarissa Luttmann

> You have heard it said to those of old, "Religion is the opium of the people," but truly, we tell you that, if exploited, religion is the vandal lurking within the people.

Introduction

The "War on Terror" has not only failed in eradicating its major target, terrorism in and from the Middle East, but terrorists flocked from the West into the Middle East (Atran and Tomass, 2017), rendering the task of cleansing the entire globe of the many distinct varieties of terrorism with one approach also impossible. Hence, we thereby stress that policymakers need to understand and distinguish between the different varieties of terrorism to devise better and more effective solutions. Fundamentally different practical and psychological motivations exist for engaging in acts of terrorism so a one-size-fits-all approach to understanding the causes of terrorist acts understandably fails to explain or enlighten those causes. By highlighting those practical and psychological motivations, this chapter criticizes such a myopic and narrow approach as inadequate to fully explore underlying catalysts.

A focus on terrorist acts committed by religious fundamentalists illuminates the argument that their terrorist acts are rooted in the religious image of a God who incinerates non-believers or sinners on Judgment Day. The belief that God is bound to inflict such terror may also cascade into practice prior to that Judgment Day. In the Bible, God is quoted using the first-person pronoun:

> Woe to the Assyrian, the rod of My anger, in whose hand is the club of My wrath. I will send him against a godless nation; I will dispatch him against a people destined for My rage, to take spoils and seize plunder, and to trample them down like clay in the streets.
>
> *(Isaiah 10: 5–6)*

God does not only terrorize the populace into submission to His Law, but may also terrorize those who had already submitted, lest they fall into apostasy. The belief that God is bound to inflict such terror may also cascade into practice prior to that Judgment Day, where believers take it upon themselves to terrorize the populace into submission. We will show in this chapter that in such religious doctrines, terrorists view power as an instrument for eliminating sin, as defined in God's Law, rather than an instrument for maintaining social peace.

Defining terrorism

While between 100 and 200 different definitions of terrorism have been identified (Bjørgo, 2004, p. 1; Kruglanski and Fishman, 2006, p. 201), there is still no agreement on a universally adopted definition of terrorism. For example, the US State Department's definition asserts that "terrorism is a premeditated, politically motivated violence perpetrated against non-combatant targets by sub-national groups or clandestine state agents, usually intended to influence an audience to advance political ends" (Title 22 of the United States Code, Section 2656f(d)). For the purpose of the following analysis, we define terrorism as violence perpetrated by individuals, groups or state agencies intended to terrorize an entire identity-sharing group indiscriminately in order to change its behaviour, the behaviour of its government, or to exact satisfaction by taking vengeance against it. The underlying violence could range from the abduction of individuals to indiscriminate mass killings to bombings of symbolic targets.

How terrorism accomplishes its aims

Terrorism can be understood as a distinct political tactic of premeditated and planned message communication rather than irrational and spontaneous acts, a tactic which might be chosen from a portfolio of different tools to achieve organizational goals (Krueger, 2007, p. 14. Hoffman, 2006, p. 229). Generally, because specific acts of terrorism are carefully designed to reflect organization ideology and capabilities, as well as characteristics of the target groups, it is increasingly accepted that there exists no single type of terrorism or primary cause thereof (Bjørgo, 2004, p. 2). Rather, the seeds and later manifestations are found in the combination of belief systems and external constraints, as well as the way in which terrorism performs compared with alternative means (North, 1991). Hence, the failure to adequately understand terrorists' distinct motives for resorting to different forms of terrorism may not only prevent us from accurately addressing the true roots of terrorism – but ill-devised policy might result in adverse outcomes (Krueger, 2007, pp. 4–5).

In its most common form, terrorism seeks to create an atmosphere of public fear. Because its primary goal is to spread societal fear beyond the circle of immediate victims, those victims are of far less concern than the overall message being publicly communicated (Krueger, 2007, pp. 14–15). This explains why many victims are civilian and usually part of a more vulnerable group that has no direct involvement with the targeted political decision-making process (Enders and Sandler, 2007, p. 2). Rather, this simulated randomness of terror operations and victims increases the difficulties faced by authorities in the anticipation of, and, hence, the ability to defend against, such terrorist attacks. Thereby, terrorist groups gain an adversarial advantage over the correspondingly stronger authorities. Finally, because people tendentiously over-respond to catastrophic emotional triggers, events manufacturing such fears constitute very effective, low-cost means of altering political preferences in the target population (Kahneman, 2011).

The political socio-economic explanation of terrorism

The political socio-economic argument explaining terrorism claims that those who are deprived from effective societal voices, lack outlets through which to defuse their socio-economic anger peacefully in the political system, anger such as absolute or relative deprivation through poverty, lack of education, political oppression, discrimination, or low social status (Kahn and Weiner, 2002). Consequently, the group leadership often exploits such frustration and anger, displacing them towards out-groups and encouraging them to carry out violent attacks against "the other", the evil enemy (Moghaddam, 2005, p. 161; Kruglanski and Fishman, 2006, p. 196). Proponents of this argument conclude that while these "root causes" of terrorism prevail, all efforts to eliminate terrorists will fail as these frustrations continue to elicit new recruits. Thus, eradicating terrorism would require adopting a democratic political system that allows people to vent frustrations towards their elected leaders rather than their neighbouring groups. For instance, this could include introduction of a "contextualized democracy" as a more effective, long-term preventive strategy "...that is, socio-political order that allows participation in decision making and social mobility through the utilization of local, culturally appropriate symbols and strategies" (Moghaddam, 2005, p. 167).

Most notably, this political socio-economic explanation of terrorism dominates most of the political class in the United States and Great Britain. It was adopted by the second Bush administration, as well as many top international institutions, advocating regime changes in the Middle East pursued with outright military conquests in Afghanistan and Iraq, and clandestine action followed by military intervention in Syria to topple its secular leadership. For example, in a 2002 speech, then President George W. Bush proclaimed, "We fight against poverty because hope is an answer to terror" (Bush, 2002). Additionally, notable figures such as Bill Clinton, his Vice President Al Gore, British Prime Minister Tony Blair, then World Bank President James Wolfensohn, Turkish Prime Minister Recep T. Erdogan, King Abdullah of Jordan, and many others, including deans of renowned universities, have claimed a similar causal relation between poverty and terrorism and thereby called for aid and educational assistance as a cure (Krueger and Malečková, 2003, p. 119).

Weaknesses of the political socio-economic explanation of terrorism

Importantly, much recent research debunks the purported causality between socio-economic deprivation and a corresponding resort to terrorism. Although a positive correlation between the incidence of terrorism and minority group economic discrimination has been identified (Piazza 2011), empirical evidence suggests that the effect of education and poverty on terrorism remains indirect and questionable (Krueger, 2007, p. 13). One argument is that socio-economic deprivation constitutes a necessary although not sufficient condition for terrorism to emerge (Kruglanski and Fishman, 2006, pp. 196–197). Alternatively, several studies have found non-existing or even opposite relationships between these socio-economic variables and participation in terrorist activities at both the individual and aggregate levels, suggesting socio-economic deprivation constitutes neither necessary nor sufficiently complete conditions to instigate terrorism (Abadie, 2006; Krueger, 2007, p. 2; Piazza, 2006, p. 159). For instance, the *9/11 Commission Report* found that terrorism is not caused by poverty, and more specifically, that impoverished and uneducated populations are especially unlikely to have strong enough political opinions to motivate participation in terrorist activity (*9/11 Commission Report*, 2004, p. 378; Krueger, 2007, p. 3). Nonetheless, they may still populate the ranks of terrorist organizations as members and thereby become contributing factors to terrorism (Kruglanski and Fishman, 2006, pp. 197, 199). The following sections examine three major causes that do not strictly fall within the political socio-economic framework of reasoning.

Findings that support the civil liberties argument

A general causal relationship appears between political oppression and terrorism. For example, political factors such as ethno-religious diversity, state repression, and the structure of party politics have been identified as significant predictors of terrorist activity (Piazza, 2006, p. 159). The underlying logic states that as non-violent democratic means to voice dissatisfaction are restrained, those in frustrated groups are more likely to utilize terrorist tactics (Krueger, 2007, p. 7). Other studies have concluded that countries that are either fully democratic or authoritarian do not experience more terrorism than the other, but those that are in-between, or hybrid regimes, are more likely to experience terrorism, potentially due to diminished state capacity (Abadie, 2006, pp. 55–56). In this context, it can be argued that the increased terrorist activity which followed the United States' 2003 violent overthrow of Saddam Hussain's regime was a result of the ensuing power vacuum left in the aftermath.

Terrorism involves instrumental reasoning

Although several studies indicate a positive correlation between terrorism and political repression, in the specific context of religiously motivated terrorism, the oppression causality argument can be rejected based on an instrumental, means-ends argument. More specifically, a rational and deliberate decision precedes an act of terrorism wherein practical, as well as moral, justifications play roles, as both direct and indirect costs and benefits of the available means. In other words, a decision to resort to terrorism follows a strategic logic where even though suicide attackers could be oblivious to their roles in the planned scheme, the leadership that directs them is comprehensively aware (Pape, 2003, p. 344). Rather than the crazed fanatics that are often portrayed in the media, more often terrorists are psychologically normal and do not display a natural inclination to resort to terrorism (Post, 2007). The choice to engage in acts of terrorism requires both an instrumental justification that terrorizing the target population advances the group's goals, and also a moral justification that the associated end is deemed superior to the moral costs of potentially lethal violence towards both oneself and the civilian targets (Kruglanski and Fishman, 2006, p. 207).

One example of such instrumental reasoning used to commit terrorist acts is detailed in a 2004, 112-page document which appeared online, in Arabic; an al-Qaida ideologue using the fictitious name of Abu Bakr Naji elaborated on the process by which "the Muslim Community [*al-Umma*] can be delivered from servility and lead humanity toward the path of divine guidance and salvation" (Naji, 2004, p. 3). Naji described the process as a "Salafi Jihadi" project, which he believed was more effective than rival projects declared by various sects of the Muslim Brothers (Brotherhood). According to Naji, the establishment of the Islamic State must proceed through three stages. In the first stage, holy warriors activate "the thorn of spite and exhaustion [*shawkat al-nikāya wa al-inhāk*]", whereby they undertake intensive terrorist operations for an extended period to exhaust the "apostate regimes" and ultimately paralyse their abilities to control the societies over which they preside. The weakening of those regimes, and their eventual fall, is bound to result in savage chaos. The second stage is "the management of savagery [*idarat al-tawahush*]", when the Jihadi organizations present themselves as new authorities that will manage the savagery that resulted from said chaos, offering themselves as enforcers of much-needed order. The holy warriors' administration would begin small, on local scales to provide essential goods and services, maintain order, provide Islamic education, raid adjacent territories, and plunder wealth, before gradually consolidating those territories. In the third stage, the "thorn of empowerment [*shawkat al-tamkīn*]", they would declare an Islamic State (Naji, 2004, p. 3).

Religious terrorism

It has been argued that religious terrorism is characterized by the ideological and fanatical interpretation of underlying religious scripture (Venkatraman, 2007, p. 5). Hence, their ultimate religious truth appeals to participants who become exalted agents of God and it supports the execution of violence and destruction as a divine duty or sacramental act (Venkatraman, 2007, p. 5; Hoffman, 2006, p. 83). As a result, the perceived cost of violence is reduced because the religious terrorist is outside an otherwise immoral system, where every non-believer represents an enemy deserving attack; thus, religious terrorism usually results in greater cruelty and destruction than secular terrorism.

Before discussing the different motivations and objectives of religious terrorism, a sample of verses from scriptures that incite, command, or condone group violence is presented to show that: (1) such scriptures have a long tradition in monotheism; (2) their holiness makes them immune from criticism; (3) they are based on the notion of a law-giver almighty God who exercises collective punishment of people for violating His laws (i.e. committing sins); (4) they inspire conquest, enslavement, and theft of neighbouring properties and lands from communities who presumably have a different image of their God (i.e. infidels, or outsiders to the perpetrators' religious identity). A reader who is not familiar with Middle Eastern theology will surely believe that these words were uttered by war criminals in times of war. However, one can easily imagine how the following verses could impact the thinking and behaviour of those who earnestly believe the words indeed emanated from an almighty creator of the universe, one who watches them from the heavens, nodding His head in approval or disapproval of the faithful's deeds. Unlike any time in the past when access to scriptures was mediated by the clerical class, today they are available at the fingertips of political entrepreneurs disguised as religious authorities and can readily be used to incite and justify group violence, holy terrorism included.

Verses from the Holy Bible

1. The Lord saw how great the wickedness of the human race had become on the earth, and [...] the Lord said, "I will wipe from the face of the earth the human race I have created – and with them the animals, the birds and the creatures that move along the ground – for I regret that I have made them" (Genesis 6: 5–7).
2. Then the Lord said, "The outcry against Sodom and Gomorrah is great. Because their sin is so grievous (Genesis 18: 20). [...] Then the Lord rained down burning sulphur on Sodom and Gomorrah – from the Lord out of the heavens [...] destroying all those living in the cities and the vegetation in the land (Genesis 19: 24–25).
3. And when the people complained, it displeased the Lord; and the Lord heard it, and His anger was kindled. And the fire of the Lord burned among them and consumed those who were in the uttermost parts of the camp (Numbers 11: 1).
4. I will strike them with a plague and destroy them – and I will make you into a nation greater and mightier than they are (Numbers 14: 12).
5. The Lord said to Moses, "Get away from this congregation so that I may consume them in an instant" (Numbers 16: 44–45).
6. Then the Lord said to Moses, "Take all the leaders of the people and execute them in broad daylight before the Lord, so that His fierce anger may turn away from Israel" (Numbers 25: 4).
7. So, Moses told the judges of Israel, "Each of you must kill all of his men who have joined in worshiping Baal of Peor" (Numbers 25: 5).

8. So now, kill all the boys, and kill every woman who has had relations with a man, but spare for yourselves every girl who has never had relations with a man (Numbers 31: 17–18).
9. When you march up to attack a city, make its people an offer of peace. If they accept and open their gates, all the people in it shall be subject to forced labour and shall work for you. If they refuse to make peace and they engage you in battle, lay siege to that city. When the Lord your God delivers it into your hand, put to the sword all the men in it. As for the women, the children, the livestock and everything else in the city, you may take these as plunder for yourselves. And you may use the plunder the Lord your God gives you from your enemies. This is how you are to treat all the cities that are at a distance from you and do not belong to the nations nearby. However, in the cities of the nations the Lord your God is giving you as an inheritance, do not leave alive anything that breathes. Completely destroy them – the Hittites, Amorites, Canaanites, Perizzites, Hivites and Jebusites – as the Lord your God has commanded you. Otherwise, they will teach you to follow all the detestable things they do in worshiping their gods, and you will sin against the Lord your God (Deuteronomy 20: 10–18).
10. Then the Lord said to Joshua, "Do not be afraid; do not be discouraged. Take the whole army with you and go up and attack Ai. For I have delivered into your hands the king of Ai, his people, his city and his land. You shall do to Ai and its king as you did to Jericho and its king, except that you may carry off their plunder and livestock for yourselves. Set an ambush behind the city" (Joshua 8: 1–2).
11. When Israel had finished killing all the men of Ai in the fields and in the wilderness where they had chased them, and when every one of them had been put to the sword, all the Israelites returned to Ai and killed those who were in it. Twelve thousand men and women fell that day – all the people of Ai. For Joshua did not draw back the hand that held out his javelin until he had destroyed all who lived in Ai. But Israel did carry off for themselves the livestock and plunder of this city, as the Lord had instructed Joshua (Joshua 8: 24–27).
12. This is what the Lord of Hosts says: "I witnessed what the Amalekites did to the Israelites when they opposed them along the way as they were coming out of Egypt. Now go and attack the Amalekites and completely destroy everything they have. Do not spare them. Kill men and women, children and infants, oxen and sheep, camels and donkeys" (Samuel 15: 2–3).
13. By the rivers of Babylon, we sat and wept when we remembered Zion. [...] Daughter Babylon, doomed to destruction, happy is the one who repays you according to what you have done to us. Happy is the one who seizes your infants and dashes them against the rocks (Psalm 137: 1, 8–9).

The Holy Gospels

Even though the Gospels lack divine commands to commit group violence, in 2003 US President George W. Bush, a Born-Again Christian, nonetheless used them to justify mass murder in Iraq, a country that was at peace with the US, under the false pretences of the operation of "Shock and Awe". His conviction that "freedom is not America's gift to the world, [but] it is the Almighty God's gift to every man and woman in this world. [... thus], we have a calling from beyond the stars to stand for freedom" (Bush, 2004). Here again, God is perceived to be the force commanding his followers to commit a violent assault on distant people. While thousands of pages of apologetic literature have been written to explain away a terrorizing and unjust God, when convenient, Christians fundamentalists reverted to "Old Testament" heroes to inspire and justify group violence, as Evangelical Franklin Graham, in an impromptu interview with National Public Radio, called for following King Solomon's example to justify war to preserve "national security", moments before his iconic father, Billy, commenced speaking at the Washington Cathedral on 14 September 2001 (Graham, 2001).

Verses from the Holy Quran

1. When your Lord revealed to the angels that I am with you, so believers brace yourselves, as I will cast terror into the hearts of those who disbelieved, so strike [them] upon the necks and strike from them every fingertip. That is because they opposed God and His Messenger. And for whoever opposes God and His Messenger, God is severe in penalizing them (Quran 8: 12–13).
2. And you did not kill them, but it was God who killed them. And you did not shoot when you shot, but it was God who shot (Quran 8: 17–18).
3. And prepare against them whatever you are able, of power and of steeds of war, by which you may terrify the enemy of God and your enemy and others besides them whom you do not know [but] whom God knows. And whatever you spend in the cause of God will be fully repaid to you, and you will not be wronged (Quran 8: 60).
4. When the sacred months have passed away, then slay the polytheists wherever you find them, and take them captives and besiege them and lie in wait for them in every ambush, then if they repent and keep up prayer and pay the poor-tax, leave their way free to them; surely God is Forgiving, Merciful (Quran 9: 5).
5. And if they break their belief after the oath they take, and they denigrate your religion, then fight the leaders of the infidels, for they do not believe, so they might cease to exist (Quran 9: 12).
6. Fight them [the apostates]; God will punish them by your hands and will disgrace them and give you victory over them and heal the breasts of believers (Quran 9: 14).
7. O you who have believed, indeed the polytheists are dirty, so let them not approach the al-Haram Mosque after this, their [final] year. And if you fear privation, God will enrich you from His bounty if He wills (Quran 9: 28).
8. Fight those who do not believe in God or in the Last Day and who do not forbid what God and His Messenger have forbidden and who do not adopt the religion of truth from those who were given the Scripture until they pay the tax on the back of their hand willingly and subdued (Quran 9: 29).
9. O believers fight those infidels adjacent to you and let them find harshness in you (Quran 9: 123).
10. And He brought down those among the People of the Scripture who supported them from their fortresses and cast terror into their hearts; made you kill some and take others captives. And He made you inherit their land and their homes and their properties and a land which you have not trodden. God is capable of everything (Quran 33: 26–27).
11. Muhammad is the messenger of God; those with him are hard against the infidels and merciful among themselves (Quran 48: 29).

The sayings of the Prophet Muhammad

1. When you meet your polytheist enemies [Christians included], invite them to three courses of action. If they respond to any one of these, accept it and withhold yourself from harming them. ... If they refuse to accept Islam, demand from them the Infidel Tax [*Jizya*]. If they

agree to pay, accept it from them and hold off your hands. If they refuse to pay the Infidel Tax, seek God's help and fight them (Sahih Muslim 19: 4294).

2. I have been commanded [by God] to fight people until they testify that there is no god but God and that Muhammad is God's Messenger, and offer the prayers perfectly and give the Charity Tax, so if they perform that, then they save their lives and property from me except for Islamic laws and then their reckoning [accounts] will be done by God (Sahih Muslim 1: 33).
3. You will fight with the Jews till some of them will hide behind stones. The stones will say, O 'Abdullah There is a Jew hiding behind me; so, kill him (Sahih al-Bukhari 52: 176).
4. Testify that there is no god but God, or else I will chop off your neck (Sahih al-Bukhari 59: 643).
5. "The Verse: 'You [true Muslims] are the best of nations ever raised up for mankind' (Quran 3: 110), means, the best of peoples for the people, as you bring them with chains on their necks till they embrace Islam" (Sahih al-Bukhari 60: 80).

In Muslim scriptures, the devout must engage in Holy War (*Jihad*) against others in the following order of priority: Apostates (*murtadoun*) or heterodox Muslims, such as Sufi (Sunni and Shia variants), Shia, Alawiyya, Isamiliyya, Duruz, and non-practising Muslims; Heathens (*kuffar*), such as people not belonging to the three monotheistic religions (albeit Christians are often considered polytheists based on belief in the trinity, and, thus, also called *kuffar*); and, lastly, the People of the Book (Jews and Christians). Generally, all people who do not acknowledge the prophecy of Muhammad are considered Infidels (*kuffar*), even though they believe in God. In a holy war, Apostate and Heathen men must be killed while their women and pre-pubescent boys must be enslaved by the holy warriors or sold as labour or sex slaves; this was seen after al-Qaida and ISIS attacks against Alawiyya and Shia Muslims and Yezidis (Tomass, 2017, pp. 108–109, 125–126).

When examining the terrorist acts committed in the Middle East, we observe that religious terrorism has become a movement in which the violence caused by the terrorist act is derived from and used to preserve literal (as opposed to fanatical) interpretations of scriptures. Perpetrators seek to enforce strict, blind devotion and obedience to the word of God throughout the population, and the terror employed functions only in totalities, ending in either total victory or total defeat. Such religiously inspired terrorist acts committed in the Middle East in the last decade are clear and specific. The perpetrators identify the target through a religious lens and then commit the terrorist act intending to: exterminate the entire group identified; force conformation to the perpetrators' value system; or to pay tribute and/or flee for their lives so that their properties can be appropriated. Which goals the terrorists pursue depends on the value accorded by scriptures to the target.

When God orders followers to terrorize people, kill men, enslave women and children, and plunder their private property through the medium of scripture, then school textbooks can certainly remind the devout of their duty to carry out those deeds. Therefore, it is of little surprise that those divine commands are part of the curriculum of al-Azhar University in Cairo, and moreover, are found inscribed in the Arab Penal Law adopted by the Arab League, as well as eventually making their way into thousands of sermons shared worldwide on YouTube and similar media outlets.

In textbooks published by al-Azhar University for contemporary Egyptian high schools, students are introduced to the works of a thirteenth-century author, accompanied with extensive contemporary annotations. The following sample is extracted from the textbook assigned in the fourth-year secondary school of al-Azhar University:

> Fighting infidels is a duty of every sane, free, and capable man. ... If Muslims besiege the people of [the Land of] War [i.e. the land that lies outside of dominion of the Muslim State] in a city or fortress, they invite them Islam; if they accept they should stop fighting them; if they do not they must pay the Infidel Tax [*Jizyah*] in the event they qualify for it ...If they refuse to pay it, they [Muslims] depend on God's assistance and fight them; they attack them by caterpillars, ruin their crops and their trees, burn them and waste them (Hanafi-al, no date, pp. 118–119. Tomass translation). [...] But the captives are taken on foot to the Land of Islam; if they become disabled [during the journey] the men are killed, and women and male children are left behind in the wilderness to die of hunger and thirst because it is forbidden to kill them (Hanafi-al, no date, p. 126. Tomass translation). [...] The Infidel Tax must be collected from them while they feel humiliated and belittled [...] those from whom we collect the Infidel Tax must be distinguished in their clothing and means of transportation (Hanafi-al, no date, pp. 139–140, Tomass translation). If a Muslim man apostates, God forbids, he is imprisoned and asked to return to Islam. He is cleared if he accepts Islam. Otherwise he is killed (Hanafi-al, no date, p. 145, Tomass translation). [...] If a woman apostates, she is not killed; she is imprisoned and beaten every day until she returns to Islam, but if one kills her, no guilt shall be laid on him and he is excused. (Hanafi-al, no date, p. 149, Tomass translation)

Religiously inspired terrorism is not born in a vacuum; it boldly enforces widely accepted and diligently taught beliefs in the Arab and Muslim world. For instance, "The Consolidated Arab Penal Law", adopted by the Arab League in 1996, defines apostasy and its punishments in Articles 162–165 of chapter 7:

> The above Articles were based on Quran 2:285 [...], Quran 4:152 [...], and on the Prophet's [...] saying: "If one changes his religion, kill him".
>
> *(The Arab League, The Council of Justice Ministers, pp. 128–129)*

One may conclude from the above legal code that apostasy from Islam is a major crime akin to grand treason or defection to enemy ranks in wartime. From this angle, the rationale of numerous suicide bombers who blow themselves up amidst Shia on pilgrimage to Karbala can be seen, for the pilgrims are perceived as apostates marching to the sight of the slaughter of al-Husayn, the Grandson of the Prophet Muhammad. That the Shia revere the burial site of al-Husayn is blasphemous to many, for nothing and no one other than God should be revered.

It is also not surprising that after consuming such literature, a cleric, like many others, concludes that engaging in terrorism is a duty of the devout: "We are terrorists and terrorism is an obligation in God's book. Let the West and East know that we are terrorists and we terrorize. 'And prepare against them whatever you are able of power and of steeds of war by which you may terrify the enemy of God and your enemy' (Quran 8: 60) for terrorism is an obligation if God's religion" (Cleric 2018). Believers in the divine source of such a verse easily sanctify doctrines and historical characters from a distant past and a different culture, beliefs that may have not been considered holy then in a literal sense. The unholy past becomes a holy present, leading the way to a clash between superstition and reason. When reason is rejected, terrorism can become one means to enforce superstition.

Religiously inspired terrorism requires a different approach

This means–ends concept and the underlying cost-benefit calculation imply three general strategies to discourage terrorism (Kruglanski and Fishman, 2006, p. 207). First, one could convince the terrorist group that the terrorism tactic is ineffective to achieve their chosen goals. Second, one could convince the terrorist group of a more effective tool to communicate their message. Third, one could convince the terrorist group that their chosen act of terrorism conflicts with other important goals, such as moral or religious codes of conduct. Based on this general prescription, it can be argued that none of these techniques are applicable to the case of fundamentalist Islamic terrorism in the Middle East. First, terrorism is highly effective in achieving public fear and, hence, potential religious submission in the Middle East. Second, strong political freedom fails to provide a valid alternative to the stated fundamentalist goal of population-wide submission to a fundamentalist Islamic doctrine and is hence fully incompatible with the democratic process itself. And third, compelling positive externalities exist, or at least a lack of negative implications, for the destruction of non-believers, or the "enemy". Such a result would not be achieved through any non-violent alternatives, as was amply evident in the destruction by ISIS and al-Qaida of pre-Islamic archaeological sites and artefacts (such as in Palmyra, Nineveh, and the Museum of Mosul), as well as religious monuments of "apostate" Muslims.

Relationships between religion and the psychology of terrorism

Although a scientific consensus exists that religion rarely constitutes a root cause of terrorism (Rogers *et al.*, 2007), in societies where religious identity trumps all social identities, inter- and intra-group dynamics can deflect social conflicts into religious ones and induce combatants to find religious justifications to commit mass murder (Tomass, 2016, Ch. 7). Based on Jones (2006), we identify six distinct ways in which specific religious characteristics can contribute to psychological preconditions for religiously motivated terrorism and group violence. These are:

1. The greater the belief in the almighty, divine punishment, and condemnation, the propensity correspondingly grows for religion to create and build upon emotions of shame, humiliation, and disgust, while directing the believer to resort to violence (Jones, 2006, p. 169). Such humiliation-driven religious violence can emerge in two ways. First, while most shame and humiliation usually develop in social and cultural contexts, heavily fanatic religious beliefs, as opposed to pacifist teachings (i.e. those of Martin Luther King or the Dali Lama), succeed in aggravating these feelings and channelling the resultant aggression for their own purposes (Jones, 2006, pp. 180–1). For example, humiliation could be interpreted as the occupation of (historic) territory by non- or other-believers. Second, religion can directly evoke and exacerbate feelings of shame and humiliation; as the perceived difference increases between finite human character and an infinite divine ideal, the propensity for such feelings commensurately follows. This is supported by the more general finding that low self-esteem paired with concrete grievances constitute major drivers of terrorism. Membership in a terrorist organization then provides an avenue in which to channel these emotions, as well as the necessary training to do so.
2. The religious tendency to think in radical totalities, all-good versus all-evil terms, can lead to an apocalyptic vision of a cosmic struggle against demonic forces, especially secularism, as displayed in many scriptures (Jones, 2006, p. 170).
3. An apocalyptic end of history is often represented through violent bloodshed (Hoffman, 1995, p. 3). This concept is thematically linked to notions of death and rebirth common to

many religions and centres on the radical change of the world order by eradicating rather than modifying the old system. Purification can solely be achieved through violent death. Climactic end of history, such as the Crusades, like Islamic terrorism, can be perceived as a Holy War which only ends when total victory has been achieved, i.e. the instigation of the Islamic State (Taheri, 1987, pp. 7–8).

4. A moral decline of the world is envisioned (Jones, 2006, p. 172). Rather than protecting just their own purity, religious terrorists assume a responsibility to purify the world from immorality. They believe that to sacrifice means to make holy; this can be achieved either by killing the enemy with a sacrificial ritual or by enacting self-sacrifice which thereby sanctifies the suicide terrorist in the eyes of the community and justifies his action as the purification of the surrounding world. Although self-sacrifice is forbidden by Islamic law, neither traditional to Islam nor supported by most Muslim clerics, martyrdom constitutes a "major theological innovation on the part of radical Islamists like bin Laden" (Jones, 2006, p. 174). With Islamist martyrs generally regarded as sacred by their communities, and martyrdom regarded as the highest form of jihad (Jones, 2006, p. 174), this nihilates the moral and social cost of dying during the act (Hoffman, 2006, p. 91). This is strongly supported by the fact that 78 per cent of all suicide terrorist incidents from 1968 to 2005 have been perpetrated between the years 2001 and 2005, a vast majority having been religiously motivated, in which Islamic terrorist groups accounted for over 80 per cent of suicide attacks in this period (Hoffman, 2006, p. 131).
5. Joining the "army of the righteous" and acquiring a sense of belonging increases self-esteem or self-aggrandizement (Jones, 2006, p. 181; Rogers *et al.*, 2007). Such a membership-based restoration of self-esteem depends on the organization's prestige and morphs into exacerbating group violence to enhance the prestige of the group itself (Post *et al.*, 2003, p. 176). Individual goals, successes, and failures become indistinguishable from those of the group, resulting in the disappearance of the sense of individual will and responsibility.
6. The prospect of being closer to God (Jones, 2006, p. 178), as well as the urge to serve and please an all-consuming God, overwhelms all connections between human beings and results in a loss of empathy for the target (Jones, 2006, p. 182). Also, a single human life becomes an insignificant casualty from a terrorist interpretation of God's eternal plan (Taheri, 1987, pp. 7–8).

Based on a central conviction of radical destruction rather than modification of the existing order, fundamentalist principles oppose negotiation, dialogue, and peaceful resolution (Gunaratna, 2002) and therefore strongly oppose the characteristics of the democratic process. In contrast, other organizations, such as the Hamas, Hezbollah, and Sinn Fein, possess more varied portfolios of political and social goals, in addition to religious motivation, so they can and do employ instruments other than terrorism, depending on the above criteria, such as diplomacy or media campaigns (Kruglanski and Fishman, 2006, p. 209). For fundamentalist Islamic groups such as ISIS and al-Qaida, terrorism is, by default, the only tactic. Hence, it can be reasonably concluded that, given the commitment of fundamentalist Islamic terrorists to goals exclusively attainable through terrorism, "it is unlikely that anything short of a total defeat will convince such groups to relinquish its use" (Kruglanski and Fishman, 2006, p. 209).

Conclusion

Religious terrorism cannot be eradicated without eroding the knowledge structures that produce terrorism. Metaphysical belief systems are ideologies and may have components that shape the internal logic of terrorism (Tomass, 2017). Those ideologies must be incorporated into a thorough analysis of terrorism – however 'irrational' these might appear from an external perspective. That said, a more targeted analysis of various forms of terrorism would result in more effective counter-terrorism strategies. Critical assumptions must be clarified within any strategic formulation, most specifically re-iterating that religious fundamentalism is not a single cause of terrorism because it establishes neither necessary nor adequate conditions for committing terrorist acts.

For the religious terrorist, violence first and foremost is a divine duty executed in direct response to a theological demand, and therefore morally justified; in this context, religion serves as a legitimizing force transmitted through holy texts and brought to bear by clerical authorities claiming to speak on behalf of God. Therefore, for the terrorist organization, group violence is defined as the only legitimate tactic for achieving its espoused goals. The threat of force against the group does not intimidate its leaders into giving up their terrorist acts. Moreover, to religious terrorists, those outside their beliefs are Infidels, not worthy to impress or seek their approval, so therefore terrorists would not consider the consequences to their self-image when they commit an indiscriminate act of violence against subhuman Infidels. For this reason, while the religious belief systems are left intact without revision, suicide attacks are most likely to continue against secular societies or religious groups that do not conform to those of the terrorist.

References

Abadie, A. (2006) Poverty, political freedom, and the roots of terrorism. *American Economic Review*, 96(2), 50–56.

Atran, S. and Tomass, M. (2017) Why are Western youth attracted to ISIS. In C. Webel and M. Tomass (eds), *Assessing the War on Terror: Western and Middle Eastern Perspectives*. London: Routledge.

Bjørgo, T. (ed.) (2004) *Root Causes of Terrorism: Myths, Reality and Ways Forward*. London: Routledge.

Bush, G. W. (2002) United States of America, Remarks by Mr. George W. Bush, President, at the International Conference on Financing for Development, Monterrey, Mexico, 22 March 2002. Online. Available www.un.org/ffd/statements/usaE.htm (accessed 6 April 2019).

Bush, G. W. (2004) George W. Bush 2004 Acceptance Speech. Video 1:12:98, posted by CSPAN, 2 September 2004. Online. Available www.c-span.org/video/?182731-2/george-w-bush-2004-acceptance-speech (accessed 6 April 2019).

'Cleric admits that terrorism is a duty in the religion of Islam, شيخ يعترف ان الارهاب فريضة في دين' YouTube video, 0:23, posted by 'سعاد الملحدة الجزائرية,' 4 October 2018. Online. Available www.youtube.com/watch?v=FcwTU_YyxwA&feature=youtu.be&fbclid=IwAR000TgGWg22OA3kRzXqSIUxxmZZojDiqXdYiVa-WBekzegSZ4EAeLsOe-E (accessed 6 April 2019).

Enders, W. and Sandler, T. (2007) An economic perspective on transnational terrorism. *The Economic Analysis of Terrorism*. London: Routledge, pp. 29–44.

Graham, B. (2001) Billy Graham's 9/11 Message from the Washington National Cathedral. (14 September 2001). Online. Available https://billygraham.org/story/a-day-to-remember-a-day-of-victory/ (accessed 6 April 2019).

Gunaratna, R. (2002) *Inside Al Qaeda: Global Network of Terror*. New York: Columbia University Press.

Hanafi-al, Abd Allah bin Mahmoud bin Mawdoud al-Moulely [1284], *Al-Ikhtiyar li Talil al-Mukhrar*, Vol 4, Curriculum for the fourth secondary year of al-Azhar University, Beirut, Lebanon: *Dar al-Kutub al-Ulmiyya* (no date).

Hoffman, B. (1995) 'Holy terror': The implications of terrorism motivated by a religious imperative. *Studies in Conflict & Terrorism*, 18(4), 271–284.

Hoffman, B. (2006) *Inside Terrorism*. New York: Columbia University Press.

Jones, J. W. (2006) Why does religion turn violent? A psychoanalytic exploration of religious terrorism. *The Psychoanalytic Review*, 93(2), 167–190.

Kahn, J. and Weiner, T. (2002) World leaders rethinking strategy on aid to poor. *The New York Times*, 18, sec. A1, 3.

Kahneman, D. (2011) *Thinking, Fast and Slow*. New York: Farrar, Straus and Giroux.

Krueger, A. B. (2007) *What Makes a Terrorist: Economics and the Roots of Terrorism*. Princeton, NJ: Princeton University Press.

Krueger, A. B. and Malečková, J. (2003) Education, poverty and terrorism: Is there a causal connection? *Journal of Economic Perspectives*, 17(4), 119–144.

Kruglanski, A. W. and Fishman, S. (2006) The psychology of terrorism: 'Syndrome' versus 'tool' perspectives. *Terrorism and Political Violence*, 18(2), 193–215.

Moghaddam, F. M. (2005) The staircase to terrorism: A psychological exploration. *American Psychologist*, 60(2), 161–169.

Naji, A. B. (2004) ادارة التوحش: أخطر مرحلة ستمر بها الأمة [*Idaret al-Tawahush: Akhtar Marhala Satamur biha al-Ummah* (*Markaz al-Dirasat wa al-Buhouth al-Islamyya*, n.d.) *The Management of Savagery: The Most Critical Stage the Muslim Community Will Pass Through*] (Centre for Islamic Studies and Research).

9/11 Commission Report (2004) Online. Available www.9-11commission.gov/report/911Report.pdf (accessed 6 April 2019).

North, D. C. (1991) Institutions. *Journal of Economic Perspectives*, 5(1), 97–112.

Pape, R. A. (2003) The strategic logic of suicide terrorism. *American Political Science Review*, 97(3), 343–361.

Piazza, J. A. (2006) Rooted in poverty?: Terrorism, poor economic development, and social cleavages. *Terrorism and Political Violence*, 18(1), 159–177.

Piazza, J. A. (2011) Poverty, minority economic discrimination, and domestic terrorism. *Journal of Peace Research*, 48(3), 339–353.

Post, J. M. (2007) *The Mind of the Terrorist: The Psychology of Terrorism from the IRA to al-Qaeda*. New York: St. Martin's Press.

Post, J., Sprinzak, E., and Denny, L. (2003) The terrorists in their own words: Interviews with 35 incarcerated Middle Eastern terrorists** This research was conducted with the support of the Smith Richardson Foundation. *Terrorism and Political Violence*, 15(1), 171–184.

Rogers, M. B., Loewenthal, K. M., Lewis, C. A., Amlôt, R., Cinnirella, M., and Ansari, H. (2007) The role of religious fundamentalism in terrorist violence: A social psychological analysis. *International Review of Psychiatry*, 19(3), 253–262.

Taheri, A. (1987) *Holy Terror: Inside the World of Islamic Terrorism*. Bethesda, MD: Adler & Adler Publishers.

The Arab League, The Council of Justice Ministers, 128–129, posted by The Arab Centre for Legal and Juridical Research, a sub-organ of the Arab League, Online. Available: http://carjj.org/node/237 (accessed 6 April 2019).

Tomass, M. (2016) *The Religious Roots of the Syrian Conflict: The Remaking of the Fertile Crescent*. London: Palgrave Macmillan.

Tomass, M. (2017) The ideological origins of ISIS: Fighting terror with common sense. In C. Webel and M. Tomass (eds), *Assessing the War on Terror: Western and Middle Eastern Perspectives*. London: Routledge.

United States Code (2004) Online. Available https://law.justia.com/codes/us/2004/title22/ (accessed February 6, 2019.

Venkatraman, A. (2007) Religious basis for Islamic terrorism: The Quran and its interpretations. *Studies in Conflict & Terrorism*, 30(3), 229–248.

13

REHABILITATION OF JIHADI TERRORISTS

Current understanding and perspectives

Kurt Braddock

At this moment, somewhere within the vast Kingdom of Saudi Arabia, a young Muslim is thinking about what to expect in his art therapy class tomorrow. Last week, he may have been playing volleyball with fellow Muslims, spoken with counsellors about his religious beliefs, or engaged in debates with Islamic scholars, all in the rooms adjacent to where he will learn to communicate his feelings through artistic expression. Perhaps after he tries his hand at painting to express his inner rage and frustration, he will request to call his family to let them know how he is progressing. He will think about how much longer he will be required to stay at the facility at which he is housed, and maybe he will consider himself lucky that he was not simply tossed in jail for what he had done.

This young man will have been arrested for terrorist offences against Saudi Arabia or for expressing opinions and intentions that are contrary to the Saudi-approved version of Islam. He is a participant in what many consider to be the gold standard of "deradicalization programmes", intended to get him to abandon his violent extremist beliefs, attitudes, intentions and behaviours, and to prepare him for reintegration into Saudi society, where he will be a happy and productive citizen of the Kingdom. Whether the programme succeeds in transforming this young man from a budding jihadi into a repentant Muslim remains to be seen. Nevertheless, the administrators of the programme will likely claim success, just as they have with countless others who came before him.

Although hypothetical, these scenes are nonetheless representative of what many individuals have gone through in their experiences with the Saudi deradicalization programme. Similarly, there are thousands more who have taken part in comparable initiatives around the world, all of which promise to "deradicalize" or "rehabilitate" those who go through them. Given the ubiquity of these programmes since the mid-2000s and the degree to which they are relied upon for treating violent extremist prisoners, it is important to regularly take stock of our understanding of these programmes and consider the impact they have.

In this vein, this chapter seeks to summarize and extend our current understanding of terrorist deradicalization and rehabilitation efforts. To accomplish these complementary goals, this chapter will be structured into multiple sections. The next section of the chapter offers a critical distinction between deradicalization and disengagement – two processes that are often confounded but have substantially different drivers and implications. Following this clarification, the chapter will turn to synopses of several past and current deradicalization programmes. Rather than review programmes in countries that have already received substantial attention by the academic community and the popular press (e.g. Saudi Arabia, Indonesia, Colombia), this chapter will feature brief synopses of lesser-known programmes to demonstrate the variability in efforts to deradicalize former jihadis around the globe. After these brief summaries, the chapter will then raise several issues that affect our understanding of deradicalization's efficacy, our interpretation of data coming out of these programmes, and our efforts for treating arrested violent extremists moving forward.

Before reflecting on the nature of specific programmes, their goals, and what it is they *actually* accomplish, let us first consider deradicalization and disengagement, as a failure to consider the differences between these two processes makes it impossible to properly evaluate the success of deradicalization programmes relative to what their administrators claim they achieve.

Disengagement and deradicalization: a critical distinction

When thinking about how and why individuals leave terrorist movements, it is crucial to understand what happens to those individuals who leave those movements, what motivates them to leave, and how we might deal with individuals who leave. In trying to address these issues, it quickly becomes clear that what we think of "leaving" terrorist movements can be multifaceted, complex and, at times, contradictory. Leaving a terrorist movement might indicate that an individual has undergone some cognitive and psychological changes that has led them to abandon the ideology that once motivated their engagement in violence. Then again, it might also mean that an individual retains the values that motivated their engagement in violence, but they were forced to leave the group because of security measures (e.g. arrest), increased responsibility outside the confines of the group (e.g. a growing family), or some other factor. It could even suggest that an individual has ceased engaging in violent activity, but remains active in the group in a non-violent role. Based on research performed by Renee Garfinkle (2007) and Helen Ebaugh (1988), John Horgan (2008) offers clarity to the situation by suggesting that leaving a terrorist movement is often the result of factors that facilitate what he calls physical disengagement and psychological disengagement.

Horgan contends that psychological disengagement involves often-gradual changes in cognitions, emotions, or attitudes towards one's involvement in terrorist activity. Fighters can undergo psychological disengagement for several reasons, including:

(1) The development of negative feelings about engaging in terrorist activity that result from the fighter's continued membership in the group (e.g. anxiety, pressure);
(2) A change in personal priorities such that the fighter's goals and needs are not being met by their membership in the terrorist movement; and
(3) Disillusionment with the terrorist movement's practices.

In contrast, physical disengagement is an explicitly identifiable phenomenon whereby an active terrorist ceases to engage in violent activity for any variety of reasons, including

(1) Apprehension by authorities;
(2) Voluntary or forced movement into a non-violent role within the group;
(3) Ostracization from the group; and
(4) Being ejected from the movement.

Note that neither physical nor psychological disengagement from terrorism requires the individual to abandon the religious, political or ideological values that may have motivated their initial interest in the movement. Indeed, interviews with current and former terrorists have shown that many individuals had ceased engagement in violent activity on behalf of a terrorist organization, but had nonetheless retained beliefs and attitudes consistent with those espoused by the organization (chapters from Bjørgo and Horgan's 2009 book).

So, consistent with these factors, and in the tradition of Horgan and others (Horgan, 2014; Horgan and Braddock, 2010), this chapter defines *disengagement* as

> ...the process whereby an individual experiences a change in role or function that is usually associated with a reduction in violent participation. It may not necessarily involve leaving the movement, but is most frequently associated with significant temporary or permanent role change. Additionally, while disengagement may stem from role change, that role change may be influenced by psychological factors such as disillusionment, burnout, or the failure to reach the expectations that influenced initial involvement.

Contrary to disengagement, the deradicalization process suggests that an individual has psychologically distanced him/herself from a terrorist ideology. In this vein, this chapter defines *deradicalization* as

> ...the social and psychological process whereby an individual's commitment to, and involvement in, violent radicalization is reduced to the extent that they are no longer at risk for involvement and engagement in violent activity.

Here, the importance of the distinction between disengagement and deradicalization becomes clear. The vast majority of efforts geared towards reducing the risk of recidivism among former terrorists are promoted as "deradicalization programmes." That is, they suggest that they are able to reduce participants' commitment to the ideology that promoted their violent radicalization. In considering the current state of "deradicalization" by describing and evaluating some of these programmes, we can make judgements about what they achieve relative to what they claim. Stated simply, by distinguishing deradicalization from disengagement, we can make more accurate claims about whether these initiatives actually reduce participants' commitment to violent extremist ideologies.

The next section offers descriptions of six initiatives around the world that have not received the same level of attention as some of the more popular programmes. For the sake of parsimony, these descriptions will be kept somewhat brief to allow for greater elaboration on key issues in the domain of terrorist rehabilitation in the final section of the chapter.

Extant "deradicalization" efforts

Before delving into the deradicalization efforts that are meant to be the focus of this chapter, it is important to recognise notable programmes that are not profiled here. Although I will not be summarizing some of the more well-known "deradicalization" initiatives geared toward rehabilitating jihadi offenders, they have been hugely influential in the evolution of these efforts, and I want to be sure to direct the interested reader to further material where they can learn about them. The programmes in Saudi Arabia, Indonesia, Yemen, and the United Kingdom are particularly fundamental to the history of deradicalization and its current state.

For information on deradicalization in Saudi Arabia, also commonly known as PRAC (Prevention, Rehabilitation, and Aftercare), see Boucek (2007), Henry (2007), Horgan and

Braddock (2010), El-Said and Barrett (2013), and Combes (2013). To learn about the Indonesian deradicalization programme designed and implemented by its special counter-terrorist force, Detachment-88, you can seek work by O'Brien (2008), Schultze (2008), Abuza (2009), and most importantly, Istiqomah (2011). Information on the programme in Yemen geared towards rehabilitating and reintegrating jihadi terrorists in the wake of the bombing of the USS Cole can be found in work by Johnsen (2004), Brandon (2005), and Boucek *et al.* (2009). Note that the earlier publication dates on these articles indicates that the Yemeni programme was largely considered a failure and has not been active in some time. Finally, readers interested in learning about the deradicalization elements of the United Kingdom's Prevent strategy can seek out work by Combes (2013), Griffith-Dickson *et al.* (2014), Elshimi (2017), and Thornton and Bouhana (2017).

With these notable efforts recognized, we now move on to lesser-known deradicalization efforts respectively implemented in Singapore, Bangladesh, Egypt and Morocco.

Singapore: the religious rehabilitation programme

Like nearby Indonesia, the deradicalization programme in Singapore was largely predicated on news related to one of the most dangerous historical terrorist threats in the region – Jemaah Islamiyah (JI). In late 2001, several Singaporeans were arrested from within the ranks of JI. Following the realization that JI posed a threat not only to Singapore's security, but also to the minds of its citizens, religious scholars in the country took it upon themselves to organize discussions, dialogue, and counselling to challenge the brand of violent Islam that JI was promoting. In 2003, these religious experts formed a group called the Religious Rehabilitation Group, who gained access to prisoners who had been arrested for terrorist offences (Gunaratna and bin Mohamed Hassan, 2011, p. 38). The original iteration of the Religious Rehabilitation Group consisted of 16 men and five women. The men engaged directly with detainees who had been arrested as part of JI, and the women worked with the wives and children who had been arrested.

Unlike some other deradicalization initiatives (see below), the Singaporean programme does not offer practical benefits (e.g. reduced jail sentences) for those who take part in deradicalization activities (IPI, 2010, p. 9). Rather than offer these kinds of incentives, the Singaporean programme features a tailored approach whereby potential participants are screened to determine how best to approach their deradicalization. Regardless of the nature of an individual's deradicalization treatment, there are elements of their treatment that are common to those in other countries. First, participants in the programme engage in discussions that help rehabilitation groups understand their interpretation of Islam and how it can be influenced. Second, individuals undergo constant psychological assessment to determine if they remain a threat to domestic security in Singapore. If they are determined to still pose such a threat, they remain in prison. Finally, and most importantly, the families of arrested individuals are provided with support to avoid feelings of neglect on the part of those families and their detained relative.

As is the case in many terrorist deradicalization programmes, detainees were initially sceptical of the Religious Rehabilitation Group, accusing its members to be agents of the government and engaging in activities that were hypocritical to the spirit of true Islam (Hassan, 2016, p. 10). Nevertheless, the Group persisted and, as of 2016, more than 40 members of JI who had been arrested for terrorist offences had been released due to their engagement with the counsellors. Interestingly, the Singaporean programme does not mandate follow-up with released prisoners; they are largely released on their own recognizance. Although prisoners are on restriction orders following their release, if an annual assessment determines them to be ready, the restriction order is lifted and the former terrorist is free.

In the time since its original activities in the early 2000s, the Religious Rehabilitation Group has expanded to create several sub-initiatives geared towards preventing the spread of violent extremism in Singapore, including a helpline through which members of the Singaporean public can receive information about ISIS and the threat it poses and a mobile application through which users can chat with members of the Religious Rehabilitation Group (Koh, 2016).

Bangladesh: grassroots education initiatives and the "true" spirit of Islam

At a basic level, the Bangladeshi programme is based on four elements: the capture and incarceration of violent extremists, gathering intelligence from those extremists, religious dialogue intended to challenge violent extremist interpretations of Islam, and the provision of money to support these three efforts. Initially established in 2005 as a response to rising violence performed by Harajat-ul-Jihad-al-Islami (HuJI) and Jama'atul Mujahideen of Bangladesh, as well as concern over what to do with those who had been arrested from those groups, the Bangladeshi deradicalization programme is largely influenced and implemented by the country's government. Despite the heavy government influence on the programme, it has still been described as a "grassroots" programme intended to dissuade jihadi violence through the spread of the "true spirit of Islam" by community leaders and religious experts, as well as the implementation of modern education initiatives intended to provide programme participants the tools they need (e.g. information technology training) to successfully integrate into Bangladeshi culture and serve as a viable contributor towards it.

The programme operates primarily in three Bangladeshi districts that have been historical bastions of violent Islamic extremism, and the participants are largely comprised of madrassa students and others whom the government has identified as being vulnerable to Islamic extremism and/or jihadi violence. In contrast to other deradicalization programmes that are formally structured, administration of the Bangladeshi programme involves attendance in seminars, symposia, and other speaking events that programme coordinators promote with seemingly harmless descriptors. For instance, in 2010, the International Peace Institute reported that some of these events were:

> ...billed as being about innocuous topics such as 'Islam and peace' or 'Islam and pluralism,' but actually focus on terrorism. There is a heavy participatory element, and a program representative described this portion of the program to a conference participant as 'a covert form of psychological warfare'
>
> *(International Peace Institute, 2010, p. 4)*

The success of the Bangladeshi deradicalization programme is not contingent only on the seminars and symposia organized by its administrators. As a complement to the psychological elements of the programme, participants are also provided with financial assistance, guidance on receiving educational support, and help for their families. The combination of the speaking engagements and logistic support offered to participants is intended to limit ill-will towards the Bangladeshi government and the state, not only on the part of the programme's participants, but their families as well.

As with all deradicalization programmes, there are no hard and fast data outlining the historical efficacy of the Bangladeshi initiative. However, participants have argued that lower levels of terrorist incidents and local violence in Bangladesh, coupled with reduced recruitment into religious extremist groups, serves as cursory evidence for the programme's efficacy. Nevertheless, the report released by the International Peace Institute warns that it is difficult to determine whether the lower levels of violent extremist incidents and phenomena in Bangladesh are the result of the deradicalization programme or the hard-line practices undertaken by the Bangladeshi government and military in dealing with terrorists within their borders.

Egypt: prisoner rehabilitation through incentives

As in Bangladesh, deradicalization efforts in Egypt have been heavily influenced by the state. Unlike in Bangladesh, however, the nature of the Egyptian programme, from the time it was first implemented up through its dealings with former Islamic State fighters, has been somewhat dubious. Despite claims from the Egyptian government that it has long had a deradicalization programme in place (suggesting that its deradicalization efforts were initiated by an ambitious Egyptian government to contend with issues that had not yet arisen), the origins of Egyptian deradicalization efforts seem to be in the 1997 ceasefire declared by the Islamic Group. More specifically, it appears that following the announced ceasefire, the government began to implement practices they believed would facilitate deradicalization among captured leaders of the Islamic Group, as well as those from Egyptian Islamic Jihad. If these groups were going to stop fighting, the Egyptian state wanted to help that process along. In this way, it appears that Egyptian deradicalization practices were not independently developed and implemented by the government from the ground up, but were instead a response to decisions made by the terrorist groups operating within Egypt (see Kaya, 2016).

The Egyptian government's deradicalization efforts aimed at former members of Egyptian Islamic Jihad and the Islamic Group were nearly exclusively focused on those members who were in prison for their offences. Rather than adopt an approach similar to, for example, the Saudi model, which emphasizes psychological rehabilitation and interpretation of ideologies, the Egyptian deradicalization model is based on the provision of rights, rewards, and benefits to prisoners. Some of these privileges included a reduction in the number of executions carried out among former terrorists, fewer prisoners being sent to solitary confinement, improved prison visits, and incarceration at a facility located near the prisoner's home. In addition to these logistic benefits, the Egyptian government also advocated prisoner education, allowing them to access media sources, as well as interaction with ideological leaders (who themselves were encouraged to espouse moderate viewpoints) and other individuals who were not involved in violent extremist activity.

It has been argued that these benefits helped to deradicalize imprisoned terrorists in Egypt by making them more sympathetic to the state. That said, leaders from Egyptian Islamic Jihad and the Islamic Group were already committed to the aforementioned ceasefire. Given this, it is difficult to determine whether the state's actions did, in fact, have any effect on whether imprisoned radicals had undergone deradicalization. Indeed, speakers at the 2010 International Peace Institute conference on deradicalization efforts in Muslim-majority states pointed out that, although the Egyptian government's efforts to improve the conditions in prisons were praiseworthy, at that point the state had not yet produced taken any tangible steps to dispossess radical prisoners from the ideologies that motivated the behaviour that landed them in prison, nor had they produced any materials to assist in the psychological rehabilitation of released terrorists.

Morocco: *Moussalaha* (reconciliation)

Rather than develop and implement a formalized, structured deradicalization programme, the Moroccan government has historically, gradually and simultaneously built up its deradicalization and counter-radicalization (i.e. efforts to challenge terrorist ideologies before they take hold) efforts while encouraging non-governmental organizations to develop their own programmes that seek to achieve these goals as well. The development of these complementary efforts has been based, in part, on "investigating grave political violations of the past" (IPI, 2010, p. 7), wherein the state committed human rights violations against suspected terrorist offenders, whom they often detained, kidnapped, or "disappeared".

In the early 2010s, the Moroccan government pursued deradicalization and counter-radicalization through several benefits provided to those suspected of or arrested for terrorist offences, including early release, pardon, and general improvement of the state's violation of human rights. More tangible benefits were afforded to arrested individuals as well, including financial compensation and employment to those who were unjustifiably persecuted by the state. In conjunction with these measures, the Moroccan government also sought to promote reconciliation between terrorist offenders and their victims by encouraging the latter to speak about their experiences. Public communication channels (i.e. television and radio) also featured programmes designed to challenge other programmes that had been espousing radical interpretations of Islam and calling for jihad.

By 2016, Moroccan authorities sought to provide more structure to its deradicalization efforts, launching a programme drafted by the General Commission for the Management of Prisons and Reintegration and a religious organization called the Mohammadia League of Ulama (Masbah, 2018, p. 5). This programme, called *Moussalaha* ("Reconciliation") involved the selection of jihadi prisoners who were willing to undergo training for three to four months that was intended to teach them about moderate Islam and reconciliation with those who do not share their beliefs. By 2018, the Reconciliation deradicalization programme had only engaged with 35 out of almost 1000 prisoners in jihadi prisons. Moreover, participation in the programme has been voluntary; only individuals who expressed a desire to change their beliefs and attitudes took part in it. This is problematic, given that, in 2018, most of those who were in Moroccan prisons for terrorist offences were unrepentant supporters of ISIS.

In addition to the blind spots the Moussalaha programme suffers in dealing with individuals who are incarcerated, there is also little assistance for those who have been released from prison. This has made their reintegration into Moroccan society difficult, given that (a) they largely do not receive training on the social skills they need to successfully engage with Moroccan communities, and (b) employers are unlikely to hire someone who has been convicted of terrorist offences under Moroccan law. A human rights activist familiar with the problems experienced by terrorist prisoners in Morocco lamented that those released from Moroccan prisons need not only psychological counselling to help them cope with what they experienced in prison, but also economic assistance to help them financially support themselves (Masbah, 2018, p. 6).

By early 2019, many of these same problems with the Moroccan initiative persisted, with only about 50 individuals having gone through the programme. Even more problematic, the programme's goal of "reconciliation" is so broad that it remains unclear what the programme seeks to accomplish, even to participants. Said one former terrorist, "reconciliation between whom and whom?" (Masbah and Ahmadoun, 2019).

Current issues in the practice of "deradicalization"

As is evident from the four cases in the previous section, approaches to jihadi deradicalization are as varied as the countries in which they are developed. Nevertheless, there remain issues common to these (and other) programmes that remain unresolved. This is particularly troubling given that some of these issues have persisted since the first deradicalization programmes emerged in the mid-2000s. In the following section, I will call attention to some of the more enduring problems with deradicalization (as it is practised) and our study of it. These issues respectively relate to the terminology we use when discussing "deradicalization" initiatives, a lack of data and transparency surrounding the efficacy of these initiatives, and a failure to evaluate salient outcomes to help illustrate what works (or does not work) when attempting to rehabilitate terrorist offenders.

Terminology

If we return to the definitions offered at the beginning of this chapter, we see that deradicalization has generally been thought of as a social and psychological process whereby an individual grows less adherent to a violent extremist ideology to the point that they are not a risk for engaging in terrorism. The key implication of this definition is that deradicalization involves some form of psychological "shift" whereby an individual's beliefs and attitudes change in such a way that they are no longer consistent with those of the terrorist group of which they were a part.

Given this definition, it becomes questionable whether the programmes profiled in this chapter (as well as other programmes around the world) are engaged in deradicalization activities. To be sure, these programmes are designed to reduce the risk that participants will re-engage in terrorism upon their reintegration into society. However, desistance from terrorism does not necessarily imply that an individual has abandoned the values that led him or her to engage in terrorism in the first place. Moreover, the majority of these programmes have not undergone formal evaluation aimed at measuring the psychological impacts of the activities (see more below), so it remains difficult to conclude that subjects have been deradicalized.

Here, it may be instructive to consider concepts from the field of criminology. Criminologists distinguish two forms of desistance from crime – primary desistance and secondary desistance. The former relates to the phase immediately following the cessation of criminal activity. During primary desistance, the criminal has stopped – at least temporarily – engaging in activities that are against the law. This might be thought of as analogous to what I have described as physical disengagement in this chapter. In contrast, secondary desistance is a much more permanent process through which an individual experiences psychological changes that reorient that individual's beliefs, attitudes and values such that they no longer support participation in criminal activity.

Using these terms, it remains impossible to say that deradicalization programmes, as currently designed, simply lead to primary desistance rather than reorient participant's values in a way that make them less likely to engage in terrorist activity. Given this, and as I have argued elsewhere (Horgan and Braddock, 2010), it seems disingenuous to refer to these programmes as "deradicalization" efforts. Instead, it is more accurate to call them "risk reduction" programmes. This term captures the essence of the activities in which participants engage, as well as the outcomes derived from those activities. Unless and until the programmes can empirically demonstrate that they fundamentally alter participants' beliefs and attitudes towards the extremist ideologies that motivated their violent behaviour, they can only be said to reduce the likelihood that someone will re-engage in terrorism; it remains unclear (and in some cases, doubtful) that the impetus for the reduction in risk is due to psychological changes.

Lack of transparency and the measurement of salient outcomes

Although it remains unclear whether "deradicalization" efforts fundamentally alter programme participants' beliefs and attitudes, this could be resolved with the advent of metrics that gauge outcomes related to the ideologies that the programmes claim to combat. More specifically, to adequately determine whether "deradicalization" programmes actually engage in deradicalization, they should seek to incorporate two practices.

First, to ensure that programme activities relate to deradicalization rather than basic disengagement, the programmes utilize measurement instruments that gauge beliefs and attitudes concerning the ideology that guided participants' behaviours. Ideally, these measurements would be employed as part of a greater empirical effort to evaluate the effects that programme interventions have. As I have argued elsewhere (Braddock, 2019), to optimize the accuracy with which the effects of interventions can be gauged, the use of experimental and quasi-experimental methods are particularly useful. In the case of deradicalization programmes, this would involve measuring participants' beliefs, attitudes, intentions, and behaviours both before and after being subjected to programme intervention activities (or through post-test only designs that allow for the inclusion of a control group against which an intervention group can be compared). Only through these kinds of evaluations can the true effect of deradicalization activities on psychological outcomes be assessed.

That said, it is not enough to only measure these outcomes. One of the most persistent problems associated with deradicalization efforts is the failure of programme personnel to be forthcoming with their findings concerning their successes and failures. These programmes have historically made grandiose statements of their achievements, declaring that incredible majorities of participants are effectively "cured" and no longer pose a threat of engaging in terrorism, that participants have assimilated a moderate ideology that renders them less likely to be re-drawn to violent interpretations of Islam, and other claims. As has been documented elsewhere, these claims are often (a) not based on actual data related to participant recidivism, (b) based on data that are not made available to the public, and/or (c) based on dubious definitions for what they perceive as success (e.g. not engaging in violence in only the country in which the programme is based). To move towards a better science of deradicalization, the data on which these claims are made need to be made transparent to evaluators, policymakers, and the general public. While reducing the risk of terrorism is unequivocally a positive outcome, only through transparent data concerning the psychologies of programme participants can we effectively argue that deradicalization is possible, let alone being effectively practised.

References

Abuza, Z. (2009) The rehabilitation of Jemaah Islamiyah detainees in Southeast Asia: A preliminary assessment. In T. Bjørgo and J. Horgan (eds), *Leaving Terrorism Behind: Individual and Collective Disengagement.* New York: Routledge.

Bjørgo, T. and Horgan, J. (eds) (2009) *Leaving Terrorism Behind: Individual and Collective Disengagement.* New York: Routledge.

Boucek, C. (2007) Extremist re-education and rehabilitation in Saudi Arabia. *Terrorism Monitor,* 5, no. 16. Available https://jamestown.org/program/extremist-reeducation-and-rehabilitation-in-saudi-arabia/ (accessed 21 July 2019).

Boucek, C., Beg, S., and Horgan, J. (2009) Opening up the jihadi debate: Yemen's Committee for Dialogue. In T. Bjørgo and J. Horgan (eds), *Leaving Terrorism Behind: Individual and Collective Disengagement.* New York: Routledge.

Braddock, K. (2019) *A Brief Primer on Experimental and Quasi-experimental Methods in the Study of Terrorism.* ICCT Policy Brief. Available https://icct.nl/wp-content/uploads/2019/01/ICCT-Braddock-Brief-Primer-on-Experimental-Methods-Study-of-Terrorism-January2019.pdf (accessed 20 August 2019).

Brandon, J. (2005) Koranic duels ease terror. *Christian Science Monitor.* Available www.csmonitor.com/2005/0204/p01s04-wome.html (accessed 12 August 2019).

Combes, W. S. (2013) Assessing two countering violent extremism programs: Saudi Arabia's PRAC and the United Kingdom's Prevent strategy. *Small Wars Journal.* Available https://smallwarsjournal.com/jrnl/art/assessing-two-countering-violent-extremism-programs-saudi-arabia%E2%80%99s-prac-and-the-united-king (accessed 21 June 2019).

Ebaugh, H. R. F. (1988) *Becoming an Ex: The Process of Role Exit.* Chicago: University of Chicago Press.

El-Said, H. and Barrett, R. (2013) Saudi Arabia: The master of deradicalization. In H. El-Said and J. Harrigan (eds), *Deradicalising Violent Extremists*. London: Routledge.

Elshimi, M. S. (2017) *Deradicalisation in the UK Prevent Strategy*. London: Routledge.

Garfinkle, R. (2007) Personal transformations: Moving from violence to peace. *United States Institute of Peace Special Report*, 186.

Griffith-Dickson, G., Dickson, A., and Robert, I. (2014) Counter-extremism and deradicalisation in the UK: A contemporary review. *Journal for Deradicalization*, Winter 2014/2015, no. 1, 26–37.

Gunaratna, R. and bin Mohamed Hassan, M. F. (2011) Terrorist rehabilitation: The Singapore experience. In R. Gunaratna, J. Jerard, and L. Rubin (eds), *Terrorist Rehabilitation and Counter-Radicalisation: New Approaches to Counter-Terrorism*. New York: Routledge.

Hassan, A. S. R. (2016) Rehabilitation & deradicalisation in Singapore: Lessons from the Religious Rehabilitation Group. Paper presented at Islam and Global Peace Forum.

Henry, T. (2007) Get out of jihad free. *The Atlantic*. Available www.theatlantic.com/magazine/archive/2007/06/get-out-of-jihad-free/305883/ (accessed 21 July 2019).

Horgan, J. (2008) Deradicalization or disengagement? A process in need of clarity and a counterterrorism initiative in need of evaluation. *Perspectives on Terrorism*, 2(4), pp. 3–8.

Horgan, J. (2014) *The Psychology of Terrorism* (2nd edn). Oxon, UK: Routledge.

Horgan, J. and Braddock, K. (2010) Rehabilitating the terrorists? Challenges in assessing the effectiveness of deradicalization programs. *Terrorism and Political Violence*, 22, 267–291.

International Peace Institute (2010) A new approach? Deradicalization programs and counterterrorism. Report on the *Countering Violent Extremism: Learning from Deradicalization Programs in Some Muslim-Majority States* meeting, 16–17 March 2010. Available www.ipinst.org/wp-content/uploads/publications/a_new_approach_epub.pdf (accessed 31 July 2019).

Istiqomah, M. (2011) Deradicalization program in Indonesian prisons: Reformation on the correctional institution. Paper presented at the Australian Counter Terrorism Conference, Edith Cowan University, Perth, Western Australia, December 2011.

Johnsen, G. D. (2004) Terrorists in rehab. *Worldview Magazine*, 17(3). Retrieved June 13 2008, from www.worldviewmagazine.com/issues/article.cfm?id=139&issue=34

Kaya, Z. (2016) Letting go: De-radicalization in Egypt. *Journal for Deradicalization*, 6 (Spring), 87–104.

Koh, J. (2016) Religious Rehabilitation Group launches mobile application to combat radicalisation. *The Straits Times*. Available www.straitstimes.com/singapore/religious-rehabilitation-group-launches-mobile-application-to-combat-radicalisation (accessed 21 July 2019).

Masbah, M. (2018) The limits of Morocco's attempt to comprehensively counter violent extremism. *Middle East Brief*, Brandeis University Crown Center for Middle East Studies. Available www.brandeis.edu/crown/publications/meb/MEB118.pdf (accessed 20 July 2019).

Masbah, M., and Ahmadoun, S. (2019) Morocco's failure to reintegrate former jihadis. *Middle East Analysis*, Carnegie Endowment for International Peace. Available https://carnegieendowment.org/sada/78313 (accessed 12 August 2019).

O'Brien, N. (2008) Interview with a former terrorist: Nasir Abbas' deradicalization work in Indonesia. *CTC Sentinel*, 1(12). Available https://researchoutput.csu.edu.au/ws/portalfiles/portal/9365260/7598postpub.pdf (accessed 2 August 2019).

Schulze, K. E. (2008) Indonesia's approach to jihadist deradicalization. *CTC Sentinel*, 1(8). Available https://ctc.usma.edu/app/uploads/2010/06/Vol.1Iss8-Art3.pdf (accessed 2 August 2019).

Thornton, A. and Bouhana, N. (2017) Preventing radicalization in the UK: Expanding the knowledge-base on the Channel Programme. *Policing: A Journal of Policy and Practice*.

PART III

Public order and organized violent crime

14

HOW CROWD VIOLENCE ARISES AND HOW IT SPREADS

A critical review of theory and evidence

John Drury, Roger Ball, Fergus Neville, Stephen Reicher and Clifford Stott

Introduction

This chapter critically reviews theory and research on the emergence and spread of crowd violence. The chapter is divided into two parts, the first focused on violence *within* crowd events, and the second concerned with the spread of conflict *between* events. Early accounts in psychology and sociology shared the view that violence was inherent in crowds, but were unable to explain the social form of that violence. Modern theoretical frameworks have focused on normative patterns in crowd conflict, and have sought to account for the fact that most crowd events are not violent. The question of the spread of rioting across locations has a more recent history. Powerful mathematical models, developed first by sociologists and then criminologists, have been able to identify clear temporal and spatial patterns, demonstrating that riots influence each other, over and above key predictors such as deprivation. Yet when attempting to explain the mechanism of this spread, social scientists have either fallen back into irrationalist psychology ("contagion") or merely re-described behaviour through use of "rational actor" models. The chapter describes research on patterns of crowd conflict across diverse events suggesting that shared social identity specifies appropriate conduct (and hence explains common limits) and is the basis of changes in relations between crowd members and out-groups (hence explaining empowered action and psychological change). Shared social identity and collective empowerment in relation to out-groups are also argued to be mechanisms through which violence spreads between events.

Violence within crowd events

Reifying the "violent crowd"?

The "violent crowd" was the social problem that prompted the first wave of crowd psychology in late nineteenth-century Europe (Barrows, 1981). Certainly, from the point of view of many in the establishment, the crowd represented a threat to their world. Workers were becoming organized in unions, and there were a number of high-profile strikes; some of these were associated with violence, although most were peaceful. More dramatically, France had seen revolutions in 1789, 1830, and 1848 in which crowds were prominent. From the perspective of the gentlemen scholars, the most shocking of all these tumultuous events – the worst "crowd horror" – was the Paris Commune of 1871, although most of the bloodshed was caused by the troops on the Communards rather than the other way round.

Faced with this threat, Gustave Le Bon (1895) and others proposed explanations for what they saw as the inherent tendencies to mindless violence in crowds. The main disagreement between these early theorists was over whether these tendencies were properties of a distinct "group mind" or were located in each individual. In Le Bon's account, when people gather together as a "psychological crowd" (i.e. any gathering having a common focus) the conscious personality disappears, to be replaced by an ancestral "racial" unconscious. Further, people become suggestible and subject to "contagion" – any behaviour or sentiment will sweep through the crowd. While crowds could be "heroic", according to Le Bon, the predominance of the primitive "racial" unconscious explained why they were always stupid and typically destructive.

Against this "transformation" account, others placed more emphasis on the (violent) *predispositions of the individuals* constituting the crowd. Thus, Sighele (1891, cited in van Ginneken, 1985) argued that crowds committed criminal acts because they were comprised of criminal individuals. Similarly, Allport (1924, p. 295) claimed that "the individual in the crowd behaves just as he would behave alone, only more so". In this account, the presence of others stimulates "fundamental (individual) drives" (self-protection, hunger, sex) to overcome the civilized values that normally regulate behaviour, leading to uncontrolled violence.

These accounts of the immanent violence of the crowd achieved popular acclaim and were dominant for so long not because of the strength of their evidence, but rather because they provided a "scientific" gloss on a prevalent anti-collectivist ideology (McClelland, 1989; Reicher and Potter, 1985; Stott and Drury, 2017). In terms of evidence, Le Bon and others relied largely on secondary sources which they used selectively, abstracting crowd violence from its social context. Events such as the Williamson county miners' strike picket violence of 1922 (to take but one example), when 18 strike-breakers were killed, were made to appear as a "typical case" of a crowd mindlessly acting out an "unsocialised drive" for destruction (Allport, 1924, p. 310). What was excluded in this case was the events leading up to the massacre (Reicher, 1987). The event was not in fact "typical" but exceptional. It was the end result of a conflict with management that had gone on since 1919. For over two years, the strikers had rejected armed violence. They only accepted the legitimacy of violence after tanks and planes had been used against them. After eight weeks of a strike over conditions described as worse than under slavery, the company brought in imported scab labour. When strikers tried to talk to them, pit guards shot and killed five of the strikers. After another shooting, the strikers marched on the mine – they then came under further attack: a plane dropped dynamite and guards shot them with machine guns. Only then did the massacre of strike-breakers occur.

An obvious problem of explanations that reify violence into a characteristic of crowd psychology is that they cannot easily explain non-violence in crowds: the most basic evidence against them is that most crowds are not violent. To take a recent example, for the 2017–2018 football season in England and Wales, where there were hundreds of crowd events, there were only 3.5 football-related arrests per 100,000 attendees (Home Office, 2018).

The example of the Williamson massacre illustrates an equally fundamental problem. These early accounts cannot explain the *social form* of crowd behaviour in violent events: they cannot explain patterns of targets and limits on violence.

A second example of a "violent crowd" will illustrate this argument further and point to the kinds of concepts needed for a social psychological model of crowd violence. The food riots that swept eighteenth-century England and France might be thought of simply as "instinctual" explosions, expressing a basic need – indeed that is precisely how Allport (1924) described them. Surely people just get desperate with hunger, and seize what grain or bread that they can? Thompson (1971) analysed around 700 food riots that occurred in England between 1750 and 1820. He showed, first, that they didn't happen at times of greatest shortage but more often when grain supplies were increasing. The precipitating cause was not hunger (though people were indeed hungry), but the perception that the millers, bakers and others had transgressed local customs – for example by transporting grain out of the locality to fetch the highest price rather than keeping it to meet local needs.

Second, behaviour in these "riots" was far from primitive and uncontrolled – nicely summarized as follows:

> mixed crowds of ordinary people gather angrily before the shops of a miller, a merchant or a baker. They complain about prices, seize the food on hand and cart it off to the market square, sell it to all comers (so long as they belong to the community) at a price they declare to be just, turn over the cash to the owner of the grain or bread, and go home saying they have done justice, as the authorities themselves should have done justice.
>
> *(Tilly et al., 1975, p. 17)*

Putting these points together, then, the food riots reflected shared conceptions of legitimacy – in terms of why they were carried out, who the targets were, and the purposes of the "violence", which was to restore justice by punishing transgression.

Norms, rationality and identities in crowd violence

The examples described above suggest that we need different kinds of concepts than "primitive drives" to understand the nature of violence in crowds. From the 1950s onwards, new approaches developed, first in sociology and then in social psychology, drawing on the constructs of norms, rationality and identity.

Emergent norm theory (Turner and Killian, 1957, 1972) suggested that crowd behaviour, including violence, was determined by the same kinds of processes shaping everyday social behaviour – namely social norms. The difference was, however, that in an "extraordinary" situation, such as a riot, the usual norms did not apply and so people had to cast around to find new norms. Turner and Killian argued that these new norms emerged gradually through processes of interaction and meaning-seeking among people in the crowd until eventually a shared understanding arose; only then was collective behaviour possible. In introducing the concept of social norms to the study of crowd behaviour, emergent norm theory represented an important advance; for the first time, crowd behaviour was understood as structured by shared meanings which provided definitions of the upper limits of behaviour. Thus, there was no "spiral" of disinhibited behaviour as the contagion concept would suggest (Turner, 1964, p. 391).

Berk (1974) agreed with Turner and Killian (1957) that crowd behaviour was based on meanings, by adopting a rationalist approach. Drawing upon game theory, he suggested that targets in riots reflected each rioter's calculation of costs and benefits. Thus, Berk and Aldridge's (1972) analysis of riots in 15 US cities found that patterns of looting and damage were selective, not random, which they suggested reflected conscious interests (personal gain and opposition to the white establishment).

Emergent norm theory was right to highlight meaning-seeking in crowds, but did not say enough about the processes or constraints in the interaction process that led to "emergent norms": why this social norm rather than another one? Berk's (1974) gaming approach similarly does not say where the "interests" behind cost-benefit analyses come from. What was needed was a theory of the "social individual" to explain why some behaviours (not others) become normative in crowds, and how interests become collective.

The *social identity model (SIM) of crowd behaviour* (Reicher, 1982, 1984, 1987) was developed not only to provide a socialized alternative to Le Bon's unsocialized crowd "barbarian" but also to fill in the gaps left by emergent norm theory and the gaming approach. The social identity approach had already been applied to, and provided a non-reductionist, non-pathologizing account of, a range of collective phenomena, including different forms of intergroup conflict (Tajfel, 1982). In the form of *self-categorization theory* (Turner *et al.* , 1987), the approach provided a set of principles explaining how it was that people could see themselves and act as a group in the first place: "social identity is the cognitive mechanism which makes group behaviour possible" (Turner, 1982, p. 21). Reicher's SIM was an application of these principles to the specificities of crowd behaviour.

The fundamental idea in the social identity approach – that we have multiple identities that each provide a basis for collective coordination – was counter-posed to the Le Bonian assumptions of then-dominant "*de-individuation*" *theory* (e.g. Zimbardo, 1970): people do not lose their sense of self in the crowd, Reicher (1984, 1987) argued; rather they shift from personal identity to an identity they share with others. This means therefore not loss of control, but rather shift to collective definitions of appropriate conduct – group norms. This suggested an explanation for why some riot behaviours become collective – such as throwing stones at police – and others – such as throwing stones at a bus – do not: influence is both enabled and constrained by the shared definition of "who we are" (Reicher, 1984).

Reicher's (1984, 1987) study of the 1980 St Pauls riot showed that even the most violent crowd displayed behavioural limits, and these limits reflected the definition of social identity shared by those in the crowd: in St Pauls, there were limits to targets (the crowd attacked the police, not passers-by; they targeted properties associated with their continued powerlessness and poverty, not local homes or shops), geographical limits (they remained within the St Pauls district), and limits in terms of who joined in (only those who identified with St Pauls). Contra "contagion", not everyone was influential and not every behaviour spread (cf. Milgram and Toch, 1969). The most influential people were those who embodied the shared identity in this context (in this case, older Rastafarians). In addition, this detailed study of the contours of a riot contradicted the most basic assumption of Le Bon and "de-individuation" theories – that people are anonymous in the crowd. In fact, most participants were among people they knew (Reicher and Potter, 1985).

While this early version of the social identity model of crowd behaviour provided a compelling account of the limits of crowd violence, it said little about the dynamics of crowd events. And yet change was evident in the St Pauls riot data; there was a process of *becoming* conflictual over time that was described but not explained. The question was how these psychological changes could be theorized without falling back into Le Bonian notions that such changes were essentially meaningless, would soon be forgotten, and had no bearing on subsequent thoughts or feelings.

How does a peaceful crowd become violent?

Methodological as well as conceptual development was required to explain the dynamics of crowd violence. Reicher's (1984, 1987) study of the St Pauls riot lacked two elements that now needed to be added to subsequent research designs. The first was the temporal dimension already mentioned. The second grew from the criticism that Le Bon and others de-contextualized crowd violence. Crowd violence could not be properly understood outside of its relationship with other agents, such as the police or troops. Thus, it was necessary to include in the analysis the perspective and actions of such out-groups as a possible contributor to the events.

By including time and out-group actions in research designs, a pattern of intergroup interaction between crowd and police was identified across a variety of conflictual crowd events, including student protests (Reicher, 1996) and football crowd conflicts (Stott and Reicher, 1998b). The observation of this pattern of interaction led to the development of the following theses that together constitute the *elaborated social identity model* (ESIM) of crowd conflict (Drury and Reicher, 2009), which we will illustrate with analysis of the 1990 poll tax riot (Stott and Drury, 1999, 2000; Stott and Reicher, 1998a).

The ESIM suggests that the *conditions* necessary for the emergence and development of conflict between a crowd and others outside the crowd (such as the police) are twofold. First there is *an asymmetry of categorical representations*. For example, on the demonstration march that preceded the poll tax riot, while crowd members understood their own behaviour in sitting down in the road as traditional and therefore legitimate protest, police saw it as a threat to public order. This contrast of perceptions is insufficient in itself for conflict, however. Second, then, there needs to be an *asymmetry of power-relations* such that the police out-group is able to physically impose its definition of legitimate practice on the in-group of crowd participants. At the poll tax demonstration, the police had the means – the technology, organization and strength in numbers – to act upon their perceptions: they moved into the crowd with horses and officers in "riot" gear, using coercion to move the crowd.

Next, there is a *dynamic*. While police at the poll tax event understood their own action as a defensive response to a situation of growing threat from the crowd, since members of the crowd understood their own action as legitimate, they perceived the police action as unprovoked, "heavy handed" and therefore *illegitimate*. This therefore legitimized crowd action against the police (first as "self-defence" but subsequently as retaliation). But where that out-group action is also experienced as *indiscriminate* (i.e. as an action against "everyone" in the crowd), that response to the police also becomes more likely. Thus, at the poll tax riot, the perception that the coercive police action threatened "everyone" (bystanders as well as those confronting police) led to a sense of common fate. This was the basis of a more inclusive in-group self-categorization among crowd participants, superseding any prior internal divisions (including between the "peaceful majority" and the "violent minority"). The formation of a single large in-group social category, along with the feelings of consensus and the expectations of mutual in-group support that are thereby engendered, *empowers* members of the crowd in-group actively to oppose the police out-group. Finally, at the poll tax riot, this empowered crowd action confirmed police fears of the inherent threat of the crowd, leading to escalation of riot-control behaviours.

The pattern described in the ESIM does not apply to all instances of crowd conflict. It does not apply where a crowd is already intent on violence, for example. However, it has been validated both by multiple observations of crowds where key elements were evidenced (Drury and Reicher, 1999, 2009; Stott and Pearson, 2007), but also by a "natural experiment" with football crowds at the 2004 European championships (Stott *et al.*, 2007, 2008). In this latter case, reducing key variables (illegitimate and indiscriminate forms of policing) led to a predicted decrease in football-related disorder. This and similar evidence has informed interventions at UK and European football policing that have contributed to a reduction in disorder (Stott and Pearson, 2007), further demonstrating the validity of the approach.

The spread of crowd violence between locations

It has long been known that riots typically occur in spatial and temporal clusters. Historians were the first to examine this, and suggested that social influence processes were involved across locations. For example, in his study of eighteenth-century rural riots, Rudé (1964) provided maps illustrating the pathways taken within each wave, and suggested that "far from being a simultaneous eruption touched off at some central point of control, they were a series of minor explosions, breaking out not only in response to local initiative but to the force of example" (Rudé, 1964, p. 29).

The wave of urban riots that took place in the USA from 1964 to 1968 prompted the largest programme of research ever undertaken on riots, beginning with the Kerner report (National Advisory Commission on Civil Disorders, 1968). Kerner noted the temporal clustering, but most of the initial explanations focused on generic causes not the relation between the riots themselves. For example, because the riots occurred typically during the summer, it was suggested that the hot weather itself caused greater aggression, perhaps by overheating people's brains. Of course, this observed correlation neglected a vital mediator, which was that the hot weather brought more people outside and onto street corners, where they were more likely to get into conflict with police.

The explanation for the riots preferred by some US politicians focused on personal characteristics of the rioters. In these *"riff-raff" explanations*, the reason that some people rioted was because they were unsocialized and not integrated into local communities. "Riff-raff" explanations allowed politicians to argue that rioters were unrepresentative of the broader society, that riots did not reflect wider problems, and that the solution was more coercive policing rather than social justice. However, reviews found little evidence for individual attitudes or characteristics as predictors of participation (Fogelson, 1971; McPhail, 1971). Indeed, those who took part were similar to others in their neighbourhood except for being slightly more educated; and the riots happened in cities where there were tight-knit and stable Black communities rather than those that were fragmented or had high levels of migration (Caplan and Paige, 1968; Feagin and Hahn, 1973).

Deprivation was another explanation. However, the earliest statistical analysis of the US riots data found only weak evidence for its role as a predictor (Spilerman, 1970). This early statistical analysis also found no evidence for interdependence – the influence of one riot on another. It is likely that both of these null results were due to limitations of statistical approach (Myers, 2000). In relation to the question of interdependence, all Spilerman did was examine whether the cities closest to where a riot occurred also saw rioting. More sophisticated techniques subsequently provided evidence for interdependence (Midlarsky, 1978; Pitcher *et al.*, 1978). Further, event history analysis of the 1960s waves – re-examining Spilerman's data – and of the Swing riots previously analysed by Hobsbawm and Rudé (1969), added to the picture, showing that influence from riots decays over time, is mitigated by geographical distance, and is conditional on the intensity of rioting (Myers, 1998, 2000). Indeed, the intensity of previous riots in a wave has now been shown to be among the most important predictors of when and where riots occur, over and above factors such as deprivation (Aidt *et al.*, 2017; Myers, 2010).

Although this work on the spread of riots took place outside psychology, researchers recognized, explicitly or implicitly, the need for a social psychological analysis (e.g. Midlarsky, 1978), and as far back as Rudé (1964) have used psychological language. The logic was clear: if there was interdependence, there had to be a social-psychological process (or process*es*) underlying this, as the mechanism of influence. We turn now to the explanations that have been offered for this.

Explaining interdependence: from "contagion" to rational choice

In speculating on the psychological substrate underlying the evidence of interdependence, Midlarsky (1978) and Pitcher *et al.* (1978) drew on an admix of primitive psychology ("contagion", "disinhibition", "imitation"; e.g. Wheeler and Caggiula, 1966) and cognition (social learning; e.g. Bandura, 1977), according to which behaviours are copied to the extent that the observer perceives that behaviour has a successful outcome.

Another kind of explanation focused instead on *communication* pathways (Rudé, 1964; Hobsbawm and Rudé, 1969). Thus, both historians (Bohstedt and Williams, 1988; Charlesworth, 1983) and sociologists (National Advisory Commission on Civil Disorders, 1968; Singer, 1970) suggested the role of word of mouth, operating via road, rivers and, later, mass media.

Work by Myers (1999, 2000, 2010) represents the logical development of these theoretical strands. Although retaining the vocabulary of "contagion" he is careful to stipulate that he does not mean the mindless, uncritical influence associated with Le Bon (1895). Based on Oberschall's (1989) *costs-benefits model* of the spread of sit-in protests, Myers defines "contagion" as "a rational form of inter-actor influence in which potential actors observe and evaluate the outcomes of others' behaviours and then make a decision for themselves about whether or not to adopt the behaviour" (Myers and Przybysz, 2010, p. 64). Thus, except in name, the primitive psychology elements of previous theorists' speculations are expunged, resulting in a consistently rationalist account. Communication, not only between events but also among people within events, is also said to be important, as a way of making judgements about outcomes (Myers, 2010).

The advantages of the 'rational choice' approach are that it offers a model of riot diffusion compatible with *resource mobilization theory* and *political opportunity structures* – and thus allows us to understand waves of riots as "movements" in some sense (Myers, 2010; cf. McAdam, 1982). But there are also profound problems associated with the approach. On the one hand, to say that rioters' actions reflect rational self-interest risks being re-description rather than explanation. As Berk (1974) conceded, by itself the approach cannot predict. What are these 'interests'? Where do they come from? What happens if someone has multiple conflicting interests? The content of the self of 'self-interest' needs to be specified.

On the other hand, however, where there is such specification, the "self" of rational choice is clearly that of the rational maximizer, or *homo economicus*. Empirically, this has been shown elsewhere to be too narrow; personal costs of collective action do not always put people off – sometimes it's the opposite (Hirsch, 1990). Here riot theory lags behind social movement theory; versions of resource mobilization theory have long moved away from instrumentalism and begun to embrace the concept of identity (e.g. Gamson, 1992), bringing them in line with both European social movement theory (Melucci, 1989) and contemporary social psychology approaches to collective action (e.g. van Zomeren *et al.*, 2008).

In short, in a similar way to Le Bon's (1895) mindless "contagion", rational-actor models do not say enough about why some people and not others join in (Milgram and Toch, 1969), why some people and not others are influential, and why some actions spread and others are suppressed (Reicher, 1984).

We suggest that, to develop an account of the process underlying riot spread, we need to follow the lead of social movement theory, and turn to the concept of *identity*, specifically by building on the social identity approach in social psychology. In the next section, we describe developments that have applied this approach, using the case of the 2011 English riots.

Forms of riot spread in the 2011 English riots

The English riots of 2011, which occurred over four days in August, involved an estimated 20,000 people, with more than 4000 arrests and costs of up to £500 million (RCVP, 2011). The wave of riots was the largest in the UK since the 1980s and the most prolonged and widespread in London since the 1780 Gordon riots (Kawalerowicz and Biggs, 2015). The first rioting took place in Tottenham, two days after the fatal shooting by police of a local mixed-heritage man, Mark Duggan. Over the next 24 hours, rioting spread to other areas of London, and the following day to other cities in England. Altogether 66 local authority areas were affected by disorder. Politically, the events represented a crisis for the government and for the police, who were seen to be unable to cope in the first few days. Interdependence of the riots was assumed in the press, which characterized the process as "copycat" behaviour (e.g. Pilkington, 2011).

While some argue that behaviour in the 2011 riots was shaped overwhelmingly by a "consumerist" ideology (Treadwell *et al.*, 2013), both data gathered prior to the events and interviews with rioters carried out afterwards suggest that anti-police sentiments were a key driver (Newburn *et al.*, 2018; Kawalerowicz and Biggs, 2015). Deprivation was a further predictor (Kawalerowicz and Biggs, 2015), and some patterns of targets were found to reflect desire to control familiar space (Tiratelli, 2017).

A number of studies have addressed the question of diffusion in the 2011 riots (see Baudains *et al.*, 2012, 2013a, 2013b; Davies *et al.*, 2013). Thus, Baudains *et al.* (2012) used crime data to show that the odds of a riot occurring in one London district in August 2011 was positively associated with the number of events occurring in the surrounding areas the previous day. Baudains and colleagues follow Myers in explaining spread in terms of rational-choice (e.g. Baudains *et al.*, 2013b). By contrast, our own approach has focused on participants' conceptions of legitimacy and empowerment.

As well as the arrest and crime figures used by Baudians and others, we have drawn upon two other types of source: archive material (including video, news, and official reports) and interviews with 240 rioters carried out shortly after the riots (*Guardian*/LSE, 2011). This extensive dataset allowed us to do two things: first to triangulate multiple sources in order to construct a detailed time-line and fine-grained narrative account of each riot; and second to analyse the phenomenology of riot participants. In this section, we summarize recent analyses of spread in Haringey, Enfield and Hackney.

The initial escalation of collective conflict in Tottenham took place after police intervention against the crowd (Stott *et al.*, 2018). The main content of the initial rioting was anti-police, judging by the targets. The rioting then spread to other locations in Haringey borough over a 12-hour period. This geographical spread occurred alongside changes in the normative content of behaviour. The major change in normative action, toward systematic looting, developed as people moved to nearby retail centres. The event went beyond a reactive riot toward proactive rioting against targets that seemed to relate to longer term structural grievances (e.g. wealth inequality, antagonism toward the "establishment"). This normative transformation corresponded with a subjective sense of collective empowerment that emerged over time directly from the ongoing identity-based intergroup dynamics of the anti-police riot. One important element of this was that long-standing "postcode rivalries" among groups of young people were superseded in their shared conflict with police. In a nutshell, then, collective action based on a shared hostility to the police both revealed and created police vulnerability, thereby forming the basis of new collective actions (Stott *et al.*, 2018).

The following day, rioting spread to Enfield, a London borough north of Haringey. What appeared to outside observers as simply looting was in fact more complex. Our analysis suggests that the rioting was a result of people converging to deliberately create conflict as a social identity-based expression of power (Ball, 2017). Some travelled from Haringey, empowered by the events the previous day; others travelled from more deprived districts of Enfield borough. After police managed to disperse them from the town centre, their motivations and the patterns of collective action changed. It was at this point that looting became more concerted and some groups systematically attacked symbols of wealth.

As Baudains *et al.* (2013a, 2013b) point out, actions by police and other authorities can inadvertently draw rioters to certain locations. In Enfield Town, police closed down the town centre based on intelligence that a riot would occur there, but in in doing so they served to communicate to potential rioters that this was indeed the place where the riot would take place (Ball, 2017).

There also seem to have been other ways that police actions had unintended consequences, hastening the spread of rioting in August 2011. Thus, in their concern to prevent rioting in Hackney, police increased "stop and searches" in the area, creating the very toxic interactions that were among the existing grievances for many people. Rioting followed shortly afterwards (Stott *et al.*, 2017).

Most of the analysis of spread described above focuses on adjacent districts or boroughs. But the diffusion of riots often occurs across non-adjoining areas and involves different populations. Here, spread is not simply a matter of individuals travelling to new locations; whole new communities get involved. Therefore, a psychological account is required to explain the involvement of these new communities. In the next section we present a social identity model of this kind of riot diffusion.

A social identity model of riot diffusion

A social identity model of riot diffusion, based upon the social identity principles described earlier, makes three key claims. The first is that since the influence of others varies with shared social identity (Turner, 1991), rioting in one location will increase support for riots in further locations as a function of the number of people in these further locations who perceive that they share a common social identity with the first rioters.

The second claim is that, insofar as the translation of pro-riot views into action depends upon a sense of empowerment based, in turn, on perceptions of agreement with and expectations support from co-present others (Drury and Reicher, 1999), then local interactions in these further locations that confirm these perceptions and expectations (Stott *et al.*, 2018) increase the probability that rioting in the first location will lead not just to supportive attitudes but also to actual rioting in the further locations.

Third, as the riots confirm the vulnerability of the police, they empower those who identify as anti-police to act in ways that are considered legitimate by rioters but which are impeded by the police in everyday life – including not only attacking police, but also looting and attacking wealth (Stott *et al.*, 2018; see also Reicher *et al.*, 1995). As well as taking place between events, there will be a homologous process *within* each location; where police are seen to be routed, this confirms their vulnerability in the local context and leads many more people to be emboldened and to converge into the area.

Arrest data from August 2011 suggest there was little travelling by riot participants across the River Thames (Baudains *et al.*, 2013b), which indicates that any diffusion of rioting from North to South London reflects psychological influence between people and events. Therefore, we examined the spread of rioting from Tottenham in the north, to Brixton, Croydon and Clapham in the south to examine the usefulness of the social identity model (Stott and Drury, 2018).

Across all three locations, we found evidence of anti-police sentiments among rioters, as well as a broader sense of alienation from "the system". Rioters often gave these common attitudes as a reason for participation. There was evidence that the shared grievance enabled collective action, through providing a sense of "we-ness", and also structured the selection of targets (first the police and then high-end shops).

However, there were also some important differences between the locations. Relatively more Brixton interviewees saw events in Tottenham as relevant to themselves, based on a common relation to the police and sometimes in terms of common identification as Black. They were more likely than other interviewees to describe their anger and sense of injustice at the killing of Mark Duggan. Relatively fewer of the Croydon and Clapham interviewees identified in this way. It therefore seems that more Brixton interviewees than those from the Croydon and Clapham riots were influenced by events in Tottenham.

Thus, there was evidence to support our first claim that the influence of rioters in one location upon the beliefs of people in other locations will vary as a function of shared social identity. In relation to the second claim, interviewees from all three riots referred to their expectations that people in their networks and communities would participate in rioting, and this seemed to have influenced their own decisions to participate.

In relation to the third claim, there was also evidence from across the three locations that, because interviewees identified as anti-police, some of them were emboldened by perceived police vulnerability created in the previous riot(s). In particular, for Croydon and Clapham interviewees, their own readiness to get involved was based on this perception.

What is more, within each location, the catalyst that transformed minor skirmishes into full-scale rioting was the actions of a relatively small group initiating conflict with police, in line with our expectation of homology. Secondary convergence occurred after this power-reversal. With this further convergence came changes in the patterns of behaviour: successful anti-police rioting created the basis for commodity rioting and attacks on property.

While the social identity model of riot diffusion is relatively new and only tested in a limited number of riot locations so far, it has the advantage over previous accounts (simple "contagion", rational-choice) of being based on evidence not only of the sequence of events (e.g. from archive and crime data), but of how participants subjectively experienced them and what their motivations were.

Conclusion

The topic of violence has historically dominated, and distorted, scholarly accounts of crowd behaviour, from its origins in late nineteenth century France. A chapter focused on explaining collective violence could give the mistaken impression that crowds and violence necessarily co-occur, perpetuating the myth of the violent crowd promoted by the early "crowd scientists". This is why it is important to finish by re-affirming that crowd violence is rare. Most of the violence in crowds historically has been committed *against* crowds not *by* them. Most crowds are not involved in struggle; but even among those that are there are usually strong norms that regulate against violence on most occasions. Some crowds in struggle adopt non-violent identities and remain peaceful when attacked. Crowds are violent when they see violence both as legitimate and as effective in meeting their particular goals. When it does occur, most crowd violence is meaningfully and normatively related to the identities of crowd participants – we know this from the selectivity in who and what is attacked. We also know that, when crowd violence spreads between people and locations, not everyone joins in and not every behaviour spreads. Shared understandings of "who we are", and who "our" enemy is, make better sense of patterns of spread than concepts such as "contagion". In order to understand crowd violence, and – where we regard it as illegitimate – to try to prevent it, we need to understand crowd members' definitions of legitimacy and illegitimacy, their sense of power, and who they include as "us". We need to understand the *identities* of the crowd.

References

Aidt, T., Leon, G., and Satchell, P. (2017) The social dynamics of riots: Evidence from the Captain Swing riots, 1830–31. Cambridge Working Paper.

Allport, F.H. (1924) *Social Psychology*. Boston, NJ: Houghton Mifflin Co.

Ball, R. (2017) The Enfield "riot": A case study for analysing the spread of urban disorder in London, August 2011. Paper presented at Annual Scientific Meeting of the International Society of Political Psychology (ISPP) June–July 2017.

Bandura, A. (1977) Self-efficacy: Toward a unifying theory of behavioural change. *Psychological Review*, 84(2), 191–215.

Barrows, S. (1981) *Distorting Mirrors: Visions of the Crowd in Late Nineteenth Century France*. Yale, CT: Yale University Press.

Baudains, P., Braithwaite, A., and Johnson, S.D. (2012) Spatial patterns in the 2011 London riots. *Policing: A Journal of Policy and Practice*, 7(1), 21–31.

Baudains, P., Braithwaite, A., and Johnson, S.D. (2013a) Geographic patterns of diffusion in the 2011 London riots. *Applied Geography*, 45, 211–219.

Baudains, P., Braithwaite, A., and Johnson, S.D. (2013b) Target choice during extreme events: A discrete spatial choice model of the 2011 London riots. *Criminology*, 51(2), 251–285.

Berk, R. (1974) A gaming approach to crowd behaviour. *American Sociological Review*, 39, 355–373.

Berk, R., and Aldrich, H. E. (1972) Patterns of vandalism during civil disorders as an indicator of selection of targets. *American Sociological Review*, 37, 533–547.

Bohstedt, J. and Williams, D. E. (1988) The diffusion of riots: The patterns of 1766, 1795, and 1801 in Devonshire. *Journal of Interdisciplinary History*, 19(1), 1–24.

Caplan, N. S. and Paige, J. M. (1968) A study of ghetto rioters. *Scientific American*, 219, 15–21.

Charlesworth, A. (1983) The spatial diffusion of rural protest: An historical and comparative perspective of rural riots in nineteenth-century Britain. *Environment and Planning D: Society and Space*, 1(3), 251–263.

Davies, T. P., Fry, H. M., Wilson, A. G., and Bishop, S. R. (2013) A mathematical model of the London riots and their policing. *Scientific Reports*, 3, 1303.

Drury, J. and Reicher, S. (1999) The intergroup dynamics of collective empowerment: Substantiating the social identity model. *Group Processes and Intergroup Relations*, 2, 381–402.

Drury, J. and Reicher, S. (2009) Collective psychological empowerment as a model of social change: Researching crowds and power. *Journal of Social Issues*, 65, 707–725.

Feagin, J. R. and Hahn, H. (1973) *Ghetto Revolts*. New York: Macmillan.

Fogelson, R. M. (1971) *Violence as Protest: A Study of Riots and Ghettos*. New York: Anchor.

Gamson, W. A. (1992) The social psychology of collective action. In A. D Morris and C. M Mueller (eds), *Frontiers in Social Movement Theory*. New Haven, CT: Yale University Press.

Guardian/LSE (2011) *Reading the Riots: Investigating England's Summer of Disorder*. London: The Guardian and LSE.

Hirsch, E. L. (1990) Sacrifice for the cause: Group processes, recruitment, and commitment in a student social movement. *American Sociological Review*, 55, 243–254.

Hobsbawm, E. and Rudé, G. (1969) *Captain Swing*. London: Phoenix Press.

Home Office (2018) Football-related arrests and banning order statistics, England and Wales, 2017–18 season. Retrieved from https://assets.publishing.service.gov.uk/government/uploads/system/uploads/attachment_data/file/756379/football-related-arrests-banning-orders-1718-hosb2818.pdf

Kawalerowicz, J. and Biggs, M. (2015) Anarchy in the UK: Economic deprivation, social disorganisation, and political grievances in the London riot of 2011. *Social Forces*, 94(2), 673–698.

Le Bon, G. (1895) *The Crowd: A Study of the Popular Mind*. London: Ernest Benn.

McAdam, D. (1982) *Political Process and the Development of Black Insurgency, 1930–1970*. Chicago: University of Chicago Press.

McClelland, J. S. (1989) *The Crowd and the Mob: From Plato to Canetti*. Abingdon, UK: Routledge.

McPhail, C. (1971) Civil disorder participation. *American Sociological Review*, 38, 1058–1073.

Melucci, A. (1989) *Nomads of the Present: Social Movements and Individual Needs in Contemporary Society*. London: Hutchinson Radius.

Midlarsky, M. I. (1978) Analyzing diffusion and contagion effects: The urban disorders of the 1960s, *American Political Science Review*, 72(3), 996–1008.

Milgram, S. and Toch, H. (1969) Collective behavior: Crowds and social movements. In G. Lindzey and E. Aronson (eds), *The Handbook of Social Psychology* (2nd ed., Vol. 4). Reading, MA: Addison-Wesley.

Myers, D. (1998) Collective violence and heterogenous diffusion processes: US racial rioting from 1964 to 1971. *American Journal of Sociology*, 106(1), 173–208.

Myers, D. (2000) The diffusion of collective violence: Infectiousness, susceptibility, and mass media networks. *American Journal of Sociology*, 106(1), 173–208.

Myers, D. (2010) Violent protest and heterogeneous diffusion processes: The spread of U.S. racial rioting from 1964 to 1971. *Mobilization: An International Quarterly*, 15(3), 289–321.

Myers, D. and Przybysz, J. L. (2010) The diffusion of contentious gatherings in the Captain Swing uprising. In S. Poole and A. Spicer (eds), *Captain Swing Reconsidered: Forty Years of Rural History from Below* (Vol. 32). Southern History Society.

National Advisory Commission on Civil Disorders (1968) *Report of the National Advisory Commission on Civil Disorders*. New York: National Advisory Commission on Civil Disorders.

Newburn, T., Diski, R., Cooper, K., Deacon, R., Burch, A., and Grant, M. (2018) 'The biggest gang'? Police and people in the 2011 England riots. *Policing and Society*, 28(2), 205–222.

Oberschall, A. (1989) The 1960 sit-ins: Protest diffusion and movement take-off. *Research in Social Movements, Conflict and Change*, 11(1), 31–53

Pilkington, D. (2011) Rioting in London sparked "copycat" behaviour, *Independent*, 14 November.

Pitcher, B. L., Hamblin, R. L., and Miller, J. L. L. (1978) Diffusion of collective violence. *American Sociological Review*, 43(1), 23–35.

Reicher, S. D. (1982) The determination of collective behaviour. In H. Tajfel (ed.), *Social Identity and Intergroup Relations*. Cambridge, UK: Cambridge University Press.

Reicher, S. D. (1984) The St Pauls' riot: An explanation of the limits of crowd action in terms of a social identity model. *European Journal of Social Psychology*, 14, 1–21.

Reicher, S. D. (1987) Crowd behaviour as social action. In J. C. Turner, M. A. Hogg, P. J. Oakes, S. D. Reicher, and M. S. Wetherell (eds), *Rediscovering the Social Group: A Self-categorisation Theory*. Oxford, UK: Blackwell.

Reicher, S. (1996) "The Battle of Westminster": Developing the social identity model of crowd behaviour in order to explain the initiation and development of collective conflict. *European Journal of Social Psychology*, 26, 115–134.

Reicher, S. and Potter, J. (1985) Psychological theory as intergroup perspective: A comparative analysis of "scientific" and "lay" accounts of crowd events. *Human Relations*, 38(2), 167–189.

Reicher, S., Spears, R., and Postmes, T. (1995) A social identity model of deindividuation phenomena, *European Review of Social Psychology*, 6, 161–198.

Riots, Communities and Victims Panel (2011) *5 Days in August – An Interim Report on the 2011 English Riots*. London: Riots, Communities and Victims Panel.

Rudé, G. F. (1964) *The Crowd in History: A Study of Popular Disturbances*. London: Lawrence and Wishart.

Singer, B. D. (1970) Mass media and communication processes in the Detroit riot of 1967. *The Public Opinion Quarterly*, 34(2), 236–245.

Spilerman, S. (1970) The causes of racial disturbances: A comparison of alternative explanations. *American Sociological Review*, 35, 627–649.

Stott, C. and Drury, J. (1999) The intergroup dynamics of empowerment: A social identity model. In P. Bagguley and J. Hearn (eds), *Transforming Politics: Power and Resistance*. London: Macmillan.

Stott, C. and Drury, J. (2000) Crowds, context and identity: Dynamic categorisation processes in the "poll tax riot", *Human Relations*, 53, 247–273.

Stott, C. and Drury, J. (2017) Contemporary understanding of riots: Classical crowd psychology, ideology and the social identity approach. *Public Understanding of Science*, 26(1), 2–14.

Stott, C. and Drury, J. (2018) The social psychology of the spread of the 2011 riots: from Tottenham to South London. Paper presented at British Psychological Society Social Psychology Section annual conference, Keele, August 2018.

Stott, C. and Pearson, G. (2007) *Football 'Hooliganism': Policing and the War on the 'English Disease'*. London: Pennant Books.

Stott, C. and Reicher, S. (1998a) Crowd action as inter-group process: Introducing the police perspective. *European Journal of Social Psychology*, 28, 509–529.
Stott, C. and Reicher, S. (1998b) How conflict escalates: The inter-group dynamics of collective football crowd "violence". *Sociology*, 32, 353–377.
Stott, C., Adang, O., Livingstone, A., and Schreiber, M. (2007) Variability in the collective behaviour of England fans at Euro2004: "Hooliganism", public order policing and social change. *European Journal of Social Psychology*, 37, 75–100.
Stott, C., Adang, O., Livingstone, A., and Schreiber, M. (2008) Tackling football hooliganism: A quantitative study of public order, policing and crowd psychology. *Psychology, Public Policy, and Law*, 14, 115–141.
Stott, C., Drury, J., and Reicher, S. (2017) On the role of a social identity analysis in articulating structure and collective action: The 2011 riots in Tottenham and Hackney. *British Journal of Criminology*, 57(4), 964–981.
Stott, C., Ball, R., Drury, J., Neville, F., Reicher, S., Boardman, A., and Choudhury, S. (2018) The evolving normative dimensions of "riot": Toward an elaborated social identity explanation. *European Journal of Social Psychology*, 48(6), 834–849.
Tajfel, H. (ed.) (1982) *Social Identity and Intergroup Relations*. Cambridge, UK: Cambridge University Press.
Thompson, E .P. (1971) The moral economy of the English crowd in the eighteenth century. *Past and Present*, 50, 76–136.
Tilly, C., Tilly, L., and Tilly, R. (1975) *The Rebellious Century: 1830–1930*. London: Dent.
Tiratelli, M. (2017) Reclaiming the everyday: The situational dynamics of the 2011 London riots. *Social Movement Studies*, 17(1), 64–84.
Treadwell, J., Briggs, D., Winlow, S., and Hall, S. (2013) Shopocalypse now: Consumer culture and the English riots of 2011. *British Journal of Criminology*, 53(1), 1–17.
Turner, J. C. (1982) Towards a cognitive redefinition of the social group. In H. Tajfel (ed.), *Social Identity and Intergroup Relations*. Cambridge, UK: Cambridge University Press.
Turner, J. C. (1991) *Social Influence*. Buckingham, UK: Open University Press.
Turner, J. C., Hogg, M. A., Oakes, P. J., Reicher, S. D., and Wetherell, M. S. (1987) *Rediscovering the Social Group: A Self-categorisation Theory*. Oxford, UK: Blackwell.
Turner, R. H. (1964) Collective behaviour. In R. E. L. Faris (ed.), *Handbook of Modern Sociology*. Chicago, IL: Rand McNally.
Turner, R. H., and Killian, L. M. (1957) *Collective Behaviour*. Englewood Cliffs, NJ: Prentice-Hall.
Turner, R. H., and Killian, L. M. (1972) *Collective Behaviour* (2nd edn). Englewood Cliffs, NJ: Prentice-Hall.
van Ginneken, J. (1985).The 1895 debate on the origins of crowd psychology. *Journal of the History of the Behavioral Sciences*, 21(4), 375–382.
van Zomeren, M., Postmes, T., and Spears, R. (2008) Toward an integrative social identity model of collective action: A quantitative research synthesis of three socio-psychological perspectives. *Psychological Bulletin*, 134, 504–535.
Wheeler, L., and Caggiula, A. R. (1966) The contagion of aggression. *Journal of Experimental Social Psychology*, 2, 1–10.
Zimbardo, P. G. (1970) The human choice: Individuation, reason and order versus de-individuation, impulse and chaos. In W. J. Arnold and D. Levine (eds), *Nebraska Symposium on Motivation 1969*. Lincoln: University of Nebraska, pp. 237–307.

15

MANAGING COLLECTIVE VIOLENCE

Policing public order and public safety events

David Marshall

Introduction

This chapter explores how current law enforcement structures respond to the wide range of public order and public safety challenges they are responsible for managing in their core duty of public protection and maintenance of the peace. Often routine and innocuous events, can, if not appropriately managed, lead to outbreaks of violence perpetrated by large groups, often, although not always, loosely or structurally affiliated by a "common purpose", driving acts of civil disobedience and group violence. These events can range from sophisticated planned actions, to spontaneous build-up of tensions and conflict. How the police respond to such situations is critical, both in the understanding of the manner in which these diverse opportunities can manifest into violent action, and in a tactical sense – what works to diffuse and control (or conversely aggravate) large-scale group violence, often seen in activities such as political protest, sporting events such as football, and other large gatherings, particularly where separate factions exist, or where a common aggravator is identified.

Understanding the interactions at play is important; after all, violence, including the spiralling effects of collective violence, requires at least one actor and one target (Adang, 2011) if it is to achieve any directed outcome. Rather than being unwieldly and operating as a mindless mass, collective violence in this context can have sagacious structures; after all those who possess the drive of such a common purpose often take steps to overcome any obstacles that impede their action and direct violence to whatever agency stands in front of the action. Violence in this sense tends to be "purposive" in nature (Waddington, 2003).

Public order policing: a historical overview

Experienced police public order commanders will regularly extol the virtues of robust planning processes and state rather confidently that the success in mitigating group violence in a public order context is 'all about the planning' and to some extent this is true. The luxury and effective use of time in this regard cannot be overstated. Planning for a football match, a political protest, or any other risk event where the event organisers have even tentatively engaged and provided a reasonable amount of notice allows police commanders time to develop plans, marshal resources of sufficient number and specialism, and crucially develop a plan around the relative threat and risk the event poses based on the available intelligence assessment. Furthermore, it allows police to assess contingencies or the 'what ifs' enabling them to build plans that address the foreseen, if sometimes assessed as unlikely, complications that may emerge during the operation, and to put steps in place to deal with these contingencies should they arise. Yet, what about those events that emerge spontaneously, where police have little time to plan and the response is more reactive than proactive? Public disorder and the associated risk of violence can and do occur spontaneously, meaning that the police have little or no prior warning that the action would take place, either through a truly unprompted event or through a failure of the "system" to identify and address at an early enough juncture. Collective violence is, in this sense, often portrayed as "unpredictable and random" (Bayley and Shearing, 2005).

In the UK context, the history of large-scale outbreaks of public disorder and violence appear at least to emerge rather spontaneously, allowing law enforcement little time to engage in robust and detailed planning processes. In fact, and although by no means an uncontested theory, there are some commentators who cited routine outbreaks of riots and "mob rule" as one of the "precipitating factors" for the introduction of Robert Peel's New Police in London in 1829 and the formation of the Metropolitan Police (Brogden, 2005), given the perceived inadequacy of the previous law enforcement structures to deal with these incidents. However, it might first be helpful to examine the historical context of serious public disorder experienced in mainland Britain over the past four or so decades in order to set the context for how policing responses have adapted and refocused in that time.

The late 1970s and 1980s saw two decades of civil unrest in many parts of the mainland UK. For the purposes of this discussion we will exclude Northern Ireland due to the separate and complex trigger points responsible for disorder occurring in that part of the UK. Without question, much of what occurred in this period on the mainland, however, was also a complex mix of concentrated social deprivation in many inner-city areas, coupled with racial tensions which existed between, in particular, the police and these same communities. The early 1980s in particular saw increasingly strained relationships between the police and black communities in inner cities in England. This manifested itself with a series of riots and civil unrest in Bristol in 1980, Brixton in 1981 followed in the same year by riots in Liverpool and Birmingham (Marshall, 2018). Until this point in history, police tactics to contain large-scale civil unrest could be described as reactionary at best, and amateurish at worst.

In the early 1980s following a series of riots, including Bristol (1980) and Brixton, London (1981), and the subsequent failure of the police in these instances to prevent this widespread disorder and injury, particularly serious injury to police officers, preparation to deal with riots, driven at government level, intensified, with dustbin lids being replaced by more sophisticated methods such as riot shields, the wearing of reinforced helmets and the emergence of more thought-out public order tactics. While some large police organizations across the globe retain permeant police specialist resources to deal with civil unrest and riots (Bayley, 2005), police forces in the UK created specialist capability in the form of Police Support Units (PSUs) to help deal with the more challenging large-scale outbreaks of public disorder. These structures remain today, and are still largely drawn from conventional officers who are trained in specialist public order tactics and equipment, and deployed away from their "day jobs" to form into organized units, with what Reiner (2000) describes as a "third force" within police organizations. In particular, there were the Broadwater Farm riots in North London, during which serious violence, including the use of firearms, was used towards the police, culminating on the brutal murder of Metropolitan Police Constable, Keith Blakelock, who was stabbed to death on the estate while deployed to the riots – the first time a police officer had been murdered in the UK in a riot situation since the Coldbath Fields incident in 1833 (Reiner, 2000).

The characterization of "rioters" in this and similar outbreaks during that period was essentially and somewhat accurately portrayed as black youths, with the flashpoint events emanating from a cocktail of perceived police oppression, racism and sustained social depravation, with violence viewed in this sense as a "symptom of collective wrath" (Waddington, 2003). This led to the Scarman Report (1982), the first to hint at "institutional racism" in policing, in the context of the trigger points for these riots. However, in the decade that followed, the nature of rioting in the UK experienced a shift and, in the early part of the 1990s, the main distinction from the previous two decades was that the rioters themselves were white (Newburn, 2014).

The Poll Tax riots in central London in 1991 were, according to some commentators, the worse of the twentieth century and symbolized the end of the Thatcher era, and with it the end of the myth that rioting was predominantly a "black thing" (Marshall, 2018). These riots saw 300 police officers injured, with hundreds of arrests made. Damage, looting, and violence "fanned out" from Trafalgar Square into other parts of London (Reiner, 2000), and the police appeared to have been taken by surprise due to the sheer scale, violence and destruction targeted towards them. Following this, there were further outbreaks of rioting in Bradford, West Yorkshire in 1995, emanating from a grievance Asian youths had with the local police; Burnley, Oldham and Bradford all in 2001; and in Birmingham in 2005, again with the trigger points being racial in nature, where racial tensions both within communities themselves and those directed specifically at the police were the catalyst for serious disorder and violence.

Causation factors: collective violence in public order situations

Before examining the most recent outbreaks of large-scale public disorder and violence in a UK context (the 2011 Summer Riots), it is important to briefly discuss the catalyst (or triggers) for riots in general which, by their nature, generally lead to large-scale acts of collective violence, destruction of property and other criminal acts. As such, it is an important factor to consider generally when understanding the catalyst(s) for such events, but, particularly in policing terms, this analysis should possibly be examined as a form of "crime prevention" as would be the approach with other "crime" types. There have been many studies and post-event analyses of what factors trigger riots, but it was Waddington (2010) who arguably created the most systemic review and analysis of this aspect in the construction of his six-point "flashpoints" model. Its fundamental premise is that "public disorder cannot be reduced to a single explanatory variable, but is best understood in terms of six interdependent, and sometimes overlapping, levels of analysis: *structural, political/ideological, cultural, contextual, situational* and *interactional*".

Waddington's model is not without criticism (see Bagguley and Hussain, 2008), although Newburn (2014) attempted to synthesize this model with other components in an attempt to bring focus not only on to the precursor events similar to Waddington's flashpoints model, but to explore those factors relevant to the aftermath of riots, as he depicts in Table 15.1.

However, it would not be doing credit to Waddington and his seminal work in this respect if we did not briefly consider his "flashpoints" hypothesis within the context of our discussion.

The six levels of Waddington's (2010) analytical framework incorporate a set of variable factors previously understood to have a contributory role to the catalysts for outbreaks of disorder (Waddington, 2010). The six levels of analysis are (Newburn, 2014): (i) *structural*, which focuses on what Waddington (2010, p. 344) describes as the "macro-sociological" factors; (ii) *political/ideological*, intergroup dynamics, and how these groups relate to and are treated by political institutions (Newburn, 2014); (iii) *cultural*, explores culture and sub-cultural (Waddington, 2010) group dynamics and their conception of social structures; (iv) *contextual*, both immediate and the longer-term immediate backdrop (Newburn 2014) in group dynamics and in particular how

Table 15.1 Riots: what to compare? (Adapted from Newburn, 2014, p. 49)

Context	*Structural*	*Political/ideological*	*Cultural*
Dynamics:	How it starts (including possible 'flashpoints')	How it matures and spreads	How long it lasts and how it ends
Nature:	Who is involved, how many and why	How the disorder is policed	What is involved: violence, arson, damage and looting
Response:	Political and public opinion	Criminal justice and penal response	Public policy response

groups interact with and view the police role in such a contextual relationship; (v) *situational*, the "spatial" and social determinant of disorder (Waddington, 2010); and (vi) *interactional*, the more direct interplay between the "group" and the police.

These six analytical variables essentially set out to quantify the "whys" of serious public disorder. That is, Waddington's model aimed to explain how these interconnecting factors contribute to the triggers that light the spark and propel and exacerbate serious group disorder, and which can be applied to the "post incident" review of such events in helping to better understand the causation factors and how significant they were. Newburn's (2014) model takes this a stage further and attempts to analyse the "aftermath" of such riots (events) in his bottom row – *Response* – in an attempt to analyse not only the triggers and factors that led to the event, but also what factors are played out post-event in respect of political/public opinion, criminal justice, and public policy response (Newburn, 2014). Components of this model with be examined more closely and contextualized considering the events of the summer of 2011, as it is helpful to identify those factors that were considered a departure from those riot events that had gone before, particularly the response to such events, as this analysis will potentially be relevant and even influential in shaping policy (including internal police policy) for managing similar outbreaks in the future.

Intelligence is key

It is perhaps useful to understand the current police methodologies in responding to the potential for serious public order situations. Much has been invested in policing terms over the past decade to ensure planning mechanisms and appropriate operational responses are in place to create a means of responding to the more routine and anticipated public-order risk, and much of this is now installed in the routine "battle rhythm" of UK policing.

Understanding what drives and motivates particular groups, including protest groups, political groups, football fans and other "common purpose" factions is crucial in how the police respond to minimize potential violent confrontations and directed action. This is relevant where police have advanced notice that a particular group or a coalition of groups (as often seen in political left-wing/right-wing gatherings) will "form up" and so can assess the relative risks these group dynamics might present, either individually or relative to contact with the "other side". Much of this will of course come from historical group behaviours, especially common in football fans where encounters tend to take place more often, and where attitudes and past behaviour will have been observed and recorded. Police would describe some of this knowledge as "information" rather than intelligence, as it may not yet be fully assessed and/or corroborated and so may not necessarily determine the outcome of the next event or encounter involving the same group dynamics.

Intelligence, on the other hand, is a collection of information from many sources (open and closed) that can be developed for specific action, and which shapes understanding of the specific encounter by identifying and developing both known and as yet unknown factors that may have a bearing on the police response. This might include meeting or gathering points, key participants and their intentions, numbers of attendees, protest site(s), areas to be frequented, whether violence is planned or anticipated (for example with a another "target" faction). Even in the more commonplace group interactions, such as those between football fans, the collection and assessment of information and intelligence is critical in shaping (i) what the police know (or what they think they know); (ii) what they still need to know in order to respond most effectively (the intelligence gaps); and (iii) how this knowledge will ultimately define the policing response strategically, tactically, and operationally.

In what has become known as one of his more infamous statements, former United States Secretary of Defence, Donald Rumsfeld, described this cycle of "knowledge", in 2002, as "Known Knowns" and "Known Unknowns". Although Rumsfeld was roundly criticized for this basic characterization at the time (particularly in the context of the public suspicion directed towards the US government post 9/11 and immediately prior to the invasion of Iraq and the search for Weapons of Mass Destruction), it does, when considered all these years later, resonate when attempting to describe the intelligence collection and assessment framework. That is, there is information that we know we know (about an event, group, objectives) and there is information that we know we don't yet know, but that we need to know (the Known Unknowns) or what would be described in policing language as "intelligence gaps". Rumsfeld took this a stage further by describing "Unknown Unknowns", or those things we do not know and do not anticipate we need to know.

This produced intelligence assessment is therefore critical in that its aim is to ultimately present police public order commanders with the best possible picture of the "knowns", and assists with the development of a plan to address the "known unknowns" (the gaps), thus helping to shape the overall assessment of risk that will, in turn, present the police with a range of tactical considerations required to mitigate risk. It is therefore the core function of those charged with developing intelligence in any given operation to ensure that their intelligence is current and accurate up to the point of operational delivery (Beggs *et al.*, 2013). Information and intelligence in essence form the first element of the *National Decision Model* (NDM) (College of Policing, 2013), the model used by police commanders to assess the response to those events that present a risk to public order and public safety (Figure 15.1).

The model was developed in the United Kingdom by the College of Policing, a professional body established in the UK in 2012 (Rowe, 2014) to support police training and the application

Police Code of Ethics
1. Gather information and intelligence
2. Assess threats and risk and develop a working strategy
3. Consider powers and policy
4. Identify options and contingencies
5. Take action and review what happened

Figure 15.1 Illustration of the Police National Decision Model (NDM).

of skills and knowledge across policing in England and Wales (College of Policing, 2013) and which replaced the previous National Policing Improvements Agency (NPIA). The NDM was fully endorsed by the then Association of Chief Police Officers (ACPO) and replaced the previous Conflict Management Model, largely to encourage use of the model in everyday police decision-making, beyond simply those situations involving conflict. Nonetheless, and particularly for our purposes, the model is considered pivotal in police decision-making as it involves the planning and execution of large-scale public order and public safety events, particularly those involving the risk of serious public disorder or violence.

The model is a six-step process, with all elements being driven by the police Code of Ethics, the ethical framework by which the police service in England and Wales operates, designed to regulate the behaviours and actions of police officers, and in effect essentially aims to professionalize policing (Rowe, 2014). As discussed, although the model is cyclical in nature in that the user is encouraged to regularly "spin" the model each time some new pieces of information are made available, the first key component is that of gathering information and intelligence. This first step is critical as each of the other subsequent assessment elements will be completely dependent on this initial assessment. In any circumstances where there is potential for group violence – protest, political unrest, clashes between rival football fans – it is this assessment that will define what risk is attached to the event, to whom this violence may be targeted or directed, and what measures therefore need to take place to help mitigate such an assessed risk.

Police Commanders at Strategic (Gold) and Tactical (Silver) level will place emphasis on this intelligence assessment, with the Gold Commander setting out their "Intelligence Requirement" at an early stage in the planning process to help inform the shape and "feel" of the operational response. Central to this Intelligence Requirement is taking the known information about an event, (i.e. in that it is already publicized or in some way fixed – i.e. event location, time, date) and building on this by developing an intelligence picture that supplements what is already known, tasking out for development what still needs to be known, and in doing so, supporting an early assessment of threat and risk, which in this instance is the risk of violence at a group level.

Assessing the threat and risk of group violence

Once an assessment has been made of all available intelligence about a public order or public safety event, or more specifically of those groups and individuals thought likely to be engaged (whether directly or indirectly) in the event, the model moves to that of assessing the threat and risks that may be posed. It is important to distinguish between threat and risk in this context, and what these mean in the assessment process. Put simply, the threat is the type of behaviour the police, based on the intelligence assessment, might reasonably expect to encounter. However, and remaining with the earlier notion of violence "target", this threat assessment will focus on what specifically the target is likely to be. This might be rival groups or factions, for example rival football supporters, competing protest groups, members of a political affiliation, or even the police themselves. Once identified, and again referencing back the intelligence assessment and what this has gleaned, the threat will be considered in line with the risk it is considered to pose.

This risk assessment will take a two-phased approach: initially the assessment will be based on the notion of no or very little police action, that is to say that no tactical measures will be applied to mitigate the threat. So, for example, if the threat is thought to be one of organized violence taking place by supporters of football Team A against supporters of football Team B, what would the likely impact be should no police measures be put in place to mitigate the threat. This will then be scored using a matrix similar to that shown at Figure 15.2. The second part of the

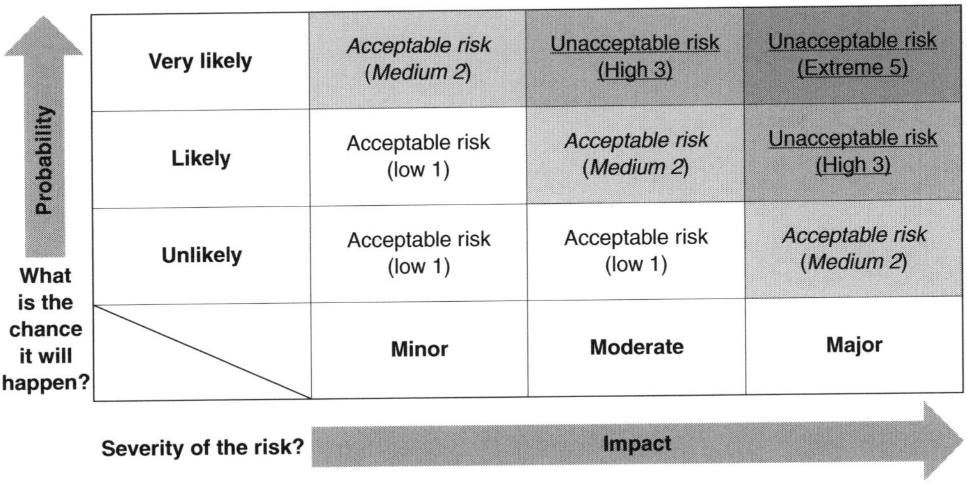

Figure 15.2 Risk matrix grid.

process examines the same threat; however, this time it assesses the risk when police measures have been applied to "treat" the threat. If we consider the football scenario, it may be assessed that should no police measures be applied to the situation then the likelihood of serious violence taking place is assessed to be high (high likelihood + major impact). However, with police tactical options introduced to mitigate this risk, ranging from basic police visibility to advanced public order tactics, the score will likely fall to either a medium or low risk.

At this stage, police commanders will outline a suite of the tactical options that they consider best mitigate against the particular threat. The Authorised Professional Practice (APP) contained within the College of Policing public order guidance (College of Policing, 2018) contains a definitive list of approved tactical options, ranging from air support to the use of mounted officers that can be considered for use by professionally competent police commanders. In their consideration of these options, commanders will need to demonstrate that these are likely to be effective and be able to address the threat with the least recourse to the use of force on the part of the police. That is, police planning processes must demonstrate that in proposing any tactical measure designed to mitigate a specific threat, they must be proportionate to the threat itself and be deployed in such a manner that minimizes the use of force in any resulting use of the tactic. Ultimately, the police strategic (Gold) commander will approve the tactical options proposed by the tactical (Silver) commander, and must be commensurate with his or her Gold strategic objectives. Depending on the situation, these objectives can be wide ranging and diverse, but in a situation where the possibility of crowd disorder or group violence is likely to be a factor, a key strategic objective will most likely be to minimize serious injury resulting from violence to all those involved.

The remaining steps in the NDM serve to develop and build upon these first two, leading ultimately to action on the ground through the use of risk-based and proportionate tactical measures and the need to demonstrate the lawful application of police powers and, crucially, public order legislation. Identifying "options and contingencies" is arguably the most critical step as it ties all other elements together and develops the plan to determine how the police response will look and feel in practice, not only to those who participate in the group, but also wider members of the public, media, political observers, and other interested stakeholders. The prism in which police action can be viewed will doubtless be different and defining the context in which the action was taken is important to capture, particularly for police commanders.

Summer 2011 riots – a game changer or wake-up call?

The fatal shooting of Mark Duggan by Metropolitan Police officers in North London on 4 August 2011 triggered a period of significant and widespread disorder, violence and looting in many parts of mainland UK. Rioting took place over a five-day period (6 to 10 August) and began in North London before spreading quickly to other parts of the UK, including Birmingham, Manchester, Liverpool and Nottingham (Newburn, 2014). This resulted in five deaths, 300 police officers were injured, and widespread damage estimated to be between £200 and 300 million (HMIC, 2011). Analysis by many commentators suggest that these riots were of a different complexion in a number of ways when contrasted with other large-scale outbreaks of urban disorder, and whilst they shared similarities in respect of a central catalyst emanating from community tension (in this case the community's perceived wrongful killing of Mark Duggan) they also differ in a number of ways to what had gone before them (Newburn, 2014).

There was such political interest (and unusually overt criticism) of how the police dealt with these outbreaks, that Her Majesty's Inspectorate of Constabulary (HMIC, now HMICFRS) was swiftly commissioned by the Home Secretary to urgently review the policing response. The Home Secretary was in fact overtly critical (a departure from the previous standard political narrative for such incidents, which was generally unanimously positive) and even described the police as having lost control, when she addressed parliament on the subject in the immediate aftermath. HMIC in describing the events of those five days of disorder, stated that "the game has changed" (HMIC, 2011) and went on to describe a number of elements and recommendations in the "post-mortem" of the police response to these events. Fundamentally however, it was the sheer speed of the events as they unfolded that was of a scale and magnitude not previously experienced in the UK context (HMIC, 2011), and which HMIC cited as one of the most unusual departures from previous events. Newburn (2014) in his analysis of the 2011 riots, cites four key areas that highlight "departure points" contrasting with previous large-scale UK post-war riots. He describes these as (i) *speed and malleability*; (ii) *looting and consumerism*; (iii) *the politics of policing*; and (iv) *the response of the penal state*.

Newburn's first two "points of departure" – *speed and malleability* and *looting and consumerism* – are considered of particular use when comparing previous riots, as they nicely define the actual actions of rioters themselves and articulate well how these actions are distinctly different from previous experience. They may therefore explain to some extent why, in a strategic and tactical sense, the police struggled to regain the streets as quickly as they might have been expected to. Two factors emerge when describing the speed with which the rioting spread; first, the rapidity of these riot incidents spreading not only across London Boroughs, but to other parts of the UK, and, second and directly connected to this, the capacity impact this created in respect of the specialist police public order resources deployed to respond to these geographically far-reaching events. This limited the opportunity for a concentration of efforts on one area, or the brigading of "mutual aid" provision. HMIC further attribute this to the police failure to properly and expeditiously deal with the Information and Intelligence picture, including a failure to manage and assess the large volume of related social media traffic to help inform strategy and deployments as the rioting began to spread to other regions.

The widespread use of mobile phones and the utilization of encrypted messaging systems (Newburn, 2014) allowed those coordinating the activity to do so with an efficacy and speed not previously experienced by UK policing in the public disorder context. HMIC was, on the whole, critical of the police's ability to properly manage the intelligence element as it related to the riots, and made a number of recommendations, principally that the rigidity of intelligence assessment models adopted by some forces (i.e. that all information required to be corroborated before it could be assessed as intelligence and therefore "actioned") hindered a sufficiently swift response, especially in the early stages of the disorder. HMIC (2011) stressed the importance of using professional experience and judgement based upon information not necessarily meeting the intelligence threshold to help inform and influence effective police deployments. Furthermore, the lack of capacity to deal with social-media related information was seen as a failing on the part of the police to properly exploit what was essentially a critical tactical option (HMIC, 2011). Other elements of intelligence (i.e. a failure to properly exploit "community intelligence") were also identified by HMIC as a missed opportunity, not only in dealing with and anticipating the emerging disorder picture but also in cascading key messages which could be circulated to communities as the incidents spread.

The second issue identified by Newburn, that of the notion of looting, is highlighted as a significant and distinct departure point from previous UK riot events. The scenes of mass looting across the country, vividly captured on CCTV, mobile phones and handheld digital cameras (Newburn, 2014) and indeed replayed on television screens as news media covered the riots, characterized for many the extent of which looting evolved as the rioting progressed. This intensified the view that the police had not used "go forward" tactics quickly enough to deal with the mass damage and looting taking place, but had instead stood back and, in some cases, withdrawn all together. Again, this element attracted unusually sharp criticism from politicians, with the Prime Minister accusing the police of treating the situation too much of a public order situation rather than as crime (Newburn, 2014). HMIC too issued criticism of the initial police tactical response, describing the initial response as "hesitant" (HMIC, 2011, p. 59) and not sufficient to deal with small but organized groups of looters (HMIC, 2011) and issued a series of recommendations in respect of the future development of police public order training and tactics. It should be stressed that whilst this level of looting in a widespread public order context was a departure from previous UK public order events, this had been experienced elsewhere in the world. For example, the United States of America experienced several public disorder outbreaks, including those in the wake of the Rodney King incident in Los Angeles in 1992, the Thompkins Park and Crown Heights riots in New York City, and the Liberty City, Miami, Florida riots (Bayley and Shearing, 2005).

It was the Los Angeles riots of 1992, in particular, that experienced large-scale violent looting similar in scale to that witnessed in London and elsewhere in 2011. Many commentators have hypothesized the reasons why looting occurred to the extent it did in 2011, but for our purposes it is sufficient to highlight that (in UK terms at least) this was a new phenomenon and challenged the police in other ways. Notably, the mass looting challenged the police's ability to stem these additional acts of criminality during the pressures of the rioting and with it the serious outbreaks of violence and destruction of property. Additionally, extensive looting introduced an additional layer of complexity and investigative demand in trying to identify those responsible for committing these acts

Conclusion

The swift and effective management and resolution of collective violence by the police in public order terms is a central function in the maintenance of the Queens Peace (HMIC, 2011). In addition, controlling such events is a central and fundamental responsibility of any police service in the protection of its citizens and their property, and in encouraging the confidence in the ability of the police in general. The role of policing in this regard is beyond simply "responding and arresting", and the structures used to manage the risk of public disorder and collective violence have, in line with the wider advances in policing, evolved and modernized over the past few decades. More structured decision-making processes (i.e. The National Decision Model), a greater emphasis on mitigation of violence and disorder through the use of information and intelligence processes, and a general professionalizing of public order training, tactics, and command has helped policing become better equipped to deal with such outbreaks, whether anticipated or otherwise.

Persistent and sustained outbreaks of collective violence can cause changes to police structures (as witnessed in the response to the 2011 Summer Riots) with the adoption, in some cases, of more militarized tactics, centralized structures, decision-making, and larger patrolling structures (a departure from lone officer patrols). It can also ultimately change the posture of policing, leading to a standing back from the more traditional community-style policing and problem-solving approaches (Bayley and Shearing, 2005). However, it must also be remembered that such instances in a UK context remain rare. Waddington (2003) asserts that we should not get violence (in this context) out of proportion, and even when such large-scale disorder does occur, the violence that is perpetrated is undertaken by relatively few within any group dynamic (Waddington, 2003).

References

Adang, O. M. J. (2011) Initiation and escalation of collective violence: An observational study. In T. Madensen and J. Knutsson (eds), *Preventing Crowd Violence*. Colorado: Lynne Rienner Publishers, pp. 69–94.

Bagguley, P. and Hussain, Y. (2008) *Riotous Citizens: Ethnic Conflict in Multicultural Britain*. Aldershot: Ashgate

Bayley, D. (2005) Police reform as foreign policy. *Australian & New Zealand Journal of Criminology*, 38(2), 206–215.

Bayley, H. and Shearing, C.D. (2005) The future of policing. In T. Newburn (ed.), *Policing: Key Readings*. Cullompton/ Devon, pp. 715–732.

Beggs, J., Thomas, G., and Rickard, S. (2013) *Public Order*. Oxford: Oxford University Press.

Brogden, M. (2005) "Horses for courses" and "thin blue lines": Community policing in transitional society. *Police Quarterly*, 8(1), 64–98.

College of Policing (2013) *National Decision Model*. Available at: www.app.college.police.uk/app-content/national-decision-model/ (accessed 6 March 2019).

College of Policing (2018) *Public Order*. Available at: www.app.college.police.uk/app-content/public-order/ (accessed 10 February 2019).

HMIC (2011) *The Rules of Engagement: A Review of the August 2011 Disorders*. Available at www.justice inspectorates.gov.uk/hmicfrs/media/a-review-of-the-august-2011-disorders-20111220.pdf (accessed 20 February 2019).

Marshall, D. (2018) Policing: Leadership, Policy & Partnerships. Available from www.my-course.co.uk/course/view.php?id=3591 (accessed 1 March 2019).

Newburn, T. (2014) The 2011 England riots in recent historical perspective. *British Journal of Criminology*, 55(1), 39–64.

Reiner, R. (2000) *The Politics of the Police*. New York: Oxford University Press.

Rowe, M. (2014) *Introduction to Policing*. London: Sage

Scarman, L. (1982) *The Scarman Report, The Brixton Disorders 10–12 April 1981*. Penguin Books.

Waddington, P. A. J. (2003) Policing public order and political contention. In T. Newburn (ed), *Handbook of Policing*. Devon: Willan, pp. 394–421.

Waddington, D. (2010) Applying the flashpoints model of public disorder to the 2001 Bradford Riot. *British Journal of Criminology*, 50(2), 342–359.

16

GANGS, VIOLENCE AND COUNTY LINES

Paul Andell

Introduction

Gang-related violence has recently appeared frequently in the media, often resulting in demands for actions to counter this. The chapter examines some of the violent actions associated with gangs and the subsequent calls for responses to these actions. It analyses the extent and causal tendencies of gang-related violence associated with drug dealing networks known as County lines, and offers a critical realist perspective to examine the complex interactions of the three modes of violence: (1) subjective; (2) objective; (3) and symbolic.

Silverman (2004) argues that when violence takes place, the broader context in which it occurs and the underlying causal forces which drive violent incidents are often concealed by the distress and trauma of horrific acts. Contextual underpinnings are often ignored by our reactions to them, due in part to the extensive ways in which these acts are mediated and understood. To the outside observer, it is difficult to understand practices which may have small fiscal rewards, disproportionate victimization of the vulnerable, and significant variations between neighbourhoods. Zizek (2008) described violence both as subjective and objective, and in doing, encourages us to think more about the objective context in which subjective violence takes place. He argues:

> ...we should learn to step back, to disentangle ourselves from the fascinating lure of this directly visible "subjective" violence, violence performed by a clearly identifiable agent. We need to perceive the contours of the background which generates such outbursts. A step back enables us to identify a violence that sustains our very efforts to fight violence and to promote tolerance.
>
> *(Zizek, 2008, p. 1)*

This chapter examines violence associated with English gangs, and in order to do so, an analyses of the definitions of gangs, the extent of gang-related violence, and explanations of how gang violence has emerged as both an expressive and functional tool for use in changing Class A drug markets in the UK will be sought. Although this chapter does not focus specifically on gender-based violence often associated with gangs (see Firmin, 2009; Pearce and Pitts 2011; Andell and Pitts, 2013), it situates the gang-associated violence of young men commonly committed against each other in a framework of subjective practices, a culture of consumerism and structural inequalities. Following this location, the chapter proceeds to make an assessment of the current concerns regarding knife crime in the UK as a "national emergency" (*The Guardian*, 6 March 2019).

Gang definitions

Discerning and explaining the behaviour of individuals and social groups in relation to social structures and culture is central to sociological analysis (Mills, 1959). However, defining what we mean by the term "gang", especially in the English context, is contentious and has been the subject of a vigorous academic discourse known as the *Gang Thesis Debate*, which involves nuanced philosophical arguments about the nature of reality, which questioned the existence of English gangs. I do not propose a full return to this debate in this chapter, suffice to say that, arguably, this debate is reminiscent of earlier deliberations about realism and idealism in critical criminology (see Lea and Young, 1984). In short, the realist critique suggests that idealists are aloof from practical policies aimed at reducing crime and victimization while the idealists contend that any improvements to the criminal justice system to combat gangs are only liberal adjustments that strengthen the grip of the capitalist system and its criminalization of the poor and disadvantaged (Tierney, 2009). While idealism tends to overplay the political importance of street culture, tending to focus on the reactions to crime by the state and media, realism focuses on the impact of crime on relatively poor neighbourhoods, but in doing so, idealists argue they precipitate heightened levels of social control by fuelling what Stanley Cohen calls "moral panics". This chapter takes a critical realist reading of gangs, which seeks to synthesize both external structural patterning of gangs and the subjective meanings of gang violence.

A definition is a requisite to the understanding of groups, regardless of what we call them or what they do. It not only allows us to categorize and differentiate social groups, but also allows us to develop interventions to respond to them. Arguably, the definition used most consistently has been the Eurogang definition, which has been subject to years of debate and empirical testing. This definition suggests a gang to be a "durable and street-oriented youth group whose involvement in illegal activity is part of its group identity" (Klein and Maxson, 2006, p. 4).

Matsuda *et al.* (2012) suggest that as gang definitions change so do the qualities of the gang and its members. In England and Wales in 2009, the Centre for Social Justice utilized the academic work of Pitts who coins the following definition:

> A relatively durable, predominantly street-based group of young people who (1) see themselves (and are seen by others) as a discernible group, (2) engage in a range of criminal activities and violence, (3) identify with or lay claim over territory, (4) have some form of identifying structural feature, and (5) are in conflict with other, similar, gangs.
>
> *(Dying to Belong, Centre for Social Justice, 2009 p. 48)*

Pitts' gang definition stems from earlier empirical work in East London where he insightfully described these groups as 'Articulated Super Gangs' (ASGs) ('articulated' meaning a vehicle consisting of flexibly connected sections, and 'super' meaning over and above a single group or entity). For Pitts, the above definition includes important aspects of observed or encountered features of English gangs, such as hierarchical networks. According to Pitts' research in East London, these hierarchies consisted of fairly closely associated groups of older career criminals linked with local criminal families, some of whose members could trace links back to the Kray brothers in the 1960s. These families were what Dick Hobbs and Geoff Pearson (2003) called 'middle market multi-commodity drug brokers who link the upper and lower levels of the market'. They maintained strong local connections, based upon mutual commercial benefit and kinship, with younger, more fluid, estate-based 'street gangs' who were involved in street crime and drug distribution. These networks were described by the police as 'fairly organised at the top but chaotic at the bottom'.

Bullock and Tilley (2008) argue that, at street level, where practitioners interact with predominantly less well organized levels of gang networks, ambiguity surrounds the term "gang". The issues involved in defining gangs have led to some abandoning the term for the purposes of less problematic operational interventions. Instead, they suggest that some aspects of gang members' behaviour, such as violence, should be focused upon. This appears to be a tenet of a Public Health approach to gangs, which is currently finding favour in policy debates (see The Youth Violence Commission, 2018, below). With arguably a more encompassing view of gangs in the US, Pyrooz and Densley (2018) discuss the differing inclusive characteristics of gangs but also point to the fact that there is no agreed-upon definition of a "gang". They suggest that the main academic concerns regarding gang definition are the issues of level of organization and involvement in crime. Specific examples arising from an English context of these two defining features are examined below in relation to violence. However, at a broad international level, it is reported (Pyrooz and Densley, 2018) that the existence of a relationship between gang membership and criminal activity has been quantified from a recent meta-analysis of 176 studies (e.g. Pyrooz *et al.*, 2016); yet, the nature of that relationship is still somewhat unclear.

The extent of gang membership in England was approximated by a study undertaken for the Children's Commissioner for England in 2019. The study estimated that up to 27,000 English children and young people were gang members, with a further 60,000 involved with gangs or siblings of gang members (Jozwiak, 2019). Before examining possible causal tendencies which underpin the realities of gang violence, the extent or scale of actual gang-related violence in the UK should first be examined.

Extent of gang-related violence in England and Wales

Early statistical studies by Bennet and Holloway (2004) utilized survey data on gang membership that was collected as part of the New English and Welsh Arrestee Drug Abuse Monitoring (NEW-ADAM) programme. The study solicited views from arrestees in 16 custody suites across England and Wales between 1999 and 2002. Putting aside methodological weaknesses due in part to the direct questioning of arrestees in a "closed system", the study was consistent with US findings, suggesting:

> Gang members tend to be involved in criminal behaviour, generalists in terms of offending pattern, responsible for a notable proportion of all offences, sometimes violent, involved in drug supply offences and have a tendency to carry weapons and guns (and sometimes use them).
>
> *(Bennet and Holloway, 2004, p. 317)*

Studies by both Pitts (2008) and Bennet and Holloway (2004) utilize Stelfox's (1998) survey work of police areas to suggest that gangs:

> ...typically engaged in a wide range of offences, although 17 per cent were described as offence specialists. Three-quarters of gangs were involved in some form of drug

> dealing. Most forces reported violence as the main problem associated with gangs. Sixty per cent of gangs allegedly possessed firearms.
>
> *(Bennet and Holloway, 2004, p. 307)*

Freedom of Information requests to the Office of National Statistics (ONS) regarding gang-related violence have drawn limited responses.

> We do not hold statistics relating to the number of active gangs. The CSEW collects some information on the proportion of children aged 10 to 15 and adults aged 16 to 29 who are a member of a street gang however it does not collect information on crimes relating to street gangs.
>
> *(ONS webpage, 21 September 2017)*

However, Andell and Pitts (2019) have reported on police data in London that suggests significant levels of gang-related violence:

> Metropolitan Police Service data also shows that between 2010 and 2013 "gang members" were responsible for 6,600 violent offences including 24 murders, 28 attempted murders, 170 other firearms offences and countless stabbings.

And,

> In its review of the Metropolitan Police Service Gangs Matrix (December 2018), MOPAC found that although "Gang-flagged" violence is a relatively small proportion of violent crime in London, it tends to be the most serious and most harmful because it is more likely to result in serious injury. Thus, for example, 57% of "Gang-flagged" stabbings in 2016/2018 resulted in serious or fatal injury, compared with 34% of non-"Gang-flagged" stabbings. Gang-related murders represented 31% of the total while 47% of gun discharges and 47% of firearms victims were gang-related.
>
> *(Andell and Pitts, 2019)*

A recent analysis of youth violence by the All Party Violence Commission in 2018 was careful to avoid the term "gang" presumably to avoid the labelling and stigma associated with so-called "Gang Talk" (Hallsworth, 2013). To date, the Commission's work is not yet complete; it has included six evidence sessions and a national "Safer Lives Survey" conducted by Warwick University in early 2018. The survey asked young people about the levels of violence that they are exposed to in their everyday lives and is the first national survey of young people's views on violence. The commission received over 2200 responses to the survey and a full analysis of the responses is due.

Initial findings suggest more than 70 per cent of young people are exposed to serious violence in real life at least once a month, with 90 per cent of young people exposed to serious violence at least once a week through media (e.g. music, television and social media). It was found that younger respondents (aged 8 to 19 years) experience the most serious violence and more than 16 per cent of young people do not feel safe at home, with less than half (46 per cent) willing to ask police for advice if they were worried about being a victim of crime. The survey also asked about drugs, with 38 per cent of young people who know at least one person who sells drugs, and almost 10 per cent who know more than 10 people who do. It was further suggested that 33 per cent know at least one person who carries a weapon, and 7 per cent know more than 10 people that do (The Youth Violence Commission Interim Report, 2018).

The Office for National Statistics (2019) states that the overall trend in violent crime over the past 20 years has declined. However, there is evidence of an increase in some lower-volume, higher-harm violent offences recorded by the police. Government figures suggest that the number of homicides recorded by the police has risen consecutively over the past four years, ending March 2018, following a long-term decline. Police recorded crime and National Health Service (NHS) data have also indicated rises in the number of offences involving knives or sharp instruments over the last four years. A recent press report (*The Guardian*, 11 March 2019) suggests that murder and manslaughter, where the attacker was aged 18 or under and used a knife, rose by 77 per cent in the last two years from 26 to 46 incidents. NHS data indicate that, in the last five years, the number of children aged 16 and under being treated for assault by a knife or other sharp object rose by 93 per cent, from 180 admissions in 2012/13, to 347 in 2017/18. What these figures suggest is an increasing knife carrying culture and/or fear of it by younger people.

The use of statistical representation of gangs and violence has the advantage of comparability, it can give estimations of scale and by measuring the rate of re-occurrence of problems it may draw closer attention to the problem. However, it has the inherent disadvantage that it does not explain the phenomenon's causal features. Young (2004, p. 13) has criticized what he terms a "fetishism of numbers" in what he calls "voodoo criminology". He argues that such approaches translate social actions and social relations into the dry language of mathematics. This mathematical approach subtracts social meaning and divides culture into a multiplicity of restricted individual choices based on predictable family traits or neighbourhood poverty indices. Additionally, it is assumed that for this type of research the evidence needs little explanation as the numbers speak for themselves. Matthews (2014) also critiques this approach and argues that the evidence needs to be interpreted and this invariably involves value judgements.

Matthews (2014) further argues that the philosophical base of empiricism used in statistical manipulation often confines the research to what is observable. He suggests that some activities are unsuitable for quantification and cannot be measured in a meaningful way. Interval scales can only be effectively developed for objects and processes that are qualitatively invariant (Sayer, 2010). Thus, we cannot measure with a linear scale the processes of socialization that influence some young men to feel safe in a street gang, or others to feel they have the opportunity to break out of mundane street existence by dealing drugs.

The role of social capital

Although official statistics are patchy with regard to gang-related violence, there are significant concerns about the role of gang members in the commissioning of violent crime in the UK. There is little long-term data on gang behaviour available; however, an overview of existing studies on gangs and gang violence by Marshall *et al.* (2005) showed that gang members committed more crime than non-gang members and they are more likely to carry weapons. Why gang members are likely to behave in such ways can be explained by ideas of social capital (Bourdieu, 1984).

Social capital can be thought of in two main forms; bonding social capital and bridging social capital. Mørch and Andersen (2012) distinguish between the social and societal functions of gangs. Gangs provide a "social" function by ensuring mutual support and maintaining social networks. In effect they offer their members "bonding social capital" which enables them to "get by". But "bridging social capital" can also be offered to young people with limited prospects as a means to a lucrative and respected position in the alternative economy by "societal" gangs operating Class A drug markets.

Violent reputation as bonding social capital

Finigan-Car *et al.* (2016) argue that for young people who live in relatively deprived neighbourhoods, street culture increases the likelihood of involvement in negative peer relationships, encounters with violent victimization, easier access to weapons, and witnessing street violence. It is suggested that this in turn increases fears for future lethal violence and reduces the ability of families and communities to manage youth aggressive behaviours.

Elijah Anderson (1990) describes how a reputation for violence in some street cultures may not return fiscal capital but can provide social capital. According to Anderson's depiction, violence is often pursued in "street" culture as respect directly produces individual satisfaction, and because a violent reputation provides protection from future assault. Simon Harding (2014) calls this reputation "street capital". A reputation for violence can offer bonding capital or a sense of belonging to similarly located peers, which serves to imbue a sense of family or "fam" but does little to elevate peers from the relatively deprived neighbourhood; for this to occur bridging capital is needed.

Involvement in drug supply networks and violence as bridging social capital

Andell and Pitts (2018) argue that there is evidence to suggest that the practices of some English street gangs have evolved into drugs distribution networks that now cover large areas of the UK. It is argued that this evolution is contingent on the global features of availability of class A drugs and the local bridging capital of pre-existing criminal networks. Pre-existing opportunity structures for crime are integral for potential transitions for contemporary English gangs. Understanding access to the middle drugs market is crucial in explaining the potential evolution of street gangs into the realms of local organized crime and the functional use of violence in the alternative market of illegal drugs.

Changes in middle market networks

Pearson and Hobbs (2003) describe the "middle market" as a level above retail whereby some participants are removed from the retail risks of the street. Andell and Pitts (2018) argue that there has been organizational transformations in some crack and heroin markets undertaken by street gangs who have distanced themselves from the streets and are now embedded in retail drug distribution networks. This calls into question contemporary understandings of definitions of street gangs (Aldridge *et al.*, 2012) and local organized crime groups (Sergi, 2018).

Increased levels of violence can be associated with new and changing arrangements in the drugs business, known as "County lines". In this business model, young people are groomed by metropolitan gangs into transporting drugs to rural locations through a mix of financial rewards and threats. Telephone lines are utilized for users to place drug orders with metropolitan gangs. A separate line is used to instruct local "runners or shotters" to deliver the order. Vulnerable recruits who are amenable to grooming for gang activities are found in children's residential homes and hostels where they are often housed; in Youth Offending Secure Estates; outside schools or pupil referral units where they have been sent after being excluded from mainstream education; or online where some vulnerable young people may spend a huge amount of time. It is suggested by some media reports (*The Guardian*, 9 March 2019) that the destabilizing influence of the County lines system has contributed to the increase in fatal stabbings to the highest levels since records began.

Andell and Pitts (2017) argue that some street gangs have placed a clear distance between themselves and the retail action, and demonstrate embedded activities over time whereby individuals may be removed from the network through enforcement but control over drug market activity is maintained by the gang. This signifies a level of sophistication equated with organized crime groups. The National Crime Agency (NCA, 2019) suggests that the majority of the country is now covered by "County line" networks and that these are a national threat.

Once drugs are in a reasonable proximity of the end user/buyer then a more flexible model of entrepreneurship takes place. Drugs are usually delivered to a residence taken over by a local gang (trap house). The "cuckooed" flats or trap houses usually belong to vulnerable substance misusers who are sometimes paid in drugs for the use of their homes or subjected to threats or violence to make it available. Gang "elders" operate and manage the franchise, ensuring that discipline is maintained and the retail end of the drugs business runs smoothly while gang "youngers" are left in the trap house to "serve up" drugs, keep the tenant under control and collect money from buyers.

Andell and Pitts (2018) report co-option of local crime families into new arrangements of County line dealing networks. Where cooperation has not happened or is challenged, increases in violence occur, which can be lethal. It would therefore appear that a new middle market is being established that combines the muscle of street gangs with the connections of the family firm. Arlacchi (1986) describes these practices as building "protective enclaves" which discourages rivals and competitors.

In order to understand the transitions of peer group to gang and then gang to local organized crime group, it is useful to consider collective subjectivities. Such groupings are not given as finished entities but as social products that are socially and locally constructed in concrete situations of action, such as violence and drug sales. Vandenberghe (2014) argues that in a realist theory of collective subjectivities, symbolic identities can transform and structure into a quasi-group and then into an organized group that can represent its members in their absence. These transformations take place as a result of collective actions in an operative chain. Such actions can be demonstrated with the coordination of violence.

County lines and the coordination of violence

Pearson and Hobbs (2003) argue the use of violence is ever-present in markets that lack formal regulation and suggest that contracts between drug sellers and customers cannot be enforced through legal recourse. Thus, grievances or non-compliance are enforced through cuts in trading ties (supply ceases), threats or as a last resort violence. Violence in stable markets is sometimes characterized as an atypical activity, the idea being that violence, albeit a functional tool, is bad for business as it attracts the attention of law enforcement agencies (Mohamed and Fritsvold, 2010; Taylor and Potter, 2013). On the other hand, destabilized markets or markets in transition can result in increased violence, which can be expressive or functional (Decker and Pyrooz, 2015).

Violence used in the collection of debts is deemed functional and is associated with higher levels of organization in crime networks. Expressive violence such as revenge killings for small reputational slights or "disrespects" is often associated with the less well organized aspects of these networks (Decker and Pyrooz, 2015). Recent reports (Office for National Statistics, 2019) of drug-related homicide (DRH) has shown that from March 2013 to March 2016, 13 per cent of both victims and perpetrators were drug dealers in all homicide cases in the UK

Andell and Pitts (2018) have analysed the causal tendencies of unevenly structured power dynamics in their analysis of gangs and County lines. They have observed changes enacted through macro-economic and cultural shifts which have resulted in the formation of new identities in the hierarchical micro-social networks of the drugs business. The resulting changes can be observed and classified as new forms of local organized crime. It is apparent that interactions in some of these new criminal organizations are symbolically regulated by violence and strategically coordinated, which has impacted on local drug dealing networks in order to meet the most profitable end, in an efficacious way through the exploitation of children and vulnerable people. It is becoming apparent that the current social and economic arrangements, ideas, values and expressions or cultural order have conditioned the institutional level of reality in which increasingly violent criminal organization takes place.

Much of the chapter has highlighted the actions of increasing forms of violence for a significant minority of young people caught up in a "world of gangs" (Hagadorn, 2008), which we argue is underpinned by the causal mechanisms of exploitative market relations, the alternative economy of drugs and the cultural capital of violence. It is suggested that the alternative market relations in which some young people become trapped are not always counter to mainstream culture but perhaps are a grotesque caricature of some of the dreams and practices of mainstream society. The same economic pushes and cultural pulls are to be found in the legitimate business world as in the alternative markets of drugs, which offer little choices in exploitative conditions to satisfy the insatiable appetites for profit and gain (Bourgeois, 1995). Reflections of the violence undertaken in criminal markets and the brutality of life in relatively deprived neighbourhoods are often mediated by refracted accounts by the participants themselves and by press reports; both of who engage in biases, deviance amplification and subsequent claims, which prompt further mediated responses.

Mediated gang violence and calls for something to be done

Metropolitan Police Commissioner, Cressida Dick, has recently laid the blame for increases in youth violence at the door of trap music and has called for videos to be removed from YouTube (*The Guardian*, 29 May 2018). Trap music (arguably a sub-genre of Hip Hop), can provide distinct cultural narratives that voice social and political concerns through lyrics and symbolism (Barron, 2013; Andell, 2015; Ilan, 2015). Lyrics can express the range and depth of expressions of gang life (Eubanks, 2017). In this continuum, exaggerated claims of violence can be made and it is difficult to discern the difference between the performative and the real. Critical realists argue it matters little how overblown the communiqués appear, as they are arguably an emergent reality, represented in video imagery and lyrics and subject to underlying causal processes (Andell 2019, in press). Hagedorn (2008) suggests that the styles and practices that gang members absorb from globalized "gangsta" culture tend to be preposterous caricatures of human behaviour in which gang violence is exaggerated and looped between real and virtual worlds (Ferrell *et al.*, 2015). Clearly, the "performative" cultural phenomena of music and lyrics cannot be ignored in the study of gang violence; however, simple content analysis of YouTube videos should be avoided in favour of a culturally nuanced analysis of "looped reality" if labelling is to be minimized .

If we are suggesting that the actions of gang violence can be refracted through a mediated lens, then it is of little surprise that so can our responses to it. With the number of fatal stabbings in England and Wales in 2017/18 totalling 55, the highest annual figure since records began (Home Office, 2018), it is little wonder that the press have called for swift repressive responses. These calls become particularly acute when images of "ideal" victims (Christie, 1986) in the form of Yousef Makki, a grammar school pupil in Manchester who was stabbed in a leafy village suburb, and Jodie Chesney, a former adventure scout, was stabbed in the back in a children's play park in North London, appeared in the press and sparked a national outcry against knife crime.

It is reported that police numbers have fallen by 22,000 police officers since 2010 (Office for National Statistics 2019). At the time of writing, Prime Minister May is reported by the BBC (2019) as saying there is "no direct correlation" between falling police numbers and a rise in violent crime. However, Metropolitan Police Commissioner, Cressida Dick, has disagreed with the Prime Minister, arguing that there is "some link" between a fall in police numbers and the rise in violent crime (BBC, 2019). Recently, the use of stop and search has been reported in the press as falling in England and Wales from a peak of 1.5 million in 2008/09 to a record low of 304,000 in 2016/17 (*The Independent*, 25 November 2018). Then Conservative MP Boris Johnson, now Prime Minister, has called for an increase in stop and search. This call was backed by ex-New Labour Home Secretary Lord Blunkett, who is reported as saying, "I can't see how you can stop someone carrying a knife if you can't search them for one" (*The Telegraph*, 8 March 2019).

Unfortunately, these calls for increases in stop and search take little notice of previous evaluations of past interventions. An evaluation of Blunt 2 by the Home Office in 2016 (McCandless *et al.*, 2016), reports that stop and search was significantly increased as a response to increased knife crime in 2008. In the last quarter of 2008/2009, the nationwide average for stop and search was one undertaken every 20 seconds. Despite significant efforts focused towards affected London boroughs, increases in stop and search achieved nothing worthy of attention to reduce knife crime.

Conclusions

In a "time of grime" (see Wheatley, 2011; Fatsis, 2018) violent events continue to unfold through mediated lenses, through which participants are likely to become further sensitized by exaggerated artistic portrayals and emotive reporting. This, in the recent past, has resulted in unrealistic demands for actions and reactions by both gang affiliates and those trying to attenuate their actions. The ensuing practices can become lethal for the protagonists in the gang's game. Politicians and moral entrepreneurs persist in arguing for more repressive measures to concretize their symbolic credentials for being tough on crime. The aforementioned ingredients of deviance and its amplification indicate a drift towards an inevitable outcome of classic moral panic (Cohen, 1972) of subsequent repressive measures which are doomed to failure. These outcomes are likely to further alienate groups of already estranged young men who are in danger of entrapment in a violent reality of gang culture.

It has been suggested that subjective and objective forms of violence are inseparably related and are played out symbolically, which have real consequences. This chapter locates gang violence in its micro- and macro- contexts, and assists us to relocate gang violence as a relational process that is not inherent in the gang, but occurs within and between peer groups, communities, and criminal cultures.

Alternative futures have been suggested through interventions based on the findings of empirical action research projects based in gang-affected neighbourhoods (Andell and Pitts, 2009, 2013, 2017) in both the micro and macro-spheres of influence (Andell, 2019). In the micro-sphere, it is suggested that social pedagogic strategies can be employed to utilize bridging capital to reclaim or re-subjectivize in order to attempt to confront and reshape the ways in which we live and enact power (Allen, 1999). In the macro-sphere, consideration should be given to a sustainable moral economy (Raworth, 2018) in order to reduce relative deprivation and ensure appropriate social spending. As Zizek (2008) suggests, the task is to change current discourse and practices in order to move from the desperate humanitarian call to stop violence to an analysis of the complex interactions of the three modes of violence; subjective, objective and symbolic. The lesson is to resist our current fascination with subjective violence in order to think and act more deeply on the real causal tendencies of violence.

References

Aldridge, J., Medina-Ariz, and Ralphs, R. (2019) *Counting Gangs: Conceptual and Validity Problems with the Eurogang Definition.* Available from: www.researchgate.net/publication/226414083_Counting_Gangs_Conceptual_and_Validity_Problems_with_the_Eurogang_Definition (accessed 20 January 2020).

Allen, J. (1999) *Spatial Assemblages of Power: From Domination to Empowerment.* In D. Massey, J. Allen, and P. Sarre (eds), *Human Geography Today*. Cambridge: Polity Press, pp. 194–218.

Andell, P. (2015) *Thinking About Gangs*. University of Bedfordshire Professional Doctorate Thesis. Bedfordshire University.

Andell, P. (2019) Addressing County lines: Praxis for community safety practitioners. *Safer Communities*. Emerald, in press.

Andell, P. and Pitts, J. (2009) West Yorkshire gangs study. *A Report for West Yorkshire Police*. Unpublished work.

Andell, P. and Pitts, J. (2013) Developing the Lambeth gangs strategy. *A Report for the Lambeth Gangs Unit*. Unpublished work.

Andell, P. and Pitts, J. (2017) Rethinking County lines. *A Report for Suffolk County Council*. ISBN 978-1-913160-03-6.

Andell, P. and Pitts, J. (2018) The end of the line? The impact of County lines drug distribution on youth crime in a target destination. *Youth and Policy*. www.youthandpolicy.org/articles/the-end-of-the-line/ (accessed 5 February 2019).

Andell, P. and Pitts, J. (2019) Book chapter. *Social Policy, Gangs and Young People*. Unitas, in press.

Anderson, E. (1990) *Streetwise: Race, Class, and Change*. Chicago, IL; Univer Press.

Arlacchi, P. (1986) *Mafia Business. The Mafia Ethic and the Spirit of Capitalism* Oxford: Oxford University Press.

Barron, L. (2013) The sound of street corner society: UK grime music as ethnography. *European Journal of Cultural Studies*, 16(5).

BBC News (2019) 5 March. www.bbc.co.uk/news/uk-47452799

Bennett, T. and Holloway, K. (2004) Gang membership, drugs and crime in the UK. *British Journal of Criminology*, 44, 305–323.

Bourgeois, P. I. (1995) *In Search of Respect: Selling Crack in El Barrio*. Cambridge; New York: Cambridge University Press.

Bullock, K. and Tilley, N. (2008) *Crime Prevention and Community Safety*, 10, 36. doi.org/10.1057/palgrave.cpcs.8150057 (accessed 27 November 2019).

Christie, N. (1986) The ideal victim. In E. A. Fattah (eds), *From Crime Policy to Victim Policy*. London: Palgrave Macmillan.

Cohen, S. (1972) *Folk Devils and Moral Panics*. London: MacGibbon and Kee.

Decker, S. and Pyrooz, D. (2015) Street gangs, terrorists, drug smugglers, and organized crime: what's the difference? In S. H. Decker and D. C. Pyrooz (eds), *The Handbook of Gangs*. Chichester, UK: John Wiley and Sons, pp. 294–308.

Dying to Belong. An In-depth Review of Street Gangs in Britain (2009) A Policy Report by the Gangs Working Group Chaired by Simon Antrobus. London: Centre for Social Justice.

Eubanks, K. (2017) After blackness, then blackness: afro-pessimism, black life, and classical hip hop as counter-performance. *The Journal of Hip Hop Studies*, 4(1), 5–22.

Fatsis, L. (2018) Grime: Criminal subculture or public counterculture? A critical investigation into the criminalization of Black musical subcultures in the UK. *Crime, Media, Culture*.

Ferrell, J., Hayward, K., and Young, J. (2015) *Cultural Criminology, An Invitation*. London: Sage.

Finigan-Carr, N. M., Gielen, A., Haynie, D. L., and Cheng, T. L. (2016) Youth violence: How gender matters in aggression among urban early adolescents. *Journal of Interpersonal Violence*, 31(19), 3257–3281. https://doi.org/10.1177/0886260515584348 (accessed 12 December 2018).

Firmin, C. (2009) Girls around gangs. *Safer Communities*, 8(2), pp. 14–16.

Hallsworth S. (2013) *The Gang and Beyond Interpreting Violent Street Worlds*. London: Palgrave Macmillan.

Harding, S. (2014) *The Street Casino: Survival in Violent Street Gangs*. Bristol: Policy Press.

Hagedorn, J. M. (2008) *A World of Gangs: Armed Young Men and Gangsta Culture*. Minnesota: University of Minnesota Press.

Home Office (2018) Homicide in England and Wales: year ending March 2018 www.ons.gov.uk/peoplepopulationandcommunity/crimeandjustice/articles/homicideinenglandandwales/yearendingmarch2018 (accessed 21 January 2020).

Ilan, J. (2015) *Understanding Street Culture Poverty, Crime, Youth and Cool*. London: Palgrave.

Jozwaik, G. (2019) Majority of child gang members unknown to councils, commissioner warns. *Children And Young People Now*, 27 February 2019. www.cypnow.co.uk/cyp/news/2006437/majority-of-child-gang-members-unknown-tocouncils-commissioner-warns (accessed 12 March 2019).
Klein, M. W. and Maxson, C. L. (2006) *Street Gang Patterns and Policies*. New York: Oxford University Press.
Lea, J. and Young, J. (1984) *What is to be Done about Law and Order?* London: Pluto Press.
Marshall, B., Webb, B., and Tilley, N. (2005) *Rationalisation of Current Research on Guns, Gangs and Other Weapons*. London: UCL, Phase One.
Matsuda, K. N., Esbensen, F. A., and Carson, D. C. (2012) Putting the "gang" in "Eurogang": characteristics of delinquent youth groups by different definitional approaches. In F. A. Esbensen and C. Maxson (eds), *Youth Gangs in International Perspective*. New York: Springer.
Matthews, R. (2014) *Realist Criminology*. London: Palgrave Macmillan.
McCandless, R., Feist, A., Allan, J., and Morgan, N. (2016) *Do Initiatives Involving Substantial Increases in Stop and Search Reduce Crime? Assessing the Impact of Operation BLUNT 2*. London: HMSO. Home Office.
Mohammad, A. R. and Fritsvold, E. R. (2010) *Dorm Room Drug Dealers: Drugs and the Privileges of Race and Class*. Boulder, CO: Lynne Reiner Publisher.
Mørch, S. and Andersen, H. (2012) Becoming a gang member: Youth life and gang. *Youth Psychology Research*, 2(9), 506–514.
Mills, C. (1959) *The Sociological Imagination*. New York: Oxford University Press.
National Crime Agency (2019) County lines drug supply, vulnerability and harm. NAC (19) 095.
Office for National Statistics (2016) Deaths related to drug poisoning in England and Wales from 1993 onwards, by cause of death, sex, age and substances involved in the death. Cardiff, UK: Office for National Statistics. www.ons.gov.uk/peoplepopulationandcommunity/birthsdeathsandmarriages/deaths/bulletins/deathsrelatedtodrugpoisoninginenglandandwales/previousReleases (accessed 22 January 2020).
Office for National Statistics (2019) *The Nature of Violent Crime in England and Wales*. Year Ending March 2018. Cardiff: Office for National Statistics.
ONS Webpage (2017) *Freedom of Information Request 21st September 2017*. www.ons.gov.uk/aboutus/transparencyandgovernance/freedomofinformationfoi/gangrelatedcrimestatisticsinlondonandengland (accessed 21 February 2019).
Pearce, J. J. and Pitts, J. M. (2011) Youth gangs, sexual violence and sexual exploitation: a scoping exercise. *The Office of the Children's Commissioner for England*. Luton: University of Bedfordshire.
Pearson, G. and Hobbs, D. (2003) King pin? A case study of a middle market drug broker. *The Howard Journal of Criminal Justice*, 42(4), 335–347. [Article]: Goldsmiths Research Online. Available at: http://eprints.gold.ac.uk/1835/
Pitts, J. (2008) *Reluctant Gangsters: the Changing Shape of Youth Crime*. Cullompten: Willan Publishing.
Pyrooz, D. C. and Densley, J. A. (2018) Gang Joining, 55: 229. https://doi-org.uos.idm.oclc.org/10.1007/s12115-018-0242-1 (accessed 27 November 2018).
Pyrooz, D. C., Turanovic, J. J., Decker, S. H., and Wu, J. (2016) Taking stock of the relationship between gang membership and offending: A meta-analysis. *Criminal Justice & Behavior*, 43, 365–397.
Raworth K (2018) *Doughnut Economics: Seven Ways to Think Like a 21st-Century Economist*. Random House Business.
Sayer, A. (2010) *Handbook of the Sociology of Morality*. S. Hitlin and S. Vaisey (eds). New York: Springer, pp. 163–178.
Sergi, A (2018) *From Mafia to Organised Crime: A Comparative Analysis of Policing Models*. London: Palgrave.
Silverman, D. (2004) Street crime and street culture. *International Economic Review*, 45(3).
Stelfox, P. (1998) Policing lower levels of organised crime in England and Wales. *The Howard Journal*, 37(4).
Taylor M. and Potter G (2013) From "social supply" to "real dealing": drift, friendship, and trust in drug-dealing careers. *Journal of Drug Issues*, 43(4), 392–406.
The Youth Violence Commission Interim Report (2018) http://yvcommission.com/wp-content/uploads/2018/07/Interim-Report-FINAL-version-2.pdf (accessed 23 January 2020).
Tierney, R. (2009) *Key Perspectives in Criminology*. Harlow: McGraw-Hill International.
Vandenberghe, F. (2014) What's critical about critical realism? *Essays in Reconstructive Social Theory (Ontological Explorations)*. London: Routledge
Wheatley, S. (2011) *Don't Call Me Urban! The Time of Grime*. Available at: https://vimeo.com/100053938 (accessed 19 March 2019).
Young, J. (2004) *Voodoo Criminology and the Numbers Game*. In J. Ferrell, K. Hayward., W. Morrison, and M. Presdee (eds), *Cultural Criminology Unleashed*. London: Glasshouse Press.
Zizek, S. (2008) *Violence*. New York: Profile Books.

17

CRIMINAL GANGS IN GLOBAL PERSPECTIVE

Motivations, transformations and functions

Moritz Schuberth

Introduction

Criminal gangs as a global phenomenon have been the object of investigation in numerous studies in various parts of the world (Dowdney, 2005; Hagedorn, 2007b; Flynn and Brotherton, 2008). Yet, despite being increasingly recognized as a global and transnational challenge, most theoretical and conceptual approaches in gang research are still derived from specific case studies from the global North (Brotherton and Barrios, 2004; Klein and Maxson, 2010; Pitts, 2013). Based on an extensive literature review and field research on violent crime in sub-Saharan Africa, Latin America and the Caribbean, this chapter provides empirical evidence on criminal gangs in the global South. Focusing on the case studies of Central America, Kenya and Haiti, this chapter discusses three aspects of contemporary global gangs: first, the motivation for members to join gangs; second, the transformation processes gangs typically undergo; and, third, the functions violence fulfils for various stakeholders of gangs, such as their politico-criminal sponsors and the community in which they are nested.

The chapter begins by discussing different approaches in gang research on the basis of a typology which categorizes motivations as either criminal or political, and as either internally or externally driven. Subsequently, it provides an overview of existing approaches to the transformation of gangs, such as *Sullivan's three-generation gang model* and *Hagedorn's concept of institutionalization*. Moreover, after debating the asserted change from criminal to political violence, it proposes to use a functionalist approach to gang violence that shifts the level of analysis from the *producers* to the *sponsors* of violence. From this point of view, gangs are seen as profit-oriented violent entrepreneurs pursuing rent-seeking activities, regardless of whether they serve the political or the criminal interests of their sponsors.

Motivations

Since 1927, the year Frederic Thrasher published his seminal work on gangs in Chicago, gang research has produced numerous approaches across a variety of academic disciplines, highlighting different motivations behind a global phenomenon. Conventional criminological definitions of gangs tend to focus on their "involvement in illegal activity" (Klein, 1995; Covey, 2010, p. 4; Klein and Maxson, 2010). For instance, according to a classic definition offered by

Klein (1971, p. 13), for a "group of youngsters" to be considered a gang, they must "have been involved in a sufficient number of delinquent incidents to call forth a consistent negative response from neighbourhood residents and/or law enforcement agencies." This definition, which criminalizes gangs, is dominating academic and media discourse and with it public opinion on gangs around the world, as recent studies on transnational gangs in Central America have shown (Manwaring, 2008; Bunker and Sullivan, 2011).

However, Mike Davis (in Hagedorn, 2008, p. xii) critiques the reduction of "complex realities and largely unexplored histories to simplistic pathologies" on the part of mainstream criminology. Likewise, Martinez (2003, pp. 97–98) remarks that such definitions criminalize the behaviour of gang members through an unbalanced focus on "violence, drugs, and sex", emphasizing the negative impact gangs have on their communities. In this respect, Hagedorn (2007a, p. 309) underlines that gangs can also "assume social, economic, political, cultural, religious, or military roles", and a number of social constructivist studies condemn the fuelling of "moral panics" (Cohen, 1972) by sensationalist media discourses, whether in Central America (Peetz, 2011) or in the United States (Tovares, 2002; Hayden, 2006).

For analytical purposes, this chapter proposes a typology that distinguishes between four subtypes of gangs, which are characterized by differing motivations and forms of criminal behaviour. The first subtype is youth gangs, which are conventionally associated with a subculture of juvenile delinquency rather than with for-profit organized criminality, and the members of which are expected to grow out of deviant behaviour when reaching maturity (Spergel, 1995; Branch, 1999). The second subtype is the more organized and institutionalized criminal gangs, which include members of various age cohorts and are committed to profit-generating criminal activities (Rodgers, 2007a; Pitts, 2013). The third subtype, politicized gangs, present themselves as ideologically motivated street organizations (Brotherton and Barrios, 2004). The fourth subtype is gangs who have been pulled into power politics by political patrons who hire them as goons to provide protection or intimidate and attack opponents (Hagedorn, 2008).

As illustrated in Table 17.1, attempts to explain why members join gangs and engage in gang-related violence can be classified along two attributes: first, whether their motivation is seen as political or criminal; second, whether their motivation is interpreted as internally driven or caused by external factors. The four subtypes can be traced back to competing schools of gang research – the ecological approach in the case of youth gangs, the rational choice approach in the case of criminal gangs, the critical theory approach in the case of street organizations, and the clientelist approach in the case of politicized gangs. Yet, it has to be recalled that the distinctions between criminal and political motivations are blurred, and that external and internal factors are inextricably intertwined and influence one another.

To begin with, the ideal-typical youth gangs are characteristic of the ecological approach, which emphasizes the criminal aspects of gangs and the impact of external or structural factors, such as cultural and societal influences, on juveniles. In this tradition, gangs are defined as

Table 17.1 Motivation of gang members in different approaches in gang research

	Criminal	*Political*
External	Ecological/cultural Youth gangs	Clientelism/patronage Politicized gangs
Internal	Rational choice Criminal gangs	Critical theory Street organizations

"unsupervised peer groups who are socialized by the streets rather than by conventional institutions" (Moore, 1998, p. 67). In his seminal work *The Gang*, which is generally considered to be the first comprehensive study on the subject (Brotherton, 2008a), Thrasher (1927) positioned the source for criminal motivation on the societal level. In the tradition of the human ecology approach of the Chicago School of sociology, gangs were treated as an organism in the urban ecosystem, caused by the social disorganization of their natural habitat (Hagedorn, 2005).

A comparable approach is taken by a number of more recent studies, which trace the emergence of gangs back to a troubled past that has disrupted the social environment. From this perspective, escalating levels of urban violence throughout Latin America – particularly in post-conflict and post-authoritarian countries – can be explained by a "culture of violence" (Adelman, 2006), "shadows of violence" (Koonings, 1999), the "banality of violence" (Pécaut, 1999), or the development of "societies of fear" (Koonings & Kruijt, 1999). According to this explanatory angle, masculinity has an important role to play and gangs are partly the result of "gendered socialization processes" in the midst of violence, to which young men are exposed (Pearce, 2010, p. 288; Baird, 2012).

The second subtype, criminal gangs, are congruent with the rational choice approach that highlights the profit-oriented dimension of gangs. From this point of view, individuals decide rationally to join criminal gangs for their own economic benefits. A number of studies from the 1980s/1990s saw the causes of gang formation in economic conditions of the American "underclass" (Hagedorn, 1988), which are characterized by "an intense competition for, and conflict over, the scarce resources that exist" in low-income neighbourhoods (Sánchez-Jankowski, 1991, p. 22). In a similar vein, Padilla (1992, p. 186) argued that gang members "view the gang as the most rational response to their social and economic circumstances." Confronted with bleak prospects for regular jobs in the formal economy, "young men began turning to the gang in search of employment opportunities", mainly in the local drug trade (Padilla, 1992, p. 101). Likewise, Venkatesh (2000, pp. 108–109) explicitly rejects pathologizing notions of a "ghetto-specific [...] culture of poverty" and instead argues that gang members aspire upward social mobility, even though through insecure and precarious "underground economies".

The third subtype, politicized gangs, are in line with the critical theory approach that focuses on the internal motivation of gang members and gives primacy to ideological conviction over economic incentives. The critical theory school of gang research emphasizes the importance of contextualizing empirical data in order to reveal the historical or socio-economic conditions that led to the emergence of gangs in the first place. For this purpose, authors in this tradition try to expose "relationships of domination" that are "contingent upon structured inequalities" (Brotherton and Barrios, 2004, p. 4). As Venkatesh (2003, p. 6) put it, the aim is to uncover "both the very real inequity that may exist among the communities as well as the numerous nondelinquent aspects" of deviant activity such as "political resistance".

The critical approach conceptualizes gang members as conscious social actors and aims to overcome the analytical divide between agency and structure by stating that "all gang subjects both make and are made by historical forces" (Brotherton, 2008b, p. 119). In this respect, Brotherton and Barrios (2004) underline aspects of political resistance and reinterpret certain gangs, such as the New York chapter of the Latin Kings, as a "street organization". A street organization is defined as:

> A group formed largely by youth and adults of a marginalized social class which aims to provide its members with a resistant identity, an opportunity to be individually and collectively empowered, a voice to speak back to and challenge the dominant culture,

> a refuge from the stresses and strains of barrio or ghetto life, and a spiritual enclave within which its own sacred rituals can be generated and practiced.
>
> *(Brotherton and Barrios, 2004, p. 23)*

Politicized gangs, the last subtype, are reflective of the clientelist approach that highlights the political function of gangs while underlining the impact of external interests. From this point of view, gangs are interpreted "as the pliant tools of corrupt, powerful city players of machine politics" (Kontos *et al.*, 2003; Brotherton and Barrios, 2004, p. 39; Hagedorn, 2008). Today, although this type of machine politics is far less pronounced in the US, it is still common practice in a number of less stable democracies across the world. In Kenya, for instance, the mobilization of politicized gangs along ethnic lines has contributed considerably to recurring post-election violence in the country (Schuberth, 2018). In the case of Haiti, gangs have long been hired as political thugs and played an important role in the country's clientelistic networks as intermediaries between local communities and politicians (Schuberth, 2017b).

Transformations

As the previous section has shown, there is an abundance of literature about the raison d'être of gangs. Yet, relatively little has been written on their transformation. One exception is the three-generation gang model, which posits that turf-based first-generation youth gangs can turn into business-oriented second-generation criminal gangs, which in turn have the potential to evolve into transnational third-generation gangs with political and social objectives (Bunker and Sullivan, 2011). This process is attributed to a combination of "politicization, internationalization, and sophistication" of the groups, whereas particular attention is given to technological advances (Sullivan, 2006, p. 487). Arguably, the ultimate goal of gangs at the final stage of this "evolutionary coup d' street [sic] process", is to take control of the state (Manwaring, 2006, pp. 506, 511).

However, Hagedorn rejects the sense of predictability and determination inherent in the three-generation model. Instead, he comes up with a concept of institutionalization in order to explain "why some gangs persist for decades despite changes in leadership and police repression" (Hagedorn, 2008, p. 9). Emphasis is given to structural factors such as urbanization, marginalization and the emergence of the drug trade, as well as to the cultural and ethnic identity of the group, which is further strengthened through mass imprisonment. From this point of view, gangs can either institutionalize into social movements, such as the *Almighty Latin King and Queen Nation* in New York City, or into highly organized drug trafficking organizations, such as the *maras* in Central America and *Comando Vermelho* in Rio de Janeiro.

Pandillas and maras in Central America

In recent years, gang research has paid particular attention to Central American gangs in North America (Zilberg, 2011; Ward, 2013) and to gangs in Central America (Bruneau *et al.*, 2011; Brenneman, 2012; Levenson, 2013). In this respect, Rodgers and Muggah (2009, p. 305) distinguish between two types of gangs in Central America: first, the "more localized, homegrown" *pandillas* are the most common type of gangs in Nicaragua. They resemble the subtype of youth gangs, which are described as unsupervised peer groups. The second type, the *maras*, have "transnational roots" and are the predominant type of gangs in the Northern Triangle.[1] *Maras* are closer to the subtype of criminal gangs. One characteristic of youth gangs is their proclivity to turn into profit-oriented criminal gangs (Sullivan, 2006), as happened with the *pandillas* in Nicaragua.

Historically, youth gangs have long been part of Nicaraguan society (Rodgers and Muggah, 2009). However, the *pandillas* have transformed significantly over the last two decades. The most detailed micro-level analysis in this respect is Dennis Rodgers' longitudinal account of how the relationship of a Nicaraguan youth gang vis-à-vis their community turned from protective to predatory as a result of the arrival of cocaine at the turn of the millennium. When first conducting research in a barrio of Nicaragua's capital, Managua, in the 1990s, Rodgers (2007c) observed that local gangs were largely viewed positively in their community because they protected inhabitants from other gangs. In fact, gangs showed a certain "community spirit" and observed the "cardinal 'golden rule'" never to victimize the local population (Rodgers, 2007c, p. 351). However, due to tightened anti-drugs efforts in the Caribbean and the improvement of infrastructure in Nicaragua, more and more Colombian cocaine was shipped through the country on its way to North America (Rodgers, 2007b). As gangs in Managua consequently became enmeshed in the local drug economy, the security situation in the barrio deteriorated significantly (Rodgers, 2007c). Instead of caring for their own community, gang members started to protect dealers and their customers, thus establishing "a predatory regime of terror" in order to protect and maximize their illicit profits (Rodgers, 2006, p. 290).

While youth gangs tend to turn into profit-oriented criminal gangs, in a few cases the latter can evolve further into powerful, institutionalized drug-trafficking organizations (DTOs) that operate on a transnational basis (Hagedorn, 2008). This happened with Central American *maras*, which Sullivan (2006) classified as politicized, internationalized and sophisticated "third-generation" gangs. The two largest *maras*, *Mara Salvatrucha* and the 18th Street Gang, were formed in Los Angeles by immigrants who had fled from the civil wars in Central America in order to protect their community against other well-established gangs (Valdez, 2011). Mass deportations of gang members from the US to their Central American countries of origin (Zilberg, 2011) and massive incarceration of alleged gang members as part of harsh *mano dura* ("firm hand") anti-gang policies in the region contributed to the expansion and institutionalization of the *maras* (Jütersonke *et al.*, 2009; Schuberth, 2016a). A number of high-profile attacks on civilians to protest *mano dura* policies and unsubstantiated rumours about links to al-Qaeda (Arana, 2005) prompted some commentators to blow the threat posed by *maras* out of proportion (Wolf, 2012).

While such sensationalist accounts need to be qualified, most analysts agree that the challenge posed by gangs increased noticeably over the last two decades and now poses a serious challenge for Central American countries (Seligson and Booth, 2010; Shifter, 2011; Farah, 2012; Rodgers and Baird, 2015). Whereas their activities were initially based on "solidarity, respect and mutual support", the *maras* have since undergone "a change in motivation, shifting towards a more sustained use of instrumental violence for economic purposes" (Cruz, 2010, p. 393). Still, it is important to distinguish between *maras* and, say, Mexican cartels. *Maras* have been found to work as local "subcontractors" for *Los Zetas* and other Mexican DTOs that are expanding their operations southward into Central America (Inkster and Comolli, 2012, p. 97). Gang members have reportedly been trained by *Los Zetas* and subsequently been hired for protection purposes, as local drug peddlers and as hitmen (Dudley, 2011). Thus, the two groups apparently do not play in the same league. In the case of certain gangs in Brazil, by contrast, this differentiation between principal and agent seems more complicated.

Comando Vermelho in Rio de Janeiro

The *Comando Vermelho* ("Red Command") in Rio de Janeiro is arguably the most well-known example of a transformed gang in Brazil. During the military dictatorship, political prisoners and common criminals who were put in the same maximum security prisons banded together to form a group called *o coletivo* (Dowdney, 2003). The 'collective' spread within Rio's prison system, fought for improved conditions of detention and enforced harsh rules among the prisoners (Penglase, 2008). Later, *o coletivo* came to be known as the *Comando Vermelho* and started to become a major player in the burgeoning drug trade. This happened in the first half of the 1980s, when Brazil was undergoing a period of democratization and as tougher anti-drug measures in Colombia turned Rio de Janeiro into South America's foremost transit point for Andean cocaine on the way to Europe and North America (Perlman, 2009).

Eventually, the *Comando Vermelho* split into rival factions, whose tough competition over the control of the drug market led to what Gay (2005, p. 55) calls "a period of intense and bloody civil war for control of the favelas." At the same time, the gang imposed itself onto the favelas, which serve as an ideal hiding place for drugs and provide a pool of unemployed young men for recruitment (Alves and Evanson, 2011). In this respect, Penglase (2005, p. 6) observes that gangs establish a "simulacrum of governmental control" in poor neighbourhoods. Yet, it has been argued that rather than constituting a parallel form of governance, gangs have established themselves as intermediaries between politicians and favela residents (Arias, 2006).

The common denominator of the two case studies of *pandillas* and *maras* in Central America and *Comando Vermelho* in Brazil is that gangs are seen as conscious social actors that undergo a process of internal transformation, which is influenced by a host of structural factors, often related to forces of globalization. Moreover, both Sullivan's three-generation gang model and Hagedorn's institutionalization model take the ecological explanation for the emergence of gangs as unsupervised peer groups as a starting point and assume that their transformation reflects a shift in the group's motivation. In some cases, however, the transformation of gangs can be traced back to interrelated and constantly changing politico-criminal ambitions of their patrons, rather than to the motivation of gang members themselves, which remains basically the same. This has been the case with politicized criminal gangs in Haiti and Kenya.

Functions

On top of the transformation of criminal gangs into more sophisticated, institutionalized, and politicized criminal groups or street organizations, another transformation that follows an inverse logic is regularly postulated in the literature on criminal violence: the transformation of politically motivated non-state armed groups (NSAGs) into economically motivated criminal gangs (Schuberth, 2015a). This trend has been associated not only with a change from rural insurgencies to urban "slum wars of the 21st century" (Rodgers, 2009), but also with a more general shift from political violence to criminal violence – or at least with increasingly blurred boundaries between the two categories (Kaldor, 1999). In the context of both Latin America (Koonings and Kruijt, 2004; Moser and McIlwaine, 2004) and sub-Saharan Africa (Bøås and Dunn, 2007; Reno, 2011), it is a common perception that political violence has been replaced by criminal or socio-economic violence in post-conflict settings and more generally in the period of democratization following the Cold War.[2]

In the case of Haiti, for instance, the official narrative brought forward was that Haiti had been in a conflict situation when the United Nations Stabilization Mission in Haiti (MINUSTAH) intervened in 2004; thus, urban gangs were perceived as having been politically motivated at that time (Schuberth, 2017a). With former President Aristide gone and in exile, the narrative continues, the country transformed into a post-conflict situation; thus, gangs were suddenly seen as being motivated by purely criminal aims (Schuberth, 2019). For instance, a United Nations Development Programme (UNDP) evaluation asserts a "shift from politically-motivated violence to purely criminal activities" (Faubert, 2006, p. 12), whereas the International

Crisis Group (2012, p. 7) states that "[g]angs today are seen as more purely criminal elements and no longer as political activists."

What proponents of the shift from political to criminal violence have in common is their focus on the motivation of *perpetrators* of violence and not on that of their *sponsors*. It is commonly taken as a given that "a perpetrator's motivations" are the decisive factor when classifying "an act of armed violence [as] politically or economically motivated" (del Frate and De Martino, 2013, p. 9). This perspective presupposes that gang members make the deliberate choice of whether to engage in violence for political ends or for purely profit-oriented, hence criminal reasons. Yet, the impact of structural constraints and external interests is not adequately taken into account. In short, it is assumed that agency of gang members trumps structure plus agency of their patrons. This assumption, however, seems difficult to maintain in consideration of the socio-economic conditions which limit the life choices of the urban poor in many countries in which gangs are present.

This is particularly evident in the case of Haiti. While an estimated 75 per cent of the country's population live below the poverty line, more than half of all Haitians live in extreme poverty (UN, 2011). But even in this unfavourable environment, popular neighbourhoods in which gangs are found are particularly worse off. According to a survey of residents in *Cité Soleil*, 83 per cent report being unemployed and 82 per cent say they would not earn "enough money to feed their households" (Marcelin, 2011, p. 25). Of course, most youth growing up in such conditions do not join gangs, so this is not their inevitable fate. Still, it has been argued that those who do join such groups are principally motivated by economic incentives rather than by political goals (Schuberth, 2016b).

Considering that the agency of gang members is limited by structural constraints, some authors suggest utilizing a functional perspective that shifts the focus of analysis from the *producers* to the *sponsors* of violence (Schuberth, 2015b). From this point of view, gangs are seen as profit-oriented violent entrepreneurs who are seeking to improve their limited life chances, regardless of whether they serve the political or the criminal interests of their sponsors. In this respect, Moser and Rodgers (2005, p. 35) define political and economic violence as "[t]he commission of violent acts [...] to obtain or maintain political power" or "economic power", respectively. What is interesting about this definition is that the categorization of armed violence as either politically or economically motivated depends not on those who *commit* the violence, but those who *commission* it. Thus, it is possible to distinguish between internal and external functions of criminal gangs.

Internally, gangs function as "potential forms of asset building and accumulation" for their members (Rodgers, 2007a, p. 180). The external function, by contrast, depends on the demands of the patron. From this perspective, gangs whose members are consistently driven by economic incentives can be paid to carry out tasks which have a political, a criminal or, for that matter, a social function for their sponsor. The functions of the violent services demanded from gangs by their sponsors tend to swing toward the political during election periods and toward the criminal in between elections. In the absence of patrons, gangs turn towards their community to generate income; that is, they turn predatory. Patrons are usually part of a country's political and economic elite, whereas members of the gangs they utilize belong to the country's most deprived social stratum (Schuberth, 2015a).

These dynamics have been observed in the case of Kenya. The slums in and around Kenya's main cities such as Nairobi and Mombasa are characterized by the presence of gangs that can assume criminal, political, or security functions, depending on the demands of their patrons. Studies demonstrated that the needs of patrons tend to depend on the political economy of the geographic area in which gangs are located. In Nairobi, the centre of political power, gangs have been found to be hired primarily for political purposes. Politicians use these groups to provide security during rallies in slum areas, to work as a mobilizing platform, or to act as goon squads in order to intimidate or eliminate political opponents (Schuberth, 2018).

The situation is different within informal settlements around Mombasa, which are littered with heroin and to a lesser degree cocaine. Over the past 30 years, hard drugs have spilled over from Mombasa's wealthy neighbourhoods into slum areas and further into other coastal towns such as Malindi and Lamu (Deveau *et al.*, 2006). Studies have shown that DTOs in Mombasa who are involved in the international and highly profitable heroin trade have both the police and criminal gangs on their payroll. In the *Likoni* slum in Mombasa, for example, gang members work in various ways for the local drug lord, such as providing security around the drug dens, looking out for clients in other parts of town, or selling drugs themselves (Schuberth, 2014). All in all, in both Kenya and Haiti, gangs evolving in an environment of poverty and high rates of unemployment fulfil different functions depending on the needs of their political or criminal sponsors.

Conclusion

Criminal gangs are an important yet understudied characteristic of many cities in the global South. Building on empirical evidence from Central America, Kenya and Haiti, this chapter provided an overview of three key elements regularly discussed in the contemporary literature on global gangs: the motivation for members to join criminal gangs; the transformation processes such groups typically undergo; as well as the functions violence fulfils for various stakeholders. Concerning motivations behind joining gangs and engaging in gang-related violence, this chapter presented four subtypes of gangs that can be traced back to competing schools of gang research – the ecological approach in the case of youth gangs, the rational choice approach in the case of criminal gangs, the critical theory approach in the case of street organizations, and the clientelist approach in the case of politicized gangs.

This chapter also discussed two approaches explaining regular shifts from one subtype to another – the three-generation gang model, which posits that youth gangs can turn into criminal gangs and further into gangs with political and social objectives, as well as the institutionalization model that explains the transformation of youth or street gangs into politicized gangs or street organizations through structural factors such as urbanization, marginalization and the international drug trade. Lastly, this chapter argued that the function of acts of violence committed by gangs regularly depends on the often overlapping criminal and political priorities of those *commissioning* these acts. Thus, while gangs can be seen as profit-oriented violent entrepreneurs who are driven by the incentive to gain income by whatever means, external interests can implicate them in power politics or organized criminal activities.

Notes

1 The Northern Triangle comprises El Salvador, Guatemala and Honduras.
2 A number of scholars, including Pearce (2010) and Rodgers (2009, p. 950), question the validity of this proclaimed shift, arguing that "contemporary urban violence can in fact be seen as a structural continuation […] of the political conflicts of the past."

References

Adelman, H. (2006) Cultures of violence. In T. Keating and W. A. Knight (eds), *Building Sustainable Peace*. Tokyo: United Nations University Press, pp. 303–330.

Alves, M. H. M. and Evanson, P. (2011) *Living in the Crossfire: Favela Residents, Drug Dealers, and Police Violence in Rio de Janeiro*. Philadelphia: Temple University Press.

Arana, A. (2005) How the street gangs took Central America. *Foreign Affairs*, 84(3), 98–110.

Arias, E. D. (2006) Trouble en route: Drug trafficking and clientelism in Rio de Janeiro shantytowns. *Qualitative Sociology*, 29(4), 427–445.

Baird, A. (2012) Negotiating pathways to manhood: Rejecting gangs and violence in Meddelins periphery. *Journal of Conflictology*, 3(1), 30–41.

Bøås, M. and Dunn, K. C. (2007) African guerrilla politics: Raging against the machine? In M. Bøås and K. C. Dunn (eds), *African Guerrillas: Raging Against the Machine*. Boulder, CO: Lynne Rienner, pp. 9–37.

Branch, C. W. (1999) *Adolescent Gangs: Old Issues, New Approaches*. Philadelphia, PA: Brunner/Mazel.

Brenneman, R. (2012) *Homies and Hermanos: God and Gangs in Central America*. New York: Oxford University Press.

Brotherton, D. (2008a) Beyond social reproduction: Bringing resistance back in gang theory. *Theoretical Criminology*, 12(1), 55–77.

Brotherton, D. (2008b) Youth subcultures, resistance, and the street organization in late modern New York. In M. Flynn and D. Brotherton (eds), *Globalizing the Streets: Cross-Cultural Perspectives on Youth, Social Control, and Empowerment*. New York: Columbia University Press, pp. 114–132.

Brotherton, D. and Barrios, L. (2004) *The Almighty Latin King and Queen Nation: Street Politics and the Transformation of a New York City Gang*. New York: Columbia University Press.

Bruneau, T., Dammert, L., and Skinner, E. (2011) *Maras: Gang Violence and Security in Central America*. Austin, TX: University of Texas Press.

Bunker, R. J. and Sullivan, J. (2011) Integrating feral cities and third phase cartels/third generation gangs research: The rise of criminal (narco) city networks and BlackFor. *Small Wars & Insurgencies*, 22(5), 764–786.

Cohen, S. (1972) *Folk Devils and Moral Panics: The Creation of the Mods and Rockers*. London: MacGibbon and Kee.

Covey, H. C. (2010) *Street Gangs Throughout the World*. Springfield, IL: Charles C Thomas.

Cruz, J. M. (2010) Central American maras: From youth street gangs to transnational protection rackets. *Global Crime*, 11(4), 379–398.

del Frate, A. A. and De Martino, L. (2013) Everyday dangers: Non-conflict armed violence. In E. Lebrun *et al.* (eds), *Small Arms Survey 2013: Everyday Dangers*. Geneva: Small Arms Survey, pp. 7–15.

Deveau, C., Levine, B., and Beckerleg, S. (2006) Heroin use in Kenya and findings from a community-based outreach programme to reduce the spread of HIV/AIDS. *African Journal of Drug & Alcohol Studies*, 5(2), 95–107.

Dowdney, L. (2003) *Children of the Drug Trade: A Case Study of Children in Organised Armed Violence in Rio de Janeiro*. Rio de Janeiro: 7 Letras.

Dowdney, L. (2005) *Neither War Nor Peace: International Comparisons of Children and Youth in Organised Armed Violence*. Rio de Janeiro: 7 Letras.

Dudley, S. S. (2011) Central America besieged: Cartels and maras country threat analysis. *Small Wars & Insurgencies*, 22(5), 890–913.

Farah, D. (2012) Central American gangs: Changing nature and new partners. *Journal of International Affairs*, 66(1), 53–67.

Faubert, C. (2006) *Evaluation of UNDP Assistance to Conflict-affected Countries: Case Study Haiti*. New York: UNDP.

Flynn, M. and Brotherton, D. (2008) *Globalizing the Streets: Cross-Cultural Perspectives on Youth, Social Control, and Empowerment*. New York: Columbia University Press.

Gay, R. (2005) *Lucia: Testimonies of a Brazilian Drug Dealer's Woman*. Philadelphia: Temple University Press.

Hagedorn, J. (1988) *People and Folks: Gangs, Crime and the Underclass in a Rustbelt City*. Chicago: Lake View Press.

Hagedorn, J. (2005) The global impact of gangs. *Journal of Contemporary Criminal Justice*, 21(2), 153–169.

Hagedorn, J. (2007a) Gangs in late modernity. In J. Hagedorn (ed), *Gangs in the Global City: Alternatives to Traditional Criminology*. Urbana/Chicago: University of Illinois Press, pp. 295–318.

Hagedorn, J. (2007b) *Gangs in the Global City: Alternatives to Traditional Criminology*. Urbana and Chicago: University of Illinois Press.

Hagedorn, J. (2008) *A World of Gangs: Armed Young Men and Gangsta Culture*. Minneapolis, MN: University of Minnesota Press.

Hayden, T. (2006) *Street Wars: Gangs and the Future of Violence*. New York: The New Press.

Inkster, N. and Comolli, V. (2012) *Drugs, Insecurity and Failed States: The Problems of Prohibition*. London: International Institute for Strategic Studies.

International Crisis Group (2012) *Towards a Post-MINUSTAH Haiti: Making an Effective Transition*. Brussels: International Crisis Group.
Jütersonke, O., Muggah, R., and Rodgers, D. (2009) Gangs, urban violence, and security interventions in Central America. *Security Dialogue*, 40(4–5), 373–397.
Kaldor, M. (1999) *New and Old Wars: Organized Violence in a Global Era*. Cambridge: Polity Press.
Klein, M. W. (1971) *Street Gangs and Street Workers*. Englewood Cliffs, NJ: Prentice-Hall.
Klein, M. W. (1995) *The American Street Gang: Its Nature, Prevalence, and Control*. Oxford: Oxford University Press.
Klein, M. W. and Maxson, C. L. (2010) *Street Gang Patterns and Policies*. Oxford: Oxford University Press.
Kontos, L., Brotherton, D., and Barrios, L. (2003) *Gangs and Society: Alternative Perspectives*. New York: Columbia University Press.
Koonings, K. (1999) Shadows of violence and political transition in Brazil: From military rule to democratic governance. In K. Koonings and D. Krujit (eds), *Societies of Fear: The Legacy of Civil War, Violence and Terror in Latin America*. London: Zed Books, pp. 197–234.
Koonings, K. and Kruijt, D. (eds) (1999) *Societies of Fear: The Legacy of Civil War, Violence and Terror in Latin America*. London: Zed Books.
Koonings, K. and Kruijt, D. (eds) (2004) *Armed Actors: Organised Violence and State Failure in Latin America*. London: Zed Books.
Levenson, D. T. (2013) *Adiós Niño: The Gangs of Guatemala City and the Politics of Death*. Durham, NC and London: Duke University Press.
Manwaring, M. G. (2006) Gangs and coups d' Streets in the new world disorder: Protean insurgents in post-modern war. *Global Crime*, 7(3–4), 505–543.
Manwaring, M. G. (2008) Sovereignty under siege: Gangs and other criminal organizations in Central America and Mexico. *Air & Space Power Journal*, 20(2), 25–41.
Marcelin, L. H. (2011) Cooperation, peace and (re-)construction? A tale from the shanties. *Journal of Peacebuilding & Development*, 6(3), 17–31.
Martinez, J. F. E. (2003) Urban street activists: Gang and community efforts to bring peace and justice to Los Angeles neighborhoods. In L Kontos *et al.* (eds), *Gangs and Society: Alternative Perspectives*. New York: Columbia University Press, pp. 95–117.
Moore, J. (1998) Understanding youth street gangs: Economic restructuring and the urban underclass. In M. W. Watts (ed.), *Cross-Cultural Perspectives on Youth and Violence*. Stamford, CT: Jai Press, pp. 65–78.
Moser, C. and Rodgers, D. (2005) *Change, Violence and Insecurity in Non-Conflict Situations*. London: Overseas Development Institute.
Moser, C. O. N. and McIlwaine, C. (2004) *Encounters with Violence in Latin America: Urban Poor Perceptions from Columbia and Guatemala*. London and New York: Routledge.
Padilla, F. M. (1992) *The Gang as an American Enterprise*. New Brunswick, NJ: Rutgers University Press.
Pearce, J. (2010) Perverse state formation and securitized democracy in Latin America. *Democratization*, 17(2), 286–306.
Pécaut, D. (1999) From the banality of violence to real terror: The case of Colombia. In K. Koonings and D. Krujit (eds), *Societies of Fear: The Legacy of Civil War, Violence and Terror in Latin America*. London: Zed Books, pp. 141–168.
Peetz, P. (2011) Youth violence in Central America: Discourses and policies. *Youth & Society*, 43(4), pp. 1459–1498.
Penglase, B. (2005) The shutdown of Rio de Janeiro: The poetics of drug trafficker violence. *Anthropology Today*, 21(5), 3–6.
Penglase, B. (2008) The bastard child of the dictatorship: The Comando Vermelho and the birth of "narco-culture" in Rio de Janeiro. *Luso-Brazilian Review*, 45(1), 118–145.
Perlman, J. (2009) Megacity's violence and its consequences in Rio de Janeiro. In K. Koonings and D. Kruijt (eds), *Megacities: The Politics of Urban Exclusion and Violence in the Global South*. London: Zed Books, pp. 52–68.
Pitts, J. (2013) *Reluctant Gangsters: The Changing Face of Youth Crime*. Cullompton: Willan Publishing.
Reno, W. (2011) *Warfare in Independent Africa*. Cambridge: Cambridge University Press.
Rodgers, D. (2006) Living in the shadow of death: Gangs, violence, and social order in urban Nicaragua, 1996–2002. *Journal of Latin American Studies*, 38(2), 267–292.
Rodgers, D. (2007a) Gangs, violence and asset building. In C. O. N. Moser (ed.), *Reducing Global Poverty: The Case for Asset Accumulation*. Washington, DC: Brookings Institution Press, pp. 179–195.

Rodgers, D. (2007b) Managua. In K. Koonings and D. Kruijt (eds), *Fractured Cities: Social Exclusion, Urban Violence and Contested Spaces in Latin America*. London: Zed Books, pp. 71–85.
Rodgers, D. (2007c) When vigilantes turn bad: Gangs, violence, and social change in urban Nicaragua. In D. Pratten and A. Sen (eds), *Global Vigilantes*. London: Hurst, pp. 349–370.
Rodgers, D. (2009) Slum wars of the 21st century: Gangs, mano dura and the new urban geography of conflict in Central America. *Development and Change*, 40(5), 949–976.
Rodgers, D. and Baird, A. (2015) Understanding gangs in contemporary Latin America. In S. H. Decker and D. C. Pyrooz (eds), *Handbook of Gangs and Gang Responses*. New York: Wiley, pp. 478–502.
Rodgers, D. and Muggah, R. (2009) Gangs as non-state armed groups: The Central American case. *Contemporary Security Policy*, 30(2), 301–317.
Sánchez-Jankowski, M. (1991) *Islands in the Street: Gangs and American Urban Society*. Berkeley and Los Angeles: University of California Press.
Schuberth, M. (2014) The impact of drug trafficking on informal security actors in Kenya. *Africa Spectrum*, 49(3), 55–81.
Schuberth, M. (2015a) The challenge of community-based armed groups: Towards a conceptualization of militias, gangs, and vigilantes. *Contemporary Security Policy*, 36(2), 296–320.
Schuberth, M. (2015b) A transformation from political to criminal violence? Politics, organised crime and the shifting functions of Haiti's urban armed groups. *Conflict, Security & Development*, 15(2), 169–196.
Schuberth, M. (2016a) Beyond gang truces and *Mano Dura* policies: Towards substitutive security governance in Latin America. *Stability: International Journal of Security & Development*, 5(1), Art. 17.
Schuberth, M. (2016b) Growing the grassroots or backing bandits? Dilemmas of donor support for Haiti's (un)civil society. *Journal of Peacebuilding & Development*, 11(1), 93–98.
Schuberth, M. (2017a) Disarmament, demobilisation and reintegration in unconventional settings: The case of MINUSTAH's community violence reduction. *International Peacekeeping*, 24(3), 410–433.
Schuberth, M. (2017b) To engage or not to engage Haiti's urban armed groups? Safe access in disaster-stricken and conflict-affected cities. *Environment and Urbanization*, 29(2), 425–442.
Schuberth, M. (2018) Hybrid security governance, post-election violence and the legitimacy of community-based armed groups in urban Kenya. *Journal of Eastern African Studies*, 12(2), 386–404.
Schuberth, M. (2019) Brazilian peacekeeping? Counterinsurgency and police reform in Port-au-Prince and Rio de Janeiro. *International Peacekeeping*, 26(4).
Seligson, M. A. and Booth, J. A. (2010) Crime, hard times, and discontent. *Journal of Democracy*, 21(2), 123–135.
Shifter, M. (2011) Central America's security predicament. *Current History*, 110(733), 49–55.
Spergel, I. A. (1995) *The Youth Gang Problem: A Community Approach*. New York: Oxford University Press.
Sullivan, J. (2006) Maras morphing: Revisiting third generation gangs. *Global Crime*, 7(3–4), 487–504.
Thrasher, F. M. (1927) *The Gang: A Study of 1,313 Gangs in Chicago*. Chicago: University of Chicago Press.
Tovares, R. D. (2002) *Manufacturing the Gang: Mexican American Youth Gangs on Local Television News*. Westport, CT: Greenwood Press.
UN (2011) *Report of the United Nations in Haiti 2011*. New York: United Nations.
Valdez, A. (2011) The origins of southern California Latino gangs. In T. Bruneau *et al.* (eds), *Maras: Gang Violence and Security in Central America*. Austin, TX: University of Texas Press, pp. 23–42.
Venkatesh, S. A. (2000) *American Project: The Rise and Fall of a Modern Ghetto*. Cambridge, MA: Harvard University Press.
Venkatesh, S. (2003) A note on social theory and the American street gang. In L. Kontos *et al.* (eds), *Gangs and Society: Alternative Perspectives*. New York: Columbia University Press, pp. 3–11.
Ward, T. W. (2013) *Gangsters without Borders: An Ethnography of a Salvadoran Street Gang*. New York: Oxford University Press.
Wolf, S. (2012) Mara Salvatrucha: The most dangerous street gang in the Americas? *Latin American Politics and Society*, 54(1), 65–99.
Zilberg, E. (2011) *Space of Detention: The Making of a Transnational Gang Crisis between Los Angeles and San Salvador*. Durham, NC and London: Duke University Press.

18

EXPLORING THE CURRENCY OF VIOLENCE IN SERIOUS ORGANIZED CRIME

Stuart Kirby, Rebecca Phythian and Laura Boulton

Introduction

Although myriad definitions exist for Serious Organized Crime (SOC), Albanese (2008) found the four most frequent characteristics to be: a continuing organizational hierarchy; the corruption of public officials to maintain immunity; obtaining rational profit through crime; and the use of force or threat. This chapter explores the latter, specifically focusing upon the currency of violence for those engaged in this environment. To do so, this chapter will examine the role of violence across a spectrum of organized crime groups (OCG), starting with the earlier studies on more formal hierarchical groups, such as the Cosa Nostra and Yakuza. It will then turn to the UK, initially looking at a study of 4109 offenders, before looking in more depth at Organized Crime Group dynamics and the views of the community. Finally, the chapter examines the characteristics of a cohort of young men, identified as being on the periphery of organized crime to establish early experiences. During this process psychological, sociological and cultural perspectives will be considered, together with an analysis of instrumental and expressive explanations. In doing so it will ultimately argue that a multitude of explanations for violence are necessary to account for the diversity found within OCGs.

At the outset, some foundations need to be laid. It is widely agreed that SOC creates a significant level of negative impact to society. This is observed at a macro level, with high level corruption associated with failed states and severe financial cost (Home Office, 2018), and also at a micro level, where widespread community fear and harm can be generated (Bullock *et al.*, 2009). Unfortunately, defining its form has proved difficult, being reported as "one of the most contested terms in academic criminology" (Sheptyki, 2003, p. 490). Much of the reason behind this has rested on the methodology used to identify and understand organized crime. There are distinct challenges associated with researching this type of violent and covert crime, which often means that academics rely upon law enforcement organizations to generate data. The quality of this may be influenced by the capacity and capability of the agencies themselves, as some offenders will be noticed whilst others remain invisible (Kirby, 2013). Further, as no country routinely categorizes information on organized crime offences or its offenders, no international comparative data are available. This limits the data in terms of representativeness and objectivity, leading to the criticism that the frequency and content of organized crime is poorly understood (von Lampe, 2012).

Nonetheless, it is important to have a definition to guide this chapter. In the UK, where the definition has evolved over recent years, it is given as, "individuals planning, coordinating and committing serious offences, whether individuals, in groups and/or as part of transnational networks" (Home Office, 2018, p. 11). Meanwhile, the United Nations defined OCGs as a "structured group of three or more persons existing for a period of time and acting in concert with the aim of committing one or more serious crimes or offences in order to obtain, directly or indirectly, a financial or other material benefit" (United Nations Centre for International Crime Prevention, UNCIP, 2000, pp. 48–49).

Research on the structure of Organized Crime Groups also generates diverse findings. Whilst some view "….crimes as very well organised" there are others who "see crimes as intermittently or more regularly networked, but not in any stable hierarchy" (Levi, 2012, p. 598). Indeed, the United Nations sought to describe Organized Crime Groups through five typologies. The "standard hierarchy" (UNCIP, 2000, p. 75), also referred to as Type 1, is aligned with Cressey's (1969) work on La Cosa Nostra in the USA (Finckenauer, 2005). This type of OCG is characterized by the reliance on violence, to achieve criminal goals and maintain internal discipline (UNCIP, 2000). Their aims are facilitated through: a rigid leadership; hierarchical structure; a strong group identity; governance of identifiable territory; and the use of corruption, racketeering and violence. However, whilst Sheptycki *et al.* (2011) points to an apparent increase in type 1 OCGs across Mexico and South America, this model appears less common than the 'enterprise model' (Smith, 1991), where profit is obtained through a series of linked criminal acts forged through the ability to engender fresh contacts. In this latter model, Sheptycki *et al.* (2011, p. 12) explain "the practices are more linked with local opportunities, deregulation or change of laws than with a strong organization… challenging the state". Finckenauer (2005, p. 65), further explains, "what we more commonly see are loosely affiliated networks of criminals who coalesce around certain criminal opportunities. The structure of these groups is much more amorphous, free floating, and flatter, and thus lacking in a rigid hierarchy". Hobbs (1998), concurs, pointing out that transnational organized crime merely comprises local groups who interact to engage in serious crime across borders. This leaves us with a varied understanding of Organized Crime, facilitated through a diverse range of structures. At one end of the continuum the boundaries are blurred, epitomized by shady business practice, whilst at the other end they morph into more locally based street gangs, who traffic drugs and other commodities, across regional boundaries. However, notwithstanding these definitional challenges a general view exists that SOC is increasing (Brocklesby, 2012); a premise that has been objectively verified in the UK's Organized Crime Group mapping project – an initiative that will be described later (National Crime Agency, 2018).

It is also pertinent to point out that a definition of violence is also contested. Iadicola and Shupe (2003, p. 23) explain, "violence is any action or structural arrangement that results in physical or nonphysical harm to one or more persons". This wide definition includes all levels of interpersonal, institutional and structural harm generated by individuals and the society they inhabit. Hawdon (2014) disregards this wider interpretation and (as we do in this chapter) focuses on physical force, including threats and attempts. However, the discussion continues to be nuanced with some questioning whether the violence used by a member of an organized crime group should be labelled as interpersonal or collective violence. Senechal de la Roche (2001) argues that collective violence can only be reported when one of the parties can attract allies, and these allies are socially close to their own group and socially distant from the other group. This process is enhanced when the groups enjoy solidarity, intimacy, cultural homogeneity, and interdependence (Senechal de la Roche, 2001). It is only when the violence involves members of the group, for the furtherance of the group, should it be considered collective.

Finally, in this section, it is also useful to set out the distinction between instrumental and expressive violence. The former relates to violence instigated to deliver a specific purpose, whilst the latter is less goal oriented and more likely to deliver greater physical injury, as it is conducted for intrinsic pleasure or gratification (McDevitt *et al.*, 2002). Topali (2006) interviewing violent offenders highlighted the positive emotions gleaned from this aggressive behaviour. This understanding is supported by cultural criminologists, who assert that some individuals living mundane and risk averse lives, engage in crime and violence for the pleasure it delivers (Katz, 1988; Lyng, 1990).

Having outlined some theoretical perspectives, the chapter will now explore the currency of violence, concentrating on the three specific areas mentioned earlier. The section on the Cosa Nostra and Yakuza comes from archived data, whilst information in relation to UK Organized Crime Groups emanates from previous research studies conducted by the authors. Readers will also observe that the information relating to each example becomes progressively more detailed, as the groups themselves run from structured hierarchies to more enterprise-based and less organized networks.

Hierarchical organized crime groups: the Cosa Nostra and Yakuza

Structured, hierarchical and mass criminal organizations have been found across the globe, including *La Eme* in Mexico, the *triad* in China, and the Russian *Mafia*. These groups form for the purpose of making money illegally (Maran, 2008), and are sustained through their ability to adapt to new opportunities in illegal markets (Hill, 2004). This particular section will focus on the Cosa Nostra and Yakuza.

The emergence of mafias have often been explained using a sociological backdrop as they are said to "emerge in societies that are undergoing a sudden and late transition to the market economy, lack[ing] a legal structure that reliably protects... disputes" (Varese, 2011, p. 193), and this can be seen in the Cosa Nostra and the Yakuza. The former can be traced back to 1838 (Paoli, 2003) and "was not created with criminal intent in mind. It started as an 'alternative' form of local government" (Maran, 2008, p. 31), although it evolved into the murderous/ sophisticated organization apparent today (Dickie, 2004). The Cosa Nostra, was built on close bonds, often bound by family, where members are "strongly bonded and secretly orientated" (Cayli, 2010, p. 387), and where betrayal was deemed unforgivable (Bolzoni, 2008). The organization had a strict and hierarchical structure. Soldiers exist at the base of the pyramid, each of whom belong to a family (Jamieson, 2000). These small families are coordinated by a *capodecina*, who in turn are led by an elected *capo* (Jamieson, 2000). Violence is reported as a critical element of the operation as it deters members who consider disloyalty, whilst also generating compliance from those who are being extorted.

The *Yakuza* emerged slightly later, in the 1920s and 1930s, although appeared less concerned with secrecy (Kaplan and Dubro, 2003). They were said to celebrate their success and endorse films that depicted, "Japanese crime bosses as benevolent patriarchs and a positive force in society" (Sheptycki, 2008, p. 24). Indeed, "after gang wars, feuding leaders have [apologized] to the public for any inconvenience caused" (Kaplan and Dubro, 2003, p. xviii). They comprise "more than 80,000 regular or associate Yakuza gang members" (Shikata, 2006, p. 416; Calderón, 2012), being based on a family structure incorporating a "unique Japanese relationship known as *oyabun-kobun* [father-son], ... providing advice, protection, and help in return receiving unswerving loyalty" (Kaplan and Dubro, 2003, p. 8). At the top of the Yamaguchi pyramid is the godfather (syndicate leader), followed by four *shatei* (younger brothers), and eight *wakashira-hosa* (assistant young leaders). Under them can be found other tiers including one executive, 83 *wakashu* (young men), each of whom commands his own legion of *kobun* (children) (Kaplan and Dubro, 2003). Kaplan and Dubro (2003, p. 8) highlight the "remarkable strength and cohesion, leading at times to a fanatic devotion to the boss".

Both the Cosa Nostra and Yakuza have been known to infiltrate public and private organizations, in particular the judiciary, politicians and law enforcement, to extend their social influence and offer wider protection (Dickie, 2004), under the "protective umbrella of the state bureaucrats and politicians" (Cayli, 2010, p. 402). Indeed, the Yakuza are said to fund and support political candidates who reciprocate with political favours (Adelstein, 2010). More relevant to this chapter is that both organizations are infamous for their use of violence (Maran, 2008). The Cosa Nostra, for example, "....survived and prospered because it intimidated witnesses, and confounded or corrupted the police and courts" (Dickie, 2004, p. 3). Further, this reputation for violence generated significant income streams for the Cosa Nostra through 'protection money' (Dickie, 2004). This approach was replicated by the Yakuza, who focused especially on the entertainment sector (Iwai, 1963), receiving protection money from, "restaurants, bars, night-clubs, and sex industry" (Hill, 2003, p. 95). Interestingly, although extremely effective in their homelands, both the Cosa Nostra and Yakuza failed to significantly extend their influence outside their native states (Hill, 2002).

Early research on hierarchical groups, such as the Cosa Nostra and Yakuza, emphasized the organization and discipline between the tiers of management. Violence was therefore legitimized through a logical process and viewed as instrumental, as it served a tangible purpose in delivering group aims. Unlike shady, but legitimate, business practice, organized crime offenders are unable to avail themselves of legal protection, nor do they have a supporting pension plan. This means violence and intimidation can be interpreted as a means to achieve a specific goal (Wieviorka, 2014), such as obtaining money through the use of threats. In this context it is often depicted as an instrumental and impersonal act, understood within the social norms of the actors involved (both perpetrators and victims).

The UK position

From here, the chapter will explore the situation in the UK, through previous research findings of the authors. It should be highlighted that UK Organized Crime Groups are generally reported to be less structured and hierarchical than the Cosa Nostra and Yakuza. Of course, as mentioned earlier, a significant methodological challenge exists in the ability to identify organized crime offenders, as no country maintains a criminal database that captures all SOC offenders. In an attempt to rectify this gap, the Home Office commissioned a study (see Francis *et al.* 2013; Kirby *et al.*, 2016), to extract a population of SOC offenders from the UK offender database (Police National Computer), over a three-year period. To separate SOC offenders from others in the database, three criteria were used: first, the individual had committed a specific organized crime (suitable offences were designated through a peer assessed process); second, the crime was committed with a co-offender; and third, it was viewed a serious crime – depicted by a custodial sentence of three years or more. A sample of 4109 organized crime offenders were extracted, together with two comparison groups: a *general crime* group ($n = 4090$), who were aligned with none of the criteria; and a *serious crime* offender group ($n = 4109$), who had previously received a custodial sentence of three years or more, but were not convicted with a co-offender nor for a specified organized crime offence.

The subsequent analysis generated a number of insights. The organized crime offenders comprised a tiny proportion of the overall offender database (0.2 per cent), with a mean prior conviction rate of 22 sanctions. This placed them as a more recidivist group than the general crime offenders, but less than the serious crime offenders (mean 27 sanctions). The SOC and serious crime offenders were also more likely to be male (95 per cent) than general offenders (78 per cent) (x^2, $p < 0.001$), and older. Whilst the modal age at the time of the inclusion offence was 27 years, for organized crime offenders, the modal age for 'serious crime' and 'general' offenders was 21 and 20 years respectively. The sample also included more non-UK nationals (14 per cent) than the serious (9 per cent) and general (10 per cent) categories (x^2, $p < 0.001$), which is higher than the 11.4 per cent level of foreign-born individuals within the UK population at that time (Rienzo and Vargas-Silva, 2013).

As such, the UK organized crime offender is predominantly a non-adolescent male, a significant number of whom are early onset and persistent offenders, with a prior conviction history dominated by drug offences (73 per cent), (serious crime offenders showed 19 per cent and general crime offenders 10 per cent drug sanctions). In fact, convictions for violence was more common with serious (26 per cent) and general crime (34 per cent) groups, than SOC offenders (9 per cent), as were acquisitive crimes (robbery, burglary and theft), which featured much less in organized crime offender history. The finding that SOC offenders have fewer convictions for violence is worthy of further exploration.

Answering this question is assisted by two other supplementary studies, both of which were assisted by the Organized Crime Group Mapping (OCGM) project. This initiative requests all police agencies in England and Wales to identify and calculate a threat score for OCGs resident in their local area (Tusikov, 2012). Over the past decade this has allowed the UK to provide a more accurate analysis on approximately 5800 OCGs containing 40,000 active offenders (Home Office, 2013). Using data from one police force, Kirby and Snow (2016) examined the characteristics of 15 OCGs, each containing between three and 15 members ($n = 99$). The OCGM requests police forces categorize offenders into three groups: principal members (who direct the group); significant members (who perform a critical role in implementing the crime and are closely linked to the principal members); and peripheral members (who are supplementary and transitory members, not involved in the planning). In this sample there were 20 principal, 42 significant, and 37 peripheral members and further analysis highlighted two specific findings. First, even within these less established enterprise models of offending it is possible to distinguish tiers of influence or hierarchy within the OCG. Second, even though the vast majority of offenders had prior convictions it was the peripheral members who were most aligned with violence. In subsequent practitioner interviews it was thought peripheral members were more dispensable and could be hired to conduct enforcement duties due to their reputation for violence. Baumeister (1999) argues some groups designate specific individuals as responsible for the violence, which separates them from the groups' decision makers, and this process was apparent here.

The other study highlights the aura of intimidation that a reputation for violence can bring. Again using the OCGM, Kirby *et al.* (2017) completed the first survey of citizens who reside in areas where Organized Crime Groups are known to proliferate, and compared these with a control group ($n = 431$). There were few demographic differences across the communities (i.e. age, number in household, settled residence, deprivation scores). However, those living in the 'OCG' locations were more likely to report low collective efficacy and generally thought their neighbours were least likely to intervene when faced with a crime in action. In contrast, those within the control site showed higher indicators of collective efficacy (trust, engagement with other residents) and also reported their fellow residents to be more likely to take action and inform the police about minor incidents of crime and disorder. However when asked about drug dealing and offences involving SOC, the control group respondents no longer reported their residents as more likely to intervene. Whilst the survey did not glean an explanation for the change in behaviour when facing SOC as opposed to low level crime, other commentators' have previously highlighted the impact of explicit and implicit OCG intimidation on the community (Crocker *et al.*, 2017). Indeed, this research shows that some locations (where OCGs proliferate), are consistently less likely to contact public authority figures, or challenge crime – what Corkrean (2013) referred to as a conflict community. As such, the ability of the police to obtain information or gain cooperation from the public in reducing organized crime and violence may be in part dependent on the location.

Young men on the periphery of organized crime

In completing this picture, the chapter now investigates the characteristics of young people who practitioners believe have the potential to become the next generation of SOC offenders. It is hoped analysis at this early stage will provide insights not noticed in more mature offenders. As these young men were found to predominantly socialize and offend within groups, it is useful to consider the term 'gang' in more detail.

Whilst some see gang membership as an evolutionary process into SOC, others view it as a completely different concept (Esbensen *et al.*, 2001). Again, "gang" definitions are contested. The Eurogang Network stated that "a street gang (or troublesome youth group corresponding to a street gang elsewhere) is any durable, street-oriented youth group whose identity includes involvement in illegal activity" (see Wood and Alleyne, 2010). In the UK, Hales *et al.* (2006) demonstrated different types of gang or crew. The first are close friendship groups, which offer safety in numbers. Second, there are associates who are all known to each other, live in close proximity and engage in criminality together. Finally, there is the criminal crew and the organized crime network, which both engage in more serious criminality including local and national drug markets. Sharp *et al.* (2006) prefer the term delinquent youth groups. These involve young people who spend a lot of time in public places in groups of three or more and have engaged in delinquent or criminal behaviour over the last 12 months. They are also said to have at least one structural feature (either a name, an area, a leader, or rules). There appear tangible differences between US and UK gang forms, with the former being more endemic and organized. However, like the UK, street gangs appear more territorial, dominated by working class males, focusing their violence on rival gang members. Gang members also have more autonomy, either acting alone to commit crime, or offending in groups when further numbers are needed.

Explanations for the formation of street gangs have often been associated with changes in wider society, such as increased competition for employment, economic contraction and immigration, social exclusion, poor education, and fragmentation of communities (see Klein and Maxson, 2006). Extending this perspective, cultural criminologists also highlight the need for kinship and purpose supported by rituals and symbols in the form of gang colours, tattoos, and graffiti. These sociological explanations are underpinned by psychological perspectives. The research by Tajfel and Turner (Tajfel *et al.*, 1971; Tajfel and Turner, 1979; Turner and Reynolds, 2010), on *social identity theory*, argued that people identify themselves with those they feel similar, whilst distancing themselves from those they feel dissimilar. They attribute their own group (in-group) with positive attributes whilst bestowing less positive attributes to others (out-group) to maintain self-esteem. This emotional connection within the in-group can mitigate individual responsibility and influence conformity to group norms. It can also generate discordance and prejudice against out-groups, whose members become depersonalized (Tajfel, 1974).

Kennedy observes that gang members are disproportionately violent when compared with other types of offenders. The dynamic of a gang inherently means allegiance to one group and hostility to others. However, he points out that the most serious violence is only associated with a small number of gang members. His study of gun-related homicide in Boston found 61 groups accounted for 60 per cent of homicides relating to those under 21 years – just 0.3 per cent of the city's population (Kennedy *et al.*, 1996; Kennedy, 2001) – and pointed out that this is similar in Cincinnati and Los Angeles. However, he argues that in each gang the members who are most likely to instigate and facilitate the most extreme violence account for 0.04 per cent, or less of the population (Kennedy, 2001). Unfortunately, being associated in areas where violence is so prevalent creates a downward spiral. Papachristos (2011), highlights the risk by pointing out that at one period, whilst the US homicide rate was 5 per 100,000, in some parts of Chicago it was 3000 in every 100,000. He argued this meant walking around certain US neighbourhoods was statistically riskier than activating a landmine in an Afghanistan war zone. Faced with this reality, gang membership brings a multitude of benefits, such as: credibility, protection, kinship and lifestyle. This sense of belonging is sustained by tattoos, initiation ceremonies, symbols and kinship. However, the cost of maintaining street credibility is violently confronting signs of disrespect, which in turn leads to reoccurring retaliatory action.

Having set out this context we can turn to our UK cohort of 'at risk' young men. The project was located in the conurbations of a large UK city and supported by data from the OCGM project and information from the police, local authority and schools. The purpose of the project was to engage with these young people in an attempt to divert them into a more legitimate lifestyle. They were initially identified through familial, or other close relationships with OCGs, albeit this was later supplemented by the use of other risk factors. Initially, many of the young people refused to engage with the process, although the eventual cohort involved 22 young people between 13 and 18 years (mean 15.18 years), of which 15 (68.2 per cent) of these were recorded as previous crime victims. All individuals were highlighted on police databases as being on the periphery of organized crime, having between 0 and 7 prior convictions. Their criminal histories encompassed various offending behaviour, although mostly for violence. Sanctions included: assault (77 per cent, $n=24$), burglary (67 per cent, $n=21$), and criminal damage (51 per cent, $n=16$), with one case of murder and three cases of sexual assault. Once agreeing to take part, all of the individuals were paired with a lead professional (often a specialist youth worker) who provided them with tailored advice in an effort to assist them into education or employment. All the young males often socialized with other troublesome youths and engaged in a wide level of aggressive behaviour in their locality. The practitioners who worked alongside them highlighted both sociological and psychological factors, facilitating their pathway into SOC.

> They all lived on the same estate. […] Those estates are creating crime because you have the worst families from all over and putting them in the one estate. Multiple generations who have been on [welfare] benefits and smoked and drank and that is the only thing the young people have known. […] The only people they know who actually have anything are drug dealers. Everyone else is poor. They want more. They see dealers in their Audi A3 and their Nikes. We all want it, but the only way they see to get it, is crime.
>
> *(P7)*

> Some kids don't have any food in the house. There's no electricity. So they rather hang around on the streets. Then they start selling bits and bobs. A bit of weed [cannabis]. Gets them enough money to buy some food from the chippy [fast food takeaway]. Where would you rather be? In a cold house, sleeping on a mattress or on the streets with the lads and you've had a portion of fish and chips. […] The older ones

> will see that, see the vulnerability. He'll do it. He'll move that. He'll hide the gun. [...] A £100 to you who has got a job and can see a future, is nothing. *£100 to someone who has nothing, wow. Millionaire for a day.*
>
> *(P1)*

Of course, not all young men on these estates became involved in crime or gangs. Psychological explanations serve to explain the difference between these and other young people who lived in the area. Specifically, the youths in the cohort exhibited a higher preponderance of risk factors and lack of protective factors.

> There was five that we worked with consistently. One had a dad in jail. One – dad passed away. Another – dad was street homeless in town. The other one's dad was not there.
>
> *(P6)*

> Things happen in their community. Stabbings. Shootings. In their street. It has become the norm in this city. No one knows how this will have affected them in later life yet. They could be traumatized. I think they will be.
>
> *(P1)*

Further, a qualitative difference could be observed across the young people within the cohort. Whilst some played a leadership role, others appeared content to be led. Similarly, as Kennedy observed, certain individuals were at the forefront of using gratuitous and extreme violence. One youth worker reported talking to one of the young people outside his house when the conversation turned to his parents. At this point he became very aggressive and lashed out at his father's car, smashing windows, tail lights and tearing off the mirrors. Police intelligence on the same individual showed his extreme unpredictability and his willingness to be at the forefront of any confrontation.

Discussion: the currency of violence

In attempting to better understand the currency of violence in organized crime, this chapter makes four specific points.

First, the obvious starting position for any discussion on this subject would be to set out the level of violence associated with SOC. However this cannot be done with any accuracy for a number of reasons. The concepts of both organized crime and violence are contested with no agreed definition for either. This issue is further hindered due to the reliance on law enforcement agencies to provide much of the data on which both concepts are measured. As such, significant elements of organized crime and violence remains invisible to the researcher. Whilst the introduction of the OCGM in the UK has assisted significantly it still remains the case that data surrounding OCGs, and the violence surrounding then, is incomplete. However, some information is available and it is on this basis that this discussion goes forward.

Second, whilst it is clear that violence plays a core role in organized crime it is more difficult to provide unambiguous theoretical perspectives which explains the phenomenon. Sociological perspectives are useful in that they turn our attention to the wider environment in which organized crime occurs. The Cosa Nostra and Yakuza emerged from the social turmoil of their region, implementing a systematic and structured approach to secure power. Similarly, the UK OCGM project highlights organized crime as more likely to emerge in areas of deprivation, a finding also replicated in street gangs. Therefore, most gang members tend to emerge from deprived and challenging urban environments where violence is used as a currency to generate respect, influence and credibility. Cultural approaches extend this understanding, explaining how OCGs and gangs generate kinship and a sense of purpose for their members. For socially excluded individuals, the social norms of the street become dominant and provide a sense of purpose that mainstream society cannot fulfil.

Nonetheless, these accounts cannot explain why some community members can resist criminal involvement, or why some offenders exert greater influence within their groups. Indeed, the research shows a certain level of hierarchy in all organized crime groups and this is most clearly illustrated in the Cosa Nostra, Yakuza, Triads and Mafia (Arsovska and Craig, 2006). Here the structure is clear and pyramidal, with leaders at the top, followed by middle tier managers, and soldiers at the base. In contrast, whilst not as structured, distinct roles are also evident in the UK OCGs, labelled as principal, significant and peripheral members, with practitioners arguing the latter were the most likely to be used as enforcers. These differences are best explained by individual characteristics and learned experiences, which will be discussed further below. However, in essence, sociological, psychological and cultural explanations all assist in providing a wider understanding as to why violent behaviour is core to SOC.

Third, this type of nuanced explanation assists when analysing instrumental and expressive accounts of violence. Put simply, violence associated with organized crime has been previously reported as instrumental, and street gang violence as expressive (Hughes and Short 2005; Papachristos, 2009). However, others argue these terms are difficult to separate and often co-occur, as violence leading to tangible goals can also generate wider pleasures through the exercise of power and dominance (Levi and Maguire, 2004, p. 811). Similarly, expressive retaliatory actions (Anderson, 1990; Bourgois, 2003) may also be aligned to a more abstract purpose. For example, whilst simple actions of disrespect can be resolved without violence, doing so may be viewed as a sign of weakness within the norms of street culture and could possibly encourage further attacks. As gang members view themselves outside of mainstream society, they must organize their own protection, which may include pre-emptive action. Felson (2009), therefore argues that violence is always instrumental, as it is always instigated to achieve some level of gain. For example, if a member of the Cosa Nostra or Yakuza face non-payment, would they view that behaviour as a breach of a financial transaction or as a sign of disrespect? It is therefore difficult for the assailant, and even more so for the academic, to accurately identify all of the factors behind the assault. A disproportionate beating could be correctly categorized as expressive in one situation, whilst in another context could be interpreted as a carefully planned action to act as a wider deterrent.

Fourth, we see from previous research, that violence (or credible threat) is central to the business of SOC. However, interestingly, we saw in the UK study that whilst violence is present in the offending history of organized crime offenders, this is to a lesser degree than other offender groups. Perhaps this can be explained by the fact that inappropriate use of violence can be bad for business. Violence, especially when it generates collateral harm, can bring unwanted scrutiny from law enforcement agencies. This enhanced surveillance brings increased risk of detection to both the organized crime offender and those they do business with. Business partners require predictability in those they engage with, therefore unpredictable and unwarranted violence can also illustrate irrational decision making. Taking the UK example, it appears offenders with a reputation for being excessively violent are less likely to be the principal and more likely to be peripheral members used specifically to enforce operations.

So where does this discussion leave us? The chapter argues that the reason both violence and organized crime are contested concepts is because they emerge in many different forms. Serious organized crime, whilst often referred to as a single crime genre, is in fact the culmination of many different crimes, conducted by many different types of people, in many different ways. Therefore if one definition cannot explain organized crime or violence, then it is perhaps unrealistic to expect we can fashion one explanation for the violence that exists within SOC. Nonetheless, these theoretical perspectives do not contradict each other, but assist in a more nuanced understanding. At a structural level, the social fabric, in terms of social change and deprivation, generates an environment from which violent organized crime offenders often emerge. The individual is then moulded by street level interactions through cultural norms and local contacts. In this developmental process, individuals forge more distinct characteristics and become less equal, having been born with different characteristics, which are advanced (positively or negatively) through life experiences. For a few of these adolescent 'troublesome youths' these experiential pathways will divert them into crime, and a few of these will become involved in organized crime, be they peripheral, significant, principal, soldier or capo members.

As such, it is an amalgam of the environment they are born into, coupled with individual characteristics and learned experiences that influences an individual's decision to use (and how to use) violence. This decision making has ramifications as it is closely aligned to how they will be viewed by their peers. When a decision to use violence is made it is the culmination of many (often subconscious) factors: individual propensity to use violence; capability and experience of the assailant to use violence; the individual character, capability and experience of the victim in defending themselves; the current context (both relating to the individuals and the group); the longer term relationship between the assailant and victim (both at individual and group levels); the ramifications of conducting or not conducting the violent act (i.e. risk and severity of retaliation).

References

Adelstein, J. (2010) The last Yakuza. *World Policy Journal*, 27(2), 63–71.

Anderson, E. (1990) *Code of the Street: Decency, Violence, and the Moral Life of the Inner City*. New York: W. W. Norton.

Arsovska, J. and Craig, M. (2006) Honourable behaviour and the conceptualisation of violence in ethnic based OCG: An examination of the Albanian Kanen and the code of the Chinese Triads. *Global Crime*, 7, 214–246.

Baumeister, R. F. (1999) *Evil: Inside Human Violence and Cruelty*. New York: Reeman/Holt.

Bolzoni, A. (2008) *White Shotgun*. Milan: RCS Libri.

Bourgois, P. (2003) *In Search of Respect: Selling Crack in El Barrio*. New York: Cambridge University Press.

Brocklesby, J. (2012) Using the Viable Systems Model to examine multi-agency arrangements for combatting transnational organised crime. *Journal of the Operational Research Society*, 63, 418–430.

Bullock, K., Chowdhury, R., and Hollings, P. (2009) *Public Concerns about Organised Crime*. Home Office. Retrieved from https://assets.publishing.service.gov.uk/government/uploads/system/uploads/attachment_data/file/116623/horr16-report.pdf

Calderón, A. (2012) Global vice: The expanding territory of the Yakuza. *Journal of International Affairs*, 66(1), 155–161.

Cayli, B. (2010) Social networks of the Italian mafia: The strong and weak parts. *CEU Political Science Journal*, 5(3), 382–412.

Cressey, D. (1969) *Theft of the Nation: The Structure and Operations of Organized Crime in America*. New York: Harper & Row Publishing.

Corkrean, J. (2013) Situational policing in rural areas. *The Police Chief*. Retrieved from www.policechiefmagazine.org/situational-policing-in-rural-areas/

Crocker, R., Garner, S., Webb, S., and Skidmore, M. (2017) The impact of organised crime in local communities. *Australian Institute of Police Management*. Retrieved from www.aipm.gov.au/engage/article/impact-organised-crime-local-communities

Dickie, J. (2004) *Cosa Nostra: A history of the Sicilian Mafia*. London: Hodder and Stoughton.

Esbensen, F., Winfree Jr., L.T., He, N., and Taylor, T.J. (2001) Youth gangs and definitional issues: When is a gang a gang, and why does it matter? *Crime and Delinquency*, 47, 105–130.
Felson, R. B. (2009) Violence, crime and violent crime. *International Journal of Conflict and Violence*, 3(1), 23–39.
Finckenauer, J. O. (2005) Problems of definition: What is organized crime? *Trends in Organized Crime*, 8(3), 63–83.
Francis, B., Humphreys, L, Kirby, S., and Soothill, K. (2013) *Understanding Criminal Careers in Organised Crime*. Home Office. Retrieved from https://assets.publishing.service.gov.uk/government/uploads/system/uploads/attachment_data/file/246392/horr74.pdf
Hales, G., Lewis, C., and Silverstone, D. (2006) *Gun Crime: The Market in and Use of Illegal Firearms*. London: Home Office.
Hawdon, J. (2014) On the forms and nature of group violence. In J. Hawdon, J. Ryan, and M. Lucht (eds), *The Causes and Consequences of Group Violence: From Bullies to Terrorists*. London: Lexington Books, pp. 3–20.
Hill, P. (2002) Tokyo: la rete della Yakuza. *Lettera Internazionale*, 71(1), 53–55.
Hill, P. (2003) *Japanese Mafia: Yakuza, Law, and the State*. Oxford: Oxford University Press.
Hill, P. (2004) The changing face of the Yakuza. *Global Crime*, 6(1), 97–116.
Hobbs, D. (1998) Going down to the "Glocal": The local context of organized crime. *Howard Journal of Criminal Justice*, 37(4), 407–422.
Home Office (2013) *Serious and Organised Crime Strategy*. Retrieved from https://assets.publishing.service.gov.uk/government/uploads/system/uploads/attachment_data/file/248645/Serious_and_Organised_Crime_Strategy.pdf
Home Office (2018) *Serious and Organised Crime Strategy*. Retrieved from https://assets.publishing.service.gov.uk/government/uploads/system/uploads/attachment_data/file/752850/SOC-2018-web.pdf
Hughes, L. and Short, J. (2005) Disputes involving youth street gang members: Micro-social contexts. *Criminology*, 43, 43–75.
Iadicola, P. and Shupe, A. (2003) *Violence, Inequality and Human Freedom*. Lanham: Rowman and Littlefield.
Iwai, H. (1963) *Byori Shudan no Kozo*. Tokyo: Seishin-Shobo.
Jamieson, A. (2000) *The Antimafia: Italy's Fight against Organized Crime*. London: Macmillan Press.
Kaplan, D. and Dubro, A. (2003) *Yakuza: Japan's Criminal Underworld*. London: University of California Press.
Katz, J. (1988) *Seductions of Crime: Moral and Sensual Attractions in Doing Evil*. New York: Basic Books.
Kennedy, D.M. (2001) *Don't Shoot: One Man, a Street Fellowship, and the End of Violence in Inner-city America*. New York: Bloomsbury Press.
Kennedy, D., Piehl, A. M., and Braga, A. (1996) Youth violence in Boston: Gun markets, serious youth offender, and a use-reduction strategy. *Law and Contemporary Problems*, 59, 147–196.
Kirby, S. (2013) *Police Effectiveness: Implementation in Theory and Practice*. Basingstoke: Palgrave Macmillan.
Kirby, S. and Snow, N. (2016) Praxis and the disruption of organised crime groups. *Trends in Organised Crime*, 19(2), 111–124.
Kirby, S., Francis, B., and Humphreys, L. (2016) Using the UK general offender database as a means to measure and analyse Organised Crime. *Policing: An International Journal of Police Strategies and Management*, 39, 78–94.
Kirby, S., McManus, M., and Boulton, L. (2017) Examining the demographic profile and attitudes of citizens, in areas where Organised Crime proliferates. *Trends in Organised Crime*, 21(2), 172–188.
Klein, M. and Maxson, C. (2006) *Street Gang Patterns and Policies*. Oxford: Oxford University Press.
Levi, M. (2012) Organised crime. In M. Maguire, R. Morgan, and R. Reiner (eds), *Oxford Handbook of Criminology* (5th edn). Oxford: Oxford University Press, pp. 595–623.
Levi, M. and Maguire, M. (2004) Reducing and preventing organised crime: An evidence-based critique. *Crime Law & Social Change*, 41, 397–469.
Lyng, S. (1990) Edgework: A social psychological analysis of voluntary risk taking. *American Journal of Sociology*, 95(4), 851–886.
Maran, A. (2008) *Mafia: Inside the Dark Heart*. California: Mainstream Publishing.
McDevitt, J., Levin, J., and Bennet, S. (2002) Hate crime offenders: An expanded typology. *Journal of Social Issues*, 58(2), 303–317.
National Crime Agency (2018) National Strategic Assessment of Serious and organised Crime. www.nationalcrimeagency.gov.uk/who-we-are/publications/173-national-strategic-assessment-of-serious-and-organised-crime-2018/file

Paoli, L. (2003) *Mafia Brotherhoods, Organized Crime, Italian Style*. New York: Oxford University Press.

Papachristos, A. V. (2009) Murder by structure: Dominance relations and the social structure of gang homicide. *American Journal of Sociology*, 115, 74–128.

Papachristos, A. V. (2011) The small world of murder. *Chicago Sun-Times*, 16 January 2011.

Rienzo, C., and Vargas-Silva, C. (2013) *Migrants in the UK: An Overview* (3rd edn). Oxford: Migration Observatory. Retrieved from https://migrationobservatory.ox.ac.uk/resources/briefings/migrants-in-the-uk-an-overview/

Senechal de la Roche, R. (2001) Why is collective violence collective? *Sociological Theory*, 19, 126–144.

Sharp, C., Aldridge, J., and Medina, J. (2006) *Delinquent Youth Groups and Offending Behaviour: Findings from the 2004 Offending, Crime and Justice Survey*. London: Home Office.

Sheptycki, J. (2003) The governance of organised crime in Canada. *The Canadian Journal of Sociology*, 28(4), 489–516.

Sheptycki, J. (2008) Transnationalism, orientalism and crime. *Asian Journal of Criminology*, 3(1), 13–35.

Sheptycki, J., Ben Jaffel, H., and Bigo, D. (2011) *International Organised Crime in the European Union*. Policy Department C: Citizens Rights and Constitutional Affairs, European Parliament. Retrieved from www.europarl.europa.eu/document/activities/cont/201206/20120627ATT47775/20120627ATT47775EN.pdf

Shikata, K. (2006) Yakuza – organized crime in Japan. *Journal of Money Laundering Control*, 9(4), 416–421.

Smith, D. (1991) Wickersham to Sutherland to Katzenbach: Evolving an 'official' definition of organized crime. *Crime, Law and Social Change*, 16(2), 134–154.

Tajfel, H. (1974) Social identity and intergroup behavior. *Social Science Information*, 13, 65–93.

Tajfel, H., Billig, M. G., Bundy, R. P., and Flament, C. (1971) Social categorization and behaviour. *European Journal of Social Psychology*, 1, 149–178.

Tajfel, H., and Turner, J. C. (1979) An integrative theory of intergroup conflict. In W. G. Austin, and S. Worchel (eds), *The Social Psychology of Intergroup Relations*. Pacific Grove, CA: Brooks/Cole, pp. 33–47.

Topali, V. (2006) The seductive nature of autotelic crime: How the seductive nature of autotelic crime neutralization theory serves as a boundary condition for understanding hardcore street offending. *Sociological Inquiry*, 76(4), 475–501.

Turner, J. C., and Reynolds, K. J. (2010) The story of social identity. In T. Postmes, and N. R. Branscombe (eds), *Rediscovering Social Identity: Key Readings*. New York: Psychology Press, pp. 13–32.

Tusikov, N. (2012) Measuring organised crime related harms: Exploring five policing methods. *Crime, Law & Social Change*, 57, 99–115.

United Nations Centre for International Crime Prevention (2000) Assessing transnational organized crime: Results of a pilot survey of 40 selected organized criminal groups in 16 countries. *Trends in Organized Crime*, 6(2), 48–49.

Varese, F. (2011) *Mafias on the Move: How Organized Crime Conquers New Territories*. Princeton: Princeton University Press.

von Lampe, K. (2012) Transnational organized crime challenges for future research. *Crime Law and Social Change*, 38, 179–194.

Wood, J. and Alleyne, E. (2010) Street gang theory and research: Where are we now and where do we go from here? *Aggression and Violent Behavior*, 15, 100–111.

19

THE USE OF VIOLENCE AND THE EVOLUTION OF ORGANIZED CRIME

Evidence from Mexico

Laura H. Atuesta

Introduction

Criminal groups use violence to operate in illegal markets. In the absence of enforceable legal contracts, violence becomes the main mechanism of communication between different groups. However, violence takes different shapes and evolves in ways that are often opaque. The evolution of organized crime in Mexico, including how rivals are threatened and territory is claimed, can be linked to the use of increasingly violent and gruesome practices. To understand the evolution of violence, we need to understand the evolution of organized crime itself. In this chapter, three dimensions of the evolution of organized crime are analysed using data from Mexico: (i) the fragmentation and alliances between criminal groups; (ii) the criminal groups' territorial control and diversification of activities; and, (iii) the way criminal groups communicate. Each of these dimensions correlate with violence and explain the ever-evolving relationship between organized crime and increasing violence in Mexico.

The evolution of organized crime can be analysed through different dimensions. For instance, we can observe the correlation between the evolution of violence and how criminal groups operate in specific territories. We can also analyse the interaction between the government and criminal groups, and the causes and consequences of these interactions, including group fragmentation and the diversification of activities. Finally, we can explore how criminal groups use different techniques to communicate with each other, for example the use of messages left next to executed bodies (known as *narcomessages*), or various killing techniques used to signal their power to rival cartels, the government, or society at large.

In what follows, the chapter summarizes the theoretical arguments that explain the evolution of organized crime. I then use data from Mexico to show how organized crime evolves through fragmentation, territorial expansion, economic diversification, and communication techniques; all provoking greater levels of more gruesome violence. Mexican organized crime has been historically linked to drug production and trafficking, however, it has not always been violent. Narcotrafficking has been observed since the end of the nineteenth century, when the Chinese community in the state of Sinaloa commercialized opium. Yet, it was not until the 1970s that narcotrafficking turned violent, as drug-trafficking groups began engaging in turf wars to control specific drug routes and territories (Valdés Castellanos, 2013).

Owing to the paucity of data, it is difficult to document the creation of new criminal groups and the fragmentation of existing ones. The most reliable sources of information are reports published by the Office of the General Attorney (PGR). The first of these reports was published in 2005, the second followed in 2013, with the last being released in 2015. In 2005, there were seven extant criminal organizations in Mexico: the cartels of Tijuana, Golfo, Juarez, Sinaloa, Pacific, Oaxaca, and Milenio. A mere seven years later in 2013, the number had grown to 88, including the cartels of La Barbie, Arellano Felix, the Knights Templar, and the Beltran Leyva, among many others. By 2015, nine main groups and 43 associated subgroups had been identified. While most of these groups had already been noted in the 2013 report, new groups such as the Cartel Jalisco Nueva Generación (CJNG) had emerged as one of the biggest and most violent cartels.

Another useful source of information for mapping organized crime in Mexico is the US Drug Enforcement Agency (DEA). However, a 2018 DEA report identified only five active cartels, including Los Zetas, the CJNG, the Sinaloa Cartel, the Juarez Cartel and the Beltran Leyva Organization. Despite mixed and incomplete information, official PGR documents, combined with DEA reports, show an interesting evolution of organized crime in Mexico. This appears not only in the shifting number of groups, but also in the different alliances and cells of each organization and their territorial control.

Turf wars and the proliferation of criminal groups in Mexican territories have increased the level of violence exponentially, measured by the homicide rate per 100,000 inhabitants. Even while violence was observed in the late 1990s, numbers did not explode until 2008 during the administration of President Felipe Calderon. Violence has been most concentrated in trafficking states (i.e. the northern states located along the US border) and in states where marijuana and poppy crops are grown (e.g. Michoacán, Sinaloa and Guerrero). For instance, the northern border state of Chihuahua saw a 1619 per cent increase in the homicide rate per 100,000 inhabitants from 2007 to 2010 (i.e. from 7.56 to 129.96). Similar growth rates have been observed in Colima, Coahuila and Nayarit. Other expressions of violence have also increased with the evolution of organized crime including extortion, kidnapping and robbery.

The literature cites several factors in explaining the increasing violence in Mexico. Some suggest that the ousting of the reigning *Partido Revolucionario Institucional* (PRI) political party in 2000 after 70 years of consistency caused a disequilibrium in the government–criminal group relationship. This disrupted the existing "protection rackets", leading to more violence (Snyder and Duran-Martinez, 2009). Others argue that the hard prohibition policies implemented in Colombia by the US government led to increasing levels of violence. In this argument, the subsequent closure of the Caribbean route to traffic cocaine to the US forced Colombian drug traffickers to negotiate alliances with Mexican criminal groups to smuggle drugs through the Mexico–US border. The amount of money and drugs entering Mexican territory fundamentally changed the nature of Mexican criminal groups, transforming them into more predatory, violent and competitive organizations, increasing drug-related violence in the country (Hope, 2013; Castillo *et al.*, 2013).

A third explanation points to the hard-line prohibitionist policies implemented by President Felipe Calderón during his 2006–2012 administration. From the outset, Calderón publicly employed military operations in several states to fight and eliminate criminal groups and drug trafficking. With their leaders and *capos* targeted, debilitated criminal organizations became an easy target for competitive groups in turf wars, and even led to factions of the same organization seeking their independence. The multiplication of groups (either through competition or fragmentation) in specific territories increased the level of violence related to organized crime (Atuesta, 2017; Phillips, 2015; Osorio, 2015).

The levels of violence associated with Mexican organized crime are too complex to be attributed to a single factor. As Alejandro Hope (2013) argues, what happened in Mexico was a "perfect storm" of several simultaneous factors triggering violence and the evolution of organized crime. We now turn to how this evolution took place and the consequences it had on the levels of violence observed in specific territories.

Theoretical arguments to explain the evolution of organized crime in Mexico

The role of the state and the prohibitionist policies on the evolution of organized crime

Public security and drug policies directly influence how organized crime evolves and behaves. The state, through the implementation of prohibitionist policies, can unintentionally create a "power vacuum" that criminal groups use to control illegal markets and territories (Skaperdas and Syropoulos, 1997). When the state declines to participate in the drug market by imposing regulations, for example, the illicit market can operate free from guidance in terms of price, product quality, or health and sanitation policies. Criminal groups therefore impose their own terms that are not always in society's interests. Thus, the buying and selling conditions are imposed by those who own the market: the criminals.

An unregulated market increases the profits of organized crime. These profits are reinvested in diversified illegal and legal businesses, allowing criminal groups to increase their profits and subsequently helping them to expand control over specific territories. In these cases, as Díaz-Cayeros (2011) explains, the government often fails to provide sufficient security to protect the population. As a result, criminal organizations impose a "parallel order" acting as a substitute to the state and receiving the support of citizens.

The evolution of organized crime: fragmentation and alliances

The literature has explored the creation of alliances and fragmentations in civil war contexts, but not as they relate specifically to organized crime (see Atuesta and Pérez-Dávila, 2017 for a review). Several factors influencing fragmentation include the number of factions within the group, external threats from competitive groups, security policies implemented in specific territories, or a lack of identity and leadership within the group. Alliances, on the other hand, arise when weaker groups decide to cooperate with each other in order to avoid external attacks, to guard against common enemies, or to seek common interests and objectives.

The dynamics of fragmentation and alliance jeopardize the organized crime equilibrium. Alliances are often unstable, since they depend on the oftentimes low credibility that each party offers and cannot rely on legal contracts to maintain order and adjudicate disagreements (Smith, 1995; Gallagher-Cunningham, 2013). Moreover, even if different parties agree to collaborate in peacetime, when imminent war or danger threatens just one of the parties, others do not have the same incentives to get involved (Smith, 1995; Hugh-Jones and Zultan, 2013).

The literature also reports mixed results regarding the effect of fragmentations and alliances on the level of violence or the duration of conflicts. As argued by Atuesta and Ponce (2017) and Atuesta and Pérez-Dávila (2017), using data from Mexico, fragmentation is stated to always increase the level of violence. However, others (e.g. Findley and Rudloff, 2012) suggest that the duration of a conflict decreases when alliances are negotiated between fragmented factions, rather than between strong and united groups. If the factors leading to cooperation are strong enough, alliances can avoid violence and lead to a negotiated peace (Atuesta and Pérez-Dávila, 2017).

The evolution of organized crime: territorial expansion and diversification

The evolution of organized crime can be tracked through the analysis of territorial expansion. The stronger criminal groups are defined through the greater the authority they impose on specific territories. Territorial control allows criminal groups to legitimize their presence with the local population by offering protection services by controlling both legal and illegal activities, and by creating alliances with other groups, thus mitigating attacks from the competition.

Skaperdas and Syropoulos (1997) describe a situation in which there is no violence monopoly because the state presence is weak, creating a power vacuum. In this case, criminal groups attempt to replace the state. Those that predominate have more weaponry, greater citizen support, and better control of specific territories. As Gambetta (1996) argues, groups controlling the market of protection through violence, trust, and threats are better able to oversee every activity (legal or illegal).

Grossman (1997) compares criminal organizations with kleptocratic states in which the main objective is to maximize profits obtained through imposing taxes on the population. Skaperdas and Syropoulos (1997) describe how these profits are then reinvested in other activities to expand territorial control to produce a multiplying effect. The more activities they control the greater territorial expansion they enjoy, in turn leading to greater profits that could then be reinvested into new activities.

The evolution of organized crime: communication and signalling

The evolution of organized crime in Mexico has been accompanied by greater levels of violence that are not only more visible but more "labelled". Violence is more "visible" because criminal groups are interested in being recognized by their rivals, society and the government. It is more "labelled" as the proportion of deaths that can be attributed to specific groups is greater than ever before (see Atuesta, 2017). Attribution correlates with both the use of "narcomessages", that is, messages left next to executed bodies, and torture.

Communication strategies of organized crime have been well-documented in the literature; specifically, the use of "street codes" used by criminals to signal to their enemies, society, or the state about specific behaviours. Street codes can include narcomessages, dress codes used by criminals, language used among them, or unique behaviours (McNeeley and Wilcox, 2015). These street codes are associated with respect, fear and recognition, which arguably allows criminals to enjoy a powerful position both in the underworld and in society.

Criminal communication is crucial to establishing trust in an environment in which no legal contracts exist. Violence, or the threat of violence, is one of the most important signals used in the criminal world. Even if criminals are unwilling to use violence, the threat alone is often enough to avoid being underestimated. This threat can be communicated directly or through reminders of previous uses of violence (Gambetta, 2011). For this reason, analysing the evolution of violence side by side with criminal communication techniques is crucial in understanding the evolution of organized crime.

The evolution of organized crime in Mexico and its relationship with violence

The history of organized crime in Mexico has been closely linked to the production and trafficking of illegal drugs. At the beginning of the twentieth century, the illegal drugs market (primarily opium and marijuana) was concentrated in the northern region of the country, in the state of Sinaloa. There, producers and traffickers were neither organized nor monopolized, and it was not accurate to talk about "organized crime" (for more on the history of narcotrafficking in Mexico, see Astorga, 2005; Valdés Castellanos, 2013; Grillo, 2011). Nonetheless, the Guadalajara Confederation was the most important organization in the 1980s. It fragmented in 1989 when its leader, Felix Gallardo, was imprisoned. Narcotrafficking routes were subsequently divided into two main groups: the Sinaloa Cartel, led by Joaquín Guzmán Loera "El Chapo" and Héctor Luis Palma Salazar "El Guero Palma"; and the Tijuana Cartel, led by the Arellano Félix brothers.

Further fragmentation was observed during the 1990s, creating groups such as the Gulf Cartel and the Beltrán Leyva Organization. However, due to arrangements between the leaders of these organizations and the government, violence remained stable and a *pax mafiosi* was established and respected. It was not until the 2000s that the proliferation of criminal groups led to the diversification of criminal activities, which consequently involved the expansion of efforts for territorial control and an increase in violence accompanied with more varied killing techniques and changes in the communication modes.

The evolution of organized crime analysed through fragmentation and alliances

To understand the evolution of organized crime in Mexico, it is important to analyse criminal groups not as unitary entities with a rigid structure and rules, but rather as various factions pursuing the same objectives. As business opportunities evolve (e.g. the drug markets), criminal groups mutate by creating alliances or fragmenting in order to adapt to new realities. Currently, Mexican criminal organizations have become even more flexible and decentralized, allowing them to expand their geographic control and economic power (Pereyra, 2012). For example, Los Zetas, one of the most prominent criminal organizations during the decade of the 2000s, employed a franchise structure, in which cells operating in specific territories were trained by the central command but were obliged to pay a fee to use the name "Zetas". They nonetheless remained independent in operation and the activities they decided to pursue (Grillo, 2011).

The flexibility of criminal organizations also fostered the creation of alliances and fragmentations. One example is the alliance of the Sinaloa Cartel with the Tijuana and Juárez Cartels, formed to control the Mexican northern border. Another example is the decision of the Beltrán Leyva Organization to collaborate with Los Zetas after clashes with their previous allies, the Sinaloa Cartel, with the objective of exploring new markets and territories (Kellner and Pipitone, 2010; Atuesta and Pérez-Dávila, 2017).

Documenting every move of organized crime in order to analyse its evolution is challenging given the rapidly changing structure of criminal groups and the continuing creation of new alliances and fragmentations. Some analyse this evolution by identifying different groups in specific territories. Beittel (2013), for instance, describes the fragmentation dynamics of 2010 and 2011 by observing which groups control what turf and drug routes. During this period, new groups such as the Knights Templar, La Resistencia, and the Cartel Jalisco Nueva Generación emerged to control territories in Nayarit, Colima and Jalisco.

Atuesta and Pérez-Dávila (2017) mapped the evolution of organized crime in Mexico focusing on six of the most important groups in the 2000s: the Cartels of Sinaloa, Juarez, Beltran Leyva, Golfo, Zetas, and La Familia Michoacana. The authors identified the Cartel leaders and the alliances they made with different gangs and groups, and their armed wings from 2007 to 2011. By analysing how these groups operate, it is possible to identify alliances and fragmentations through time. Most of the information was obtained from the CIDE-PPD database that gathered information about violent events related to organized crime in Mexico from December 2006 to November 2011.

Atuesta and Pérez-Dávila (2017) identified more than 200 active groups in different territories between 2007 and 2011. Some of them disappeared shortly after their creation, while others persisted for longer periods through structural changes and cooperation with other organizations. Most of the fragmentations observed during the period were caused by military operations in specific territories. As widely documented (Phillips, 2015; Atuesta and Ponce, 2017; Atuesta and Pérez-Dávila, 2017), when the government captures leaders or lieutenants of organizations, the structure of the group devolves as new factions break away and competitive groups attack in turf wars. Other fragmentations result when factions of the same group with different interests decide to become independent and a change in leadership is rejected by group members, or previously created alliance become too weak and members leave. Alliances, on the other hand, are often created for different reasons: seeking territorial expansion and protection, consolidating weakened factions after a fragmentation, or unifying to attack a common enemy.

By coding violent events gathered in the CIDE-PPD database, Atuesta and Pérez-Dávila (2017) attributed violence to fragmentations and alliances observed in Mexico from 2007 to 2011. The fragmentation that led to the greatest number of executions was the clash between the Sinaloa and the Juarez Cartels, with 1922 homicides, followed by the fragmentation between the Beltran Leyva Organization and the Sinaloa Cartel, with 377 homicides. Due to the fragmentations it experienced, the Sinaloa Cartel saw the greatest number of attributable homicides with 3059, corresponding to 75 per cent of the total number attributed to fragmentations.

According to the information gathered from the CIDE-PPD database, the number of homicides attributed to fragmentations was greater than those attributed to alliances. However, it is difficult to conclude that fragmentations are more violent than alliances because often the violence generated by the alliances is not as "visible" as those attributed to fragmentations. For instance, when a criminal is killed by enemies belonging to a different group post-fragmentation, a narcomessage is often left next to the executed body, which makes attribution to fragmentation easier. On the other hand, when executions are conducted as a result of an alliance, violent or more torturous killing techniques are rarely used, and the killing is not always attributed or labelled.

There are specific cases in which an alliance can demonstrate extreme levels of violence. This was the case in the alliance between the Gulf Cartel and Los Zetas, where the latter was created as an armed wing of the Cartel. Several years after their creation, Los Zetas detached and declared war on the Gulf Cartel. According to information from the CIDE-PPD database, 229 homicides were attributed to the alliance and 144 were attributed to the fragmentation. When Los Zetas became independent, the Gulf Cartel was not their only enemy, they also had to fight the Sinaloa Cartel in Durango and La Familia Michoacana in Michoacán. In fact, Los Zetas became a "public enemy", forcing several groups to collaborate with each other to survive Los Zetas' attacks.

The evolution of organized crime analysed through territorial expansion

According to a report presented in the Mexican National Senate in 2010, cited by Buscgalia (2008), 63 per cent of the municipalities in Mexico are currently "feudalized" by organized crime. "Feudalization" refers to the situation in which organized crime has completely corrupted the municipal, state or federal authorities, or where alliances between public officers and criminal groups have been observed (La Jornada, 2008). Feudalization is also observed through the growth of illegal activities in a municipality such as piracy, child prostitution, and human and drug trafficking.

Kellner and Pipitone (2010) document how the expansion of organized crime in Mexico began in the 1990s when drug-related groups began fighting amongst themselves to control drug routes and turf. Other authors instead argue that the expansion began in the 2000s when groups became more independent and sought territorial control and diversification of their activities (Oyarvide, 2011). Barttolotta and Gago (2011) point specifically to 2001 when the government of President Vicente Fox received a document from the Senate identifying the presence of drug-related groups in different municipalities in the country.

According to official Mexican and US sources, the territorial expansion of Mexican organized crime has not been limited only to Mexico. Since narcotrafficking is a transnational business, criminal groups have sought to expand to neighbouring countries, including the US and Guatemala. According to a US Justice Department report published during the Bush administration, Mexican criminal organizations are currently active in 195 US cities (Barttolotta and Gago, 2011). This presence is measured by the number of arrests of Mexican criminals (mostly from the Sinaloa and the Gulf Cartels) during two US Drug Enforcement Agency investigations: "Project Reckoning" (175 arrests) and "Operation Xcellerator" (755 arrests). Nonetheless, this definition of "organized crime presence" is problematic, since groups can be active in a specific territory without being detained.

Other sources documenting the presence and territorial expansion of organized crime in Mexico include the "Red Zone Maps" published by the Federal Electoral Institute, the report prepared by Beittel (2013) for the US Congress, the *Transcrime* report prepared by Dugato *et al.* (2014), and maps published by Stratfor Global Intelligence (2012) about criminal group activity in Mexico. According to the Federal Electoral Institute Red Zone Maps, 70 per cent of the 300 electoral districts experienced electoral risk in 2009 as security forces were absent and criminal groups had some control over the territory. Maps of the presence of criminal organizations published by Beittel (2013) and Stratfor Global Intelligence (2012) coincide on the territories in which Los Zetas and the Sinaloa Cartel are present: in the east and northeast of the country, respectively. Dugato *et al.* (2014) use a principal component method involving more than 20 different sources of information to measure criminal presence and organized crime threats. They found that the states with the greatest criminal presence were Guerrero, Chihuahua, Nayarit, and Colima, while the states with the lowest criminal presence included Veracruz, Puebla, Chiapas, and Tlaxcala.

Reports published by the Office of the General Attorney in 2005, 2013 and 2015 also provide context on the evolution of organized crime in Mexico by tracking the territorial expansion of criminal groups. In 2005, seven main groups were identified, as illustrated in Table 19.1.

By 2013, these groups and their territories had changed: eight main groups with 80 subgroups active in different territories, as shown in Table 19.2.

According to the 2005 PGR report, organized crime in Mexico was concentrated in 26 of the 32 states. Yet, this number decreased to 24 in 2013. In 2013, criminal groups were observed in states that previously had none, such as Guerrero, Baja California Sur, the state of Mexico, and San Luis Potosí. Such differences, both in the number of groups as well as in the number of states with an organized crime presence, revealed rapid changes in the evolution of organized crime.

Finally, the 2015 PGR report documented the presence of nine criminal groups and 43 subgroups present in 20 states, as shown in Table 19.3.

As Beittel (2013) argues, organized crime should be understood as a dynamic phenomenon. The CIDE-PPD database allows us to analyse these changes from 2007 to 2011 with a yearly frequency. Organized crime presence is measured by the involvement of specific groups in violent events. Forty main groups and 200 smaller groups, cells, armed wings, and gunmen were identified during the five years. Six main groups were involved in more than half of the total number of identified events: the Juarez, Beltran Leyva, Sinaloa and the Gulf Cartels, La Familia Michoacana, and Los Zetas. The Sinaloa Cartel and Los Zetas accounted for the majority of violent actions during this time period.

Los Zetas is an interesting case; in contrast to other groups, its expansion is not based only on drug trafficking. Los Zetas are comprised of ex-military personnel recruited by the Gulf Cartel for protection. The advantage of military training and their knowledge of the government's modus operandi allowed them to quickly gain control of different municipalities. As

Table 19.1 Presence of criminal groups according to the PGR report of 2005.

Name	*Territorial control*
Tijuana Cartel	Mexicali, Tecate, Ensenada and El Valle-Baja California
Colima Cartel	Baja California, Nuevo León, Aguascalientes, Jalisco, Colima, Michoacán, Distrito Federal
Juárez Cartel	Chihuahua, Sonora, Coahuila, Sinaloa, Durango, Zacatecas, Nuevo León, Tamaulipas, Jalisco, Michoacán, Querétaro, Morelos, Distrito Federal, Puebla, Oaxaca, Veracruz, Tabasco, Chiapas, Campeche, Yucatán and Quintana Roo
Sinaloa Cartel	Baja California, Sonora, Sinaloa, Durango, Zacatecas, Nayarit, Nuevo León, Tamaulipas, Jalisco, Colima, Guanajuato, Estado de México, Morelos, Distrito Federal, Guerrero, Chiapas and Quintana Roo
Golfo Cartel (in Alliance with Los Zetas)	Nuevo Laredo, Matamoros, Reynosa, Miguel Alemán (Tamaulipas) and Morelia (Michoacán)
Cacique Oaxaqueño Group	Chihuahua, Durango, Tamaulipas, Distrito Federal, Veracruz, Oaxaca and Chiapas
Milenio Cartel	Nuevo León, Tamaulipas, Jalisco, Colima, Michoacán and Distrito Federal

Source: Barttolotta and Gago (2011).

Table 19.2 Presence of criminal groups according to the PGR report of 2013.

Name	*Territorial control*
Los Zetas (three subgroups)	Tamaulipas, Quintana Roo, San Luis Potosí, Zacatecas, Nuevo León
The Pacific Cartel (12 subgroups)	Chihuahua, Sinaloa, Jalisco, Colima, Michoacán, Veracruz, Durango, Guerrero, Coahuila, Baja California
The Arellano Félix (14 subgroups)	Baja California, Baja California Sur
La Familia Michoacana (five subgroups)	Morelos, Guerrero, Estado de México, Jalisco, Michoacán
The Knight Templar (two subgroups)	Morelos, Estado de México
New Cartel of Juárez (two subgroups)	Chihuahua
La Barbie (23 subgroups)	Chiapas, Distrito Federal, Estado de México, Guerrero, Morelos, Quintana Roo
Beltrán Leyva Organization (19 subgroups)	Nuevo León, Nayarit, Jalisco, Sinaloa, Baja California Sur, Sonora, Guerrero, Morelos, Aguascalientes, Distrito Federal, Estado de México, Oaxaca, Baja California

Source: PGR (2013).

Table 19.3 Presence of criminal groups according to the 2013 PGR report.

Criminal groups	*Subgroups*	*Territorial control*
Pacifico	Gente Nueva, Los Cabrera, La Barredora, Poniente Cartel, El Aquiles, El Tigre, Los Artistas Asesinos, Los Mexicles	Chihuahua, Sinaloa, Durango, Guerrero, Coahuila, Baja California
Arellano Felix	El Chan, El Jorquera, El Kieto	Baja California
La Familia Michoacana	Guerreros Unidos (La Nueva Empresa)	Morelos, Guerrero, state of Mexico
Carrillo Fuentes	La Linea, Los Aztecas	Chihuahua
Beltran Leyva	Los Mazatlecos, El 2 mil, Los Granados, Los Rojos, La Oficina, Los Ardillos, Independent Cartel of Acapulco	Sinaloa, Baja California Sur, Guerrero, Aguascalientes
Los Zetas	Sangre Zeta, Zetas Operational Group, Zetas Command, El Círculo, el Extranjero, Zetas Unit, Néctar Lima, Zetas Delta Group, Los Negros, Zetas Special Forces	Coahuila, Nuevo León, Tamaulipas, Guanajuato, Tabasco, Quintana Roo
Gulf Cartel	Metros, Rojos, Lacoste Group, Dragones Group, Bravo Group, Pumas Group, Apoyo Ceros M3 Group, Los Fresitas, Los Sierra, Los Pantera, Ciclones, Los Pelones	Tamaulipas, Quintana Roo
The Knights Templar	No subgroups identified	Michoacán, Guerrero, Guanajuato, Morelos, state of Mexico, Jalisco, Colima, Querétaro, Baja California
Cartel Jalisco Nueva Generación	No subgroups identified	Jalisco, Colima, Michoacán, Guanajuato, Nayarit, Guerrero, Morelos, Veracruz, Mexico City

Source: PGR (2013).

a result, Los Zetas have been the criminal organization with the greatest territorial expansion in Mexico. According to Coscia and Rios (2012), in 2010, Los Zetas operated in 405 municipalities, while La Familia Michoacana and the Gulf Cartel were active in 227 and 244 municipalities, respectively.

In 2008, Los Zetas were active in 29 municipalities. By 2010, this number was 121; an expansion of 317 per cent in two years. In contrast to groups with a rigid structure, such as the Sinaloa and the Gulf Cartels, Los Zetas' decentralized structure gave them the flexibility to rapidly expand to new territories. Additionally, they generated comparatively more revenue than their rivals by controlling most of the legal and illegal activities in their territories, including drug trafficking and production, migrant trafficking, extortion and oil robbery (Dudley and Rios, 2013).

In contrast, the territorial expansion of the Sinaloa Cartel has been slower and of a different tenor than that of Los Zetas. A strongly centralized enterprise, the Sinaloa Cartel was established as a family organization. According to Coscia and Rios (2012), the Sinaloa Cartel was only present in the state of Sinaloa, and in 14 of the 18 municipalities therein. Although the Cartel tried to control other territories, engaging in turf wars with the Juarez Cartel and Los Zetas, their activities have been concentrated in the northwest side of the country (Osorno, 2009). According to Grillo (2011), the Sinaloa Cartel is also the organization with the greatest influence internationally, with a presence in more than 50 countries located in North America, Europe, Western Africa, Australia, and Southeast Asia. According to the CIDE-PPD database, the Sinaloa Cartel expanded from nine states in 2008 (in 16 municipalities) to 83 municipalities located in 10 states by 2010.

Not all criminal groups in Mexico have expanded geographically. For instance, the Juarez Cartel solely concentrated its activities in Chihuahua. Out of a total of 1475 events reported in Chihuahua (for which a group could have been identified), the Juarez Cartel participated in 1433 (97 per cent). In 2008, the municipalities with the greatest number of active groups were Culiacan (Sinaloa, 11 groups), followed by Tijuana (Baja California, nine groups). By 2011, the municipalities with the greatest number of groups were Acapulco (Guerrero, 27 groups) and the city of Juarez (Chihuahua, 11 groups).

Unsurprisingly, these data show that territories with the most groups also experienced increased violence related to organized crime. For instance, Chihuahua, Jalisco and Guerrero, the states with the greatest number of groups, also exhibited a significant growth in organized-crime-related homicides (e.g. from 2007 to 2011 these were 1707, 735 and 266 per cent, respectively).

The evolution of organized crime analysed through communication strategies: a review of Atuesta (2017)

The evolution of organized crime can also be analysed through criminal communication. The CIDE-PPD database provides data on how violence has increased and mutated over time. For instance, homicides related to organized crime are more visible and attributable to specific groups. From 30,982 events gathered in the 'Executions' category of the CIDE-PPD database, 8.54 per cent had messages left next to executed bodies. Whilst only 3 per cent of the events had a narcomessage in 2007, this figure increased to 11 per cent by 2011. However, not all narcomessages had a clear target: in 2007 only 29 per cent of the narcomessages were attributable, but this percentage increased to 70 per cent in 2011.

The total number of executions reported in the CIDE-PPD database from December 2006 to November 2011 was 43,801, and the total number of narcomessages found was 2680. However, the use of narcomessages increased exponentially over time. For example, from 2007 to 2008 the number of narcomessages increased by more than 400 per cent. In 2010 and 2011, the annual growth rates were of 80 and 75 per cent, respectively.

According to Eiss (2014), the first narcomessage published by the press in Mexico was found in Guerrero on 20 April 2006 when two police officers were executed and decapitated. However, the first narcomessages recorded in the CIDE-PPD database were registered in March 2007; two in the state of Nuevo Leon and one in Quintana Roo. These messages were addressed to public officers who were alleged to be cooperating with the Sinaloa Cartel. One month later, in April 2007, messages were found in Tabasco, Nuevo Leon, and Guerrero. Over the five years analysed, the practice of using narcomessages expanded to 25 of the 32 Mexican states, with these being more frequently used in Guerrero, Sinaloa, Chihuahua, and the state of Mexico.

While narcomessages reveal how criminals communicate in Mexico, no single reason can explain why organized crime related violence has become more visible and attributable. One possibility, however, is that as competition between groups increased, narcomessages were more frequently employed to engender fear and respect. Atuesta (2017) classified all messages included in the CIDE-PPD database (shown in Table 19.4) to understand how such modes of communication can help track the evolution of violence and organized crime in

Table 19.4 Classification of narcomessages according to Atuesta (2017).

	Directed to the government	*Directed to snitches*	*Vigilante messages*	*Rivalry between groups*	*Drug related or related to territorial control*
2007	5	5	9	31	3
2008	42	32	40	143	11
2009	59	111	148	192	62
2010	84	107	222	342	123
2011	79	135	193	508	87

Mexico. These categories are not exclusive; for instance, a message could be directed to the government and also to "snitches" (i.e. a criminal who cooperates with the government to earn a lighter punishment).

The temporal evolution of the narcomessages provides insight into the evolution of organized crime in Mexico. For instance, while at the beginning of the analysis period most narcomessages were directed to a specific group (rivalry between groups); the content changed as the country became more violent. Los Zetas were the first to use narcomessages, "signing" their messages by changing all of the letters "s" to "z" or by tattooing a "Z" on the victim's body.

The appearance of vigilante messages marked an important change in the content of narcomessages from 2008 to 2009. In 2008, most of the messages were directed to other groups, the government, or society. By 2009, new criminal groups formed that (ironically) repudiated the violence generated by organized crime. Groups such as the "Narco Killer Priest" or the "People's Avenger" in Chihuahua and Guerrero, respectively, tried to justify their executions using narcomessages. For instance, several messages were found justifying the killing as victims were selling drugs to children or next to schools, because they were kidnappers, or they were found extorting or stealing from the population.

Why do criminal groups feel the need to justify their violent acts? One hypothesis is the desire to obtain support from the population. In some regions, such as Chihuahua, Michoacán and Guerrero, these messages could signal the appearance of self-defence groups that were created as an alternative solution in territories where the presence of the state is weak and governmental institutions were unable to stop the organized-crime-related violence.

The analysis of narcomessages also reveals clashes for territorial control. For instance, the state with the greatest number of messages found was Guerrero, where La Familia Michoacana and the Beltran Leyva Organization were involved in a protracted territorial war. Moreover, La Familia Michoacana is considered one of the most territorial groups. In 2009, La Familia was identified as either a victim or perpetrator in 118 narcomessages, with most of them found in states under their territorial control. La Familia attempted to seek control of Veracruz in 2010, starting turf wars with other groups. Their messages were focused on territorial control and on the monopoly of drug production and trafficking.

Figure 19.1 summarizes the evolution of Mexican organized crime from 2007 to 2011 through the analysis of narcomessages. Over this period, violence became more visible and more attributable, marked by a rise in the use of signed narcomessages. These changes were accompanied by an increase in the number of groups, the appearance of new 'vigilante' groups, and the method by which groups executed their victims. The use of torture became more frequent, the number of executions per event increased, and groups frequently employed varied, yet often sadistic killing techniques.

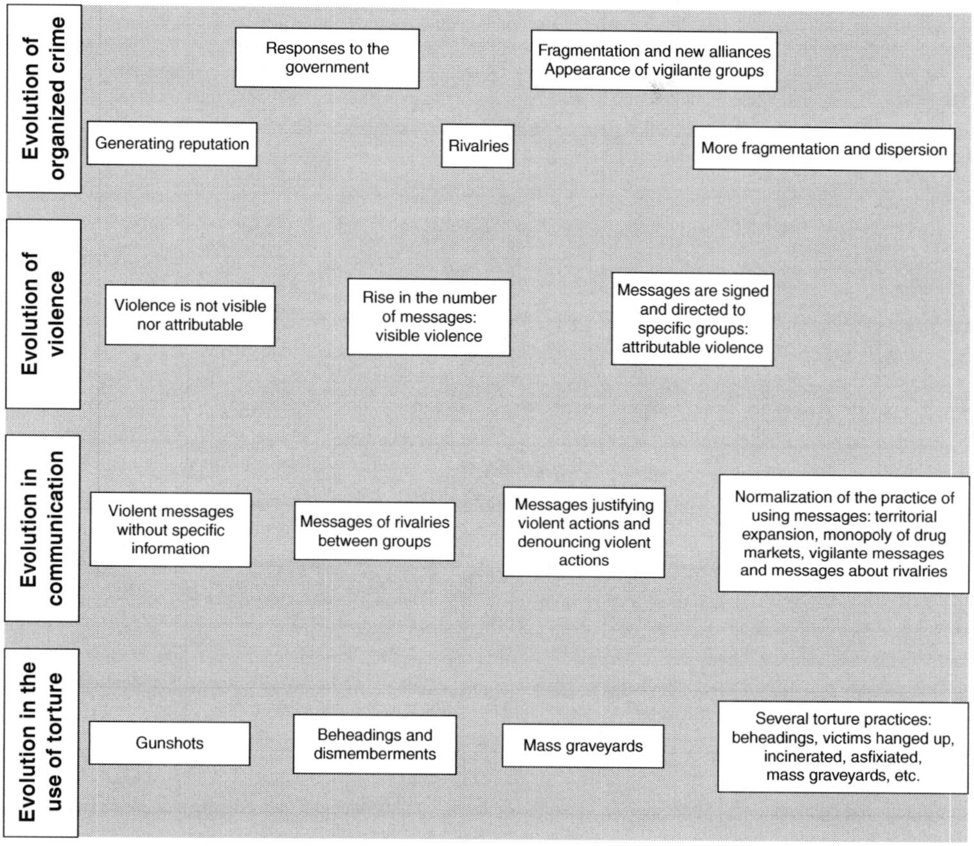

Figure 19.1 Evolution of organized crime (figure made by the author).

Conclusion

This chapter analyses the evolution of organized crime from different perspectives, through the creation of alliances and fragmentations, the territorial expansion of criminal groups, and the methods criminal groups use to communicate. Each of these factors has been related to an evolution of violence.

One cannot analyse the increase of violence in Mexico without understanding how organized crime has evolved in the country. Violence has increasingly become the method these groups use to interact with one another. For instance, if the government designs security policies to confront criminal groups, such groups may react by fragmenting themselves and increasing violence between them. If the government focuses their efforts on eliminating drug production and trafficking, groups will find other illegal markets to derive profit, such as human trafficking, oil theft, or extortion. This diversification of activities is accompanied by greater territorial control and more violence to compete with rival groups. Finally, although criminal groups are able to use various modes of communication, narcomessages left next to victims tend to be the most common (and, arguably, effective) method of relaying their message.

In sum, the evolution of violence and organized crime are not isolated phenomena. If Mexico aims to cease the wave of violence related to organized crime, policymakers need to understand the factors that are generating this violence and mitigate them. In this sense, it may prove useful to analyse the security and drug policies implemented in the country, such as the militarization of public security or the prohibitionist drug policies, and evaluate their effects in terms of the evolution of organized crime. Although it is not the objective of this chapter to conduct this analysis, the different dimensions analysed here may arguably prove helpful in implementing more effective public policies.

References

Astorga, L. (2005) *El siglo de las drogas. El narcotráfico, del Porfiriato al nuevo milenio*. Mexico, DF: Plaza Janes.

Atuesta, L. H. (2017) Narcomessages as a way to analyse the evolution of organised crime in Mexico. *Global Crime*, 18(2), 100–121.

Atuesta, L. H., and Pérez-Dávila, Y. S. (2017) Fragmentation and cooperation: The evolution of organized crime in Mexico. *Trends in Organized Crime*, 21(3), 1–27.

Atuesta, L. H., and Ponce, A. F. (2017) Meet the Narco: Increased competition among criminal organisations and the explosion of violence in Mexico. *Global Crime*, 18(4), 375–402.

Barttolotta, L., and Gago, A. F. E. I. (2011) Violencia social, crisis estatal y políticas de excepción: notas sobre la "guerra al narcotráfico en México". *Dossier México*, 48.

Beittel, J. S. (2013) Mexico's drug trafficking organizations: Source and scope of the violence. *United States Congressional Research Service*, 7–5700.

Buscgalia, E. (2008) The paradox of expected punishment: Legal and economic factors determining success and failure in the fight against organized crime. *Review of Law & Economics*, 4(1), 290–317.

Castillo, J. C., Mejia, D., and Restrepo, P. (2013) Illegal drug markets and violence in Mexico: The causes beyond Calderón. http://cie.itam.mx/SEMINARIOS/MarzoMayo_2013/Mejia, 3(10), 2013.

Coscia, M. and Rios, V. (2012) Knowing where and how criminal organizations operate using web content. In *Proceedings of the 21st ACM International Conference on Information and Knowledge Management*, pp. 1412–1421.

Díaz-Cayeros, A., Magaloni, B., Matanock, A., and Romero, V. (2011) Living in fear: Social penetration of criminal organizations in Mexico. Working paper. http://irps.ucsd.edu/assets/001/502967.pdf.

Dudley, S. and Rios, V. (2013) Why Mexico's Zetas expanded faster than their rivals. *Insight Crime, Organized Crime in the Americas*, 21 April 2013. www.insightcrime.org/news-analysis/why-mexicos-zetas-expanded-faster-rivals.

Dugato, M., De Simoni, M., and Savona, E. U. (2014) *Measuring OC in Latin America. A methodology for developing and validating scores and composite indicators for measuring OC at national and subnational level.* Report elaborated by Transcrime and the Center of Excellence in Statistical Information on Government, Crime, Victimization and Justice.

Eiss, P. K. (2014) The narcomedia: A reader's guide. *Latin American Perspectives*, 41(2), 78–98.

Findley, M. and Rudloff, P. (2012) Combatant fragmentation and the dynamics of civil wars. *British Journal of Political Science*, 42(4), 879–901.

Gallagher-Cunningham, K. (2013) Actor fragmentation and civil war bargaining: How internal divisions generate civil conflict. *American Journal of Political Science*, 57(3), 659–672.

Gambetta, D. (1996) *The Sicilian Mafia: The Business of Private Protection*. Cambridge, MA: Harvard University Press.

Gambetta, D. (2011) *Codes of the Underworld: How Criminals Communicate*. Princeton, NJ: Princeton University Press.

Grillo, I. (2011) *El Narco: Inside Mexico's Criminal Insurgency*. New York: Bloomsbury Publishing.

Grossman, H. I. (1997) Rival kleptocrats: the mafia versus the state. In G. Fiorentini and S. Peltzman (eds), *The Economics of Organised Crime*. Cambridge, UK: Cambridge University Press, pp. 143–160.

Hope, A. (2013) La Tormenta Perfecta, Revista Nexos. 1 November 2013. www.nexos.com.mx/?p=15547.

Hugh-Jones, D. and Zultan, R. I. (2013) Reputation and cooperation in defense. *Journal of Conflict Resolution*, 57(2), 327–355.

Kellner, T. and Pipitone, F. (2010) Inside México's drug war. *World Policy Journal*, 27(1), 29–37.

La Jornada (2008) El narco ha feudalizado 60% de los municipios, alerta ONU. www.jornada.unam.mx/2008/06/26/index.php?section=politica&article=013n1pol (accessed 8 May 2018).

McNeeley, S. and Wilcox, P. (2015) Street codes, routine activities, neighbourhood context and victimization. *British Journal of Criminology*, 55(5), 921–943.

Osorio, J. (2015) The contagion of drug violence: Spatiotemporal dynamics of the Mexican war on drugs. *Journal of Conflict Resolution*, 59(8), 1403–1432.
Osorno, D.E. (2009) El Cártel de Sinaloa. *Una historia del uso político del narco*. Mexico: Grijalbo.
Oyarvide, C. M. (2011) La Guerra contra el narcotráfico en México. Debilidad Del estado, orden local Y fracaso de Una estrategia.
Pereyra, G. (2012) México: violencia criminal y guerra contra el narcotráfico. *Revista Mexicana de Sociología*, 74(3), 429–460.
PGR (2013) Células delictivas con presencia en el país. Information request 0001700011613 to the PGR.
PGR (2015) No title. Information request 0001700202114 to the PGR.
Phillips, B. J. (2015) How does leadership decapitation affect violence? The case of drug trafficking organizations in Mexico. *The Journal of Politics*, 77(2), 324–336.
Skaperdas, S. and Syropoulos, C. (1997) 3 gangs as primitive states. *The Economics of Organised Crime*, 61.
Smith, A. (1995) Alliance formation and war. *International Studies Quarterly*, 39(4), 405–425.
Snyder, R. and Duran-Martinez, A. (2009) Does illegality breed violence? Drug trafficking and state-sponsored protection rackets. *Crime, Law and Social Change*, 52(3), 253–273.
Stratfor Global Intelligence (2012) Cartel activity in Mexico. 30 October 2012. www.stratfor.com/sites/default/files/styles/full_width/public/main/images/Cartels_2012_year_end_0.jpg?itok=UOUJ-IAQ.
Valdés Castellanos, G. (2013) *Historia del narcotráfico en México*. Santillana Ediciones.

20
ORGANIZED VIOLENCE
The mafia

Gianmarco Daniele and Marco Le Moglie

Introduction

This chapter reviews our knowledge of the relationship between violence and organized crime. Our focus is on Italian criminal organizations, as they represent a well-studied case of how violence can shape the origins, success and impact of criminal groups. We explore interconnected theories that explain why organized crime develops in some areas rather than others, and then discuss how criminal organizations can expand and migrate to new areas. Finally, we document the detrimental effects of organized criminal violence on firms, politicians and ordinary citizens.

The origins of organized violence: a history of protection

Investigations of why criminal organizations arise are crucial for our understanding of how they shape our societies. In recent decades, scholars from different fields (e.g. economics, sociology, criminology, anthropology and political science) have proposed complementary explanations for the surge in organized crime. One strain of literature investigates the economic determinants of organized crime and emphasizes organized crime's goal of establishing a monopoly in the use of violence to control illegal markets. In those markets, the lack of an authority entitled to use force may encourage agents to pursue profits through predation and violence rather than through economic competition (Reuter, 1983; Skaperdas, 1992; Hirshleifer, 1995; Grossman and Kim, 1995; Grossman, 1998; North *et al.*, 2009; van Besouw *et al.*, 2016; Castillo *et al.*, 2018).

However, violence is a "good", the production of which involves high fixed costs in terms of the resources needed (e.g. purchase weapons) and the opportunity cost of carrying it out (e.g. retaliation by other agents). At the same time, the average cost of violence is likely to decrease as the quantity produced increases. In fact, once the high fixed costs have been overcome, the cost of producing more violence falls drastically, as the resources initially invested to start production can be employed in multiple activities at almost no cost. For example, the equipment bought to undertake one robbery can be employed to undertake another one. These dynamics may ultimately mean that only one (big) agent (or very few) can actually produce violence in an efficient manner (Schelling, 1984; Bates *et al.*, 2002; Grossman, 2002; Duran-Martinez, 2015). Therefore, criminals organize themselves into groups in order to afford the high fixed costs of producing violence and to take advantage of the decreasing average costs associated with the production of this 'good'.

A second line of literature focuses on the sociological determinants of organized crime, especially cultural environments that offer fertile contexts for this type of crime. These environments are typically characterized by a low level of social trust, which discourages stable cooperation among agents. In this context organized crime arises as a substitute for trust. As such, it can be used to guarantee transactions among agents (Banfield, 1958; Black, 1983; Gambetta, 1988; Putnam, 1993; Varese, 1994; Glaeser *et al.*, 1996). For instance, Gambetta (1988) argues that the high degree of social distrust fostered by the strategy of "divide et impera" adopted by the Spanish branch of the Habsburgs in their rule of southern Italy strongly contributed to creating the conditions that allowed for the rise of the Sicilian mafia. Similarly, Varese (1994) suggests that the rise of organized crime in Russia was an effect of the Communist period, which removed society's trust in government and institutions.

Although these economic and sociological explanations are fascinating, they only provide partial explanations of the actual determinants of organized crime. On the one hand, if the presence of organized crime is assumed to reflect a desire to achieve and maintain a monopoly on violence in illegal markets, the phenomenon's persistence, especially after a legitimate competitor (i.e. the state) challenges that monopoly, remains unexplained. This is, for example, the case for Italian mafia groups as well as Colombian and Mexican cartels, which persist even though governments have attempted to defeat them (Abello-Colak and Guarneros-Meza, 2014; Dell, 2015). Moreover, it cannot explain the rise of organized crime in environments where the state has a monopoly over violence, as in the case of Chinese triads after the return of Hong Kong to mainland China in 1997 (Chu, 2000; Lintner, 2004), or its emergence in systems where incentives and constraints limit the use of violence, as in the case of Italian mafia organizations operating in northern Italy (Moro and Sberna, 2018). On the other hand, viewing organized crime as a substitute for trust fails to address the fact that some criminal organizations are active in contexts that do not require risky transactions because they are formally supported by the legal system, or the presence of organized crime in countries with societies rooted in social trust, such as Japan (Milhaupt and West, 2000; Hill, 2003).

Several scholars have tried to overcome inconsistencies in the economic and sociological explanations by adopting a more integrated institutional approach that shows how the rise of organized crime is significantly shaped by institutional incentives and disincentives (Gambetta, 1993; Milhaupt and West, 2000). The institutional approach tends to suggest that organized crime originates from societal demands for order and control that formal institutions are unable to fully satisfy. In other words, according to the institutional approach, organized crime arises as a result of the adaptation of parts of society to institutional weaknesses. This may be due to the complete absence of legal institutions, as in the case of illegal markets, or to institutional discontinuities, such as a dramatic change in the political or economic system.

The adoption of the institutional approach has substantial implications. First, violence is no longer viewed as an end but rather as a means through which organized crime provides a tradeable good (i.e. protection) in the form of secure property rights and contract enforcement (Tilly, 1985; Gambetta, 1993). Second, the institutional approach provides a framework in which the rise of organized crime is considered not as a matter of the supply of violence but rather as a result of the interaction between the demand for private protection and the supply of protection through violence. Third, organized crime does not act as a monopolist in the market for protection. Instead, it competes with formal institutions (Konrad and Skaperdas, 2012).

These three elements allow us to reconcile the inconsistencies of the economic and sociological explanations, and to develop an operative framework for understanding the origins of organized crime. This framework can be applied to a wide variety of contexts, including licit (Alexander, 1997; Buonanno *et al.*, 2015; Dimico *et al.*, 2017) and illicit activities (Dell, 2015); different local situations (Varese, 2001; Hill, 2003; Weinstein, 2008); and illegal activities other than organized crime (Suárez, 2000; Schneider and Schneider, 2002; Shah, 2006; Sánchez de la Sierra, 2018).

A seminal application of the institutional approach is found in Bandiera (2003), who studies the origins of the Sicilian mafia. According to her model, the mafia arose as an equilibrium in a non-cooperative two-stage game between a set of landlords and a mafia group in a context characterized by weak protection of property rights. More specifically, each landlord faced a positive probability of having his income stolen through predatory attacks, while the mafia group could successfully commit to protecting some landlords by diverting the attacks towards other landlords. By buying protection, each landlord redirected thieves to others' properties, thereby decreasing his or her probability of being attacked while increasing that likelihood for the other landlords. This essentially meant that by purchasing protection, each landlord generated a negative externality for the other landlords. The existence of this negative externality made each landlord better off if he or she was the only landlord (or one of the few) to be protected because the thieves would target property without protection. This implies that the landlords competed for the protection offered by mafia. In this type of competitive setting, there is a non-cooperative equilibrium in which every landlord buys protection from the mafia, although the results are sub-optimal for the class of landlords as a whole (Bandiera, 2003). In fact, everyone would be better off if no landlord purchased protection, but this does not happen because the landlords do not fully internalize the social costs generated by their decisions to buy protection from the mafia.

The predictions of this model credibly reflect the situation in which the Sicilian mafia arose during the second half of the nineteenth century. In fact, the abolition of feudalism in 1812 and the dissolution of the feudal armies pushed soldiers to look for new occupations. At the same time, the fall of the feudal order generated a new set of landowners who increasingly demanded protection for their newly acquired plots. Given the institutional vacuum that followed the troubled transition from the Bourbons to a unified Italy (1861), the newly founded state was unable, at least in the initial years following its establishment, to deal with requests for protection from new landowners. This ultimately led those landowners to search for private protection, which a group of people equipped with the right skills was willing to provide.

Another set of interesting insights produced by Bandiera's (2003) model concerns the size of the rent that the mafia can extract from the market for protection. In fact, the model predicts a positive correlation between this rent and both the number of people competing for protection and the value of the goods to be protected. The same study provides an empirical test of the first prediction and finds that the mafia's presence was indeed stronger in areas with greater land fractionalization, which implied a higher number of landowners demanding protection. The second prediction is in line with the view of many historians that mafia groups emerged in areas where Sicily's wealth was concentrated, especially in the richer, export-oriented areas around Palermo, the former capital of the Bourbon kingdom (Lupo, 1996, 2011; Dickie, 2004).

Along similar lines, Buonanno *et al.* (2015) and Dimico *et al.* (2017) provide robust evidence on the relationship between the surge in the Sicilian mafia and the presence of valuable natural resources. In particular, the former study proves the causal link between the origins of the Sicilian mafia and the distribution of sulphur mines across Sicily, while the latter assesses the link between the mafia's origins and areas of citrus production. At the time of Italian unification, Sicily was one of the biggest global exporters of both goods. Moreover, during the troubled times of the institutional transition, they were also the goods most worthy of protection. For instance, sulphur had to be transported from the mines in the Girgenti area to Palermo and that transportation had to be secured. Citrus production, which requires several years of investments before the trees generate fruits as well as uninterrupted irrigation, also needed extensive protection.

Beyond the protection of tangible goods such as land and natural resources, the need for protection of less tangible goods, such as political rents, is a major determinant of organized crime. Findings in this regard shed light on the collusion between organized crime and politics. Acemoglu *et al.* (2019) show how the mafia spread from its original surroundings in the most urban and wealthy parts of Sicily, where it had proven its value as an enforcer, to the more rural parts of the island. Local politicians made intensive use of the mafia's service to protect their rents from the socialist Sicilian Fasci movement, which violently called for a substantial redistribution of the land by the new Italian state.

The reliability of the institutional approach primarily builds on its capacity to be easily extended to other settings with specific environmental characteristics. For instance, Milhaupt and West (2000) and Hill (2003) adopt this approach to investigate the rise of Japanese *yakuza*. They show that, as in Sicily, organized crime in Japan developed in the post-feudal period (i.e. the Meiji period, 1868–1911) due to a dramatic increase in private property rights that was not followed by sufficient state protection. This empowered groups of criminals and disenfranchised samurai, who were willing and able to fulfil the rising demand for private protection. In the same fashion, Varese (2001) tracks the origins of the Russian mafia (i.e. the *Vory v Zakone*) to the Russian transition from the communist system to the market economy at the end of the 1980s and in the early 1990s. This period was characterized by the spread of property ownership without clear property rights legislation, and by an increasing number of dismissed officers and soldiers ready to provide private protection.

Finally, if the origins of organized crime mainly lie in its role as a provider of protection and enforcer of property rights in the presence of valuable resources and weak institutions, it is fair to ask whether organized crime is just another form of what economists call the "resource curse". This concept refers to the propensity of countries with an abundance of natural resources to have worse development outcomes than those with fewer natural resources. Pinotti (2015b) tries to address this question at a cross-country level, and finds a positive, robust relationship between primary export intensity – a raw measure of the economic relevance of natural resources in each country[1] – and the presence of organized crime. Specifically, higher values for primary export intensity at the country level during the 1970s are associated with a greater presence of organized crime in the following years. This relationship is driven by the fact that those countries have weak institutions, while the relationship is absent for countries with medium- and high-quality institutions.

Organized crime on the move: strategy or adaptation?

Are criminal organizations sedentary or mobile groups? Morselli *et al.* (2011) distinguish between two kinds of dynamics that may shape the mobility of criminal groups. On the one hand, organized crime organizations may want to expand their activities to new areas and new markets with the aim of increasing their revenues and profits. On the other hand, the emergence of criminal groups in contexts different from those in which they originated depends on the presence of specific characteristics that favour the transplantation of these groups. In both cases, a set of "pull" factors (i.e. forces drawing criminal groups to certain settings) and "push" factors (i.e. forces driving criminal groups away from certain settings) can be identified.

The push factors include the intensity of repression policies and law enforcement, and the degree of competition among criminal groups in the area. Examples of pull factors include the demand for goods typically traded by organized crime organizations, the presence of poorly regulated economic sectors with low levels of human capital, a lack of a proper law enforcement, a high degree of impunity and corruption, proximity to trafficking routes and flawed border controls. Morselli *et al.* (2011) conclude that the mobility of organized crime typically reflects the presence of specific constraints and opportunities in both the home and host countries rather than a strategic choice.

Varese (2011), who provides a different view of the mobility of organized crime, describes it as a strategic adaptation to bad luck in a suitable environment. This view relies on two main aspects of the migration of organized crime. First, even strategic decisions to move might be the outcome of non-strategic motivations. Second, strategic thinking might be present even when organized crime is forced to move. In particular, he suggests a need to reclassify the motivations for the mobility of organized crime proposed by Morselli *et al.* (2011) into two main categories: (1) those related to the supply of organized crime; and (2) those related to the local conditions in the new context, which may create a demand for the goods and services offered by organize crime. In the former category, we can distinguish between factors leading to a change in the supply of organized crime, such as the search for new resources, investments or markets, and those factors that may induce unintended variations in that supply, as in the case of generalized migration and/or repressive policies in the home environment. The latter category includes low levels of social trust, institutional weakness, booming markets, large illegal markets and the presence of other criminal groups.

Anecdotal evidence of these dynamics can be found in the recent migration of Mexican cartels to other Central American countries, such as Guatemala, Belize, Honduras and El Salvador, and the migration of the Sicilian mafia to the United States at the beginning of twentieth century. In the former case, the displacement of criminal groups reflected the "war on drugs" launched by the Mexican government as well as the local characteristics of Central American countries, including widespread impunity and corruption as well as their strategic location along major drug-trafficking routes. These dynamics led the Mexican cartels to increasingly look at these weak countries as possible hosts for parts of their activities, especially drug production and smuggling (Dudley, 2011; UNODC, 2012). Similarly, the repressive policies implemented in Sicily during the Fascist regime as well as the significant increase in Italian migration to the US contributed to an unintended movement of Sicilian criminals into the New World. Once in the US, the Sicilian mafia took advantage of certain contingencies in the new environment, such as the introduction of prohibition and favourable police reforms in major cities (Varese, 2011; Critchley, 2009).

A more quantitative exploration of the framework proposed by Varese (2011) is provided by Buonanno *et al.* (2015), who investigate the expansion of mafia organizations from southern to northern Italy. The study demonstrates that the combination of two key factors was responsible for the mafia's move to northern Italy during the late 1960s. The first was the unintended variation in the supply of organized crime induced by a certain repressive policy in Italy known as Confino.[2] During the 1960s and 1970s, this policy imposed the resettlement of mobsters across northern Italy. The second factor was the "Italian economic miracle", which occurred between the late 1950s and the early 1970s, and was responsible for massive migration from southern Italy to northern Italy. The dramatic increase in internal migration affected the supply of organized crime across all of Italy and created the local conditions necessary for the effective transplantation of mafia-type organizations. In other words, it resulted in a cultural environment that was closer to the environment in which the mafia had originated and it provided access to a cheap workforce.

The economic consequences of organized violence

In the previous sections, we examined some of the theories that help explain the origins of organized crime. However, there is no comprehensive theory on the socio-economic consequences of organized crime, probably due to the many direct and indirect ways in which the mafia can affect society. In this section, we examine studies on the overall effects of organized crime on economic growth and local development.

Estimating the economic effects of mafia activity is challenging because, as we discussed above, the distribution of criminal organizations is far from random. Therefore, correlational studies linking the presence of a mafia to economic growth are likely to be biased. The most reliable contributions exploit natural experiments in order to reduce concerns about reverse causality and omitted variables, which could simultaneously affect the spread of organized crime and economic growth. Pinotti (2015a) focuses on the spread of organized crime to two regions in southern Italy in the 1970s. While criminal organizations had traditionally been active in Calabria, Sicily and Campania, their influence had been marginal in the neighbouring regions of Basilicata and Apulia. However, this equilibrium changed after the closure of the free port of Tangier in 1960, which had been a central hub for tobacco smuggling. This led to the closure of the Tyrrhenian smuggling route (from Morocco to Sicily and Naples) in favour of the Adriatic route (from Albania to Apulia). As tobacco smuggling was the most important business for the mafia in the 1970s, criminals gradually extended their presence in these areas.

A second relevant factor was a major earthquake that hit the area in November 1980. In the ensuing months, massive inflows of public aid attracted mafia groups, which misappropriated relief money through ad-hoc criminal firms. Pinotti (2015a) exploits these two exogenous events to compare the actual and counterfactual development of these regions (i.e. the development of Apulia and Basilicata with and without mafia groups). Over a 30-year period, he finds that the mafia's presence lowered Gross Domestic Product (GDP) per capita in the next decades by 16 per cent. This estimate shows the significant effect that mafia groups can have on communities. Unfortunately, we do not have similar reliable estimates for the effects of organized crime in other countries (estimates are available only for Mexico and Colombia).[3] Nevertheless, as shown at the end of the first section, correlational studies based on national data seem to confirm that organized crime is negatively correlated with different proxies of economic development, as shown by Pinotti (2015b).

The next question is how the mafia's presence curbs local development. Scholars have identified several mechanisms that may explain such effects. First, although criminal organizations typically use criminal firms to launder illegal revenue, the legal activities of those firms also serve as an additional source of profit (Le Moglie and Sorrenti, 2018). This is the case when these organizations aim at monopolizing a sector and excluding "clean" firms, which are negatively affected by violence and extortion. For instance, Mexican drug cartels diversified their businesses by entering the food sector, where they took control over profitable commodities, such as limes, whiskey and avocados (Aranda, 2013; Garcıa-Ponce and Lajous, 2014). In Europe, criminals rely on even more sophisticated activities. In Italy and Eastern Europe, for example, criminal firms prosper thanks to corruption, which channels public funds (i.e. firms' subsidies and public procurements) to mafia-connected firms (Daniele and Dipoppa, 2018; Barone and Narciso, 2015).

Second, the uncertainty created by mafia threats deters local and international investments, which further depresses productivity and economic growth (Albanese and Marinelli, 2013; Daniele and Marani, 2011). An exemplary case is the liberalization of the Mexican oil sector, which took place in 2013. Until the reform, the oil sector was controlled by Pemex, a state-owned company. The liberalization aimed at promoting competition, attracting international investors and increasing Pemex's productivity. However, the new policy also reduced gasoline subsidies, which led to anti-government demonstrations and to the development of a new business among Mexican cartels (Payan and Correa-Cabrera, 2016). Criminals started to tap pipelines in order to steal gasoline and resell it at a higher price. Attacks against Pemex's employees and its infrastructure quickly increased, and the Mexican government found itself unable to stop oil thefts. Pemex's losses due to illegal tapping from 2013 to 2016 are estimated at approximately US$6.4 billion (Duhalt, 2017). This uncertain and risky environment deterred foreign investors interested in entering this sector. In a paradoxical way, a policy aimed at pulling in foreign investors ended up attracting organized crime to the business.

Third, organized violence may alter development by directly affecting ordinary people's decision-making. Gutiérrez-Romero (2015) shows that cartels' violence spreads fear among the local population, which increases the perception of insecurity. In fact, from 2006 to 2010, 34,550 murders were officially linked to organized crime in Mexico, which represents a significant increase from previous years (2000–2006), when only 8901 murders were linked to organized crime. This was a strong push factor, especially for those individuals living in cities close to the US border where violence reached dramatic levels. Rios (2014) shows that such an increase in perceived insecurity does increase migration outflows from most violent cities, estimating that 264,692 Mexicans migrated to avoid organized crime. Conversely, Basu and Pearlman (2017) find little evidence of such a displacement due to organized violence, neither internally, nor towards the US. Orozco-Aleman and Gonzalez-Lozano (2018) suggest a solution to this empirical puzzle by distinguishing between local violence and violence along migration routes: they state that while the former increases migration the latter may actually deter it.

Finally, organized crime's violence may also have a long-lasting impact by affecting new generations. Brown (2018) demonstrates how exposure to Mexican violent crime in utero substantially influences birth weight, especially for children of mothers with a low socio-economic status and/or poor mental health. Or rather, Sviatschi (2017) proves that youth exposure to drug violence significantly increases the probability to commit violent and drug-related crimes later in life due to the accumulation of "illegal" human capital.

Organized crime and the use of violence

The numerous negative consequences that organized criminal violence may have on both economy and society make the understanding of why and when criminals turn to the use of violence of primary importance for all the actors aimed at fighting criminal organizations. In particular, such violence may target either rival groups or specific members of the civic society, such as for example national or local politicians. Concerning the violence between different criminal organizations, sudden changes in the profitability of a market are a first important determinant of conflict among them. Castillo *et al.* (2018) examine the Mexican cocaine trade. Since the early 2000s, Mexican municipalities near the US border have been the main point of entry for cocaine being moved into the US. At that time, most of the cocaine was produced in Colombia. In 2006, shortages in the supply of cocaine increased sharply due to the introduction of a more effective drug-enforcement policy in Colombia. Scarcity increased cocaine prices, which led to more conflicts among Mexican cartels as they competed to control the increasingly valuable good. Castillo *et al.* (2018) show that these dynamics explain a substantial share of the rise in homicides in Mexico between 2006 and 2009. In a related study on why violence has escalated in Mexico in recent years, Dell (2015) documents how anti-cartel crackdowns, which weaken the incumbent criminal group, may lead to more violence owing to rival traffickers' attempts to replace incumbent criminals. Shocks in the criminal power structure are a second predictor of future intra-group conflicts and violence.

Organized criminal violence is not only aimed at controlling illegal markets; it can also extend to politics. A crucial factor to make it possible is that mafia groups are able to credibly threaten politicians. In contexts characterized by weak law enforcement and powerful criminal groups, politicians may face some level of risk. For instance, in the past decade, Mexican cartels killed about 100 mayors (Grillo, 2016). In Colombia, the FARC (Fuerzas Armadas Revolucionarias de Colombia) attempted to sabotage opposition leaders through violence and intimidation, which led to the murder of five politicians and the resignation of 222 of the country's 463 mayors in 2002 (Dal Bó *et al.*, 2006). In Italy, 134 politicians were killed between 1974 and 2014 (Lo Moro *et al.*, 2015). Daniele and Geys (2015) and Daniele (2017) directly test this theory in relation to local Italian politicians, exploiting variations in organized crime's political influence across time and space. In the first study, they focus on a law (no. 164/1991) that enables the national government to dissolve a city council if there are ties between municipal politicians and the mafia. As this law has been used each year since 1991 across a variety of cities, the authors can compare elected politicians in treated cities before and after the law's enforcement. They find a strong increase in local politicians' abilities (measured in terms of their level of education) after the law had been brought into play, which suggests a gain in the expected payoffs from engagement in politics. As the expected payoffs increase, the most competent individuals are motivated to return to the political arena.[4] Along the same lines, we would expect a decrease in politicians' abilities when mafia threats become more visible. This is what Daniele (2017) finds when studying the effects of mafia murders of politicians in Italian municipalities. After the murder of a local politician (a strong display of mafia power), there is a substantial decline in the ability level among local elected officials.

The fact that we have little knowledge about the political effects of mafia violence is closely linked to the lack of reliable data. By definition, data on illegal activities are partial and underreported. In an attempt to overcome this limitation, Daniele and Dipoppa (2017) collected the first dataset on violent threats against politicians. Their dataset covers all reported attacks against Italian politicians from 2010 to 2014; most of which can be attributed to criminal organizations. The reliability of these data lies in the fact that some types of attacks cannot go unreported, as they take place in public spaces (e.g. physical assaults, arson, murder, property damage). Most of the attacks are concentrated in southern Italy, which is generally more affected by organized crime. The most common types of attacks are arson and threat letters, while mayors are the most targeted category. They represent an ideal target – on the one hand, they hold direct power at the local level and, on the other hand, they are not widely exposed to national media. This is important, as Italian criminal organizations work hard to avoid media exposure – any such exposure increases police presence in the focal area.

There are two possible explanations of why criminals use violence against politicians: their aim might be to influence policymaking while politicians are in office or to ensure the election of mafia-connected politicians. Empirical evidence supports both theories. Daniele and Dipoppa (2017), who use data on local elections from 2010 to 2014, found that attacks against politicians peak in the first few weeks after a local election. This evidence is in line with the idea that criminals want to discourage any adverse policies from the very beginning of the politician's term in office. Moreover, the effect is mostly driven by attacks on newly elected mayors, who constitute new agents with whom to negotiate. In contrast, Alesina *et al.*'s (2018) study of the historic role of mafia organizations from the nineteenth century onwards identified that political violence increased before national elections, as mafias use violence to discourage honest politicians. Violence appeared to be an effective signal – after mafia-driven political murders, there was a decline in the saliency of mafia-related topics in parliamentary debates. In addition, criminals might be interested in influencing politicians to direct public funds to their connected firms and in avoiding anti-crime law enforcement. This pressure may affect accountability mechanisms and distort politicians' payoffs, thereby changing the pool of candidates running for office. Dal Bó *et al.*'s (2006) model shows that when organized crime is politically active, politicians' payoffs decrease. Consequently, more competent candidates leave politics to pursue better options in other sectors.

However, related studies demonstrate that politicians may benefit from negotiations with the mafia. Acemoglu *et al.* (2013) show that Colombian paramilitary groups can have significant effects on elections, as they provide votes to political parties that support paramilitary-friendly policies. This suggests a possible "quid pro quo" relationship between criminals and politicians. Similar evidence is provided by De Feo and De Luca (2017) in the Italian context. For the period from 1946 to 1992, they document how the Sicilian mafia supported the leading national party (the Christian Democratic Party), especially when elections were contested. These authors also highlight a similar relationship, as criminals obtained economic advantages in the construction sector in exchange for their electoral support.

Conclusions

In the last two decades, our knowledge on organized crime has considerably improved. This is noticeable especially concerning the understanding of the mafia's roots due to the institutional approach, whose predictions have been supported by several empirical contributions. The availability of new measures of illegal activities is also triggering a rich set of studies on the effects of organized crime, which valuably tracks the dynamics shaping the mobility of criminal groups.

The release of accurate administrative data will allow for a systematic adoption of evaluations to understand those policies that are more likely to counter organized crime in specific contexts. As criminal organizations are ever evolving in a changing world, this line of research will follow the development of organized crime in a world shaped by uncertain borders, unstable political scenarios and unprecedented empowering technologies.

Nevertheless, data unavailability still deters a clear understanding of the dynamics within and across criminal groups. While, just in the European Union, there are currently about 5000 operating criminal organized groups (Ugelvik *et al.*, 2019), scholars have been able to study just a few of them. Future studies may be able to systematically collect novel data on the spread and power of emerging mafias around the world. This will allow a better understanding of the criminal market structure, a mostly unexplored topic, including promising research questions concerning how competition dynamics among and within groups affect power equilibria in the illegal market, and understanding which shocks or policies are more likely to trigger violence among groups and which, instead, are more likely to promote cooperation.

Notes

1 This measures exports of primary products relative to total exports, as described by Sachs and Warner (1997).
2 Established by law n. 1423, which was passed in 1956 and subsequently modified in 1965 by law n. 575.
3 Concerning Mexico, see for instance Gutiérrez-Romero and Oviedo (2017), while regarding Colombia, see Angrist and Kugler (2008).
4 In two related studies, Galletta (2017) and Di Cataldo and Mastrorocco (2018) find that the enforcement of this law reduces expenditures in mafia-infiltrated sectors (e.g. construction) as well as inefficient investments in nearby cities.

References

Abello-Colak, A. and Guarneros-Meza, V. (2014) The role of criminal actors in local governance. *Urban Studies*, 51(15), 3268–3289.
Acemoglu, D., De Feo, G., and De Luca, G. (2019) Weak states: Causes and consequences of the Sicilian mafia. *Review of Economic Studies* (forthcoming).
Acemoglu, D., Robinson, J. A., and Santos, R J. (2013) The monopoly of violence: Evidence from Colombia. *Journal of the European Economic Association*, 11(s1), 5–44.
Albanese, G. and Marinelli, G. (2013) Organized crime and productivity: Evidence from firm-level data. *Rivista italiana degli economisti*, 18(3), 367–394.
Alesina, A., Piccolo, S., and Pinotti, P., (2018) Organized crime, violence, and politics. *The Review of Economic Studies*, 86(2), 457–499.
Alexander, B. (1997) The rational racketeer: Pasta protection in depression era Chicago. *The Journal of Law & Economics*, 40(1), 175–202.
Andreas, P. and Wallman, J. (2009) Illicit markets and violence: What is the relationship? *Crime, Law and Social Change*, 52(3), 225–229.
Angrist, J. D. and Kugler, A. D. (2008) Rural windfall or a new resource curse? Coca, income, and civil conflict in Colombia. *The Review of Economics and Statistics*, 90(2), 191–215.
Aranda, S. (2013) Stories of drug trafficking in rural Mexico: territories, drugs and cartels in Michoacan. In *European Review of Latin American and Caribbean Studies/Revista Europea de Estudios Latinoamericanos y del Caribe*, pp. 43–66.
Bandiera, O. (2003) Land reform, the market for protection, and the origins of the Sicilian mafia: Theory and evidence. *The Journal of Law, Economics, and Organization*, 19(1), 218–244.
Banfield, E. (1958) *The Moral Basis of a Backward Society*. New York: The Free Press.
Bates, R., Greif, A., and Singh, S. (2002) Organizing violence. *Journal of Conflict Resolution*, 46(5), 599–628.
Barone, G. and Narciso, G. (2015) Organized crime and business subsidies: Where does the money go? *Journal of Urban Economics*, 86, 98–110.
Basu, S. and Pearlman, S. (2017) Violence and migration: evidence from Mexico's drug war. *IZA Journal of Development and Migration*, 7(1), 18.
Berg, L.-A. and M. Carranza (2018) Organized criminal violence and territorial control: Evidence from northern Honduras. *Journal of Peace Research*, 55(5), 566–581.
Black, D. (1983) Crime as social control. *American Sociological Review*, 48(1), 34–45.
Brown, R. (2018) The Mexican drug war and early-life health: The impact of violent crime on birth outcomes. *Demography*, 55(1), 319–340.
Buonanno, P., Durante, R., Prarolo, G., and Vanin, P. (2015) Poor institutions, rich mines: Resource curse in the origins of the Sicilian mafia. *The Economic Journal*, 125(586), F175–F202.
Castillo, J. C., Mejía, D., and Restrepo, P. (2018) Scarcity without leviathan: The violent effects of cocaine supply shortages in the Mexican drug war. *The Review of Economics and Statistics* (forthcoming).
Chu, Y. K. (2000) *The Triads as Business*. New York: Routledge.
Critchley, D. (2009) *The Origin of Organized Crime in America: The New York City Mafia, 1891–1931*. New York, London: Routledge.
Dal Bó, E., Dal Bó, P., and Di Tella, R. (2006) "Plata o Plomo?": Bribe and punishment in a theory of political influence. *American Political Science Review*, 100(1), 41–53.
Daniele, G. (2017) Strike one to educate one hundred: Organized crime, political selection and politicians' ability. *Journal of Economic Behavior & Organization*, 159, 650–662.
Daniele, G. and Dipoppa, G. (2017) Mafia, elections and violence against politicians. *Journal of Public Economics*, 154, 10–33.
Daniele, G. and Dipoppa, G. (2018) Doing business below the line: Screening, mafias and public funds. Baffi Carefin Centre Research Paper, (2018–98).
Daniele, G. and Geys, B. (2015) Organised crime, institutions and political quality: Empirical evidence from Italian municipalities. *The Economic Journal*, 125(586), F233–F255.
Daniele, V. and Marani, U. (2011) Organized crime, the quality of local institutions and FDI in Italy: A panel data analysis. *European Journal of Political Economy*, 27(1), 132–142.
De Feo, G. and De Luca, G. D. (2017) Mafia in the ballot box. *American Economic Journal: Economic Policy*, 9(3), 134–167.
Dell, M. (2015) Trafficking networks and the Mexican drug war. *American Economic Review*, 105(6), 1738–1779.

Di Cataldo, M. and Mastrorocco, N. (2017) *Organised Crime, Captured Politicians and the Allocation of Public Resources*. Available at SSRN: https://ssrn.com/abstract=3124949 or http://dx.doi.org/10.2139/ssrn.3124949

Dickie, J. (2004) *Cosa Nostra: A History of the Sicilian Mafia*. New York: Palgrave Macmillan.

Dimico, A., Isopi, A., and Olsson, O. (2017) Origins of the Sicilian mafia: The market for lemons. *The Journal of Economic History*, 77(4), 1083–1115.

Dudley, S. (2011) The zetas in Guatemala. *InSight Crime Special Report*.

Duhalt, A. (2017) Looting fuel pipelines in Mexico. *Issue Brief* (23 June 2017).

Duran-Martinez, A. (2015) To kill and tell? State power, criminal competition, and drug violence. *Journal of Conflict Resolution*, 59(8), 1377–1402.

Galletta, S. (2017) Law enforcement, municipal budgets and spillover effects: Evidence from a quasi-experiment in Italy. *Journal of Urban Economics*, 101, 90–105.

Gambetta, D. (1988) Mafia: The price of distrust. In D. Gambetta (ed.), *Trust: Making and Breaking Cooperative Relations*. Oxford: Basil Blackwell, Chapter 10, pp. 158–175.

Gambetta, D. (1993) *The Sicilian Mafia: The Business of Private Protection*. Cambridge, MA: Harvard University Press.

Garcıa-Ponce, O. and Lajous, A. (2014) How does a drug cartel become a lime cartel. *Washington Post*, 20 May.

Glaeser, E. L., Sacerdote, B., and Scheinkman, J. A. (1996) Crime and social interactions. *The Quarterly Journal of Economics*, 111(2), 507–548.

Grillo, I. (2016) Why cartels are killing Mexico's mayors. *New York Times*. 17 January.

Grossman, H. I. (1998) Producers and predators. *Pacific Economic Review*, 3(3), 169–187.

Grossman, H. I. (2002) "Make us a king": Anarchy, predation, and the state. *European Journal of Political Economy*, 18(1), 31–46.

Grossman, H. I. and Kim, M. (1995) Swords or plowshares? A theory of the security of claims to property. *Journal of Political Economy*, 103(6), 1275–1288.

Gutierrez-Romero, R. (2015) Estimating the impact of Mexican drug cartels and drug-related homicides on crime and perceptions of safety. *Journal of Economic Geography*, 16(4), 941–973.

Gutiérrez-Romero, R. and Oviedo, M. (2017) The good, the bad and the ugly: The socioeconomic impact of drug cartels and their violence. *Journal of Economic Geography*, 18(6), 1315–1338.

Hill, P. (2003) *The Japanese Mafia: Yakuza, Law, and the State*. Oxford: Oxford University Press.

Hirshleifer, J. (1995) Anarchy and its breakdown. *Journal of Political Economy*, 103(1), 26–52.

Konrad, K. A. and Skaperdas, S. (2012) The market for protection and the origin of the state. *Economic Theory*, 50(2), 417–443.

Lintner, B. (2004) Chinese organised crime. *Global Crime*, 6(1), 84–96.

Lo Moro, D., Gualdani, M., Zizza, V., and Cirinnà, M. (2015) Commissione Parlamentare d'inchiesta sul fenomeno delle intimidazioni nei confronti degli amministratori locali, Relazione Conclusiva. Senato della Repubblica Italiana.

Lupo, S. (1996) *Storia della Mafia*. Roma: Donzelli Editore.

Lupo, S. (2011) *L'unificazione italiana. Mezzogiorno, Rivoluzione, Guerra civile*. Roma: Donzelli Editore.

Milhaupt, C. J. and West, M. D. (2000) The dark side of private ordering: An institutional and empirical analysis of organized crime. *University of Chicago Law Review*, 67(1).

Moro, F. N. and Sberna, S. (2018) Transferring violence? Mafia killings in nontraditional areas: Evidence from Italy. *Journal of Conflict Resolution*, 62(7), 1579–1601.

Morselli, C., Turcotte, M., and Tenti, V. (2011) The mobility of criminal groups. *Global Crime*, 12(3), 165–188.

North, D., Wallis, J. J., and Weingast, B. (2009) *Violence and Social Orders*. Cambridge, UK: Cambridge University Press.

Orozco-Aleman, S. and Gonzalez-Lozano, H. (2018) Drug violence and migration flows lessons from the Mexican drug war. *Journal of Human Resources*, 53(3), 717–749.

Payan, T. and Correa-Cabrera, G. (2016) *Security, the Rule of Law, and Energy Reform in Mexico*. James A. Baker III Institute for Public Policy of Rice University: www.bakerinstitute.org/research/security-mexicos-energy-reform/

Pinotti, P. (2015a) The economic costs of organised crime: Evidence from Southern Italy. *The Economic Journal*, 125(586), F203–F232.

Pinotti, P. (2015b) The causes and consequences of organised crime: Preliminary evidence across countries. *The Economic Journal*, 125(586), F158–F174.

Putnam, R. D. (1993) What makes democracy work? *National Civic Review*, 82(2), 101–107.
Reuter, P. (1983) *Disorganized Crime: The Economics of the Invisible Hand*. Cambridge, MA: MIT Press.
Rios, V. (2014) The role of drug-related violence and extortion in promoting Mexican migration: Unexpected consequences of a drug war. *Latin American Research Review*, 49(3), 199–217.
Sachs, J. D. and Warner, M. W. (1997) Fundamental sources of long-run growth. *The American Economic Review*, 87(2), 184–188.
Sánchez de la Sierra, R. (2018) On the origin of states: Stationary bandits and taxation in eastern Congo. *Journal of Political Economy* (forthcoming).
Schelling, T. C. (1984) *Choice and Consequence*. Cambridge, MA: Harvard University Press.
Schneider, J. and Schneider, P. (2002) The mafia and al-Qaeda: Violent and secretive organizations in comparative and historical perspective. *American Anthropologist*, 104(3), 776–782.
Shah, A. (2006) Markets of protection: The terrorist Maoist movement and the state in Jharkhand, India. *Critique of Anthropology*, 26(3), 297–314.
Skaperdas, S. (1992) Cooperation, conflict, and power in the absence of property rights. *The American Economic Review*, 82(4), 720–739.
Suárez, A. R. (2000) Parasites and predators: Guerrillas and the insurrection economy of Colombia. *Journal of International Affairs*, 53(2), 577–601.
Sviatschi, M. M. (2017) Making a narco: Childhood exposure to illegal labor markets and criminal life paths. Unpublished manuscript, Columbia University.
Tilly, C. (1985) *War Making and State Making as Organized Crime*. Cambridge, UK: Cambridge University Press, pp. 169–191.
Ugelvik, S., Aas, G., Runhovde, S., Strype, J., Bjørgo, T., Aas, G., … and Aas, K. F. (2019) EU serious and organised crime threat assessment. In *Police Cooperation and Sovereignty in the EU: Norway's Lessons for Europe*. Oslo: Willan, Vol. 10, No. 1, pp. 1–23.
UNODC (2012) *Transnational Organized Crime in Central America and the Caribbean: A Threat Assessment*. United Nation Office on Drug and Crime.
van Besouw, B., Ansink, E., and van Bavel, B. (2016) The economics of violence in natural states. *Journal of Economic Behavior & Organization*, 132, 139–156.
Varese, F. (1994) Is Sicily the future of Russia? Private protection and the rise of the Russian mafia. *European Journal of Sociology*, 35(2), 224–258.
Varese, F. (2001) *The Russian Mafia: Private Protection in a New Market Economy*. Oxford: Oxford University Press.
Varese, F. (2011) Mafia movements: A framework for understanding the mobility of mafia groups. *Global Crime*, 12(3), 218–231.
Weinstein, L. (2008) Mumbai's development mafias: Globalization, organized crime and land development. *International Journal of Urban and Regional Research*, 32(1), 22–39.

21

DISRUPTING ORGANIZED CRIME IN THE UK

Tackling violence, intimidation and coercion

Michael Lewis, Daniel T. Beaumont and Rob Ewin

Interventions are increasingly being designed to disrupt ongoing criminal activity rather than identify crimes that have already been committed (Innes and Sheptycki, 2004). The emerging emphasis on disrupting organized criminal groups can be contrasted with older enforcement-led approaches, which were resource intensive and limited in their success (Kirby and Nailer, 2013). *Rational choice theory* (Cornish and Clarke, 1986) assumes that individuals adopt a rational perspective when engaging in illicit activity and can therefore be diverted away if the cost of doing so outweighs the benefits. This holds some premise for the disruption of organized criminal groups, providing that the complexities of this phenomena are better understood. Organized criminal networks are heterogeneous and operate at varying levels (Kirby and Nailer, 2013), engage with other known associates and diversify into different types of crime (Galeotti, 2005), making assessment of their strategies problematic. There is a common understanding, nevertheless, that criminal groups are ultimately driven by profit, with violence, intimidation and coercion administered to further their criminal purpose and obstruct the policing response to them (Dean *et al.*, 2010; Stelfox, 1998). Yet, it is this behaviour that makes members of organized criminal groups visible and susceptible to intervention, thereby making disruption viable.

The chapter will expand on this approach, defining organized crime before identifying a number of multi-agency strategies adopted to tackle behaviours, such as violence, often thought to be a vessel for maximizing criminal entrepreneurship. There will be a focus on organized crime manifesting in the United Kingdom, solely making reference to other countries for comparison purposes.

Defining organized crime

Organized crime has received considerable attention in recent years as Governments have become increasingly aware of its scope, costs and dangers. Indeed, "organized crime" as a phenomenon has been integrated into the vocabulary of politicians and the wider public, yet there remains no agreed reference point for which it can be defined while satisfying all parties (Woodiwiss and Hobbs, 2009). Definitions vary according to their sources, and although politicians and law enforcement are likely to delineate organized crime in a manner that is conducive to their operations and risk management, social scientists prefer a deeper, more theoretical basis for their analysis (Wright, 2006). The focus of the term appears to depend on who is defining it and for what means (Sergi, 2016). Thus, achieving a unified definition of organized crime may, at present, prove challenging, and instead a review of the reoccurring themes within existing definitions is recommended.

The term "organized crime" has readily been applied, albeit subjectively, to a certain type of more sophisticated, complex set of criminal activities embedded within a network of illicit markets. Activities are known to involve a plethora of financially-rewarding crimes, including firearms, drugs, child sexual exploitation (CSE), modern slavery and human trafficking, which are often "enabled" through violence, corruption and intimidation (Albanese, 2008; Hauck and Peterke, 2010; Wright, 2006). However, restricting the definition of organized crime to a simple list of serious illegal activities does not provide any meaningful information on the "organized" element of the crime, or the characteristics of the group that are initiating these activities. Such a view essentially depicts organized crime as an indicator of criminality, which is problematic as organized crime is heterogeneous, dependent on context, persons involved, and the market within which it subscribes; activities are therefore likely to vary across groups. Engagement in such activities does not automatically indicate involvement in organized criminality (Hauck and Peterke, 2010), and ignoring this would make organized crime impossible to measure, let alone respond to (Crocker *et al.*, 2017).

Organized crime has also been conceptualized through the defining characteristics of the organizations themselves (Hagan, 2006), with groups falling into either a hierarchical or enterprise model. It is the former that has been associated with organizations, such as the Italian Mafia and Mexican drug cartels (Paoli, 2006), and recognized in Finckenauer's (2005) approach to organized crime. He listed eight analytic defining variables of organized crime, which included "lack of ideology, structure/organized hierarchy, continuity, violence/use of force or use of threat, restricted membership, illegal enterprises, penetration of legitimate businesses and corruption" (Longo, 2010, p. 17). According to Longo (2010), it is the hierarchical structure and continuity of the organization that gives organized crime its collective identity. If specific individuals leave, or indeed are detained by law enforcement, they are simply replaced by others. This therefore enables organizations to continue and adapt to changes in the external environment, thus making disruption problematic. Organized criminality, much like legitimate businesses, have distinct enterprises such as those handling recruitment, cash flow, communications and the management of people (Wright, 2013). Law enforcement activity can fail where interventions only focus on specific elements of the enterprise, or seek to detain only 'high profile' members without a focus on their wider business, recovery of criminally gained assets, and removal of money laundering capability.

The use of force, violence and intimidation have been considered as strategies to gain power and control territory, and have readily been associated with hierarchical organizations, such as the Italian Mafia. These strategies have been viewed as 'anti-state' activity that threaten national institutions and, as such, have been coined a political concern (Longo, 2010). Whilst some scholars believe that a hierarchical structure is necessary to exercise this "anti-state" activity, others have suggested that a centralized structure is suffice, providing that any violence, as a form of territorial control, occurs solely at a sub-national level to avoid direct conflict with the state (e.g. Catanzaro, 1993, as cited in Longo, 2010).

Arguably, there has been an evolution in organized crime, with a shift from traditional definitions relating to structure towards "entrepreneurial crime", which focuses on a financial or economic objective. Traditional forms of organized crime predominantly utilized power to protect specific interests whereas entrepreneurial crime is said to have transformed itself into the national economy, accumulating profit through the production of services and goods, and using violence and intimidation more so to sustain competitive advantage (Dean *et al.*, 2010; Longo,

2010). Smith (1975) conceptualized entrepreneurial crime as a response to a latent illicit demand that extended beyond the legal market. However, Paoli (2002) rejected this, claiming that definitions of organized crime cannot be narrowed down to the provision of illegal goods and services. She argued that illicit market dynamics were often unorganized, lacking rules, security and controls, and were therefore not conducive to organized crime. Instead, Paoli (2002) referred back to the traditional viewpoint, stating that there is more to organized crime than the illegal entrepreneurial activities, making reference to several non-economic roles, such as protection and the supplying of votes.

The enterprise model, nevertheless, was proposed in response to an increase in the effect of organized crime on member states of the European Union (EU, 1998; Smith, 1980). As such, a joint report of the European Commission and Europol was published in 2001 outlining a working definition of organized crime (Wright, 2006). This demarcates organized crime through 11 characteristics (Elvins, 2003, p. 34):

> 1). *Collaboration of more than two people*; 2). Each with own appointed tasks; 3). *For a prolonged or indefinite period of time*; 4). Using some form of discipline or control; 5). *Suspected of the commission of serious criminal offences*; 6). Operating at an international level; 7). Using violence or other means for intimidation; 8). Using commercial or business-like structures; 9) Engaged in money laundering; 10). Exerting influence on politics, the media, public administration, judicial authorities or the economy; and 11). *Determined by the pursuit of profit and/or power.*

Of these characteristics, six have to be identified, with the four in italics needing to be among the six for a case to be viewed as organized crime.

These characteristics place significant emphasis on the formation of structured links to allow for a range of criminal acts or exploitation that generate profit. Article 2 of the United Nations (UN) Convention against Transnational Organized Crime (United Nations Office on Drugs and Crime, 2004, p. 5) supported this view and defined an organized criminal group as:

> A structured group of three or more persons, existing for a period of time and acting in concert with the aim of committing one or more serious crimes or offences… in order to obtain, directly or indirectly, a financial or material benefit.

Thus, there are similarities between the EU and UN definitions of organized criminal groups, with organizational structure depicted as an important concept. This is not to say, however, that organizations adopt the same characteristics or structures, rather there are more subtle, implicit differences across groups that relate to function, and this facilitates a range of organized criminal activity.

Although organizational structure has long been associated with more traditional forms of organized crime, its importance seems to have extended to entrepreneurial crime, suggesting that the hierarchical and enterprise models are less distinct than initially thought. Adopting a social network analytical approach offers further insight into the structural systems underpinning organized criminal groups, and according to Mcillwain (1999), such organizations are underpinned by a social system comprising a multiplex set of relationships among individuals (and with other groups) whose overall aim is to provide illicit goods and services. These connections are stated to be fluid and interdependent, largely influenced by the context in which the organized criminal activity takes place (Longo, 2010). The provision of services by organized crime groups should not be underestimated as many current forms involve human trafficking as a key element to service the sex, agricultural, drug production, domestic and beauty demands of western cultures (Aronowitz, 2001; FitzGerald, 2012).

It becomes apparent that there is little consensus on the meaning of the term "organized crime". Whilst conceptualizations share common features, there are also differences, and it is arguably these differences that further convey organized crime as a heterogeneous construct. Definitions of organized crime should not be abandoned, rather they are to be viewed as a foundation for continual dialogue between academics and practitioners where theoretical understandings can be merged with worked experience. It is this relationship that will aid the generation of vital knowledge aimed at improving the effectiveness of counter-organized crime policies, and the consequent disruption of organized criminal groups (Longo, 2010).

However, there are notable limitations with the aforementioned definitions in that organized crime has been conceptualized in such a manner to facilitate both law-enforcement and political interest and, as such, there are theoretical features or characteristics that have likely been omitted. Definitions, such as the enterprise model, provide a focus for the policing of organized crime so as to avoid an ineffective use of resources. The inclusion of illicit activities, whilst fitting with modern criminal law (i.e. individuals are punished for what they do, not what they belong to), also supports the detection of organized crime, which only tends to become apparent during further investigation (Hauck and Peterke, 2010). Attending to illicit activities, such as violence, somewhat increases the visibility of organized criminal networks and may prove to be one method of identifying and deterring such groups. Yet, this method of detection is by no means straightforward and challenges remain, which are highlighted in the ensuing section.

Organized crime and gang violence

The National Crime Agency (NCA), formally known as the Serious Organized Crime Agency (SOCA) until October 2013, is responsible for tackling organized crime at a national and international level in England and Wales. Their policing model is mostly consistent with the enterprise model and views organized crime as a set of varying illicit activities committed by a group. The emphasis on criminal activities as a defining feature distinguishes organized crime in England and Wales from that occurring in other countries, such as Italy, which Sergi (2015) associates more with the hierarchical (structural) model. There are also deviations from the enterprise model, albeit to a lesser extent, in that organized crime in England and Wales is linked to gang-related activity, such as violence (Hobbs, 2013), which on the surface does not necessary fit with the model's entrepreneurial focus. The English conceptualization of organized crime as local gang-style enterprises has thus been disputed (e.g. Klein *et al.*, 1991). However, there is now general acceptance that it is the "seriousness" of the criminal activity that differentiates local gangs from established organized criminal groups, with the latter associated more with increased bouts of severe activity (Home Office, 2014), which, unsurprisingly, is likely to result in disproportionate harm (Kirby *et al.*, 2016). Both groups, nevertheless, are reported to be rooted in their local territories and linked to drugs and violence manifesting at street-level (Sergi, 2015).

As such, violence, intimidation and coercion have readily been associated with both street gangs and organized criminal groups (e.g. Decker and Curry, 2000; Ratcliffe, 2016). Reference to violence in this instance, however, does not involve that which manifests on an individual basis for personal gain, rather it relates to violence occurring in the context of membership specific to the gang or organized criminal group. There is much debate as to whether street gangs evolve into criminal business organizations, with scholars proposing that gangs may form, but not necessarily reach the highest developmental stage and commit more serious offences for profit (Densley and Harding, 2018; Pitts, 2019). It is at the highest level where gangs are said to shift from the recreational and criminal stages to financial goal orientation. Yet, this mutation is likely to be determined by the opportunities available, pre-existing forms of criminality in the area, gang member attributes and local enforcement (Pitts, 2019). In areas of weaker local enforcement, with criminality unfamiliar to the policing control, there are distinct opportunities for organized criminality; for example, the current trajectory of County lines drug supply chains, and Cuckooing. In these instances, law enforcement has to learn of the criminality, its context and boundaries, and then respond. This can be time consuming. Evolutionary trajectories may therefore differ across gangs, resulting in varying levels of organization and commitment to instrumental goals.

Regardless of level or sophistication, violence, intimidation and coercion are prevalent in gang life. Wright (2006), however, makes a distinction between tactical and strategic forms of violence, noting the latter to be utilized both directly and indirectly by well-established crime groups. Strategic violence is adopted to fulfil longer-term goals, which may directly relate to growth, survival, and the need to protect the organization from competitors or law-enforcement. This may also occur indirectly, for example, where adults belonging to an established organized crime group mentor younger members through the business-like restructuring of street gangs, thus resulting in entrepreneurial expansion to rural and coastal areas; formally known as County lines (Hesketh and Robinson, 2019). The emergence of County lines over the past six years has resulted in a dramatic rise in violence, specifically knife crime, due to street gangs attempting to protect their territory and enhance market growth (usually for the supply of drugs). The involvement of children and young people as vulnerable gang members also raises issues surrounding criminal exploitation (Pitts, 2019), and therefore becomes a safeguarding concern requiring a proactive policing response.

Violence, intimidation and coercion occurring at a more tactical level focuses on achieving short-term goals, such as encouraging legitimate businesses to part with money or provide a service (Wright, 2006). In some instances there is little need for tactical violence and, instead, the reputation of the organized criminal group is sufficient to coerce others to succumb to their demands and/or deter local citizens from providing valuable intelligence to the police (Crocker *et al.*, 2017). As such, coercion in this respect may be viewed as an instrumental form of illegitimate power (Wright, 2006), and to some extent resembles the traditional characteristics of mafia-like organized crime. It is this power that also enables the more sophisticated organized criminal groups to become less visible as the "players" at the top, whose reputation has established them as influential, instruct younger individuals to execute duties on their behalf. Areas where legitimate employment opportunities are rare become an attractive hunting ground for organized criminal groups to enlist vulnerable adults or young people. A case study of a London borough found that established organized criminals, commonly identified as older foreign nationals (usually over the age of 26 years; NCA, 2015) partaking in more serious crime for a sustained period of time (Francis *et al.*, 2013), coerced local youths into conducting retail-level drug dealing activities, in some instances using intimidation to force them (Hales and Hobbs, 2010).

Drug markets, such as those observed with County lines, are linked to a high prevalence of violence, or threat of violence, which is usually administered to enforce the payment of drug debts, disrupt local drug markets, sanction informants and resolve competition (Hesketh and Robinson, 2019; Lupton *et al.*, 2002). This approach to business is known to circumvent further bouts of violence, often in retaliation; thus exacerbating the problem and causing significant damage to an area's reputation. Whilst some residents may be too intimidated to report the occurrences, others may feel compelled to take action in an attempt to protect their community (Crocker *et al.*, 2017; Lupton *et al.*, 2002). However, the recruitment of local youths to facilitate the dealing of drugs works well here in diverting police attention from the activities of the key "players" within the organized group (Stelfox, 1998). Local law enforcement may respond to smaller sub-elements of the organization, depending on resource availability, and simply offer intelligence to the wider policing community which may not serve longer-term interests or tackle other elements of the criminal business. There may become an intense policing response to victims, which may require more resources, diverting further attention from the core crime business.

Despite conflicting views (e.g. Sergi, 2015), this approach tentatively conveys a role for the hierarchical model within organized crime in England and Wales, although networks seem to be dynamic and less formal (Levi, 2003) in comparison to those associated with more traditional mafia-type organizations. The pursuit of profit also continues to support the application of the entrepreneurial model. Indeed, the presence of overlapping hierarchical and entrepreneurial features suggest that the configuration of an organized criminal group is fluid, dependent on context and desired outcome. One would assume that this flexibility also allows for diversification when there is a need to evade police detection, form new alliances and extend geographical scope (Galeotti, 2005). Pitts (2019) provides an example of the well-organized Beaumont gang in Waltham Forest who were "going county" (a reference to County lines), recruiting younger people via mobile communication to traffic and sell drugs in the South East and South West of England, and South Wales. They were also found "Cuckooing" homes (i.e. the use of violence and abuse to target the homes of others and use them as bases for drug dealing) belonging to vulnerable adults in Waltham Forest, turning them into "crack houses". When police intervened, the gang diversified into the robbery of high value motor vehicles.

Conceptually and operationally, organized crime is becoming more complex. The ability to diversify into a range of legitimate and illicit activities gives rise to challenges when establishing associated harms, in turn making it difficult to prioritize crimes and offenders (Kirby, 2013). In the "absence of law" (i.e. "the actual or perceived inability of the police to counter the threat posed"; Pitts, 2019, p. 69), individuals are becoming increasingly anxious and assume responsibility for managing risk themselves. This method of informal social control is known to result in an escalation of violence, and maintains a perceived lack of both protection and police legitimacy (Pitts, 2019; Wilson, 2012). However, authorities are attempting to combat this view, requesting that communities report suspicious activity; yet, those at most risk are arguably hard to reach and intelligence is often poor, thus limiting the effectiveness of detection at a local level (Crocker *et al.*, 2017).

In a recent study, Kirby *et al.* (2018) emphasized the challenges of policing hostile environments. Individuals residing in areas associated with higher concentrations of organized criminal groups were found to perceive their neighbours as less likely to intervene in scenarios relevant to organized crime (e.g. drug dealing). However, there was subtle disparity between these areas, which suggests that communities interpret and respond to incidents in different ways and would therefore benefit from tailored community engagement programmes. Low levels of collective efficacy consistently reported by those living in areas where organized criminal groups proliferate was also a particular concern (Kirby *et al.*, 2018), and interventions should arguably focus on improving resilience through fostering trust, social integration and motivation among residents. Consistent with the *broken windows theory* (Wilson and Kelling, 1982), communities that are able to work together and involve the police are likely to prevent low-level crime escalating into more serious forms. Indeed, with regards to organized crime, this level of severity has already been reached and instead there should be an emphasis on encouraging community support, where residents feel collectively able to provide intelligence without fear of retribution.

The complexities outlined so far arguably warrant further attention. The presence of organized criminal groups within local areas are noted to impinge on community confidence, and indeed, increase opportunities for impressionable youths to be drawn into abnormal patterns of criminality. Low levels of collective efficacy act as a barrier to disruption strategies, where a lack of informal community policing inhibits the sharing of information and perpetuates a culture that favours little contact with law enforcement. An innovative, tangible and urgent intervention is thus warranted that considers societal, cultural and environmental factors, and supports the development of more resilient and cooperative communities that proactively help to deter and disrupt organized crime. This moves the chapter on to explore the role of policing in organized crime, specifically in terms of "disruption".

Policing organized crime: a shift towards disruption

Defining organized crime is complex and as a result gives rise to challenges for law-enforcement when developing proactive strategies surrounding detection, disruption and investigation (Coyne and Bell, 2011). It is their inherent flexibility that provides organized criminal groups with the ability to identify risks and opportunities for exploitation at a pace that exceeds law enforcement response. The processing of criminal technology, recording of witness statements, interviewing of suspects, obtaining of any necessary expert testimony, all add to the complexity of policing organized criminality. This has led to law enforcement agencies having to consider alternative policing approaches to tackle this growing national and international concern, with some agencies preferring surveillance, remote technology, and the use of informants to accrue substantial intelligence and evidential material. These resources are more complex to administer, offer higher risk, and can be politically sensitive.

At present, particularly at a local level, the response to organized crime in England and Wales is governed by the police and their partners. Although not a strict requirement, it is recommended that individual police forces, of which there are 44 in England and Wales, including the British Transport Police, produce profiles of organized crime within their geographical jurisdiction and develop a plan based on CONTEST (i.e. Pursue, Protect, Prevent and Prepare), the UK's counter-terrorism strategy (Crocker *et al.*, 2017). Policing organized crime in this manner conveys it as a national security threat similar to that of terrorism. Whilst organized crime and terrorism have distinctly different characteristics and motives, they are both sociologically classified as specific forms of group crime (Zubrzycki, 2015) and, as such, applying a counter-terrorism initiative may aid interventions in dealing with organized crime, specifically when aiming to reduce harm. Kirby (2013) indicates that prevention is central to the policing of terrorism, and the investigative process therefore revolves around the ability to understand who the terrorists are and how they function within and as a group. He further notes that there are several means of preventing terrorist incidents, which include the arrest or deportation of the offender and target hardening (i.e. increasing the difficulty to execute an act of terrorism through removing facilitating mechanisms, such as funding and personal contacts). In applying this approach to organized crime, Kirby (2013) conveys the importance of first understanding the parts forming the criminal process and then using this information to prevent it from happening by disrupting criminal networks and plans.

Thus, disruption and prevention appear to be key concepts when tackling organized crime. Although prevention focuses on the crime itself and explores methods of removing the opportunity for this to occur, it is disruption that takes action to manage the risks that stem from the social domain (Wright, 2006), that is the offender's network, lifestyle and routine, which are all important for the growth of the organized criminal group. Disruption has been described as a "more flexible, transitory and dynamic tactic that can be used more generally to make the environment hostile for the organized crime" (Kirby, 2013, p. 160), and concentrates predominantly on the offender. Yet, as highlighted, organized criminal groups consist of members with varying seniority and capability; all of whom collectively exhibit a range of legitimate and illegitimate activities. Certain members of the criminal group may be more visible than others, which provides an additional obstacle to overcome. Consider the Beaumont gang for instance, the more established members are likely to be hidden and protected whilst the younger recruits are exposed, trafficking and selling drugs at street-level. These extra layers enhance the complexity of the response required and, consequently, a tailored intervention is warranted that considers offence type(s), offender characteristics and the context within which crimes are being committed (Kirby and Snow, 2016).

According to Bright and colleagues (2017), law enforcement strategies may be able to disrupt and dismantle organized criminal networks by attending to social (i.e. connections between key members in the group) and human capital (i.e. key members with specific attributes or skills that facilitate the group's goals). Strategies that endeavour to remove key members with high social capital aim to fragment the organized network. The removal of members with high human capital, however, targets functioning (e.g. the illicit production of substances; Robins, 2009). Disruption strategies that focus on social and human capital have been found to be more effective than opportunistic law enforcement methods, such as "stop and search" (Bright *et al.*, 2017). It is the latter, nevertheless, that may prove useful for targeting recruits working at street-level.

Interventions that focus on more integral members of an organized criminal group are likely to encounter challenges relating to network characteristics. To overcome these, Duxbury and Haynie (2019) emphasize the importance of recognizing criminal network resilience when developing disruption strategies. They state that organized groups who prioritize security and limit their visibility through minimizing connections are likely to be more robust to disruption than groups who are more efficient, involving highly connected members responsible for relaying tasks and information. It is the security-orientated networks, however, that take longer to recover following disruption due to the smaller pool of eligible replacements (Duxbury and Haynie, 2019). Following disruption, organized criminal networks are likely to reflect on vulnerabilities and reshape their structure to prevent further damage (Morselli, 2009). Interventions should therefore be flexible in their approach whilst also being aligned to the type of criminal network. Intelligence becomes crucial when tailoring such interventions, as does obtaining information from those who have disengaged from involvement in organized crime (Douglas and Smith, 2018).

As noted, knowledge obtained through intelligence-led approaches, can be used to develop and inform disruption strategies. Through intelligence, the NCA for example, is able to make an assessment of threat that can then be used to inform policing strategies more locally (Sergi, 2015). However, this so-called "golden-thread" of policing (Home Office, 2010, p. 23) has received considerable criticism, with law enforcement agencies accused of focusing on what is already known, using recorded and investigated criminal activity to subsequently predict what is not known (Ratcliffe, 2008). There is a demand to move away from this predictive methodology to gathering intelligence that is anticipative and accounts for broader factors, such as environment and type of criminal network, which are central to understanding how organized criminal groups operate (Coyne and Bell, 2011). Reverting back to the onus on the offenders themselves, Verfaillie and Beken (2008) reflect on the importance of detecting rather than targeting, identifying opportunities from the criminal perspective so as to allow for new intelligence to be obtained. Revisiting the Protect and Prevent strands of the UK counter-terrorism strategy may assist with this, extending covert and overt surveillance to also include the monitoring of vulnerable groups who are deemed at risk of being recruited by organized criminal networks (Crocker *et al.*, 2017). Focusing solely on historic information is likely to limit disruption strategies by solely attending to known suspects and old ways of working, neglecting the notion of organized criminal activity as an evolving and resilient construct, and indeed, the harm suffered by communities and businesses through which groups operate (Innes and Sheptycki, 2004).

Intelligence-led disruption strategies place significant emphasis on joint working, where there is an expectation that law enforcement agencies share information to aid the detection of organized crime. However, for this to be effective, Crocker *et al.* (2017) call for clearer guidance on individual roles and responsibilities to avoid confusion or overlap across agencies when collecting information, which has historically proven difficult to implement (Leong, 2007). Rather, there was a preference for an enforcement-orientated approach whereby organized criminals were prosecuted. Whilst this method is still used today, it tends to only be implemented for lower level offences (e.g. Kirby and Snow, 2016), simply due to the estimated number of active offenders being far greater than those facing prosecution at any one time. It has therefore been deemed an inefficient and unsustainable use of police resources, especially as many organized criminals will continue to operate and exploit others whilst in prison.

As such, there has been a shift from prosecution to the reduction of organized crime, with disruption strategies becoming central to this. There are an increasing number of proposals conveying disruption as an effective intervention for tackling organized crime, yet few have received empirical attention (Kirby and Nailer, 2013). Rather, it would appear that such suggestions are based on "gut instinct" or anecdotal evidence. Kirby and Snow (2016), however, sought to systematically analyse organized crime disruption and investigated the manner in which English police forces tackled 15 organized criminal groups, which comprised a total of 99 individuals. One hundred and sixty-one interventions were identified, ranging from one to 29 for each organized criminal group. For analysis purposes, Kirby and Snow (2016) categorized the interventions into five broad themes, which were as follows: (1) policing behaviours; (2) specific investigative activity (e.g. search warrants); (3) the use of the Criminal Justice System (e.g. prosecution of low level offending); (4) the control of assets (e.g. the repossession of property); and (5) activity that controls or modifies the behaviour of the suspect.

In this instance, "policing behaviours" refer to activities that explicitly make suspects aware that they are being targeted. Despite fear of inducing displacement (i.e. crime directed from one target to another, or to a new location, due to the removal of an opportunity for crime or seeking to prevent it; Clarke, 2012), similar deterrence strategies have been adopted in the United States (US) with promising results (e.g. Braga *et al.*, 2018). Legal options for prevention also exist with the creation of preventative orders such as the Slavery and Trafficking Risk Orders (STRO, Pt 2 The Modern Slavery Act 2015) designed to create criminal sanctions based on cumulative evidence and perceived risk. Based on *rational choice theory*, which posits that crime is likely to be prevented when offenders perceive costs to outweigh the benefits (Cornish and Clarke, 1986), focused deterrence strategies adopt a multi-agency approach to communicate incentives and disincentives to targeted gang members (Kennedy, 2008) whilst also enhancing procedural justice and police legitimacy. Explicit messages are conveyed directly to gangs, informing them that any use of violence will be met with a rapid and severe policing response (Braga and Weisburd, 2012). At the same time, an emphasis is also placed on the benefits of non-violent behaviour to encourage a change in offender perception.

This approach alone is unlikely to disrupt organized crime as group members may purposely reduce their criminal activity during active interventions to avoid detection (especially those networks who are conscious of security). Other proactive crime prevention mechanisms are therefore expected to be at play to assist with this process. Yet, the diverse array of disruption techniques highlighted by Kirby and Snow (2016) arguably go some way to tackle organized crime as a heterogeneous construct and block opportunities to sustain illicit activities across contexts, thus increasing the perceived cost of committing crime. It is important at this stage to also recognize that police agencies operating at a local, national or international level have varying levels of resources and, as such, their response to organized crime is determined by both capacity and capability. Identifying the most appropriate disruption strategy would help with resource allocation, but research in this area remains limited due to methodological and ethical concerns, concerns that view the disruption process as intrusive and manipulative, and difficult to evaluate due to a lack of predetermined outcome variables. This section therefore concludes with a recommendation that academics and practitioners work together to consider an alternative means of ethically determining the effectiveness of specific disruption strategies when tackling organized crime.

Conclusion

Organized crime as a theoretical and operational entity is becoming more complex and thus requires a policing response that focuses on organized networks at varying levels and across contexts. There needs to be an emphasis on intelligence-led approaches that predict developments in organized crime rather than relying on known information as a means of detection. Proactively identifying those vulnerable to exploitation may prove valuable in disrupting gang-related enterprises in England and Wales, with a partnership approach between law enforcement and community agencies further strengthening this. A range of disruption strategies have been found to be useful in deterring organized crime, and indeed violence and intimidation, beyond resource-intensive enforcement methods. However, further empirical investigation is required to more effectively align disruption strategies with organized crime and, in doing so, tailoring interventions to account for varying offender characteristics, offence types, and the context within which organized networks are functioning.

References

Albanese, J. S. (2008) Risk assessment in organized crime: Developing a market and product-based model to determine threat levels. *Journal of Contemporary Criminal Justice*, 24, 263–273.

Aronowitz, A. A. (2001) Smuggling and trafficking in human beings: The phenomenon, the markets that drive it and the organisations that promote it. *European Journal on Criminal Policy and Research*, 9(2), 163–195.

Braga, A. A. and Weisburd, D. L. (2012) The effects of focussed deterrence strategies on crime: A systematic review and meta-analysis of the empirical evidence. *Journal of Research in Crime and Delinquency*, 49, 323–358.

Braga, A. A., Weisburd, D. L., and Turchan, B. (2018) Focussed deterrence strategies and crime control: An updated systematic review and meta-analysis of the empirical evidence. *Criminology and Public Policy*, 17, 205–250.

Bright, D., Greenhill, C., Britz, T., Ritter, A., and Morselli, C. (2017) Criminal network vulnerabilities and adaptations. *Global Crime*, 18, 424–441.

Clarke, R. V. (2012) Opportunity makes the thief. Really? And so what? *Crime Science*, 1, 1–9.

Cornish, D. B. and Clarke, R. V. (1986) *The Reasoning Criminal: Rational Choice Perspectives on Offending*. New York: Springer.

Coyne, J. W. and Bell, P. (2011) The role of strategic intelligence in anticipating transnational organised crime: A literary review. *International Journal of Law, Crime and Justice*, 39, 60–78.

Crocker, R., Webb, S., Skidmore, M., Gill, M., and Graham, J. (2017) *The Impact of Organised Crime in Local Communities*. Surrey: Police Federation of England and Wales.

Dean, G., Fahsing, I., and Gottschalk, P. (2010) *Organised Crime: Policing Illegal Business Entrepreneurialism*. Oxford: Oxford University Press.

Decker, S. H. and Curry, G. D. (2000) Responding to gangs: Comparing gang member, police and task force perspectives. *Journal of Criminal Justice*, 28, 129–137.

Densley, J. and Harding, S. (2018) *Gangs in Europe*. Oxford: Oxford Research Encyclopaedia of Criminology and Criminal Justice.

Douglas, K. and Smith, R. G. (2018) Disengagement from involvement in organised crime: Processes and risks. *Trends and Issues in Crime and Criminal Justice*, (542), 1–15.

Duxbury, S. W. and Haynie, D. L. (2019) Criminal network security: An agent-based approach to evaluating network resilience. *Criminology*, 57, 314–342.

Elvins, M. (2003) Europe's response to transnational organised crime. In A. Edwards and P. Gill (eds), *Transnational Organised Crime: Perspectives on Global Security*. London: Routledge, pp. 28–41.

European Union (1998) *Article 1 of the Joint Action of the Justice and Home Affairs Council to Create a Criminal Offence to Participate in a Criminal Organisation*. Brussels: European Union, Council of Justice and Home Affairs Ministers.

Finckenauer, J. O. (2005) Problems of definition: What is organised crime? *Trends in Organized Crime*, 8, 63–83.

FitzGerald, S. A. (2012) Vulnerable bodies, vulnerable borders: Extraterritoriality and human trafficking. *Feminist Legal Studies*, 20(3), 227–244.

Francis, B., Humphreys, L., Kirby, S., and Soothill, K. (2013) *Understanding Criminal Careers in Organised Crime*. Crime Research and Analysis, 64. London: Home Office.

Galeotti, M. (2005) *Global Crime Today: The Changing Face of Organised Crime*. London: Routledge.

Hagan, F. E. (2006) "Organized Crime" and "organized crime": Indeterminate problems of definition. *Trends in Organized crime*, 9, 127–137.

Hales, G. and Hobbs, D. (2010) Drug markets in the community: A London borough case study. *Trends in Organized Crime*, 13, 13–30.

Hauck, P. and Peterke, S. (2010) Organized crime and gang violence in national and international law. *International Review of the Red Cross*, 92, 407–436.

Hesketh, R. F. and Robinson, G. (2019) Grafting: "The boyz" just doing business? Deviant entrepreneurship in street gangs. *Safer Communities*, 18, 54–63.

Hobbs, D. (2013) *Lush Life: Constructing Organised Crime in the UK*. Oxford: Oxford University Press.

Home Office (2010) *Policing in the 21st Century: Reconnecting Police and the People*. London: The Stationary Office.

Home Office (2014) *Serious and Organised Crime Local Profiles: A Guide*. London: The Stationary Office.

Innes, M. and Sheptycki, J. W. E. (2004) From detection to disruption: Intelligence and the changing logic of police crime control in the United Kingdom. *Interpersonal Criminal Justice Review*, 14, 1–24.

Kennedy, D. M. (2008) *Deterrence and Crime Prevention: Reconsidering the Prospect of Sanction*. London: Routledge.

Kirby, S. (2013) *Effective Policing? Implementation in Theory and Practice*. London: Palgrave Macmillan.

Kirby, S., Francis, B., Humphreys, L., and Soothill, K. (2016) Using the UK general offender database as a means to measure and analyse organized crime. *Policing: An International Journal of Police Strategies and Management*, 39, 78–94.

Kirby, S., McManus, M., and Boulton, L. (2018) Examining the demographic profile and attitudes of citizens, in areas where organized crime groups proliferate. *Trends in Organized Crime*, 21, 172–188.

Kirby, S. and Nailer, L. (2013) Reducing the offending of a UK organized crime group using an opportunity reducing framework: A three year case study. *Trends in Organized Crime*, 16, 397–412.

Kirby, S. and Snow, N. (2016) Praxis and the disruption of organized crime groups. *Trends in Organized Crime*, 19, 111–124.

Klein, M., Maxson, C., and Cunningham, L. (1991) "Crack", street gangs and violence. *Criminology*, 31, 623–650.

Leong, A. V. M. (2007) *The Disruption of International Organised Crime: An Analysis of Legal and Non-legal Strategies*. Hampshire: Ashgate Publishing.

Levi, M. (2003) The organization of serious crimes. In M. Maguire, R. Morgan, and R. Reiner (eds), *The Oxford Handbook of Criminology*. Oxford: Oxford University Press, pp. 878–913.

Longo, F. (2010) Discoursing organized crime: Towards a two-level analysis. In F. Allum, F. Longo, D. Irrera, and P. A. Kostakos (eds), *Defining and Defying Organised Crime: Discourse, Perceptions and Reality*. Abingdon: Routledge, pp. 15–28.

Lupton, R., Wilson, A., May, T., Warburton, H., and Turnbull, P. J. (2002) *A Rock and a Hard Place: Drug Markets in Deprived Neighbourhoods*. London: Home Office.

Mcillwain, J. S. (1999) Organized crime: A social network approach. *Crime, Law and Social Change*, 32, 301–323.

Morselli, C. (2009) *Inside Criminal Networks*. New York: Springer.

National Crime Agency (2015) *National Strategic Assessment of Serious and Organised Crime 2015*. London: NCA.

Paoli, L. (2002) The paradoxes of organised crime. *Crime, Law and Social Change*, 37, 51–97.

Pitts, J. (2019) The evolution of the English street gang. *Safer Communities*, 18, 64–78.

Ratcliffe, J. H. (2008) *Intelligence-led Policing*. Oxfordshire, Willan Publishing.

Ratcliffe, J. H. (2016) Central American police perception of street gang characteristics. *Policing and Society*, 26, 291–311.

Robins, G. (2009) Understanding individual behaviors within covert networks: The interplay of individual qualities, psychological predispositions, and network effects. *Trends in Organized Crime*, 12, 166–187.

Sergi, A. (2015) Divergent mind-sets, convergent policies: Policing models against organized crime in Italy and in England with international frameworks. *European Journal of Criminology*, 12, 658–680.

Sergi, A. (2016) National security vs criminal law: Perspectives, doubts and concerns on the criminalisation of organised crime in England and Wales. *European Journal on Criminal Policy and Research*, 22, 713–729.

Smith, D. C. (1975) *The Mafia Mystique*. New York: Basic Books.

Smith, D. C. (1980) Paragons, pariahs and pirates: A spectrum-based theory of enterprise. *Crime and Delinquency*, 26, 358–386.

Stelfox, P. (1998) Policing lower levels of organised crime in England and Wales. *The Howard Journal*, 37, 393–406.

United Nations Office on Drugs and Crime (2004) *Article 2: United Nations Convention against Transnational Organized Crime*. New York: United Nations.

Verfaillie, K. and Beken, T. (2008) Proactive policing and the assessment of organised crime. *Policing: An International Journal of Police Strategies and Management*, 31, 534–552.

Wilson, W. J. (2012) *The Truly Disadvantaged: The Inner City, the Underclass, and Public Policy* (2nd edn). Chicago: Chicago University Press.

Wilson, J. W. and Kelling, G. L. (1982) Broken windows: The police and neighbourhood safety. *Atlantic Monthly*, 249, 29–38.

Woodiwiss, M. and Hobbs, D. (2009) Organized evil and the Atlantic alliance: Moral panics and the rhetoric of organized crime policing in America and Britain. *British Journal of Criminology*, 49, 106–128.

Wright, A. (2006) *Organised Crime*. Abingdon: Willan.

Wright, A. (2013) *Organised Crime*. Abingdon: Willan.

Zubrzycki, W. (2015) Similarities and differences between organized crime and terrorism. *International Security*, 7, 53–70.

PART IV

Gang and multiple offender groups

22

DISTINGUISHING BETWEEN AGGRESSION IN GROUPS AND IN GANGS

Are gangs always violent?

Matthew Valasik and Shannon E. Reid

Introduction

Conflict is a principal driver for sustaining gang life. The extant research on street gangs has regularly shown a strong, positive relationship between gangs and violence, existing across places and over time (Howell and Griffiths, 2018; Papachristos, 2013; Pyrooz *et al.*, 2016; Valasik *et al.*, 2017). Starting with Thrasher's (1927) foundational work in Chicago, the last century's research has revealed that street gangs thrive in areas where social discord, perceived or real, between groups is present (Howell, 2015; Howell and Griffiths, 2018; Papachristos, 2009; Taniguchi *et al.*, 2011). Two vital ingredients for the establishment and preservation of street gangs are: the threat of violence and actual conflict. Being a victim of violence, or the fear of being a victim of violence, facilitates the group bonds, promotes solidarity, and increases cohesion among members (Decker *et al.*, 2014; Hagan, 1993; Hennigan and Spanovic, 2012; Pyrooz *et al.*, 2013; Wood, 2014). For example, the threat of being attacked by members of a rival group encourages at-risk youth to join a street gang in their community, strengthens solidarity among gang members, and provides an outlet for members to engage in gang violence (Hughes and Short, 2014; Klein and Crawford, 1967; Melde and Esbensen, 2011; Papachristos, 2009; Short and Strodtbeck, 1965). Additionally, there is a myth-making quality to gang-related violence as incidents are told, retold and embellished, with each telling increasing a gang's street reputation/status and strengthening the group's identity, while also having the activities of the group be exaggerated by the press or on social media (Patton *et al.*, 2019; Esbensen *et al.*, 2001; Felson, 2006; Gravel *et al.*, 2018; Howell and Griffiths, 2018). The process of socializing new members into a gang is facilitated by experiences with violence that are shared by the group, allowing for the gang's mythology to be integrated into these individuals' identities (Decker, 1996; Hennigan and Spanovic, 2012). Over time, as more experiences are shared within the gang, members embrace and adhere more to the group's mores, norms, and behaviours encouraging violence as a means of resolving conflict (Anderson, 1999; Decker, 1996; Klein, 1995a; Short and Strodtbeck, 1965). Studies routinely find that when compared with non-gang members, including other delinquent groups, gang members have a greater likelihood of participating in violent and or/criminal acts, engage in intergroup violence, carry and possess a firearm or weapon, and be at an increased risk of violent victimization (Battin *et al.*, 1998; Decker, 1996; Melde and Esbensen, 2013; Taylor *et al.*, 2007; Thornberry et al., 2003; Wu and Pyrooz, 2016).

This chapter investigates the complexities of group violence, focusing specifically on the importance of violence in the subculture of street gangs (e.g. social identity). The chapter begins by unpacking what gang-related violence involves. The risk/protective factors that contribute to an individual participating in gang-related violence or being violently victimized are then discussed. This leads into a discussion about gang members' exposure to being a victim of violence, with attention to gender differences. Then, the two unique features, social and spatial dependence, which delineate gang-related violence from non-gang violence are discussed. The chapter ends by comparing conventional street gangs to the emerging phenomenon of Alt-Right gangs (e.g. racist skinheads, Proud Boys) and how their appropriation of violence is analogous to conventional street gangs (see Reid and Valasik, 2018a; 2020; Valasik and Reid, 2018a; 2019).

What is gang-related violence?

Despite recent declines in overall violence, gang-related violence accounts for a substantial amount of the overall violence in large metropolitan areas (Papachristos, 2014; Petersen, 2016). For instance, gang-related homicides account for 30 to 50 per cent of lethal violence in urban centres (Howell *et al.*, 2011; Howell and Griffiths, 2018). However, tension still exists about how to classify criminal acts as being gang-related (see Esbensen *et al.* 2001; Klein and Maxson 2006; Maxson, 1999; Maxson and Klein, 1990; 1996; Rosenfeld *et al.*, 1999). Gang-related crimes have traditionally been described as being either motive- or member-based incidents. A criminal act of violence that directly relates to gang-related activities (e.g. recruitment, retaliation, territoriality, etc.) satisfies the motive-based definition (Klein and Maxson, 1989; Maxson, 1999; Maxson *et al.*, 1985; Maxson and Klein, 1990; 1996; 2002; Rosenfeld *et al.*, 1999). Conversely, an act of violence where any participant, suspect or victim, is associated with a gang is considered to be a gang-related crime under the affiliated- or member-based definition (Klein and Maxson, 1989; Maxson, 1998; Maxson et al., 1985; Maxson and Klein, 1990; 1996; Rosenfeld *et al.*, 1999). Using a member-based definition errs on the side of inclusion of criminal incidents that could be attributed to a motive (e.g. domestic dispute) that is unrelated to an individual's status as a gang member, "after all, gang members can and do act of their own accord" (Papachristos, 2009, p. 86). In contrast, utilizing a motive-based definition samples "too heavily on the dependent variable by capturing only those cases in which a group motive was determined" (Papachristos, 2009, p. 86). Furthermore, if an act of gang violence satisfies the motive-based definition then it would also meet the requirements of the member-based definition, representing only a subsample of gang-related violence. Relying on only a subsample of gang-related violence has the potential to ignore or exclude valuable information (see Pyrooz, 2012). Additionally, previous studies find that regardless of employing either a motive- or member-based definition to gang violence, the characteristics (e.g. offender, victim, location) in a gang-related homicide are significantly different than a non-gang incident, and comparison between motive- or member-based definitions are essentially identical (Maxson and Klein, 1996). Beyond the theoretical importance of how gang violence is defined by academia, there are also practical implications to how police agencies and policymakers understand and react to gang-related violence within any given jurisdiction (Rosenfeld *et al.*, 1999).

Similarly, law enforcement classifies gang-related violence by definitions that are analogous to those just discussed. Under the "Chicago definition", an incident is considered to be gang-related only if the motivation driving the act is beneficial to the gang as a group (e.g. recruitment, retaliation, or territoriality). As such, the "Chicago definition" is restrictive since an incident must satisfy the criteria of being dependent upon the group concerns of the gang for that incident to be considered a gang-related crime (Decker and Curry, 2002). Conversely, under the "Los Angeles definition" an incident is defined as a gang-related offence if either the victim or suspect is an actively affiliated member (see Maxson *et al.*, 1985; Valasik *et al.*, 2016) of a street gang, or if the context of a criminal act is in line with gang activity (Klein and Maxson, 2006). The definition employed by a law enforcement agency will impact the amount of gang-related crime and violence recorded within a jurisdiction. For example, Maxson and Klein (1990) find that under the "Chicago definition" there is half as much gang-related violence compared with classifying incidents based upon the "Los Angeles definition". Thus, it is necessary to consider such a disparity when deciding the manner in which to address gang-related violence within a municipality (Esbensen *et al.*, 2001).

In the United States, there is a lack of consensus on the definition of gang violence across law enforcement agencies. Due to the lack of a uniform definition, each jurisdiction (of which there are over 18,000 in the US) may be counting gang violence in a different manner, making comparisons or even an accurate count of gang violence impossible (Decker and Pyrooz, 2010; Rosenfeld *et al.*, 1999). Additionally, the lack of definitional consensus between academics, law enforcement, and policymakers on what is considered an act of gang-related violence makes it difficult to develop and adhere to meaningful public policies (Decker and Pyrooz, 2010; Esbensen *et al.*, 2001; Klein and Maxson, 2006). For example, how and which resources are allocated to gang-related violence within a municipality will look very different based upon the amount estimated. An underestimate of gang-related violence would leave communities vulnerable to violence, while an overestimate of gang-related violence results in the wasting of valuable resources, which is not trivial for jurisdictions with limited finances. Lastly, definitional vagueness also contributes to the publics' fear of gangs and gang-related violence through media depictions and how police agencies report gang-related crimes (Blasko *et al.*, 2015; Esbensen *et al.* 2001; Lane, 2002; Lane and Meeker, 2003).

Gang members' risk factors

Another principal theme investigated by gang researchers is understanding why individuals decide to join a gang. Prior studies have revealed that two main elements drive individuals towards joining a gang. Circumstances that propel an individual towards gang life are termed push risk factors. Motivations which attract an individual into becoming a gang member are referred to as pull risk factors. Such risk factors that generally pull an individual into becoming a gang member include the need to fill a void, gain respect, and entertainment (Gibson *et al.*, 2012; Klein and Maxson, 2006; Moore, 1991; Sutton, 2017). Male gang members are customarily seeking excitement and adventure, while female members are searching for a familial group that is emotionally more satisfying and meaningful than what is provided by their own kin (Klein and Maxson, 2006; Moore, 1991). It is not uncommon for there to be domestic discord (e.g. violence or abuse) in gang members' home life, or to reside in a non-traditional household (e.g. female-headed household) (Hill *et al.*, 1999; Thornberry *et al.*, 2003). Push factors that are a recurring theme in the extant literature that press individuals into gang life are searching for a shared social identity (Decker, 1996; Hennigan and Spanovic, 2012), residing in an economically depressed community (Curry and Spergel, 1988; Hill *et al.*, 1999; Thornberry *et al.*, 2003) and strong financial incentives (Densley, 2013; Padilla, 1992; Stephenson, 2015). Probably the most important push risk factor that propels individuals into a becoming a gang member is the desire to feel safe and be protected from rival groups or bullies in the local neighbourhood or from abusive family members (Hill *et al.*, 1999; Short and Strodtbeck, 1965).

The existing gang literature has revealed that individuals associated with a gang are more likely to engage in criminal activities (Katz *et al.*, 2011; Pyrooz *et al.* 2016). Additionally, when compared with non-gang members, gang-related crimes have a great likelihood of being more serious in nature (Decker *et al.*, 2008). These patterns are quite robust with multiple studies using various methodological approaches revealing analogous findings. The majority of gang research that focuses on violence tends to emphasize gang members' role as the purveyor of violence, ignoring the reality that gang members are also victims of violence. While studies consistently reveal that gang members are more likely to participate in violent criminal acts, gang members are also at significantly greater risk of experiencing violent victimization (Wu and Pyrooz, 2016). For example, in any given year, gang-related homicides account for 13 per cent of total homicides in the United States. In large urban areas (i.e. population greater than 200,000) they account for 20 per cent (Howell and Griffiths 2018). Even though gang researchers have clearly ascertained that non-gang members have lower rates of victimization than gang members, our knowledge of the social processes that increase gang members' vulnerability of becoming a victim of violence remain an understudied domain in gang research. One exception is the work of Wu and Pyrooz (2016), which reveals that becoming a gang member (i.e. the selection model) and actively associating with gang members (i.e. facilitation model) are both (i.e. enhancement model) associated with gang members experiencing victimization at greater frequencies. While, "gang membership increases the victimization beyond sources of selection" it is important to keep in mind that gang members participating in acts of delinquency also make it more likely for that gang member to be a victim (Wu and Pyrooz, 2016, p. 548).

Furthermore, as gang members abide by the norms of the gang, particularly to the acceptance and use of violence, antagonistic situations where minor disrespect is presented (e.g. insults, derogatory stares, etc.) may easily escalate into serious violence (Decker, 1996). As violence is used as the default reaction in response to symbolic threats, maintaining one's status and reputation reinforces these acts as "norms of reciprocity" (Papachristos 2009, p. 76). In fact, upon analysing gang-related homicides in the city of Los Angeles, Klein and Maxson (1989, p. 224) found that these "norms of reciprocity" were so central to gang life that gang-related violence was almost three times more likely to be driven by fear of retaliation than any other type of homicide. As violence between rival street gangs becomes intergenerational, younger members are promptly supplied with an already established adversary to attack. With group solidarity being a fundamental characteristic connected to gang-related violence, street gangs follow a principle of collective responsibility in which any sole member is a representative of the entire group (see Densley, 2013). Such that, if one gang member is attacked by a rival gang member it is treated as if the entire gang is being assaulted by the entire rival gang. Thus, gang members have greater levels of entitativity and tend to view any individual residing within a rival gang's territory as being associated with that rival gang, and viewed as a potential target for retaliatory violence (see Vasquez *et al.* 2015). It is not surprising then that retaliatory gang-related violence tends to spill over into the non-gang population. Leovy (2015, p. 206) observes this exact phenomenon in South Central Los Angeles stating that "a black assailant looking to kill a gang rival is looking before anything else, for another black male … a presumed combatant, conscripted into a dismal existence 'outside the law' whether he wanted to be or not."

Compared with non-gang individuals, gang members increased involvement in criminal and delinquent behaviours would produce lifestyle differences that could explain a gang member's greater risk of being a victim of violence (Gover *et al.*, 2009; Peterson *et al.*, 2004; Taylor *et al.*, 2007; 2008). Additionally, gang studies find that an overlap prevails between both gang membership and criminal offending and criminal offending and victimization (Pyrooz *et al.*, 2016; Taylor *et al.*, 2007; 2008). Through the transitive property, this suggests that gang membership should be associated in a strong and positive direction with being violently victimized. In addition to the elements associated with a subculture of violence, there are other important risk factors that make gang members more vulnerable to being victimized. These include characteristics at the individual-, family- and school-level (Craig *et al.*, 2002; Hill *et al.*, 1999; Taylor *et al.* 2007; 2008). For instance, at the individual-level, risk factors include the level of self-control or demographic measures (e.g. gender, age, etc.) (see Sutton, 2017). At the family-level, characteristics like the level of attachment an individual has to his parents or the degree of parental monitoring are impactful (Taylor *et al.*, 2007; 2008; Wu and Pyrooz, 2016). Lastly, at the school-level, measures could include items such as commitment to school, level of academic achievement, or school atmosphere (Craig *et al.*, 2002; Sutton, 2017; Taylor *et al.*, 2007).

Risk of victimization

Despite aggravating risk factors being present, the fact that gang members are associating with a gang may make them a more suitable target for victimization (Gover *et al.*, 2009; Peterson *et al.*, 2004; Taylor *et al.*, 2007). Prior studies have highlighted that contextual characteristics may increase the likelihood of gang member violent victimization. For example, loitering in places where there is greater accessibility to alcohol and drugs significantly amplifies the propensity of gang member being victimized (Taylor *et al.*, 2007). Being involved in violent and criminal acts also increases a gang member's vulnerability of being a victim of violence as there are a greater number of situations where exposure to a motivated offender (i.e. a rival gang member) is exacerbated and the number of capable guardians is diminished (Taylor *et al.*, 2007; 2008; Wu and Pyrooz, 2015). There is also a greater likelihood that gang members abstain from contacting law enforcement agencies about being the victim of crime so as to not make their gang status known or attract attention to illegal activities they are involved in; either of which could increase their risk of being victimized (Barnes *et al.*, 2012). Additionally, the ongoing cycle of retaliatory violence between rival gang members only fosters the belief that violence is a regular part of everyday gang life (Katz *et al.*, 2011; Papachristos, 2009).

Gang members, however, may actually have greater vulnerability to being violently victimized by their fellow gang members than from rivals. For instance, initiations (i.e. being "jumped in" to the gang) are common occurrences where gang recruits endure violent victimization from veteran members (Decker and Van Winkle, 1996; Short and Strodtbeck, 1965; Klein and Maxson, 2006; Vigil, 2003). Gang members are also at risk of violent victimization if they decide to leave their group (Decker, 1996; Decker and Van Winkle, 1996; Vigil, 2003). Gang members may also use violence to strengthen norms in the gang or to enforce the group's rules (Decker, 1996; Taylor *et al.*, 2007). Unfortunately, a common reason that motivates many individuals to join a gang is the desire for protection and to achieve a sense of safety in their local neighbourhood (Hill *et al.*, 1999; Katz *et al.*, 2011; Klein and Maxson, 2006; Short and Strodtbeck, 1965).

Violent victimization within the gang is not equally distributed across men and women. Studies have revealed that significant differences exist in both the type of victimization and an individual's vulnerability to being victimized based on the gender of the gang member (Miller, 1998; Sutton, 2017). Research discerns that prior to becoming a gang member, female recruits endure excessive amounts of victimization (Bell, 2009; Fleisher and Krienert, 2004; Moore, 1991; Sutton, 2017). For instance, it is common for parents or guardians of female members to have problems with substance abuse (Peterson and Howell, 2013; Sutton, 2017). Additionally, female gang members are also more likely to experience abuse in their home, both sexual and physical, either from older male family members or acquaintances (Fleisher, 1998; Hunt and

Joe-Laidler, 2001; Miller, 1998, 2001; Moore and Hagedorn, 2001; Schalet *et al.*, 2003; Sutton, 2017). Besides residing in unstable homes, many female gang members live in communities that have greater levels of socio-economic deprivation and community isolation, which act as a push risk factor that encourages them to join a gang (Gibson *et al.*, 2012; Sutton, 2017). While female recruits seek out gangs to serve as a refuge, protecting them from being victimized by loved ones or to avoid family pressures, research clearly reveals that such safety is not to be found (Gibson *et al.*, 2012; Sutton 2017). In fact, female gang members are even more vulnerable to being victims of violence and, in particular, sexual abuse, assault and rape by male fellow gang members (Gibson *et al.*, 2012; Sutton, 2017).

The predominantly male-orientation of gangs makes them hypermasculine groups (Chesney-Lind *et al.*, 1996; Howell and Griffiths, 2018; Swart, 1991). Not surprisingly, the prevalence of unequal gender norms within a gang results in a power imbalance between a gang's female and male members (Bjerregaard and Smith, 1993; Howell and Griffiths, 2018; Hayward and Honegger, 2014; Peterson *et al.*, 2004). For instance, in gangs where males are in greater numbers, female gang members are then relegated to subservient roles and treated as inferiors. Furthermore, within these gangs, female members are thought of as nothing more than objects to be sexually exploited (Gibson *et al.*, 2012; Sutton, 2017; Ulloa *et al.*, 2012). As such, a female initiate in a predominantly male gang is more likely to be sexually assaulted or be required to have sex with numerous male members (Gibson *et al.*, 2012; Gover *et al.*, 2009; Hayward and Honegger, 2014). Additionally, these female members are also significantly more likely to endure intimate partner violence and sexual assault (Gibson *et al.*, 2012; Gover *et al.*, 2009).

Gang studies have clearly indicated that gender differences exist in not only the types of victimization experienced by male and female members but also their levels of vulnerability to victimization. While the primary risk factor influencing the violent victimization of male gang members is their exposure to neighbourhood violence, female gang members are most likely to be victimized by their fellow male gang members, including their significant others (Minnis *et al.*, 2008; Nydegger *et al.*, 2017; Sutton, 2017; Ulloa *et al.*, 2012). Given that the risk factors and forms of victimization are different for females than for males, the implementation of gender-specific prevention and intervention programmes is necessary (Howell and Griffiths, 2018). Additionally, as the proportion of female members in gangs continues to increase, balancing out a more equitable gender ratio, the types of victimization that female members will endure is likely to shift (see Howell and Griffiths, 2018). As such, further research is necessary to reveal how changing patterns in gang membership are impacting patterns of violent victimization.

The social and spatial patterns of gang violence

A core theme examined by gang researchers, and more broadly the field of criminology, is how space influences the geographic distribution of violence in an area. Since, the time of Thrasher's (1927) influential work nearly a century ago, gang researchers have remained interested in understanding the relationship between gangs and space (see Valasik and Tita, 2018). Even though space is a crucial component to examine gang-related violence (e.g. territoriality, retaliation, etc.), it was not until Geographic Information Software (GIS) emerged in the early 1990s that practitioners, researchers and policymakers could expediently create maps and analyse the spatial relationship between the distribution of crime/violence and the characteristics of a neighbourhood, including the territories of street gangs (Anselin *et al.*, 2000; Block, 2000). Coincidently, at the same time that GIS software was advancing, many urban centres throughout the United States were experiencing an epidemic of lethal violence. In 1991, the annual number of homicides peaked to 24,700 in the United States. Additionally, street gangs at this time began to diffuse both within "chronic" gang cities and to "emergent" gang cities across the United States (Howell *et al.*, 2011; Howell and Griffiths, 2018; Spergel and Curry, 1993). As GIS improved, it allowed for researchers to analyse the role that street gangs play on the diffusion of violence, homicide in particular (Cohen and Tita, 1999; Rosenfeld *et al.*, 1999; Morenoff and Sampson, 1997; Tita and Cohen, 2004). Utilizing spatial analytical techniques to examine gang-related violence is particularly germane given the fact that gangs have an orientation towards space (i.e. a claimed territory) and the retaliatory nature of gang violence (see Papachristos *et al.*, 2013; Tita and Radil, 2011; Valasik and Tita, 2018).

The vast majority of research that exists on gang-related homicide examines the phenomenon at the micro-level, emphasizing the differences between gang-related and nongang-related incidents (e.g. Curry and Spergel, 1988; Klein and Maxson, 1989; Maxson, 1998; Maxson *et al.*, 1985; Maxson and Klein, 1990; 1996; Rosenfeld *et al.*, 1999). These studies greatly improved the field of criminology's knowledge base about the characteristics (i.e. victim, suspect and incident setting) that distinguish gang homicides from non-gang homicides. Furthermore, the findings from this avenue of research have aided policymakers with a more generalized understanding about the dynamics of a gang-related homicide. Gang-related homicides are localized phenomenon that are concentrated in specific communities, leading researchers to focus their efforts on the macro-level characteristics that are associated with these acts of lethal violence. For instance, studies have investigated the relationship between gang-related homicide and the city- (Pyrooz, 2012) and neighbourhood-level (Curry and Spergel, 1988; Rosenfeld *et al.*, 1999; Valasik *et al.*, 2017) correlates (e.g. unemployment, poverty, youth population, etc.). For decades, the fields of criminology and sociology have stressed that to better understand the patterns of gang-related violence it is important that the spatial concentration of individual, group and community characteristics be accounted for in research (Valasik and Tita, 2018). In their argument, Curry and Spergel (1988) suggest that neighbourhoods with greater levels of residential mobility and lower levels of social control had an increased likelihood of sustaining a gang-related homicide, whereas economically depressed areas endured a greater risk of gang-related crime and delinquency (Curry and Spergel, 1988). The findings from Curry and Spergel's (1988) study emphasize just how distinctive gang-related homicides are from other types of violence, along with challenging traditional theories related to poverty and social disorganization (see Bursik and Grasmick, 1993; Short and Strodtbeck, 1965). For instance, Valasik *et al.* (2017) reveal that gang-related homicides actually remain affixed to economically depressed neighbourhoods, not just for a few years, but are actually geographically concentrated in these communities for decades. Conversely, non-gang homicides seem to be less embedded in a neighbourhood's social problems, while also being without the social (i.e. rivalries) and spatial (i.e. turf) structure to generate any significant geographic patterning (Valasik *et al.*, 2017).

Yet, trends in gang-related crime and violence observed at the city-level (e.g. Pyrooz, 2012) may obscure patterns that may deviate at the neighbourhood-level (Densley, 2013; Klein, 1995b). Gang scholars have suggested using a more meaningful ecological areal unit, smaller than the neighbourhood (i.e. census tract), when analysing gang-related activities due to the fact that street gangs are not active in every part of their claimed turf and regularly limit their activities and loitering to sub-neighbourhood locales, termed "set spaces" (Tita *et al.*, 2005, p. 273) (see also Klein, 1995a; Taniguchi *et al.*, 2011; Valasik, 2018). Furthermore, Valasik and Tita (2018) warn that it is important to control for gang presence in an area, not only to be able to understand where gang-related violence clusters in space, but also to begin to unpack why it transpires and diffuses across space. Many criminological studies cite the existence of street gangs in a neighbourhood to explain clustering of gang-related violence in certain communities, but they fail to explicitly measure the presence of street gangs (see exceptions Brantingham *et al.*, 2012; Grannis, 2009; Huebner *et al.*, 2016; Katz and Schnebly, 2011; Valasik, 2018). Gang research employing Risk Terrain Modeling (RTM) has revealed that the places most vulnerable to gang-related homicides have a concentration of gang set space locations (i.e. hangouts) and local gang members' residences (Valasik, 2018). Both types of places are well known spaces which gang members regularly inhabit. Places most at risk of experiencing gang-related assault have residential concentrations of local gang members but are also in proximity to Metro rail stops (e.g. train/subway stops) and places where gang members have been observed loitering by police (Valasik, 2018). These spaces act as "activity hubs" where rival gang members are more likely to come into contact with each other and where a dispute can escalate into an altercation.

Clearly, as highlighted here, the existing gang literature shows that an important predictor of gang-related violence is geography. For example, findings from Papachristos *et al.* (2013) indicate that rival street gangs that have claimed turfs that share a common boundary are more vulnerable to experiencing intergang conflicts and violence. Yet, social distance is also an important contributing factor (Papachristos *et al.*, 2013; Radil *et al.*, 2010; Tita and Greenbaum, 2009), such that rival street gangs, without spatially adjacent turfs, also have a greater likelihood of enduring subsequent acts of gang-related violence (Papachristos *et al.*, 2013). Thus, "the lives of gang members are woven into the larger social fabric of the neighbourhoods, social networks, families, and friends" (Papachristos *et al.* 2015, p. 627). Gang members are entangled within their local communities both socially and spatially. Furthermore, gang-related violence does not remain contained solely within a street gang's spatial boundaries of their claimed turf, but is enmeshed in gang members' social connections. Both spatial and social proximity are important to understand the patterns and dynamics of gang-related violence (Brantingham *et al.*, 2012; Papachristos, 2009; Papachristos *et al.*, 2013; 2015). The interactive influence of reciprocity and spatial adjacency actually amplifies intergang conflict and violence with combining social exchanges and geographic proximity (Papachristos *et al.*, 2013). Therefore, it is important to incorporate both the spatial and social features of street gangs and their membership fully to understand the patterns and trends associated with gang-related violence. More and more gang researchers are incorporating the relationships between social spaces and physical places to better predict where gang-related violence is most likely to occur (see Valasik, 2018).

Gangs compared to Alt-Right groups

Over the course of the last few years a wave of identity politics and culture wars have emerged in the United States, and throughout much of Europe. Scholars and policymakers have grown concerned that these social movements are radicalizing youth not only domestically, but also internationally (Dandurand, 2014; Decker and Pyrooz, 2011, 2015; Pyrooz *et al.*, 2018; Valasik and Phillips, 2017). Of particular concern has been an upsurge in the public presence of the far-right. The recent manifestation of the "Alt-Right", a moniker originally coined by Richard Spencer in 2008, is of particular concern (see Hawley, 2017; 2019; Lyons, 2018; Main, 2018; Neiwert, 2017, Waring, 2018; 2019; Wendling, 2018; Winter, 2019). The Alt-Right portray themselves as a leaderless, loosely organized group of young, white identitists in a "fun movement, one using Internet jargon familiar to tech-savvy millennials" that tries to alter the political landscape (Hawley, 2017, p. 20). While originally emerging from the digital realms of the internet and social media, the Alt-Right has since then manifested in the real world. Through "free speech" rallies and demonstrations – like those documented in Charlottesville, VA, Berkeley, CA and Portland, OR, crowds of young white males gather together with other white nationalists/white supremacists to protest against some perceived slight. The results of these protests have regularly resulted in hate-related crimes, violence, and even murder (ProPublica, 2018; VICE news, 2017). Even with this growing visibility and overt use of violence by Alt-Right groups, there has been a tendency by scholars and local law enforcement to treat this phenomenon as just anomalous individuals or some form of radical youth subculture (see Curry *et al.*, 2014; Etter, 1999; Hamm, 1993; Reitman, 2018). Yet a substantial subset of the Alt-Right are members of delinquent, street-oriented youth groups which include various racist skinheads (e.g. 211 Bootboys, B49, etc.), Proud Boys, Rise Above Movement (R.A.M.) and Atomwaffen Division (Aljezeera, 2018; Bromwich, 2018; DeCook, 2018; Lopez, 2017; Reid and Valasik, 2018b; 2020; Roose and Winston, 2018; Thompson *et al.*, 2017; 2018; Valasik and Reid, 2018a; Wood, 2017). It is these types of Alt-Right groups that Reid and Valasik (2020) term as "Alt-Right gangs" (see also Valasik and Reid, 2018b). A modification of the traditional Eurogang definition, which "has become widely adopted and appears regularly in publications" is one of the most prevalent modern definitions used to evaluate membership in a street gang (Maxson and Esbensen, 2016, p. 7). As such, an Alt-Right gang is defined by Reid and Valasik (2020) as

> A durable, public-oriented group (both digitally and physically) whose adoption of signs and symbols of the white power movement and involvement in illegal activity is part of its group identity.

Under this definition, the contention that white power youth groups, including street gangs (e.g. Public Enemy Number One [PEN1], Nazi Low Riders) and other troublesome youth groups (e.g. racist skinheads), would not qualify as an Alt-Right gang is removed (see also Klein, 1996; 2001; 2009; Klein and Maxson, 2006; Pyrooz et al., 2018; Reid and Valasik, 2018a; 2020; Simi, 2006; Simi *et al.*, 2008; Valasik and Reid, 2018b; 2019).

Risk factors

The criminological field's current knowledge base about the risk factors that influence Alt-Right gang membership is currently limited, similar to the challenges faced by early gang research. This includes not having consistent definitions, secluded populations, limits with official data, and an overreliance on initial studies (e.g. Hamm, 1993; Klein, 1995a), which have obstructed progress on examining these Alt-Right youth and limited the ability to establish effective interventions to counter these groups. While there is an overall lack in the generalizable push and pull factors driving Alt-Right gang membership, many of the themes that have emerged are based upon qualitative studies (ADL, 1995; Baron, 1997; Klein, 2009; Shashkin, 2008; Simi, Smith and Reeser, 2008).

For push risk factors, youth involved in racist skinheads typically ranges from adolescence into early adulthood (i.e., 12–25 years of age) (see ADL, 1995; Baron, 1997; Klein, 2009; Shashkin, 2008; Simi *et al.*, 2008). These crime-prone years (see Farrington *et al.*, 2009; Hirschi and Gottfredson, 1983) are also consistent with when youth are observed joining a conventional street gang (Curry, 2000; Hughes, 2013; Klein and Maxson, 2006; Pyrooz, 2014; Pyrooz and Sweeten, 2015). Also, analogous to conventional street gangs, males are at greater risk of becoming a member of an Alt-Right gang (ADL, 1995; Ezekiel, 2002; Pollard, 2016). The caveat being that limited studies exist examining female membership in Alt-Right gangs and the white power movement more broadly, with the exception of Blee's (2002; 2017) research. It is not uncommon for Alt-Right gang members to reside in households with single-parents, irregular parental employment, and domestic discord (e.g. abuse, neglect, violence) (ADL, 1995; Baron,

1997; Ezekiel, 2002; Kinsella, 1996; Miller-Idriss, 2018; Pilkington *et al.*, 2010; Siedler, 2011; Valasik and Reid, 2018a). Another pattern analogous with conventional street gangs is the greater likelihood that Alt-Right gang members are unemployed, to have dropped out of high school, to abuse alcohol and drugs, and have substantial amounts of time that is unsupervised (Baron, 1997; Shashkin, 2008; Simi and Windisch, 2018; Wooden and Blazak, 2001).

In regards to pull risk factors, the motivations for a youth to join an Alt-Right gang are also comparable to the documented patterns observed in the broader literature on conventional street gangs (Reid and Valasik, 2018a; 2020; Valasik and Reid, 2018a, 2018b). Additionally, joining an Alt-Right gang provides a "sense of strength, group belonging, and superiority" (ADL, 1995, p. 5). The fact is that many youths that join an Alt-Right gang do so to escape feeling marginalized and being fearful of potential violent victimization. Becoming a member of an Alt-Right gang, just as with conventional street gangs, serves as a strategy to gain safety, defence and protection from local bullies or other street gangs (Baron, 1997; Ezekiel, 2002; Picciolini, 2018; Simi *et al.*, 2008). Lastly, it is not uncommon for Alt-Right gangs to engage in a variety of profit-oriented crimes, including burglary, counterfeiting, drug sales, identity theft and robbery, which provides a financial motivation to join (Simi *et al.*, 2008).

Normalization of criminality and violence

Analogous to conventional street gangs, Alt-Right gangs also participate in symbolic and instrumental acts of violence (Moore, 1994). That being said, much of the extant literature on patterns of violence and criminality of Alt-Right gangs focuses on the group ideology, and hate-based criminal acts (Curry *et al.*, 2014; Etter, 1999; Klein, 1995a). Yet, Alt-Right gangs regularly engage in crimes and violence that are unassociated with their political ideology (Baron, 1997; Berlet and Vysotsky, 2006; Blee, 2002; Borgeson and Valeri, 2005; Pollard, 2016; Sarabia and Shriver, 2004; Simi and Futrell, 2015; Simi *et al.*, 2008). While public displays of violence are believed to reaffirm one's identity to the group and bolster the symbolic solidarity of the group (ADL, 1995; Baron, 1997; Moore, 1994), much of the violence that Alt-Gangs pursue is retributive in nature for either real or perceived slights by out-groups (Baron, 1997; Simi *et al.*, 2008). Furthermore, most disputes are often interpersonal in nature and frequently involve other white street youth (Baron, 1997; Ridgeway, 1990; Simi, 2006; Simi *et al.*, 2008). Alt-Right gangs, like conventional street gangs, have high levels of entitativity, or the perception that rival group's members are a unified and cohesive group, considering any member of the offending group (e.g. Jewish individuals, immigrants, non-whites, etc.) as responsible and blameworthy. As such, any violent behaviour (e.g. hate-based crimes) directed broadly at these out-groups lacks discretion and spreads into the broader non-white population (Mills *et al.*, 2017; Perry and Scrivens, 2016). Simi and colleagues (2008) stress that despite much of the focus on bias-motivated violence (e.g. Curry *et al.*, 2014; Etter, 1999; Klein, 1995a) these acts are quite infrequent compared with other criminal acts. Most Alt-Right gang violence is analogous to patterns observed among conventional gang rivalries (Baron, 1997; Simi *et al.*, 2008; Valasik and Reid, 2018a). In fact, Alt-Right gangs engage in much of the same type of "cafeteria-style offending", versatile criminal and/or anti-social behaviour that lacks any specialized pattern, as conventional street gangs, which includes profit-oriented crimes, identify theft, and various property crimes (ADL, 1995; Baron, 1997; Freilich *et al.*, 2009; Perry and Scrivens, 2016; Pilkington *et al.*, 2010; Simi, 2006; Simi *et al.*, 2008). Lastly, it is important to note that no evidence has indicated that Alt-Right gangs are amassing the profits from their criminal endeavours to support larger political initiatives (Simi, 2006).

Conclusion

Violence is a complex phenomenon that is integral to gang members' group identity, use of space, group subculture, social interactions other groups, and relationship to victimization. Conventional street gangs regularly employ violence for both symbolic purposes (e.g. increasing their group's status) and instrumental purposes (e.g. generating revenue). The increased exposure to violence and the accepted use of it as a means to fulfil a gang's goals greatly facilitates its normalization among group members. Violence and conflict play a critical role in the creation and maintenance of gangs. Yet, this process is not solely unique to conventional street gangs. As highlighted by Reid and Valasik (2018a; 2018b; 2020), Alt-Right gangs have substantial overlap with conventional street gangs when it comes to the factors that push and pull individuals into joining the group, along with how violence is used and accepted by the group. For instance, Proud Boys provides a clear illustration of just how similar Alt-Right gangs are to conventional street gangs, when it comes to the use of violence. Analogous to conventional street gangs, Proud Boys have a violent, yet bizarre initiation process to "jump in" new members (see Hawley 2019; Reid and Valasik, 2020; Vigil 1988; 1996). Proud Boys are also encouraged to use violence to settle disputes and when confronting rival groups and adversaries, which has resulted in numerous street brawls and criminal acts of violence (Coaston, 2018; DeCook, 2018; First Vigil 2019). Both Alt-Right and conventional gangs, have a high degree of entitativity, and tend to view any individual that opposes their point of view as being associated with a rival group, and liable to violent victimization (see Vasquez *et al.*, 2015). Additionally, both conventional gangs and Alt-Right gangs are more likely to be the victims of violence, besides being "jumped in" but also through having greater exposure to violence, as seen through numerous public demonstrations and rallies over the last few years (e.g. Charlottesville, New York City, Berkeley, Portland, etc.). As Alt-Right gangs become more and more prominent and confrontational in society it becomes imperative that systematic research is employed investigate these groups to better ascertain possible intervention strategies that policymakers and law enforcement can employ to avoid public violence. Understanding and intervening in group-based violence is critical to our ability to reduce violence and victimization within gangs.

References

Anti-Defamation League (ADL) (1995) *The Skinhead International: A Worldwide Survey of Neo-nazi Skinheads*. New York: ADL.

Aljezeera (2018) Charlottesville: Four white supremacists charged over 2017 rally. (2 October). Retrieved from www.aljazeera.com/news/2018/10/charlottesville-4-members-white-supremacist-ram-group-charged-181002215128738.html

Anderson, E. (1999) *Code of the Street: Decency, Violence and the Moral Life of the Inner City*. New York: W. W. Norton.

Anselin, L., Cohen, J., Cook, D., Gorr, W., and Tita, G. E. (2000) Spatial analyses of crime. *Crime Justice*, 4, 213–262.

Barnes, J. C., Boutwell, B. B., and Fox, K. A. (2012) The effect of gang membership on victimization: A behavioral genetic explanation. *Youth Violence and Juvenile Justice*, 10(3), 227–244.

Baron, S. W. (1997) Canadian male street skinheads: Street gang or street terrorists? *Canadian Review of Sociology*, 34(2), 125–154.

Battin, S. R., Hill, K. G., Abbott, R. D., Catalano, R. F., and Hawkins, J. D. (1998) The contribution of gang membership to delinquency beyond delinquent friends. *Criminology*, 36(1), 93–116.

Bell, K. E. (2009) Gender and gangs: A quantitative comparison. *Crime & Delinquency*, 55(3), 363–387.

Berlet, C., and Vysotsky, S. (2006) Overview of US white supremacist groups. *Journal of Political and Military Sociology*, 34(1), 11.

Bjerregaard, B., and Smith, C. (1993) Gender differences in gang participation, delinquency, and substance use. *Journal of Quantitative Criminology*, 4, 329–355.

Blasko, B. L., Roman, C. G., and Taylor, R. B. (2015) Local gangs and residents' perceptions of unsupervised teen groups: Implications for the incivilities thesis and neighborhood effects. *Journal of Criminal Justice*, 43(1), 20–28.
Blee, K. M. (2002) *Inside Organized Racism: Women in the Hate Movement*. Berkeley, CA: University of California Press.
Blee, K. M. (2017) *Understanding Racist Activism: Theory, Methods, and Research*. London, New York: Routledge.
Block, R. L. (2000) Gang activity and overall levels of crime: A new mapping tool for defining areas of gang activity using police records. *Journal of Quantitative Criminology*, 16(3), 369–383.
Borgeson, K., and Valeri, R. (2005) Examining differences in skinhead idealogy and culture through an analysis of skinhead websites. *Michigan Sociological Review*, (Fall), 45–62.
Brantingham, P. J., Tita, G. E., Short, M. B., and Reid, S. E. (2012) The ecology of gang territorial boundaries. *Criminology*, 50(3), 851–885.
Bromwich, J. E. (2018) What is Atomwaffen? A neo-nazi group, linked to multiple murders. *The New York Times*, 12 February. Retrieved from www.nytimes.com/2018/02/12/us/what-is-atomwaffen.html
Bursik, R. J., Jr., and Grasmick, H. G. (1993) *Neighborhoods and Crime: The Dimensions of Effective Community Control*. Lanham, MD: Lexington Books.
Chesney-Lind, M., Shelden, R. G., and Joe, K. A. (1996) Girls, delinquency, and gang membership. *Gangs in America, 2*(1), 185–204.
Coaston, J. (2018) 4 members of an alt-right "fight club" charged with inciting a riot in Charlottesville. *Vox*. Retrieved from www.vox.com/2018/10/2/17928174/charlottesville-unite-the-right-alt-right-violence-federal-charges
Cohen, J., and Tita, G. E. (1999) Diffusion in homicide: Exploring a general method for detecting spatial diffusion processes. *Journal of Quantitative Criminology*, 15(4), 451–493.
Craig, W. M., Vitaro, F., Gagnon, L., and Tremblay, R. E. (2002) The road to gang membership: Characteristics of male gang and nongang members from ages 10 to 14. *Social Development*, 11(1), 53–68.
Curry, G. D. (2000) Self-reported gang involvement and officially recorded delinquency. *Criminology*, 38(4), 1253–1274.
Curry, G. D., and Spergel, I. A. (1988) Gang homicide, delinquency, and community. *Criminology*, 26(3), 381–406.
Curry, G. D., Decker, S. H., and Pyrooz, D. C. (2014) *Confronting Gangs: Crime and Community* (3rd edn). New York: Oxford University Press.
Dandurand, Y. (2014) Social inclusion programmes for youth and the prevention of violent extremism. In M. Lombardi, M. Ragab, V. Chin, Y. Dandurand, V. de Divitiis, and A. Burato (eds), *Countering Radicalisation and Violent Extremism Among Youth to Prevent Terrorism*. Amsterdam: IOS Press.
Decker, S. H. (1996) Collective and normative features of gang violence. *Justice Quarterly*, 13(2), 243–264.
Decker, S. H., and Curry, G. D. (2002) Gangs, gang homicides, and gang loyalty: Organized crimes or disorganized criminals. *Journal of Criminal Justice*, 30(4), 343–352.
Decker, S. H., and Pyrooz, D. C. (2010) On the validity and reliability of gang homicide: A comparison of disparate sources. *Homicide Studies*, 14(4), 359–376.
Decker, S. H., and Pyrooz, D. C. (2011) Gangs, terrorism, and radicalization. *Journal of Strategic Security*, 4(4), 151–166.
Decker, S. H., and Pyrooz, D. C. (2015) "I'm down for a Jihad": How 100 years of gang research can inform the study of terrorism, radicalization and extremism. *Perspectives on Terrorism*, 9(1), 2014–2112.
Decker, S. H., and Van Winkle, B. (1996) *Life in the Gang: Family, Friends and Violence*. New York: Cambridge.
Decker, S. H., Katz, C. M., and Webb, V. J. (2008) Understanding the black box of gang organization: Implications for violence, drug sales, and violent victimization. *Crime & Delinquency*, 54, 153–172.
Decker, S. H., Pyrooz, D. C., Sweeten, G., and Moule, R. K. (2014) Validating self-nomination in gang research: Assessing differences in gang embeddedness across non-, current, and former gang members. *Journal of Quantitative Criminology*, 30(4), 577–598.
DeCook, J. R. (2018) Memes and symbolic violence: #proudboys and the use of memes for propaganda and the construction of collective identity. *Learning, Media and Technology*, 43(4), 485–504.
Densley, J. (2013) *How Gangs Work*. New York: Palgrave Macmillan.
Esbensen, F. A., Winfree Jr, L. T., He, N., and Taylor, T. J. (2001) Youth gangs and definitional issues: When is a gang a gang, and why does it matter? *Crime & Delinquency*, 47(1), 105–130.

Etter, G. W. (1999) Skinheads: Manifestations of the warrior culture of the new urban tribes. *Journal of Gang Research*, 6(3), 9–21.

Ezekiel, R. S. (2002) An ethnographer looks at Neo-Nazi and Klan groups: The racist mind revisited. *American Behavioral Scientist*, 46(1), 51–71.

Farrington, D. P., Ttofi, M. M., and Coid, J. W. (2009) Development of adolescence-limited, late-onset, and persistent offenders from age 8 to age 48. *Aggressive Behavior: Official Journal of the International Society for Research on Aggression*, 35(2), 150–163.

Felson, M. (2006) *Crime and Nature*. Thousand Oaks, CA: Sage.

First Vigil. (2019) Cases by right-wing group. *First Vigil*. Retrieved from https://first-vigil.com/

Fleisher, M. S. (1998) *Dead End Kids: Gang Girls and the Boys they Know*. Madison, WI: University of Wisconsin Press.

Fleisher, M. S., and Krienert, J. L. (2004) Life-course events, social networks, and the emergence of violence among female gang members. *Journal of Community Psychology*, 32, 607–622.

Freilich, J. D., Chermak, S. M., and Caspi, D. (2009) Critical events in the life trajectories of domestic extremist white supremacist groups: A case study analysis of four violent organizations. *Criminology & Public Policy*, *8*(3), 497–530.

Gibson, C. L., Swatt, M. L., Miller, J. M., Jennings, W. G., and Gover, A. R. (2012) The causal relationship between gang joining and violent victimization: A critical review and directions for future research. *Journal of Criminal Justice*, 40(6), 490–501.

Gover, A. R., Jennings, W. G., and Tewksbury, R. (2009) Adolescent male and female gang members' experiences with violent victimization, dating violence, and sexual assault. *American Journal of Criminal Justice*, 34(1–2), 103–115.

Grannis, R. (2009) *From the Ground Up: Translating Geography into Community through Neighbor Networks*. Princeton, NJ: Princeton University Press.

Gravel, J., Allison, B., West-Fagan, J., McBride, M., and Tita, G. E. (2018) Birds of a feather fight together: Status-enhancing violence, social distance and the emergence of homogenous gangs. *Journal of Quantitative Criminology*, 34(1), 189–219.

Hagan, J. (1993) The social embeddedness of crime and unemployment. *Criminology*, 31(4), 465–491.

Hamm, M. S. (1993) *American Skinheads: The Criminology and Control of Hate Crime*. Westport, CT: ABC-CLIO.

Hawley, G. (2017) *Making Sense of the Alt-Right*. New York: Columbia University Press.

Hawley, G. (2019) *The Alt-Right: What Everyone Needs to Know*. New York: Oxford University Press.

Hayward, R. A., and Honegger, L. (2014) Gender differences in juvenile gang members: An exploratory study. *Journal of Evidence-based Social Work*, 11(4), 373–382.

Hennigan, K. M. and Spanovic, M. (2012) Gang dynamics through the lens of social identity theory. In F.-A. Esbensen and C. L. Maxson (eds), *Youth Gangs in International Perspective*. New York: Springer, pp. 127–149.

Hirschi, T., and Gottfredson, M. (1983) Age and the explanation of crime. *American Journal of Sociology*, 89(3), 552–584.

Hill, K. G., Howell, J. C., Hawkins, J. D., and Battin-Pearson, S. R. (1999) Childhood risk factors for adolescent gang membership: Results from the Seattle Social Development Project. *Journal of research in Crime and Delinquency*, 36(3), 300–322.

Howell, J. C. (2015) *The History of Street Gangs in the United States: Their Origins and Transformations*. Lanham, MD: Lexington Books.

Howell, J. C. and Griffiths, E. (2018) *Gangs in America's Communities* (3rd edn). Thousand Oaks, CA: Sage Publications.

Howell, J. C., Egley Jr, A., Tita, G. E., and Griffiths, E. (2011) *US Gang Problem Trends and Seriousness, 1996–2009*. Bureau of Justice Assistance, US Department of Justice, Office of Juvenile Justice and Delinquency Prevention.

Huebner, B. M., Martin, K., Moule Jr, R. K., Pyrooz, D., and Decker, S. H. (2016) Dangerous places: Gang members and neighborhood levels of gun assault. *Justice Quarterly*, 33(5), 836–862.

Hughes, L. A. (2013) Group cohesiveness, gang member prestige, and delinquency and violence in Chicago, 1959–1962. *Criminology*, 51(4), 795–832.

Hughes, L. A. and Short, J. F. (2014) Partying, cruising, and hanging in the streets: Gangs, routine activities, and delinquency and violence in Chicago, 1959–1962. *Journal of Quantitative Criminology*, 30(3), 415–451.

Hunt, G. P. and Joe-Laidler, K. (2001) Alcohol and violence in the lives of gang members. *Alcohol Research and Health*, 25(1), 66–71.

Katz, C. M., and Schnebly, S. M. (2011) Neighborhood variation in gang member concentrations. *Crime and Delinquency*, 57(3), 377–407.
Katz, C. M., Webb, V. J., Fox, K., and Shaffer, J. N. (2011) Understanding the relationship between violent victimization and gang membership. *Journal of Criminal Justice*, 39, 48–59.
Kinsella, W. (1996) *Web of Hate: Inside Canada's Far Right Network*. New York: HarperCollins Publishers.
Klein, M. W. (1995a) *The American Street Gang*. New York: Oxford University Press.
Klein, M. W. (1995b) "Street gang cycles." In J. Q. Wilson and J. Petersilia (eds), *Crime*. San Francisco, CA: Institute for Contemporary Studies Press, pp. 217–236.
Klein, M. W. (1996) Gangs in the United States and Europe. *European Journal on Criminal Policy and Research*, 4(2), 63–80.
Klein, M. W. (2001) Resolving the Eurogang paradox. In M. W. Klein, H. Kerner, C. L. Maxson, and E. G. M. Weitekamp (eds), *The Eurogang Paradox*. Dordrecht: Springer, pp. 7–19
Klein, M. W. (2009) *The Street Gangs of Euroburg: A Story of Research*. Bloomington, IN: iUniverse.
Klein, M. W. and Crawford, L. Y. (1967) Groups, gangs, and cohesiveness. *Journal of Research in Crime and Delinquency*, 4(1), 63–75.
Klein, M. W. and Maxson, C. L. (1989) Street gang violence. *Violent Crime, Violent Criminals*. Newbury Park, CA: Sage, pp. 198–234.
Klein, M. W. and Maxson, C. L. (2006) *Street Gang Patterns and Policies*. New York: Oxford University Press.
Lane, J. (2002) Fear of gang crime: A qualitative examination of the four perspectives. *Journal of Research in Crime and Delinquency*, 39(4), 437–471.
Lane, J., and Meeker, J. W. (2003) Fear of gang crime: A look at three theoretical models. *Law & Society Review*, 37(2), 425–456.
Leovy, J. (2015) *Ghettoside: A True Story of Murder in America*. New York: Spiegel & Grau.
Lopez, G. (2017) The radicalization of white Americans. *Vox*, 18 August. Retrieved from www.vox.com/identities/2017/8/18/16151924/radicalization-white-supremacists-nazis
Lyons, M. N. (2018) *Insurgent Supremacists: The U.S. Far Right's Challenge to State and Empire*. Montreal, Quebec: Kersplebedeb.
Main, T. J. (2018) *The Rise of the Alt-Right*. Washington, DC: Brookings Institution Press.
Maxson, C. L. (1999) Gang homicide: A review and extension of the literature. In M. Dwayne Smith and M. A. Zahn (eds), *Homicide: A Sourcebook of Social Research*. Newbury Park, CA: Sage Publications, pp. 197–220.
Maxson, C. L. and Esbensen, F. A. (2016) Participation in and transformation of gangs (and gang research) in an international context: Reflections on the Eurogang research program. In C. L. Maxson and F. A. Esbensen (eds), *Gang Transitions and Transformations in an International Context*. New York: Springer, pp. 1–11.
Maxson, C. L. and Klein, M. W. (1990) Street gang violence: Twice as great, or half as great? In C. R. Huff (ed.), *Gangs in America*. Newbury Park, CA: Sage, pp. 71–100.
Maxson, C. L. and Klein, M. W. (1996) Defining gang homicide: An updated look at member and motive approaches. In C. R. Huff (ed.), *Gangs in America* (2nd edn). Thousand Oaks, CA: Sage Publications, pp. 3–20.
Maxson, C. L. and Klein, M. W. (2002) "Play groups" no longer: Urban street gangs in the Los Angeles region. In M. J. Dear (ed.), *From Chicago to L.A.: Making Sense of Urban Theory*. Thousand Oaks, CA: Sage Publications, pp. 239–266.
Maxson, C. L., Gordon, M. A., and Klein, M. W. (1985) Differences between gang and nongang homicides. *Criminology*, 23, 209–222.
Melde, C. and Esbensen, F. A. (2011) Gang membership as a turning point in the life course. *Criminology*, 49(2), 513–552.
Melde, C. and Esbensen, F. A. (2013) Gangs and violence: Disentangling the impact of gang membership on the level and nature of offending. *Journal of Quantitative Criminology*, 29(2), 143–166.
Miller, J. (1998) Gender and victimization risk among young women in gangs. *Journal of Research in Crime and Delinquency*, 35(4), 429–453.
Miller, J. (2001) *One of the Guys: Girls, Gangs, and Gender*. New York: Oxford University Press.
Miller-Idriss, C. (2018) *The Extreme gone Mainstream: Commercialization and Far Right Youth Culture in Germany*. Princeton, NJ: Princeton University Press.
Mills, C. E., Freilich, J. D., and Chermak, S. M. (2017) Extreme hatred: Revisiting the hate crime and terrorism relationship to determine whether they are "Close Cousins" or "Distant Relatives". *Crime & Delinquency*, 63(10), 1191–1223.

Minnis, A. M., Moore, J. G., Doherty, I. A., Rodas, C., Auerswald, C., Shiboski, S., and Padian, N. S. (2008) Gang exposure and pregnancy incidence among female adolescents in San Francisco: Evidence for the need to integrate reproductive health with violence prevention efforts. *American Journal of Epidemiology*, 167(9), 1102–1109.

Moore, D. (1994) *The Lads in Action: Social Process in an Urban Youth Subculture*. Aldershot: Arena.

Moore, J. (1991) *Going Down to the Barrio: Homeboys and Homegirls in Change*. Philadelphia, PA: Temple University Press.

Moore, J. W. and Hagedorn, J. (2001) *Female Gangs: A Focus on Research*. Washington, DC: US Department of Justice, Office of Justice Programs, Office of Juvenile Justice and Delinquency Prevention.

Morenoff, J. D. and Sampson, R. J. (1997) Violent crime and the spatial dynamics of neighborhood transition: Chicago, 1970–1990. *Social Forces*, 76(1), 31–64.

Neiwert, D. (2017) *Alt-America: The Rise of the Radical Right in the Age of Trump*. London, UK: Verso.

Nydegger, L. A., DiFranceisco, W., Quinn, K., and Dickson-Gomez, J. (2017) Gender norms and age-disparate sexual relationships as predictors of intimate partner violence, sexual violence, and risky sex among adolescent gang members. *Journal of Urban Health*, 94(2), 266–275.

Padilla, F. M. (1992) *The Gang as an American Enterprise*. New Brunswick, NJ: Rutgers University Press.

Papachristos, A. V. (2009) Murder by structure: Dominance relations and the social structure of gang homicide. *American Journal of Sociology*, 115(1), 74–128.

Papachristos, A. V. (2013) *48 Years of Crime in Chicago: A Descriptive Analysis of Serious Crime Trends from 1965 to 2013*. New Haven, CT: Institution for Social and Policy Studies, Yale University.

Papachristos, A. V. (2014) Chicago is far from being the murder capital of the U.S. *LSE American Politics and Policy*. Retrieved from http://bit.ly/MoVMQi

Papachristos, A. V., Braga, A. A., Piza, E., and Grossman, L. S. (2015) The company you keep? The spillover effects of gang membership on individual gunshot victimization in a co-offending network. *Criminology*, 53(4), 624–649.

Papachristos, A. V., Hureau, D. M., and Braga, A. A. (2013) The corner and the crew: The influence of geography and social networks on gang violence. *American Sociological Review*, 78, 417–447.

Patton, D. U., Pyrooz, D. C., Decker, S., Frey, W. R., and Leonard, P. (2019) When Twitter fingers turn to trigger fingers: A qualitative study of social media-related gang violence. *International Journal of Bullying Prevention*, 1(3), 205–217.

Perry, B. and Scrivens, R. (2016) Uneasy alliances: A look at the right-wing extremist movement in Canada. *Studies in Conflict & Terrorism*, 39(9), 819–841.

Petersen, N. (2016) Neighborhood context and media constructions of murder: A multilevel analysis of homicide newspaper coverage in Los Angeles County. *Homicide Studies*, 20, 25–52.

Peterson, D., Taylor, T. J., and Esbensen, F. A. (2004) Gang membership and violent victimization. *Justice Quarterly*, 21(4), 793–815.

Petersen, R. D. and Howell, J. C. (2013) Program approaches for girls in gangs: Female specific or gender neutral? *Criminal Justice Review*, 38(4), 491–509.

Picciolini, C. (2018) *White American Youth*. New York: Hachette Books.

Pilkington, H., Garifzianova, A. B., and Omel'chenko, E. (2010) *Russia's Skinheads: Exploring and Rethinking Subcultural Lives*. London, New York: Routledge.

Pollard, J. (2016) Skinhead culture: The ideologies, mythologies, religions and conspiracy theories of racist skinheads. *Patterns of Prejudice*, 50(4–5), 398–419.

ProPublica (2018) Documenting Hate: Charlottesville (Television Series Episode). *Frontline*, 20 November.

Pyrooz, D. C. (2014) "From your first cigarette to your last dyin' day": The patterning of gang membership in the life-course. *Journal of Quantitative Criminology*, 30(2), 349–372.

Pyrooz, D. C. (2012) Structural covariates of gang homicide in large US cities. *Journal of Research in Crime and Delinquency*, 49(4), 489–518.

Pyrooz, D. C. and Sweeten, G. (2015) Gang membership between ages 5 and 17 years in the United States. *Journal of Adolescent Health*, 56(4), 414–419.

Pyrooz, D. C., LaFree, G., Decker, S. H., and James, P. A. (2018) Cut from the same cloth? A comparative study of domestic extremists and gang members in the United States. *Justice Quarterly*, 35(1), 1–32.

Pyrooz, D. C., Sweeten, G., and Piquero, A. R. (2013) Continuity and change in gang membership and gang embeddedness. *Journal of Research in Crime and Delinquency*, 50(2), 239–271.

Pyrooz, D. C., Turanovic, J. J., Decker, S. H., and Wu, J. (2016) Taking stock of the relationship between gang membership and offending: A meta-analysis. *Criminal Justice and Behavior*, 43(3), 365–397.

Radil, S. M., Flint, C., and Tita, G. E. (2010) Spatializing social networks: Using social network analysis to investigate geographies of gang rivalry, territoriality, and violence in Los Angeles. *Annals of the Association of American Geographers*, 100(2), 307–326.

Reid, S. E., and Valasik, M. (2018a) Ctrl+ ALT-RIGHT: Reinterpreting our knowledge of white supremacy groups through the lens of street gangs. *Journal of Youth Studies*, 21(10), 1305–1325.

Reid, S. E. and Valasik, M. (2018b) To deter violence, let's treat Alt-Right Groups as street gangs. *The Crime Report*, 14 August. Retrieved from https://thecrimereport.org/2018/08/14/to-deter-violence-why-not-consider-alt-right-groups-as-street-gangs/

Reid, S. E. and Valasik, M. (2020) *Alt-Right Gangs: A Hazy Shade of White*. Berkeley, CA: University of California Press.

Reitman, J. (2018) U.S. law enforcement failed to see the threat of white nationalism. now they don't know how to stop it. *The New York Times*, 3 November 2018, Magazine. Retrieved from www.nytimes.com/2018/11/03/magazine/FBI-charlottesville-white-nationalism-far-right.html.

Ridgeway, J. (1990) *Blood in the Face: The Ku Klux Klan, Aryan Nations, Nazi skinheads, and the Rise of a New White Culture*. New York: Thunder's Mouth Press.

Roose, K. and Winston, A. (2018) Far-right internet groups listen for Trump's approval, and often hear it. *The New York Times*, 4 November. Retrieved from www.nytimes.com/2018/11/04/us/politics/far-right-internet-trump.html

Rosenfeld, R., Bray, T. M., and Egley, A. (1999) Facilitating violence: A comparison of gang-motivated, gang-affiliated, and nongang youth homicides. *Journal of Quantitative Criminology*, 15(4), 495–516.

Sarabia, D. and Shriver, T. E. (2004) Maintaining collective identity in a hostile environment: Confronting negative public perception and factional divisions within the skinhead subculture. *Sociological Spectrum*, 24(3), 267–294.

Schalet, A., Hunt, G., and Joe-Laidler, K. (2003) Respectability and autonomy: The articulation and meaning of sexuality among the girls in the gang. *Journal of Contemporary Ethnography*, 32(1), 108–143.

Shashkin, A. (2008) Origins and development of racist skinheads in Moscow. In F. van Gemert, D. Peterson and I. Lien (eds), *Street Gangs, Migration, and Ethnicity*. New York: Routledge, pp. 97–114.

Short, J. F. and Strodtbeck, F. L. (1965) *Group Process and Gang Delinquency*. Chicago: University of Chicago Press.

Siedler, T. (2011) Parental unemployment and young people's extreme right-wing party affinity: Evidence from panel data. *Journal of the Royal Statistical Society: Series A (Statistics in Society)*, 174(3), 737–758.

Simi, P. (2006) Hate groups or street gangs? Emergence of racist skinheads. In J. F. Short, Jr. and L. A. Hughes (eds), *Studying Youth Gangs*. Lanham: AltaMira Press, pp. 145–160.

Simi, P. and Futrell, R. (2015) *American Swastika: Inside the White Power Movement's Hidden Spaces of Hate*. Lanham, MD: Rowman & Littlefield.

Simi, P., and Windisch, S. (2018) Why radicalization fails: Barriers to mass casualty terrorism. *Terrorism and Political Violence*, DOI: 10.1080/09546553.2017.1409212.

Simi, P., Smith, L., and Reeser, A. M. (2008) From punk kids to public enemy number one. *Deviant Behavior*, 29(8), 753–774.

Spergel, I. A., and Curry, G. D. (1993) The national youth gang survey: A research and development process. In A. P. Goldstein and C. R. Huff (eds), *The Gang Intervention Handbook*. Champaign, IL: Research Press, pp. 359–400.

SPLC (2019) "Proud Boys." *Southern Poverty Law Center*. Retrieved from www.splcenter.org/fighting-hate/extremist-files/group/proud-boys

Stephenson, S. (2015) *Gangs of Russia: From the Streets to the Corridors of Power*. Ithaca: Cornell University Press.

Sutton, T. E. (2017) The lives of female gang members: A review of the literature. *Aggression and Violent Behavior*, 37, 142–152.

Swart, W. J. (1991) Female gang delinquency: A search for "acceptably deviant behavior". *Mid-American Review of Sociology*, XV(1), 43–52.

Taniguchi, T. A., Radcliffe, J. H., and Taylor, R. B. (2011) "Gang set space, drug markets, and crime around drug corners in Camden." *Journal of Research in Crime and Delinquency*, 48(3), 327–363.

Taylor, T. J., Freng, A., Esbensen, F. A., and Peterson, D. (2008) Youth gang membership and serious violent victimization: The importance of lifestyles and routine activities. *Journal of Interpersonal Violence*, 23(10), 1441–1464.

Taylor, T., Peterson, D., Esbensen, F., and Freng, A. (2007) Gang membership as a risk factor for adolescent violent victimization. *Journal of Research in Crime and Delinquency*, 44, 351–380.

Thompson, A. C., Winston, A., and Bondgraham. (2017) Racist, violent, unpunished: A white hate group's campaign of menace. *ProPublica*. Retrieved from www.propublica.org/article/white-hate-group-campaign-of-menace-rise-above-movement

Thompson, A. C., Winston, A., and Hanrahan, J. (2018) Ranks of Notorious Hate Group Include Active-Duty Military. *ProPublica*. Retrieved from www.propublica.org/article/atomwaffen-division-hate-group-active-duty-military

Thornberry, T. P., Krohn, M. D., Lizotte, A. J., Tobin, K., and Smith, C. A. (2003) *Gangs and Delinquency in Developmental Perspective*. Cambridge, UK: Cambridge University Press.

Thrasher, F. M. (1927) *The Gang*. Chicago: University of Chicago Press.

Tita, G. E. and Cohen, J. (2004) Measuring spatial diffusion of shots fired activity across city neighborhoods. In M. F. Goodchild and D. G. Janelle (eds), *Spatially Integrated Social Science*. New York: Oxford University Press, pp. 171–204.

Tita, G. E. and Greenbaum, R. T. (2009) Crime, neighborhoods, and units of analysis: Putting space in its place. In D. Weisburd, W. Bernasco, and G. J. N. Bruinsma (eds), *Putting Crime in Its Place: Units of Analysis in Geographic Criminology*. New York: Springer, pp. 145–170.

Tita, G. E. and Radil, S. M. (2011) Spatializing the social networks of gangs to explore patterns of violence. *Journal of Quantitative Criminology*, 27, 521–545.

Tita, G. E., Cohen, J., and Engberg, J. (2005) An ecological study of the location of gang "set space". *Social Problems*, 52(2), 272–299.

Ulloa, E. C., Dyson, R. B., and Wynes, D. D. (2012) Inter-partner violence in the context of gangs: A review. *Aggression and Violent Behavior*, 17(5), 397–404.

Valasik, M. (2018) Gang violence predictability: Using risk terrain modeling to study gang homicides and gang assaults in East Los Angeles. *Journal of Criminal Justice*, 58, 10–21.

Valasik, M., and Reid, S. E. (2018a) White nationalist groups are really street gangs, and law enforcement needs to treat them that way. *The Conversation*, 4 December. Retrieved from https://theconversation.com/white-nationalist-groups-are-really-street-gangs-and-law-enforcement-needs-to-treat-them-that-way-107691

Valasik, M. and Reid, S. E. (2018b) Alt-Right gangs and white power youth groups. *Oxford Bibliographies Online: Criminology*.

Valasik, M. and Reid, S. E. (2019) The Schrödinger's Cat of gang groups: Can street gangs inform our comprehension of skinheads and Alt-Right groups? *Deviant Behavior*, 40(10), 1245–1259.

Valasik, M. and Phillips, M. D. (2017) Understanding modern terror and insurgency through the lens of street gangs: ISIS as a case study. *Journal of Criminological Research, Policy and Practice*, 3(3), 192–207.

Valasik, M. and Tita, G. (2018) Gangs and space. In S. D. Johnson and B. Gerben (eds), *The Oxford Handbook of Environmental Criminology*. Oxford: Oxford University Press, pp. 843–871.

Valasik, M., Barton, M. S., Reid, S. E., and Tita, G. E. (2017) Barriocide: Investigating the temporal and spatial influence of neighborhood structural characteristics on gang and non-gang homicides in East Los Angeles. *Homicide Studies*, 21(4), 287–311.

Valasik, M., Reid, S. E., and Phillips, M. D. (2016) CRASH and burn: Abatement of a specialised gang unit. *Journal of Criminological Research, Policy and Practice*, 2(2), 95–106.

Vasquez, E. A., Wenborne, L., Peers, M., Alleyne, E., and Ellis, K. (2015) Any of them will do: In-group identification, out-group entitativity, and gang membership as predictors of group-based retribution. *Aggressive Behavior*, 41(3), 242–252.

VICE News (2017) Charlottesville: Race and Terror (Television Series Episode). *Vice News Tonight*, 14 August.

Vigil, J. D. (1988) Group processes and street identity: Adolescent Chicano gang members. *Ethos*, 16(4), 421–445.

Vigil, J. D. (1996) Street baptism: Chicano gang initiation. *Human Organization*, 55(2), 149–153.

Vigil, J. D. (2003) Urban violence and street gangs. *Annual Review of Anthropology*, 32(1), 225–242.

Waring, A. (2018) *The New Authoritarianism – Volume 1: A Risk Analysis of the US Alt-Right Phenomenon*. Stuttgart, Germany: ibidem-Verlag.

Waring, A. (2019) *The New Authoritarianism – Volume 2: A Risk Analysis of the European Alt-Right Phenomenon*. Stuttgart, Germany: ibidem-Verlag.

Wendling, M. (2018) *Alt-right: From 4chan to the White House*. London: Pluto Press.

Winter, A. (2019) Online hate: From the far-right to the "Alt-Right" and from the Margins to the Mainstream. In K. Lumsden and E. Harmer (eds), *Online Othering*. Cham: Springer International Publishing, pp. 39–63.

Wood, G. (2017) His Kampf. *The Atlantic*, 28 May. Retrieved from www.theatlantic.com/magazine/archive/2017/06/his-kampf/524505/
Wood, J. L. (2014) Understanding gang membership: The significance of group processes. *Group Processes & Intergroup Relations*, 17(6), 710–729.
Wooden, W. S. and Blazak, R. (2001) *Renegade Kids, Suburban Outlaws: From Youth Culture to Delinquency* (2nd edn). Belmont: Wadsworth.
Wu, J. and Pyrooz, D. C. (2016) Uncovering the pathways between gang membership and violent victimization. *Journal of Quantitative Criminology*, 32(4), 531–559.

23

CURRENT UNDERSTANDING OF MULTIPLE PERPETRATOR SEXUAL OFFENDING

Teresa Ferraz-da-Silva

Introduction

Sexual violence committed by multiple perpetrators is not a recent phenomenon; however, in the last couple of decades there has been an increase in the media reporting of these cases (Franklin, 2013). While this has served to draw attention to this topic, in many cases it does not portray a representative picture of this type of crime. In an examination of high-profile media cases of sexual assaults committed by multiple perpetrators, Franklin (2013) found that only cases that are considered newsworthy make headlines. The elements that make them newsworthy include the level of brutality, unusual features, young age of victims, number of perpetrators involved, notoriety of the perpetrators, and political factors. It is necessary to examine the academic literature to gain a true understanding of this type of sexual offending. In this chapter an overview will be provided of what is currently known about multiple perpetrator sexual offending, examining the theories and research conducted to date.

Definition of multiple perpetrator sexual offending (MPSO)

A number of different terms have been used to describe sexual violence committed by multiple perpetrators (Horvath and Kelly, 2009). These terms vary across different countries and contexts (da Silva *et al.*, 2013). In the academic literature the most common utilized terms are "gang rape" and "group rape". Horvath and Kelly (2009) discuss the difference between these two terms and their connotations. There is a lack of consensus regarding what constitutes a gang (Alleyne and Wood, 2010) and the term is usually associated with a "street-oriented youth group whose identity includes involvement in illegal activity" (Weerman *et al.*, 2009, p. 20). However, this definition is not representative of the majority of sexual assaults committed by multiple perpetrators. In relation to the term "group" there is an on-going debate within social psychology regarding what constitutes a group. Whereas some authors believe that two people can be considered a group (Williams, 2010), others argue that a dyad should not be considered a group because some of the group processes in larger groups do not occur in dyads (Moreland, 2010). This is important because research has shown that a large number of sexual assaults, committed by multiple perpetrators, are carried out by dyads or duos (Hauffe and Porter, 2009; Horvath and Kelly, 2009; Porter and Alison, 2004, 2006; Woodhams, 2008). Horvath and Kelly

(2009, p. 94) proposed the use of the term multiple perpetrator rape as an overarching term when referring to a "sexual assault which involves two or more perpetrators". The authors believe that this could facilitate the development of subtypes, which could be specific to local contexts, or found transnationally. In this chapter, the term multiple perpetrator sexual offending (MPSO) will be used instead of multiple perpetrator rape as it is the term utilized in the main theory examined.

Prevalence and contexts of MPSO

It is believed that MPSO has been present throughout history and can be found in many countries (Brownmiller, 1975; Sanday, 2007). The exact incidence and prevalence is difficult to determine due to differences in the definitions of rape and study designs utilized (Harkins and Dixon, 2010). Furthermore, in the majority of official records of rates of sexual offending it is not possible to distinguish between lone and MPSO (Hauffe and Porter, 2009; Porter and Alison, 2006). Additionally, rape is one of the most under-reported crimes, with recent numbers suggesting that 83 per cent of victims did not report their experiences to the police (Office for National Statistics, 2018).

There are a number of studies that have been carried out in different countries, which have reported incidence and prevalence rates. From these we can conclude that MPSO is a significant problem. However, due to different study designs and sample sizes used it is difficult to directly compare rates, but it is possible to conclude that, internationally, approximately 9 to 33 per cent of sexual assaults are perpetrated by multiple assailants. It was found that in the United Kingdom, between 11 and 19 per cent of sexual offences involved multiple perpetrators (Curran and Millie, 2003; Kelly *et al.*, 2005; Wright and West, 1981). This upper prevalence rate seems to be higher in other countries. For example, in the United States, the rate of rape committed by multiple assailants is estimated to lie between 10 per cent and 33 per cent (Franklin, 2004), and in South Africa between 8.9 per cent (Jewkes *et al.*, 2009) and 27 per cent (Swart *et al.*, 2000). Additionally, the National Crime and Safety Survey (2002) in Australia found that 23 per cent of adult female and male victims of sexual violence were assaulted by multiple assailants (Australian Bureau of Statistics, 2004).

Not only is MPSO found throughout the world, it also seems to occur in many different contexts. Harkins and Dixon (2010) identify several subcategories of MPSO that they divide into two main categories: MPSO of peers and adults, and MPSO against children. The most common type is MPSO of peers and adults, which includes a number of sub-categories: rape in street gangs; fraternity rape; rape in sports settings either by coaches or players; rape during war; prison rapes; group date rapes not associated with fraternities; rape in countries under corrupt governments; human sex trading. The sub-categories of MPSO against children category include: paedophile organizations; child sex rings; rape in sports settings either by coaches or players; day care centres; residential care. For some of these sub-types there is a paucity of research. For an overview of the contexts where there is more research see da Silva *et al.* (2013, pp. 16–29).

Due to the fact that there are few studies on the prevalence and incidence of MPSO, it is not possible to yet conclude whether this type of sexual violence is more prevalent in some countries than in others. In order to draw any concrete conclusions, further international research is required. To facilitate this research it is necessary to separate out lone and multiple perpetrator sexual offences in official government reports, and in prevalence studies on sexual violence, which currently is not commonly done.

Theories and explanations of MPSO

Earlier theories/explanations of MPSO tended to offer simple individual or sociological explanations and were influenced by the dominant theories of general sexual offending of the era. The majority of those earlier explanations developed from a feminist perspective (Brownmiller, 1975; Groth and Birnbaum, 1979; Scully and Marolla, 1985). These authors proposed that factors such as power, control, male bonding, and validation of masculinity contributed to MPSO. Many of these factors were believed to also be present in lone sexual offending, but what was seen as a unique dynamic in MPSO was the camaraderie and co-operation between co-offenders (Groth and Birnbaum, 1979). These explanations placed great emphasis, almost exclusively, on socio-cultural factors. At that time, only the *Patterns of Forcible Rape* of Amir (1971) proposed an interaction of various factors to explain MPSO, which included: negative/stereotypical attitudes towards women and sexual identity; group processes; a precipitating event; situational factors and a leader in the group that facilitated the mobilization of the other members.

The *Multi-Factorial Model of MPSO* developed by Harkins and Dixon (2010, 2013) represents the most comprehensive theory to date that combines the factors proposed by the earlier theories and includes others. In this chapter a general overview of this model will be provided; for a more in-depth description of this model and other earlier explanatory theories of MPSO see da Silva *et al.* (2015) and Harkins and Dixon (2010, 2013). The Multi-Factorial Model of MPSO proposes that this type of sexual assault occurs due to an interaction between various factors, namely individual, socio-cultural and situational. Individual factors include biological predispositions, personality traits, developmental factors, and sexual preferences. Socio-cultural factors include norms, myths, values and beliefs held at the societal, cultural, and community level about women, violence and sexuality. Examples of these are rape culture, rape myths, and patriarchy. Situational factors such as unique settings are thought to act as a trigger or help to overcome inhibiting factors. Harkins and Dixon (2010, 2013) considered that some unique settings are conducive to MPSO (e.g. where there are power imbalances between groups, where hostile masculinity or exaggerated sexuality is acceptable, or where there is anonymity in action, such as during war). This model suggests that the likelihood of an individual taking part in MPSO would depend on their individual characteristics (e.g. personality traits and sexual interests), their beliefs about women and violence, and specific contexts that could help them overcome inhibitions.

Harkins and Dixon (2010, 2013) also proposed that individual, socio-cultural and situational factors interacted in a number of ways, which further contributed to the probability of the occurrence of MPSO. Three possible interactions were identified, labelled as follows: internalization of socio-cultural factors; group processes; and sub-cultural context. The internalization of socio-cultural factors occurs between the individual and the socio-cultural context and is related to the level to which socio-cultural norms are internalized and how these influence an individual's cognitions and beliefs. The group processes occur between the individual and situational factors. The authors highlighted the importance of the group processes and identified a number of group dynamics they believe are applicable to MPSO, such as social comparison, social dominance, conformity, obedience to authority, social corroboration, de-individuation, and groupthink. The sub-cultural context takes place between the situational context and socio-cultural factors. Some subcultures have accepted norms or beliefs about dominance and sexual aggression, and in favourable situations these could lead to MPSO.

The Multi-Factorial Model of MPSO meets a number of the criteria proposed by Ward *et al.* (2006) when evaluating a theory. In their critical review of the Multi-Factorial Model of MPSO, da Silva *et al.* (2015) found that it is consistent with some of the earlier MPSO theories as well as with other theories of general sexual offending, which propose the interaction of individual, socio-cultural and situational factors (Ward and Beech, 2006). It is able to explain some existing empirical findings and phenomena such as group processes. Furthermore, it unifies research on group sexual offending with research related to group processes, which permits the generation of new predictions in the area of MPSO. However, there are some gaps in knowledge, with the model also lacking explanatory depth in some factors. Overall, some empirical evidence can be found that supports the Multi-Factorial Theory of MPSO and it could be used as a guide to researchers and practitioners who could contribute to its testing and further development.

Research on MPSO

Research and literature on sexual offending is substantial and continually developing (Ward *et al.*, 2006). However, most of the research conducted has been on lone sexual offending. When sexual offences committed by multiple perpetrators have been included in samples, they are rarely separated out from lone offences. In the last decade there has been a surge in interest in MPSO that has resulted in the publication of a number of articles (Adolfsson *et al.*, 2017; Alleyne *et al.*, 2014; Bamford *et al.*, 2016; Chambers *et al.*, 2010, 2013; da Silva *et al.*, 2014, 2015, 2018; 't Hart-Kerkhoffs *et al.*, 2011; Morgan *et al.*, 2012; Woodhams *et al.*, 2012) and even the first book dedicated to MPSO (Horvath and Woodhams, 2013). Nevertheless, compared to research conducted on lone sexual offending, MPSO still remains a relatively under-researched area with gaps in academic knowledge clearly remaining (Harkins and Dixon, 2010; Horvath and Woodhams, 2013). Thus, it is perhaps of value to present here what the research is able to tell us currently, focusing on the characteristics of MPSO, group size, motivations, and women involved as perpetrators.

Characteristics of MPSO

The majority of the research on MPSO has examined the characteristics of the perpetrators, victims and their offences. The samples utilized in this research range from archival data, such as police reports and victim statements (Amir, 1971; Chambers *et al.*, 2010; da Silva *et al.*, 2014; Horvath and Kelly, 2009; Woodhams, 2008; Wright and West, 1981), Court files (Bijleveld and Hendriks, 2003; Bijleveld *et al.*, 2007), and law reports (Hauffe and Porter, 2009; Porter and Alison 2006). Some of these studies specifically examined characteristics of perpetrators of MPSO while others compared lone and multiple perpetrator sexual offenders.

A systematic review and meta-analysis was conducted by Bamford *et al.* (2016) in which they examined demographic and offence variables in male MPSO in English-speaking Western countries. In relation to the perpetrators, they found that the majority were in their early 20s and over a third had a previous conviction. Only 11 per cent of previous convictions were related to sexual offending in comparison to lone offenders, who possessed more previous sexual convictions (25 per cent). Duos were found to be the most common group size. In relation to victims, they found that they were on average younger than the perpetrators and, similar to the perpetrators, there were high frequencies of drug and alcohol use by the victims. Substance use was a reported factor in just under half of all MPSO offences, which may reflect the social contexts where victims were obtained. In terms of offence characteristics, the most frequent offence behaviour reported was vaginal rape (87 per cent), followed by multiple penetration (48 per cent) and fellatio (38 per cent). It was found that in 61 per cent of the cases further violence was indicated. Victims were more likely assaulted indoors, but approached outdoors. This differed from the lone perpetrators where victims were more likely to be approached indoors. Overall, when the multiple perpetrator and lone offences were compared, they were significantly different in relation to 65 per cent of their offence behaviours.

A number of studies have also been carried out in Western countries, outside of the UK, such as Belgium (De Wree, 2004), the Netherlands (Bijleveld and Hendriks, 2003; Bijleveld *et al.*, 2007; Hooing *et al.*, 2010; 't Hart-Kerkhoffs *et al.*, 2011), Sweden (Kjellgren *et al.*, 2006), Switzerland (Aebi *et al.*, 2012), and in non-Western countries, namely Ghana (Quarshie *et al.*, 2018), South Africa (Jewkes *et al.*, 2015; Vetten and Haffejee, 2005), and South Korea (Park and Kim, 2016). In general, there are a number of similarities across the studies in terms of age of perpetrators and victims, group size, and sexual acts, which was similar to the findings of Bamford *et al.* (2016). However, it is important to highlight that there are also some differences, particularly in relation to offence behaviours. For example, in terms of the approach and location of the rape, in the UK the majority of victims were approached outside and raped indoors (Horvath and Kelly, 2009; Woodhams, 2008; Wright and West, 1981), whereas in South Africa, even though the victims were also mainly approached outdoors, the majority were raped outdoors in open spaces (Vetten and Haffejee, 2005). Differences have also been found in the use of violence; studies from the United States (Gidycz and Koss, 1990; Ullman, 1999, 2007) and the UK (Woodhams, 2004, 2008; Woodhams *et al.*, 2007; Wright and West, 1981) report more violence in MPSO than studies in the Netherlands and Belgium (Bijleveld *et al.*, 2007; Boelrijk, 1997; De Weer, 2004). It was not possible to conclude if there were differences in MPSO between countries, or if the differences found were due to the diverse methodologies used. Further research across countries utilizing similar methodologies is required to obtain a clearer picture. There also seem to be differences between juvenile and adult MPSO. For example, adults are more likely to engage in MPSO with just one other perpetrator whereas adolescents are more often part of bigger groups (da Silva *et al.*, 2014). Additionally, adults stated more frequently than adolescents that alcohol played a part in their offence (da Silva *et al.*, 2015). More research comparing these two groups is needed because if differences do exist it is likely that juvenile and adult perpetrators of MPSO could also have different motivations, risk levels and treatment needs.

A number of the studies examining the characteristics of MPSO characterize the typical perpetrator as a young ethnic minority male, from a single parent household, with low education, poor employment prospects, and an average non-deviant personality profile (Bijleveld and Hendriks, 2003; Bijleveld *et al.*, 2007; De Wree, 2004; 't Hart-Kerkhoffs *et al.*, 2011; Hooing *et al.*, 2010). Nevertheless, a few studies found that some perpetrators of MPSO were from higher socio-economic backgrounds (Franklin, 2013; Jewkes and Sikweyiya, 2013) and some had psychopathic traits (Jewkes and Sikweyiya, 2013). Differences and inconsistencies found in the characteristics of MPSO could suggest that it is likely that there are different types of perpetrators of MPSO. Indeed, a typology of four types of MPSO or pathways (i.e. violence, criminality, intimacy and sexuality), related to crime scene behaviours and victim and offender characteristics, was proposed by Chambers *et al.* (2010). The intimacy, violence and sexuality types are characterized by social contact between the victim and at least one of the perpetrators. However, they have different main themes. The intimacy type involves targeting through a deceptive romantic relationship. In the violence type the naivety of the victim is used by the perpetrators to coerce them in a violent and sexual manner. The sexuality type usually includes extreme sexual behaviour and overt displays of masculinity. The criminal type does not include social contact and the victim is physically forced to the crime scene. It is possible that the offenders seek a quick thrill through the enactment of extreme criminal behaviour. Chambers *et al.* (2010) suggested that there could be an association between these four types and offender characteristics (e.g. age). Further research is necessary to test this typology and to possibly identify more types of perpetrators of MPSO. A significant limitation of the research conducted on the characteristics of MPSO is the lack of studies conducted in the community with non-convicted perpetrators. More research conducted with community samples (e.g. Jewkes and Sikweyiya, 2013) would be of assistance and provide a clearer picture of MPSO, including perhaps assisting with a refinement of MPSO perpetrator typology.

Group size

As demonstrated earlier, there appears to be differences between lone and MPSO; however, little is known about differences *within* MPSO. Even though it seems as if duos are the most common group size (Bamford *et al.*, 2016), the number of perpetrators involved in MPSO can range from 2 to 14, or more (Hauffe and Porter, 2009; Horvath and Kelly, 2009; Porter and Alison, 2004, 2006; Woodhams, 2008). Taking into consideration the debate in social psychology regarding the differences in dynamics between duos and bigger groups (Moreland, 2010), it is important therefore to examine the effect of differences in group size.

This area remains under-researched, with only a small number of studies that have either examined duos and larger groups (Amir, 1971; Lambine, 2013), or differences between lone, duo and 3+ groups (da Silva *et al.*, 2014; Park and Kim, 2016). Significant differences were found between duo and larger groups (Amir, 1971; Lambine, 2013), and between lone, duo and 3+ groups in relation to offender, victim and offence characteristics (da Silva *et al.*, 2014; Park and Kim, 2016). Furthermore, it was possible to predict the likelihood of an offence being committed by a lone, duo, or 3+ group offender based on certain socio-demographic (e.g. age, ethnicity) and offence (e.g. planning, use of vehicle, approach, location, sexual acts performed) characteristics. Although there are similarities between research in the UK (da Silva *et al.*, 2014) and in other jurisdictions, such as South Korea (Park and Kim, 2016), there remain differences, such as age between lone and duo perpetrators, and use of verbal threats. It is not possible to conclude if these differences relate to cultural differences or different methodologies used. Additionally, it is also unclear whether duos are more similar to lone or 3+ group offenders, or to what extent they fall along a continuum (da Silva *et al.*, 2014). In future research on sexual violence it would be useful to separate out lone, duos and 3+ group offences. This would allow a clearer picture to emerge regarding these subtypes. It would be possible then to examine if they differ in terms of intervention and treatment needs.

Motivations

There is very little research that has examined the motivations and reasons behind these offences. The most direct means of gaining insight into this area is to interview the perpetrators of MPSO. There are a few studies where perpetrators provide some (limited) information about aspects of their offending, but this information appeared as a by-product of research focusing on other issues (e.g. Etgar and Ganot-Prager, 2009; Hooing *et al.*, 2010; Jewkes *et al.*, 2006; 2011; Scully and Marolla, 1985). Of that which has been able to at least comment on motivation, a common reason given for involvement in MPSO was responding to group processes, such as social acceptance and group pressure (Etgar and Ganot-Prager, 2009; Hooing *et al.*, 2010). Furthermore, compared with lone perpetrators, the reasons given by juvenile perpetrators of MPSO were more often non-sexual, such as those related to sociability and social dominance (Hooing *et al.*, 2010). Participating in this type of sexual offending for recreation, fun, and male camaraderie were also reported (Jewkes *et al.*, 2006; 2011; Scully and Marolla, 1985). Additionally, in

South Africa, some perpetrators of MPSO admitted that they were involved in this type of assault because they wanted to punish girls or women who they considered did not conform to stereotypical gender norms (e.g. they were considered promiscuous or drank alcohol and smoked).

To date, there are only two published studies that focused exclusively on interviewing perpetrators of MPSO (Blanchard, 1959; da Silva *et al.*, 2018). Blanchard's (1959) sample consisted of seven teenage boys who had participated in two different multiple perpetrator offences (three belonged to one group and four to the other). Psychodynamic theory was utilized to explain their assault and it was argued by the authors that sexual orientation may have featured as a factor. The author, in this somewhat dated study, concluded that in one of the groups the sexual feelings identified seemed to be between the perpetrators instead of between the perpetrators and victim. However, he thought that the sexual feelings in the other group were focused on the leader appearing to defending himself against the fear of being perceived as weak or not masculine enough. Blanchard (1959) identified a clear leader in both groups and highlighted the importance of the leaders and their ability to direct the attention of the other members in the group to sexual issues. Furthermore, he found that the group dynamics between the leaders and the rest of the members during the group evaluations were very similar to the dynamics present during the actual assault.

da Silva *et al.*'s (2018) sample consisted of 25 juvenile and adult convicted perpetrators of MPSO, who were interviewed regarding their involvement and reasons for participating in the offence. The authors identified six themes for an individual's involvement in MPSO, namely; it started as something else; the influence of others (direct or indirect); lack of awareness; victim blaming; influence of alcohol and or drugs; and normalized sexual violence. In most cases the participants did not provide just one reason as they considered that various factors played a role in their offence. The authors concluded that the results supported the existence of some of the factors proposed by the Multi-Factorial Model of MPSO (Harkins and Dixon, 2010; 2013). The themes *influence of others* and *lack of awareness* provided evidence for the existence of group processes and dynamics. In the *influence of others* theme it was possible to identify group processes, such as social conformity and social comparison, which were proposed by Harkins and Dixon (2013). This was evident in some of the interviews, where participants stated that they did not want to "look bad", to have problems with the group, or be rejected by the others. Some declared that they obeyed an order that was given without questioning it, and others admitted that they participated after the co-offenders either insisted they do so or taunted them. Modelling was another group process found in the *influence of others* theme, with some participants stating that they took part after seeing their co-offenders assault the victim. O'Sullivan (1991) suggests that by watching peers sexually assault a victim, members of the group learn that it is acceptable, and also how to do it. The descriptions made by the perpetrators of the offence happening in a fast and confusing manner, and of not being aware of thoughts and feelings, in the theme *lack of awareness*, could point to the presence of the group process of deindividuation, where the group begins to act more as a collective. Harkins and Dixon (2013) proposed that deindividuation could help explain how a person could lose their sense of identity and responsibility and effectively "go along" with the group action.

Socio-cultural factors related to beliefs and attitudes about gender norms and sexuality were also identified in the theme *victim blaming*. Some participants judged the female victim by her past behaviour and assumed that if she had, or was believed to have had, many past sexual partners or participated in group sex, she would be willing to have sex with all the group members. In the theme *normalized sexual violence*, it was possible to identify the sub-cultural context proposed by Harkins and Dixon (2013), where socio-cultural factors seem to be interacting with situational factors. Participants who came from crime-prone neighbourhoods, known for their gang culture, explained how they considered their actions as "normal" because it was something that they had witnessed and was acceptable in their circle of friends and acquaintances. The theme *influence of alcohol and/or drugs* was suggestive of situational factors. Some participants believed that they would not have committed the assault if they were not under the influence of alcohol or drugs. Finally, in the theme *started as something else*, the majority of participants explain that they had not planned a sexual assault but that "somehow" it had happened. This theme suggested a combination of individual, socio-cultural and situational factors contributed to the assault. For example, in situations where the participants said they were socializing, there may have been an interaction between individual traits (e.g. personality or sexual interests), beliefs about stereotypical masculinity and a situation where co-offenders are present and are drunk, excited and/or aroused, as well as there being an available victim.

In conclusion, the limited research examining reasons and motivations suggests that a number of factors seem to contribute to MPSO, which provides some support for the Multi-Factorial Model of MPSO. Additionally, group processes and dynamics seem to play an important part and represent a unique feature of this type of sexual offending. More research where perpetrators of MPSO are interviewed, including community samples, is certainly needed.

Female MPSO

The majority of the research conducted on MPSO has focused on male perpetrators. However, evidence suggests that females are more likely than males to perpetrate a sexual crime with a co-offender (Gillespie *et al.*, 2015; Vandiver, 2006; Williams and Bierie, 2015). Therefore, it is important to include female MPSO when examining this area. There are a small number of studies that have compared the characteristics and offending patterns of female lone and multiple perpetrator sexual offenders (ten Bensel *et al.*, 2019; Budd *et al.*, 2017; Gillespie *et al.*, 2015; Muskens *et al.*, 2011; Vandiver, 2006; Wijkman *et al.*, 2010). These studies found some similarities, differences, and mixed results between the two groups.

In relation to offender characteristics, most studies found that female lone and multiple perpetrator sexual offenders were similar in age and ethnic background. However, ten Bensel *et al.* (2019) reported that lone offenders were significantly younger than multiple perpetrators. Furthermore, lone offenders appeared more often single (ten Bensel *et al.*, 2019) and less often mothers (Wijkman *et al.*, 2010).

There have been some inconsistent findings regarding clinical characteristics; Muskens *et al.* (2011) found that female lone compared with multiple offenders were more likely to have received a diagnosis of a mood disorder. This was in line with what Gillespie *et al.* (2015) found, namely with lone offenders presenting with a greater number of personal vulnerabilities, such as mental health issues and substance abuse. Multiple perpetrators, however, reported more environmentally-based factors, such as a current partner who was a sexual offender and involvement with other know offenders. However, Wijkman *et al.* (2010) reported that lone offenders were less often diagnosed with personality disorders, with ten Bensel *et al.* (2019) not finding any differences in the self-reporting of mental health issues or prior sexual abuse victimization. In relation to previous convictions Vandiver (2006) found that multiple perpetrator sexual offenders were, however, more likely to have previous convictions for non-sexual offences than lone offenders. This contradicted ten Bensel *et al.*'s, (2019) findings that lone offenders were more likely to have been arrested multiple times before the index offence.

In terms of offence and victim characteristics, multiple perpetrators were more likely than lone perpetrators to have multiple victims, familial victims, and victims of both sexes (Vandiver,

2006; Wijkman *et al.*, 2010). Lone perpetrators also tended to target older male victims, whereas, multiple perpetrators targeted younger female victims (ten Bensel *et al.*, 2019; Muskens *et al.*, 2011; Wijkman *et al.*, 2010). Lastly, Wijkman *et al.* (2010) reported that offences involving penetration were more frequently committed by multiple perpetrators.

As with male MPSO, little is known about differences *within* female MPSO. There is only one study that examined different sized groups with different sex compositions (Budd *et al.*, 2017). These authors analysed sexual offences committed by four groupings: lone female sexual offenders; co-ed pairs consisting of one male and one female sexual offender; all-female; and multiple perpetrator groups that consist of a combination of three or more female and male sexual offenders. A key finding was that the offences involving lone female sexual offenders and all-female groups had similar characteristics, while co-ed pairs and multiple perpetrator mixed groups had similar characteristics. In line with Vandiver (2006) and Wijkman *et al.* (2010), they found that offences involving co-ed pairs were more likely to involve female victims than lone offences. Furthermore, they also found that co-ed pairs were more likely to target dependent children and intrafamilial family members. The multiple perpetrator mixed groups were more likely than other groupings to involve stranger victims, more injury, and more diverse offending beyond sexual crimes. Contrary to Vandiver (2006), who found no significant differences in relation to the sexual assault location, it was found that the all-female group sexual offences were more likely to occur in prison than those involving one or more male co-offenders.

To date, there are no published studies that directly compare female and male multiple perpetrator sexual offenders. Williams *et al.* (2019) compared female and male child sexual abusers; however, only their female sample included multiple perpetrators. They found significant differences between the offender characteristics of lone female offenders (LFO), female multiple perpetrators (FMP), and lone male offenders (LMO) in their psychological dispositions, environmental niche, and factors preceding the offence. For example, LFO tended to have the highest level of personal problems. FMP had poorer self-management than LMO, but better sexual self-regulation. LMO had more sexual abuse supportive cognitions.

Even though there are some inconsistencies in the research, it is nevertheless possible to conclude that there are a number of differences between female lone and multiple perpetrator offenders, victims and offences. Furthermore, there also seem to be some differences between different sized groups with distinctive sex compositions. More research is required to better understand those differences as they could provide information regarding motivations and risk factors important for prevention, assessment and treatment purposes.

Implications for practice

The research conducted to date on MPSO has a number of practical implications for prevention, assessment and treatment purposes. In relation to prevention, research has shown that a great number of multiple perpetrator sexual offences are committed by young people. This means that prevention programmes should be targeted at young adolescents from school level onward. Furthermore, since there is clear empirical evidence for the role of group processes and dynamics in MPSO, these should be incorporated into prevention programmes, where issues such as peer pressure and group behaviours could be addressed. In these programmes young people could learn how to recognize and react appropriately to group processes and dynamics within their own peer group, and challenge their peers that plan or initiate sexual violence.

In relation to risk assessment, when assessing an individual that has committed a MPSO, the factors of young age and socio-economic conditions should be considered as potential risk factors worthy of further exploration, along with any cultural issues of relevance. If these factors are indicated, they should be taken into account when planning intervention.

Additionally, group processes should also be taken into account; the risk level of an offender who participates in a sexual assault in a group setting, where group processes such as peer pressure are involved, is likely to be different to that of a lone sexual offender.

It is likely that some perpetrators of MPSO would not have committed the crime on their own and that group contexts could represent a potential risk factor for them. This means that, on their own, these offenders could be less risky than lone sexual offenders, but in certain group contexts their risk levels for re-offending could be higher. It is important to note that some studies ('t Hart-Kerkhoffs *et al.*, 2011; Woodhams *et al.*, 2012) have identified the presence of leaders and followers in MPSO groups. It is not certain if these leaders have different characteristics to the followers, which could influence their risk of re-offending, but further research is necessary. The research findings overall certainly suggest that MPSO is a heterogeneous crime with diverse perpetrators with varying motivations, which also suggests that there may be differential risk factors. This points to more individualized approaches to intervention based on the unique characteristics of the case under review. Further research is necessary to better understand the individual and situational factors that play a role in MPSO.

In terms of implications for treatment, since group processes and dynamics have been identified as being unique to this type of sexual offending they should be specifically addressed in treatment programmes. Blanchard (1959) and Etgar and Ganot-Prager (2009) reported on the dynamics that they observed between individuals who had participated in the same multiple perpetrator sexual assault, with whom they were working. They found that the dynamics present within the treatment group were similar to those that were present during the assault.

This means it is crucial to analyse a perpetrator's social role within a group and their interactions whilst in a group setting (Etgar, 2013). By analysing the offence, practitioners can gain a better understanding of how the offender interacted with other perpetrators and what their specific role(s) were during the offence. This information could help the practitioner plan an intervention tailored to the offender where they could learn how to recognize group dynamics and react to them in more appropriate ways.

Currently, treatment programmes for sexual offenders do not distinguish between lone and multiple perpetrator sexual offenders. However, the findings summarized in the current chapter clearly demonstrated some differences between these types of sexual offenders. Consequently, they are likely to have different treatment needs. This implies that changes may be needed to adapt existing treatment programmes so that the needs of MPSO offenders are met; elements such as learning to identify and pro-socially react to group dynamics and processes.

Conclusions and future directions

In this chapter, an overview of what is currently known about MPSO theory and research was provided. In relation to theory, there is some empirical support for the Multi-Factorial Theory of MPSO (da Silva *et al.*, 2015). Even though there are still some evidence gaps and more research is necessary to develop it further, this model can be used by researchers and practitioners to help guide their work in the area of MPSO and potentially advance its development. In terms of research, it is possible to conclude that MPSO is a significant global problem that is under-researched. More cross-cultural studies using similar methodologies need to be conducted to gain a better understanding of the extent and characteristics of MPSO. This could be facilitated by separating out lone and multiple perpetrator sexual offences in official government reports, and in studies on sexual violence, extending it also to capture in more detail the role of group process. As illustrated here, research suggests that there are a number of differences between lone, duo, and 3+ group sexual offending. More studies are needed to further examine these differences in diverse samples to determine any differences in typologies, risk levels and motivations, which have implications for assessment and treatment.

Finally, there is also a need for research conducted with community samples, which would provide us with much needed information about unconvicted perpetrators of MPSO. This research could take advantage of more qualitative approaches so that a richer account of this under-researched area could be obtained.

References

Aebi, M., Vogt, G., Plattner, B., Steinhausen, H., and Bessler, C. (2012) Offender types and criminality dimensions in male juveniles convicted of sexual offences. *Sexual Abuse: A Journal of Research and Treatment*, 24(3), 265–288.

Adolfsson, K., Stromwall, L., and Landstrom, S. (2017) Blame attribution in multiple perpetrator rape cases: The impact of sympathy, consent, force, and beliefs. *Journal of Interpersonal Violence*, 1–29. doi: 10.1177/0886260517721171

Alleyne, E., Gannon, T., Ó Ciardha, C., and Wood G. (2014) Community males show multiple-perpetrator rape proclivity: Development and preliminary validation of an interest scale. *Sexual Abuse: A Journal of Research and Treatment*, 26(1), 82–104.

Alleyne, E. and Wood, J. (2010) Gang involvement: Psychological and behavioral characteristics of gang members, peripheral youth and non-gang youth. *Aggressive Behavior*, 36(6), 423–436.

Amir, M. (1971) *Patterns in Forcible Rape*. Chicago, IL: University of Chicago Press.

Australian Bureau of Statistics (2004) *Sexual Assault in Australia: A Statistical Overview, 4523.0*. [Online] Available at: www.abs.gov.au/AUSSTATS/abs@.nsf/DetailsPage/4523.02004 [Accessed 4 Feb 2019].

Bamford, J., Chou, S., and Browne, D. (2016) A systematic review and meta-analysis of the characteristics of multiple perpetrator sexual offences. *Aggression and Violent Behavior*, 28, 82–94.

Bijleveld, C. and Hendriks, J. (2003) Juvenile sex offenders: Differences between group and solo offenders. *Psychology, Crime and Law*, 9(3), 237–245.

Bijleveld, C., Weerman, M., Looije, D., and Hendriks, J. (2007) Group sex offending by juveniles: Coercive sex as group activity. *European Journal of Criminology*, 4(1), 5–31.

Blanchard, H. (1959) The group process in gang rape. *Journal of Social Psychology*, 49(2), 259–266.

Boelrijk, M. (1997) *Minderjarige zedendelinquenten en het strafrecht: de strafrechtelijke aanpak van minderjarige plegers van seksuele delicten*. Amsterdam: VU Uitgeverij.

Brownmiller, S. (1975) *Against Our Will: Men, Women and Rape*. Bowie, MD: Robert Brady.

Budd, M., Bierie, M., and Williams, K. (2017) Deconstructing incidents of female perpetrated sex crimes. *Sexual Abuse: A Journal of Research and Treatment*, 29(3), 267–290.

Chambers, J., Horvath, M., and Kelly, L. (2010) A typology of multiple-perpetrator rape. *Criminal Justice and Behavior*, 37(10), 1114–1139.

Chambers, J., Horvath, M., and Kelly, L. (2013) Reconstructing and sequencing behaviours in multiple perpetrator rape. *Psychology Crime & Law*, 19(3), 253–275.

Curran, K. and Millie, A. (2003) *Rape and Indecent Assault: Incidence and Service Provision in Southwark*. Project Report. London: Safer Southwark Partnership.

da Silva, T., Harkins, L. and Woodhams, J. (2013) Multiple perpetrator rape as an international phenomenon. In M. Horvath, and J. Woodhams (eds), *Handbook on the Study of Multiple Perpetrator Rape: A Multidisciplinary Response to an International Problem* (1st edn). Abingdon: Routledge, pp. 10–36.

da Silva, T., Woodhams, J., and Harkins, L. (2014) Heterogeneity within multiple perpetrator rapes: A national comparison of lone, duo and 3+ perpetrator rapes. *Sexual Abuse: A Journal of Research and Treatment*, 26(6), 503–522.

da Silva, T., Woodhams, J., and Harkins, L. (2015) Multiple perpetrator rape: A critical review of existing explanatory theories. *Aggression and Violent Behavior*, 25(Part A), 150–158.

da Silva, T., Woodhams, J., and Harkins, L. (2018) "An adventure that went wrong": Reasons given by convicted perpetrators of multiple perpetrator sexual offending for their involvement in the offense. *Archives of Sexual Behavior*, 47(2), 443–456.

De Wree, E. (2004) *Perpetrators of Group Rape*. Ghent, Belgium: Ghent University.

Etgar, T. (2013) Multiple perpetrator rape offenders: Treatment issues. In M. Horvath, and J. Woodhams (eds), *Handbook on the Study of Multiple Perpetrator Rape: A Multidisciplinary Response to an International Problem* (1st edn). Abingdon: Routledge, pp. 10–36.

Etgar, T. and Ganot-Prager, K. (2009) Advantages of group therapy for adolescent participants in the same gang rape. *Journal of Child Sexual Abuse*, 18(3), 302–319.

Franklin, K. (2004) Enacting masculinity: Antigay violence and group rape as participatory theatre. Sexuality research and social policy. *Journal of NSRC*, 1(2), 25–40.

Franklin, K. (2013) Masculinity, status, and power: implicit messages in Western media discourse on high-profile cases of multiple perpetrator rape. In M. Horvath, and J. Woodhams (eds), *Handbook on the Study of Multiple Perpetrator Rape: A Multidisciplinary Response to an International Problem* (1st edn). Abingdon: Routledge, 37–66.

Gidycz, C. A. and Koss, M. P. (1990) A comparison of group and individual sexual assault victims. *Psychology of Women Quarterly*, 14, 325–342.

Gillespie, S., Williams, R., Elliott, I., Eldridge, H., Ashfield, S., and Beech, A. (2015) Characteristics of females who sexually offend: A comparison of solo and co-offenders. *Sexual Abuse: A Journal of Research and Treatment*, 27(3), 284–301.

Groth, A. and Birnbaum, H. (1979) *Men who Rape: The Psychology of the Offender*. New York: Plenum.

Harkins, L. and Dixon, L. (2010) Sexual offending in groups: An evaluation. *Aggression and Violent Behavior*, 15(2), 87–99.

Harkins, L. and Dixon, L. (2013) A multi-factorial approach to understanding multiple perpetrator sexual offending. In J. Wood and T. Gannon (eds), *Crime and Crime Reduction: The Importance of Group Processes* (1st edn). New York: Routledge, pp. 75–95.

Hauffe, S. and Porter, L. (2009) An interpersonal comparison of lone and group rape offences. *Psychology, Crime and Law*, 15(5), 469–491.

Hooing, M., Jonker, M., and van Berlo, W. (2010) Juvenile sex offenders in a mandatory educational programme: Subtypes and characteristics. *Journal of Sexual Aggression*, 16(3), 332–346.

Horvath, M. and Kelly, L. (2009) Multiple perpetrator rape: Naming an offence and initial research findings. *Journal of Sexual Aggression*, 15(1) 83–96.

Horvath, M. and Woodhams, J. (eds) (2013) *Handbook on the Study of Multiple Perpetrator Rape: A Multidisciplinary Response to an International Problem*. Abingdon: Routledge.

Jewkes, R., Dunkle, K., Koss, M., Levin, J., Nduna, M., Jama, N., and Sikweyiya, Y. (2006) Rape perpetration by young, rural South African men: Prevalence, patterns and risk factors. *Social Science and Medicine*, 63(11), 2949–2961.

Jewkes, R. and Sikweyiya, Y. (2013) Streamlining: understanding gang rape in South Africa. In M. Horvath and J. Woodhams (eds), *Handbook on the Study of Multiple Perpetrator Rape: A Multidisciplinary Response to an International Problem* (1st edn). Abingdon: Routledge, pp. 116–131.

Jewkes, R., Sikweyiya, Y., Dunkle, K., and Morrell, R. (2015) Relationship between single and multiple perpetrator rape perpetration in South Africa: A comparison of risk factors in a population-based sample. *BMC Public Health*, 15(616), 1–10.

Jewkes, R., Sikweyiya, Y., Morrell, R., and Dunkle, K. (2009) *Understanding Men's Health and Use of Violence: Interface of Rape and HIV in South Africa*. Medical Research Council Policy Brief: Pretoria. Retrieved from South African Medical Research Council. [Online.] Available at: www.mrc.ac.za/sites/default/files/attachments/2016-07-08/violence_hiv.pdf (accessed 5 February 2019).

Jewkes, R., Sikweyiya, Y., Morrell, R., and Dunkle, K. (2011) Gender inequitable masculinity and sexual entitlement in rape perpetration in South Africa: Findings of a cross-sectional study. *PloS One*, 6(11): e29590 [online]. Available at: https://journals.plos.org/plosone/article?id=10.1371/journal.pone.0029590#s1 (accessed 5 February 2019).

Kelly, L., Lovett, J., and Regan, L. (2005) *A Gap or a Chasm? Attrition in Reported Rape Cases*. Home Office Research Study, No. 293. London: Home Office.

Kjellgren, C., Wassberg, A., Carlberg, M., Langstrom, N., and Svedin, C. (2006) Adolescent sexual offenders: A total survey of referrals to Social Services in Sweden and subgroup characteristics. *Sexual Abuse: A Journal of Research and Treatment*, 18(4), 357–372.

Lambine, M. (2013) Numbers matter: characteristic differences between lone, duo and 3+ group rapes. In M. Horvath and J. Woodhams (eds), *Handbook on the Study of Multiple Perpetrator Rape: A Multidisciplinary Response to an International Problem* (1st edn). Abingdon: Routledge, 67–81.

Moreland, R. (2010) Are dyads really groups? *Small Group Research*, 41(2), 251–267.

Morgan, L., Brittain, B., and Welch, J. (2012) Multiple perpetrator sexual assault: How does it differ from assault by a single perpetrator? *Journal of Interpersonal Violence*, 27(12), 2415–2436.
Muskens, M., Bogaerts, S., van Casteren, M., and Labrijn, S. (2011) Adult female sexual offending: A comparison between co-offenders and solo offenders in a Dutch sample. *Journal of Sexual Aggression*, 17(1), 46–60.
Office for National Statistics (2018) *Sexual Offences in England and Wales: Year Ending March 2017*. [Online.] Available at: file:///C:/Users/ab8217/Downloads/Sexual%20offences%20in%20England%20and%20 Wales%20year%20ending%20March%202017%20(1).pdf (accessed 10 January 2019).
O'Sullivan, C. (1991) Acquaintance gang rape on campus. In A. Parrot and L. Bechhofer (eds), *Acquaintance Rape: The Hidden Crime* (1st edn). New York: Wiley, 140– 156.
Park, J. and Kim, S. (2016) Group size does matter: Differences among sexual assaults committed by lone, double, and groups of three or more perpetrators. *Journal of Sexual Aggression*, 22(3), 342–354.
Porter, L. and Alison, L. (2004) Behavioural coherence in violent group activity: An interpersonal model of sexually violent gang behaviour. *Aggressive Behavior*, 30(6), 449–468.
Porter, L. and Alison, L. (2006) Examining group rape: A descriptive analysis of offender and victim behaviour. *European Journal of Criminology*, 3(3), 357–381.
Quarshie, E., Davies, P., Badasu, M., Tagoe, T., Otoo, P., and Afriyie, P. (2018) Multiple perpetrator rape in Ghana: Offenders, victims and offence characteristics. *Journal of Sexual Aggression*, 24(1), 125–141.
Sanday, P. (2007) *Fraternity Gang Rape: Sex, Brotherhood, and Privilege on Campus* (2nd edn). New York: New York University Press.
Scully, D. and Marolla, J. (1985) "Riding the bull at Gilley's": Convicted rapists describe the rewards of rape. *Social Problems*, 32(3), 251–263.
Swart, L., Gilchrist, A., Butchart, A., Seedat, M., and Martin, M. (2000) Rape surveillance through district surgeon offices in Johannesburg, 1996–1998: Evaluation and prevention implications. *South African Journal of Psychology*, 30(2), 1–10.
't Hart-Kerkhoffs, L., Vermeiren, R., Jansen, L., and Doreleijers, T. (2011) Juvenile group sex offenders: A comparison of group leaders and followers. *Journal of Interpersonal Violence*, 26(1), 3–20.
ten Bensel, T., Gibbs, B., and Burkey, R. (2019) Female sex offenders: Is there a difference between solo and co-offenders? *Journal of Interpersonal Violence*, 34(19), 4061–4084. doi: 10.1177/0886260516674202.
Ullman, S. E. (1999) A comparison of gang and individual rape incidents. *Violence and Victims*, 14, 123–133.
Ullman, S. E. (2007) Comparing gang and individual rapes in a community sample of urban women. *Violence and Victims*, 22, 43–51.
Vandiver, D. (2006) Female sex offenders: A comparison of solo offenders and co-offenders. *Violence and Victims*, 21(3), 339–354
Vetten, L. and Haffejee, S. (2005) Gang rape. A study in inner-city Johannesburg. *S. A. Crime Quarterly*, 12, 31–36.
Ward, T. and Beech, A. (2006) An integrated theory of sexual offending. *Aggression and Violent Behavior*, 11(1), 44–63.
Ward, T., Polaschek, D., and Beech, A. (2006) *Theories of Sexual Offending*. Chichester: John Wiley & Sons Ltd.
Weerman, F., Maxson, C., Esbensen, F., Aldridge, J., Medina, J., and van Gemert, F. (2009) *Eurogang Program Manual: Background, Development, and Use of the Eurogang Instruments in Multi-site, Multi-method Comparative Research*. [Online.] Available at: www.umsl.edu/ccj/Eurogang/EurogangManual.pdf (accessed 23 January 2019).
Wijkman, M., Bijleveld, C., and Hendriks, J. (2010) Women don't do such things! Characteristics of female sex offenders and offender types. *Sexual Abuse: A Journal of Research and Treatment*, 22(2), 135–156.
Williams, K. (2010) Dyads can be groups (and often are) *Small Group Research*, 41(2), 268–274.
Williams, K. and Bierie, D. M. (2015) An incident-based comparison of female and male sexual offenders. *Sexual Abuse: A Journal of Research and Treatment*, 27(3), 235–257.
Williams, R., Gillespie, S., Elliott, I., and Eldridge, H. (2019) Characteristics of female solo and female co-offenders and male solo sexual offenders against children. *Sexual Abuse: A Journal of Research and Treatment*, 31(2), 151–172.
Woodhams, J. (2004) Characteristics of juvenile sex offending against strangers: Findings from a non-clinical study. *Aggressive Behavior*, 30, 243–253.
Woodhams, J. (2008) *Juvenile Sex Offending: An Investigative Perspective*. (Unpublished doctoral dissertation). Retrieved from British Library Electronic Theses Online Service (uk.bl.ethos.517673).

Woodhams, J., Gillett, R., and Grant, T. (2007) Understanding the factors that affect the severity of juvenile stranger sex offences: The effect of victim characteristics and number of suspects. *Journal of Interpersonal Violence*, 22, 218–237.

Woodhams, J., Cooke, C., Harkins, L., and da Silva, T. (2012) Leadership in multiple perpetrator stranger rape. *Journal of Interpersonal Violence*, 27(4), 728–752.

Wright, R., and West, D. (1981) Rape: A comparison of group offences and lone assaults. *Medicine, Science and the Law*, 21(1), 25–30.

24

COLLECTIVE VIOLENCE ONLINE

When street gangs use social media

James Densley

Introduction

The internet in general and social media in particular are central to the lives of young people in ways that have developed so rapidly that it is difficult for families, law enforcement, teachers and other statutory professionals to keep pace. A recent Pew Research Centre survey found that fully 95 per cent of US teens have access to a smartphone, and 45 per cent say they are online "almost constantly" (Anderson and Jiang, 2018). The internet provides a space that is less regulated than most other areas of young people's lives, which has obvious benefits for self-expression and creativity (Boyd 2014). Social media can be a powerful platform for young people to craft identity, or to present themselves how they want to be seen – what Ervin Goffman (1959) called, "impression management". However, the absence of "capable guardianship" that somewhat defines the online environment also results in "routine activities", where violent offending and victimization are tangible (Cohen and Felson, 1979). Hence why social media has been described as "a vector for youth violence" (Patton *et al.*, 2014).

Longitudinal survey research has found that gang membership peaks around age 14 (Pyrooz and Sweeten, 2015), thus we can safety say that gang members are, first and foremost, young people. It should come as no surprise, therefore, to learn that gang members are online and that they use the internet for a variety of prosocial and antisocial purposes (e.g. Balasuriya *et al.*, 2016; Densley 2013; Moule *et al.*, 2014; Pyrooz *et al.*, 2015; Van Hellemont, 2012; Womer and Bunker, 2010). Like non-gang members, gang members use the internet for shopping and socializing (Lane, 2018; Moule *et al.*, 2013). Unlike non-gang members, they use the web for "internet banging" (Patton *et al.*, 2013), that is, inciting rival gangs by posting threats and insults and otherwise managing individual and collective gang reputations (Décary-Hétu and Morselli, 2011; Irwin-Rogers and Pinkney, 2017; Irwin-Rogers *et al.*, 2018; Johnson and Schell-Busey, 2016; Lauger and Densley, 2018; Morselli and Décary-Hétu, 2013). This chapter aims to examine some of the finer points of the 'internet banging' phenomena because they can be overstated, or at the very least oversimplified, by the media and policymakers. It will discuss how social media has changed gangs' relationship with each other and with gang territory and how the internet has created new incentives for gang violence and new avenues for its perpetration, with implications for policy and practice.

Gang "set space" in the digital age

Territory has always played an important role in the history of gang life (Thrasher, 1927) and research shows that the physical locations where gang members routinely socialize (i.e. set spaces) or encounter rival gang members (e.g. territorial boundaries) exhibit disproportionately high levels of violence (Brantingham *et al.*, 2012; Huebner *et al.*, 2016; Radil *et al.*, 2010; Taniguchi *et al.*, 2011; Tita *et al.*, 2005). It is well known that a street corner can be a "staging area" for gang violence (Anderson, 1999, p. 76). However, the development of the internet has provided a virtual space in which gang members can interact and foster collective identity. The question thus becomes, does this equally constitute a staging area for violent interactions?

As gangs moved from the analogue world to the digital world, gang members began posting threats and insults online that functioned similarly to threats and insults in the real world (e.g. Johnson and Schell-Busey, 2016; Lauger and Densley, 2018; Patton *et al.*, 2017c). Gang members are sensitive to public insults (Harding, 2010; Horowitz, 1983; Hughes and Short, 2005; Lauger, 2012, Papachristos, 2009), but given that many disputes in physical space do not result in actual violence (Jacobs and Wright, 2006), it is likely that the same is true in virtual space. In fact, social media may even provide a platform upon which gangs can simulate conflict as a cathartic alternative to street-based violence. Arguably, posting online releases the build-up of "destructive energy" that in days past might have escalated to serious violence for those involved, thus echoing the potential views of Lorenz (1966). Further, it allows those watching the action unfold to live vicariously through the participants, safe from any consequences or retaliation.

Alternatively, if someone is attacked online and they cannot sufficiently defend themselves with the digital tools to hand, then the sense of humiliation and shame could mount (Scheff and Schorr, 2017), which would obviously be devastating to a young person's sense of identity and self-worth (see Erikson, 1977). If a fight breaks out on a street corner or school playground, for example, it invariably attracts an audience (Collins, 2008). But when someone films that fight and uploads it to social media, the audience is no longer time and space bound. Social media transforms everyday violence into dramatic spectacle that lives in perpetuity (Surette, 2015). Gang youth are repeatedly victimized each and every time any initial victimization is replayed, shared, or repurposed on the internet (e.g. Frey, 2018). Overexposure could potentially incite them to retaliatory violence in an effort to save face (i.e. avoid embarrassment and preserve reputation), especially when perceived taunts and insults remain "live" and can be rerun indefinitely. Consistent with Gilligan (1997), if they fight back against the treatment they have received and against those who have shamed them, revenge becomes an act of justice and a reassertion of selfhood and pride.

Gang embeddedness and disengagement in the digital age

In many ways, social media has changed what it means to be a "member" of a gang. While the typical gang member only stays active for about two years (Pyrooz and Sweeten, 2015), virtual proximity has the potential to prolong involvement in and exposure to gang life. Even without the internet, incarcerated or ex-gang members maintain social and emotional ties to their former gangs (Pyrooz *et al.*, 2014). With the internet, however, "gang embeddedness" and participation feel different (Pyrooz *et al.*, 2013). Take, for instance, incarcerated gang members, who are physically detached from day-to-day gang activity, but now able to post to social media using concealed mobile phones (for an example, see Storrod and Densley, 2017).

For the collective gang, social media from prison showcases global reach and security threat level, which can simultaneously impress friends and intimidate rivals. For the individual gang member, a prison selfie or fight video is the "holy grail" because the setting validates their "criminal credentials" and the medium demonstrates additional contempt for the law because they shouldn't have a cell phone in the first place (Densley, 2013; Gambetta, 2009). On the streets, reputation is everything (Harding, 2014; Lauger, 2012) and while prison has been described as a "badge of honour" for some gang members, prisoners do fear being forgotten. Therefore, correspondence from the inside helps the incarcerated gang member stay more than just connected; they stay *relevant* to the outside and achieve expressive status goals (Storrod and Densley, 2017).

For the first time in history, gang reputations can now be quantified, so every new follower or like or retweet becomes a measure of their success. But what happens to all that demonstrable "street capital" (Harding, 2014) once an individual disengages from the gang? A visual record of one's past life could easily be used to disqualify ex-gang members from full social acceptance or from accessing social services such as education, employment, training, and housing (Pager, 2007). Within the European General Data Protection Regulations that became law in May 2018, there is the "right to erasure", more commonly known as "the right to be forgotten", which means that an individual has the right to have all of their personal data erased without undue delay, especially if it is causing them undue harm. Perhaps by deleting their entire social media profile, ex-gang members can now credibly "signal" their disengagement from the gang better than ever before (Densley and Pyrooz, 2017). Alternatively, social media also provides a powerful public platform to denounce or renounce gang membership and to evidence ongoing "recovery" (Flores, 2013). Either way, there is something about social media that redefines the "ties that bind" people to gangs (Pyrooz *et al.*, 2014).

The cycle of gang violence online

Online social networks supplement face-to-face sociability, rather than replace it (Chayko, 2008), and on the "digital street" the real and the virtual routinely overlap to create a "networked life" (Lane, 2018). For example, gang-involved youth will physically trespass into areas associated with rival gangs, film themselves defacing or disrespecting those areas, then post these videos online to expose the security breach and taunt and humiliate the opposing gang, who, in turn, might respond in kind (Densley, 2013; Irwin-Rogers and Pinkney, 2017). There are many examples of conflict enacted online spilling out into real world violence, such as when threatening Twitter activity preceded the murder of one Chicago gang member (Patton *et al.*, 2017b). While physical conflicts in the street are sporadic, social media is continuous, which means a victim of abuse may find it difficult to escape or hide. HM Inspectorate of Probation (2017, 18) reported one UK case whereby "a young person had appeared in a gang video filmed outside of his home. A rival gang identified the location of the home and a group arrived one evening to intimidate and cause damage to the home". Such an example demonstrates how the internet has changed what it means to be a victim of gang violence today, not least because it thrusts people into the spotlight with or without their consent.

In their extension of Decker's (1996) cycle of gang violence model, Moule *et al.*, (2017) account for some of the contextual-, group- and individual-level factors that may predict when insults thrown online translate to violence in real life. They argue, for example, that close proximity to other gangs in physical space may increase the likelihood that online threats escalate into violence on the street. Likewise, particular responses to online provocations may correlate with individual levels of immersion or "embeddedness" in the culture of the gang (Pyrooz *et al.*, 2013). Core gang members, or gang youth with tenuous "street capital" (Harding, 2014), may feel more inclined (or compelled) to back up their fighting words with violent deeds compared with periphery gang members, for example. Dispositional characteristics already tied to violent offending, such as adherence to street code (Anderson, 1999) or low levels of self-control (Gottfredson and Hirschi, 1990), may also help explain differential reactions to online slights. Consistent with retaliatory violence offline (Decker, 1996; Papachristos, 2009), Moule and colleagues (2017) found that gang members were more likely than non-gang members to report that: (a) online provocations led to offline violence; (b) they would respond to instances of gang disrespect; and (c) they would retaliate for violence against their gang. Part of the need to retaliate stems from the need to develop a dangerous reputation that can intimidate others to not interfere in the gang's business (Felson, 2006). Such reputations are hard earned and often established via status-seeking violent performances (Gambetta, 2009), which, as the following section describes, take new forms in the digital age.

Status-seeking violence online

"If it bleeds, it leads" wrote journalist Eric Pooley in 1989. The phrase was primarily a critique of mass media sensationalism and how, in the process of commanding higher ratings, coverage of murder and mayhem had suppressed any real news. Ultimately, "if it bleeds, it leads", was a statement about the public's fear of, and fascination with, violence. In the digital age, this phrase takes on an even deeper meaning.

Scholars and practitioners of violence understand well that violence is difficult to perform, which is why most of us abstain from it (Collins, 2008). Even those who do not (e.g. gang members), spend far more time *talking* about it than actually doing it (Lauger, 2014). Since its peak in the mid-1990s, moreover, interpersonal violence, as measured by traditional crime statistics, is generally in decline (Sharkey, 2018). This makes the rise of "cyber violence" so intriguing (Peterson and Densley, 2017a). On YouTube, Facebook, Twitter, or Instagram, there are thousands of examples of people, including gang members, engaged in violent deeds that in days past would have remained hidden from public view (Ferrell *et al.*, 2015; Sandberg and Ugelvik, 2016; Surette, 2015).

The question is, why? Why do people post at times deadly and extravagant acts of violence online knowing that in this digital age of perfect remembering, it can and will be used as evidence against them? The simple answer may be because people are watching. Indeed, we can map the trajectory of so-called performance violence from the advent of videotape in the 1980s, to the "reality television" and sex tape celebrities of the 1990s, to the self-made influencers who become "instafamous" online and leverage that fame into book deals and corporate sponsorships. The internet can turn nobody into somebody very quickly. For people who may already feel that the world ignores them or fails to see them as they wish "to be seen" (Yar, 2012), this can be seductive.

An electronically-mediated world gives new meaning to William Shakespeare's observation that, "All the world's a stage, and all the men and women merely players" (for a discussion see Surette, 2015). For the first time in history, young people carry with them a (video) camera at all times. Thanks to smart phones, people can live even the most intimate moments of their private lives in public. And, thanks to social media, there are powerful incentives to do so. If people see something they like, they post it. If they see something they don't like, they often post it more. This "will to representation" (Yar, 2012) means that one's *subjective* reality becomes *objectively* quantified and validated by the number of likes, views, retweets, friends, and followers they accumulate. People start to behave as though, should a tree fall in the woods with nobody there to capture it for Instagram, it wouldn't make a sound (Peterson and Densley, 2017b).

It is arguably exhausting living like this – the pressures to perform in "the age of the selfie" (Jurriëns, 2016; Sandberg and Ugelvik, 2016); the fear of missing out; the need to create a constant stream of content in order to keep up with the Joneses – or the Kardashians; to continue being "the best" by being the most talked about and outdoing oneself each time. But, as noted earlier, "If it bleeds, it leads". What better way to *win the internet* than through violence? Violence has proven display value (Densley, 2013; Gambetta, 2009) and as any prize fighter or street corner youth can testify, violence is a route to respect and social status (Anderson, 1999; Felson, 1982; Messerschmidt, 1993). Wilkinson (2001, p. 232) explains, "Violence often is used to perpetuate and refine the pursuit of 'toughness,' and to claim the identity of being among the toughest". To the extent that gang membership is itself an identity "performance" (Garot, 2010), the performance of violence online makes sense. The internet is the new public square.

We all want to be acknowledged, confirmed, and celebrated. Arguably our deepest need is to be seen (Goffman, 1959). To be seen how they want to be seen, gang members' perform more than just violence online (Van Hellemont, 2012), but violence best meets the definition of "clickbait", that is, something designed to entice users to follow that link to other online content. Such explains why someone would be willing to fatally shoot her own boyfriend from about a foot away whilst he held a book to his chest during a stunt intended for YouTube (Stevens, 2017). Why an 18-year-old girl would livestream the rape of her 17-year-old friend on Periscope, allegedly because she "got caught up on the likes" the video was receiving (McPhate, 2016). And why, the white supremacist who killed 50 people at two mosques in Christchurch, New Zealand, livestreamed his shooting rampage to Facebook from a head-mounted camera (Densley and Peterson, 2019).

With time, visual recognition algorithms will be able to recognize violent imagery as it is uploaded and "hash" (electronically censor) it to prevent it from being reposted, possibly disincentivizing the performance of violence (Densley and Peterson, 2019). In the meantime, incessantly bombarded with the sights, sounds, and emotions of shootings, stabbings, and sexual assaults posted online, youth risk becoming desensitized to violent acts; or worse, learn to think of them as viable solutions to life's problems. Watching unedited, unpredictable, and sometimes disturbing violence on auto-play and continuous loop can arguably create "vicarious traumatization" for young people (Lerias and Byrne, 2003). So too can being constantly reminded of dead friends and "fallen soldiers" lost to gang warfare (see Frey, 2018; Patton *et al.*, 2018a). Analyses of Twitter content have even found that expressions of grief and loss predict increased future aggression among gang-involved youth (Patton *et al.*, 2018b).

The threat of violence, both real and perceived, is what drives gang recruitment for protection (Melde *et al.*, 2009). In the digital age, that threat is always present and always looming. Immersion in violence can feed a belief system that our neighbourhoods and communities are unsafe, that violent crime rates are rising, that our odds of being a victim are greater than they really are, and that the world is a dangerous place. This fear and anxiety can normalize joining gangs and carrying weapons, building on traditional notions of gang identity that promise both excitement and protection (Densley, 2013), thus creating a "copycat" or snowball effect – a theory that holds people will act out violence in patterns similar to the violence they see (Surette, 2017).

Violent performances achieve mostly expressive goals, but they can also feed the instrumental activity of gangs, such as drug dealing via "County lines".

Instrumental violence and County lines

"County lines" is a term used by the police to describe a growing practice among UK gangs: travelling from major cities to remote rural areas, market towns, or coastal locations in search of new customers for illicit goods and services, especially heroin and crack cocaine (Andell and

Pitts, 2018; Coomber and Moyle, 2018; Robinson *et al.*, 2018; Windle and Briggs, 2015). Technology is the central organizing feature of the County lines business model because drugs are sold over a network of dedicated mobile phone "lines" (McLean *et al.*, 2020, p. 4). County lines have also initiated ugly forms of technologically-enabled coercion and exploitation. First, marginalized and vulnerable young people are recruited over social media, with gang members, who have amassed huge followings online like local celebrities and influencers (Scotter, 2019), luring them by showing off images of the alleged proceeds of crime – cash, designer clothing, and luxury cars (Storrod and Densley, 2017).

Young girls and women are also targeted by men who create the impression of a romantic relationship before subjecting them to coercive control (Densley *et al.*, 2013). Control of young men and women extends to them being filmed whilst being abused, beaten and humiliated (by their own gang), or whilst allegedly fraternising with the enemy (such as being in places where they should not be). Sextortion and revenge porn (i.e. the sharing of private sexual photographs or films) are other concerns, for young women especially (Boyle 2010). Owing to its intrinsic potential for damage, this *kompromat* becomes "digital collateral" (Storrod and Densley, 2017) that can be employed as a hostage in establishing a credible commitment to the gang (Gambetta, 2009). This is where gang violence overlaps with other forms of "cyber violence" (Peterson and Densley, 2017a), such as cyberstalking and harassment, humiliation porn (Boyle, 2010), and online exposing and shaming known as "doxing".

Next, GPS location tags and popular apps such as *Find iPhone* or *Find Friends* are routinely used to keep young recruits in constant contact and under constant surveillance as they travel far from home (Storrod and Densley, 2017). Youngsters may be asked by higher-ranking gang members to provide photo or video evidence of their journeys, their surroundings, and their activities. They get asked to livestream (via FaceTime, Snapchat and WhatsApp) not only where they are and who is with them, but also that they still have drugs they were given to sell or money they have earned through selling. This round-the-clock surveillance, known as "remote mothering" but tantamount to remote controlling (Storrod and Densley, 2017), makes it difficult for young people to focus on anything other than the gang or to seek help without arousing suspicion from gang leaders.

On platforms such as Snapchat and Instagram, violent images can be posted momentarily and taken down instantly, leaving little trace evidence. The temporary nature of these communications and the end-to-end encryption provided by messaging tools such as WhatsApp, however, only partially safeguard gang members from law enforcement or social service intervention. Every message sent or image posted leaves a digital fingerprint (Goodman, 2015). A time-stamped record of an incident shared can make it harder to cast doubt upon evidence later drawn from memory – something that sexual violence survivors routinely encounter (Riedel and Welsh, 2015). By making violent victimization visible, social media forces practitioners and policymakers to rethink violence prevention and intervention for the digital age (Frey, 2018). However, over-interpretation of some online content has collateral consequences – perhaps best illustrated by the debate over the veracity of gang-related rap music videos.

Expressive violence and rap music videos

Gangs have long used music videos to present gang life as aspirational. As technology has improved, the look and feel of these videos has changed from amateurish and freeform to professional and crafted (Densley, 2012; Irwin-Rogers and Pinkney, 2017; Lauger and Densley, 2018; Storrod and Densley, 2017; Urbanik and Haggerty, 2018). For gangs involved in County lines, a good rap video can both promote a fearsome reputation that will warn off competitors and create brand recognition of the illicit goods and services that the gang provides to potential customers (Storrod and Densley, 2017) and, like professionals on LinkedIn or celebrities on Twitter, gang members must create their own brand.

However, too much exposure can run the risk of evidence that can be used against you, hence why some gangs openly use social media as a means of advertising, whilst others eschew it as attracting unwanted attention (Whittaker *et al.*, 2018). Videos posted online tend to feature younger gang members, who have the most to gain from "signalling" their reputations (Densley, 2013). The videos tend not to feature the most senior members of the gang, who have already accumulated "street capital" (Harding, 2014) and prefer to maintain a low public profile to avoid police attention.

Drill music, a subgenre of trap rap that originated in Chicago but is popular in the UK, has come in for heavy criticism by Metropolitan Police Chief Cressida Dick, who in 2018 called on platforms such as YouTube to remove content which "glamourizes" violent crime (Waterson, 2018). Trap (short for "trap house") is a slang term for a place where drugs are produced and sold, but the idea of being "trapped" on the streets is also present (Storrod and Densley, 2017). Like gangster rap before it, trap and drill blur the line between realism, sensationalism, and social commentary (Chang, 2005). Some trap and drill rappers are so popular and influential that they create a looped reality whereby, "the street scripts the screen and the screen scripts the street" (Ferrell *et al.*, 2015, p. 259).

For young people who make music, video is a key way to share their work with a wider audience and potentially make money from doing so (Irwin-Rogers and Pinkney, 2017; Storrod and Densley, 2017). Online platforms such as SBTV, LinkUp TV, and GRM Daily are all popular urban music sites in Britain that feed YouTube and other commercial outlets. These videos primarily offer a means of enhancing personal reputations and pursuing *expressive* goals such as identity, friendship, and (in the case of "diss tracks") revenge that are separate from *instrumental* concerns (Storrod and Densley, 2017). But the right video at the right time can further the material interests of the gang, both in terms of enhancing its collective reputation and, in rare cases where they go viral and attract subscribers, through ad views. For both reasons, music videos are now routinely analysed in terms of both lyrics and behaviour and scanned for evidence of wrongdoing.

Individual sharing of drill or trap music on YouTube is now potential criteria for adding names to the Metropolitan Police Service's database of purported gang members (the "Gangs Matrix"), because music videos featuring gang names or signs are considered an indicator of likely gang affiliation (Densley and Pyrooz, 2019b). Civil liberties groups and internet scholars worry that YouTube is becoming a mode of surveillance and intelligence gathering for control agents, whereby activities on social media create guilt by association (see Amnesty International, 2018; Lane *et al.*, 2019; Patton *et al.*, 2017a). Making a music video to upload and share online is an everyday pursuit for many young people. The majority of youth who do so are not gang members or committing any crime, yet they are increasingly rendered as troublesome and subject to suspicion and censorship.

In many ways, the current debate about drill and trap is only the latest in a long series of panics about rap songs and music videos (see Kubrin and Nielson, 2014). Performance personas adopted by rap MCs often articulate experiences of life on the margins and, therefore, reflect the crime and violence that is seen and heard in their everyday surroundings (Harkness, 2014). Some artists rap about gangs because they come from gang backgrounds – reflecting, not shaping, the reality of marginalized youth. As with other genres and art forms, however, this creative expression includes a mix of fantasy and reality. Myth-making is a recognized characteristic of gang culture (Howell, 2007; Lauger, 2012; Van Hellemont and Densley, 2019), therefore, it can be difficult to distinguish between content that uses artistic licence to comment on and reference criminal acts and content that is alleged to be a visual record of actual wrongdoing or an incitement to wrongdoing. The internet certainly complicates what Felson (2006) referred to as "big gang theory", whereby lesser-known gangs borrow established signs and symbols from large, notorious gangs, such as Bloods and Crips, in an effort to establish reputations as groups to be feared, without ever having to actually develop those reputations through violent action (see also, Densley, 2012).

Still, the implication is that as easy as it is for gangs to monitor their members via smart phones and social media, law enforcement can do the same. As easy as it is for individuals to post material online that can leave them vulnerable to intimidation, so it is that they can post content that leaves them open to arrest and prosecution. There are some legal and ethical questions about whether police can enter into an online relationship with an alleged gang member (e.g. by "friending" them on Facebook) without first disclosing their true identity, but in reality it happens all the time (e.g. Densley, 2013, p. 99). Law enforcement and social service providers monitor social media for warning signs of escalating tensions between rival gangs so that the transmission of violence can be interrupted (Patton *et al.*, 2016). As technology improves, much like how Netflix can predict the movies we like to watch, deep learning algorithms will be able to read for signs that people wish to do others grievous harm, and therefore potentially intervene even earlier. However, we cannot leave it all to the computer scientists. An algorithm is only as good as its trainer and deep learning is only as good as its data. Gang experts, community violence specialists, and, importantly, young people who understand both the code of the street and the context-specific language of social media are needed to help design fair, impartial, and responsive AI systems (Frey, 2018; Patton *et al.*, 2018a).

Concluding remarks

This chapter has presented some of the ways in which the internet and social media influence and facilitate gang life and gang violence. Everything described herein meets the definition of "problematic internet use" (Moreno, 2013, p. 113). As social media becomes a stronger and less predictable driving force in young people's lives, it is vitally important that (a) researchers continue to study how gangs and the internet intersect and (b) practitioners and policymakers take the power of social media seriously. Hospital admissions for injuries caused by stabbings, like the total number of knife offences, have been rising across the UK since 2014 (HM Government, 2018). In 2018, 285 killings involving knives took place, the highest number in a single year since 1946, and 39 of these deaths were young people under the age of 20. Gangs and/or social media are not the *only* or even the *primary* drivers of rising weapon-enabled youth violence in the UK; but the analysis presented in this chapter suggests that we ignore them at our peril. Gang life is constantly evolving (Densley, 2014) and a digital overlay on what has always been an "interstitial" phenomena (Thrasher, 1927) has the potential to define collective violence.

References

Amnesty International UK (2018) *Trapped in the Matrix*. London: Author.

Andell, J. and Pitts, J. (2018) The end of the line? The impact of county lines drug distribution on youth crime in a target destination', *Youth and Policy*. Online. Available www.youthandpolicy.org/articles/the-end-of-the-line/

Anderson, E. (1999) *Code of the Street*. New York: W. W. Norton and Company.

Anderson, M. and Jiang, J. (2018) Teens, social media and technology 2018. *Pew Research Centre*. Online. Available www.pewinternet.org/2018/05/31/teens-social-media-technology-2018/

Balasuriya, L., Wijeratne, S., Doran, D., and Sheth, A. (2016) Finding street gang members on Twitter. *2016 IEEE/ACM International Conference on Advances in Social Networks Analysis and Mining (ASONAM)*, pp. 685–692.

Boyd, D. (2014) *It's Complicated: The Social Lives of Networked Teens*. New Haven, CT: Yale University Press.

Boyle, K. (ed.) (2010) *Everyday Pornography*. London: Routledge.

Brantingham, P. J., Tita, G. E., Short, M. B., and Reid, S. E. (2012) The ecology of gang territorial boundaries. *Criminology*, 50, 851–885.

Chang, J. (2005) *Can't Stop, Won't Stop*. New York: St. Martin's Press.

Chayko, M. (2008) *Portable Communities*. Albany, NY: SUNY Press.

Cohen, L. and Felson, M. (1979) Social change and crime rate trends: A routine activity approach. *American Sociological Review*, 44, 488–608.

Collins, R. (2008) *Violence: A Micro-Sociological Theory*. Princeton, NJ: Princeton University Press.

Coomber, R. and Moyle, L. (2018) The changing shape of street-level heroin and crack supply in England: Commuting, holidaying and cuckooing drug dealers across 'county lines'. *The British Journal of Criminology*, 58, 1323–1342.

Décary-Hétu, D. and Morselli, C. (2011) Gang presence in social network sites. *International Journal of Cyber Criminology*, 5, 876–890.

Decker, S. (1996) Collective and normative features of gang violence. *Justice Quarterly*, 13, 243–264.

Densley, J. (2012) The organisation of London's street gangs. *Global Crime*, 13, 42–64.

Densley, J. (2013) *How Gangs Work*. New York: Palgrave Macmillan.

Densley, J. (2014) It's gang life, but not as we know it: the evolution of gang business. *Crime & Delinquency*, 60, 517–546.

Densley, J., Davis, A., and Mason, N. (2013) Girls and gangs: preventing multiple perpetrator rape. In M. Horvath and J. Woodhams (eds), *Handbook on the Study of Multiple Perpetrator Rape*. Abingdon, UK: Routledge, pp. 255–281.

Densley, J. and Peterson, J. (2019) Terrorism is a performance. Don't watch. *Star Tribune*. Online. Available www.startribune.com/terrorism-is-a-performance-don-t-watch/507322442/

Densley, J. and Pyrooz, D. C. (2019a) A signaling perspective on disengagement from gangs. *Justice Quarterly*, 36, pp. 31–58.

Densley, J. and Pyrooz, D. (2019b) The Matrix in context: taking stock of police gang databases in London and beyond. *Youth Justice*. Online. Available 10.1177/1473225419883706

Erikson, E. (1977) *Toys and Reasons*. New York: W. W. Norton.

Felson, M. (2006) The street gang strategy. In M. Felson (ed.), *Crime and Nature*. Thousand Oaks, CA: Sage, pp. 305–324.

Felson, R. B. (1982) Impression management and the escalation of aggression and violence. *Social Psychological Quarterly*, 45, pp. 245–254.

Ferrell, J., Hayward, K., and Young, J. (2015) *Cultural Criminology: An Invitation*. Thousand Oaks, CA: Sage.

Flores, E. O. (2013) *God's Gangs*. New York: NYU Press.

Frey, W. (2018) Humanizing digital mental health through social media: Centering experiences of gang-involved youth exposed to high rates of violence. *Biomedical Informatics Insights*, 10, 1–5.

Gambetta, D. (2009) *Codes of the Underworld*. Princeton, NJ: Princeton University Press.

Garot, R. (2010) *Who you Claim: Performing Gang Identity in School and on the Streets*. New York: New York University Press.

Gilligan, J. (1997) *Violence*. New York: Vintage Books.

Goodman, M. (2015) *Future Crimes*. New York: Doubleday.

Goffman, E. (1959) *The Presentation of Self in Everyday Life*. New York: Anchor.

Gottfredson, M. and Hirschi, T. (1990) *A General Theory of Crime*. Stanford, CA: Stanford University Press.

Harding, D. J. (2010) *Living the Drama*. Chicago: University of Chicago Press.

Harding, S. (2014) *The Street Casino*. Bristol: Policy Press.

Harkness, G. (2014) *Chicago Hustle and Flow*. Minneapolis, MN: University of Minnesota Press.

HM Inspectorate of Probation, (2017) The work of youth offending teams to protect the public. Online. Available www.justiceinspectorates.gov.uk/hmiprobation.

HM Government (2018) *Serious Violence Strategy*. Online. Available www.gov.uk/government/publications/serious-violence-strategy

Horowitz, R. (1983) *Honor and the American Dream*. New Brunswick, NJ: Rutgers University Press.
Howell, J. C. (2007) Menacing or mimicking? Realities of youth gangs. *Juvenile and Family Court Journal*, 58, 39–50.
Huebner. B. M., Martin, K., Moule R. K., Pyrooz, D., and Decker, S. H. (2016) Dangerous places: Gang members and neighborhood levels of gun assault. *Justice Quarterly*, 33, 836–862.
Hughes, L. A. and Short, J. F. (2005) Disputes involving youth street gang members: Micro-social contexts. *Criminology*, 43, 43–76.
Irwin-Rogers, K. and Pinkney, C. (2017) *Social Media as a Catalyst and Trigger for Youth Violence*. London: Catch22.
Irwin-Rogers, K., Densley, J., and Pinkney, C. (2018) Gang violence and social media. In J. L. Ireland, P. Birch, and C. A. Ireland (eds), *The Routledge International Handbook of Human Aggression*. Abingdon, UK: Routledge, pp. 400–410.
Jacobs, B. A. and Wright, R. (2006) *Street Justice*. New York: Cambridge University Press.
Johnson, J. and Schell-Busey, N. (2016) Old message in a new bottle: Taking gang rivalries online through rap battle music videos on YouTube. *Journal of Qualitative Criminal Justice and Criminology*, 4, 42–81.
Jurriëns, E. (2016) Intimate video? Creative bodies in the age of the selfie. *Continuum*, 30, 1–19.
Kubrin, C. and Nielson, E. (2014) Rap on trial. *Race & Justice*, 4, 185–211.
Lane, J. (2018) *The Digital Street*. New York: Oxford University Press.
Lane, J., Ramirez, F., and Pearce, K. E. (2019) Guilty by visible association: Socially mediated visibility in gang prosecutions. *Journal of Computer-Mediated Communication*, 23, 354–369.
Lauger, T. (2012) *Real Gangstas*. New Brunswick, NJ: Rutgers University Press.
Lauger, T. (2014) Violent stories: Personal narratives, street socialization, and the negotiation of street culture among street-oriented youth, *Criminal Justice Review*, 39, 182–200.
Lauger, T. and Densley, J. (2018) Broadcasting badness: Violence, identity, and performance in the online gang rap scene. *Justice Quarterly*, 35, 816–841.
Lerias, D. and Byrne, M. K. (2003) Vicarious traumatization: symptoms and predictors. *Stress and Health*, 19, 129–138.
Lorenz, K. (1966) *On Aggression*. New York: Harcourt, Brace & World, Inc.
McLean, R. Robinson, G., and Densley, J. (2020) *County Lines: Criminal Networks and Evolving Drug Markets in Britain*. Cham, Switzerland: Springer.
McPhate, M. (2016) Teenager is accused of live-streaming a friend's rape on Periscope. *New York Times*, 18 April. Online. Available www.nytimes.com/2016/04/19/us/periscope-rape-case-columbus-ohio-video-livestreaming.html
Melde, C., Taylor, T. J. and Esbensen, F. A. (2009) "I've got your back": An examination of the protective function of gang membership. *Criminology*, 47, 565–594.
Messerschmidt, J. W. (1993) *Masculinities and Crime*. Lanham, MD: Roman and Littlefield.
Moreno, M. A. (2013) *Sex, Drugs n Facebook*. Alameda: Hunter House.
Morselli, C. and Décary-Hétu, D. (2013) Crime facilitation purposes of social networking sites: A review and analysis of the "cyberbanging" phenomenon. *Small Wars and Insurgencies*, 24, 152–170.
Moule, R. K., Pyrooz, D. C., and Decker, S. H. (2013) From "what the f#@% is a Facebook" to "who doesn't use Facebook?": The role of criminal lifestyles in the adoption of the use of the Internet. *Social Science Research*, 42, 1411–1421.
Moule, R. K., Pyrooz, D. C. and Decker, S. H. (2014) Internet adoption and online behaviour among American street gangs: Integrating gangs and organizational theory. *British Journal of Criminology*, 54, 1186–1206.
Moule, R. K., Decker, S. H., and Pyrooz, D. C. (2017) Technology and conflict: Group processes and collective violence in the Internet era. *Crime, Law and Social Change*, 68, 47–73.
Pager, D. (2007) *Marked*. Chicago, IL: University of Chicago Press.
Papachristos A. (2009) Murder by structure: Dominance relations and the social structure of gang homicide. *American Journal of Sociology*, 115, 74–128.
Papachristos, A., Hureau, D., and Braga, A. (2013) The corner and the crew: The influence of geography and social networks on gang violence. *American Sociological Review*, 78, 417–447.
Patton, D. U., Eschmann, R. D., and Butler, D. A. (2013) Internet banging: New trends in social media, gang violence, masculinity and hip hop. *Computers in Human Behavior*, 29, A54–A59.
Patton, D. U., Hong, J. S., Ranney, M., Patel, S., Kelley, C., Eschmann, R., and Washington, T. (2014) Social media as a vector for youth violence: A review of the literature. *Computers in Human Behavior*, 35, 548–553.

Patton, D. U., Eschmann, R., Elsaesser, C., and Bocanegrad, E. (2016) Sticks, stones and Facebook accounts: What violence outreach workers know about social media and urban-based gang violence in Chicago. *Computers in Human Behavior*, 65, 591–600.

Patton, D. U., Brunton, D-W., Dixon, A., Miller, R. J., Leonard, P., and Hackman R. (2017a) Stop and frisk online: Theorizing everyday racism in digital policing in the use of social media for identification of criminal conduct and associations. *Social Media and Society*, 3, 1–10.

Patton, D. U., Lane, J., Leonard, P., Macbeth, J., and Smith Lee, J. R. (2017b) Gang violence on the digital street: Case study of a South Side Chicago gang member's Twitter communication. *New Media and Society*, 19, 1000–1018.

Patton, D. U., Patel, S., Sung Hong, J., Ranney, M. L., Crandall, M. and Dungy, L. (2017c) Tweets, gangs, and guns: a snapshot of gang communications in Detroit. *Violence and Victims*, 32, 919–934.

Patton D. U., MacBeth, J., Schoenebeck, S., Shear, K., and McKeown, K. (2018a) Accommodating grief on twitter: an analysis of expressions of grief among gang involved youth on twitter using qualitative analysis and natural language processing, *Biomedical Informatics Insights*, 10. doi: 10.1177/1178222618763155.

Patton D. U., Rambow, O., Auerbach, J., Li, K., and Frey, W. (2018b) Expressions of loss predict aggressive comments on Twitter among gang-involved youth in Chicago. *NPJ Digital Medicine*, 1. Online. Available www.nature.com/articles/s41746-018-0020-x

Peterson, J. and Densley, J. (2017a) Cyber violence: What do we know and where do we go from here? *Aggression and Violent Behavior*, 34, 193–200.

Peterson, J. and Densley, J. (2017b) Why the trend of posting gruesome acts online? *Star Tribune*. Online. Available www.startribune.com/why-the-trend-of-posting-gruesome-acts-online/419900553/

Pooley, E. (1989) Grins, gore, and videotape: The trouble with local TV news. *New York Magazine*, 9 October. Online. Available https://books.google.com/books?id=_OcCAAAAMBAJ&printsec=frontcover&source=gbs_ge_summary_r&cad=0#v=onepage&q&f=false

Pyrooz, D. C., Decker, S. H., and Moule, R. K. (2015) Criminal and routine activities in online settings: Gangs, offenders, and the Internet. *Justice Quarterly*, 32, 471–499.

Pyrooz, D. C., Decker, S., and Webb, V. (2014) The ties that bind: Desistance from gangs. *Crime & Delinquency*, 60, 491–516.

Pyrooz, D. C. and Sweeten, G. (2015) Gang membership between ages 5 and 17 years in the United States. *Journal of Adolescent Health*, 56, 414–419.

Pyrooz, D. C., Sweeten, G., and Piquero, A. R. (2013) Continuity and change in gang membership and gang embeddedness. *Journal of Research in Crime and Delinquency*, 50, 239–271.

Radil, S. M. Flint, C., and Tita, G. E. (2010) Spatializing social networks: Using social network analysis to investigate geographies of gang rivalry, territory, and violence in Los Angeles. *Annals of the Association of American Geographers*, 100, 307–326.

Riedel, M. and Welsh, W. (2015) *Criminal Violence* (4th edn). New York: Oxford University Press.

Robinson, G., McLean, R., and Densley, J. (2018) Working county lines: child criminal exploitation and illicit drug dealing in Glasgow and Merseyside. *International Journal of Offender Therapy and Comparative Criminology*. Online. Available 10.1177/0306624X18806742.

Sandberg, S. and Ugelvik, T. (2016) Why do offenders tape their crimes? Crime and punishment in the age of the selfie. *British Journal of Criminology*, 57, 1023–1040.

Scheff, S. and Schorr, M. (2017) *Shame Nation*. Naperville, IL: Sourcebooks.

Scotter, K. (2019) The gang killers who are YouTube celebrities. *BBC News*. Online. Available www.bbc.com/news/uk-england-suffolk-45749043

Sharkey, P. (2018) *Uneasy Peace*. New York: W. W. Norton & Company.

Stevens, M. (2017) Woman who fatally shot boyfriend in YouTube stunt pleads guilty. *New York Times*, 19 December. Online. Available www.nytimes.com/2017/12/19/us/youtube-shooting-minnesota-guilty-plea.html

Storrod, M. and Densley, J. (2017) 'Going viral' and 'Going country': The expressive and instrumental activities of street gangs on social media. *Journal of Youth Studies*, 20, 677–696.

Surette, R. (2015) Performance crime and justice. *Current Issues in Criminal Justice*, 27, 195.

Surette, R. (2017) Copycat crime. *Oxford Research Encyclopaedia in Criminology and Criminal Justice*. Online. Available 10.1093/acrefore/9780190264079.013.33

Taniguchi, T. A., Ratcliffe, J. H., and Taylor, R. B. (2011) Gang set space, drug markets, and crime around drug corners in Camden. *Journal of Research in Crime and Delinquency*, 48, 327–363.

Thrasher, F. (1927) *The Gang*. Chicago: University of Chicago Press.

Tita, G. E., Cohen, J., and Engberg, J. (2005) An ecological study of gang "set space". *Social Problems*, 52, 272–299.

Urbanik, M. and Haggerty, K. (2018) #It's dangerous: The online world of drug dealers, rappers and the street code, *The British Journal of Criminology*, 58, 1343–1360.

Van Hellemont, E. (2012) Gangland online: Performing the real imaginary world of gangstas and ghettos in Brussels, *European Journal of Crime, Criminal Law and Criminal Justice*, 20, 159–173.

Van Hellemont, E. and Densley, J. (2019) Gang glocalization: How a global mediascape creates and shapes local gang realities. *Crime, Media, Culture*, 15, 169–189.

Waterson, J (2018) YouTube deletes 30 music videos after Met link with gang violence. *Guardian*. Online. Available www.theguardian.com/uk-news/2018/may/29/youtube-deletes-30-music-videos-after-met-link-with-gang-violence

Wilkinson, D. (2001) Violent events and social identity: Specifying the relationship between respect and masculinity in inner-city youth violence. *Sociological Studies of Children and Youth*, 8, 231–265.

Yar, M. (2012) Crime, media and the will-to-representation. *Crime, Media, Culture*, 8, 245–260.

Whittaker, A., Cheston, L., Tyrell, T., Higgins, M., Felix-Baptiste, C., and Havard, T. (2018) *From Post-codes to Profits: Changes in Gang Activity in Waltham Forest*. London: LSBU. https://doi.org/10.18744/PUB.002234

Windle, J. and Briggs, D. (2015) 'It's like working away for two weeks': The harms associated with young drug dealers commuting from a saturated London drug market. *Crime Prevention and Community Safety*, 17, 105–119.

Womer, S. and Bunker, R. J. (2010) Sureños gangs and Mexican cartel use of social networking sites. *Small Wars and Insurgencies*, 21, 81–94.

25
BIKER GANGS
Evolution, motivation and applying function to management

Carol A. Ireland, Jane L. Ireland and Sören Henrich

Introduction

This chapter will consider important components of biker gangs, specifically those most often referred to as Outlaw Motorcycle Gangs (OMGs). There is academic debate concerning how such groups are labelled and how to further define the organized crime that they arguably form part of. Increased research in this area has only added confusion to this. However, whilst acknowledging the difficulties in definition, the focus of the current chapter is on current understandings of the evolution and motivation of such biker groups.

Evolution I: how Outlaw Motorcycle Gangs have developed and been defined

The majority of motorcycle groups are considered law-abiding, with members enthusiastic about being part of such groups as a means of promoting their interest, values and positive social engagement with like-minded others. Whilst not restricted just to the United States and the United Kingdom, examples would include the American Motorcyclist Association (American-motorcyclist.com, 2019), which has over 212,000 members, and where over 71 per cent of members have 25 years of driving experience. Although substantially smaller in numbers, the British Motorcyclists Federation (2019), notes around 260 associated motorcycle clubs, 6500 full members and 53,000 affiliated members. All of these mainstream groups aim to support members to drive safely whilst encouraging engagement in a large social group of individuals who have a passion for motorbikes.

There are, however, a much smaller number of motorcycle groups that now function more as gangs, linked to organized crime/collective violence: Outlaw Motorcycle Gangs (OMGs). These groups embrace pro-offending ideals, engaging in a range of criminal and antisocial behaviours, where they reject mainstream motorcycle groups as dissimilar to themselves, but still hold a passion for motorbikes. Such groups present international concern, with Europol classifying them as a national threat (Europol, n.d.).

It is less clear as to the initial development of these groups, yet it is felt they developed sometime between the First and the Second World Wars (Piano, 2017). Such groups consist predominantly of white men who feel they do not fit mainstream society. Instead they feel alienated, seeking identity with an "outlaw status", with a fearlessness to defend this identity at all costs, and with the addition of pro-offending attitudes (Piano, 2017). Further, Piano (2017) and Quinn (2001) argue that, during the inception of such groups, the initial members consisted of ex-veterans who were seeking to meet their addiction to the excitement of violence and conflict, with the added bonus of a sense of comradeship by being part of such groups, referred to as the "saloon society". It is argued that the OMGs offered the closest substitute to army life at this time, linking to a sense of brotherhood, patriotism, discipline (of sorts), masculinity, violence and technical knowledge (Veno, 2010). There was a noted "golden age" of OMGs beginning after the Second World War, and as veterans returned home (Piano, 2017). However, such claims can also be observed as contradictory, and it is noted that some aspects and symbols of the OMGs' way of life can contrast with the value of veterans (Piano, 2017). Yet, it is further argued that such individuals initially set up OMGs following unsuccessful attempts to join the more mainstream motorcycle groups (Piano, 2017).

Over past decades, however, such OMGs have evolved considerably; the groups initially set up by veterans to support a shared identity have now developed into groups that engage in nationally and, more recently, internationally organized crime. Further, and as OMGs have evolved, two factions are observed within them: the conservative and the radical. The conservative faction would fit most closely to the veterans, where their values are focused on the ideals of what is "morally right", with the freedom that the lifestyle offers and the camaraderie of the brotherhood. This faction is now notably on the decline. Alternatively, the radical faction is that which shows greater interest in the opportunities for profit by engagement in criminal activities that the OMG can offer, and which has arguably now evolved the groups into international organized crime (Piano, 2017). It is the radical group that appears now to comprise the largest components of OMGs, and where engagement in crime is now a requirement for membership (Piano, 2017).

These minority OMGs have been referred to as the "one percenters", which was a phrase first used by the American Motorcyclist Association when they made a statement that 99 per cent of their members were law abiding. The phrase "one percenters" was then proudly used by these OMGs (Shields, 2012; Piano, 2017). This general term, subsequently used by law enforcement in the United States, has now been adopted into the academic literature. However, this term is rejected by some as misleading (e.g. Barker, 2005) and there remains an interchange between terms such as "one percenter groups" and "motorcycle/biker gangs". In 2015, the United State Department of Justice offered one of the most comprehensive definitions of such gangs, and one that paralleled further with wider definitions of organized crime (United States Department of Justice, 2015). They defined an OMG as an association of three or more individuals, which collectively identify as creating fear and intimidation, such as through a common name, slogan, physical marking and/or attire. They are further defined as having a purpose that, at least in part, comprises criminal activity achieved through violence or intimidation, with the aim of preserving or furthering the power, reputation or economic resources of the OMG.

In addition, OMGs do develop an identified structure. For instance, they may utilize rules for joining and have defined expectations of its members, including regular engagement with the group by members. The OMG further supports and protects its members from other criminal groups, where it is intended for the OMG to have a degree of control over a particular area/region, or to protect its perceived interests from other rivals (United States Department of Justice, 2015).

Whilst there are various local, regional, national and international OMGs, the four main groups are considered to be the Hells' Angels, Outlaws, Bandidos and Pagans, referred to as the "Big Four". This terminology dates back to the 1970s, when they were considered to be the most powerful groups (Quinn and Forsyth, 2011). These groups were further amplified by law enforcement's reference in the 1980s and 1990s to the "Big Four" (Piano, 2017). Across time, the Pagans have reportedly reduced both territory and status, whereas a newer group called the "Mongols" have emerged as a powerful OMG. Furthermore, the Hells' Angels are noted to be overtly hostile to any OMG they do not have any influence over, with an overall aim to acquire full control; the Mongols have been considered their "arch-rivals" (Quinn and Forsyth, 2011). As noted earlier, there are the more "traditional" (the conservative faction) or "purist" (the radical faction) sub-groups within these groups, where the traditional bikers prefer to maintain their original focus of being a biker, cruising on their bikes and dealing with conflict in a more traditional manner, such as physical assault with knives, fists or chains. Yet, the more radical faction have a more entrepreneurial and enhanced focus on engagement in organized crime (Quinn and Forsyth, 2011). Yet, it would be too simplistic to suggest that a member is in only one of these groups, as there can be transferring between the two, with each sub-group able to appreciate the other. Quinn and Forsyth (2011), for example, argue that membership to either faction is a reflection more of what is a priority to that member at that time.

Regarding the nature of the criminal activity of OMGs, this has been varied, involving drug and firearm trafficking, violence, money laundering, theft, exploitation (e.g. prostitution), gambling and extortion (Shields, 2012). This activity is not restricted just to a particular region, but as commerce has become more global, so too has the global reach of such OMGs. They have now extended their gangs internationally. Consequently, they have therefore evolved in order to exploit an international criminal opportunity, which brings with it a range of concerns regarding their global reach, use of violence and efforts to evade law enforcement (Shields, 2012). This is not the only aspect of their evolution; there has also been evolution within the culture of the OMGs, including regarding rivalry with others and the more developed use of a "uniform".

Evolution II: the development of rivalry and identity

A key cultural component of OMGs is the observation that rivalry toward other groups is akin to warfare (Quinn and Forsyth, 2011), and one that can dictate how groups interact with each other. This may be further a reflection of the origins of such groups, specifically from veterans, where it was earlier noted that there was a desire to continue the excitement of violence and conflict, which can mirror their experience of war. Quinn and Forsyth (2011) argue that, as a result of such perceived warfare, OMGs can regard themselves as soldiers, with their gang as their "nation-tribe", with their apparel developing more into a uniform. LeShan (2002) argues further that a focus on "warfare" can suspend normal expectations regarding moral and social rules, leading instead to entitlement and that absence of more rational thought, which would be expected outside of a period of "war". Expectations and thought processes can be further negatively amplified by emotions such as anger and fear, justifying a need to be self-focused and to focus on the immediate. This can be further influenced by the culture of the OMGs, which are arguably designed to shock non-members, to actively reject values of mainstream society, and to demonstrate an inability to adjust to economic advances post Second World War (Piano, 2017).

This is further observed by a focus on extreme belief sets, where for the first few decades of the OMGs' emergence they adopted openly racist and white-supremacist ideals, as well as a focus on Nazi ideology, with reference to such ideology often indicated through tattoos or attire. Yet, there is the further suggestion that the wearing of Nazi memorabilia was simply an effort to annoy others (Piano, 2017), which did not necessarily suggest a close affiliation with the ideals of the Nazi view. More so, it was arguably an attempt to further distance themselves from mainstream society through the use of shock, intimidation, distaste, and to further amplify a need to be seen as dangerous. However, there is more recent evidence to suggest that the OMGs may be trying to create less distance between themselves and mainstream society. This includes the Hell's Angels banning Nazi memorabilia. It is felt that this may be linked to its changing direction as a more highly structured criminal organization (Piano, 2017), and where perhaps they are seeking respect from other criminal organizations, focusing more on the financial gain from the use of violence. This would suggest that, as they are adopting a more international reach of criminal activity, they are again evolving in their culture and that, as a result, their motivation for engaging in organized crime is also evolving.

Motivations for criminal action

It is no surprise that, due to a focus on violence and criminality, OMGs have been found involved in a high proportion of offences. Research has certainly indicated that OMGs comprise more criminal convictions and a higher frequency of offending (Klement, 2016) than other groups, which can be a product of their group affiliation. For example, Klement (2016) reported that across two time periods they observed that 38 per cent and 56 per cent of OMG members already had more than one conviction within a 12 month period, with 5 per cent of the OMG population being responsible for between 27 per cent and 32 per cent of all OMG convictions in a 12 month period. This seems to suggest that a smaller proportion of the membership is responsible for a greater proportion of offences. There were also differences across OMGs, with most convictions relating to the Hells Angels and the Bandidos (Klement, 2016).

The motivations for a more *organized* approach to offending, including violent offending, in OMGs, however, can be complex and varied. The current chapter cannot hope to capture this area in full but it is worth noting in brief the value of a seminal sociological theory that offers some potential understanding, namely *Social Action Theory* (Weber, 1978). Weber (1978) argued that societies can encourage certain motives for action, identifying four types of social action: *Traditional*, an action derived from habit – the "way things have always been"; *Affective*, an action driven by emotion, feelings or affect, and where the consequences are not considered; *Value-Rational*, an action consciously determined by a belief in a specific value of a type of behaviour; and *Instrumental-Rational*, an action where the means, ends and consequences are all considered, that a goal wants to be achieved and an action is engaged in to achieve this.

Alach (2011) argued that the motives for OMGs related to the Value-Rational social action and where the OMG is focused on status and cohesion; that to engage in criminality and violence within the group is part of what is expected, it is part of the cohesion and commonality within the group. It is not, for example, motivated by a need to deal with any negative emotion and neither is it driven by a need only for profit, which would fit more of the Instrumental-Rational type of social action. However, OMGs may be driven by a combination of two of these four types of social action, specifically the Value-Rational, such as defending the lifestyle of the group and the protection of territory, as well as some elements of Instrumental-Rational, such as engaging in crime for monetary gain (Alach, 2011).

The importance of membership and protection of group cohesion/expectations

Clearly, adopting a social action explanation for behaviour suggests a group that identifies as a social collective with a shared identity. Without this, social action could not be achieved as a group. Identity, notably shared identity, becomes a pivotal component of how an OMG secures, protects and facilitates membership. Joining an OMG can be initially considered via the lens of

Social Identity Theory (Tajfel *et al.*, 1979). Here, it is argued that the social group an individual belongs to can be regarded as a source of pride and self-esteem. An OMG is not an exception to this, especially as a substantial amount of effort is required in order to become part of and accepted by this social group. Thus, the *investment* in the social group becomes enhanced. The *shared* social identity that such groups offer provides members with a sense of belonging. In an effort to protect self-image and to enhance group cohesion in such groups, efforts can be made to increase the status of the OMG (the "in-group") by promoting negative or prejudicial views toward those that are not part of the group (the "out-group"). Thus, there is an expectation that an OMG could hold prejudicial/negative views toward other OMG groups, to protect self-image, group cohesion and shared self-identity. At a very basic level of understanding, therefore, social identity becomes focused on maintenance and strengthening of current membership to the OMG because of attitudes and values held. This includes those that support a use of aggression and/or criminal activity, as one example.

In a group that places considerable value on shared social identity and group cohesion, personal loyalties to the group become key (Vergani and Collins, 2015). Yet, as a group becomes larger there can be a fracturing within groups, essentially an out-group within an in-group can develop. This then requires the process of group cohesion and shared social identity to be strengthened as a remedy to such a development to ensure that no out-group within its main body evolves. Within OMGs there has been this internal conflict where dominance within the group is fought, which then poses a threat to the entire group (Quinn and Forsyth, 2011). For example, Quinn and Forsyth (2011) noted repeated rivalry in the 1960s between the Gypsy Jokers and the Oakland chapter of the Hells Angels, leading to violence. Yet, the San Francisco chapter of the Hells Angels would socialize with the Gypsy Jokers. However, since the 1970s, there became greater group cohesion, with conflict within the groups themselves being handled more diplomatically owing to clearer structures and mechanisms for managing disagreements. As a result, focus could instead be directed again toward rival gangs (Quinn and Forsyth, 2011), which in itself arguably strengthens group cohesion and a shared social identity by massing forces against a shared enemy.

When considering the use of aggression by an OMG, it would perhaps fit the notion of "habitual aggression" (Huesmann, 1998; Martens, 2000). This refers to aggression occurring more than once, and is indicative of a continuation of an aggressive pattern of behaviour underpinned by core beliefs, including normative beliefs (Ireland, 2018). Normative beliefs represent those held by an individual, which they believe others hold as well. In an OMG it could include beliefs such as "You fight to protect the group". This could drive the use of aggression, which could be either *reactive* or *proactive* in nature. *Reactive aggression* is regarded as a more uncontrolled form of aggression, driven by negative emotion, and serving as a means of securing a blocked goal (Ireland, 2018; Berkowitz, 1989). *Proactive aggression*, however, is regarded as more planned aggression, devoid of a negative emotion and linked more to social learning models of aggression, where aggression is learnt from observations within the environment (Berkowitz, 1989). Whilst an OMG member can, of course, demonstrate both forms of aggression, and thus be mixed-motive, it is arguably more likely that their predominant use would be that of proactive aggression. Here, the aggression has a clear goal attached to it, such as the use of violence to gain financial profit from a criminal act, to maintain status and/or respect within the group and/or to protect the group. The use of proactive aggression is also likely to be positively reinforced within the group, and thus viewed more positively than a more uncontrolled (reactive) act. The uncontrolled, reactive aggression may be less supported in the group as it can be harder to manage. As such, the use of aggression within the OMG toward non-members can have adaptive qualities. The concept of aggression having adaptive qualities is not a new one (Ireland,

2018). This is not to be supportive of aggression on moral grounds, but rather to note that it can have reinforcing qualities and serve a pragmatic purpose, particularly to the continued cohesion of a group with a shared social identity and where clear gains can be made from displays of aggression.

Indeed, when membership of the OMG is considered, the individual must possess values and beliefs that aggression can be helpful. These need to be well-established beliefs prior to involvement in such groups. Their absence would make it unlikely, or certainly more difficult, for group-affiliation to occur. Further reinforcement of the use of aggression within the group may be found through the observational learning of aggression, and where the individual observes the use of aggression in an individual they value and identify with (Ireland, 2018; Bandura, 1989), in this case the other members of the OMG.

When further considering what maintains membership to the OMG, one essential aspect are the resources that it provides to members. Resources or "goods" are critical not just in securing membership with the promise of what can be achieved, but also in maintaining membership. As such groups consist of those that arguably feel detached from mainstream society, the OMG membership offers "brotherhood", connection and comradeship, where members support one another without fear of ridicule or rejection. This fits closely with theories of motivation, specifically self-determination theory (Deci and Ryan, 2000). In brief, this theory argues that humans have three psychological needs that are important and which we all strive to achieve: autonomy, competence and relatedness. *Autonomy* relates to the ability for an individual to be self-directed, to make choices, and to be able to act on their own interests and values. *Competence* relates to an individual feeling effective in what they do, and to feel they are capable. Finally, *relatedness* focuses on the need to interact, connect with others in a meaningful and caring way, and to feel a sense of belonging with those around them. This is also consistent with Social Identity Theory (Tajfel *et al.*, 1979).

Two of these needs match particularly closely with the 'goods' offered by the OMG: Competence and Relatedness. Competence can be met in a variety of ways, such as the demonstration of technical skill in bike repair amongst their peers, which is held in high regard (Piano, 2017), and through proficiency in aggression use. Relatedness is strongly met within the OMG via companionship, and where there is an expectation to support members if needed, both financially and emotionally, as well as through accommodation, if required (Piano, 2017). Ultimately there is a strong sense of belonging and camaraderie within the group. It could arguably be this particular need that presents as one of the most highly regarded "goods" that can be offered to those who have, until that point, felt a disconnect from society.

Once group membership is achieved, intimidation can become a key tool to further assert greater status within the group. Gomez del Prado (2011) argues that, at an initial level, there are individuals who aspire to be part of the group, regarded as "relations", who intimidate in the hope to obtain the status of a "hanger-on", and in the hope they can then work to become regular members of the group. Gomez del Prado (2011) further noted that members of the OMG are rarely alone, that they always have these "relations" with them, who are attempting to climb the hierarchy within the group. It is further noted that such "relations" can represent 65 per cent of suspects in criminal activity within these groups, and where they have "little to lose" and a need to prove to the group that they do not fear law enforcement. As such, they are expected to show a degree of confidence in their ability to engage with law enforcement, either at the direction of OMG members, or on their own initiative (Gomez del Prado, 2011).

Yet, expectations within the group for membership are not purely a need for lower members to utilize intimidation and to demonstrate their loyalty. There is, additionally, an expectation for members to maintain membership by the generation of income. Failure to do so can threaten their membership. For instance, Quinn and Forsyth (2011) note that the rivalry (or warfare) between OMGs requires the generation of finances, with a need to purchase weapons, protective equipment and to pay for required legal fees. The expected income and when it is due is set by each group, with each member expected to apply their own skill to acquire such funds. Members are not expected to discuss how they are acquiring these funds within the group, as ultimately the funds boost the financial status of the group and protect assets (Quinn and Forsyth, 2011). However, they are expected not to abuse the support of OMGs, as to do so would threaten their own membership (Piano, 2017).

The level of criminal activity noted within OMGs, which is captured earlier, would also fit with the wider (non-OMG) gang literature, which allows for three hypotheses for membership to be considered: the *Selection Hypothesis*, the *Facilitation Hypothesis* and the *Enhancement Hypothesis* (Melde and Esbenson, 2011; Thornberry *et al.*, 2003). The Selection Hypothesis argues that gang members commit crime as they already have relatively stable criminal history prior to joining the group, which would be consistent with Klement (2016). The Facilitation Hypothesis argues that membership to the group, in this case the OMG, can serve to increase the use of criminal activity for the duration that the member is affiliated to the group. This would appear to also fit with the OMG, where there is a heightened focus on criminal activity, with the use of aggression forming a strong component of the group values, and where there is a need to provide income to support the group, which could include through criminal means. Finally, the Enhancement Hypothesis is a combination of the Selection and Facilitation Hypotheses, where prior history and current involvement in offending serve to naturally continue the offence cycle. When considering the values of the OMG, and especially their more current attention to international criminal activity and a focus on profit through crime, the facilitation hypothesis would appear to fit particularly well. It also perhaps contributes to the public negative perception of OMGs, which has been described as a form of "moral panic" (Gomez del Prado, 2011).

Public and professional perceptions: intimidation as a tool

Moral panic is defined as anxiety or alarm from the public, commonly referred to as a society-level fear since it is felt by a large number of the population as something "sinister" or threatening to society. This fear can be amplified by media coverage of troubling events, and the message they wish to portray. This is arguably well applied to OMGs, where there has been an active attempt to present them as intimidating to non-members as a tactic to create distance from non-members, but also to further criminal activity. This is not, however, without basis; the OMG groups have been involved in actions that have clearly threatened professionals and the public, but it is the level of panic that then begins to emerge that can be problematic. It is troubling not only in terms of creating moral panic but also in emphasizing to those interested in membership to OMGs that their reputation of harnessing fear and intimidation as a collective is justified. For some, this could make membership more attractive and also help to convince rival groups that they have a valid basis to be feared by them.

For instance, it was noted in the 1990s that groups of individuals such as prison officers, journalists, law enforcement, prosecutors and bartenders were victims of OMGs. This reached a peak of reported fear when, in 1997, two prison officers were murdered, there was an attempted assassination of a journalist, and a bartender murdered for refusing to serve individuals associated with criminal organizations (Gomez del Prado, 2011). Such problems continue more recently. Vergani and Collins (2015), for example, described how one "unit" (or "chapter") in an Australian based OMG (the Comanchero MC) is called the "Wrecking Crew", with the members' sole role to intimate and terrorize adversaries of the club. The "Finks MC" are also further reported to have the "Terror Team", utilized for extreme violence, intimidation, and to monitor criminal operations (Vergani and Collins, 2015). Further, the Australian OMGs have been noted to utilize military-grade explosives, sophisticated communication devices, and intelligence/counterintelligence methods and, in 2012, the Comanchero MC in New South Wales attempted to blow up a hotel. Aggressive actions have been directed in the main toward rival gangs, but invariably the public have been at risk, which has contributed to the "moral panic" concerning OMGs and the level of threat that they pose to wider society.

This also redirects back to the earlier references as to the importance of intimidation within OMGs in order to meet their needs, and to influence significant others, including those connected to the criminal justice system. Such intimidation by OMGs has a psychological component to its approach and is an attempt to *destabilize* law enforcement and other components of the judicial process, essentially as a form of protection for the group (Gomez del Prado, 2011). There have been, for example, reports of the intimidation of jury members and witnesses by the Hell's Angels, with this referred to this as "emotional terrorism" (Lavigne, 1999). The nature of intimidation of witnesses has been long researched, with Graham (1985) offering three types of intimidation that continue to add value. The first type is considered the more traditional, occurring the most frequently, and where there is a clear and obvious use of *intimidation with physical violence* to instil fear. The second type is subtler, *using family members or others to deter the witness from giving evidence.* The final type focuses on the *anticipation that intimidation may take place,* leading the witness to disengage from the legal process. Such approaches have been used by OMGs (Vergani and Collins, 2015) and is suggestive of a more organized approach to criminal engagement and successful avoidance of the legal consequences.

Indeed, the research of Gomez del Prado (2011) noted a variety of subtle and vague intimidation approaches by OMGs against law enforcement, making it difficult to proceed with allegations through the Court process. This has served to maximize the ability of the OMG to continue their engagement in criminal activity. This was noted especially when efforts were made by law enforcement to intervene on their activities. This included OMG members intimidating by:

- Making law enforcement officers feel vulnerable by referring to their personal life and significant others;
- Noting personal characteristics of law enforcement officers or significant others, with the aim to destabilize;
- Following the law enforcement officer, driving past their home, contacting them on personal numbers;
- Making threats to destroy their careers and/or undermine their credibility, including attempting to sue the law enforcement officer, knowing that if there is an investigation then the law enforcement officer is removed from duty and suspended. This includes making complaints focusing on minor issues, such as the law enforcement officer wearing sunglasses during a police intervention.

Promoting fear in an officer of becoming involved in proceedings, and the intrusion into their private life, present the most valuable means of intimation that the OMGs possess (Gomez del Prado, 2011). It is further argued that there is an increased chance of intimidation toward law enforcement officers who are newer to their post, with some law enforcement officers actively choosing not to engage with OMGs. However, some of the more experienced investigating officers are affected less by acts of intimidation, and do not always recognize them as such unless they are significant (Gomez del Prado, 2011). As such, the experience of the officers is noted as key when considering the potential impact of such intimidation in disrupting them in the course of their duties. This will be returned to later when capturing the approaches to management of OMGs but, first, a model is outlined that draws together the core components of how an OMG has evolved and how it operates, with a view to considering how their management can be most pro-socially achieved.

Proposing a preliminary functional understanding of Outlaw Motorcycle Gangs and applying this to management

A common thread through this chapter has been the need to consider the functions of the OMG by accounting for its evaluation across time, membership and motives for existence. Considering the functional elements will undoubtedly assist with the management of OMGs by moving towards an understanding as to their existence and maintenance as opposed to focusing purely on their believed symptoms (e.g. offending). Presented in Figure 25.1 is an attempt to provide a functional understanding of OMGs using the *Functional Model of Outlaw Motorcycle Gangs* (FM-OMG). This attempts to illustrate more clearly the evolution, factions, focus and function of OMGs.

Figure 25.1 is a preliminary depiction or representation as to the key functions of OMGs, such as the different factions and the motives for membership to such factions. This preliminary depiction summarizes the motivation for initial engagement in the OMG by its members, such as a rejection of society's mainstream values. It then considers how this can evolve over time, such as the importance of gaining social identity within the group, and where over time the strong group connection and need for comradeship solidifies continued membership. Of importance can be how this model could then be utilized when applied to intervention and management of such groups. Consequently, the following initial ideas could be considered.

First, there is a need to *be aware of the history of the OMGs, and their evolution:* The importance of understanding the history of the development so that it can be caste more into an evolutionary understanding is critical if efforts are then made to manage such groups. For instance, knowing the make-up of the groups and how they have evolved is important in helping management approaches, considering them as more organized groups that have a shared social identity. These are not chaotic groups but organized, which needs to be fully understood and respected. If there is to be any effort to intervene and manage such groups, they first need to be fully understood and appreciated.

Second, *not all motorcycle groups are the same.* A considerable risk in management is to regard them as one collective group. It is important to identify that the only ones of interest are those engaging in offending. A helpful approach may be to recognize the more positive and peaceful factions, working with these effectively in communities to help offset moral panic. Therefore, and arguably, a large criminal component of these groups is the radical faction, linking to the preliminary depiction in Figure 25.1.

Third, there is the importance of *seeking realistic peaceful alternatives to achieving their purposes.* This may be a more radical strategy to other management approaches, yet the key is to consider if their group needs can be met and maintained without the use of criminality, and which also recognizes the experience, skills and expertise of the membership.

Finally, there is a need to *interrupt the use of intimidation by the OMG.* Here Gomez del Prado (2011) identified a number of initial solution, with a key area being specific training for law enforcement to manage their expectations of what could occur and prepare them accordingly. This includes specialized training on OMGs and the tactics utilized, which may also reduce less experienced officer's negative response to intimidation. Such training should focus on the structure of OMGs, their organizational system, their overall network, as well as methods of intimidation. Further, OMGs are status driven and, consequently, there is a role to be played by more senior officers (Gomez del Prado, 2011), who may be more respected by the OMG. In addition, Gomez del Prado (2011) argues the importance of networked communication, namely that which recognizes OMGs as a more global network. As such, ensuring clearer communication

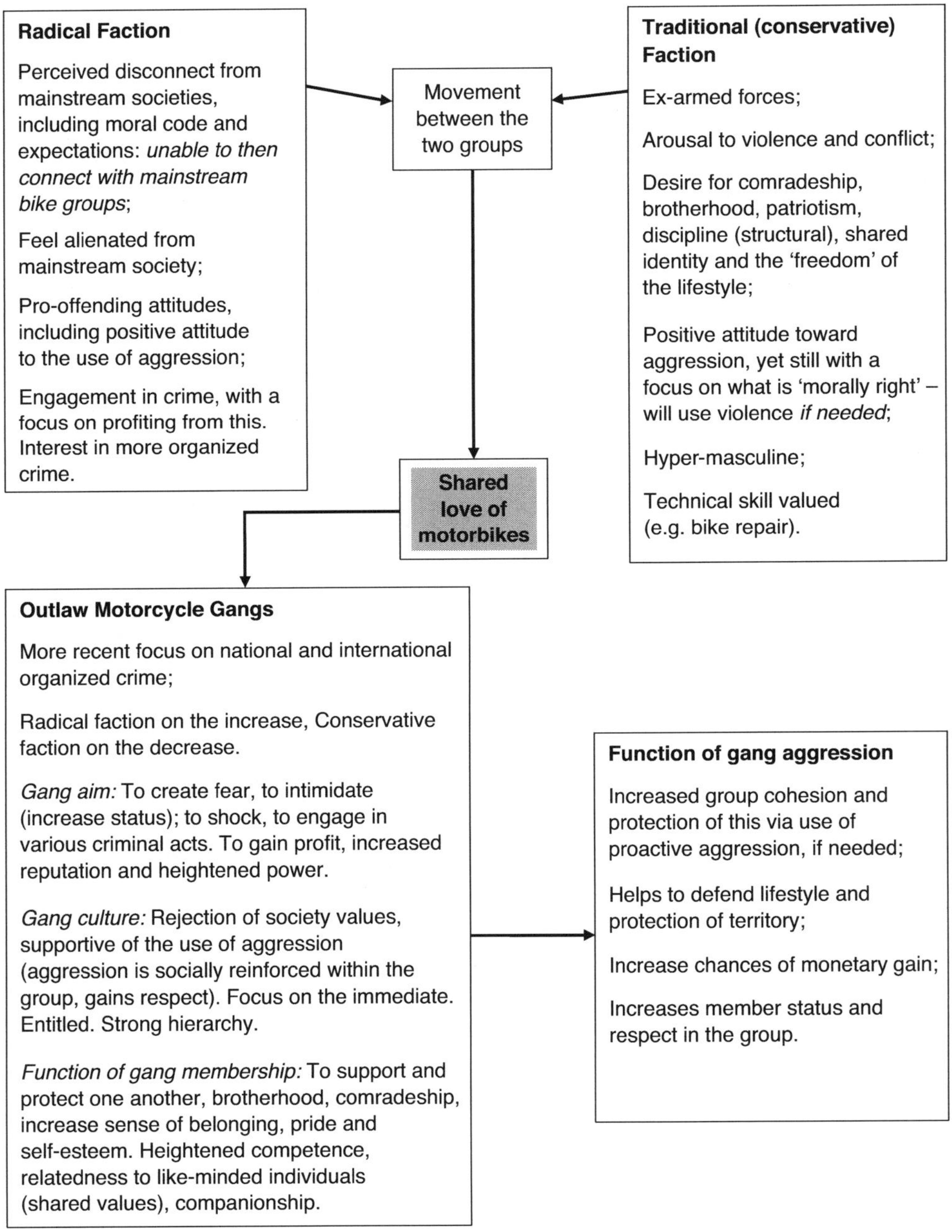

Figure 25.1 Functional Model of Outlaw Motorcycle Gangs (FM-OMG).

across law enforcement, including within service, nationally and internationally, becomes a key element of good quality intelligence on OMGs, whilst recognizing their increasing reach. Finally, Gomez del Prado (2011) argues the need to provide a thorough understanding of the standard law and police powers, to combat any tendency for OMGs to sue law enforcement officers. Fundamentally, greater knowledge and awareness is key (Gomez del Prado, 2011). Gomez del Prado (2011) further argues that efforts to control such groups cannot just be via law enforcement officers, as more should be done at a governmental level, where the government is able to maximize on the protection offered to officers who are sued without clear evidence, as well as greater measures to protect the personal data of officers.

Conclusion

In summary, the function of the OMG has evolved over time, progressing more to engagement in organized criminal activity. Whilst the more traditional factions of these groups exist, they are reducing, and the majority of members now appear to direct the OMG more towards the business of organized criminal activity.. However, to fully understand and manage such groups, their functions and needs require continual consideration: to interrupt such groups in their criminal activity, the functions of the groups needs to be fully understood for *each group*. Only then can efforts be made to interrupt such functions and to direct the groups to less criminal solutions to meeting their needs. Arguably the focus should be on them maintaining a social identity that is not conducive with criminality, whilst maintaining a shared passion for motorbikes.

References

Alach, Z. J. (2011) An incipient taxonomy of organised crime. *Trends in Organized Crime*, 14(1), 56–72.

Americanmotorcyclist.com (2019) *American Motorcyclist Association > Home*. [Online.] Available at: www.americanmotorcyclist.com/ (accessed 9 May 2019).

Bandura, A. (1973) *Aggression: A Social Learning Analysis*. New Jersey: Prentice-Hall.

Barker, T. (2005) One percent bikers clubs: A description. *Trends in Organized Crime*, 9(1), 101–112.

Berkowitz, L. (1989) Frustration-aggression hypothesis: Examination and reformulation. *Psychological Bulletin*, 106(1), 59.

British Motorcyclists Federation (2019) *Home » British Motorcyclists Federation*. [Online.] Available at: www.bmf.co.uk/ (accessed 9 May 2019).

Deci, E. L. and Ryan, R. M. (2000) The "what" and" why" of goal pursuits: Human needs and the self-determination of behavior. *Psychological Inquiry*, 11(4), 227–268.

Europol (n.d.) *Outlaw Motorcycle Gang*. [Online.] Available at www.europol.europa.eu/crime-areas-and-trends/crime-areas/outlaw-motorcycle-gangs (accessed 8 May 2019).

Gomez del Prado, G. (2011) Outlaw motorcycle gangs' attempted intimidation of Quebec's police forces. *Police Practice and Research: An International Journal*, 12(1), 66–80.

Graham, M. H. (1985) *Witness Intimidation: The Law's Response*. Westport, CT: Quorum Books.

Huesmann, L. R. (1998) The role of social information processing and cognitive schema in the acquisition and maintenance of habitual aggressive behavior. In *Human Aggression*. San Diego, CA: Academic Press, pp. 73–109.

Ireland, J. L. (2018) Individual assessments of aggression: Accounting for core factors. In *Violent and Sexual Offenders*. London: Routledge, pp. 231–255.

Klement, C. (2016) Outlaw biker affiliations and criminal involvement. *European Journal of Criminology*, 13(4), 453–472.

Lavigne, Y. (1999) *Hells Angels at War*. Toronto, Ontario: Harpercollins Canada.

LeShan, L. (2002) *The Psychology of War: Comprehending its Mystique and its Madness*. New York: Skyhorse Publishing.

Martens, W. H. (2000) Antisocial and psychopathic personality disorders: Causes, course, and remission – A review article. *International Journal of Offender Therapy and Comparative Criminology*, 44(4), 406–430.

Melde, C. and Esbensen, F. A. (2011) Gang membership as a turning point in the life course. *Criminology*, 49(2), 513–552.
Piano, E. E. (2018) Outlaw and economics: Biker gangs and club goods. *Rationality and Society*, 30(3), 350–376.
Quinn, J. F. (2001) Angels, Bandidos, Outlaws, and Pagans: The evolution of organized crime among the big four 1% motorcycle clubs. *Deviant Behavior*, 22(4), 379–399.
Quinn, J. F. and Forsyth, C. J. (2011) The tools, tactics, and mentality of outlaw biker wars. *American Journal of Criminal Justice*, 36(3), 216–230.
Shields, D. (2012) The infamous 'one percenters': A review of the criminality, subculture, and structure of modern biker gangs. *Justice Policy Journal*, 9(1), 1–33.
Tajfel, H., Turner, J. C., Austin, W. G., and Worchel, S. (1979) An integrative theory of intergroup conflict. In W. G. Austin and S. Worchel (eds), *The Social Psychology of Intergroup Relations*. Monterey, CA: Brooks/Cole, pp. 33–47.
Thornberry, T. P., Krohn, M. D., Lizotte, A. J., and Chard-Wierschem, D. (1993) The role of juvenile gangs in facilitating delinquent behavior. *Journal of Research in Crime and Delinquency*, 30(1), 55–87.
United States Department of Justice (2015) *Outlaw Motorcycle Gangs (OMGs)*. [Online.] Justice.gov. Available at: www.justice.gov/criminal-ocgs/gallery/outlaw-motorcycle-gangs-omgs (accessed 9 May 2019).
Veno, A. (2010) *The Brotherhoods: Inside the Outlaw Motorcycle Clubs*. Crows Nest, NSW, Australia: Allen & Unwin.
Vergani, M. and Collins, S. (2015) Radical criminals in the grey area: A comparative study of Mexican religious drug cartels and Australian outlaw motorcycle gangs. *Studies in Conflict & Terrorism*, 38(6), 414–432.
Weber, M. (1978) *Economy and Society*, 1st ed., Berkeley, CA: University of California Press.

26
OUTLAW BIKER CLUBS
A case study exploration of collective violence

Mohammed Rahman

Introduction

In the academic epoch, *outlaw* motorcycle clubs are known as the "one-percenters", an established sub-culture that is not recognized by the American Motorcyclist Association as a law-abiding motorcycle organization (Barker and Human 2009). Indeed, this has resulted in several biker clubs being labelled as "organized crime" groups, and in other cases as "gangs". In the global north, academically and politically, the terms are used interchangeably when describing such clubs (Barker 2007). In regards to a motorcycle club (MC), the label "organized crime" was first associated with the Hells Angels Motorcycle Club (HAMC), an international club, which formed in 1948 in California, USA. By 1969, the HAMC had established itself in London, England, after being chartered by its founder, Ralph "Sonny" Barger (Barger *et al.*, 2001). Across the Atlantic, the United States Federal Government indicted Barger and several of his associates under the Racketeering Influenced and Corrupt Organizations Act (RICO); a US federal law passed in 1970 with extensive focus on racketeering crimes, and one that allowed identified leaders of an organization to be tried for crimes that they ordered others to do, or assisted them in doing.

Of note, contemporary research on outlaw clubs gravitates towards the perception that such fraternities are indeed "gangs", given their explicit symbolic nature, which is often displayed through garment "patches". Scholars note how patches identify club membership, ranking, and territorial location (Quinn and Koch 2003). However, clubs that wear such insignias refute patches as gang emblems, which is reinforced by research that argues how biker apparels contribute towards the construction of identity and organizational branding. So too, through the cultivation of a deviant image, outlaw organizations have been able to successfully commercialize themselves, with many of the self-proclaimed one-percenters "trademarking" their brand (Kuldova 2017). The trademark's symbolic power within consumer culture is global, which therefore illustrates the paradoxical nature of outlaw clubs. By default, they are anti-establishment, yet their utilization of licit services enables them to promote their organization on an international scale, which in turn finances growth in legal and illegal markets (Schouten and McAlexander, 1995). Crucially, Kuldova (2019) argues that growth of anti-establishment movements under the spell of neoliberalism is not accidental, but inevitable. Nonetheless, discussions of whether such clubs are street gangs or criminal organizations continue to dominate scholarly work (see Wolf, 1991; Bjørgo, 2019; Lauchs, 2019), yet Rahman and Lynes (2018) posit that it is difficult to distinguish authoritatively gangs from organized crime groups, given the blurred and indistinct nature of actors and their interactions.

Rather than contributing towards the ongoing academic debate on defining gangs and organized crime groups, this chapter explores spontaneous collective violence, which is generally overlooked in collective violence scholarship. In doing so, through case examples, it illustrates how spontaneous acts of collective violence are welcomed by outlaw clubs, as they contribute towards the clubs' maintenance of symbolic boundaries and "brotherhood", a keystone concept that will be critically explored later.

Collective violence, the legitimation of violence and brotherhood

In everyday discussions, violence is viewed as an undesirable or illegal act. Gangland conflict, for example, is typically described as violent practice, whereas soldiers who maim or kill in the battlefield are likely to be described as war heroes or patriots. While official and unofficial statements underline the conceptuality of violence, we can see how euphemisms distort our perceptions of actors of harm. Globally, collective violence is a unified approach towards employing violent practice. Commentators who have extensively explored the phenomenon align their discussion towards extreme organized or institutionalized forms of violence, which include student protests, riots, revolutions, wars and genocide (Apter, 1997; Tilly, 2003; Brewer, 2010). Indeed, as Ray (2018, p. 181) eloquently says, "the role of state or quasi-state agents in pursuing collective violence requires different analysis from that of spontaneous violence". So, before considering spontaneous violence that emerges from outlaw biker clubs, this section will first consider key arguments in relation to collective violence and the legitimation of violence.

Tilly (2003) considers collective violence to encompass at least two perpetrators of physical damage, which results at least in part from coordination among persons who perform the damaging acts. Collective violence, through a definition of this nature, omits individual acts and non-material damage. For Tilly, the concept is relational, which therefore means that violence conventionally emerges from social interactions and settings. Politically, we are often exposed to unified acts of violence because of "broken negotiations" whereby a bargaining process that was non-violent has skewed. These types of violent practice usually involve little coordination; however, their implications can be catastrophic. Often, violent rituals require high coordination, as their priorities involve inflicting maximum damage to others, so as to be able to receive priority within a recognized locale. Tilly (2003) recognizes gang rivalry to be associated with violent rituals, yet opportunism often acts as a catalyst for gangland rivalries, especially for those that are considered to be "outlaw bikers" (Kuldova and Quinn, 2018; Bjørgo, 2019; Lauchs, 2019). While opportunistic violence resonates with politically oriented violence, in that they both involve little coordination, what separates them is that opportunistic violence is, in some cases, driven by behavioural disposition. All violence that is public or involves the public can be viewed as "political" as it may be a threat to public order, but it is not always political in its core motivations. Hence, violence may have depoliticized connotations, and this is a prevalent feature for collective violence that is employed by outlaw clubs.

In relation to outlaw biker clubs, violence is a defining characteristic of club identity, and a commodity that is used to start, maintain and advance legitimate and illegitimate enterprises (Barker, 2007). Commentators of one-percenter clubs draw together case examples of violence within a collective nature (Marsden and Sher, 2007), and note how enmity between such clubs is global. Accounts of violence employed by one-percenter organizations are often secondary and, given the clandestine nature of club members, there is little to go by with regards to primary narratives. Of note, the biographical account of the founder of the HAMC – Ralph "Sonny" Barger (Barger *et al.*, 2001) – is perhaps the most celebrated and reliable account of the outlaw biker world, especially when it concerns the HAMC. Here, it is worth noting that the significance of research on serious violence has stemmed from "true crime" genre and investigative journalism (Clarkson, 2003, 2008; Thompson, 2008, 2011). Such texts often offer thought-provoking accounts of criminal careers, which most academic works fail to achieve. While texts such as Barger *et al.* (2001) are often dismissed by social scholars, Durham *et al.* (1995, p. 144) state that "the true crime genre is an important, yet understudied, aspect of popular representations of crime". So too, it should be highlighted that true crime accounts may misrepresent the crimes that they attempt to "reveal". Rahman (2019) makes clear how this also extends from general popular understandings to official narratives. Nonetheless, the fact that true crime offers the understanding of offending through an alternative account provides a distinctive type of insight that is advantageous for case study work. Thus, below are some narratives of violence from Sonny Barger's biography.

Throughout his biography, Sonny alludes to the importance of how members of the HAMC are obliged to support fellow members under any circumstances, that is: "a very select brotherhood of men who will fight and die for each other" (Barger *et al.*, 2001, p. 67); "a Hell's Angel should never break and run" (Barger *et al.*, 2001, p. 146). During the early years of the HAMC, the Oakland HAMC chapter would go on regional and national runs as a pack, which inevitably led to violent confrontations with rival gangs, which only helped gain nationwide notoriety. Intra-gang violence was also an active issue for the HAMC during Sonny's presidency, as there was once a period when "Oakland and Frisco Hell's Angels would fuck each other up" (Barger *et al.*, 2001, p. 148).

While the reasons of these violent encounters were often trivial, all members were required to partake in brawls in order to maintain themselves as "righteous" bikers (Katz, 1988). Here it is important to note that the propensity to violence is what separates "patched" bikers from mainstream bikers. Hence, the former is labelled as what has already been described as the one-percenters, those that "engage in unconventional behaviour, often criminal behaviour" (Barker and Human, 2009, p. 174). Quinn and Koch (2003, p. 286) consider how status frustration and endless quest for power drives the agenda for "establishing and maintaining an image as dangerous, unpredictable, and outrageous". Barker and Human (2009, p. 174) further clarify that the one-percenters are of all one race, sex, or sexual orientation. Indeed, the tension between intense allegiance and hierarchal control on the one hand, and the autonomous violent masculinity is perplexing to the "outsider" (Becker, 1997). As Quinn and Koch (2003, p. 289) observe, "loyalty to a national hierarchy reinforces deeply felt tribal solidarity and power". Indeed, based on the above, violence is a "legitimated" function that is used for clarifying issues, solving problems, and promoting intergroup communication.

Before critically exploring the legitimation of violence in the outlaw biker world, it is worthwhile first defining legitimacy, which Ball-Rokeach (2017, p. 101) considers to be "a collective judgement that attributes the qualities of 'goodness' or 'morality' or 'righteousness' to behaviour". It can be argued that individuals who are engaged in legitimated forms of violence are often embraced by others through praise and acceptance. In return, they may view themselves as righteous individuals who carried out an act for the sake of "Good" (Katz, 1988). Legitimacy is a complex social phenomenon, and given its political construct, it is only in some cases that the use of violence is "legitimate" in the eyes of all concerned. However, it is the outlaw characteristic of brotherhood, and the paradoxical nature of biker clubs that help outlaw members identify when violence can be employed in a legitimate manner (Barker, 2007). For instance, members tend to separate themselves from the opposite gender when it comes to business imperatives but they are prepared to exploit women for their intrinsic desires (Bjørgo, 2019). Members tend to also separate themselves from mainstream society, yet are unable to do so economically, be it due to legitimate or illegitimate means. It is these paradoxes that serve as clear boundaries, which leads to the rationalization and justification of violence.

In relation to the justification of violence, the term justification alludes to the explanation or reasoning of behaviour. Ball-Rokeach (2017, p. 102) argues that "justifications for violent actions are not inherently properties of events, but develop as part of events in process". Thus, when legitimacy of a violent act is cleared from scrutiny, evaluation in the form of justification is integrated into the event. Indeed, when this is not achieved, justification becomes problematic. In the context of outlaw clubs, the justification of violence, and violence itself is underpinned by "brotherhood" (Wolf, 1991) – a keystone characteristic in the biker subculture.

The notion of brotherhood is commonplace in academic literature (Reynolds, 1967; Thompson, 2011), yet there is no consensus as to what it means. Some scholars have viewed the concept functionally, in the sense that brotherhood means being dependent on each other on a day to day basis (Quinn, 1987; Marsden and Sher, 2007). Others view it as a default value that can be used when a fellow biker needs help, especially in compromising situations (Barker, 2007; Barker and Human, 2009). While the term remains ambiguous, it generally considers the relationship between brothers, which seemingly excludes women. Indeed, this reinforces, Barger's stance on how outlaw clubs such as the HAMC are elite men's club, and the participation of women is contingent upon club rules as opposed to state laws. The meticulous ethnographic work of Wolf (1991) provides persuasive accounts of how, through brotherhood, an outlaw club fulfils a member's personal search for identity and community. The author epitomizes brotherhood as the bedrock of the outlaw community, and considers it to be a lengthy process that reveals the true nature of a biker. In relation to brotherhood, Wolf (1991, pp. 98–99) notes:

> The prospective member discovers that his involvement in the club is expected to go beyond institutional participation (love of the club) and beyond motorcycling (love of biking) to include the formation of friendship ties – 'love for your brothers'. In a parallel manner, the participation of members as a collective transcends formal organizational tasks to include the generation and maintenance of group solidarity.

The term "prospect" is often used to denote bikers who have joined a club and are on a probationary period. During this period, the individual will be tested by "patched" (established, full-time) members to determine his devotion towards the club and its followers. During the prospect stage of a biker, Barker (2007, p. 69) notes that "the man's attitude is conditioned so that he displays a sense of responsibility and respect towards the patchholders of the club, without which he will not develop a sense of brotherhood". Interestingly, this resonates with the above passage from Wolf (1991), in that a group social network – the "brotherhood" – becomes a means for underlying realities of group association. Indeed, because of the subculture nature of such clubs; the social network element for the prospect biker – a byproduct of brotherhood – serves as a buffer to isolate oneself from outside social ties, so as to be able to build allegiances within club quarters. This reinforces the clandestine nature of such organizations. In sum, brotherhood is characterized by a combination of a high degree of connectedness, the construction and strengthening of interpersonal commitment, and the scope of interpersonal contact.

Based on this, it is evident that the premise which triggers brotherhood is support. Support is contingent upon collectivity and welfare – of collective fate – without which an outlaw club cannot function. Scholarly works on biker clubs have commented on how such fraternities institutionalize the "all for one, one for all" support ethos, by incorporating it into their club rules, which in turn is often displayed through deviant or criminal behaviour against rival clubs or members of mainstream society (Barger *et al.*, 2001; Thompson, 2011; Bjørgo, 2019; Lauchs, 2019). The mutual-support ethos, namely in relation to public awareness, acts as a defensive group border marker and functions effectively to impede any conflict between the club and host society. As Wolf (1991, p. 98) notes: "The knowledge that a violator faces retribution from the whole club serves to restrain assaults by outsiders". Such sentiments are echoed by Sonny Barger, who states in his biography: "when a Hell's Angel fights a citizen or a rival club member, everybody rat-packs to his side" (Barger *et al.* 2001, 148).

As mentioned, prospect members can face testing times to measure their fidelity towards club members and the club itself. In some cases, these involve violent encounters. Below is a narrative account from Gypsy, a North American motorcycle club road captain and his recollection of how his club reacted when a prospect failed to live up to his commitment:

> We were an outlaw club, but that doesn't mean that we went looking for trouble. But when it came, we didn't back down from it … We were walking down an alley and there were these five Italians … They came at us, one of them grabbed a two-by-four. Stu took away the two-by-four and we beat them. They could have been dead for all we knew. We didn't have time to find out cause the sirens began, and we hit the road. And we had this striker [prospect] with us. While we were there fighting like fucking cats and dogs this fucker stood back and watched. When we got back to the clubhouse, Stu said: 'You Fucker! Get out of the building. Either get out, or I'll drag you out! If you're in a fight with us it's all for one and one for all. If we're getting the shit kicked out of us, you get in there and get the shit kicked out of you. You're no fucking blood special!' Stu took that poor fucker outside and he beat the supreme shit out of him. Stu left him lying outside the clubhouse. When we came the next morning, he was gone.
>
> *(Wolf, 1991, pp. 99–100)*

The excerpt above charts the significance of brotherhood; an uncompromising commitment from club members, which in turn is rewarded through unwavering comradeship and support. For the biker, the acquisition of brotherhood means the surrender of past friendships. In this subculture, by default and design, there is an expectation for all newcomers to embrace the outlaw way of life, or what is deemed to be "all for one, one for all". So too, collective nature requires members to be on constant standby, so as to be able to help a fellow comrade pragmatically or combatively. Based on the passage above, while outlaw MCs may not actively look for trouble, retreating from conflict is never an option. As Ellis (2014, p. 23) explains, "the need for men to achieve, and appear to be in possession of, a particular masculinity has relevance for understanding violent criminality, which can represent a means to exert dominance and power over others". Outlaw MCs are like most subcultures, in the sense that their belief system or interests are at variance with the larger culture. The legitimation of violence is a politically laden construct (Apter, 1997), yet in relation to outlaw MCs, the legitimation of violence, especially in regards to spontaneous acts of violence, is an ingrained disposition that is reinforced through brotherhood, a quality that advocates unity and support in compromising or conflictual situations.

This chapter has thus far alluded to how collective violence within outlaw MC settings is an extension of brotherhood. This will now be elaborated on in relation to two airport brawls that involved outlaw fraternities.

Two airport brawls

The public display of violence of outlaw members is unique in contrast to other organizations that are deemed to be criminally inclined. In addition, the public violence carried out by such MCs are "glocal", in that their crimes are not conducted in fixed terrain, rather they are manifested because of local and global networks of opportunities (Hobbs, 2013; Rahman, 2019). The HAMC is the biggest outlaw MC in the world and, at the time of writing, the MC is spread across five continents, 58 countries, 85 areas, with a total of 466 charters (Hells Angels, 2019). The MC is notorious for its violent feuds with rival MCs, especially in North America and other regions of the global north. Often, however, the violent feuds take place in public domains, which Rahman (2019) considers to be *spectator violence*; that is, physical violence which is exhibited in a public capacity. Indeed, there is another paradox to consider here; while the intrinsic interactions of MCs are clandestine, their violent interactions are often openly displayed in public settings.

In England, spectator violence or public displays of violence in a collective sense is hardly associated with outlaw biker clubs. While outlaw clubs are spread across England, their nefarious actions rarely make news headlines. So, when members of the HAMC and Outlaw Motorcycle Club (OMC) brawled on 20 January 2008, at Birmingham International Airport, Birmingham, England, the incident became national headline news. The brawl started when a few members from both clubs noticed each other on the same flight back from Alicante, Spain. According to court information, both clubs rang for reinforcements prior to landing at Birmingham airport. Those that came as reinforcements brought with them various weapons, including a meat cleaver. Almost 30 members from both sides clashed, with some wielding knuckledusters and hammers (*The Telegraph* 2009).

In the airport, passengers had to take cover from the violence that proceeded in the arrivals terminal. In total, four OMC members – Mark Mosely, Neale Harrison, Mark Price and Jeremey Ball were found guilty of rioting. Three HAMC members – Paul Artlett, Sean Timmins and Leonard Hawthorne were found guilty of rioting. Once the trial ended, the West Midlands Police said that the "horrendous" violence during the riot was unprecedented in the history of the airport. According to the BBC (2009), Bill Holland, who was Assistant Chief Constable of Warwickshire Police at the time, said the following:

> It is a matter of official record that over many years, outlaw motorcycle clubs have been actively engaged in organised crime.

While the above reiterates the global narrative that outlaw clubs are indeed organized crime groups, the Birmingham airport brawl depicts the unique spontaneous nature of their collective violence. Criminologically, the case is an iconic "signal crime", a concept coined by Innes and Fielding (2002) that argues how certain criminal or disorderly acts have a disproportionate impact upon the fear of crime. Indeed, airport disorders, especially those that involve rival fraternities, are uncommon.

Of note, another example of spectator violence, in an airport, within a collective capacity, is the murder of Hells Angels bikie Anthony Zervas. Zervas was clubbed with a 17 kg metal bollard and stabbed with a pair of scissors at a domestic airport terminal in Sydney, Australia on 22 March 2009. According to news reports, Zervas got off a flight with his brother, a senior Hells Angels member, and the president of the Hells Angels Guildford chapter, Derek Wainohu (Sutton, 2018). He was killed by the president of the Comancheros biker club, Mahmoud "Mick" Hawi. Before the fatal incident, several members of the Hells Angels and the Comancheros brawled in the airport terminal after a chance encounter between Hawi and Wainohu. Similar to the Birmingham airport case, the Comancheros requested back up. During the trial, the jury heard evidence from airport staff, passengers and CCTV footage was also shown. In total, six Comanchero members stood trial for murder, while a Hells Angels member was tried for riot and affray. After a four-month trial, the jury took 21 days to deliver its verdict. While part of the defence case was that the victim approached Hawi with an offensive weapon, the Comanchero leader was found guilty of murder and affray in 2011 (Wells, 2011). He was sentenced to 28 years in prison, with a non-parole period of 21 years. While the sole Hells Angel, David Padovan, was found not guilty, four of the five Comancheros were convicted for several violent acts. Christian Menzies, Zoran Kisacanin and Usama Potrus were acquitted of manslaughter and murder, but were found guilty of rioting. Menzies and Kisacanin were also found guilty of affray (Welch, 2009).

Like most one-percenter club presidents, Hawi was a notorious figure who was feared in the biker underworld. Born in Beirut, Lebanon, Hawi emigrated with his family to Australia. Before murdering Zervas, Hawi lived a flamboyant lifestyle and was known to recruit young men from Middle Eastern backgrounds into the biker fold. After serving three years for Zervas' murder, the New South Wales Court of Criminal Appeal set aside the conviction and Hawi was released on bail. Soon after, he pleaded guilty to manslaughter and was given a six-year sentence, but was immediately released because of the time he had already served. However, in February 2018, Hawi was assassinated in his car outside a gym in Rockdale, Sydney. At the time of writing, several individuals have been charged with murder and are awaiting trial (AAP, 2019).

In relation to the two cases above, there are some commonalities to consider. Both depict spontaneous acts of collective violence, as the encounters were not premeditated, albeit both cases offer descriptions of reinforcement. The reinforcement aspect should be of interest. It elucidates the notion of brotherhood, and portrays the fraternal nature of outlaw clubs – one that is contingent on comradeship – irrespective of how difficult or compromising the task ahead may be. In addition, both brawls occurred in a public place, two international airports. Violent disorder in a collective capacity is usually a redundant phenomenon; however, within the space of 14 months, two chapters of the HAMC were involved in extreme violence that served to be spectator violence. Some scholars have argued that a spectator approach towards violence is a means of "doing gender" and "doing masculinity", especially in the presence of both peers (Muncie, 2009; Deuchar, 2013). While in both cases the HAMC members were outnumbered, it can be argued that their participation in spectator violence, irrespective of purpose, was an "honour contest", which therefore required MC members to exert dominance in order to acclaim honour. So too, the notion of honour is often achieved through the consumption of violence, which in turn provides a means of maintaining symbolic boundaries. It is for this reason that this chapter now moves on to consider symbolic boundaries, and their significance for the growth and progression of outlaw MCs.

The consumption of collective violence: maintaining symbolic boundaries

This chapter started by considering how collective violence, like most violence, involves symbolic-expressive action. In the political sense, the upshot of collective violence encompasses the expectation of instrumental gain, which Ray (2018, p. 182) argues includes a "complex play of control, policing, and mobility through space". In this work on the sociology of collective violent action, Hartman (2015) notes that symbolic boundaries constitute the "missing link", thus filling the micro-macro "gap" in violence. By "symbolic boundaries", Hartman considers the relational elements of cognitive, affective and cultural resources that actors mobilize, so as to be able to act within a violent capacity individually and on behalf of a group.

As Tilly (1998) describes, symbolic boundaries are selective representational re-descriptions embedded and constrained by socially organized speech, which are often produced and reproduced as oral or written "stories" in terms of "standard stories". By standard stories, he means "stories in which connected, self-propelled actors, individual or collective, cause events, outcomes, and each other's actions" (Tilly, 1998, pp. 42–43). Indeed, for Hartman (2015), the measurements of violence are of significance, and symbolic boundaries serve as a marker to frame an individual's identification with another person and their intentional or mental state.

According to Ray (2018, p. 183), "maintaining and mobilizing status differences and boundaries involves narratives especially of past dramatic events including defeats, through which actors become drawn into mobilization processes". Narratives are crucial for the creation of symbolic boundaries, and in turn they set patterns of relationships and conceptual distinctions. For example, violence in the motorcycle world is not exclusively an outlaw phenomenon; however, the narratives that are constructed by media or popular culture suggest otherwise. For outlaws, narratives of the past are based on interactions which inform, educate and shape the temperament of a MC member. While the two cases discussed in this chapter may come across as merely spontaneous acts of collective violence, it is worth noting that outlaw violence is often instrumental, in that "violence [is] used to achieve a recognised objective" (D'Cruze *et al.* 2006, p. 125). This means that the execution of violence is used for gain.

Moreover, D'Cruze *et al.* (2006, p. 130), alludes to how particular murders connected with organized crime can be viewed as "expressive than rational – gestures of power, which assert (masculine) identity and authority through their very recklessness or the excess of violence". This is evident in the Sydney airport brawl, whereby Hawi's penchant for violence offset any "reasoning", a characteristic that is integral for all leaders, even those that represent criminal fraternities. In addition, this exemplifies the symbolic nature of outlaw members; individuals who take "special liberties", whose motivation centre on self, and therefore it allows them to deprive, rob, and destroy with impunity without ever acknowledging the harms placed upon others (Hall, 2012). As Winlow (2014) notes, rather than acknowledging such harms, the individuals who believe that they are entitled to special liberty remain attached to an image of themselves as the most useful circulators of commodities and the most transcendent free individuals, the creators of a prosperous future and the pioneers of the free expression of the full spectrum of drives and desires.

Irrespective of motive or opportunity, the consumption of violence is an indicator that separates outlaw MC's from other motorcycle clubs. Indeed, for criminal organizations, violence serves as a basis for achieving masculine honour. In their research on collective identity in the MC underworld, Rahman and Lynes (2018) discuss how masculine honour is conventionally focused on cultural factors to assist explaining that men from certain societies may express overt masculine qualities. Johnson and Demetriou (2016) argue that masculine honour has usually been thought to depend on a man's virility and willingness to defend with violence. Indeed, honour that is achieved through collective violent interactions represents the understanding of solidarity, and subsequently cultivates the creation, maintenance and advancement of symbolic boundaries.

Here, it is important to note the twofold aspect of collective violence and symbolic boundaries in the outlaw realm. In the micro (individual) sense, MC members, especially prospect members, are expected to develop, hone and display their physical prowess via intra-gang violence, which in many ways serves as invaluable conditioning for violent encounters with external groups. As Sonny recalls, 'Oakland and Frisco Hell's Angels would fuck each other up at every occasion' (Barger *et al.* 2001, p. 148). Most MCs are territorial, which means that each club has various *chapters* that spread regionally across a country. Thus, given the territorial nature, Barker (2007) describes how concerns of honour and financial issues converge to ignite inter-club warfare. This reinforces the importance of all members being on standby, as the preservation of a chapter is paramount, regardless of it being due to intra-club rivalry. In addition, the protection of a chapter via violence symbolizes those that are deemed to be what Hall (2012) calls "criminal undertakers", individuals who aim to journey from the ranks of the exploited to the exploiters.

From a non-violent perspective, in relation to symbolic boundaries, members are expected to represent themselves in ways that leave no doubt of who they are and what they epitomize. This chapter has already highlighted that there is an expectation for members to unequivocally devout themselves to their club, its members and their needs. In doing so, this displays club commitment, mutual support ethic and a protective mechanism that transcends into an impregnable social network. For instance, Wolf (1991) considers the significance of a clubhouse, which is a building space that members occupy and share for formal business. This makes the clubhouse a sacred place, and, from a logistical perspective, members who operate from an established clubhouse are "required to provide a place of refuge and hospitality for touring patch holders or visiting clubs" (Wolf, 1991, p. 165). Thus, it is through the notion of brotherhood whereby ties become multi-layered and serve an array of interests.

Political or spontaneous collective violence is spread by communication and behaviour. From a collective (macro) perspective, this chapter has revealed how violence is a crucial commodity that is used to maintain or advance the violent reputation of outlaw clubs. Additionally, from a masculine standpoint, the consumption of violence is imperative. For these kinds of organizations, retaliation is perceived as an alternative form of criminal justice, which is obligatory to undertake to defend their status of honour and masculinity. In other words, to not act antagonistically may produce a form of social stigmatization, because "responding with toughness and strength becomes imbedded in the definition of being a man" (Gilbert and Andrews, 1998, p. 266). It can be argued that those involved in the airport brawls merely saw their rivals as "objects" that would enable them to defend and advance their "masculine honour". For as Johnson and Demetriou (2016, p. 4) state, "what really matters for male honour is performance, especially on the battlefield".

The symbolic boundaries of outlaw clubs are explicit, in so far that permanent members of a club are required to represent themselves collectively in public settings via "patched" garments, which serve as keynote insignias, and which are always maintained, honoured and respected. In simple terms, the patches are treated in the manner that military personnel would treat their service stripes. This chapter has highlighted the symbolic capital that outlaw clubs such as the HAMC acquire based on their image, and while outlaw clubs are vilified in media and popular culture based on their physical appearance, Kuldova (2019) notes how recently large numbers of people have gravitated towards outlaw groups. For instance, following the 2019 Christchurch terrorist attack, which was carried out by far-right extremist Brenton Tarrant, who killed 50 Muslims whilst they prayed at a mosque, the president of the Waikato Mongrel Mob, Sonny Fatu vowed to guard mosques with members of his chapter. According to news coverage by Kerr (2019), he was quoted to have said: "we will support and assist our Muslim brothers and sisters for however long they need us". This reiterates the paradoxical and anti-establishment nature of outlaw clubs, but highlights the relevance of brotherhood, which Maas (2013) found in her empirical study is a quality that is shared by some bikers between anyone, irrespective of their walk in life.

Conclusion

This chapter highlights the politically driven notion of collective violence, and how it can be employed when considering spontaneous acts of violent practice. Through case study examples, it is evident that the common thread that runs through collective violence and symbolic boundaries is brotherhood; which also serves as a guiding principle for the functionalities of club member, and what is expected from them individually and collectively. Violence is a legitimated function in the outlaw realm, which therefore makes it a viable commodity that is used to create, maintain and advance operations or activities deemed to be deviant or criminal. In summary, outlaw clubs are mainly in warfare with the "mirror image", as both fraternities occupy men who, in the capitalist era, undertake "special liberties" (Hall, 2012), by configuring their ethical codes to employ harm so as to be able to elevate themselves within an asocial hierarchy.

References

Apter, D. (1997) *The Legitimization of Violence*. London: Palgrave Macmillan.

AAP (2019) *Third Man Charged with Mick Hawi's murder*. [Online.] Australian Associated Press. Available at: www.9news.com.au/2019/03/14/18/37/man-charged-with-mick-hawi-s-murder (accessed 12 March 2019).

Ball-Rokeach, S. (2017) The legitimation of violence. In J. F. Short, Jr and M. E. Wolfgang (eds), *Collective Violence*. New York: Routledge, pp. 100–112.

Barger, S., Zimmerman, K., and Zimmerman K. (2001) *Hell's Angel: The Life and Times of Sonny Barger and The Hell's Angels Motorcycle Club*. London: Harper Collins.

Barker, T. (2007) *Biker Gangs and Organised Crime*. Newark: LexisNexis.

Barker, T., and Human, K. (2009) Crimes of the big four motorcycle gangs. *Journal of Criminal Justice*, 37(2), 174–179.

BBC (2009) *Public 'At Risk' from Rival Gangs*. [Online.] British Broadcasting Corporation. Available at: news.bbc.co.uk/1/hi/england/west_midlands/8109883.stm (accessed 12 February 2019).

Becker, H. (1997) *Outsiders: Studies in the Sociology of Deviance*. New York: Free Press.

Bjørgo, T. (2019) Preventing organised crime originating from outlaw motorcycle clubs. *Trends in Organized Crime*, 22(1), 84–122

Brewer, J. (2010) *Peace and Processes*. London: Wiley.

Clarkson, W. (2003) *Moody: The Life and Crimes of Britain's Most Notorious Hitman*. Edinburgh: Mainstream Publishing.

Clarkson, W. (2008) *Gangs of Britain*. London: John Blake.

D'Cruze, S., Walklate, S., and Pegg, S. (2006) *Murder*. Cullompton: Willan.

Deuchar, R. (2013) *Policing Youth Violence: Transatlantic Connections*. London: Trentham Books/ IOE Press.

Durham, A. M., Elrod, H. P., and Kinkade, P. T. (1995) Images of crime and justice: Murder and the "true crime" genre. *Journal of Criminal Justice*, 23(2), 143–152.

Ellis, A. (2016) *Men, Masculinities and Violence: An Ethnographic Study*. London: Routledge.

Gilbert, P. and Andrews, B. (1998) *Shame: Interpersonal Behavior, Psychopathology and Culture*. New York: Oxford University Press.

Hall, S. (2012) *Theorizing Crime and Deviance: A New Perspective*. London: Sage.

Hartman, E. (2015) Symbolic boundaries and collective violence: A new theoretical argument for an explanatory sociology of collective violent action. *Journal for the Theory of Social Behaviour*, 46(2), 166–186.

Hells Angels (2019) *Club History*. [Online.] Hells Angels official website. Available at: hells-angels.com/our-club/history/ (accessed 17 March 2019).

Hobbs, D. (2013) *Lush Life: Constructing Organized Crime in the UK*. Oxford: Oxford University Press.

Innes, M. and Fielding, N. (2002) From community to communicative policing: 'Signal crimes' and the problem of public reassurance. *Sociological Research Online*, 7(2), 1–12.

Johnson, L. and Demetriou, D. (2016) *Honour in the Modern World: Interdisciplinary Perspectives*. Maryland: Rowman and Littlefield.

Katz, J. (1988) *Seductions of Crime*. New York: Basic Books.

Kerr, F. (2019) *Mongrel Mob Gang Members to Stand Guard at Local Mosque, in Support of Muslim Kiwis*. [Online.] Stuff Limited. Available at: www.stuff.co.nz/national/christchurch-shooting/111395229/mongrel-mob-gang-members-to-stand-guard-at-local-mosque-in-support-of-muslim-kiwis?cid=app-iPhone (accessed 26 March 2019).

Kuldova, T. (2017) Hells Angels: Motorcycle corporation in the fashion business: Interrogating the fetishism of the trademark law. *Journal of Design History*, 30(4), 389–407.

Kuldova, T. (2019) *How Outlaws Win Friends and Influence People*. London: Palgrave Macmillan.

Kuldova T. and Quinn, J. (2018) Outlaw motorcycle clubs and struggles over legitimation. In T. Kuldova and M. Sánchez-Jankowski (eds), *Outlaw Motorcycle Clubs and Street Gangs*. London: Palgrave Macmillan.
Lauchs, M. (2019) Are outlaw motorcycle gangs organized crime groups? An analysis of the Finks MC. *Deviant Behavior*, 40(3), 287–300.
Maas, K. (2013) Making sense of motorcycle brotherhood: Women, branding, and construction of self. *All Theses, Dissertations, and Other Capstone Projects*. Paper 238.
Marsden, W. and Sher, J. (2007) *Angels of Death: Inside the Bikers' Global Crime Empire*. London: Hodder and Stoughton.
Muncie, J. (2009) *Youth and Crime*. London: Sage.
Quinn, J. (1987) Sex roles and hedonism among members of 'outlaw' motorcycle clubs. *Deviant Behavior*, 8(1), 47–63.
Quinn, J. and Koch, S. (2003) The nature of criminality within one-percent motorcycle clubs. *Deviant Behavior*, 24(3), 281–205.
Rahman, M. (2019) *Homicide and Organised Crime: Ethnographic Narratives of Serious Violence in the Criminal Underworld*. London: Palgrave Macmillan.
Rahman, M. and Lynes, A. (2018) Ride to die: Understanding masculine honour and collective identity in the motorcycle underworld. *Journal of Criminological Research, Policy and Practice*, 4(4), 238–252.
Ray, L. (2018) *Violence and Society* (2nd edn). London: Sage.
Reynolds, F. (1967) *Freewheelin Frank*. New York: Grove.
Schouten, J. and McAlexander, J. (1995) Subcultures of consumption: An ethnography of the new bikers. *Journal of Consumer Research*, 22(1), 43–61.
Sutton, C. (2018) *Life and Times of Slain Bikie Prince Mick Hawi*. [Online.] news.com.au. Available at: www.news.com.au/national/crime/life-and-times-of-slain-bikie-prince-mick-hawi/news-story/8da2669ff2d85411831b1aab60dc4a39 (accessed 11 January 2019).
The Telegraph (2009) *Hells Angels and Outlaws Biker Gangs Jailed for Airport Riot*. [Online.] *The Telegraph*. Available at: www.telegraph.co.uk/news/uknews/law-and-order/5579341/Hells-Angels-and-Outlaws-biker-gangs-jailed-for-airport-riot.html (accessed 12 December 2018).
Thompson, T. (2008) *Gangs: A Journey into the Heart of the British Underworld*. London: Hodder and Stoughton.
Thompson, T. (2011) *Outlaws: Inside the Violent World of Biker Gangs*. London: Hodder and Stoughton.
Tilly, C. (1998) Micro, macro, or megrim? In J. Schlumbohm (ed), *Mikrogeschichte – Makrogeschichte: komplementär oder inkommensurabel?* Göttingen: Wallstein Verlag, pp. 33–52.
Tilly, C. (2003) *The Politics of Collective Violence*. Cambridge: Cambridge University Press.
Welch, D. (2009) Hells Angel killed in airport attack. [Online.] *The Sydney Morning Herald*. Available at: www.smh.com.au/national/hells-angel-killed-in-airport-attack-20090322-95om.html (accessed 11 March 2019).
Wells, J. (2011) *Bikie Boss Guilty of Murder over Airport Brawl*. [Online.] Australian Broadcasting Corporation. Available at: www.abc.net.au/news/2011-11-02/comancheros-boss-guilty-of-murder-over-airport-brawl/3610910 (accessed 11 March 2019).
Winlow, S. (2014) Trauma, guilt and the unconscious: some theoretical notes of violent subjectivity, *The Sociological Review*, 62(2), 32–49.
Wolf, D. (1991) *The Rebels: A Brotherhood of Outlaw Bikers*. Toronto: University of Toronto Press.

27
PRISON GANGS
Re-examining their existence, reframing their function

Jane L. Ireland, Philip Birch, Sören Henrich, Michael Lewis and Carol A. Ireland

Introduction

This chapter considers prison gangs by outlining definitional challenges that concern this social phenomenon before examining the importance of accounting for the specifics of prison environments. As a consequence, the chapter presents a social eco-system approach to understanding prison gangs and, in doing so, accounts for theories of importation, strain and deprivation, incorporating these into a proposed Gang Social-Ecosystem Model (G-SEM). Adopting the core principles of such theories, consideration is given to both "pull" and "push" variables and how these may apply to the G-SEM. In conclusion, the chapter draws to a close by challenging the more pejorative approach to defining and understanding gangs, particularly in prisons.

The term "gang" can invite a view of violence, broader criminality and a range of dissocial acts designed to drive forward a shared group agenda. This is, however, arguably a populist view that resides within media depictions and helps drive myths and misunderstandings. It is, nevertheless, the case that gangs have been associated with violent and illegal acts (e.g. Fortune, 2004; Gaes *et al.*, 2002), including within the confines of a prison (e.g. Pyrooz *et al.*, 2011; Drury and DeLisi, 2011; Griffin and Hepburn, 2006). The relationship between aggression and prison gang membership is certainly not in dispute (e.g. Griffin and Hepburn, 2006; Scott, 2001). Scholars have argued that gang members are responsible for the majority of prison violence (Cox, 1996; Camp and Camp, 1985), with some estimates indicating that 50 per cent of prison violence is driven by gangs (Camp and Camp, 1985). These estimates are dependent on how gangs are defined and, as such, there is a need to recognize the considerable complexity in this area. This includes accounting not just for the negative aspects of gangs but also the positives; a recognition that can be considered troubling by some practitioners, researchers and policymakers. Nevertheless, acceptance of *all* aspects of gang membership becomes important as we proceed to outline their role in potentially stabilizing changing, chaotic and threatening environments, such as prisons.

Defining prison gangs

Defining prison gangs is complex; trying to fix on a definition of gangs has, without doubt, served to complicate the area (Ireland and Power, 2012). It has served to distract from the true focus of work, namely understanding why gangs operate and using this to intervene in neutralising and/or limiting their negative impacts. At the most basic level, gangs are perhaps best described as social groups (Decker, 2004), labelled by some sectors as "gangs". The concept of a gang is certainly not new, although other terms have been used to describe them, such as "Security Threat Group" and "Inmate Disruptive Groups" (Fleisher, 2011). The conceptualization of the term gang has also been aligned to prison bullying (Ireland, 2017). Indeed, a predecessor to the term bullying was "mobbing", a sociological term specifically described as the targeting of an individual by a group, regardless of context. The term "ganging up" has a basis here and, across time, appears to have developed into other terms, such as harassment. "Mobbing" is not a human specific term, however, and has a basis in the work of Lorenz (1966) who described such behaviour among birds and other (non-human) animals as a collective attack driven by hate. The latter aspect was removed from the original German translation, with the sole focus becoming that of a *collective* attack. This has had increasing application to human behaviour, including to "gang up" in the workplace, where it is described as a form of group bullying (Leymann, 1996).

Regardless, the origins of the concept of a group attack, seemingly for a shared aim, are clear. It was originally attributed to animals attempting to *thrive*, a Darwinian concept underpinned by a need to survive by *protecting* yourself and those connected to you. *Thriving* and *protection* are crucial components to acknowledge since it is accepted that gangs commonly engage in behaviours connected to thriving, whether this be via turf (area) acquisition, other material acquisition and/or to protect or grow their membership. Protection and avoiding deprivation through material acquisition have been recognized as important driving features for gang membership, both of which appear key to prison environments and commonly described as variables "pushing" individuals to join a gang (Decker, 1996).

The term "gang" is perhaps a more media-friendly term, however, serving to provide a certain image that appears attractive to a populist readership; if gangs were instead referred to as a "group" then perhaps it would garner less interest. The function of gangs can also be lost as there is a focus on the symptoms of their presence. Take for example the following definition:

> a social division in a traditional society consisting of families or communities linked by social, economic, religious, or blood ties, with a common culture and dialect, typically having a recognized leader.
>
> *(Oxford Dictionary, 2019)*

Aspects of a community link, culture and leadership all resonate with the definition of a gang. However, the definition presented above is that of a tribe and yet the similarity to a gang description is notable. Nevertheless, it has different connotations and is arguably less pejorative. Interestingly, the term gang appears to have become aligned more with a *moral* description focusing on the dissocial behaviour thought primarily linked to it. Consider, for example, the following definition of a gang offered by the Eurogang network;

> A youth gang, or troublesome youth group, is a durable, street-oriented youth group whose involvement in illegal activity is part of their group identity.
>
> *(Weerman et al., 2009. p. 20)*

This clearly focuses on the negative aspects of gang membership. Illegal activity is a judgement by a State in terms of what constitutes an offence and is arguably influenced by morals. Such a definition automatically assumes that all gang members are criminals. Thus, there appears a moral layer placed over earlier aligned definitions (e.g. tribes) that makes no mention of the more positive elements that would be expected with a tribe (e.g. community, family, other related ties). This point is made since definitions are important; they have a developed history that evolves over time and allow us to draw differences between what is a "gang" and what has the same organized structure, and yet is described using distinctly different terminology. Lost within the definitions is, perhaps, the impact the environment has within which a gang is operating, with a need to adopt a more neutral stance with descriptions and not one loaded towards negative connotations. However, Weerman *et al.* (2009) make a strong argument for the inclusion of the word "illegal" in their gang definition, on the grounds of policy. They argue that, without this inclusion, the attention given to gangs by policymakers would diminish. Thus, it would appear the definition is a strategic decision and not one driven by the specifics of an empirically-based definition. The importance of accounting for policy in definition development may have been lost as the term "gang" takes on an ever-developing pejorative label. Focusing on definition alone perhaps becomes more futile, with a need instead to shift towards understanding their presence as a group with a shared social identity. Thus, the issue that academics, and increasingly practitioners, are aiming to address with regards to prison gangs is their structure, how they develop and are maintained, as well as how this can be positively impacted on. To do this, there needs to be less focus on the popularized symptoms of gang *membership* (e.g. aggression; drugs; indiscipline) and a greater understanding of their *organization* and function within certain environments, for example, the ability of gangs to foster and enable discrimination and prejudice, which feeds into gang behaviour (Smithson *et al.*, 2012).

The words membership and organization are chosen deliberately; both suggest a degree of entry requirement, similar to employment, to a group that has both structure and performance indicators. Thus, they operate as we would expect a business. We know that gangs, including prison gangs, are highly organized (Orlando-Morningstar, 1997) and, yet, the organizational structure and more positive elements of gang membership, namely affiliation, friendship and community that it brings are not as well considered. However, these positive elements are increasingly being recognized (Skarbek, 2014), including within prisons (Ireland and Power, 2012). Membership of a group is in itself protective (Ireland and Power, 2012) and required for group-living species, such as humans. The term "gang" fails to give credit to the deeper level of organization and adaptive function that a gang can present with. Indeed, if we focus briefly on the definition applied to prison gangs we find ones such as: "…social organizations that resist authority, violate rules, and promote violence" (Griffin and Hepburn, 2006, p. 444). Focus does not move towards the words 'social organization' but rather the symptoms – resist, violate, promote violence. There are many ways in which to question these definitions; for example, do gangs really promote violence or are they just violent to acquire their aims? The *promotion* of violence falls within the domain of other groups, or perhaps forms part of initiation processes to join a group where prowess to both administer and tolerate aggression is judged. Or is the promotion simply part of an image that is cultivated in order to protect?

The point being made here is that focusing on a simple association between aggression/indiscipline and gang membership may lead to assumptions being made when in fact the association is more complex. Successful species have the ability to adapt to surroundings and to demonstrate the *potential* to be aggressive if required; this potential should not be confused with actuality since a highly aggressive species is more than likely to be selected out of existence, usually a result of a high-risk lifestyle where their risk for injury and/death is simply enhanced. Put simply, to create a *perception* of being aggressive has more advantages than to *actually be* highly aggressive if the ultimate aim is one of survival. This arguably places the development of all gangs into a social ecosystem, which in a prison is perhaps magnified by the specifics of the environment and the need to adapt. The term "ecosystem" is deliberately chosen since focus is on a community *coexisting with non-living aspects* of their environment, in this instance a prison environment, to which they are unavoidably linked. Essentially they are interacting as a system comprising of non-living (i.e. physical/organizational) and living (i.e. social) aspects.

We certainly should not be surprised by the existence of "gangs" within prisons. Prisons are threatening environments, where membership to a named group is likely to confer protection (Egan and Beadman, 2011) and provide a social identity (Fong and Buentello, 1991), which perhaps becomes lost when described merely as a "prisoner". Add to this the economic advantage of being in a group in an environment that is materially deprived compared with the community (e.g. Egan and Beadman, 2011; Scott, 2001) and a recipe for gang creation starts to emerge. Understanding the development and maintenance of gangs is perhaps of more value in managing them than becoming too focused on definition, prevalence and symptoms. The ensuing section thus focuses on the development and maintenance of gangs, presenting them as part of a social ecosystem within prisons.

Understanding how prison gangs form: introducing the Gang Social-Ecosystem Model (G-SEM)

The development of prison gangs remains poorly understood, with research limited, descriptive and largely atheoretical. There is a need to avoid focus on myths concerning development (Biondi, 2017) and to concentrate more on the specifics of the environment and the role of direct importation (and life course importation; DeLisi *et al.*, 2011) and adaption/deprivation. Importation reflects the characteristics that prisoners bring with them to the prison and represents commonly referred to theories in this area (DeLisi *et al.*, 2004). There is a need to apply these models more broadly, by exploring membership characteristics on a group/network and not individual level, and by reflecting on how these groups have been imported into prisons and adapted. This is also in keeping with the prison bullying literature, which moved away some decades ago from the concept of individual pathology to consider the wider environment and how prisoners are attempting to adapt to this (Ireland, 2017). It is only through understanding development through the lens of the environment that individuals find themselves housed in, that a fuller understanding of gangs can perhaps be considered. Understanding gang development also allows us to focus more on holistic approaches to management that account for the group and not just the individual.

Before introducing the theoretical model that aims to understand how gangs are embedded within a wider social ecosystem structure, we will first consider some grounding principles that apply to how individuals become involved in indiscipline within prison settings. These principles underpin the model that will be presented. Key elements include avoiding individual conceptualizations; deprivation and importation; avoiding a strained environment; and consideration of the drivers underpinning the decision to join a prison gang.

Moving away from individual conceptualizations

There is increasing acceptance, both empirically and theoretically, that prisoners become involved in challenging behaviours because of an interaction between what they bring with them to the environment (e.g. intrinsic factors) and the environment itself. A salient illustration is the *Multifactor Model of Bullying in Secure Settings* (MMBSS: Ireland, 2012), which highlights how pre-existing individual factors (e.g. attitudes supportive of aggression, prior history of violence) interact with social aspects of prisons (e.g. presence of dominance and power hierarchies among prisoners; a prisoner code supporting aggression), to encourage involvement in aggression, either on an individual or group level. Custodial experience, and thus prison social experience, has represented the only distinguishing factor repeatedly recognized in the literature, with bullies presenting with more experience of institutional care than non-bullies (Ireland, 2017). This shares some similarities with prison gang research, which also reflects the importance of custodial experience (Wood *et al.*, 2009), extending it to further capture pre-existing family gang connections (Rufino *et al.*, 2012). Custodial experience and/or prior family experience with gangs are noted correlates of familiarization with societal rules and expectations, within a gang, that are then transferred to a prison setting. "Gang codes" are well recognized as is the "inmate code" (Ireland, 2017). They are both products of groups forming with an identity, even if the membership routinely alters. In prisons, the "inmate" code comprises a range of expectations, such as the need to protect, to use aggression when necessary and not to inform (to "grass") on others (Ireland, 2005). These elements are shared with gang codes. The formation of codes is a further indication of the role of the wider social environment that begins to operate, extending beyond the individual. Adoption of codes, either explicitly or implicitly, is recognized as a survival mechanism (Paterline and Petersen, 1999) and forms part of "prisonization" (Thomas and Petersen, 1977), where an individual becomes *assimilated* into prison culture. Part of this culture, it is argued, includes gangs and could represent a natural assimilation into an environment where membership of a gang develops as a means of meeting a range of needs, including survival and a sense of protection (Ireland and Power, 2012).

Countering deprivation and the pains of imprisonment

Deprivation theory (Goffman, 1961; Sykes, 1958) describes how, when an individual is placed into an environment as restrictive as a prison, their needs have to be met through maladaptive means (Sykes, 1958). Lack of resources, crowding and increased risk of aggression exposure, are just examples of factors that form part of the "pains of imprisonment" (Morris and Worrall, 2014; Sykes, 1958), which a prisoner will seek to manage. The development of gangs in such a situation becomes clearly adaptive on the grounds that it is a means of organizing access to increased resources, developing territory to protect the little space available, offering protection against aggression and ensuring all of this is protected via a "code" that is consolidated by a social identity being afforded to a gang. Thus, there is a clear advantage in a deprived environment to join a named group that can offset some of the pains, even if the cost of membership is notable. None of this is new: the concept of a "gorilla role" was first proposed by Sykes (1958), in which a prisoner overcame deprivation at the expense of other prisoners, through exploitation. Although this role has been aligned to the concept of a prison bully, it equally applies to the head of a gang. An issue that is not, however, addressed with deprivation is the role of wider society factors; it is suggested that gang development can mirror a state structure and essentially represent a response to wider societal issues (Biondi, 2017), which are then transferred into a prison, where the gang structure simply continues. This consideration lends itself to examine the role for pre-existing factors. Societal factors can be offered as an illustration of such pre-existing factors, including social exclusion. However, individual factors should not be overlooked, factors such as family gang membership prior to imprisonment (Rufino *et al.*, 2012). Pre-existing factors cannot be downplayed, since some prison gangs are a clear extension of community based gangs. The characteristics thus imported into the environment become key.

Why is importation important?

Importation theory, a valuable consideration at this point, refers to the pre-existing characteristics of prisoners (e.g. Irwin and Cressey, 1962). As noted, with gang membership there are pre-existing connections that can be transferred to the prison setting (Rufino *et al.*, 2012). This aligns with the notion of importation, which further recognizes that culture is not a sole product of the environment but influenced by pre-existing beliefs and attitudes. Importation theory has been one of the most commonly applied theories to understanding the development of prison gangs (DeLisi *et al.*, 2004; 2011). At its simplest application is the notion that you bring your connections with you into an environment that allows for the gang to continue, to have a presence and/or flourish. What is essentially being considered, however, is the *life course importation model*, where you are bringing with you a generation of deprivation experiences and delinquency (DeLisi *et al.*, 2011). This could extend to a *state* importation model in those environments where deprivation and challenges are not family-restricted but state-specific, leading to prison gangs essentially mirroring the structure of a state (Biondi, 2017). This is an important consideration since what is being argued here is that gangs in prison can be an importation not just of the individual but of a culture that is responding to wider societal issues (e.g. poverty, reliance on crime to survive). Thus, what enters a prison is far more entrenched in its development, which begins to suggest that an intervention approach focused on tacking attitudes and beliefs underpinning membership is futile in the absence of addressing the wider environmental and societal issues.

Avoiding a strained environment

Although deprivation and importation can offer some explanation as to why gangs may start to operate in prisons, on their own they are too simplistic to account for the continued development and reinforcement of gangs. Casting gangs as an adaptive approach to managing the strains of prison life becomes valuable. Viewing them perhaps as a means of bringing order to a chaotic social structure, where the risk of uncontrolled aggression and/or misconduct is raised, becomes important.

General Strain Theory (GST, Agnew, 1992, 2001) considers exposure to *strain* in prison as a likely risk factor for involvement in prison indiscipline, including aggression. Strain includes the deprivation of the environment, risk of harm, residing with threatening others, having an inability to acquire what you need to function (e.g. access to drugs), and losing a sense of identity and belonging. Gangs become a solution to this strain by providing an antidote; they offer a means of providing goods (governed by a code of conduct), a sense of belonging, identity and protection. The costs for belonging to and/or seeking the support of a gang may be high but this may outweigh the overall strain a prisoner is trying to manage. Indeed, strain theorists argue that it is the exposure to strain that produces a drive to offend (Agnew, 1992, 2001) and to cause an individual to exceed their usual responses. Consequently, it could be argued that you may not be a member of a gang in the community but the specific strain of the prison environment pushes you towards gang membership in a prison. Protective factors against strain include supportive relationships and coping resources (Steiner *et al.*, 2014), both of which could arguably be obtained via gang connections in prison.

Deciding to join a prison gang: pull or push?

Two core principles are commonly referred to in the street gang literature, namely "pull" and "push" variables in motivating membership of a gang. Pull variables reflect drivers, such as a need to join a gang to obtain a sense of fulfilment, respect or for stimulation (e.g. excitement), or for a sense of networked belonging, as you would achieve with a family (Gibson *et al.*, 2012; Sutton, 2017; Valasik and Reid, Chapter 22, this volume). Pull variables capture more individually led motivators and argue for membership as a means of achieving positive reinforcement (i.e. a gain). Conversely, push variables are more environmentally driven and attempt to replace or repair a feature of the social or wider environment that is missing or insufficient. These include a need to acquire a shared social identity (Decker, 1996), to make advancements financially (Stephenson, 2015), as a solution to residing in a materially deprived area (Thornberry *et al.*, 2003) and/or to afford protection from an actual and/or perceived threat, thereby enhancing safety (Hill *et al.*, 1999). The latter has been described as the most significant of the variables pushing membership (Valasik and Reid, this volume).

The application of these principles to a prison environment would appear a logical one considering all that has been outlined. Although reputation, excitement and a sense of belonging are important (i.e. pull variables), it seems push variables may be more significant. The principles of strain and deprivation theories support a role for push variables, with pull variables arguably informed primarily by importation. However, a prior history of exposure to abuse, deprivation and economic disadvantage, which are not uncommon within prisoner samples, would suggest that *life course importation* variables of this nature will actually serve to present as push variables. Thus, it would seem push variables, namely circumstance, are the primary driving features in comparison to pull variables. This is an important consideration since it points to a focus on circumstances as a means of intervening with gang membership. It is not suggesting that pull variables are not important; they are, but pull variables are more likely to appear further down the gang development line, perhaps as a facilitating factor to determine continued involvement in an established gang where a sense of belonging and reputation is well-developed. Rather, it is being suggested here that push variables are particularly important drivers for the initial joining and assimilation into a prison gang.

Gang Social-Ecosystem Model (G-SEM)

Bringing all these features together into a model that can begin to offer an understanding as to the genesis of prison gangs becomes of value, both in offering an understanding but also in directing future research. What is undoubtedly missing from the research to date is any attempt to outline the *pathway* of gang development, accounting for its formation and organization, integration into a prison, avenues for growth and how it adapts. The G-SEM attempts to do this by nesting these aspects into a social-ecosystem context out of which the gang journey is born and then reinforced as a continued product of the social-ecosystem it finds itself in. A key factor to acknowledge, however, is that gangs differ in their development, and whereas some may be an extension of a gang from the community, others are not. The G-SEM draws on circumstance and situational factors, importation, deprivation and evolutionary influences. It is shown in Figure 27.1.

G-SEM outlines the wider context within which a prison gang may form and be maintained, noting the role of wider circumstance contexts, such as state influences and prior factors of relevance. These are then imported into a prison and include prior gang membership and the experience of being victimized. Processes of importation, deprivation, strain, mirroring and a need to maintain an identity are all key background factors before prison placement, with these processes serving as a bridge between the wider context and the prison facilitating variables.

The prison environment then serves to facilitate gang development/maintenance through the continuing presence of deprivation and strain, with importation variables allowed to further

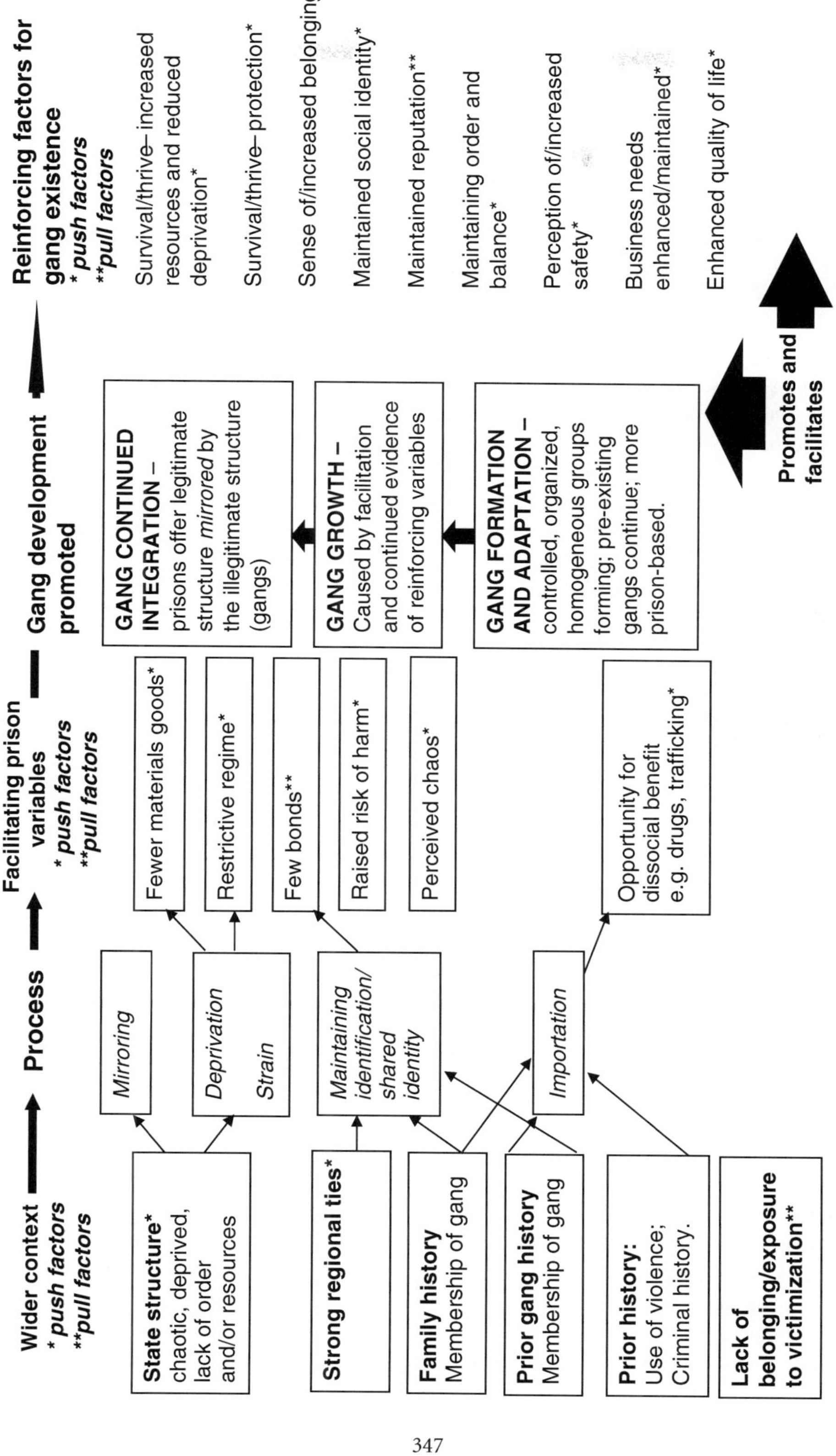

Figure 27.1 Gang Social-Ecosystem Model (G-SEM).

manifest. The concept of push and pull variables become important within a discussion of these facilitators. Push variables are the most prevalent in comparison to pull and appear as a continuation of the wider pre-prison environment. Push variables that then facilitate within the prison include deprivation and fear of/risk of harm and chaos, all of which occur within the context of a restricted regime, and arguably push for the further development of prison gangs. The pull variable of "few bonds" should not be lost within the push variables, however, since G-SEM argues for a need to compensate for this as a crucial component for gang development, particularly in an environment where bonding can serve as a means of protecting against harm and thereby creating a pull–push variable. Indeed, it is well recognized that gangs will thrive where there is a threat of/actual violence (push variable) since this serves to promote bonds and group cohesion (Decker *et al.*, 2014; Howell and Griffiths, 2018), making an argument for a closer push–pull association and returning us to the Darwinian concept of thrive and protection as important for the collective action of groups.

G-SEM provides further argument that the majority of reinforcing factors connected to gang development are push factors. It presents prison gangs as serving as a *solution to unpleasant circumstances* by either removing these or moderating them. They could, for example, be providing a solution to material deprivation by making goods more accessible to those connected to the gang; they could be removing the perceived fear of being harmed; and/or providing order to an arguable chaotic environment, to name but a few. Nevertheless, pull factors are also indicated as reinforcing, where the gains of gang membership focus on reputational enhancement and/or a sense of belonging. In this sense, pull factors are acting as positive reinforcers and thus as "gains".

What G-SEM cannot explain is how these reinforcing factors can be weighted. For example, are the push factors, although greater in number, more significant than the pull factors, or do certain pull factors override push factors? Regardless, both push and pull factors relate to prison gang membership, with the G-SEM embedding itself in a more circumstance-driven model of understanding prison gang membership, which attends to the processes of importation, deprivation and strain. It does not, however, discount the potential for factors that have *both* a push and a pull component. This is an area that future research could perhaps focus attention on to determine in more discrete terms the distinction between these components and their dynamic interplay within the specifics of a prison environment.

Conclusion

The current chapter has highlighted difficulties in the definition of gangs and how these are informed by a changing history. Labels are never of value and focus should instead be fixed on the notion of a group forming with a shared social identity and shared aims. Shifting focus from definitions also allows us to centre attention more on the role and function of gangs, particularly in prison environments, where importation, deprivation and strain become key, coupled with the role of a wider social and circumstance context that is often neglected. The G-SEM is presented as an initial theoretical model that aims to bring together these concepts and to recognize also what moves an individual towards gang membership. It further avoids any discussion of the symptoms of gangs. It is accepted that they play a role in aggression and indiscipline, including illegal acts, but equally that any attempt at intervention needs to focus less on the symptoms and more on the factors driving their formation and facilitation. Within this understanding of (prison) gangs, there needs to be an acceptance that humans are a group-living species and we will attempt to gravitate towards groups, particularly those that will protect us and assist us to thrive. This accounts again for the more positive elements of gangs. The G-SEM argues that in a threatening and sometimes chaotic environment, such as a prison, there is a clear argument for the adaptive elements of a gang to be acknowledged. Without the presence of a "gang" another named group would simply appear. Consequently, attention to "gang intervention" should acknowledge all aspects of their function, both negative and positive. Focus should perhaps move instead to fostering more of a "community" than a "gang" to drive prosocial aims. Removing gangs may not be the answer but reframing their presence and role may be.

References

Agnew, R. (1992) Foundation for a general strain theory of crime and delinquency. *Criminology*, 30, 47–87.

Agnew, R. (2001) Building on the foundation of general strain theory: Specifying the types of strain most likely to lead to crime and delinquency. *Journal of Research into Crime and Delinquency*. 38, 319–361.

Biondi, K. (2017) Prison violence, prison justice: The rise of Brazil's PCC: Could the origins and code of ethics of São Paulo's largest prison gang offer a new way to think about prison security policy in Brazil? *NACLA Report on the Americas*, 49(3), 341–346.

Camp, G. M. and Camp, C. G. (1985) *Prison Gangs: Their Extent, Nature, and Impact on Prisons*. Washington, DC: U.S. Government Printing Office.

Cox, V. (1996) Prison gangs: Inmates battles for control. *Corrections Compendium*, 10, 6–9.

Decker, S. H. (2004) *From the Street to the Prison, from the Prison to the Street: Understanding and Responding to Prison Gangs* (2nd edn). Richmond, KY: National Major Gang Task Force. American Correctional Association.

Decker, S. H. (1996) Collective and normative features of gang violence. *Justice Quarterly*, 13(2), 243–264.

Decker, S. H., Pyrooz, D. C., Sweeten, G., and Moule, R. K. (2014) Validating self-nomination in gang research: Assessing differences in gang embeddedness across non-, current, and former gang members. *Journal of Quantitative Criminology*, 30(4), 577–598.

DeLisi, M., Berg, M. T., and Hochstetler, A. (2004) Gang members, career criminals and prison violence: Further specification of the importation model of inmate behavior. *Criminal Justice Studies*, 17(4), 369–383.

DeLisi, M., Trulson, C. R., Marquart, J. W., Drury, A. J., and Kosloski, A. E. (2011) Inside the prison black box: Toward a life course importation model of inmate behavior. *International Journal of Offender Therapy and Comparative Criminology*, 55(8), 1186–1207.

Drury, A. J. and DeLisi, M. (2011) Gangkill: An exploratory empirical assessment of gang membership, homicide offending, and prison misconduct. *Crime & Delinquency*, 57, 130–146.

Egan, V. and Beadman, M. (2011) Personality and gang-embeddedness. *Personality and Individual Differences*, 51, 748–753.

Fleisher, M. S. (2011) Gang management in corrections. In P. Carlson and J.S. Garrett (eds), *Prison and Jail Administration: Practice and Theory* (3rd edn). Gaithersburg, MD: Aspen Publishing, 232–245.

Fong, R. S. and Buentello, S. (1991) The detection of prison gang development: An empirical assessment. *Federal Probation*, 55, 66–69.

Fortune, S. (2004) Prison gang leadership: Traits identified by prison gangsters. *Journal of Gang Research*, 11, 25–46.

Gaes, G. G., Wallace, S., Gilman, E., Klein-Saffran, J., and Suppa, S. (2002) The influence of prison gang affiliation on violence and other prison conduct. *Prison Journal*, 82, 359–386.

Gibson, C. L., Swatt, M. L., Miller, J. M., Jennings, W. G., and Gover, A. R. (2012) The causal relationship between gang joining and violent victimization: A critical review and directions for future research. *Journal of Criminal Justice*, 40(6), 490–501.

Goffman, E. (1961) *Asylums*. New York: Anchor Books.

Griffin, M. L. and Hepburn, J. R. (2006) The effect of gang affiliation on violent misconduct among inmates during the early years of confinement. *Criminal Justice and Behaviour*, 33, 419–448.

Hill, K. G., Howell, J. C., Hawkins, J. D., and Battin-Pearson, S. R. (1999) Childhood risk factors for adolescent gang membership: Results from the Seattle Social Development Project. *Journal of research in Crime and Delinquency*, 36(3), 300–322.

Howell, J. C. and Griffiths, E. (2018) *Gangs in America's communities* (3rd edn). Los Angeles: Sage Publications.

Ireland, J. L. (ed.) (2005) *Bullying Among Prisoners: Innovations in Theory and Research.* Cullompton, Devon: Willan Publishing.

Ireland, J. L. (2012) Understanding bullying among younger prisoners: Recent research and introducing the Multifactor Model of Bullying in Secure Settings. *International Journal of Adolescent Medicine and Health*, 24(1).

Ireland, J. L. (2017) Understanding and managing bullying among those detained in secure settings: Moving beyond the individual. In J. L. Ireland, C. A. Ireland, M. Fisher, and N Gredecki (eds), *Routledge International Handbook of Forensic Psychology in Secure Settings.* New York: Routledge.

Ireland, J. L. and Power, C. L. (2012) Propensity to support prison gangs: Its relationship to gang membership, victimisation, aggression and other disruptive behaviors. *Psychology, Crime and Law*, 19(9), 801–816.

Irwin, J. K. and Cressey, D. R. (1962) Thieves, convicts and the inmate subculture. *Social Problems*, 10, 142–155.

Leymann, H. (1996) The content and development of mobbing at work. *European Journal of Work and Organizational Psychology*, 5(2), 165–184.

Lorenz, K. (1966) *On Aggression.* York, UK: Methuen Publishing.

Morris, R. G. and Worrall, J. L. (2014) Prison architecture and inmate misconduct: A multilevel assessment. *Crime and Delinquency*, 60, 1083–1109.

Orlando-Morningstar, D. (1997) Prison gangs. *Special Needs Offender Bulletin*, 2, 1–13.

Oxford Dictionary (2019) Oxford University Press. Oxford.dictionaries.com.

Paterline, B. A. and Petersen, D. M. (1999) Structural and social psychological determinants of prisonization. *Journal of Criminal Justice*, 27(5), 427–441

Pyrooz, D., Decker, S. H. and Fleisher, M. S. (2011) From the street to the prison, from the prison to the street: Understanding and responding to prison gangs. *Journal of Aggression, Conflict and Peace Research*, 3, 12–24.

Rufino, K. A., Fox, K. A., and Kercher, G. A. (2012) Gang membership and crime victimization among prison inmates. *American Journal of Criminal Justice*, 37(3), 321–337.

Scott, G. (2001) Broken windows behind bars: Eradicating prison gangs through ecological hardening and symbolic cleansing. *Corrections Management Quarterly*, 5, 23–36.

Skarbek, D. (2014) *The Social Order of the Underworld: How Prison Gangs Govern the American Penal System.* Oxford: Oxford University Press.

Smithson, H., Ralphs, R., and Williams, P. (2012) Used and abused: The problematic usage of gang terminology in the United Kingdom and its implications for ethnic minority youth. *British Journal of Criminology*, 53(1), 113–128.

Steiner, B., Butler, H. D., and Ellison, J. M. (2014) Causes and correlates of prison inmate misconduct: A systematic review of the evidence. *Journal of Criminal Justice*, 42, 462–470.

Stephenson, S. (2015) *Gangs of Russia: From the Streets to the Corridors of Power.* Ithaca: Cornell University Press.

Sutton, T. E. (2017) The lives of female gang members: A review of the literature. *Aggression and Violent Behavior*, 37, 142–152.

Sykes, G. M. (1958) *The Society of Captives: A Study of a Maximum Security Prison.* Princeton, NJ: Princeton University Press.

Thomas, C. W. and Petersen, D. M. (1977) *Prison Organization and Inmate Subcultures.* Indianapolis, IN: Bobbs-Merrill.

Thornberry, T. P., Krohn, M. D., Lizotte, A. J., Tobin, K., & Smith, C. A. (2003) *Gangs and Delinquency in Developmental Perspective.* Cambridge, UK: Cambridge University Press.

Weerman, F. M., Maxson, C. L., Esbensen, F. A., Aldridge, J., Medina, J., and van Gemert, F. (2009) *Eurogang Programme Manual: Background, Development, and use of the Eurogang Instruments in Multi-Site, Multi-Method Comparative Research.* www.umsl.edu/ccj/Eurogang/EurogangManual.pdf (accessed 24 April 2019).

Wood, J., Moir, A., and James, M. (2009) Prisoners' gang-related activity: The importance of bullying and moral disengagement. *Psychology, Crime & Law*, 15(6), 569–581.

INDEX